THE VICTORIA HISTORY
OF THE
COUNTIES OF ENGLAND

—————

A HISTORY OF
OXFORDSHIRE

VOLUME XIII

Oxford University Press, Walton Street, Oxford OX2 6DP
Oxford New York
Athens Auckland Bangkok Bombay
Calcutta Cape Town Dar es Salaam Delhi
Florence Hong Kong Istanbul Karachi
Kuala Lumpur Madras Madrid Melbourne
Mexico City Nairobi Paris Singapore
Taipei Tokyo Toronto

and associated companies in
Berlin Ibadan

Oxford is a trade mark of Oxford University Press

Published in the United States
by Oxford University Press Inc., New York

© University of London 1996

British Library Cataloguing in Publication Data
A catalogue record for this book is available
from the British Library

ISBN 0 19 722790 2

Printed by H Charlesworth & Co Ltd
Huddersfield, England

THE VICTORIA HISTORY
OF THE
COUNTIES OF ENGLAND

EDITED BY C. R. J. CURRIE

THE UNIVERSITY OF LONDON
INSTITUTE OF
HISTORICAL RESEARCH

INSCRIBED TO THE

MEMORY OF HER LATE MAJESTY

QUEEN VICTORIA

WHO GRACIOUSLY GAVE THE TITLE TO

AND ACCEPTED THE DEDICATION

OF THIS HISTORY

A HISTORY OF THE COUNTY OF

OXFORD

EDITED BY ALAN CROSSLEY

VOLUME XIII

BAMPTON HUNDRED (PART ONE)

PUBLISHED FOR

THE INSTITUTE OF HISTORICAL RESEARCH

BY

OXFORD UNIVERSITY PRESS

1996

The cost of research for this volume was met largely by
Oxfordshire County Council,
whose support is gratefully acknowledged

CONTENTS OF VOLUME THIRTEEN

LIST OF ILLUSTRATIONS

For permission to reproduce pictures in their possession and for loan of photographic prints thanks are rendered to Berkshire Record Office, the Bodleian Library, the British Library, the President and Fellows of Magdalen College, Oxford, the Centre for Oxfordshire Studies, Dr. J. Blair, and Mr. R. Rosewell.

Plates between pages 104 and 105:

LIST OF ILLUSTRATIONS

LIST OF MAPS AND PLANS

Thanks are offered to Dr. J. Blair for the reconstruction of Bampton's Early Topography and for the plans of Bampton and Standlake churches and Standlake rectory house. The plan of Cokethorpe House was prepared by A. P. Baggs. All other maps, except plate 39 and that on page 126, were drawn by the Oxfordshire editorial staff.

EDITORIAL NOTE

THE partnership between the University of London and the Oxfordshire County Council, as described in the Editorial Note to Volume IX of the History of Oxfordshire, has continued, and the University of London, for which the *Victoria County History* is published, again records its thanks to the Oxfordshire County Council for the generosity with which it has met the costs of compilation, aided by important contributions from the University of Oxford.

In Oxfordshire the work has been supervised by an Advisory Sub-Committee which reports to the County Council's Museums, Arts, Libraries, and Leisure Committee, the staff of the Oxfordshire V.C.H. being part of the Department of Leisure and Arts.

Almost all the research and writing for this volume was done in the years 1990–5. The help of many institutions and private persons who gave information and advice, or granted access to houses or to documents in their care, is acknowledged with gratitude. Many are mentioned in footnotes, and others are named in the preamble to the lists of illustrations and maps, but special thanks are rendered here to Bodley's Librarian and the staff of the Bodleian Library, to the Oxfordshire County Archivist and his staff, the Oxfordshire County Library service, particularly the staff of the Centre for Oxfordshire Studies, the Oxford Archaeological Unit, the staffs of the Public Record Office, the Department of Manuscripts of the British Library, and of the National Monuments Record, the archivist of Berkshire, his Grace the duke of Norfolk and the archivist of Arundel Castle, the most Hon. the marquess of Bath and the archivist of Longleat House, the Dean and Chapter of Exeter cathedral and their archivist, the governing bodies and archivists of Balliol, Brasenose, Christ Church, Exeter, Jesus, Lincoln, Magdalen, Mansfield, New, Regent's Park, St. John's, Wadham, and Worcester Colleges, Oxford, Mrs. H. Babington Smith, Mr. P. Best, Dr. J. Blair, Major R. A. Colvile, Dr. A. Millard, Mr. R. Rosewell, Miss S. Stradling, and Mr. D. Sturdy.

The *General Introduction* to the *Victoria County History*, published in 1970, and its *Supplement* published in 1990 give an outline of the structure of the series as a whole, with an account of its progress.

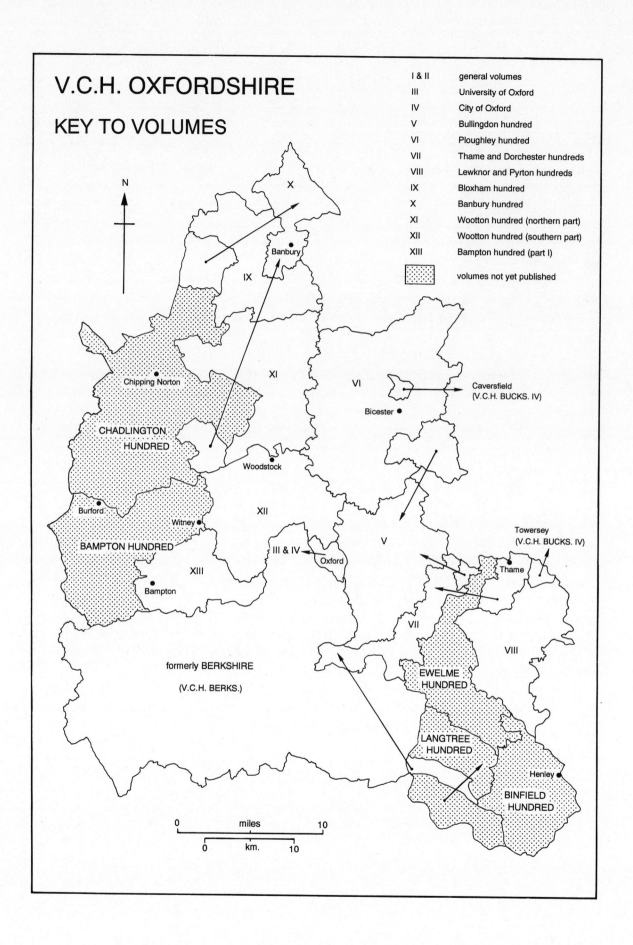

V.C.H. OXFORDSHIRE

KEY TO VOLUMES

I & II	general volumes
III	University of Oxford
IV	City of Oxford
V	Bullingdon hundred
VI	Ploughley hundred
VII	Thame and Dorchester hundreds
VIII	Lewknor and Pyrton hundreds
IX	Bloxham hundred
X	Banbury hundred
XI	Wootton hundred (northern part)
XII	Wootton hundred (southern part)
XIII	Bampton hundred (part I)

volumes not yet published

N

Banbury

IX

X

Chipping Norton

XI

VI

Bicester

Caversfield
(V.C.H. BUCKS. IV)

CHADLINGTON
HUNDRED

Woodstock

XII

Burford

Witney

Towersey
(V.C.H. BUCKS. IV)

V

BAMPTON HUNDRED

III & IV

Oxford

Thame

XIII

Bampton

VII

VIII

EWELME
HUNDRED

formerly BERKSHIRE

(V.C.H. BERKS.)

LANGTREE
HUNDRED

Henley

BINFIELD
HUNDRED

0	miles	10
0	km.	10

LIST OF CLASSES OF DOCUMENTS
IN THE PUBLIC RECORD OFFICE

USED IN THIS VOLUME
WITH THEIR CLASS NUMBERS

Chancery

		Proceedings
C	1	Early
C	2	Series I
C	3	Series II
C	5	Six Clerks Series, Bridges
C	54	Close Rolls
C	60	Fine Rolls
C	66	Patent Rolls
C	78	Decree Rolls
		Inquisitions post mortem
C	132	Series I, Henry III
C	133	Edward I
C	134	Edward II
C	135	Edward III
C	136	Richard II
C	137	Henry IV
C	138	Henry V
C	139	Henry VI
C	140	Edward IV
C	142	Series II
C	143	Inquisitions ad quod damnum

Court of Common Pleas

CP	25/1	Feet of Fines, Series I
CP	25/2	Series II
CP	40	Plea Rolls
CP	43	Recovery Rolls

Exchequer, King's Remembrancer

E	134	Depositions taken by Commission
E	142	Ancient Extents
E	150	Inquisitions post mortem, Series II
E	152	Enrolments of Inquisitions
E	179	Subsidy Rolls &c.
E	310	Particulars for Leases
E	315	Miscellaneous Books
E	317	Parliamentary Surveys
E	318	Particulars of Grants
E	321	Proceedings of the Court of Augmentations

Home Office

| HO | 67 | Agricultural Returns |
| HO | 107 | Population Returns |

Justices Itinerant &c.

| JUST | 1 | Eyre Rolls |
| JUST | 2 | Coroners' Rolls |

Court of King's Bench

| KB | 27 | Coram Rege Rolls |

Probate

| PROB | 11 | Registered copies of P.C.C. wills |

Court of Requests

| REQ | 2 | Proceedings |

General Register Office

RG	9	Census Returns 1861
RG	10	1871
RG	11	1881
RG	12	1891

Special Collections

SC	1	Ancient Correspondence
SC	2	Court Rolls
SC	6	Ministers' and Receivers' Accounts
SC	8	Ancient Petitions

State Paper Office

| | | State Papers Domestic |
| SP | 12 | Elizabeth I |

Court of Star Chamber

		Proceedings
STAC	2	Henry VIII
STAC	4	Mary

SELECT LIST OF BODLEIAN LIBRARY MANUSCRIPTS

USED IN THIS VOLUME

MS. Ch. Oxon.	Oxfordshire charters
MS. d.d. Ch. Ch.	Medieval deeds from the archives of Christ Church, Oxford
MS. d.d. Dew	Deeds collected by G. J. Dew
MS. d.d. Fitt	Papers of the Cary family
MS. d.d. Harcourt	Papers of the Harcourt family, chiefly 16th–20th-century
MS. d.d. Shrewsbury	Deeds relating to estates of the earls of Shrewsbury
MS. Dep.	
d 72, 78	John Dunkin's collections for Oxfordshire, formerly Dunkin MSS.
MS. Don.	
b 14, c 90–1, e 108	Oxfordshire church notes by James Hunt
MS. Dodsworth 143	Copies, 17th-century, of medieval deeds, including some of the Goldsborough family relating to Bampton
MS. Eng. th. e 49	Sermons 1718–29 by John Conybeare, later bishop of Bristol
MS. Rawl.	
B 103	Miscellaneous papers, including Oxfordshire church notes
B 250	Miscellaneous papers, some relating to Northmoor inclosure, 1666
D 384	Papers probably belonging to Edmund Warcupp of Northmoor, mainly 17th-century
MS. Rolls Oxon.	Miscellaneous Oxfordshire rolls
MS. Tanner 32, 115	Collections of letters and papers, 16th- and 17th-century
MS. Top. Gen.	
a 11	Topographical drawings by R. C. Buckler
c 85	Collection of probate documents, 17th–19th-century
MS. Top. Oxon.	
a 37	Oxfordshire prints and drawings, 18th- and 19th-century
a 64–9	Oxfordshire drawings 1797–1830 by J. C. Buckler
b 21	Court rolls, some of Northmoor and Hardwick, 16th-century
b 75	Historical notes and papers relating to Oxfordshire, probably collected by D. T. Powell and C. F. Wyatt
b 78	Collections for Ducklington, Hardwick, and Cokethorpe by the Revd. W. D. Macray
b 89–91	Drawings of Oxford and neighbourhood, mainly 19th-century
b 169	Legal papers, mainly abstracts of title, some relating to Oxfordshire
b 220	Monumental inscriptions and drawings of Oxfordshire buildings, early 19th-century
b 256	Notes and drawings of Oxfordshire buildings, 19th-century
b 265	Transcripts and papers, some relating to Northmoor inclosure 1666–73
c 55, 60	Oxfordshire collections of W. H. Turner
c 103–5	Papers relating to church restorations, mainly 1860–70
c 118	Notes and transcripts by Thomas Napkyn, curate of Standlake, early 17th-century
c 224	Oxfordshire legal papers 1573–1738
c 290	Miscellaneous Oxfordshire papers 1753–1875
c 378	Historical notes and a diary by Thomas Wyatt (d. 1652), rector of Ducklington
c 484–99	Photographs of Oxfordshire listed buildings from 1956
c 532	Drawings, 19th-century, including some of Oxfordshire buildings by J. C. Buckler

NOTE ON ABBREVIATIONS

Among the abbreviations and short titles used, the following may require elucidation:

A.-S.	Anglo-Saxon
Abbrev. Plac. (Rec. Com.)	*Placitorum Abbreviatio* (Record Commission, 1811)
Abbrev. Rot. Orig. (Rec. Com.)	*Rotulorum Originalium Abbreviatio, temp. Hen. III, Edw. I* (Record Commission, 1805)
Acts of P.C.	*Acts of the Privy Council of England* (H.M.S.O. 1890–1964)
Acts of P.C. (Rec. Com.)	*Proceedings and Ordinances of the Privy Council of England, 1386–1542* (Record Commission, 1834–7)
Alum. Oxon. 1500–1714; 1715–1886	*Alumni Oxonienses, 1500–1714; 1715–1886*, ed. J. Foster (Oxford, 1888–92)
B.L.	British Library
B.N.C. Mun.	Muniments of Brasenose College, Oxford
Bampton Hund. R.	*Oxfordshire Hundred Rolls of 1279 (Bampton Hundred, Witney Borough)*, ed. E. Stone, P. Hyde (O.R.S. xlvi)
Baptist Union Corpn.	Records of the Baptist Union Corporation at Baptist House, Didcot, Oxon.
Besse, *Sufferings*	J. Besse, *A Collection of the Sufferings of the People called Quakers, from 1650 to 1689* (1753)
Bk. of Fees	*The Book of Fees* (H.M.S.O. 1920–31)
Blenheim Mun.	Muniments of the duke of Marlborough at Blenheim Palace, Woodstock, Oxon.
Blk. Prince's Reg.	*Register of Edward the Black Prince* (H.M.S.O. 1930–33)
Bodl.	Bodleian Library
bp.	bishop
Bp. Fell and Nonconf.	*Bishop Fell and Nonconformity: Visitation Documents, 1682–3*, ed. Mary Clapinson (O.R.S. lii)
Brewer, *Oxon.*	J. N. Brewer, *A topograghical and historical description of the county of Oxford* (1819)
Burke, *Peerage; Ext. & Dorm. Baronetcies; Land. Gent.*	J. Burke and others, *A Genealogical and Heraldic Dictionary of the Peerage, Baronetage and Knightage*; *A History of the Extinct and Dormant Baronetcies*; *A Dictionary of the Landed Gentry*
C.B.A. Group 9	Council for British Archaeology, Regional Group 9
C.C.C. Mun.	Muniments of Corpus Christi College, Oxford
C.J.	*Journals of the House of Commons*
C.O.S., OPA; PRN; SMR	Centre for Oxfordshire Studies, Central Library, Westgate, Oxford, Oxfordshire Photographic Archive; Primary Record Number; Sites and Monuments Record
Cal. Chart. R.	*Calendar of the Charter Rolls preserved in the Public Record Office* (H.M.S.O. 1903–27)
Cal. Close	*Calendar of the Close Rolls preserved in the Public Record Office* (H.M.S.O. 1892–1963)
Cal. Cttee. for Compounding	*Calendar of the Proceedings of the Committee for Compounding, etc.* (H.M.S.O. 1889–92)

Cal. Cttee. for Money	*Calendar of the Proceedings of the Committee for Advance of Money, 1642–56* (H.M.S.O. 1888)
Cal. Doc. France, ed. Round	*Calendar of Documents preserved in France, illustrative of the History of Great Britain*, ed. J. H. Round (H.M.S.O.1899)
Cal. Fine R.	*Calendar of the Fine Rolls preserved in the Public Record Office* (H.M.S.O. 1911–62)
Cal. Inq. Misc.	*Calendar of Inquisitions Miscellaneous (Chancery) preserved in the Public Record Office* (H.M.S.O. 1916–68)
Cal. Inq. p.m.	*Calendar of Inquisitions post mortem preserved in the Public Record Office* (H.M.S.O. 1904–87)
Cal. Inq. p.m. Hen. VII	*Calendar of Inquisitions post mortem, Henry VII* (H.M.S.O. 1898–1955)
Cal. Lib. R.	*Calendar of the Liberate Rolls preserved in the Public Record Office* (H.M.S.O. 1917–64)
Cal. Papal Reg.	*Calendar of Papal Registers: Papal Letters* (H.M.S.O. and Irish MSS. Com. 1893–1986)
Cal. Pat.	*Calendar of the Patent Rolls preserved in the Public Record Office* (H.M.S.O. 1891–1986)
Cal. Q.S.	Calendar of quarter sessions records in the Oxfordshire Record Office by W. J. Oldfield
Cal. S.P. Dom.	*Calendar of State Papers, Domestic Series* (H.M.S.O. 1856–1972)
Camd., Camden Soc.	Camden Series, Camden Society
Cart. Sax. ed. Birch	*Cartularium Saxonicum*, ed. W. de Gray Birch (1883–99)
Cart. St. Frid.	*The Cartulary of the Monastery of St. Frideswide at Oxford*, ed. S. R. Wigram (O.H.S. xxviii, xxxi)
Cat. Anct. D.	*Descriptive Catalogue of Ancient Deeds in the Public Record Office* (H.M.S.O. 1890–1915)
Cath. Rec. Soc.	Catholic Record Society
Ch. and Chapel, 1851	*Church and Chapel in Oxfordshire, 1851. The Return of the Census of Religious Worship*, ed. Kate Tiller (O.R.S. lv)
Ch. Bells Oxon.	F. Sharpe, *The Church Bells of Oxfordshire* (O.R.S. xxviii, xxx, xxxii, xxxiv)
Ch. Ch. Arch.	Archives of Christ Church, Oxford
Ch. Com. Rec.	Records of the Church Commissioners at Millbank, London
Chant. Cert.	*Chantry Certificates and Edwardian Inventories of Church Goods*, ed. Rose Graham (O.R.S. i)
Char. Com.	Charity Commission
Char. Don.	*Abstract of Returns relative to Charitable Donations for the Benefit of Poor Persons*, H.C. 511 (1816), XVI
chwdn.	churchwarden
Close R.	*Close Rolls of the Reign of Henry III preserved in the Public Record Office* (H.M.S.O. 1902–15)
Complete Peerage	G. E. C[okayne] and others, *The Complete Peerage* (2nd edn. 1910–59)
Compton Census, ed. Whiteman	*The Compton Census of 1676*, ed. A. Whiteman (Records of Social and Economic History, N.S. x)
Courage Arch., Bristol	Courage Brewery archives at Counterslip, Bristol
Crockford	*Crockford's Clerical Directory*
ct.	court
Cur. Reg. R.	*Curia Regis Rolls preserved in the Public Record Office* (H.M.S.O. 1922–79)
D. & C. Exeter	Archives of the dean and chapter of Exeter cathedral
D.N.B.	*Dictionary of National Biography*

Davis, *Oxon. Map* (1797)	R. Davis, *A New Map of the County of Oxford* (1797)
Dep. Kpr's. Rep.	*Annual Report of the Deputy Keeper of the Public Records* (1840–1958)
Deserted Villages of Oxon.	K. J. Allison, M. W. Beresford, and J. G. Hurst, *Deserted Villages of Oxfordshire* (Leicester Univ. Dept. of English Local History, Occasional Papers, no. 17)
Dir.	*Directory*
Dugdale, *Mon.*	W. Dugdale, *Monasticon Anglicanum*, ed. J. Caley and others (1817–30)
E.E.T.S.	Early English Text Society
E.H.R.	*English Historical Review*
E.P.N.S.	English Place-Name Society
Econ. H.R.	*Economic History Review*
Educ. of Poor Digest	*Digest of Returns to the Select Committee on the Education of the Poor*, H.C. 224 (1819), ix (B)
Emden, *O.U. Reg. to 1500*	A. B. Emden, *Biographical Register of the University of Oxford to* A.D. *1500* (1957–9)
Emden, *O.U. Reg. 1501–40*	A. B. Emden, *Biographical Register of the University of Oxford* A.D. *1501 to 1540* (1974)
Evans, *Ch. Plate*	J. T. Evans, *Church Plate of Oxfordshire* (1928)
Ex. e Rot. Fin. (Rec. Com.)	*Excerpta e Rotulis Finium, Hen. III* (Record Commission, 1835–6)
Eynsham Cart.	*Cartulary of Eynsham Abbey*, ed. H. E. Salter (O.H.S. xlix, li)
Farrar, *Honors*	W. Farrar, *Honors and Knights' Fees* (3 vols. 1923–5)
Feud. Aids	*Inquisitions and Assessments relating to Feudal Aids preserved in the Public Record Office* (H.M.S.O. 1899–1920)
G. E. C. *Baronetage*	G. E. C[okayne], *Complete Baronetage* (1900–9)
Gent. Mag.	*Gentleman's Magazine*
Geol. Surv.	Geological Survey
Giles, *Hist. Bampton*	J. A. Giles, *History of the Parish and Town of Bampton* (2nd edn. with supplement, 1848)
Glasscock, *Subsidy 1334*	R. E. Glasscock, *The Lay Subsidy of 1334* (1975)
Godstow Eng. Reg.	*English Register of Godstow Nunnery*, ed. A. Clark (E.E.T.S. orig. ser. 129, 130, 149)
Grundy, *Saxon Oxon*	G. B. Grundy, *Saxon Oxfordshire* (O.R.S. xii)
H.C.	House of Commons
H.L.	House of Lords
H.M.S.O.	Her (His) Majesty's Stationery Office
Harl. Soc.	Harleian Society
Hearth Tax Oxon.	*Hearth Tax Returns for Oxfordshire, 1665*, ed. Maureen Weinstock (O.R.S. xxi)
Hist. MSS. Com.	Historical Manuscripts Commission
Hodgson, *Q.A.B.*	C. Hodgson, *Account of the Augmentation of Small Livings by the Governors of the Bounty of Queen Anne* (2nd edn. 1845)
Incl.	Inclosure
Inq. Non. (Rec. Com.)	*Nonarum Inquisitiones in Curia Scaccarii* (Record Commission, 1807)

Jefferys, *Oxon. Map* (1767)	T. Jefferys, *The County of Oxford* (1767)
Jnl. R. Agric. Soc.	*Journal of the Royal Agricultural Society*
L. & I. Soc.	List and Index Society
L. & P. Hen. VIII	*Letters and Papers, Foreign and Domestic, of the Reign of Henry VIII* (H.M.S.O. 1864–1932)
L.J.	*Journals of the House of Lords*
L.R.S.	Lincoln Record Society
Land Util. Surv.	*Reports of the Land Utilisation Survey of Britain*: pt. 56, *Oxfordshire*, by Mary Marshall (1943)
Leland, *Itin.* ed. Toulmin Smith	*Itinerary of John Leland*, ed. L. Toulmin Smith (1907–10)
Lewis, *Topog. Dict. Eng.* (1840)	S. Lewis, *Topographical Dictionary of England* (1840)
Linc. Coll. Mun.	Muniments of Lincoln College, Oxford
Lond. Gaz.	*London Gazette*
Lunt, *Val. Norw.*	*Valuation of Norwich*, ed. W. E. Lunt (1926)
Magd. Coll. Mun.	Muniments of Magdalen College, Oxford
McClatchey, *Oxon. Clergy*	D. McClatchey, *Oxfordshire Clergy, 1777–1869* (1960)
Misc. Gen. et Her.	*Miscellanea Genealogica et Heraldica*, ed. J. J. Howard, W. B. Bannerman, and A. W. Hughes Clarke (1868–1938)
N. & Q.	*Notes and Queries*
N.M.R.	Royal Commission on Historical Monuments (England): National Monuments Record
N.R.A.	National Register of Archives
O.A.H.S. *Proc.*	*Proceedings* of the Oxford Society for Promoting the Study of Gothic Architecture, 1839–59; and of the Oxford Architectural and Historical Society, 1860–1900
O.A.S. *Rep.*	*Reports and Transactions* of the North Oxfordshire Archaeological Society, 1853–86, and of the Oxfordshire Archaeological Society 1887–1949
O.H.S.	Oxford Historical Society
O.R.C.C.	Oxfordshire Rural Community Council
O.R.O.	Oxfordshire Archives, formerly the Oxfordshire County Record Office
O.R.S.	Oxfordshire Record Society
O.S.	Ordnance Survey
Oldfield, 'Clerus Oxf. Dioc.'	MS. index to clergy of Oxford diocese by W. J. Oldfield in Oxfordshire Archives
Orr, *Oxon. Agric.*	J. Orr, *Agriculture in Oxfordshire* (1916)
Oseney Cart.	*Cartulary of Oseney Abbey*, ed. H. E. Salter (O.H.S. lxxxix–xci, xcviii, ci)
Oxf. Chron.	*Oxford Chronicle*
Oxf. Jnl.	*Jackson's Oxford Journal*
Oxf. Jnl. Synopsis	'Chronological Synopsis and Index to Oxon. Items in Jackson's Oxford Journal 1753–80', ed. E.C. Davies; '1781–90', ed. E. H. Cordeaux (Typescripts 1967, 1976: copies in Central Library, Westgate, Oxford and the Bodleian Library)

Oxon. Fines	*Feet of Fines for Oxfordshire, 1195–1291*, ed. H. E. Salter (O.R.S. xii)
Oxon. Poll, 1754	*The Poll of the Freeholders of Oxfordshire, taken at Oxford on 17–23 April 1754*
Oxon. Visit.	*Visitations of Oxfordshire in 1566, 1574, and 1634*, ed. W. H. Turner (Harl. Soc. v)
P.N. Oxon. (E.P.N.S.)	Margaret Gelling, *Place-Names of Oxfordshire* (English Place-Name Soc. xxiii–xxiv)
P.O. Arch.	Post Office archives at Mount Pleasant, London
P.R.O.	Public Record Office
P.R.S.	Pipe Roll Society
Par. Colln.	*Parochial Collections by Anthony Wood and Richard Rawlinson*, ed. F. N. Davis (O.R.S. ii, iv, xi)
Parker, *Eccl. Top.*	J. H. Parker, *Ecclesiastical and Architectural Topography. Oxfordshire* (1850)
Parker, *Guide*	*Guide to the Architectural Antiquities in the Neighbourhood of Oxford* [ed. J. H. Parker and W. Grey] (1846)
Pat. R.	*Patent Rolls of the Reign of Henry III preserved in the Public Record Office* (H.M.S.O. 1900–3)
Pevsner, *Oxon.*	Jennifer Sherwood and Nikolaus Pevsner, *Buildings of England: Oxfordshire* (1974)
Pipe R.	*Pipe Roll*
Plac. de Quo Warr. (Rec. Com.)	*Placita de Quo Warranto* (Record Commission, 1818)
Poor Abstract, 1777; 1787	*Reports of Select Committees on Poor Laws, 1775–7 and 1787*, H.C. Series 1, vol. ix
Poor Abstract, 1804; 1818	*Abstract of Answers and Returns relative to the Expense and Maintenance of the Poor*, H.C. 175 (1804), i; H.C. 82 (1818), xix
Protestation Rtns. and Tax Assess.	*Oxfordshire and North Berkshire Protestation Returns and Tax Assessments 1641–2*, ed. J Gibson (O.R. S. lix)
R.O.	Record Office
Reading Cart.	*Reading Abbey Cartularies*, i, ed. B. R. Kemp (Camden 4th ser. xxxi)
Rec. Com.	Record Commission
Red Bk. Exch. (Rolls Ser.)	*Red Book of the Exchequer*, ed. H. Hall (Rolls Series, 1896)
Reg. Regum Anglo-Norm.	*Regesta Regum Anglo-Normannorum 1066–1154*, ed. H. W. C. Davies and others (1913–69)
Rep. Com. Char.	*Reports of the Commissioners for Charities* (1819–40), indexed in H.C. 279 (1840), xix (2)
Rot. Chart. (Rec. Com.)	*Rotuli Chartarum, 1199–1216* (Record Commission, 1837)
Rot. Cur. Reg. (Rec. Com.)	*Rotuli Curiae Regis, 6 Richard I to 1 John* (Record Commission, 1812–18)
Rot. de Ob. et Fin. (Rec. Com.)	*Rotuli de Oblatis et Finibus* (Record Commission, 1835)
Rot. Hund. (Rec. Com.)	*Rotuli Hundredorum temp. Hen. III & Edw. I* (Record Commission, 1812–18)
Rot. Lib. (Rec. Com.)	*Rotuli de Liberate, regnante Johanne* (Record Commission, 1844)
Rot. Litt. Claus. (Rec. Com.)	*Rotuli Litterarum Clausarum, 1204–27* (Record Commission, 1833–44)
Rot. Litt. Pat. (Rec. Com.)	*Rotuli Litterarum Patentium, 1201–16* (Record Commission, 1835)

NOTE ON ABBREVIATIONS

Rot. Parl.	*Rotuli Parliamentorum* [1783]
Sanders, *Eng. Baronies*	I. J. Sanders, *English Baronies, 1086–1327* (Oxford, 1960)
Secker's Corresp.	*The Correspondence of Thomas Secker, bishop of Oxford 1737–58*, ed. A. P. Jenkins (O.R.S. lvii)
Secker's Visit.	*Articles of Enquiry at the Primary Visitation of Dr. Thomas Secker, 1738*, ed. H. A. Lloyd Jukes (O.R.S. xxxviii)
Ser.	Series
Skelton, *Antiq. Oxon.*	J. Skelton, *Illustrations of the Principal Antiquities of Oxfordshire* (1823)
Stapleton, *Cath. Miss.*	B. Stapleton, *Oxfordshire Post-Reformation Catholic Missions* (1906)
Subsidy 1526	*Subsidy Collected in the Diocese of Lincoln in 1526*, ed. H. E. Salter (O.H.S. lxiii)
Tax. Eccl. (Rec. Com.)	*Taxatio Ecclesiastica Anglie et Wallie ... circa* A.D. *1291* (Record Commission, 1801)
Trans.	*Transactions*
Univ. Brit. Dir. ii	*Universal British Directory* [1793]
V.C.H.	*Victoria County History*
Valor Eccl. (Rec. Com.)	*Valor Ecclesiasticus, temp. Hen. VIII* (Record Commission, 1810–34)
Visit. Dioc. Linc.	*Visitations in the Diocese of Lincoln 1517–31*, ed. A. Hamilton Thompson (L.R.S. xxxiii, xxxv, xxxvii)
Wilb. Letter Bks.	*The Letter Books of Samuel Wilberforce 1843–68*, ed. R. K. Pugh (O.R.S. xlvii)
Wilb. Visit.	*Bishop Wilberforce's Visitation Returns, 1854*, ed. E. P. Baker (O.R.S. xxxv)
Witney Ct. Bks.	*Calendar of the Court Books of the Borough of Witney 1538–1610*, ed. J. L. Bolton and Marjorie M. Maslen (O.R.S. liv)
Wood's Life	*The Life and Times of Anthony Wood, antiquary, of Oxford 1632–95*, ed. A. Clark (O.H.S. xix, xxi, xxvi, xxx, xl)
Young, *Oxon. Agric.*	A. Young, *General View of the Agriculture of Oxfordshire* (1809 and 1813)

BAMPTON HUNDRED

UNTIL 1844 Bampton hundred, on the west side of the county, covered *c.* 48,500 a., divided among 16 ancient parishes; its population in 1841 was 15,628.[1] The hundred formed a compact block of land, bounded on part of the north and much of the east by the river Windrush, on the south by the river Thames, and on part of the south-west by the river Leach. From an early date, however, three parishes within those bounds belonged wholly or partly to other counties, and two to another Oxfordshire hundred.[2] In the south and south-east the hundred lay chiefly on alluvium and on the oolitic gravels of the Upper Thames, in parts of the east on Oxford Clay, and in the north and the west on Cornbrash, Forest Marble, and oolitic White Limestone. The land is gently undulating with few prominent hills, rising from *c.* 65 m. by the Thames in the extreme south-east to *c.* 150 m. along parts of the western boundary towards the Cotswolds.[3]

Though not named in Domesday book, the hundred may be identified with two hundreds attached in 1086 to the large royal manor of Bampton. In the 12th century it was still occasionally called a double hundred, but the two parts may never have been separately administered and by the 13th century had been combined.[4] Their composition in 1086 was probably little different from that in the 13th century, when the combined hundred already contained the 16 parishes (with their constituent hamlets) included later:[5] the Domesday assessment of those places was *c.* 201 hides,[6] and in the carucage of 1220 the hundred, excluding the exempt ecclesiastical manors of Bampton Deanery, Shifford, Hardwick and Brighthampton, and Witney, paid on 207 ploughs.[7] The composition of the separate Domesday hundreds may have been reflected in the later hundred's division into east and west parts, each of which accounted for *c.* 100 Domesday hides.[8] Among places later excluded from the hundred, Langford and, probably, Little Faringdon and Shilton were held in 1086 by Aelfsige of Faringdon with the manor of Great Faringdon (then Berks.); by the 13th century all three formed part of the Berkshire hundred of Faringdon, though Langford's hamlets of Grafton and Radcot remained in Oxfordshire and in Bampton hundred. Widford, owned by St. Oswald's priory in Gloucester, belonged in 1086 to the Gloucestershire hundred of Barrington and later to Slaughter hundred, and Northmoor, as an outlier of Taynton manor, belonged probably to the three hundreds attached to Shipton under Wychwood, later Chadlington hundred. Tenurial connexions probably also explain Minster Lovell's and Little Minster's inclusion in Chadlington hundred by 1220.[9]

[1] *V.C.H. Oxon.* ii. 215–16 and n. Figs. here given exclude Langford, Little Faringdon, and Shilton (then Berks.), and Widford (then Glos.). [2] Below.

[3] O.S. Maps 1/25,000, SP 20/30, 21/31, 40/50, 41/51 (1977–83 edns.); Geol. Surv. Map 1/50,000, solid and drift, sheet 236 (1982 edn.).

[4] *V.C.H. Oxon.* i. 400; *Pipe R.* 1182 (P.R.S. xxxi), 126; 1183 (P.R.S. xxxii), 102 and n.; *Bk. of Fees,* i. 316–17; ii. 822–3; *Oxon. Domesday, Intro. and Translation* (Alecto edn. 1990), 21–3.

[5] *Bk. of Fees,* i. 316–17; i. 822–3; *Bampton Hund. R.* 17 sqq.; *Feud. Aids,* iv. 162–3; P.R.O., E 179/161/8–9.

[6] *V.C.H. Oxon.* i. 400 sqq.; the figure excludes 15 hides at Langford (later Berks.), but includes 2 hides at Grafton. Another

3 ungelded hides were later attached to Bampton Deanery manor: below, Bampton: Bampton and Weald, manors.

[7] *Bk. of Fees,* i. 316–17. Some unlisted hamlets were probably assessed with the manor or parish to which they belonged; cf. *Bull. Inst. Hist. Res.* xli. 212–16.

[8] P.R.O., E 179/255/4, pt. i, ff. 19–33v.; pt. iii, ff. 243–51; cf. *V.C.H. Oxon.* i. 400 sqq.

[9] *V.C.H. Oxon.* i. 401, 427; *V.C.H. Berks.* i. 292–3 (wrongly identifying 'Rocote' with Radcot), 319–20; *V.C.H. Glos.* vi. 3–4; *Bk. of Fees,* i. 317; *Feud. Aids,* iv. 162–3, 165; *Oxon. Domesday, Intro. and Translation* (Alecto edn. 1990), 26; below, Northmoor, intro. Langford, Shilton, and Widford are reserved for treatment in a future volume.

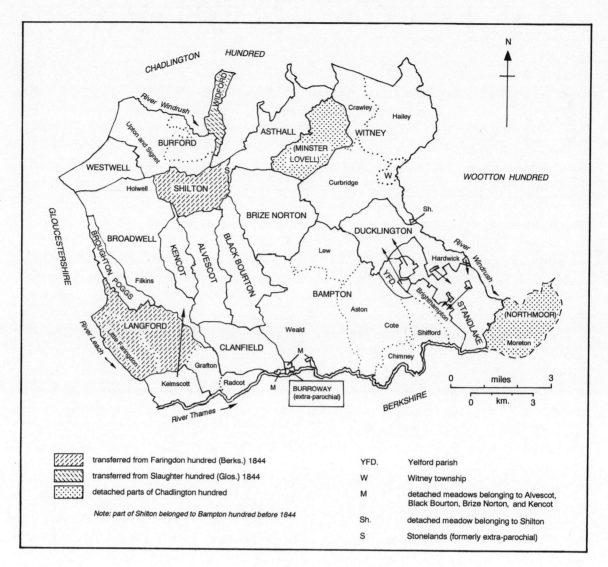

BAMPTON HUNDRED *c.* 1880

In the later 13th century Bampton hundred contained *c.* 45 separate settlements,[10] among them the later lost or shrunken settlements of Benney and Puttes in Clanfield, Alwoldsbury in Clanfield or Alvescot,[11] Putlesley, Eggesley, and East Weald (later Claywell) in Ducklington, and Caswell in Witney. Denleghe (later Delly End) in Witney's hamlet of Hailey was separately listed in 1316.[12] Thirty-five places were mentioned in 1642, and 30 townships, some including more than one settlement, were included in 1841.[13] In 1844 Langford, Little Faringdon, and Shilton were transferred to the hundred from Berkshire, and Widford from Gloucestershire, and a detached farm of 244 a. belonging to Broughton Poggs parish was transferred to Gloucestershire. The extra-parochial Stonelands (*c.* 20 poles) and Burroway (31 a.) were counted as part of the hundred by 1841 and 1881 respectively, and in 1881 the total area was 54,022 a. (21,871 ha.).[14]

In the later 12th century and earlier 13th the hundred was evidently granted at

---

[10] *Bampton Hund. R.* 17 sqq., omitting Burford (with Upton and Signet) evidently in error; cf. *Bk. of Fees*, i. 317; *Feud. Aids*, iv. 162–3. A small portion of Langford included in 1279 belonged to Radcot manor: *Bampton Hund. R.* 58.

[11] *Bampton Hund. R.* 55 n.; cf. *Deserted Villages of Oxon.* 30, wrongly associating it with Burroway.

[12] *Feud. Aids*, iv. 162; *P.N. Oxon.* (E.P.N.S.), ii. 321.

[13] *Protestation Rtns. and Tax Assess.* 1–33; *Census*, 1841; cf. *Hearth Tax Oxon.* 210–34. Brighthampton and Brittenton formed one settlement: below, Standlake, intro.

[14] *Census*, 1841–81; Act to Annexe Detached Parts of Counties, 7 & 8 Vic. c. 61.

pleasure with Bampton manor, with which it passed in 1248 to Henry III's half-brother William de Valence.[15] It descended with the manor to the Talbots, later earls of Shrewsbury, and was divided with it in 1660. Lords of the two, unequal moieties remained joint lords of the hundred thereafter: courts were held in both names and the profits were divided.[16] In 1382 the hundred was leased with the manor for 7 years to Sir Robert Tresilian,[17] and in the later 16th century the right to hold the court was sometimes let with the demesne to the earl's steward.[18]

The bailiff of Bampton was mentioned in 1248, and the bailiff of the liberty of Bampton in 1320.[19] In the later 13th century the lord claimed return of writs, pleas of withernam, gallows, pillory and tumbrel, assize of bread and ale, and probably (as in the 17th century) waifs, strays, and felons' goods, though in 1285 the Crown denied that return of writs and withernam could be held without special warrant.[20] Hundred courts were held every three weeks and the view or court leet twice a year, in 1362 at Hock day and Michaelmas, and in the 1670s in April and in September or October.[21] Perquisites were valued at 20s. in 1296, and income from the two views at 100s. in 1362;[22] in 1652 certainty money, payable at Michaelmas, totalled 13s. 4d. a year, and profits of the courts leet and three-weekly courts £6.[23]

Numerous franchises were claimed within the hundred by the later 13th century,[24] though not all survived in the 17th century and later. Before 1248 Richard, earl of Cornwall (d. 1272) transferred to his court of North Osney the suit of his tenants at Brize Norton, Astrop, Clanfield, Puttes, Asthall, and Black Bourton, for which he established separate views and claimed assize of bread and ale.[25] Bishops of Winchester claimed extensive franchises in their borough of Witney and its hamlets, including view of frankpledge, quittance of suit from the hundred and shire courts, and return of writs,[26] and in Burford the earl of Gloucester or his mesne tenant claimed return of writs, assize of bread and ale, and 'other liberties'.[27] At Westwell the lord claimed view of frankpledge and the right of excluding royal bailiffs, at Hardwick and Standlake lords claimed, among other franchises, gallows and tumbrel, at Radcot the lord claimed infangthief and outfangthief, and at Bampton and Aston Exeter cathedral claimed waifs and strays and other royalties. Views were claimed in the manors of Broadwell, Hardwick and Brighthampton, Alvescot, Ducklington, and Bampton Deanery, though in the last three the earl's bailiff held the view for a fixed annual payment.[28] Several lords owing suit to the hundred court had by 1279 transferred the obligation to a tenant as part of their services.[29]

In the 16th and 17th centuries the Bampton view elected tithingmen and sometimes other officers for Bampton, Weald, Lew, Aston, Lower Haddon, Shifford, Kencot, Black Bourton, Clanfield, Alwoldsbury, and Kelmscott, and

[15] *Pipe R.* 1187 (P.R.S. xxxvii), 66–7; 1188 (P.R.S. xxxviii), 7, 149; 1230 (P.R.S. N.S. iv), 245; *Bk. of Fees*, i. 588; ii. 1396; *Plac de Quo Warr.* (Rec. Com.), 668; *Cal. Chart. R.* 1226–57, 339; below, Bampton: Bampton and Weald, manors.

[16] Bodl. MS. d.d. Harcourt c 1/7 (13); B.L. Map C 7 e 16 (3), p. 36; below, Bampton: Bampton and Weald, manors.

[17] *Cal Close*, 1381–5, 108.

[18] P.R.O., REQ 2/198/14, m. 2.

[19] *Berks. Eyre 1248* (Selden Soc. xc), no. 193; *Sel. Cases in K.B.* iv (Selden Soc. lxxiv), pp. 95–6.

[20] Giles, *Hist. Bampton*, 130–2, Suppl. p. 2; *Rot. Hund.* (Rec. Com.), ii. 30; *Bampton Hund. R.* 17. For return of writs, *Close R.* 1247–51, 518; 1251–3, 98.

[21] P.R.O., E 317/Oxon./1; Longleat House (Wilts.),

NMR 3315; *Bampton Hund. R.* 50, 52, 60, 65; Giles, *Hist. Bampton*, 138–9.

[22] P.R.O., C 133/76, no. 2; Giles, *Hist. Bampton*, 138–9; cf. *Rot. Hund.* (Rec. Com.), ii. 30.

[23] P.R.O., E 317/Oxon./1.

[24] Para. based on *Bampton Hund. R.* 17–77.

[25] *Rot. Hund.* (Rec. Com.), ii. 30; *Ministers' Accts. of Earldom of Cornwall, 1296–7*, i (Camden 3rd ser. lxvi), 143–8; *V.C.H. Oxon.* iv. 279.

[26] *Bampton Hund. R.* 71, 74–5, 89; *Cal. Chart. R.* 1226–57, 145–6; *Cal. Fine R.* 1445–52, 57.

[27] *Rot. Hund.* (Rec. Com.), ii. 37.

[28] Cf. ibid. 30; Giles, *Hist. Bampton*, 131–2; below, Bampton: Bampton and Weald, local govt.

[29] *Bampton Hund. R.* 25, 50–1, 55, 65.

retained varying jurisdiction over all those places.[30] Separate annual lawdays were held reportedly until the 19th century for Black Bourton and Broughton Poggs, for Broadwell and its hamlets, for Alvescot, and for Ducklington and Standlake.[31] By 1789 there was only one annual court at Bampton, which presumably still exercised hundredal jurisdiction;[32] it continued in the early 19th century but had lapsed by 1848.[33] Hundredal rights were sold with the two portions of Bampton manor in the later 19th century[34] but were not mentioned later.

For purposes of county administration the hundred was divided into east and west divisions before the mid 17th century, and a chief constable for each was appointed at the sessions.[35]

This volume treats the south-eastern part of Bampton hundred, and the adjoining parish of Northmoor, a detached part of Chadlington hundred. The land is low lying, and in the south especially is cut by numerous small streams flowing into the Thames, a landscape which has prompted comparison with the Dutch polderlands.[36] There was intensive prehistoric, Iron-Age, and Romano-British settlement of the riverside gravels,[37] and evidence of early Anglo-Saxon activity includes a prominent barrow at Lew. Bampton was an important royal centre possibly by the 8th century, and estates and presumably settlements existed at Aston, Lew, Ducklington, Brighthampton, Chimney, and Shifford by the early 11th century; the landscape was by then highly organized and included some open fields, apportioned moorland, woodland interspersed with clearings, and, at Ducklington, a park or game enclosure (*haga*).[38] By the 13th century the area was chiefly one of nucleated villages surrounded by open fields, but there were several small hamlets and groups of farmsteads, many of them later shrunk or deserted. Some, notably in Ducklington, resulted probably from woodland assarting, and others, such as Lower Haddon in Bampton or Ramsey in Northmoor, may indicate late colonization of marginal land, but hamlets such as Hardwick and Cokethorpe were evidently more ancient. Parochial development was impeded by the establishment of a late Anglo-Saxon royal minster at Bampton: most of the area here treated formed part of Bampton's early *parochia*, and boundaries hardened relatively late, in some parishes remaining unusually complex until 19th-century rationalization.

Most parishes here treated were agricultural communities supported from mixed farming; they looked to markets at Oxford, Witney, and Great Faringdon (formerly Berks.), and earlier to Bampton, which had a market by 1086 but which by the later Middle Ages was itself predominantly agricultural. Standlake had a small market in the Middle Ages. There was some early inclosure at Lower Haddon, Chimney, and Shifford (all in Bampton), and at Northmoor, but elsewhere parliamentary inclosure was delayed until the early or mid 19th century. Fast-flowing rivers prompted early building of mills both for corn-grinding and for fulling, and until the late 17th century there was textile and leather working notably at Standlake and Bampton. Fishing rights in the rivers and numerous streams were noted frequently.

[30] Arundel Castle, MS. M 535; Longleat House, NMR 3315.

[31] P.R.O., E 317/Oxon./1; B.L. Add. MS. 27535, f. 45; ibid. Map C 7 e 16 (3), p. 36; Longleat House, NMR 3315; Arundel Castle, MS. TP 100.

[32] B.L. Map C 7 e 16 (3), p. 36.

[33] Arundel Castle, MS. TP 100; Pigot, *Lond. & Prov. Dir.* (1830); Giles, *Hist. Bampton*, 53; cf. *Rtns. of Co., Hund. and Borough Cts.*, H.C. 338 (1839), xliii, omitting Bampton.

[34] O.R.O., Tice I/vii/3; ibid. Crowdy I/51, lot 20.

[35] P.R.O., E 179/255/4, pt. i, ff. 19–33v.; ibid. pt. iii, ff. 234–51; O.R.O., QSM II/7, p. 456; *Oxon. Justices* (O.R.S. xvi), 20, 47, 65.

[36] F. Emery, *Oxon. Landscape*, 156; below, Bampton, general intro.

[37] e.g. D. Benson and D. Miles, *Upper Thames Valley, an Arch. Surv. of the River Gravels*, 30–51.

[38] Cf. J. Blair, *A.-S. Oxon.* 130–2.

The villages are built chiefly of local limestone rubble with thatched or stone-slated roofs, but several late-medieval timber-framed houses survive, including some of high status at Standlake and Yelford. Other high-status medieval buildings were of stone, from Taynton and elsewhere. Later houses of note, all stone-built, include Cokethorpe House, Cote House, and, in Bampton, Weald Manor and Bampton Manor House. Brick was introduced on a small scale in the 19th century, some of it locally manufactured at Aston in Bampton parish, and during the 20th century several villages were enlarged in a variety of building materials, chiefly to accommodate newcomers working in Witney or Oxford. A concentration of moated sites at Standlake, Yelford, and Northmoor presumably reflected drainage rather than defensive requirements.

BAMPTON

BAMPTON,[1] the centre of an Anglo-Saxon royal estate and hundred, site of a late Anglo-Saxon minster, and formerly a market town, lies close to the river Thames *c.* 12½ miles (20 km.) west of Oxford and 4½ miles (7½ km.) south-west of Witney.[2] The ancient parish, part of a much larger *parochia* dependent on Bampton minster,[3] was the largest in Oxfordshire, comprising 11,238 a. in 1877[4] and including the townships

Bampton and Standlake until the 20th century, is treated under Standlake. Bampton, Weald, and Lower Haddon, called townships in the Middle Ages[5] and each with their own fields, were combined for most civil purposes from the 17th century, and in the 19th became a civil parish of 4,491 a.[6] Shilton meadow (36 a.) by the Thames, a detached part of Shilton parish (formerly Berks.), seems to have been included in

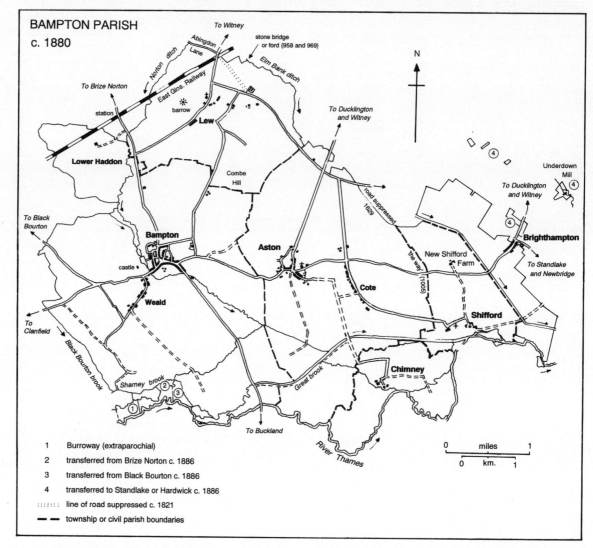

BAMPTON PARISH c. 1880

1	Burroway (extraparochial)
2	transferred from Brize Norton c. 1886
3	transferred from Black Bourton c. 1886
4	transferred to Standlake or Hardwick c. 1886

∷∷∷∷ line of road suppressed c. 1821

– – – township or civil parish boundaries

or hamlets of Bampton, Weald (from an early date physically part of Bampton), Lew, Aston and Cote, Shifford, Chimney, and Lower Haddon, the last three all shrunk or deserted settlements. All those townships are treated below, and Brighthampton, divided between

Bampton for civil purposes by the early 19th century,[7] and detached meadows belonging to Brize Norton (12 a.) and Black Bourton (27 a.) were added in 1886 under the Divided Parishes Act, bringing the total acreage to 4,530 a. (1,832 ha.).[8] Aston and Cote, a single township with a

---

[1] The help of Dr. J. Blair of The Queen's College, Oxford, who made available extensive unpublished work on Anglo-Saxon and early medieval Bampton, is gratefully acknowledged. This article was completed in 1992, and includes minor revisions until 1995.

[2] The principal O.S. maps used were 1/2,500, Oxon. XXXI. 14–16, XXXVII. 2–4, 6–8, 10–12, 14–16, XXXVIII. 1, 5–6, 9–10, 13 (1876 and later edns.); 1/2,500, SP 3002–3102, 3003–3103 (1971 edn.); 6", Oxon. XXXI, XXXVII–XXXVIII (1884 and later edns.); 1/25,000, SP 20/30 (1977 edn.).

[3] Below, this section; below, Bampton and Weald, churches.

[4] O.S. *Area Bk.* (1877).

[5] e.g. P.R.O., E 179/161/10; *Select Coroners' Rolls* (Selden Soc. ix), 93.

[6] *Census*, 1881, 1911; below, Bampton and Weald, econ. hist., local govt.; Lower Haddon, econ. hist.

[7] *Census*, 1801–81; O.S. *Area Bk.* (1877); cf., however, O.R.O., Shilton tithe award (1841) and amendment (1857).

[8] O.R.O., RO 277; *Census*, 1891, 1981; O.S. Map 6", Oxon. XXXVII (1884 edn., revised after 1886): copy in Bodl.

shared field system, became in the 19th century a civil parish of 2,997 a.; Lew (1,642 a.), Shifford (775 a.), and Chimney (668 a.), all independent townships, became separate civil parishes. In 1931 Aston and Cote was united with Chimney to form a new civil parish of Aston Bampton, enlarged to 4,440 a. (1,797 ha.) in 1954 by the addition of Shifford. Lew (664 ha.) remained unaltered in 1981.[9] Burroway, an area of meadow by the Thames also treated below, was artificially delineated in 1851 as an extraparochial area of 31 a., evidently less than its earlier extent. It was added to Clanfield c. 1886.[10]

The boundaries of Bampton's perhaps already diminished *parochia* were described in 1318, when they coincided only partly with later parish boundaries and included Clanfield, Black Bourton, parts of Alvescot and Ducklington, Yelford, Standlake, part of Northmoor, and a small area later in Stanton Harcourt. Presumably those boundaries reflected earlier arrangements, though they departed in some details from known pre-Conquest estate boundaries, and by 1318 seem to have been tendentious; by then some later parish boundaries within the former *parochia* were already hardening.[11] The later ancient parish of Bampton[12] was bounded on the south and south-west by the Thames, as in 1318, and by Burroway, Sharney, and Black Bourton brooks; at the south-west corner the boundary through intermixed meadows between the brooks was defined by the inclosure commissioners in 1839 and 1851, and was revised in 1886.[13] The rest of the western boundary followed furlongs and old inclosures, and, further north, Norton ditch, evidently the Marsh Haddon brook mentioned in the boundaries of 1318.[14] The ancient parish's northern boundary followed part of an ancient route called Abingdon Lane, and, by 1767, a zig-zag line between Lew and Curbridge heaths, which ran to Elm Bank ditch; in 969, however, the boundary seems to have run from the lane (then called the 'old way') to the ditch along a lost branch road, which continued across a stone bridge or ford mentioned in 10th-century charters.[15] That part of the boundary may have been adjusted before 1044 when an account of Witney's contiguous boundaries ignored both the ford and the road and mentioned only a 'new ditch', but the account seems to have omitted several boundary points[16] and it seems more likely that the later

parish boundary resulted from a post-medieval division of common pasture. *Horninga maera* (the boundary of the *Horningas*), mentioned in descriptions of Witney's bounds both in 969 and 1044, was preserved in the medieval name Horningmere, denoting land apparently in Lew; Lew slade, also mentioned in 1044, may have been an alternative name for Norton ditch.[17] 'Annieslou', mentioned in 1318 and referring probably to a marshy place (O.E. *sloh*), was apparently at the intersection of Norton ditch and Abingdon Lane.[18]

Elm Bank ditch formed the north-eastern boundary as far as the southern edge of Barley Park wood (in Ducklington parish) in the 10th century and later,[19] though in 1318 deponents alleged that the boundary of Bampton's *parochia* followed a path, apparently Abingdon Lane, which met the ditch (then called 'Bernelesdych' or Barley ditch) apparently also near the wood. The boundary described may thus have excluded the north-eastern corner of the later parish, but there is no further evidence for boundary changes in that area, and deponents may, as in Ducklington, have cited a convenient road merely as an approximate landmark.[20] From Elm Bank ditch, called the brook of Aegel's spring in 958, the boundary of the ancient parish followed a complex series of field boundaries between the later Claywell and Newhouse Farms, partly described in a 10th-century account of Ducklington's boundaries;[21] from there it followed the line of early roads towards Shifford and Brighthampton, preserved in a notably straight stretch of Aston township's eastern boundary near Yelford, and in Shifford township's straight northern boundary.[22] The ancient parish's eastern boundary with Standlake remained ill defined until the 19th century except through Brighthampton hamlet, where it followed tenurial divisions; a new boundary was established at Standlake's inclosure c. 1853, and detached parts of Bampton parish defined at that date were transferred to Standlake or Hardwick c. 1886.[23] Combe Hill, in Lew township's southern part, was said in 1708 to be tithable to Yelford, but remained part of Bampton and later of Lew parish.[24]

The ancient parish was mostly flat and low lying (c. 65–70 m.), though a steep rise near Lew's southern boundary, reflected in early furlong names,[25] attains over 80 m., and Lew

9 O.R.O., RO 277, RO 615; *Census*, 1881–1991, giving Lew's area in 1991, without comment, as 663 ha.; O.S. Map 6", Oxon. XXXVII (1884, revised after 1886). For the part of Brighthampton in Bampton parish, below, Standlake, intro.

10 O.R.O., Burroway incl. and tithe awards; O.S. Map 6", Oxon. XXXVII (1884 edn.); *Census*, 1881–91.

11 D. & C. Exeter, MS. 2865; *V.C.H. Oxon.* xii. 267; below, Ducklington, Northmoor, Standlake, Yelford. Alvescot, Black Bourton, and Clanfield are reserved for treatment in a future vol.

12 O.S. Maps 6", Oxon. XXXI, XXXVII–XXXVIII (1883–4 edn.); above, map on p. 6.

13 O.R.O., Clanfield and Burroway incl. awards; O.S. Map 6", Oxon. XXXVII (1884 edn., revised after 1886).

14 B.L. Map C 7 e 16 (3), between pp. 34–5; D. & C. Exeter, MS. 2865.

15 Jefferys, *Oxon. Map* (1767); Grundy, *Saxon Oxon.* 80; *Oxoniensia*, lvii. 342–8; below, Lew, intro.

16 Grundy, *Saxon Oxon.* 82–3; below, Ducklington,

intro.

17 Grundy, *Saxon Oxon.* 80, 83; *Oxoniensia*, lvii. 344; *P.N. Oxon.* (E.P.N.S.), ii. 316 n.; D. & C. Exeter, MSS. 5100–1; cf. J. Blair, *A.-S. Oxon.* 131.

18 D. & C. Exeter, MS. 2865; *P.N. Elements* (E.P.N.S.), ii. 129.

19 Grundy, *Saxon Oxon.* 31–2; O.S. Map 6", Oxon. XXXI (1884 edn.); below, Ducklington, intro.

20 D. & C. Exeter, MS. 2865; below, Ducklington, intro.

21 Grundy, *Saxon Oxon.* 30–1; below, Ducklington, intro. A short stretch SW. of the wood was adjusted probably at Ducklington's inclosure: O.R.O., Bampton incl. award, plan VI; O.S. Map 6", Oxon. XXXI (1884 edn.).

22 Below, Aston and Cote, intro.; Shifford, intro.

23 Below, Standlake, intro.

24 O.R.O., QS/1708 Epiph./20; ibid. incl. award; O.S. Map 6", Oxon. XXXI (1884 edn.).

25 e.g. D. & C. Exeter, MS. 2931 ('Abovehulle' and 'Bynythehyll'); cf. B.L. Add. MS. 31323 III; O.R.O., MS. d.d. Par. Bampton a 2 (R).

barrow stands at 107 m. There are smaller hills south of Lower Haddon Farm, north of Bampton town, and south-east of Weald Lane. Much of the parish's southern part lay on alluvium,[26] which flooded frequently but provided some rich meadow and pasture; a large tongue of alluvium between Aston and Cote, used as commons until inclosure, reaches the parish's north-eastern edge. Along the southern boundary, the Thames splits into numerous small streams, a feature which has prompted comparison with the Dutch polderlands, and which was reflected in medieval fieldnames such as Rowney, described with adjoining meadows in the 13th century as an 'island'.[27] The parish's northern part, including most of Lew and Lower Haddon townships, lay chiefly on Oxford Clay, which caused drainage problems but provided some 'strong corn-growing land',[28] and there are smaller areas of Oxford Clay around Weald Lane, north of Aston village, and immediately north of Old Shifford. Lew village, Lower Haddon Farm, and houses along Weald Lane lie on clay, though most settlements, including the core of Bampton town and the outlying sites of the castle and the Beam, are sited on gravel terraces composed of Summertown–Radley or Flood Plain Terrace deposits. Gravel also underlay some of Weald's and Aston and Cote's open fields, and in the 19th century provided soils of varying quality.[29]

BAMPTON AND WEALD

THE townships of Bampton and Weald, together c. 4,034 a.,[30] adjoined the parish boundary on the south and south-west. Highmoor brook formed the north-western boundary presumably by the 15th century, when quitrents for a meadow on its west bank belonged to the lord of Haddon.[31] The northern boundary in the 18th century followed furlongs and old inclosures, the division in the north-west chiefly corresponding to that between demesne closes owned by Exeter cathedral (in Bampton), and closes attached to Bampton Earls manor (wholly or partly in Lew);[32] some sections may have corresponded with the boundaries of an estate at Bampton granted in the 10th century,[33] though the inclusion in Lew field in 1298 of 'Hangindelonde', presumably Hanging Lands, later in Bampton, suggests adjustment in the later Middle Ages.[34] The open-field section of the boundary was revised at inclosure between 1812 and 1821,[35] and by the later 19th century three closes in the north-west, belonging to Bampton Earls manor and perhaps formerly in Lew, were included in Bampton civil parish.[36] The township's eastern boundary was marked in the 18th century by hedges and fences dividing Aston and Cote's fields from Bampton's; a straight section south-west of Aston village resulted from partition of Aston's West moor between Aston and Bampton before the later 17th century, and the boundary west of Aston village may reflect a similar partition of shared pasture at Truelands.[37] Straight artificial boundaries in the south-east between Bampton's and Aston's meadows and around Shilton parish's detached lot meadow seem to have been established before inclosure,[38] though a map of 1789, perhaps in error, showed the later Bampton Inmead south of Isle of Wight brook as belonging to Aston.[39] Queenborough meadow, west of Tadpole bridge and tenurially part of Aston manor, seems to have been regarded in 1859 as within Bampton township.[40]

The boundary between Bampton and Weald ran in the 18th and 19th centuries up Cheapside from the Talbot Inn in the market place, along Church Street, and around the west side of the churchyard, bringing the Deanery, Churchgate House (the former south vicarage house), and much of the south-west part of the town into Weald, but leaving the church, Bampton Manor House, and all of Broad Street in Bampton.[41] With some notable exceptions that boundary corresponds to the early division of the town between the chief manors of Bampton Deanery and Bampton Doilly (north-west and south-east, mostly in Bampton), and Bampton Earls (mostly · south-west, and with lands lying mostly in Weald), and may indicate a planned distribution of land among different lords when the townships' later medieval fields were established.[42] Weald's fields, north-west and south of the town, were separated from Bampton's by Shill and Highmoor brooks and, further south, by a wedge of old inclosures, formerly part of Bampton moor.[43]

A unitary estate said in 1069 to have been granted to Bampton minster between 955 and 957 lay apparently in Bampton, Aston, and possibly parts of Weald and Lew, suggesting that the later township boundaries were

[26] Geol. Surv. Map 1/50,000, solid and drift, sheet 236 (1982 edn.).
[27] F. Emery, *Oxon. Landscape*, 156; *Cal. Chart. R. 1226–57*, 235, 246; cf. *P.N. Oxon.* (E.P.N.S.), ii. 304, s.v. Rushey.
[28] Ch. Ch. Arch., MS. Estates 74, ff. 132–5; below, Lew, econ. hist.
[29] e.g. Jesus Coll. Mun., box 15, list 3, farm rep. 16 May 1873; ibid. list 4, surv. and valuation 14 Nov. 1864.
[30] Excluding Lower Haddon: O.S. *Area Bk.* (1877); O.R.O., incl. award, s.v. Haddon. For boundaries, below, map on p. 32.
[31] O.R.O., incl. award; D. & C. Exeter, MSS. 5100–6.
[32] B.L. Add. MS. 31323 III; ibid. Map C 7 e 16 (3), p. 35; O.R.O., incl. award, plans II and VI.
[33] Below, this section.
[34] B.L. Add. Ch. 67114; cf. ibid. Add. MS. 31323 III.
[35] O.R.O., MS. d.d. Par. Bampton a 2 (R).
[36] Ibid. incl. award, s.v. Quy closes; O.S. Map 6", Oxon. XXXI (1884 edn.); cf. below, Lew, econ. hist.
[37] B.L. Map C 7 e 16 (3), p. 35; ibid. Add. MSS. 31323 HHH, III; O.R.O., Misc. WA I/1, f. 9. The name Truelands occurs on both sides of the boundary.
[38] O.R.O., MS. d.d. Par. Bampton a 2 (R); ibid. incl. award, plan IV; ibid. Shilton tithe award (1841); ibid. Aston and Cote tithe map (1841).
[39] D. & C. Exeter, MS. M 1.
[40] *Cal. Chart. R. 1226–57*, 235, 246; O.R.O., MS. Oxf. Dioc. c 457/1, tithe award 1859.
[41] P.R.O., HO 107/872; ibid. RG 9/905; RG 11/1514; B.L. Map C 7 e 16 (3), map between pp. 34–5.
[42] B.L. Map C 7 e 16 (3), map between pp. 34–5; ibid. Add. MS. 31323 III; O.R.O., incl. award; below, this section; manors.
[43] Below, econ. hist. (agric.).

established after the mid 10th century.[44] From Kingsbridge, a crossing of Shill brook either at the end of modern Bridge Street or further north near the Deanery, the estate's boundary ran up the brook to its confluence with the hollow or sunken brook, evidently Highmoor brook, which is in places deeply sunk and steep-sided. At Cynstane's tree it left the hollow brook to follow 'the way' until the foul brook's head, then followed that brook to the stone bridge, which later field names suggest was in Aston over a watercourse south-west of Newhouse Farm.[45] Presumably 'the way' was a road on or near the later northern boundary, perhaps running along the ridge on the northern edge of later Lew Leaze; the foul brook, whose name derived from the underlying clay, was presumably a stream, later lost, flowing south-eastwards from Lew into Aston. From the stone bridge the boundary followed another 'way' to the *burh* ditch, presumably south of the town, which it followed to rejoin Shill brook; that 'way' is unidentified, but may have survived as a north–south track to Aston village which crossed Stone Bridge furlong in Aston's Kingsway field.[46]

It has been suggested that the chief east–west route through Bampton formed part of an inferred minor Roman road which crossed the river Windrush at Gill Mill and continued through Weald towards Lechlade (Glos.), entering Bampton from the north-east perhaps along the later Kingsway Lane, and passing just south of the later market place. The name Kingsway implies that the lane, a minor track in the 19th century, was an important route to the Anglo-Saxon royal *tūn*, and its projected course south of the later market place passes close to the sites of an early Anglo-Saxon *Grubenhaus* and of a medieval manor house.[47] Another inferred early road ran north-eastwards from Cowleaze Corner to cross the site of the Lady well and skirt the northern perimeter of the Deanery. Both roads may have formed part of a more extensive Roman and early medieval network running north-east to south-west and north-west to south-east, which was partly preserved in the later road and field pattern, and which influenced Bampton's early topography.[48] The road from Brize Norton, and a pre-inclosure road from Witney and Lew which formerly intersected it north of the town, were probably also ancient, and like the inferred Roman road seem to have been diverted to funnel into the market place perhaps in the 13th century;[49] the

Brize Norton road represented the end of a medieval saltway from Droitwich (Worcs.), where Bampton had salt rights in 1086.[50] Barcote way, south of the town, a small lane in 1789,[51] originated possibly as a southwards continuation of those roads, crossing the Thames at or near Rushey weir and continuing to Barcote in Berkshire; Burroway ford, mentioned in 1671,[52] was presumably a river crossing further west.

The chief southerly route by the mid 18th century was that to Buckland and Abingdon, which crossed Isle of Wight brook by a ford and the Thames by a recently built wooden bridge at Tadpole or Kent's weir; it flooded frequently.[53] Heavy traffic passed presumably over Radcot bridge to the west or Newbridge to the east, so that from the later Middle Ages Bampton was bypassed both by the chief north–south routes, and by east–west ones between London and the Cotswolds, though traffic westwards to Lechlade and beyond was mentioned in the 16th century and later.[54] In the late 18th century there were reportedly no stoned roads to any of the surrounding hamlets, travellers 'striking across the common by which the town was surrounded and finding their way to Witney, Burford [or] Oxford ... in the best way they could'.[55] The name Bampton in the Bush, however, recorded from the 17th century,[56] referred probably to extensive heath and scrubland in the north of the parish rather than to its inaccessibility, and there is no evidence that Bampton's roads were worse than elsewhere.

A turnpike road from Witney was established in 1771, meeting the Brize Norton road in Lew township and continuing through Bampton to Clanfield to meet the Burford–Faringdon road.[57] The Brize Norton–Buckland road was turnpiked in 1777, and stone bridges were built over Isle of Wight and Meadow brooks and, *c.* 1789, at Tadpole bridge. Fines were instituted for those avoiding tolls by cutting across fields or meadows to Chimney, to cross the Thames presumably at Duxford ford.[58] The Bampton sections of both turnpikes, in 'excellent repair' *c.* 1793, were confirmed at inclosure in 1821 when the older road to Lew and Witney was suppressed; a new road to Lew and Yelford via later Coalpit Farm was established across former open fields, and a track from Cowleaze Corner to Black Bourton was confirmed as a 40-ft. carriageway.[59] Fisher's bridge, at the east end of the town and so called by 1672,[60] was rebuilt in 1825, Isle of Wight bridge in 1835, and Mill brook bridge, at the

44 *Jnl. Brit. Arch. Assoc.* xxxix (1883), 299–301; cf. J. Blair, *A.-S. Oxon.* 131.

45 O.R.O., Aston and Cote tithe map; B.L. Add. MS. 31323 HHH.   46 Below, Aston and Cote, intro.

47 J. Blair, 'Ecclesiastical Topography' (Bampton Research Paper 3, priv. print. 1990), 1–3: copy in C.O.S.; *S. Midlands Arch.* xix (1989), 49–50; below, this section; manors (Bampton Doilly). For Kingsway Lane, O.R.O., Aston and Cote incl. award [roads]; J. Blair, *A.-S. Oxon.* 131, which misplaces it.

48 Blair, 'Eccl. Topog.' 1–2.

49 Ibid. 1–2. For those and other roads, below, map on p. 32.

50 *P.N. Oxon.* (E.P.N.S.), i. 3; *Trans. Birmingham Arch. Soc.* liv (1929–30), 14; *V.C.H. Oxon.* i. 400.

51 B.L. Map C 7 e 16 (3), map between pp. 34–5.

52 Longleat House (Wilts.), NMR 3315, ct. 27 Sept. 1671.

53 O.R.O., P4/2/MS 1/5, f. 5; Asthall–Buckland Turnpike Act, 17 Geo. III, c. 105, pp. 1, 15: copy in Bodl.; Oxf. Jnl. Synopsis, 11 June 1777, 30 Oct. 1789; Jefferys, *Oxon. Map* (1767).

54 P.R.O., REQ 2/198/14; O.R.O., Cal. Q.S. viii, p. 662; Oxf. Jnl. Synopsis, 12 May 1757; below, econ. hist. (agric.).

55 Giles, *Hist. Bampton*, 17 n.

56 e.g. *Writings and Speeches of O. Cromwell*, ed. W. C. Abbott, i. 343.

57 Witney–Clanfield Turnpike Act, 11 Geo. III, c. 73: copy in Bodl.; below, Lew, intro.

58 Asthall–Buckland Turnpike Act, 17 Geo. III, c. 105; Oxf. Jnl. Synopsis, 11 June 1777, 30 Oct. 1789.

59 *Univ. Brit. Dir.* ii [1793], 252–3; O.R.O., incl. award; above, map on p. 6.

60 Longleat House, NMR 3315, ct. 9 Apr. 1672.

town's west end, in 1877, when it was found to have been near collapse, and repairs to Meadow Arch bridge were required in 1878.[61] Roads in 1864 were 'not in the best condition',[62] and the two turnpikes were disturnpiked in 1874.[63]

River transport was important from the early Middle Ages.[64] An artificial watercourse west of the Deanery, 16 m. wide and rubble-revetted on its west side, may have been part of a navigable canal feeding into Great brook, and thence to the Thames at Shifford; its course north of the Deanery is marked by shallow depressions and, probably, by a notably straight stretch of Highmoor brook. It had been backfilled by the end of the Middle Ages.[65] A 'considerable' coal wharf near Tadpole bridge existed perhaps by 1808 and certainly by 1854, and continued reportedly until 1877.[66]

From the 1840s carriers linked Bampton with Faringdon Road Station on the G.W.R.,[67] but in the 1860s rail links westwards remained circuitous, and proposed improvements were enthusiastically supported by townspeople.[68] The East Gloucestershire Railway from Witney to Fairford, with a station, called Bampton Station, just north of the parish boundary, opened in 1873. It became part of the G.W.R. in 1890 and closed in 1962.[69]

Commercial inns existed in Bampton by the 18th century,[70] but no coaches are known before 1842 when there was a daily service from the Talbot Inn to Moreton-in-Marsh (Glos.) via Bourton on the Water and Stow (Glos.), and another to London using the railway.[71] Carriers from Bampton to London were mentioned in the 17th century,[72] and in the early 19th century carriers travelled to Oxford, with passengers also, and to Witney, Burford, and Faringdon (then Berks.).[73] In the 18th century letters were collected from Witney or Wantage (then Berks.) by private arrangement, but a receiving office was opened in Bampton in 1796, and a penny post from Witney was established in 1817.[74] The office dealt with money orders by 1864 and had a telegraph office by 1877.[75] Until the 1840s it was on Broad Street, in Waterloo House or its predecessor; thereafter until *c.* 1883 it was run by the printer George Holloway from premises on the west side of the market place, moving later to no. 7 High Street, before 1918 back to the market place, and by 1971 to the former Wheatsheaf public house on Bridge Street.[76] It remained open in 1994.

Groups of prehistoric cropmarks, some suggesting settlement, have been identified on the Thames-side gravels in the southern part of the townships.[77] A Bronze-Age ring ditch surrounding the medieval Deanery west of the church seems to be respected by the boundary ditch of the later minster enclosure, and presumably survived as a visible earthwork in the Anglo-Saxon period.[78] Burroway (i.e. *burh-īeg*), a gravel island in the Thames alluvium, is named from an Iron-Age defensive enclosure, whose ramparts, incorporating much burnt clay, survive as substantial earthworks,[79] and a large Iron-Age and Romano-British settlement existed east of the later town around Aston road and Calais Farm.[80] Other Roman settlements have been identified south-west of the town in Primrose field, where a stone altar carved with a figure of the goddess Fortuna was found,[81] at the Royal Signals Station south-east of Weald Lane,[82] and near Meadow Farm.[83]

An early Anglo-Saxon *Grubenhaus* was excavated south of the market place in the grounds of Folly House,[84] but the most extensive finds of that date have been further east near Calais Farm, on the edge of the Iron-Age and Romano-British site. Besides settlement remains,[85] they include scattered burials from a probably mid-Saxon cemetery, including one with a 7th-century bronze pin and another with a bone pin-beater. Beam Cottage, nearby, was the site of the medieval chapel of St. Andrew 'of Beme', so called by 1317; an early 12th-century shaft base was found built into the cottage, and burials around it produced radiocarbon dates from the 11th century to the 13th. The 'beam' itself (O.E. *bēam*, 'tree', 'post', or 'pillar') may have been an upstanding ritual landmark, possibly a cross; the

[61] H. J. Tollit, *County Bridges Rep.* (1878), 12–14, 30–2, 51–2, 69–71; *List of County and other Bridges* (1845): copies in Bodl.

[62] *Oxf. Chron.* 23 Jan. 1864.

[63] Turnpike Acts, 37 & 38 Vic. c. 95; *Return of Roads Disturnpiked*, H.C. 353, p. 7 (1878), lxvi.

[64] e.g. B.L. MS. Cotton Nero A xii, ff. 47v.–50, mentioning river traffic from Radcot; *Oxoniensia*, lii. 93 n.; below, Aston and Cote, intro.; Chimney, intro.; Shifford, intro.

[65] *S. Midlands Arch.* xxii (1992), 55–6.

[66] Bodl. MS. Ch. Oxon. 5273; *P.O. Dir. Oxon.* (1854); *Dutton, Allen & Co.'s Dir. Oxon.* (1863); F. S. Thacker, *Thames Highway* (1968), ii. 67.

[67] *P.O. Dir. Oxon.* (1847 and later edns.); *Oxf. Chron.* 20 June 1840; cf. E. T. MacDermot and C. R. Clinker, *Hist. G.W.R.* i. 53–4.

[68] *Oxf. Chron.* 25 Oct., 8 Nov. 1845, 23 Jan., 28 May 1864.

[69] MacDermot and Clinker, *Hist. G.W.R.* ii. 13–15, 40 and n.; C. R. Clinker, *Reg. Closed Passenger Stns.* ii. 16; O.S. Map 6", Oxon. XXXI (1884 edn.).

[70] Below, this section.

[71] Pigot, *Royal Nat. & Comm. Dir.* (1842).

[72] D. & C. Exeter, MS. 1979, p. 2; J. Taylor, *Carriers Cosmographie* (1637), s.v. Bampton, probably but not certainly Oxon.: copy in Bodl.

[73] Pigot, *Lond. & Prov. Dir.* (1830); *Royal Nat. &*

[...] *Comm. Dir.* (1842); T. S. Allen, *Original Rhymes* (1826), 28–9: copy in Bodl.

[74] D. & C. Exeter, MS. 6016/6, R. Coxeter to D. & C. 16 May 1711; P.O. Arch., POST 40/37, no. 50K; POST 42/71, pp. 436–7; POST 42/104, pp. 438–9, 473.

[75] *P.O. Dir. Oxon.* (1864 and later edns.); cf. P.O. Arch., POST 35/78, p. 100; POST 35/103, p. 189.

[76] O.R.O., incl. award, no. 432; P.R.O., HO 107/872, HO 107/1731; Jesus Coll. Mun., box 15, list 7, *Sale Cat.* (1918); *P.O. Dir. Oxon.* (1854 and later edns.); *Kelly's Dir. Oxon.* (1883 and later edns.); O.S. Maps 1/2,500, Oxon. XXXVII. 7 (1876 and later edns.); SP 3003–3103 (1971 edn.).

[77] D. Benson and D. Miles, *Upper Thames Valley, an Arch. Survey of the River Gravels*, 36–9. This and the following two paragraphs are based on a draft by J. Blair.

[78] *S. Midlands Arch.* xxii (1992), 55–7.

[79] Ibid. xi (1981), 103; C.O.S., PRN 2426, 5483.

[80] *S. Midlands Arch.* xvii (1987), 80; xviii (1988), 73; Ashmolean Mus., Dept. of Antiquities, Bampton file; C.O.S., PRN 1531, 2247, 3265, 3301.

[81] *S. Midlands Arch.* xviii. 73–4; xix. 47–9.

[82] Royal Signals Arch. Club, *Report* (1967); C.O.S., PRN 1528, 2572, 4243–4, 4270, 4293.

[83] C.O.S., PRN 8199.

[84] *S. Midlands Arch.* xxii (1992), 56.

[85] Ibid. xvii. 80; xviii. 73.

name Bampton (*tūn* by the *bēam*) suggests that it was an early and important focus, from which the later, probably mid Anglo-Saxon royal and ecclesiastical centre further west was named.[86]

By the early 8th century Bampton may have been important: it featured prominently in 12th-century accounts of the life of St. Frideswide which drew probably on earlier traditions,[87] and its possession of salt rights in Droitwich (Worcs.) suggests links with the distribution network of 8th- and 9th-century Mercia.[88] A minster on the site of the later church existed probably by 955–7, when King Eadwig reportedly granted land 'to the holy man of Bampton and the community';[89] presumably the holy man was St. Beornwald, to whom the church was later dedicated and who may have been an early head of the community.[90] By the 11th century a *tūn* in the area of the later town formed the centre of a considerable royal demesne, which besides the later royal manor included Clanfield, said in 1086 to be 'of the king's first fee', and Brize Norton (Bampton's north *tūn*), divided before 1066 into 1-hide holdings for royal thegns.[91] Though no archaeological evidence has been found a royal manor house may have occupied the site of the later castle on the town's western edge, and castle and church face each other across Shill brook, which in the 10th century separated their respective core lands.[92]

Weald, denoting woodland and, later, open country, was recorded by name from the late 12th century, and was a separate township by the 13th.[93] Possibly it originated as a separate settlement along the putative east–west route from Gill Mill, though in the later Middle Ages Weald Lane seems to have led only to commons along the parish's western edge.[94] There was settlement at the lane's northern end probably by *c.* 1170, when Osney abbey acquired a house apparently on the site of Weald Manor Farm.[95]

Domesday Book did not generally differentiate tenants in Bampton and Weald from those in other hamlets, though the total of 111 *villani*, *buri*, *bordarii*, and *servi* on the three chief manors in 1086 may indicate a large population in the town.[96] Fifteen freeholders, some probably non-resident, and 95 villeins and cottagers were listed in 1279, but at least 30 cottagers mentioned in 1317 were omitted, and in all there may have

been over 120 households.[97] Despite the recent grant of a market and fair the economy may even then have been predominantly agricultural, and widespread division of holdings suggests pressure on resources.[98] The population probably continued to rise in the early 14th century, and in 1377 poll tax was paid by 367 inhabitants over 14;[99] the impact of the Black Death may therefore have been relatively limited.

By the early 15th century there were signs of contraction, and the population was apparently falling, several holdings remaining unoccupied for long periods and some being abandoned.[1] Bampton remained a relatively small and impoverished community of farmers and small tradesmen with a few resident gentry,[2] though 91 inhabitants contributed to the subsidy of 1542–3,[3] and from the 1580s the population seems to have increased slowly but steadily despite temporary falls in the birth rate.[4] Over 200 male inhabitants were named in the Protestation Return of 1641–2, and in 1662 a total of 96 householders were taxed on 268 hearths,[5] suggesting a 17th-century population of over 500 and rather more than 100 houses. Estimates by 18th-century vicars implied a falling number of houses in the parish as a whole,[6] but the birth rate continued to rise and usually to exceed the death rate, and by 1801 there were 215 houses in Bampton and Weald, 8 of them unoccupied, and 1,003 inhabitants.[7] Mortality was unusually high in 1546, 1610, 1729, and 1768, the last year marked by an outbreak of 'contagious fever', and a lesser peak in 1819 was perhaps caused by choleraic fever which had broken out among the Witney poor the previous year.[8] Other references to fever or smallpox in the late 17th century and the 18th[9] were not reflected in mortality rates.

From the 1820s poverty and unemployment[10] prompted large scale emigration to America and the British colonies, which was actively promoted by the vestry and continued in the 1850s.[11] The population nevertheless rose sharply until 1831 and more slowly until 1861, when it reached 1,713 accommodated in 393 houses, with another 15 unoccupied. It fell steadily to 1,104 in 1921, returning to mid 19th-century levels only from the 1960s as limited expansion took place, and in 1991 the population was 2,459.[12]

86 Ibid. xvi. 87; xvii. 80; J. Blair, 'Eccl. Topog.' *passim*; below, churches.   87 *Oxoniensia*, lii. 90–3.
88 *V.C.H. Oxon.* i. 400; J. Blair, *A.-S. Oxon.* 84–6.
89 Recited in a confirmation of 1069: *Jnl. Brit. Arch. Assoc.* xxxix (1883), 299–301.
90 *Oxoniensia*, xlix. 47–55; below, churches; cf., however, *Early Med. Europe*, iv (1), 103 and n.
91 *V.C.H. Oxon.* i. 400, 415–16; below, manors. For the east *tūn*, below, Aston and Cote, intro.
92 Above, this section [boundaries]; below, manors (castle); cf. D. & C. Exeter, MS. M 1; B.L. Add. MS. C 7 e 16 (3), map between pp. 34–5.
93 *P. N. Oxon.* (E.P.N.S.), ii. 305, 470; above, this section. For East Weald (later Claywell), below, Ducklington.
94 Below, econ. hist. (agric.).   95 Below, Lew, manor.
96 *V.C.H. Oxon.* i. 400, 402, 414, including tenants in Aston and Cote, Chimney, and Lew: below, manors.
97 D. & C. Exeter, MS. 2931; *Bampton Hund. R.* 18–20, 23–4, 28–9.   98 Below, econ. hist.
99 P.R.O., E 179/161/8–10; E 179/161/42.
1 Below, econ. hist. (agric.); churches [vicarage hos.].

2 Below, econ. hist.
3 P.R.O., E 179/162/234; cf. ibid. E 179/161/173, E 179/161/179, E 179/162/341.
4 C.O.S., par. reg. transcripts, analyzed in 'Bampton: a Demographic Hist. Geography' (Leicester Univ. Centre for Urban Hist. unpubl. research project, 1990).
5 P.R.O., E 179/255/4, pt. i, ff. 19–20; *Protestation Rtns. and Tax Assess.* 6–7; cf. *Hearth Tax Oxon.* 221–3; *Compton Census*, ed. Whiteman, 417, 422.
6 O.R.O., MSS. Oxf. Dioc. d 555, f. 29; d 558, f. 33; d 564, f. 29.   7 *Census*, 1801.
8 C.O.S., par. reg. transcripts; O.R.O. MS. d.d. Par. Bampton b 10, f. 34v.; C. Creighton, *Hist. Epidemics in Britain*, ii (1894), 170.
9 O.R.O. MSS. d.d. Par. Bampton b 10, f. 44v.; b 11, ff. 128 and v., 177v.; b 12, ff. 20v., 28v., 29v., 92v.; b 13, f. 28; *Secker's Corresp.* 74.
10 Below, econ. hist. (agric.); local govt. (par. govt.).
11 O.R.O. MS. d.d. Par. Bampton c 8, ff. 105, 131, 133, 149v., 150v., 173v., 177v., 203v.; *Oxf. Chron.* 16 Feb. 1850; *Oxf. Jnl.* 6 Nov. 1858.
12 *Census*, 1801–1991.

The former minster estate at Kingsbridge seems to have included virtually the whole of the later town,[13] and Bampton is a classic instance of a 'monastic town' formed around an important church. Almost certainly the minster occupied the site of the later parish church, on a small natural hillock in the Gravel Terrace: human bones excavated in the churchyard pro-

medieval (and possibly late 11th-century) chapel in the Deanery west of the church, and a 15th-century chantry chapel on Catte (later Queen) Street.[18] Though not all those sites were necessarily pre-Conquest, the basic arrangement was probably a relic of the Anglo-Saxon minster, and may help to explain the complexity of the town subsequently superimposed on it.

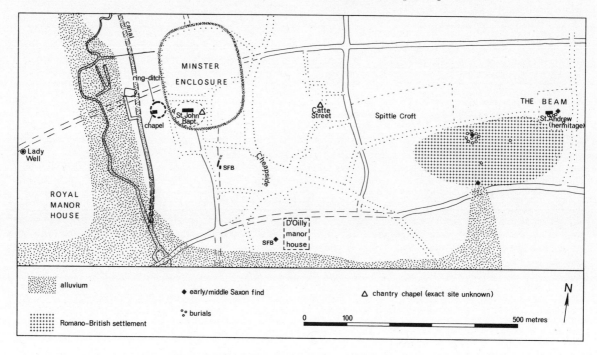

BAMPTON'S EARLY TOPOGRAPHY
Inferred roads in broken line; later roads in dotted line.

duced radiocarbon dates in the 9th or early 10th century, and a pre-Conquest church or chapel may underlie the north transept.[14] A large oval enclosure of a kind widely recognized on monastic sites in Britain and Ireland,[15] and whose outline is preserved in the line of Landells Lane and in the curving south churchyard-wall, surrounded the later churchyard, the site of the houses on its east and north sides, and further north the site of Bampton Manor House; excavations in the churchyard's north-west corner revealed a perimeter ditch 4 metres wide with 11th-century pottery in its fill.[16] In the late 11th century or the 12th the ditch was backfilled, and a north–south road bounded by ditches was laid out across its western edge, crossing the western part of the later churchyard and apparently continuing Landells Lane, named from the 14th-century Laundels family, southwards to Mill bridge.[17] An early alignment of holy sites running from west to east included, besides the church and the Beam chapel, the Lady well in the north-west corner of the castle moat, a

Church View, running south from the churchyard, may have been the site of the 11th-century market before encroachment on its eastern side reduced it to a narrow lane. On topographical grounds it almost certainly formed a major thoroughfare linking the Brize Norton road with Barcote way, and excavations to the east revealed a sunken-floored building of a type associated with late Anglo-Saxon urban frontages.[19] The market may thus have originated on minster land, though by 1066 the Crown had seized it with the rest of the minster estate, and it remained attached to the royal manor thereafter.[20]

The town seems to have been replanned probably in the 12th or 13th century. A large triangular market place was laid out south-east of the church enclosure, perhaps in 1241 when a new market was granted by Henry III; roads apparently diverted to funnel into it included the Brize Norton road, which thereafter ran along Broad Street, and the east–west route passing near the sites of the Anglo-Saxon *Grubenhaus* and of an early manor house, which thereafter

[13] Above, this section [boundaries]. This and the following two paragraphs were written by J. Blair.
[14] *S. Midlands Arch.* xxii (1992), 55; below, churches.
[15] Cf. *Pastoral Care before the Parish*, ed. J. Blair and R. Sharpe, 229–35.
[16] *S. Midlands Arch.* xviii. 89–90.
[17] Ibid. xxii (1992), 55–8; below, other estates.

[18] Blair, 'Eccl. Topog.' *passim*; below, this section; churches.
[19] Excavations by J. Blair (1994); above, this section [roads]. An unexplained curving ditch was excavated immediately NW. of the building in 1995.
[20] *V.C.H. Oxon.* i. 400; below, manors (Bampton Deanery); econ. hist. (markets and fairs).

ran along High and Bridge Streets.[21] The churchyard was extended westwards to the Deanery boundary, obliterating the road which had replaced the early enclosure ditch, the other churchyard boundaries were squared up, and by the mid 13th century roads with cottage tenements existed along the north and east sides of the churchyard.[22] In that modified state the former oval enclosure retained a distinct identity as a settlement around the church, and in the late 13th century the northern part of its boundary was refortified with a timber palisade.[23]

The intricate network of back lanes was established by the later Middle Ages. Bushey Row, formerly New Inn Lane from a 19th-century public house near its southern end, may represent the original line of the road from Curbridge,[24] and Queen Street, so called (though not at first consistently) by 1830, was Catte Street in 1402.[25] Houses on Samford or Sandford Lane existed by the later 15th century.[26] Church Street, which in the 18th and 19th centuries marked part of the boundary between Bampton and Weald townships and whose north side was lined with houses held of the former minster estate, was presumably also early, and a house of possibly 15th-century origin survives on its south side.[27] Cheyne and Mill Green Lanes, leading from Bridge Street to the top of Weald Lane, and Rosemary Lane, from the market place to Church View, existed by the 18th century[28] and are probably also medieval.

Late medieval depopulation may have caused physical contraction, notably around the churchyard, where several cottages fell derelict and were absorbed into neighbouring curtilages.[29] In 1767[30] the limit of expansion was marked on the west by Ham Court and Bampton mill, on the north by Landells Lane and by later New Road, and on the east by Calais, earlier Callace, Farm. Houses on Rowles Lane, apparently the stretch of the Aston road near Calais Farm, were mentioned in the late 16th century,[31] but as the east end of High Street near Bushey Row was called Town (or Down) End in the 17th century,[32] expansion eastwards may have been relatively recent. Buckland road remained largely unsettled until the 19th century,[33] and until inclosure the only outlying houses were the former chapel

at the Beam, from the 17th century a copyhold cottage,[34] and the farmsteads and cottages along Weald Lane, some of them of 17th-century origin.[35] The market place suffered encroachment before the mid 18th century, when an island of buildings on its northern edge included tradesmen's premises and an inn,[36] and encroachment continued in the 19th century with the building of the National school, later demolished, at the top of Bridge Street, and of the town hall.[37] A market house, 'much ruined' in 1669,[38] was not mentioned later, and an 'ancient' market cross near the centre of the market place, apparently standing in 1777, had disappeared by 1848, as had a large hawthorn tree nearby.[39] The later war memorial cross, on the market place's north side east of the village hall, was erected in the early 1920s on the site of a house and wheelwright's shop.[40] Lavender Square, an open space where Queen Street enters the market place on the north, was so called by 1826.[41]

During the 19th century new building and improved amenities gradually transformed the town's appearance, said in 1847 to have been recently much improved.[42] An incoming vicar in 1872 noted the 'broad and clean' streets and 'tidy' rows of shops,[43] though High Street residents were still depositing household rubbish in the gutters in 1883,[44] and there was no permanent street lighting until c. 1887.[45] Some areas of apparently slum housing were cleared only in the early 20th century.[46]

From the late Anglo-Saxon period there seems to have been a high concentration of royal servants and officers in the Bampton area, several holding Crown land apparently in reward for their services.[47] Late 10th- and early 11th-century landholders in Bampton or its hamlets included Theoderic the goldsmith, Aelfwine the king's *scriptor* and minister, the thegn Bundi the forester, and Aretius the king's minister,[48] and in the later Middle Ages several Bampton inhabitants, some of them holders of modest estates and others bailiffs for non-resident lords, were active in royal service or local government, among them the king's buyer Paulinus of Bampton (fl. 1250),[49] Thomas Fettiplace (d. by 1446), M.P. for Oxfordshire,[50] and some members of

21 Blair, 'Eccl. Topog.'; below, manors (Bampton Doilly); econ. hist. (markets and fairs); maps on pp. 12, 18.
22 J. Blair, 'Medieval Clergy' (Bampton Research Paper 4, priv. print. 1991), 25-9: copy in C.O.S.; below, churches [vicarage hos.].
23 S. Midlands Arch. xvi (1986), 88-90.
24 Blair, 'Eccl. Topog.' fig. 2; O.S. Map 1/2,500, Oxon. XXXVII. 7 (1876 edn.); below, this section [inns].
25 D. & C. Exeter, MS. 6016/a; O.R.O., Mor. XIII/i/1-2; P.R.O., HO 107/872; ibid. RG 9/905.
26 Exeter Coll. Mun., M. II. 1: deeds re Sandford Ho.
27 O.R.O., incl. award; S. Midlands Arch. xxii. 57, 62; above, this section [boundaries].
28 Jefferys, Oxon. Map (1767); B.L. Add. MS. 31323 III.
29 Below, churches [vicarage hos.].
30 B.L. Add. MS. 31323 III; Jefferys, Oxon. Map (1767).
31 O.R.O., D.Y. II/i/1; cf. P.R.O., HO 107/872; ibid. RG 9/905.
32 O.R.O., Acc. 2184, New Inn deeds; ibid. D.Y. XV/i/1.
33 Ibid. incl. award.   34 Below, churches.
35 e.g. Old Farmhouse, at the lane's southern end.
36 B.L. Add. MS. 31323 III; ibid. Map C 7 e 16 (3), betw. pp. 34-5; O.R.O., incl. award.
37 Below, this section (buildings); educ.

38 Longleat House, Coventry pps. CVI, f. 87v.
39 Giles, Hist. Bampton, 15 n.; Asthall-Buckland Turnpike Act, 17 Geo. III, c. 105, pp. 1, 5, 7.
40 O.R.O., incl. award; O.S. Map 1/2,500, Oxon. XXXVII. 7 (1876 and later edns.); Kelly's Dir. Oxon. (1924).
41 T.S. Allen, Original Rhymes, 16.
42 P.O. Dir. Oxon. (1847); cf. Oxf. Chron. 25 Nov. 1838, 19 Nov. 1853; below, this section (buildings); local govt. (public services).
43 [E. G. Hunt], Music of a Merry Heart [1886], 191: copy in Bodl.
44 O.R.O., MS. d.d. Par. Bampton c 12, item k, s.a. 1883; cf. Oxf. Jnl. 8 Jan. 1859.
45 Below, local govt. (public services).
46 Below, this section (buildings).
47 For a possible royal palace at Bampton, above, this section; below, manors (castle).
48 Below, manors (Bampton); Aston and Cote, manors [other estates]; Shifford, manor.
49 Cal. Chart. R. 1226-57, 241; Oxon. Fines (O.R.S. xii), pp. 239-40; Rot. Hund. (Rec. Com.), ii. 30; Cal. Pat. 1247-58, index s.v. Bampton.
50 Complete Peerage, xii (1), 619-20 and n.; Cal. Pat. 1429-36, 623; 1436-41, 588.

the Laundels family.[51] John Walker (fl. 1380), Nicholas Wrenne (fl. 1442) and John Folkes (fl. 1449) were tax collectors for the county,[52] and in the 14th century royal inquisitions post mortem were held frequently at Bampton.[53] Letters patent or close were dated there in 1270, 1277, and 1328, after the manor had passed from royal hands.[54] The presence of a small but significant group of resident gentry, many of them local landowners and some still active in local government, continued throughout the 16th and 17th centuries, with families such as the Palmers, Coxeters, and Gowers,[55] and some other inhabitants called themselves gentleman or bachelor.[56]

Increasingly there was a professional element. Lawyers resident from the early 18th century included members of the Coxeter family,[57] Gascoigne Frederick (d. 1780) of Bampton Deanery Manor,[58] John Mander (d. 1809) of Bampton House,[59] and Robert Kirke (d. 1800) of Weald Manor, who served as consul at Algiers,[60] and from the early 19th century there were resident solicitors with businesses in the town.[61] By the mid 18th century there were two practising surgeons,[62] and another retired to Bampton in the late 1760s.[63] The leisured, landowning, and professional element continued into the 19th century,[64] and though numerically small exercised an important influence on the town's appearance, institutions, and general tone: an advertisement for a house in 1761 commented on its position in a 'genteel neighbourhood' and in good sporting country, listing among the town's advantages a weekly card assembly and the presence of resident apothecaries and physicians.[65] Bampton nevertheless remained too isolated, relatively poor, and agriculturally orientated ever to become especially fashionable, and in 1793 was described as a town chiefly of 'farmers and numerous poor, with several gentlemen and some reputable tradesmen'.[66] A

further aspect of its social character was the presence, from the Middle Ages, of West-Country immigrants, presumably servants or followers of the parochial clergy, who were mostly high-status ecclesiastics of Devon origin.[67] The name Devenish was recorded from the 14th century,[68] and in the 16th a man was accused of marrying in Bampton despite having a wife and children in Devon.[69] The Dotyn family, prominent later in the century, followed two vicars of that name,[70] and even in the mid 19th century a few inhabitants had been born in Devon.[71]

An inn was mentioned in 1573,[72] and from the mid 18th century there were usually c. 10 or more licensed alehouses and inns.[73] The Talbot Inn, on the south side of the market place, was so called by 1668 after the lords of the manor to which it belonged,[74] and in 1870 had stabling for 10 horses.[75] Though rebuilt or remodelled in the early 18th century[76] it was described in 1789 as 'very old' with 'small and inconvenient rooms', and c. 1811–13 a new room was added over the carriage entry.[77] The Bell, on the site of the later village hall, the Fleur de Lis, on the south-east side of the market place, and the Horse Shoe, at the top of Bridge Street, were inns probably by 1753.[78] The Bell was mentioned frequently, with the Talbot, as a venue for public meetings and auctions in the later 18th century,[79] and was a 'very regular inn' in 1826; it closed in the 1880s.[80] The Fleur de Lis closed in the early 1870s and was demolished in the early 20th century,[81] and the Horse Shoe, rebuilt c. 1925,[82] remained open in 1994. The Hermitage and Old Priory on Broad Street, let to a baker as the Red Lion in the 1780s and 1790s,[83] may have offered accomodation, and an undated sign found at the Morris Clown on High Street, opened as the George c. 1811 and called the New Inn from c. 1821 to 1975, described it as a posting house with livery stables.[84] Unidentified inns included the Roebuck, mentioned

51 Below, other estates.
52 *Cal. Fine R.* 1377–83, 58; 1437–45, 217; 1445–52, 124; *Cal. Pat.* 1381–5, 351; *Cal. Close,* 1385–9, 666–7. For Wrenne and Folkes, cf. D. & C. Exeter, MS. 6016/2/1; B.L. Harl. Roll L. 6–7, L. 10.
53 e.g. *Cal. Inq. p.m.* iv, p. 102; viii, p. 161; xi, p. 70; xiii, p. 161; xv, p. 39; xvi, p. 176; cf. *Cal. Pat.* 1272–81, 433.
54 *Cal. Pat.* 1266–72, 458–9,; 1272–81, 187–8; *Cal. Close,* 1272–9, 366–7, 409; 1327–30, 365; below, manors.
55 P.R.O., PROB 11/214, ff. 230–2; PROB 11/234, ff. 215v.–217; PROB 11/322, ff. 333v.–334; PROB 11/256, ff. 219–20; PROB 11/314, ff. 333v.–334v.; Bodl. MS. Top. Oxon. c 118, f. 11; *Bp. Fell and Nonconf.* p. xxiv; *Oxon. Visit.* (Harl. Soc. v), 335.
56 e.g. O.R.O., MSS. Wills Oxon. 78/4/1, 20/5/17, 128/1/7, 28/1/29, 173/2/52; *Cal. Fine R.* 1422–30, 180; *L. & P. Hen. VIII,* i (1), p. 822.
57 *Alum. Oxon. 1500–1714,* s.v. Coxeter; Bodl. MS. d.d. Harcourt c 3/9 (11); *Country Life,* c (1946), 257–8.
58 *Oxf. Jnl.* 29 Jan. 1780; below, manors.
59 *Univ. Brit. Dir.* ii [1793], 252–3; below, this section (buildings).
60 B.L. Map C 7 e 16 (3), p. 66; *Oxf. Jnl. Synopsis,* 13 Mar. 1790; C.O.S., par. reg. transcripts.
61 Below, econ. hist. (trade and ind.).
62 *Oxf. Jnl. Synopsis,* 3 Apr. 1756, 23 May 1761, 20 Aug. 1768, 6 Nov. 1773; *Univ. Brit. Dir.* ii [1793], 252–3.
63 Bodl. MS. Top. Gen. c 85/71; *Oxf. Jnl. Synopsis,* 2 Oct. 1776; *Alum. Oxon. 1715–1886,* s.v. Fortescue.
64 P.R.O., RG 9/905; *P.O. Dir. Oxon.* (1847 and later edns.).
65 *Oxf. Jnl. Synopsis,* 14 Mar. 1761.
66 *Univ. Brit. Dir.* ii [1793], 252–3; cf. Brewer, *Oxon.* 481.

67 Below, churches.
68 P.R.O., E 179/161/10; D. & C. Exeter, MS. 2931.
69 *Visit. Dioc. Linc.* i. 131.
70 O.R.O., MSS. Wills Oxon. 17/1/58, 17/1/61; Exeter Coll. Mun. M. II. 1; below, churches.   71 P.R.O., HO 107/1731.
72 *Oxon. Ch. Ct. Depositions,* ed. J. Howard-Drake, no. 129.
73 O.R.O., QSD V/1–4.
74 Longleat House, NMR 3315, ct. 4 Oct. 1668; Arundel Castle, MS. TP 288, no. 19; below, manors (Bampton Earls).
75 O.R.O., Crowdy I/51, lot. 52.
76 Arundel Castle, MS. TP 288, no. 19.
77 Ibid. MS. TP 91, s.a. 1811–13; B.L. Map C 7 e 16 (3), pp. 50–1, map between pp. 34–5; O.R.O., Bampton incl. award, plan I.
78 O.R.O., QSD V/1–4; ibid. DY XXXI/i/1; ibid. incl. award.
79 *Oxf. Jnl. Synopsis,* indexes s.v. Bell, Talbot, Wal. King, Onesimus Taylor.
80 T. S. Allen, *Orig. Rhymes* (1826), 5–6; *Kelly's Dir. Oxon.* (1883 and later edns.); cf. O.R.O., D.Y. XVI/iii/1; ibid. Misc. Me I/1; B.L. Add. Ch. 38955–7; C.O.S., OPA 4823.
81 *P.O. Dir. Oxon.* (1869, 1877); O.S. Map 1/2,500, Oxon. XXXVII. 7 (1876 and later edns.); cf. Bodl. MS. Top. Oxon. c 522, f. 21v.; C.O.S., OPA 82/764.
82 W. J. Monk, *Ramble in Oxon.* [c. 1925], advertisement in endpapers; cf. below, plate 4.
83 D. & C. Exeter, Ch. Comm. 13/74354, p. 34; ibid. 13/74363a, 80/134543.
84 O.R.O., Acc. 2184, New Inn deeds; ibid. incl. award, no. 919; ibid. QSD V/4; ibid. QSD L.22; sign on gable end 1992; local inf.

from 1660 to 1681,[85] the Three Compasses, mentioned in 1787, and the Crown, mentioned from 1774 to 1787.[86] The 'White Hart inn', mentioned from 1700 to 1715, was in a cottage, and may not have offered accommodation.[87] Numerous alehouses included one at Rushey weir licensed from 1796 to 1814,[88] the Plough on Broad Street, closed in 1923,[89] and the Lamb in the market place, associated with a smithy and other buildings and demolished following its closure c. 1956.[90] There were seven public houses in 1994, all of 19th-century origin except for the Talbot, the Horse Shoe, and the Romany, opened after 1946.[91]

A friendly or benefit society founded in 1751 was rescued from insolvency in 1797 by a subsidy from the poor rate.[92] Another was established in 1795,[93] and from the 1840s there were usually two: the Old Club, meeting at the Talbot and occasionally at the Fleur de Lis, and the Victoria Club, meeting at the Horse Shoe and later at the Wheatsheaf on Bridge Street.[94] A Court of the Ancient Order of Foresters met by 1869 at the Fleur de Lis and later at the New Inn, and continued into the later 20th century.[95] Penny readings (including musical items) and other entertainments were held frequently in the town hall or National school in the later 19th century, performers and organizers including local clergy, gentry, and farmers, and were well attended.[96] A Philharmonic Society was formed in 1870,[97] and Bampton brass band, established by 1869 when disagreement erupted with the vicar over custody of its new bass drum, continued in the early 20th century.[98] Holloway's 'theatre' near the church, mentioned in 1871 when *Hamlet* proved more popular than the competing harvest festival,[99] was not mentioned later and was perhaps a temporary sideshow. A cricket club, with its own ground, existed by 1859, and a football club by 1907,[1] and a horticultural society established in 1860 continued in the 20th century.[2] A reading society with its own librarian was mentioned in 1828 and revived in 1847,[3] and in the late 1860s and again in 1884 a subscription news and reading room was opened

in the town hall;[4] a charitable bequest in 1905 provided for annual payments of c. £5 to the men's and £2 to the boys' reading room.[5] A lending library mentioned from 1891 seems to have closed in the early 1920s;[6] a public library run by the County Council was opened in Rosemary House on the west side of the market place before 1957, and in 1964 was moved to the former grammar school on Church View.[7]

Rogation-week circuiting, mentioned in 1713,[8] continued until inclosure in the early 19th century. Beer and victuals were provided by the vicars and by farmers of the tithes, the circuiters' route reportedly taking them on the first day to Clanfield, where the farmer of Bampton's tithes provided breakfast, on the second to Lower Haddon and 'Heart's Yat' on Lew heath, and on the third to Aston and Cote; Shifford and Brighthampton were not explicitly mentioned. In the early 19th century the circuit was marked by crosses cut with a paddle, traditionally carried by a woman who had never been married.[9] The vicars' and tithe-owners' obligation to provide a breakfast of beer, beef, and bread on St. Stephen's day (26 December), also mentioned in 1713, similarly continued until inclosure, though an obligation to provide the 'harvest bottle' may have lapsed by the later 18th century.[10] May day celebrations, in which local children dressed as Lord, Lady, and Jack-in-the-Green, lapsed in the mid 19th century but survived in modified form at Whitsuntide in 1897,[11] and in the early 1990s children still paraded with wild flower garlands for which prizes were awarded.[12] A backsword contest and fair held on Whit Wednesday in 1753[13] suggest earlier Whitsuntide festivities. Payments in 1741 for ringing the church bells on Coronation day, the king's birthday, and 'Gunpowder Treason' day may indicate local celebrations on those occasions, and a local 'Gunpowder Plot Rhyme' was still current in 1894.[14]

Morris dancing in Bampton may be traced to the early 19th century and probably the late 18th, though claims that the Bampton Morris is the oldest in England with a continuous history

85 Longleat House, Coventry pps. CVI, ff. 35v., 87v.; O.R.O., MS. Wills Oxon. 7/2/28.
86 O.R.O., MS. Oxf. Dioc. c 654, ff. 90–1, 95 and v.; ibid. QSD V/2; cf. ibid. MS. Wills Oxon. 24/1/1.
87 Arundel Castle, MS. TP 288, no. 3; O.R.O., Cal. Q.S. iii, p. 440; cf. Bodl. MSS. d.d. Shrewsbury c 2/8 (16), c 3/9 (4), c 3/9 (22), c 4/10 (12).
88 O.R.O., QSD V/2–4; cf. F. S. Thacker, *Thames Highway* (1968), ii. 62–5.
89 O.R.O., Pocock III/38/1–2; Courage Arch., Bristol, EK/E/4, p. 127; C.O.S., OPA 4837, 4842.
90 O.R.O., Acc. 2184, Lamb deeds; ibid. incl. award, no. 458; P.R.O., RG 9/1451; C.O.S., OPA 4820, 19026; local inf.
91 *Country Life*, c (1946), 119; cf. O.R.O., incl. award; P.R.O., HO 107/872; ibid. RG 11/1514; Pigot, *Lond. & Prov. Dir.* (1830); *P.O. Dir. Oxon.* (1847 and later edns.); *Kelly's Dir. Oxon.* (1883 and later edns.).
92 O.R.O., MS. d.d. Par. Bampton c 8, ff. 13v.–14.
93 Ibid. Cal. Q.S. iii, p. 615.
94 *Oxf. Chron.* 8 July 1837, 6 June 1846, 17 June 1848, 17 Aug. 1850, 14 June 1851, 8 June 1855; *Witney Express*, 8 June 1871, 23 May 1872; *Oxf. Jnl.* 20 May, 3 June 1871.
95 *Witney Telegraph*, 26 Dec. 1868; J. L. Hughes-Owens, *The Bampton We Have Lost*, 98: copy in C.O.S.
96 *Oxf. Jnl.* 19 Nov., 26 Nov., 3 Dec. 1859; *Witney Telegraph*, 27 Oct. 1866, 24 Oct. 1868; *Witney Express*, 27

Oct. 1870; *Oxf. Jnl.* 25 Feb. 1871.
97 *Witney Express*, 17 Nov. 1870.
98 O.R.O., MS. d.d. Par. Bampton c 12, item g; *Kelly's Dir. Oxon.* (1907 and later edns.).
99 *Oxf. Jnl.* 30 Sept. 1871.
1 Ibid. 28 May, 23 July 1859; *Kelly's Dir. Oxon.* (1907 and later edns.).
2 *Witney Express*, 11 Aug. 1870; *Oxf. Mail*, 25 Aug. 1972.
3 Bodl. MS. Top. Oxon. e 632, f. 1; *Oxf. Chron.* 20 Mar. 1847.
4 *P.O. Dir. Oxon.* (1869); *Kelly's Dir. Oxon.* (1887).
5 O.R.C.C. Kimber files, bequest of Amelia Carter by will proved 1905.
6 *Kelly's Dir. Oxon.* (1891 and later edns.).
7 Bodl. MS. Top. Oxon. c 484/1, no. 4049; inf. from Major R. A. Colvile. 8 P.R.O., PROB 11/551, f. 252v.
9 Giles, *Hist. Bampton*, 57–8; Blenheim Mun., shelf J 4, box 19, legal opinion *re* Lower Haddon 8 Oct. 1842.
10 P.R.O., PROB 11/551, f. 252v.; Exeter Coll. Mun., M. II. 1, cert. 13 Oct. 1750; Giles, *Hist. Bampton*, 56–7; *Char. Don.* 966–7.
11 *Folklore*, viii, no. 4 (1897), 308–9.
12 *Bampton Beam*, viii, no. 2 (1993), 4: copy in C.O.S.; cf. *Oxf. Times*, 30 May 1958.
13 *Oxf. Jnl.* 26 May 1753.
14 O.R.O., MS. d.d. Par. Bampton b 10, f. 4v.; Bodl. MS. Top. Oxon. d 192, f. 115.

of over 300 years lack documentary support. By 1848 and probably earlier the side performed regularly at Whitsuntide, and by the 1870s appeared frequently in neighbouring villages; in the early 20th century it attracted visitors from as far as London and Birmingham. A rival side was established after the First World War, and there were three sides in 1995[15] when Whitsuntide dancing and other festivities continued. Christmas mummers were recorded in 1848, reportedly continuing an earlier, probably 18th-century tradition but with a new script, and the practice was revived in the later 20th century.[16] An annual Shirt Race established in 1953 continued in the 1990s.[17] A curfew bell, mentioned from the later 18th century, was rung in the 1950s but not by 1992.[18]

The Lady well, on the town's western edge, was known for its supposed healing properties apparently by the later 18th century, and it seems likely that the tradition was of medieval origin, reflecting the well's probable importance as an early religious site.[19] Its association with eye ailments suggests connections with the cult of St. Frideswide,[20] but in the 19th century it was associated with the Virgin, and in 1886 it was called Good Queen Anne's well.[21] Stonework survived in the mid 19th century, but the site was then overgrown and the tradition reportedly in decline; the well's restoration and 'inauguration' in 1848 reflected a more Romantic interest, perhaps inspired by a recently published account.[22] By the 1880s it was again 'choked up with tangled growths and rubbish', though bathing of infected eyes in its waters continued into the 20th century.[23]

The king's prison in Bampton was mentioned in 1259.[24] Social control may, as claimed in the 19th century,[25] have been facilitated by the presence of J.P.s and earlier of other officers, but Bampton experienced the usual outbreaks of occasional unrest: local gangs attacked Bampton mill in 1264 and one of the manor houses in 1353,[26] and in 1398 Bampton men were prominent in a treasonable uprising in west Oxfordshire; others may have been implicated in Bishop Merke's rebellion in 1400.[27] In the late 16th century the earl of Shrewsbury's bailiff at Ham Court (for-

merly Bampton castle) was persistently threatened by a rival's supporters, and claimed that his wife died of fright after a gun was fired.[28] Controversy over a surgeon's use of inoculation in the 1770s allegedly resulted in violence and intimidation, which drove him first to Aston and later out of the parish.[29] In 1835 there were riots following changes in the poor law,[30] and in 1872 use of soldiers to break strikes in the area reportedly 'envenomed a dispute hitherto carried on ... without the least desire ... of violence', provoking social antagonism which persisted ten years later.[31] A county prosecution association had Bampton subscribers by 1756, and a local association with a committee comprising leading gentry and clergy was set up c. 1778, when crime was said to be especially prevalent. It met usually at the Talbot or Bell inns and continued in the 1850s.[32]

The identification of Bampton with *Beandun*, where Cynegils allegedly defeated over 2,000 Britons in 614, lacks evidence.[33] King Stephen stormed Bampton in 1142 after the empress Maud established a garrison and fortified the church tower.[34] Forces under Cromwell, bound for Witney, skirmished near the town on 27 April 1645 with c. 300 royalist infantry returning to Faringdon; the royalists withdrew to a 'pretty strong house', presumably the castle, and barricaded the town. They surrendered the following day, and a local tradition that Cromwell slighted the castle is unsubstantiated.[35] In 1649 Fairfax marched through Bampton in pursuit of the Levellers.[36] Prominent Bampton men were accused in 1648–9 of having supplied the royalist garrison at Oxford,[37] and in 1661 John Hanks (d. 1669), seeking restoration of Bampton Deanery manor, claimed to have been in arms for the king at Oxford.[38] Relics with Jacobite slogans, bearing the name of Martha Frederick (d. 1768), were found at Bampton Manor House, but there is no evidence that other family members were implicated.[39]

The poet John Philips (d. 1709) was born at Bampton in 1676, a son of one of the vicars.[40] Sir Frederick Whitaker (d. 1891), premier of New Zealand, was born there in 1812, a son of the lessee of Bampton Deanery manor.[41] F. W.

15 K. Chandler, 'Morris Dancing at Bampton until 1914' (priv. print. 1983): copy in C.O.S.; C. J. Sharp and H. C. MacIlwaine, *Morris Bk.* iii. 37–9; *Folklore*, viii, no. 4 (1897), 309–10, 317–24; local inf.

16 Giles, *Hist. Bampton*, 60, 177–8; local inf.

17 *Bampton Beam*, vi, no. 1 (1992), 2: copy in C.O.S.

18 O.R.O., MS. d.d. Par. Bampton, ff. 53, 64; P.C.C. min. bk. 1949–67, in custody of vicar and par. officers; local inf.

19 Bodl. MSS. Top. Oxon. d 190, f. 225; d 191a, f. 89; Giles, *Hist. Bampton*, 66–8; above, this section [settlement].

20 *Oxoniensia*, lii. 91.

21 Giles, *Hist. Bampton*, 67; [E. G. Hunt], *Music of a Merry Heart*, 214.

22 *Oxf. Chron.* 12 Aug. 1848; Giles, *Hist. Bampton*, 66–8.

23 [Hunt], *Music of a Merry Heart*, 214; J. L. Hughes-Owens, *The Bampton We Have Lost*, 13–14. The well remained inaccessible in 1994.

24 *Close R.* 1259–61, 12, 32. 25 Giles, *Hist. Bampton*, 54.

26 *Cal. Pat.* 1258–66, 339; 1350–4, 453.

27 *Oxon. Sessions of the Peace* (O.R.S. liii), 10, 42–4, 72–4, 82–9; *Cal. Pat.* 1399–1401, 385; *Sel. Cases in K.B.* vii (Selden Soc. lxxxviii), no. 3.

28 P.R.O., REQ 2/198/14.

29 Oxf. Jnl. Synopsis, 15 Feb. 1772, 17 July, 28 Aug., 24 Sept. 1773, 30 Apr., 25 Sept. 1774, 11 Feb., 25 Mar. 1775, 26 June 1776, 2 May 1778.

30 Below, econ. hist. (agric.).

31 *Agric. Trade Unionism in Oxon.* (O.R.S. xlviii), 12, 132; *Witney Express*, 15 Aug. 1872; [Hunt], *Music of A Merry Heart*, 210–12.

32 *Oxf. Jnl.* 24 Apr. 1756; Oxf. Jnl. Synopsis, 10 Feb. 1778, 17 Oct., 16 Nov., 30 Nov. 1782, 24 Oct., 6 Nov. 1783, 7 July 1790; *Oxf. Chron.* 12 May 1838, 20 Jan. 1855; cf. below, local govt. (par. govt.).

33 *A.-S. Chron.* ed. D. Whitelock, 16; cf. *D.N.B.* s.v. Cynegils; J. Blair, *A.-S. Oxon.* 38.

34 *Gesta Stephani*, ed. K. R. Potter, 138–40.

35 *Writings and Speeches of O. Cromwell*, ed. W. C. Abbott, i. 343; J. Sprigge, *Anglia Rediviva* (1647), 12.

36 H. Cary, *Mems. of the Gt. Civil War* (1842), ii. 137.

37 *Cal. Cttee. for Money*, ii. 999, 1028.

38 D. & C. Exeter, MS. 1981.

39 E. D. Longman and S. Loch, *Pins and Pincushions* (1911), 171; C.O.S., par. reg. transcripts.

40 C.O.S., par. reg. transcripts, s.a. 1677; *D.N.B.*

41 C.O.S., par. reg. transcripts, s.a. 1814; *D.N.B.*; below, manors.

Taunt (d. 1915) of Waterloo House on Broad Street, prominent in Bampton's musical life in the late 19th century and early 20th,[42] was distantly related to the Oxford photographer Henry Taunt, who photographed Bampton extensively, though there is no evidence that they knew each other.[43] In 1918 the novelist John Buchan visited and contemplated buying Weald Manor, the model for 'Fullcircle' in *The Runagates Club*.[44]

The Royal Signals Regiment established a listening station south-east of Weald Lane in 1939. It was taken over by the R.A.F. in 1969[45] and continued in 1993.

BUILDINGS.[46] A cruck-framed cottage north of the churchyard was mentioned in 1440,[47] and the discovery of encased timber frames in some surviving houses suggests that timber construction was common in medieval Bampton. Bell Cottage on Bell Lane,[48] formerly fronting the market place, Thatched Cottage on Church Street,[49] and Knapps Farm on Bridge Street, described below,[50] all began as small, timber-framed, three-bayed houses with open halls: Bell Cottage, the most archaic, retains a cruck truss, and Thatched Cottage and Knapps Farm are of similar, cruck-derived construction. All were later encased in rubble, Thatched Cottage possibly *c.* 1700 when 'a great deal' of building was noted there.[51] Cromwell House and the Old Forge at Cheapside, in origin a substantial late 16th-century house with a later wing aligned along Church Street at the northern, probably service, end, retain a principal post suggesting that they, too, were timber-framed, though the house was encased in stone before the 18th century. A mutilated, four-centred fireplace survives in the large central room, but 19th-century subdivision has obscured the earlier arrangement. The house was let from 1683 to Richard Coxeter's relict Jane, who may have lived there, and was held with 1½ yardland in the 18th century.[52]

Most surviving houses are 17th-century or later, of local limestone rubble with stone-slated or, less commonly, thatched roofs.[53] Much stone

for 17th- and 18th-century rebuilding came presumably from Bampton castle, demolished about that time:[54] several rubble-built cottages incorporate blocks of dressed stone in quoining or door-surrounds, and the Elms on Broad Street includes a re-used arrow slit low down in its north side-wall. Stone for such high-status medieval buildings as the church, Deanery, and castle[55] came perhaps from the Burford or Taynton quarries,[56] and in the 19th century Brize Norton and, for higher quality work, Milton stone was used for bridge repairs and presumably other purposes.[57] Brick seems not to have been used until the 1880s following the opening of Bampton station, and then only rarely.[58] Fires necessitated occasional rebuilding: one in 1467 damaged or destroyed houses on Exeter cathedral's manor,[59] and an evidently more widespread one in 1607 prompted a relief fund.[60] Cromwell House and the Old Forge were called Burnt House in 1789 and apparently in the 17th century.[61] In the 1960s fire destroyed the thatched roof of the Elephant and Castle public house on Bridge Street.[62]

Several houses of 17th- or early 18th-century origin, most of them former farmsteads,[63] line the principal streets. Manor Cottage, on the corner of Broad Street and Landells Lane, was built shortly before 1654,[64] and Leighton Cottage, on Church View, was 'much altered' between 1686 and 1789.[65] Wood House (formerly Southside) north of the church, built in the later 17th century reportedly for the Wood family,[66] has a symmetrical, five-bayed front of semi-dressed stone, and retains an original staircase and other fittings; it was occupied from *c.* 1798 to 1810 by a minister of Cote Baptist chapel,[67] and was reroofed[68] and extended in the 19th century. Nos. 1–3 Church View, in origin a single, probably 17th-century house with a later staircase wing at the rear and a single-storeyed addition on the north, was held in 1686 by another of the Coxeter family.[69] Grayshott House, on the south side of High Street near the market place, was built *c.* 1700 probably by the wealthy maltster and farmer Jethro Bunce (d. 1726),[70] originally with a symmetrical front of 5 bays and with a hipped, stone-slated roof. A sixth bay was added on the

42 *Oxf. Jnl.* 25 Feb. 1871; *Kelly's Dir. Oxon.* (1907); commem. window in church.
43 C.O.S., OPA Bampton photos.; inf. from Mr. M. G. Cook, Wallingford.
44 *Country Life,* c (1946), 256; J. Adam Smith, *John Buchan*, 218.   45 *Witney Gaz.* 26 Feb. 1976.
46 For manor and vicarage hos., below, manors; churches.
47 D. & C. Exeter, MS. 4756; *S. Midlands Arch.* xxii. 59.
48 Unpubl. surv. by J. Blair (1993).
49 *S. Midlands Arch.* xxii. 59, 62.
50 Ibid.; below, Aston and Cote, manors (Golofers).
51 Arundel Castle, MS. TP 288, no. 14; cf. B.L. Map C 7 e 16 (3), p. 58, map between pp. 34–5.
52 Bodl. MSS. d.d. Shrewsbury c 2/8 (16), c 3/9 (4), c 3/9 (22), c 4/10 (12); Arundel Castle, MS. TP 288, no. 3; B.L. Map C 7 e 16 (3), map between pp. 34–5; ibid. pp. 42–3, s.v. Burnt Ho.
53 Cf. C.O.S., OPA 4819, 4829, 4837, 19015, 76/2797.
54 Below, manors (castle).
55 Ibid.; below, manors (Bampton Deanery); churches.
56 e.g. D. & C. Exeter, MS. 5105, mentioning Taynton stone for repairs at the Deanery.
57 H. J. Tollit, *County Bridges Rep.* (1878), 31–2, 52, 69, 71: copy in Bodl.   58 Below.

59 D. & C. Exeter, MS. 3774, ff. 139, 143v.
60 *Oxf. Council Acts, 1583–1626* (O.H.S. lxxxvii), 180.
61 B.L. Map C 7 e 16 (3), pp. 42–3, map between pp. 34–5; Bodl. MS. d.d. Shrewsbury c 2/8 (16), mentioning Burnt Ho. close. No fire damage was found.
62 Bodl. MS. Top. Oxon. c 484/1, nos. 4038, 5226–7; local inf.
63 Cf. B.L. Map C 7 e 16 (3), pp. 36–73; D. & C. Exeter, MS. 4544; ibid. MS. M 1; O.R.O., incl. award.
64 P.R.O., PROB 11/284, f. 352, mentioning ho. lately built on Calves close; cf. O.R.O., D.Y. VII/ii/3, VII/iv/1–6; ibid. incl. award, no. 101.
65 B.L. Map C 7 e 16 (3), pp. 58–9, no. 9; cf. O.R.O., D.Y. XVII/i/1–3.
66 Giles, *Hist. Bampton,* 23, 61–2; though the fam. was omitted from hearth taxes, cf. C.O.S., par. reg. transcripts, s.a. 1674.
67 O.R.O., QSD L.22, s.a. 1799–1812; cf. ibid. incl award; J. Stanley, *Church in the Hop Garden,* 170: copy in Bodl.   68 Giles, *Hist. Bampton,* 64.
69 O.R.O., D.Y. XVII/i/1, mentioning Anne Coxeter's ho. to the south; cf. B.L. Map C 7 e 16 (3), p. 58, no. 9.
70 O.R.O., Acc. 2184, deeds *re* New Inn and nos. 9–11 High St., locating Bunce's ho. west of no. 11; cf. ibid. MS. Wills Oxon. 117/1/13; ibid. incl. award, nos. 917, 925.

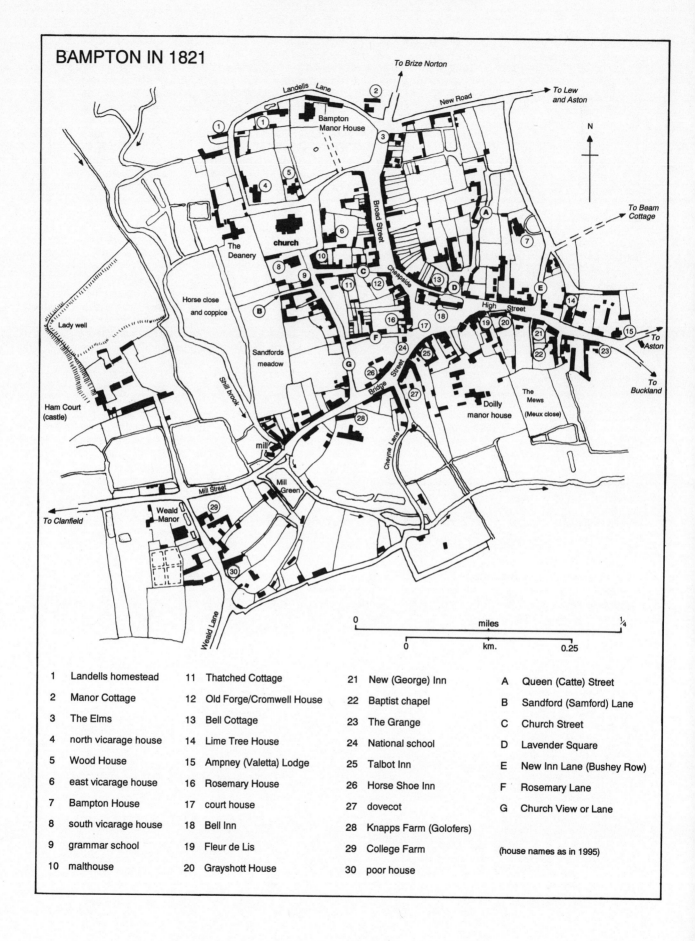

BAMPTON IN 1821

1	Landells homestead	11 Thatched Cottage	21 New (George) Inn	A Queen (Catte) Street
2	Manor Cottage	12 Old Forge/Cromwell House	22 Baptist chapel	B Sandford (Samford) Lane
3	The Elms	13 Bell Cottage	23 The Grange	C Church Street
4	north vicarage house	14 Lime Tree House	24 National school	D Lavender Square
5	Wood House	15 Ampney (Valetta) Lodge	25 Talbot Inn	E New Inn Lane (Bushey Row)
6	east vicarage house	16 Rosemary House	26 Horse Shoe Inn	F Rosemary Lane
7	Bampton House	17 court house	27 dovecot	G Church View or Lane
8	south vicarage house	18 Bell Inn	28 Knapps Farm (Golofers)	
9	grammar school	19 Fleur de Lis	29 College Farm	(house names as in 1995)
10	malthouse	20 Grayshott House	30 poor house	

east soon after, and in the early 19th century a scullery was added beyond and a short rear wing was built on the original house's central axis, perhaps when the lower part of the staircase was replaced. Another notable 17th-century building is the former grammar school on Church View, built on the site of an earlier cottage.[71]

Weald Manor,[72] at the north end of Weald Lane, originated as the farmhouse for 3 copyhold yardlands on Bampton Earls manor.[73] From the late 16th century to the early 19th it was let to local gentry, including, probably, members of the Snoddenham family from the 1560s, in 1609 Bartholomew Peisley,[74] and from c. 1675 or earlier members of the Coxeter family.[75] It was drastically remodelled allegedly in 1742, when the lease was held by Thomas Coxeter (d. 1755) in trust for his mother, with reversion to his wife Elizabeth;[76] she lived elsewhere by 1765,[77] and in 1774 the lease passed apparently through marriage to Robert Kirke (d. 1800) of Clements Inn.[78] The house, called a mansion house in 1738 and the Manor House from the earlier 19th century when it housed a private school,[79] was sold with manorial rights in 1870, perhaps through a misconception resulting from the name.[80]

The house as remodelled, of coursed limestone with ashlar dressings, is quadrangular, of 2 storeys with an attic, and with a hipped, stone-slated roof. The east front, remodelled to appear symmetrical and with earlier dormers concealed behind an 18th-century parapet, seems formerly to have been a hall range flanked by short cross wings, a plan which suggests a date before the mid 17th century; in 1662 the earlier house was taxed possibly on 8 hearths.[81] Presumably in 1742 it was refaced and refenestrated: the central, pedimented porch and eastern gateway with rusticated piers were built, then or soon after the central hall and rooms to its south were refitted, and the hall was extended westwards to accommodate a staircase, the work necessitating reroofing of the main range. Presumably at the same time the cross wings were extended westwards to form a central courtyard: the north front, of six bays, retains a building line with quoins between the fourth and fifth bays. The south-east bedroom on the first floor retains 17th-century wooden panelling, and 18th-century

interior decoration includes a fireplace and cornice in the first-floor drawing room on the south.[82]

In the earlier 19th century the house was 'dilapidated',[83] and repairs were carried out c. 1859 and c. 1880.[84] The west range appears to have been remodelled during the 19th century, and in the early 20th extensive alterations were carried out for Ernest Blackburne,[85] who in 1903 added a small studio at the south-west corner. Perhaps at the same time the central courtyard was roofed over, a canted bay window of 2 storeys was added to the library at the south end of the east range, the dining room was enlarged, and some interior decoration was refurbished and some fenestration renewed. The drawing room was panelled with beading on bare walls in the late 1920s or 1930s.[86]

The grounds were landscaped presumably c. 1742, and in 1789 included fishponds, an 'avenue', and, south-west of the house, a formal pleasure garden incorporating a sundial which survives. Plantations of elms added 'to the ornament of the place'.[87] Fishponds east of the house were filled in between 1821 and 1876, and in the early 20th century the grounds were relandscaped presumably by Blackburne, who introduced various stone garden ornaments. A fishpond west of the house was extended into a large artificial lake, and a new main driveway, with its own lodge, was made to Clanfield road on the north. A stable block, later Stable Cottage, was built east of the lodge before 1876.[88] A reset medieval cross base within a circle of yews south-west of the house seems to have been in that position by 1789.[89]

Bampton House off Bushey Row, in its own grounds, is a substantial square house of the earlier 18th century, the date of surviving staircases, and was remodelled c. 1800 for the lawyer John Mander (d. 1809).[90] A canted bay window was added on the south, most other windows were renewed, and much of the interior was refitted. The house was later let to members of the Whitaker family, and passed before 1851 to the Southbys, who lived there until the early 20th century.[91] Lime Tree House on High Street, owned with other houses in 1821 by Revd. William Joseph Walker, son of the surgeon Joseph Walker (d. 1803),[92] is also of the earlier

71 Below, educ.; below plate 8.
72 Cf. *Country Life*, c (1946), 256–9; Pevsner, *Oxon.* 433–4; D.o.E., *Revised Hist. Bldg. List: Bampton* (1989), 57–8: copy in C.O.S.; below, plate 10.
73 Arundel Castle, MS. TP 288, no. 2; B.L. Map C 7 e 16 (3), pp. 66–8.
74 P.R.O., REQ 2/268/53; B.L. Add. MS. 27535, f. 39, both referring to a ho. and 3-yardland fm.; cf. Arundel Castle, MS. TP 288; B.L. Map C 7 e 16 (3), pp. 36–73; O.R.O., MS. Wills Oxon. 173/2/52.
75 Arundel Castle, MS. TP 288, no. 2; Bodl. MSS. d.d. Shrewsbury c 3/9 (11), c 3/9 (15), c 3/9 (17), c 4/10 (1), c 4/10 (15).
76 B.L. Map C 7 e 16 (3), p. 67; P.R.O., PROB 11/708, ff. 344v., 346 and v.; PROB 11/819, ff. 177 and v.
77 Conveyance 19 June 1765, in possession of Group Capt. P. Dainty, Bampton; P.R.O., PROB 11/977, f. 161v.
78 Arundel Castle, MS. TP 19, lease 25 Mar. 1774; Oxf. Jnl. Synopsis, 13 Jan. 1787; C.O.S., par. reg. transcripts.
79 P.R.O., PROB 11/708, f. 344v.; Giles, *Hist. Bampton*, 22; *P.O. Dir. Oxon.* (1847 and later edns.); below, educ.
80 O.R.O., Crowdy I/51, lot 20.
81 P.R.O., E 179/255/4, pt. i, f. 19, s.v. Ric. Coxeter.

82 Pevsner, *Oxon.* 434 suggests that the fireplace is not *in situ*, but it predates 20th-century alterations: *Sale Cat.* 4 June 1880, in possession of Major R. A. Colvile.
83 Arundel Castle, MS. TP 100, s.v. Chas. Tunstall.
84 *Appeal of Behalf of St. Mary's College, Bampton* (1860): copy in Bodl. G.A. Oxon. c 22 (2); *Sale Cat.* 4 June 1880.
85 So called in deeds; cf. *Kelly's Dir. Oxon.* (1903 and later edns.), naming Edw. Blackburne.
86 Datestone 1903; inf. from Major R. A. Colvile; cf. *Country Life*, c (1946), 257, 259; Pevsner, *Oxon.* 434.
87 B.L. Map C 7 e 16 (3), pp. 66–7, map between pp. 34–5.
88 O.R.O., incl. award, plan III; O.S. Map 1/2,500, Oxon. XXXVII. 6 (1876 and later edns.); ibid. SP 3002–3102 (1971 edn.).
89 B.L. Map C 7 e 16 (3), map between pp. 34–5; *Sale Cat.* 4 June 1880, plan; *Country Life*, c (1946), 259.
90 B.L. Map C 7 e 16 (3), map between pp. 34–5; *Univ. Brit. Dir.* ii [1793], 252–3; cf. Bodl. MS. Top. Oxon. a 37, ff. 67–8.
91 O.R.O., D.Y. XXXIV/i/1–2; ibid. Welch XCVII/ii/1; P.R.O., HO 107/1731; *Kelly's Dir. Oxon.* (1883 and later edns.).
92 O.R.O., incl. award, no. 410; C.O.S., par. reg. transcripts; Bodl. MS. Ch. Oxon. 3222; illust. in *Country Life*, c (1946), 119.

18th century. Its symmetrical front includes a central doorway with pilasters and an elaborate shell hood, and the interior retains a staircase of similar date.[93] The Elms, at the north end of Broad Street, incorporates part of a 17th-century house on the north, but the principal range fronting the street is of the mid 18th century with a symmetrical ashlar front of three bays, Venetian windows to both floors, and a central pedimented doorway.[94] A large first-floor room has an enriched plaster cornice and plaster panelling, and similar decoration survives on the staircase. Possibly it was the house on Broad Street occupied until c. 1772 by Mrs. (probably Sara) Mander (d. 1786),[95] and in 1821 it was owned with other houses by the surgeon Joseph Andrews (d. 1828).[96] In the early 1840s it was occupied by the wealthy farmer Jonathan Arnatt (d. 1844), formerly of Lew House,[97] for whom, perhaps, the ground floor rooms were refitted and a back wing and stair turret added behind the main stair. An extension on the south, later South Elms, was added presumably while the house was being used as a boarding school,[98] and in 1895 the 17th-century wing was remodelled and probably extended by F. and M. Staples-Browne, who seem, however, to have resided only after 1899. The house was remodelled in the 20th century, and in the 1980s several features were introduced from other buildings.[99]

Prospect House to the north and Waterloo House (formerly St. Oswald) to the south were built in the earlier 19th century on the site of earlier cottages.[1] Prospect House, a tall, narrow building set well back from the street, was a private school in the 1850s, and in 1881 was occupied by a clergyman's widow; Waterloo House was occupied by the 1880s by the organist and music teacher F. W. Taunt.[2] Haytor House in Lavender Square, a detached L-shaped building with a symmetrical front of 3 bays and a porticoed porch, was built between 1821 and 1841 by the solicitor James Rose (d. 1864), who lived there until his death.[3] Oathurst, a substantial three-storeyed house west of Lime Tree House, was built after 1821 on the site of former outbuildings, and from the 1860s until c. 1909 was occupied by general practitioners who ran a surgery there. In 1939 it housed a language school for foreign students and c. 1976 it became an old people's home;[4] a local tradition that it was a railway hotel lacks evidence.

Several lesser houses, notably around the market place, were rebuilt during the 18th century, reflecting continued modest wealth from trade and agriculture. The Talbot Inn was rebuilt shortly after 1700,[5] and adjoining houses on the east, owned in 1821 by a maltster, a grocer, and a butcher,[6] were rebuilt later in the century. A long, low range on the market place's west side bears the inscription TP 1795, probably for Thomas Peck (d. 1814), who held it of Bampton Earls manor.[7] Wheelgate House, south-east of the market place, owned by the maltster Richard Haskins (d. 1770)[8] and of 18th-century origin, was remodelled in the early 19th century when a third storey was added. A large, ashlar-fronted house to its west, occupied successively by a butcher and farmer, by the mercer and haberdasher Thomas Bryan, and from c. 1794 by the owner of Bampton Doilly manor, was 'newly fitted up' before 1800, when it was sold to the corndealer Thomas Collins (d. 1842);[9] a canted bay shop-window was added later, and an extension was built over the cart entry.[10] Nos. 9–11 High Street, east of Grayshott House, were rebuilt c. 1735 on the site of two earlier houses, possibly by the milliner Laurence Bishop (d. 1739), and were divided, as later, into three.[11] They were again remodelled or rebuilt in the later 18th century and early 19th, and shortly after 1821 no. 8 was built onto the west side of the later Morris Clown to form a continuous line of buildings, occupied by tradesmen in the 19th century.[12]

During the earlier 19th century some houses were refronted in modest imitation of grander buildings. Lesta House on High Street was remodelled perhaps after it was acquired by the mason and builder Robert Oakey in 1837,[13] and includes a notable stone doorcase similar to that of Waterloo House. A shop adjoining the Talbot Inn south of the market place, owned by the maltster John Bateman (d. 1849),[14] acquired an ashlar colonnade of Doric columns, while Rosemary House on the west side, remodelled perhaps by the tailor Levi Robins (d. 1852),[15] has a central doorway with a semicircular fanlight and an open-pedimented stone hood on scroll brackets. Box House on the corner of Bridge Street and Rosemary Lane, a symmetrical two-storeyed house of three bays with a semicircular hood over the doorway, was built perhaps by the mason and publican Charles Lord; he owned the site with the Horse Shoe

93 *Country Life*, c (1946), 119, 169.
94 Below, plate 6.
95 Oxf. Jnl. Synopsis, 12 June 1772, 14 Oct. 1786; C.O.S., par. reg. transcripts.
96 O.R.O., incl. award; C.O.S., par. reg. transcripts.
97 P.R.O., HO 107/872; O.R.O., QSD L.22; *Oxf. Chron.* 24 May 1845; C.O.S., par. reg. transcripts; below, Lew, intro.   98 Below, educ.
99 Datestone; *Kelly's Dir. Oxon.* (1895 and later edns.); inf. from owners (1992).   1 O.R.O., incl. award.
2 P.R.O., HO 107/872; ibid. RG 11/1514; *Kelly's Dir. Oxon.* (1883 and later edns.); below, educ.
3 O.R.O., incl. award, no. 461; ibid. Crowdy I/51, town plan (which omits ho.); P.R.O., HO 107/872; ibid. RG 10/1451; C.O.S., par. reg. transcripts.
4 O.R.O., incl. award; ibid. Pocock III/35; P.R.O., RG 9/905; RG 11/1514; *Kelly's Dir. Oxon.* (1887 and later edns.); *Witney Gaz.* 13 Mar. 1980.   5 Above [inns].
6 O.R.O., incl. award; cf. P.R.O., HO 107/872; *Univ. Brit. Dir.* ii [1793], 252–3; Pigot, *Lond. & Prov. Dir.* (1830).

7 O.R.O., incl. award; cf. ibid. MS. Wills Oxon. 237/1/15.
8 O.R.O., D.Y. XXXI/i/1; ibid. MS. Wills Oxon. 36/2/4.
9 Ibid. Mor. XIII/iv/1–5; ibid. MS. Wills Oxon. 140/3/28; ibid. incl. award, no. 906; *Oxf. Jnl.* 9 Aug. 1800.
10 Cf. O.R.O., incl. award, plan I; O.S. Map 1/2,500, Oxon. XXXVII. 7 (1876 edn.).
11 O.R.O., Acc. 2184, deeds re New Inn and nos. 9–11, esp. mutilated mortgage of 1735; ibid. MS. Wills Oxon. 162/1/42.
12 Ibid. incl. award, plan I; P.R.O., HO 107/872; O.S. Map 1/2,500, Oxon. XXXVII. 7 (1876 edn.).
13 O.R.O., Welch XCVII/i/1–6; cf. ibid. incl. award, no. 417; D.o.E., *Revised Hist. Bldgs. List, Bampton*, 39, suggesting an earlier date: copy in C.O.S.
14 O.R.O., incl. award, no. 902; P.R.O., HO 107/872; C.O.S., par. reg. transcripts.
15 O.R.O., incl. award, no. 499; ibid. Crowdy I/51, plan; P.R.O., HO 107/872; deeds for neighbouring ho., in private possession.

public house and had yards adjoining, and may have built nearby Sherborne Villas and Fernlea.[16]

There were cottages at the north end of Buckland road by 1821, and during the 19th century small artisans' dwellings were built as far as Fisher's bridge. The Swan, built south of the bridge before 1842, marked the limit of expansion.[17] From the 1830s and 1840s there were a few outlying farmhouses and cottages,[18] and some existing farmhouses were rebuilt, among them Weald Manor Farm in 1884.[19] Within the town there was much rebuilding of artisans' and labourers' dwellings, mostly by local builders. New cottages at Mill Green and possibly on the east side of Queen Street were built by the mason Samuel Spencer (d. 1841) in the 1820s or 1830s,[20] and from the 1850s several houses on the earl of Shrewsbury's manor were rebuilt by the carpenter and builder Robert Plaster (d. 1877), who acquired beneficial leases. They included Westbrook House on Bridge Street, built on Plaster's own holding, and on Broad Street the stone terrace later called Matthew House, no. 5, and Clovelly, which replaced earlier houses and yards and was occupied by tradesmen in 1881.[21] Other new houses included Windsor Cottages (1887) and Victoria Cottages (1893) on Broad Street, both brick-fronted terraces replacing stone and thatched cottages,[22] Oban (c. 1835) and Albion Place (1875) on Bridge Street, Belgrave Cottages (1903) and Bourton Cottages (1906) on Church Street, Eton Villas (1907) on the corner of Church and Broad Streets, and Folly View (1906) and Fleur de Lis Villas (c. 1910) south of the market place.[23] Areas of crowded and probably insanitary labourers' accommodation north of Rosemary Lane and south of the market place in Kerwood's Yard, called Jericho in 1841, were cleared apparently in the early 20th century.[24]

A Baptist meeting house was built south of High Street c. 1778. Institutional buildings of the 19th century included the National school, later demolished, at the top of Bridge Street, and its successor on Church View, the Particular Baptist chapel on Buckland road, and the Methodist chapel on Bridge Street, built on the site of earlier cottages.[25] The town hall in the centre of the market place, built by subscription in 1838

to designs by George Wilkinson, is a rectangular Italianate building of two storeys, whose ground floor originally formed an open arcade for use as a market house.[26] Some or all of the arches were blocked presumably by the 1870s, when the ground floor included a lockable fire-engine house.[27] A small, single-storeyed extension on the east was added in 1906 at the expense of Philip Southby;[28] a clock built on the roof perhaps at that time was moved in 1971 to the motor repair garage to the north.[29] Following the opening of a purpose-built fire station on New Road c. 1971[30] the large engine-doors were blocked, and in 1992, when the upper floor housed the Bampton Arts Centre, most of the arches were glazed.

The most notable building of the late 19th century and the 20th is the Grange,[31] so called by 1891, on the south side of High Street, an extensive house which reached its present size as a result of successive enlargement and remodelling, much of it by W. G. Lindup (d. c. 1930).[32] At the north-east corner it incorporates part of a late 17th- or early 18th-century house owned in the 18th century by the Dewe family, and later by the Hawkinses and Townsends;[33] extensions to the south and west, in a variety of styles, may incorporate some walls of earlier buildings. Re-used on the first floor are a number of later 18th-century wooden doorcases of high quality, similar in style to Robert Adam's work and perhaps brought from Eynsham Hall following its demolition in 1903,[34] though confirmation is lacking.

Council houses were being built by the 1930s, but Bampton's slow population growth during the earlier 20th century meant that new building was chiefly confined to small estates north of New Road and between Bushey Row and Beam Cottage.[35] A planning report in 1966 concluded that large scale expansion was impractical and undesirable, and recommended that future building should remain confined to those areas, with no further building on Weald Lane.[36] A new primary school was built north of New Road in 1961,[37] old people's flats between Queen Street and Bushey Row were opened in 1969, and a few houses were built at the lower end of Bridge Street in the early 1980s and north of New Road in 1994.[38]

16 O.R.O., Tice I/vii/5; Jesus Coll. Mun., box 15, list 7, *Sale Cat.* 14 Sept. 1864, lots 5–10; P.R.O., RG 9/905; RG 11/1514.
17 O.R.O., incl. award, plans I–II; O.S. Map 1/2,500, Oxon. XXXVII. 7 (1876 edn.); Pigot, *Royal Nat. & Comm. Dir.* (1842), s.v. Swan.
18 Below, econ. hist. (agric.); O.S. Map 1/2,500, Oxon. XXXVII. 7 (1876 edn.).
19 Datestone WB 1884, for Wm. Blackburne, owner of Weald Manor; cf. Ch. Ch. Arch., MS. Estates 60, ff. 72–104.
20 Jesus Coll. Mun., box 15, list 11; O.R.O., Mor. XIII/i/1.
21 Bodl. MSS. d.d. Shrewsbury c 4/12 (5–7); O.R.O., Crowdy I/51, lots 38–9, 48–9; P.R.O., RG 11/1514; below, econ. hist. (trade and ind.).
22 Datestones; C.O.S., OPA 4837.
23 Datestones; for Fleur de Lis villas, *Kelly's Dir. Oxon.* (1907, 1911); for Oban, deeds in private possession.
24 O.R.O., incl. award, nos. 937–52; P.R.O., HO 107/872; ibid. RG 9/905; RG 11/1514; O.S. Map 1/2,500, Oxon. XXXVII. 7 (1876 and later edns.).
25 O.R.O., Crowdy I/51, lot 38; below, educ.; nonconf.
26 *Oxf. Chron.* 5 May, 11 Aug. 1838; *Oxoniensia*, xxxv. 56; Giles, *Hist. Bampton*, 21, 54–5; inscription on N. wall.

27 O.R.O., MS. d.d. Par. Bampton c 12, item k, s.a. 1880; *P.O. Dir. Oxon.* (1877); J. L. Hughes-Owens, *The Bampton We Have Lost*, 88: copy in C.O.S.; below, plate 3.
28 *Kelly's Dir. Oxon.* (1907); inscription on E. wall.
29 C.O.S., OPA 1916–17; local inf.
30 O.S. Map 1/2,500, SP 3003–3103 (1971 edn.); local inf.
31 Cf. Pevsner, *Oxon.* 435, wrongly calling it the Gables.
32 O.R.O., incl. award, no. 927; ibid. Mor. XIII/ix/1, 8, 10; C.O.S., OPA 11990; *Sale Cat.* (1930): copy in C.O.S.; O.S. Map 1/2,500, Oxon. XXXVII. 7 (1876 and later edns.); *Kelly's Dir. Oxon.* (1891 and later edns.).
33 O.R.O., incl. award, no. 927; Bodl. MS. d.d. Fitt c 4.
34 *V.C.H. Oxon.* xii. 121–2.
35 C.O.S., OPA 19028; O.S. Maps 1/2,500, Oxon. XXXVII. 6–7 (1921 edn.); SP 3002–3102, 3003–3103 (1971 edn.); ibid. 6", SP 30 SW (1960 edn.).
36 M. W. Robinson, 'Bampton, Rep. on Survey and Plan' (TS. 1966): copy in C.O.S., SMR Bampton file; cf. *Bampton, an Appraisal, 1982–85*: copy in C.O.S.
37 Below, educ.
38 Jesus Coll. Mun., box 15, list 11, planning application 1982; local inf.

MANORS AND CASTLE. Until the late Anglo-Saxon period the royal manor of *BAMPTON* included all the ancient parish and much land outside it.[39] From the 10th century or earlier it was diminished by piecemeal grants, described below,[40] and in 1086 totalled 27½ hides; another ½ hide held by Ilbert de Lacy of the bishop of Bayeux's gift, a 'parcel' held by Walter son of Ponz, unspecified woodland held by Henry de Ferrars and formerly by a thegn, Bundi the forester, and 60 a. in Stockley (in Asthall) were said to be of the king's demesne.[41] A separate 3-hide estate held by Ilbert de Lacy of the bishop of Bayeux has not been traced later, and was presumably reabsorbed into the royal manor, perhaps c. 1100 when Ilbert's son Robert was expelled from the country.[42]

Bampton manor was held in 1156, apparently at pleasure, by Thierry (d. 1163), count of Flanders, from c. 1167 by Thierry's son Matthew, count of Boulogne, who forfeited his lands in 1173, and from c. 1175 by Matthew's brother Philip (d. 1191), count of Flanders, whose lands were held in custody from 1180 by William de Mandeville, earl of Essex.[43] On Philip's death the manor was briefly held by the sheriff of Oxfordshire towards ward of Oxford castle, and was granted in 1196 to John, count of Mortain, and in 1198 to Reginald de Dammartin, count of Boulogne, who had married Count Matthew's daughter.[44] Following Reginald's defection in 1203 it passed in custody to Geoffrey FitzPeter, but was restored in 1212. Though still regarded as part of Reginald's honor of Boulogne after his capture in 1214 at the battle of the Bouvines, it was granted at pleasure in 1217 to Fawkes de Breauté, and in 1227 for life to Philip Daubeny, who in 1235 granted it to Cirencester abbey for three years.[45] Philip died before 1238, when the land in Aston and Cote was granted to Imbert de Pugeys, and in 1248 Henry III granted the rest of the manor, in Bampton, Weald, Lew, and probably Lower Haddon, to his half-brother William de Valence, earl of Pembroke.[46]

On William's death in 1296 that reduced manor, later *BAMPTON EARLS*, *KING'S BAMPTON*, or *BAMPTON TALBOT* and

assessed at 1 knight's fee, passed to his son Aymer (d. *s.p.* 1324).[47] In 1325 it was assigned with other of Aymer's lands to his niece and coheir Elizabeth Comyn, who before 1327 married Richard Talbot (d. 1356), later Lord Talbot,[48] and the manor remained with the Talbots, later earls of Shrewsbury. In 1355 Richard granted it in survivorship to John Carreu, John Laundels, and Thomas Talbot, clerk, on whose death in 1362 it reverted to Richard's son Gilbert (d. 1387), Lord Talbot; he leased it in 1382 to Sir Robert Tresilian for 7 years.[49]

Gilbert's son Richard, Lord Talbot, died seised in 1396.[50] His son Gilbert, a minor, had possession by 1405 and died in 1418, leaving an infant daughter, Ankaret.[51] Gilbert's relict Beatrice (d. 1447) received a third in dower and married Thomas Fettiplace, living at Bampton in the 1430s;[52] in 1419 she received custody of the other two thirds, but following Ankaret's death in 1421 she surrendered her dower in return for a tenancy. Gilbert's lands and titles passed to his brother John (d. 1453), created earl of Shrewsbury in 1442 and of Waterford in 1446,[53] to John's son John, killed at the battle of Northampton in 1460, and in 1464 to his son John, who died seised of a third in 1473, the rest being held by dowagers.[54]

John's son George, a minor in 1473, entered on the reunited manor probably in 1486.[55] On his death in 1538 it seems to have passed to his relict Elizabeth (d. 1567) as jointure,[56] and by 1569 to his grandson George Talbot (d. 1590); he settled it for life on his wife Elizabeth (d. 1608), who leased it.[57] By 1609 it had reverted to George's son Gilbert (d. 1616), from whom it passed with the earldom to his brother Edward.[58] Edward died in 1618, and following a series of disputes the manor was apparently divided between, among others, his sister Grace, relict of Henry Cavendish, his sister Mary's grandson Sir George Savile Bt. (d. *s.p.* 1626), and Earl Gilbert's daughter Elizabeth (d. *s.p.* 1651) and her husband Sir Henry Grey (d. 1639), earl of Kent; Henry and Elizabeth held courts as lords of Bampton in 1623.[59] Before 1640 Elizabeth acquired an interest in Grace's

39 Above, intro.
40 Below, this section; Aston and Cote, manors; Chimney, manor; Lew, manor; Lower Haddon, manor; Shifford, manor; Ducklington, manor; Northmoor, manor; Standlake, manor.
41 *V.C.H. Oxon.* i. 375 n., 376, 400; *P.N. Oxon.* (E.P.N.S.), ii. 301. Ferrars's woodland was perhaps that later in Standlake: below, Standlake, intro.; econ. hist.
42 *V.C.H. Oxon.* i. 405; ibid. v. 284.
43 *Pipe R.* 1156–8 (Rolls Ser.), 36, 82, 149; 1162 (P.R.S. v), 26; 1168 (P.R.S. xii), 205; 1173 (P.R.S. xix), 166–8, 171; 1175 (P.R.S. xxii), 11; 1181 (P.R.S. xxx), 64, 110; 1188 (P.R.S. xxxviii), 7; J. Dunbabin, *France in the Making* (1985), 322, 391.
44 *Pipe R.* 1191–92 (P.R.S. N.S. ii), 268; 1194 (P.R.S. N.S. v), 7, 88; 1196 (P.R.S. N.S. vii), 211–12; 1198 (P.R.S. N.S. ix), 189; J. H. Round, *Studies in Peerage and Fam. Hist.* (1901), 176–7.
45 *Pipe R.* 1202 (P.R.S. N.S. xv), 203–4, 206; 1212 (P.R.S. N.S. xxx), 18–19; 1220 (P.R.S. N.S. xlvii), 23; *Rot. Lib.* (Rec. Com.), 91; *Rot. Litt. Claus.* (Rec. Com.), 116, 300; *Cal. Chart. R.* 1226–57, 54, 184; *Close R.* 1234–7, 68; Round, *Peerage and Fam. Hist.* 178–9.
46 *Close R.* 1237–42, 70; 1247–51, 133, 277; below, Aston and Cote, manors; Lower Haddon, manor. Imbert had meanwhile farmed the whole manor.

47 *Cal. Inq. p.m.* iii, p. 221; xi, p. 337.
48 *Cal. Fine R.* 1319–27, 338; *Cal. Inq. p.m.* vi, pp. 314 sqq., 328; vii, pp. 287, 292; *Complete Peerage*, xii (1), 612–14 and n.
49 *Cal. Pat.* 1354–8, 268; *Cal. Inq. p.m.* x, p. 277; xi, pp. 337–8; *Cal. Close* 1381–5, 108; cf. *Oxon. Sessions of the Peace* (O.R.S. liii), 102.
50 *Cal. Inq. p.m.* xvii, pp. 336, 339.
51 P.R.O., C 138/41, no. 68; *Cal. Pat.* 1405–8, 139.
52 P.R.O., C 139/42, no. 86; *Complete Peerage*, xii (1), 619; *Cal. Pat.* 1429–36, 623; 1436–41, 588.
53 P.R.O., C 138/58, no. 44; *Cal. Fine R.* 1413–22, 284; *Cal. Close*, 1447–54, 11; *Complete Peerage*, xi. 698–704; xii (1), 620.
54 P.R.O., C 139/179, no. 58, m. 14; C 140/46, no. 52, m. 15; *Cal. Pat.* 1467–77, 397, 421, 541; *Complete Peerage*, xi. 704–6.
55 *Complete Peerage*, xi. 706–7; cf. *Cal. Pat.* 1467–77, 400, 421, 561–2; 1476–85, 120–1, 369.
56 P.R.O., REQ 2/268/53; ibid. C 142/143, no. 51.
57 Ibid. C 142/380, no. 128; C 142/231, no. 106; Bodl. MS. Tanner 115, f. 180 and v.; *Complete Peerage*, xi. 712–14.
58 B.L. Add. MS. 27535, f. 37; P.R.O., C 2/Jas. I/W 20/37.
59 P.R.O., C 2/Jas. I/W 20/37; ibid. C 142/380, no. 128; C 142/424, no. 90; O.R.O., Tice I/i/1; Bodl. MSS. d.d. Shrewsbury c 1/6; c 3/9 (12b); *Complete Peerage*, vii. 173; xi. 715–17; G.E.C. *Baronetage*, i. 49–50; Burke, *Peerage* (1878), 361.

share, which she granted in reversion to Sir William Savile Bt. (d. 1644) of Thornhill (Yorks. W.R.), Sir George's brother and heir;[60] the Savile share, later two thirds, passed thereafter to Sir William's son Sir George (d. 1695), and before 1660 to Sir William's brother-in-law Sir William Coventry (d. 1686),[61] the other third having passed by 1654 to Francis Talbot (d. 1668), earl of Shrewsbury.[62] The manor was formally partitioned in 1660.[63]

The Talbots' third passed to Francis's son Charles (d. s.p. 1718), created duke of Shrewsbury in 1694, who settled his Oxfordshire lands on his cousin George Talbot (d. 1733), brother of the 13th earl. From him they passed to his son George (d. 1787), earl of Shrewsbury, and, with the earldom, to George's nephew Charles (d. 1827), Charles's nephew John (d. 1852), and John's cousin Bertram Arthur (d. 1856), who devised the family estates to Lord Edmund Bernard Howard (later Talbot), son of the duke of Norfolk.[64] In 1870 the estate, then c. 570 a. in Bampton, Weald, and Lew, was sold by trustees established under an Act of 1803;[65] Ham Court or Castle Farm (110 a.), including the former castle or manor house, was bought by Jesus College, Oxford, and the land in Lew (73 a.) by Christ Church, Oxford, the rest being divided among many purchasers.[66] Manorial rights were sold with Weald Manor.[67]

The Coventrys' two thirds, c. 980 a. in Bampton, Weald, Lew, and Clanfield,[68] were bequeathed by Sir William (d. 1686) to his nephew Henry Savile for life, with reversion to his cousin's son William Coventry who was lord by 1700.[69] William inherited the earldom of Coventry in 1719 and died in 1751, leaving the estate to his younger son John Bulkeley Coventry (d. 1801); it passed later to John's elder brother George (d. 1809), earl of Coventry, and to George's younger son, the Hon. John Coventry of Spring Hill (Worcs.) and later of Burgate House (Hants), who in 1824 sold it to Thomas Denton of Ashford Lodge (Mdx.) and later of Lew.[70] Denton died in 1851 and his relict Elizabeth in 1859, when the estate passed to trustees under Denton's will.[71] The land in Lew was sold to John Jones of Worcester before 1863, when

he sold it to Christ Church, Oxford; in 1865 the rest of the estate was sold with the manorial rights also to Jones, who conveyed much of it to Jesus College, Oxford.[72] Jones died in 1875 leaving the residue of his estates in trust to be sold, and manorial rights evidently lapsed.[73]

CASTLE. The castle, later Ham Court,[74] was built on the town's western edge by Aymer de Valence c. 1315, in which year he received a licence to crenellate. It remained the manor house for Bampton Earls manor, and was divided between the two moieties from the 17th century until 1871.[75] A 13th-century window surviving in 1821[76] suggests that the castle succeeded a house built by Aymer's father William c. 1256, when he received oaks and beams for his new hall,[77] and presumably there was an earlier royal manor house on or near the site:[78] wine was sent to Bampton as well as to the royal palace at Woodstock in 1210, and letters close and patent were dated from Bampton in 1236 and later.[79] The castle was partly ruined by 1664 and was mostly demolished before 1789;[80] surviving remains, all of c. 1315, comprise the lower half of the west gatehouse, abutted on the north by a rectangular lodging range of 2 storeys, and on the south by c. 10 m. of curtain wall. Before 1660 the gatehouse and lodging range were converted into a farmhouse, called Ham Court presumably from nearby Ham field,[81] and further alterations were made in the 18th and 19th centuries. It remained a farmhouse in 1994.

A drawing of the west front in 1664[82] shows the gatehouse crenellated, with, over the gate passage, a tall, two-light transomed window, presumably with curvilinear tracery similar to that in the northern lodging range. The gatehouse formed the centrepiece of a symmetrical front of 4 bays, which extended north and south to round corner-towers with 3 tiers of arrowslits, and which had 2 intermediate projecting turrets supported on pillars 'partly … within the wall, and partly standing without'.[83] The castle was said to be quadrangular, with round towers at each corner and similar gatehouses on the east and, possibly, north and south, implying a symmetrical plan grouped around a courtyard. A

60   O.R.O., Tice I/i/1; P.R.O., C 142/774, no. 17; G.E.C. *Baronetage*, i. 50.

61   P.R.O., C 142/774, no. 17; Bodl. MS. d.d. Shrewsbury c 1/7 (13); Giles, *Hist. Bampton*, Suppl. p. 2; G.E.C. *Baronetage*, i. 50; *D.N.B.* s.v. Thos. Coventry, 1st Baron Coventry.

62   Bodl. MS. Top. Oxon. b 169, ff. 26–28v.; ibid. MS. d.d. Shrewsbury c 1/7 (1–10); O.R.O., Misc. Lancs. VI/12, some describing his share as a half.

63   Bodl. MSS. d.d. Shrewsbury c 1/7 (11), c 1/7 (13).

64   Ibid. c 2, c 3, c 4, *passim*; Act for vesting … estates of Charles, earl of Shrewsbury … in trustees, 43 Geo. III, c. 40 (Local and Personal); *Complete Peerage*, xi. 720–27, 731.

65   *Sale Cat., Shrewsbury Settled Estates* (1870): copy in O.R.O., Crowdy I/51; Act for vesting … estates … in trustees, 43 Geo. III, c. 40 (Local and Personal).

66   Jesus Coll. Mun., box 15, list 4, conveyance 5 May 1871; Ch. Ch. Arch., MS. Estates 74, ff. 144–5; ibid. Lew, C 1, C 2; below, Lew, manor; cf. O.R.O., Misc. Me I/3–4; ibid. Adkin II/2; Bodl. G.A. Oxon. b 92 (41).

67   *Sale Cat.* (1870), lot 20; above, intro. (buildings).

68   O.R.O., incl. award; ibid. Tice I/vii/5; Arundel Castle, MS. TP 104.

69   P.R.O., PROB 11/384, f. 14; Arundel Castle, MS. TP 288.

70   P.R.O., PROB 11/787, f. 62; O.R.O., Tice I/v/1–4, 6–7; *Complete Peerage*, iii. 473; Burke, *Peerage* (1878), 291–2; below, Lew, manor.

71   O.R.O., Tice I/vii/1, 3.

72   Ibid. Tice I/vii/3, 5–7; Ch. Ch. Arch., MS. Estates 74, ff. 134–138v.; ibid. Lew, B 1–2; Jesus Coll. Mun., box 15, list 4, conveyances 6 Jan. 1865, 21 June 1865; list 5, conveyance 26 Oct. 1865.

73   O.R.O., Tice I/vii/10; cf. *P.O. Dir. Oxon.* (1877), mistakenly calling him lord.

74   Cf. Pevsner, *Oxon.* 433; *Country Life*, c (1946), 120–1; J. Blair, 'Bampton Castle' (Bampton Research Paper 1, priv. print. 1988), on which the following account is partly based: copy in C.O.S.

75   *Cal. Pat.* 1313–17, 278; below.

76   B.L. Add. MS. 36372, f. 119v., erased drawing visible under ultra-violet light.

77   *Close R.* 1254–6, 259, 305, 351.

78   Above, intro. [settlement]; this section (Bampton manor).

79   *Pipe R.* 1210 (P.R.S. N.S. xxvi), 193; *Close R.* 1234–7, 400; above, intro.

80   Below.

81   Below, econ. hist. (agric.).

82   *Wood's Life*, ii, p. 21 and pl. 1.   83   Ibid.

projection based on surviving remains, corroborated by earthworks to the west and north and by watercourses to the east and west, suggests a frontage of *c.* 110 m. (360 ft.), far larger than Aymer's castle at Goodrich (Herefs.), which may indicate that Bampton castle was planned as the *caput* for his barony.[84] Surviving ditches and a residual scarp to the west suggest a broad moat *c.* 30 m. wide.[85]

dower awards, having evidently been set aside for domestic use: the only other parts of the castle granted were half a building (*domus*) called 'Longstable', with the enclosure between it and the gatehouse, the west garden, and an east garden which extended from the 'Knyhton' chamber eastwards to the mill pond and southwards to the road into Bampton. A fishpond in the west garden and a dovecot were also men-

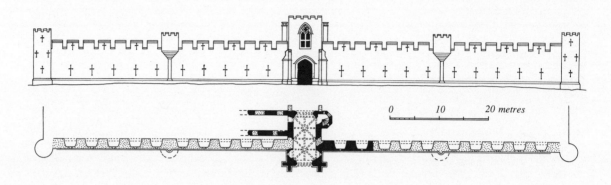

BAMPTON CASTLE: WEST FRONT
Reconstruction based on A. Wood's drawing of 1664 and surviving remains

The gatehouse,[86] projecting forward from the line of the curtain wall, retains pairs of angle buttresses on the external corners, with scars for similar buttresses on the east. Small embrasures for arrow-slits survive in the side walls at the west end of the gate passage, and at the east end are a pair of two-centred doorways, the northern leading to the ground floor of the lodging range, and the southern to a polygonal stair turret with tiny cusped-headed single-light windows, which rises to the level of the demolished upper chamber over the gate passage. Internally the gate passage comprises two square, rib-vaulted bays, each with a much-damaged foliage boss. The lodging block's upper storey retains a fireplace of high quality with moulded jambs and a corbelled stone hood, and in the east wall a two-light transomed window with curvilinear tracery. Its ground floor has no medieval features, and its north end has been truncated or rebuilt.

Despite its size, the castle seems to have been used only as an occasional residence. Aymer stayed at Bampton in 1307 and 1312 but is not known to have visited after 1315,[87] and Gilbert, Lord Talbot (d. 1387), leasing the manor to Sir Robert Tresilian in 1382, reserved the right to stay for a day and night if the lessee and his wife were absent.[88] In 1397 and 1420 the west gatehouse and rooms adjoining were included in

tioned.[89] Other parts of the castle and its associated buildings may already have been derelict, since in 1422 the remaining two-thirds of the manor included a stone house with granges and other 'ruined' buildings.[90] Some bailiffs in the 15th century[91] may have been accommodated in the castle, and by the later 16th century the whole site, variously described as the castle or mansion house or as Ham Court, was let with the demesne to the lord's steward or to local gentry, some of whom probably sublet it. In the earlier 17th century the demesne and some agricultural buildings were sometimes let separately.[92]

The buildings were partitioned with the manor in 1660, by which time the west gatehouse and lodging block were the only habitable parts, and the gate passage had been blocked and divided into two storeys.[93] The earl of Shrewsbury's tenant received the first two floors, comprising a hall and parlour on the ground floor of the gatehouse with one long room above, and a chamber and service rooms in the lodging range. William Coventry's tenant received two upper storeys apparently over the former gate passage, and adjoining offices perhaps in a 'little cabin' north of the gatehouse, built against the curtain wall before 1664 and supported in part apparently by the lodging block.[94] The kitchen was

84 Blair, 'Bampton Castle', 1, 4–6, figs. 5 and 7.
85 Ibid. 5–6; *Wood's Life*, ii. 21.
86 Para. based on Blair, 'Bampton Castle', 2–4.
87 D. & C. Exeter, MS. 3672, pp. 17–18; J. S. Phillips, *Aymer de Valence, Earl of Pembroke*, 35 and n.
88 *Cal. Close*, 1381–5, 108.
89 P.R.O., C 136/95, no. 17; C 139/42, no. 86; cf. B.L. Map C 7 e 16 (3), map between pp. 34–5, showing a small pond SE. of the gateho.
90 P.R.O., C 138/58, no. 44.

91 Cf. *Cal. Pat.* 1467–77, 400, 421; 1476–85, 369; *Complete Peerage*, xii (1), 620 n.
92 e.g. P.R.O., REQ 2/44/6; REQ 2/105/15; REQ 2/198/14; ibid. C 2/Jas. I/W 20/37; ibid. PROB 11/121, ff. 18–20; PROB 11/214, ff. 230–2; B.L. Add. Ch. 38960; O.R.O., MS. Wills Oxon. 17/1/61; Bodl. MS. d.d. Shrewsbury c 1/7 (13); Longleat House (Wilts.), Coventry pps. CVI, ff. 35v., 83, 85.
93 Bodl. MS. d.d. Shrewsbury c 1/7 (13).
94 *Wood's Life*, ii, plate 1.

evidently free standing. A 'great door' leading to the main stairs in 1660 was perhaps that on the gatehouse's east side near the south-east stair turret, which in the early 19th century had a small, projecting porch in classical style, with an arched opening, keystone, and cornice.[95] A great barn of 7 bays, mentioned in 1592 and also partitioned in 1660,[96] may have been the cruck-framed barn surviving in 1821, presumably one of three long ranges north-east and south-east of the gatehouse which were aligned from west to east and lay within the putative medieval enclosure.[97] The north and south curtain walls were ruinous presumably by 1664, when it was unclear whether they included gatehouses, and surviving walls were demolished before 1789.[98]

Ham Court was let from the later 17th century to resident farmers.[99] The gatehouse's upper half was demolished perhaps before 1789, when the Coventrys' tenant was no longer accommodated there: by 1821 the gatehouse comprised only the lower two storeys with attics lit by dormer windows, the upper stage having been replaced by a steep-pitched roof of stone slate.[1] The Coventrys' tenant in 1789 occupied a later-demolished line of buildings on the south, which in the mid 19th century included a south-facing, stone-built house of two storeys with a pitched gabled roof and attic dormers.[2] That was demolished probably after Jesus College, Oxford, acquired the whole farm,[3] and before 1876 a plain, square extension of two storeys, with stone-mullioned windows and a canted bay window on the south, was built onto the gatehouse's south side behind the curtain wall, whose south end was rebuilt.[4] Presumably about that time the north lodging range was refurbished, a battlemented parapet was added to the polygonal stair turret at the gatehouse's south-east corner, and windows in the blocked carriageway on the west were renewed.[5]

The manor of *BAMPTON DEANERY* or *BAMPTON EXETER*, otherwise the rectory manor, originated in King Eadwig's grant to Bampton minster between 955 and 957 of lands in Bampton, Aston, and Chimney.[6] Before 1066 the estate was granted probably by Edward the Confessor to his clerk Leofric (d. 1072), later bishop of Exeter; he gave it in 1069 to the newly founded Exeter cathedral chapter, and in 1086 it was assessed at 6 hides.[7] Three additional ploughlands, which paid no geld and were later held in demesne, were claimed in the 13th century to have been given by King Athelstan (d. 939),[8] but there is no evidence that the cathedral or its predecessors owned land in Bampton before Leofric's gift, and probably the whole manor derived from the former minster estate.[9] Except for a brief period during the Interregnum the chapter held the manor until 1862 when it was vested in the Ecclesiastical Commissioners, who sold or exchanged the Aston land and some of that in Bampton and Weald in 1866, and made later piecemeal sales. In 1990 the Church Commissioners retained 487 a. in Bampton and Weald.[10]

In 1086 Robert Losinga, bishop of Hereford, held the 6 hides and possibly all 9 at farm.[11] In the mid 12th century probably the whole estate, including tithes and other ecclesiastical revenues, was used to endow two prebends in Exeter cathedral, but before the 1180s there was some reorganization: a 'prebend' or farm mentioned from 1189 × 96 and confirmed to the chapter before 1220 seems to have been the later rectory manor, which included the glebe and house, some tithes, and half the offerings, and in the early 13th century the remaining ecclesiastical revenues were used to endow perpetual vicarages.[12] The manor was leased until 1382, when all the chapter's estates were taken in hand;[13] early lessees included the royal clerks Godfrey de Lucy and Richard Marsh,[14] but from the 1220s all were canons of Exeter.[15]

From the late 14th century the manor was let in parcels, resulting in the emergence of two, and later three, distinct estates. That later called the 'parsonage' or 'rectory', made up wholly or partly of former demesne and including the medieval manor house, was let from 1398–9 or earlier,[16] and was estimated at *c.* 200 a. in 1662.[17] Fifteenth-century lessees included bailiffs and vicars or their relatives,[18] but from the 16th century the estate was held by local gentry, notably the Mores of Lower Haddon from 1538, in the early 17th century the Peisleys, from

95 Below, plate 2; cf. Bodl. MS. Top. Oxon. d 218, f. 47.
96 P.R.O., REQ 2/198/14; Bodl. MS. d.d. Shrewsbury c 1/7 (13).
97 B.L. Add. MS. 36437; ibid. Map C 7 e 16 (3), between pp. 34–5; Blair, 'Bampton Castle', 6, fig. 8.
98 B.L. Map C 7 e 16 (3), between pp. 34–5; *Wood's Life*, ii. 21; cf. Bodl. MS. Don. c 90, f. 367.
99 Bodl. MSS. d.d. Shrewsbury c 3/9 (1), (10); c 4/10 (12); Arundel Castle, MS. TP 98, pp. 25–7.
1 B.L. Map C 7 e 16 (3), p. 42, map between pp. 34–5; Bodl. MS. Top. Oxon. a 65, no. 62; ibid. MS. Top. gen. a 11, f. 115; below, plate 2.
2 B.L. Map C 7 e 16 (3), map between pp. 34–5; O.R.O., incl. award; Bodl. MS. Top. Oxon. c 522, f. 21; Giles, *Hist. Bampton*, 64; cf. Jesus Coll. Mun., box 15, list 4, *passim*.
3 Below, other estates.
4 O.S. Map 1/2,500, Oxon. XXXVII. 6 (1876 edn.).
5 Cf. Bodl. MS. Top. Oxon. a 65, nos. 61–2; C.O.S., OPA 4806; *Country Life*, c (1946), 120.
6 *Jnl. Brit. Arch. Assoc.* xxxix (1883), 298–301; after 957 Eadwig ruled in Wessex only.
7 *Jnl. Brit. Arch. Assoc.* xxxix. 298–301; *Cod. Dipl.* ed.

Kemble, iv, no. 940; *V.C.H. Oxon.* i. 402; *D.N.B.* s.v. Leofric.
8 D. & C. Exeter, MSS. 641, 643, 2931; ibid. MS. 3672, pp. 17–18; *Bampton Hund.* R. 23, 76. Cf. J. Blair, 'Medieval Clergy' (Bampton Research Paper 4, priv. print. 1991), 5 n.: copy in C.O.S.
9 For appurtenant houses in Oxford, Blair, 'Medieval Clergy', 2, 5, 9.
10 Ch. Com. Rec. L 7, pp. 399, 445; ibid. 22529A–D; D. & C. Exeter, Ch. Comm. 80/134557; *Lond. Gaz.* 5 Sept. 1862, pp. 4364–5; inf. from Church Commissioners.
11 *V.C.H. Oxon.* i. 402.
12 Below, this section; churches.
13 *Jnl. Soc. Archivists*, ii (1960–4), 258.
14 *Rot. Welles*, i (L.R.S. iii), p. 129; cf. *Rot. Litt. Pat.* i (Rec. Com.), p. 87; *Reg. Antiquiss.* iii (L.R.S. xxix), p. 265; *D.N.B.*
15 J. Blair, 'Bampton Deanery' (Bampton Research Paper 2, priv. print. 1988), 20–2: copy in C.O.S.
16 D. & C. Exeter, MS. 5100, referring to the 18th year of the farm.
17 Ibid. MS. 4030, p. 13; ibid. MS. 2028.
18 Ibid. MSS. 6016/2/1–2; ibid. MS. 3498 (35); cf. ibid. MS. 2727; *Oxoniensia*, lvi. 116–18.

c. 1624 the Dewes, and from 1778 to *c.* 1813 the Hawkinses,[19] all of whom seem to have sublet the land to local farmers.[20] A small part, later 70 a., was let separately from 1619.[21] In 1651 the estate was bought from the trustees for sale of Church lands by John Fielder of Borough Court in Odiham (Hants), but was recovered by the cathedral at the Restoration.[22]

The rest of the manor, in Bampton, Aston, Cote, Chimney, and Clanfield,[23] was let with the manorial rights in 1549 to John Southcott of Bovey Tracey and Thomas Deane of Dartington (Devon), who in 1552 assigned their right to Thomas More (d. 1561), lord of Haddon. It descended with Haddon until 1617 when John More sold the lease to William Hanks of Aston and Robert Veysey of Taynton.[24] Chimney was held by the Veyseys and their successors thereafter,[25] and the rest of the manor by the Hankses and their successors, manorial rights being shared until 1838 when it was agreed to lease them with the Bampton moiety only.[26]

William Hanks (d. 1627) was succeeded by his relict Jane (d. 1658),[27] who from 1641 held jointly with her son John[28] and in 1650 bought her moiety from the trustees for the sale of Church lands following the cathedral's deprivation.[29] John (d. 1669) succeeded her, and obtained a renewal of the chapter's lease after the Restoration.[30] The estate passed to his relict Dorothy (d. 1702), who married John Loder of Hinton Waldrist (Berks.), to Dorothy's sister Mary Croft (d. 1719), and perhaps before Mary's death to their nephew John Frederick (d. 1739) of Bampton and Gray's Inn; he held it from 1726 with his son John (d. 1775) of Wellingborough (Northants.), and left his lands in trust to his younger son Gascoigne.[31] The estate was settled on Gascoigne in 1754 following the discharge of legacies under earlier family settlements.[32] Gascoigne's sister Mary succeeded him in 1780 and died in 1785, leaving her lands to her sisters Elizabeth Snell (d. 1788) and Susannah Frederick (d. 1798); both left their share to their relative Edward Whitaker (d. 1825),[33] succeeded in 1828, following a dispute over his will, by his son Frederick (d. 1854),

deputy-lieutenant of Oxfordshire. In 1866 Frederick's trustees acquired the freehold of much of the estate, including the post-medieval manor house and apparently manorial rights, from the Ecclesiastical Commissioners by purchase and exchange;[34] the house was acquired later by the Bampton solicitor Robert Hockley Bullen (d. 1870), whose relict Emily (d. 1894) was called lady of the manor in 1891,[35] but manorial rights were not mentioned later.

William I's confirmation to Leofric and Exeter cathedral in 1069 included 'all the king's tithes', later interpreted by the chapter as those arising from ancient demesne within the former Bampton manor.[36] Rectorial tithes, owed in 1317 from lands in Brize Norton, Shilton, Yelford, Ducklington, Hardwick, Standlake, Black Bourton, and Clanfield as well as from Bampton, Weald, Lew, Haddon, Aston, and Shifford,[37] remained with the cathedral except during the Interregnum, when they were sold with the 'parsonage' estate.[38] In the 14th century most were farmed with the manor, and in the earlier 15th they were administered by the cathedral's bailiff;[39] from the late 15th and the 16th they were let in parcels, those from the 'parsonage' lands descending with that estate from 1476, and corn tithes, oblations, and a third of Bampton and Weald's hay tithe being held from 1753 with the Bampton moiety.[40] Under a private agreement in the 1560s Exeter College, Oxford, paid 26s. 8d. annually towards the marriage of poor women of Bampton and 13s. 4d. to the poor while holding corn and hay tithes.[41] Eynsham abbey retained most demesne tithes in Shifford until the early 15th century, when the demesne was farmed and became fully tithable,[42] and *c.* 1074 Robert d'Oilly gave two thirds of his demesne tithes of Bampton to the chapel of St. George in Oxford castle, from which they passed to Osney abbey and were exchanged with the vicars in 1433.[43] Moduses in the 17th century and later included 5d. (formerly 4d.) for calves, 1½d. for cows, 1d. for heifers, 2d. for lambs, and, by the 19th century, 2 eggs per hen on Good Friday, though some other tithes were still then collected in kind.[44] Tithes in Bampton, Weald,

[19] D. & C. Exeter, MSS. 6016/2/3–40; ibid. Ch. Comm. 14/74394–9; O.R.O., D.Y. VII/i/1, D.Y. VII/ii/1; Oxf. Jnl. Synopsis, 30 Dec. 1778.

[20] D. & C. Exeter, MS. 2028; ibid. MS. 4030, p. 13; ibid. Ch. Comm. 13/74363, p. 27; P.R.O., E 179/255/4, pt. i, f. 20; O.R.O., QSD L.22; Bodl. MS. d.d. Fitt c 4.

[21] O.R.O., D.Y. VII/ii/1–3; ibid. incl. award.

[22] P.R.O., C 54/3603, no. 40; D. & C. Exeter, MS. 4030, p. 14; *V.C.H. Hants*, iv. 93.

[23] D. & C. Exeter, MSS. 4030, 4544; cf. *Oxoniensia*, l. 209–14.

[24] O.R.O., D.Y. VII/i/1; cf. below, Lower Haddon, manor.

[25] Below, Chimney, manor.

[26] D. & C. Exeter, Ch. Comm. 13/74373a, 13/74354–5; ibid. MS. 2031. For leases and partitions, ibid. MSS. 6016/1/1–45; B.L. Add. Ch. 38928–9, 38933–4, 38937, 38941, 38943, 38954–8, 38951.

[27] P.R.O., PROB 11/152, ff. 424v.–425; PROB 11/284, ff. 351–3.

[28] O.R.O., D.Y. VII/i/3; D. & C. Exeter, MS. 4777.

[29] P.R.O., E 134/1656–7/Hil. 4; ibid. E 134/1656–7/Hil. 20; Giles, *Hist. Bampton*, 147–50.

[30] D. & C. Exeter, MSS. 658–9, 1980–2, 4030; O.R.O., MS. Wills Oxon. 33/3/16.

[31] O.R.O., D.Y. VII/vi/4; D.Y. VII/vi/9; P.R.O., PROB 11/464, ff. 153–4; B.L. Add. Ch. 38934–6, 38944; Bodl. MS. Ch. Oxon. 3001; C.O.S., par reg. transcripts.

[32] O.R.O., D.Y. VII/vi/8–9.

[33] B.L. Add. Ch. 38952–4; D. & C. Exeter, Ch. Comm. 80/134558, 80/134561; cf. *Oxon. Anecdotes* [*c.* 1826], 3–4: copy in Bodl. Mary held in trust for Gascoigne from 1761.

[34] D. & C. Exeter, Ch. Comm. 80/134561, 80/134557; Ch. Com. Rec. L 7, pp. 399, 455; *D.N.B.* s.v. Whitaker.

[35] O.R.O., Crowdy I/51, town plan; P.R.O., RG 11/1514; *Kelly's Dir. Oxon.* (1891 and later edns.); C.O.S., par reg. transcripts.

[36] *Jnl. Brit. Arch. Assoc.* xxxix. 299; *Oxon. Local Hist.* ii (2), 37–8.

[37] D. & C. Exeter, MS. 2931; cf. ibid. MS. 6016/6, rents of Bampton; ibid. Ch. Comm. 13/74360. For the vicars' share, below, churches.

[38] P.R.O., C 54/3603, no. 40; above, this section.

[39] D. & C. Exeter, MSS. 2931, 5100–6.

[40] Ibid. MSS. 6015/2–3, 6016/2/2–40, 6016/3/1–9; ibid. Ch. Comm. 14/74394–74401.

[41] Exeter College Mun., M. II. 1.

[42] *Eynsham Cart.* i, pp. 4, 306; ii, pp. 5–6; D. & C. Exeter, MSS. 2931, 5101–2.

[43] *Oseney Cart.* iv, pp. 3, 26–7, 496–8; *V.C.H. Oxon.* ii. 160; cf. D. & C. Exeter, MS. 640.

[44] O.R.O., MS. Oxf. Archd. Oxon. c 31, f. 135v.; ibid. Aston and Cote tithe award (1841), p. 2; B.L. Add. Ch. 38921; D. & C. Exeter, Ch. Comm. 13/74360; Bodl. MS. d.d. Harcourt c 296, deposition of Thos. Banister 1766; A. Young, *Oxon. Agric.* 40.

and Lew, excepting those from the 'parsonage' estate, were commuted at inclosure in 1821, when the chapter received in exchange 212½ a. and, in Haddon, a corn-rent charge of £85 to be reassessed every 14 years.[45] The chapter's tithes in Aston and Cote, Brighthampton, and Shifford were commuted between 1841 and 1849 for rent charges totalling £142 16s., which in 1862 were vested in the Ecclesiastical Commissioners with the rest of the estate.[46]

The medieval manor house, west of the church, was called the Deanery by the mid 19th century.[47] In the 14th it was kept in demesne by farmers of the manor presumably for bailiffs and as an occasional residence,[48] and was later let with the 'parsonage' estate. Right of accommodation was reserved for the chapter and their officers, and in the late 15th century the dean stayed there during a journey from London.[49] In the 17th century and the 18th it was occupied probably by some of the Dewes and Hawkinses,[50] and in the 19th became a farmhouse;[51] it was sold without its farmland in 1921.[52]

The surviving building,[53] of coursed limestone rubble with ashlar dressings, is two-storeyed with a basement and attics, and pitched, stone-slated roofs. The plan is irregular, with projecting north, east, and south-west wings of different dates. At basement level on the house's south side the east end of a later-truncated range of the late 11th or early 12th century retains two symmetrically-disposed windows with rounded heads and wide splays; the sill of a third window and one splay of another in the south wall also survive. An east range was built to the north-east in the later 12th century, with an overlapping abutment which blocked the northernmost of the three windows. Its thick basement walls each contain at least one window with wide splays and ashlar quoins, and three sets of rubble voussoirs on its external north wall are evidently the relieving arches for more windows. The range's west wall was probably rebuilt c. 1200, and includes remains of a lancet window high in the gable end and of a pointed doorway leading into the basement. The north wing, much altered and of uncertain date, retains opposing doorways which may be evidence for a late medieval plan.

In the late 16th or early 17th century, perhaps after the lease passed from the the non-resident Mores to Bartholomew Peisley and the Dewe family,[54] the surviving portions of the house were extensively remodelled. The north wing may have been rebuilt with a large internal chimney stack, the south and east walls of the east wing were rebuilt, and a large stack was added to the south range, whose upper part was rebuilt and and whose west end may have been demolished. Later in the 17th century a staircase with corkscrew balusters was built into the central area. Building work was noted in 1814,[55] but most 19th-century alterations appear to have been destructive as the house was reduced in size, notably through truncation of the house's west end and north wing,[56] to whose north gable diagonal buttresses were added in imitation of those on the east wing. A two-storeyed extension in Tudor style was added in the north-west angle in the mid 19th century, and in the earlier 20th the porch was rebuilt and the south range extended, shortly before dormers were added to the roof.[57] A major restoration and renovation was carried out in 1990 and 1991.

A thatched 'old hall' mentioned in 1317 may have been free-standing and linked to the other buildings by a covered way or *claustrum*.[58] It was derelict by 1381 when a new hall with a chamber at its west end was built by the chapter's farmer. A stone-slated first-floor chapel with glazed windows, mentioned in the 14th and 15th centuries, was presumably in one of the surviving medieval ranges, both aligned on the church;[59] the abutting range apparently contained two chambers in 1317, both with chimneys and garderobes, and one in 1381. Service rooms in 1317 included a buttery, larder, kitchen, bakehouse, and dairy, all stone-slated, and a thatched malt-drying house. A substantial stone-built gatehouse, evidently on the site of the modern gate near Cobb House, was ruinous in 1317, when it had a chamber over, and a granary or bailiff's chamber formed one side; the chamber was removed c. 1389 and the gate was reroofed. Buildings flanking the gateway in the late 18th century and early 19th but demolished before 1876 were perhaps its remains. A possible inner gateway immediately north of the house, shown on a map of 1789 when it formed part of a north range running westwards from the north wing, may have been an earlier entrance before the curtilage was extended northwards, perhaps in the 13th century. Both it and the north range were demolished before 1876.[60]

Agricultural buildings in 1317 included a thatched tithe barn 129 ft. long, ordered to be demolished in 1389, and a 156-ft. demesne barn adjoining a 136-ft. byre. All lay presumably north of the house as in 1789, within a 4-a. court and barnyard. An 8-a. garden mentioned in 1317 would have fitted into the later curtilage south

45 Bampton Incl. Act, 52 Geo. III, c. 46 (Local and Personal, not printed); O.R.O., Bampton incl. award.

46 O.R.O., tithe awards; Bodl. MS. d.d. Harcourt c 296, copy of Shifford tithe award; Ch. Com. Rec. L 7, pp. 365–83.

47 Giles, *Hist. Bampton*, 25.

48 D. & C. Exeter, MS. 2931.

49 Ibid. MSS. 5100, 6016/2/1–2; *Oxoniensia*, lvi. 113.

50 e.g. P.R.O., PROB 11/388, f. 107; D. &. C. Exeter, Ch. Comm. 13/74363, p. 27; O.R.O., Cal. Q.S. viii, p. 593; Bodl. MS. d.d. Fitt c 4; Oxf. Jnl. Synopsis, 30 Dec. 1778; C.O.S., par. reg. transcripts.

51 P.R.O., HO 107/1731; ibid. RG 9/905.

52 Ch. Com. Rec. 335687.

53 Cf. Blair, 'Bampton Deanery', on which the following acct. is partly based; Pevsner, *Oxon.* 432–3. Illust. in *Country Life*, c (1946), 168–9; Bodl. MS. Top. Oxon. c 6, p. 63;

C.O.S., OPA 4803–4; below, plate 7. For maps, D. & C. Exeter, MS. M 1; O.R.O., incl. award, plan I.

54 Above. Peisley, formerly of Aston and Haddon, lived in Bampton by 1616: Jesus Coll. Mun., box 15, list 1 (bdle. 1), no. 16.

55 D. & C. Exeter, MS. 6016/7, bdle. 2, letter from W. Higgons 25 Feb. 1814.

56 Cf. O.R.O., incl. award, plan I; O.S. Map 1/2,500, Oxon. XXXVII. 6 (1876 edn.).

57 Cf. O.R.O., incl. award, plan I; Bodl. MS. Top. Oxon. c 6, p. 63; C.O.S., OPA 4803–4.

58 Two paras. based on Blair, 'Bampton Deanery'; cf. D. & C. Exeter, MSS. 2857, 2931.

59 Cf. Blair, 'Bampton Deanery', 18, suggesting that it may have originated as an 11th-century double chapel.

60 O.S. Map 1/2,500, Oxon. XXXVII. 6 (1876 edn.).

and south-east of the house, including Horse close and coppice which were later confused with the lessee's freehold.[61] Fishpools in the garden in 1317 were probably in the canalized streams of Shill brook, and a dovecot in the garden was mentioned in leases until 1538.[62] A formal garden laid out south of the house before 1789 was obliterated during the 19th century.[63]

The manor house for the Bampton and Aston moiety from the early 17th century was that west of Broad Street, called Bampton Manor House by the mid 19th century.[64] In origin the farmhouse for an amalgamation of 3 copyhold yardlands,[65] it was adopted as the manor house presumably during the 1620s when William Hanks, formerly of Aston, settled in Bampton;[66] thereafter it was occupied successively by the Hankses, Fredericks, and Whitakers,[67] and was substantially rebuilt probably by Edward Whitaker c. 1806. In 1669 it was two-storeyed and included a hall, a study, great and little parlours, and a kitchen, brewhouse, and buttery; in 1767 it comprised a main north–south range, presumably the hall, with symmetrical cross wings projecting eastwards.[68] Early in the 19th century, presumably after Edward Whitaker complained that the house would have to be 'nearly all taken down and rebuilt',[69] the main range was replaced by a large 3-storeyed block with a hipped, Stonesfield-slated roof; the remodelled 17th-century cross wings were retained at the north and south ends of the east front, forming a symmetrical composition. Both wings retain 18th-century panelling, of which that in the southern rooms is of soon after 1700, and there are some re-used 17th-century fittings. The line of the southern cross wing was continued westwards to provide a south entrance front perhaps also c. 1806: the central doorway stands at the base of a 3-storeyed stair tower with a gabled roof, which in 1848 had an arcaded entrance porch with a tall round-headed window above.[70] The porch was replaced by one in Gothic style and the tall window by an oriel in the later 19th century. A 2-storeyed south-west wing with a gabled roof, probably also 19th-century, was replaced c. 1904–5 by a single-storeyed wing with a parapet, creating an approximately sym-metrical south front.[71] The house was refurbished in the early 1980s and the stucco was renewed.

A stable block and carriage house on the north were built by Gascoigne Frederick in 1755,[72] and in 1767 there was a small formal garden immediately west and south of the house, the outline of which remained visible in 1876.[73] A carriageway leading southwards from the house, lined in 1841 with a 'beautiful avenue of elm trees',[74] was replaced by one to Broad Street in the 20th century, and in the later 20th century the gardens were relandscaped and a small pond created.[75]

Four hides in Bampton, Weald, and Aston, later *BAMPTON DOILLY* manor, were held in chief in 1086 by Robert d'Oilly (d. c. 1093) and of him by Roger, possibly a relative.[76] The overlordship, which descended with the barony of Hook Norton, was recorded on the death of Hugh de Plessis in 1363 but had apparently lapsed by 1428,[77] and in the 16th century the manor was held as of Bampton manor, to which quitrents of probably 6s. were owed.[78]

The undertenancy, assessed with Kencot at 2 knights' fees,[79] passed before 1142 to Roger d'Oilly and before c. 1150 to his son Roger, who by separate gifts granted ½ hide and one yardland in Aston to Eynsham abbey.[80] The manor was held thereafter by a succession of d'Oillys, all called Roger, until the early 14th century, a small portion being held in dower in 1222.[81] In 1268 Roger son of Roger d'Oilly granted the reversion to Roger son of John d'Oilly, but on the former's death c. 1309 the manor was divided between his two coheirs and their husbands Richard of Goldsborough (Yorks. W.R.) and John de Meaux, whose rights were upheld against Roger son of John's heir.[82]

The Goldsborough moiety, apparently held in dower in 1395,[83] descended through the male line to Richard Goldsborough (d. 1504), and to his son Richard (d. 1508) and grandson Thomas (d. 1566).[84] Some lands and rents were held by relatives in the 14th century, and in the earlier 15th the manor was apparently leased.[85] Thomas settled the moiety in 1564 on his son Richard,[86] who in 1570 sold it to Charles Matthew of

61 D. & C. Exeter, MS. 6016/7, bdle. 1, letter from F. Whitaker 18 Dec. 1815; O.R.O., incl. award, plan I.
62 D. & C. Exeter, MSS. 6016/2/1–4.
63 Ibid. MS. M 1; O.S. Map 1/2,500, Oxon. XXXVII. 6 (1876 edn.).
64 Giles, *Hist. Bampton*, frontispiece; O.S. Map 1/2,500, Oxon. XXXVII. 6 (1876 edn.); below, plate 9.
65 D. & C. Exeter, MSS. 2933, p. 15; 2934, p. 3; Giles, *Hist. Bampton*, 148.
66 O.R.O., D.Y. VII/ii/1, D.Y. I/iii/1–2.
67 B.L. Add. MS. 31323 III; *Oxf. Jnl.* 29 Jan. 1780; Giles, *Hist. Bampton*, 22; datestone with name of G. Frederick, on stables.
68 B.L. Add. Ch. 38926; ibid. Add. MS. 31323 III.
69 D. & C. Exeter, MS. 6016/5 (1800–10 bdle.), letter 30 Aug. 1806.
70 Giles, *Hist. Bampton*, frontispiece.
71 D.o.E. *Revised Hist. Bldg. List: Bampton* (1989), 21: copy in C.O.S.; *Country Life*, c (1946), 169; C.O.S., OPA 4809–12; below, plate 9.
72 Datestone on stables.
73 B.L. Add. MS. 31323 III; O.S. Map 1/2,500, Oxon. XXXVII. 6 (1876 edn.).
74 *Sale Cat.* 25 Sept. 1841: copy in Blenheim Mun., shelf

J 4, box 20; O.R.O., MS. d.d. Par. Bampton a 2 (R).
75 O.S. Maps 1/2,500, Oxon. XXXVII. 6–7 (1876 and later edns.); SP 3003–3103 (1971 edn.); A. Lees-Milne and R. Verey, *The Englishwoman's Garden* (1980), 92–6.
76 *V.C.H. Oxon.* i. 414.
77 *Bampton Hund. R.* 28; *Cal. Inq. p.m.* xi, p. 354; *Feud. Aids*, iv. 194; Sanders, *Eng. Baronies*, 54.
78 P.R.O., C 142/143, no. 51, recording a 3s. quitrent for one moiety; *Cal. Inq. p.m. Hen. VII*, ii, p. 593.
79 *Bk. of Fees*, ii. 823, 837; *Feud. Aids*, iv. 194.
80 *Eynsham Cart.* i, pp. 73, 75–7.
81 B.L. Add. Ch. 56458; *Oxon. Fines*, p. 66; *Bk. of Fees*, ii. 823, 837; *Bampton Hund. R.* 28.
82 Bodl. MS. Dodsworth 143, ff. 28, 32v.–33v., 37v.; *Oxon. Fines*, p. 197; *Feud. Aids*, iv. 162, 182.
83 Bodl. MS. Dodsworth 143, f. 34.
84 Ibid. ff. 26–51; *Cal. Inq. p.m.* ix, p. 184; cf. A. Goldsbrough, *Memorials of the Goldesborough Fam.* (priv. print. 1930), between pp. 30–1.
85 Bodl. MS. Dodsworth 143, ff. 33v.–35v.; D. & C. Exeter, MSS. 4755; 4756, m. 3.
86 P.R.O., C 142/143, no. 51; Goldsbrough, *Goldesborough Fam.* 100–3.

Oxford;[87] from him most of it passed presumably by sale to Thomas Reed in 1571, and in 1576 to Thomas Yate, who in 1588 conveyed it to Leonard Yate of Witney.[88] An agreement between Leonard Yate and Michael Jobson in 1596 to divide the manorial profits[89] referred apparently to a subdivision of the moiety, since in 1624 Jobson's relict Margaret vested her right in Richard Blower, who held the moiety in common until 1658.[90] The other share was held probably in 1609 and certainly in 1620 by presumably another Thomas Yate, who with his wife conveyed it in 1635, evidently much diminished, to John Palmer of Bampton.[91] On Palmer's death in 1650 it was divided between his nieces Elizabeth, Katherine, and Ruth, who with their husbands John Young, William Nabbs, and Thomas Tremaine partitioned it in 1660.[92]

The Meaux moiety passed on John de Meaux's death after 1331[93] to his son Thomas (d. 1361), whose grandson and heir Thomas, a minor, entered on it in 1370, and in 1395 it was held by that Thomas's relict Alice.[94] In 1428 it was held by John Anthony, perhaps a lessee,[95] but before 1439 it passed apparently through marriage to the Spanby family of Spanby (Lincs.), descending to Arthur Spanby (d. 1509), and to Arthur's sister Joan and her husband James Saunders or Standish (d. 1557).[96] They seem to have conveyed it c. 1510 to the Haydock or Haddock family, which in the mid 16th century let all or part of it.[97] In 1595 William Haydock conveyed it to his relative Thomas Smallpage (d. 1597) of Gray's Inn,[98] who left it to his nephew Percival Smallpage (d. 1616); in 1617 Percival's sister Anne Smallpage and others sold it under earlier agreements to Thomas Ward and Thomas Willear of Bampton and possibly other tenants,[99] who sold much of it piecemeal.[1]

The later descent of both moieties is obscure, but by 1764 the manor, then a single farm of c. 230 a. centred on the manor house and no longer described as a moiety, was owned by Richard Lissett (d. 1764), vicar of Oundle (Northants.) and a native of Bampton. It passed to Richard's

nephew William Lissett (d. 1791) and niece Jane Lissett (d. 1799), whose trustee Edward Whitaker, of Bampton Deanery manor, evidently bought it under the terms of her will.[2] Though described as a manor in 1800 and occasionally thereafter, the farm seems by 1821 to have been absorbed into Whitaker's other freeholds, with which it was sold after his death, and by the mid 19th century it had been broken up.[3]

The d'Oillys had a manor house in Bampton possibly in 1086, when land was held in demesne, and certainly by 1247, when their 'court' included a house, barn, and fishpools.[4] Following the manor's partition either the curtilage was divided or another house was built: John de Meaux had a house in Bampton in 1349 and 1353, and in 1653 Thomas Willear's sale of part of his moiety included half of Meux close with a dovehouse and fishponds,[5] while the non-resident Goldesboroughs leased the 'site' of their manor probably in 1404 and in 1564.[6] The manor house in the 18th century and early 19th stood south of the market place on the site of modern Folly House,[7] and though it is uncertain to which moiety it belonged that may have been the site of the d'Oillys' medieval house: the surviving building includes a thick, possibly medieval wall, and excavation in 1989 revealed a concentration of medieval features, including 12th- and 13th-century pottery and, south of the house, traces of a possibly medieval wall running east–west along the edge of the gravel terrace, perhaps marking a southern boundary.[8] The curtilage's other boundaries are preserved perhaps in the lines of Cheyne Lane and of a former watercourse on the west, and of the southern edge of the market place on the north, suggesting a large inclosure c. 30 metres square.[9] Both moieties apparently included a dovecot, one of them perhaps the large, 17th-century stone dovecot west of Folly House, separately owned in the 19th century.[10]

Buildings in the early 19th century included a 'handsome, substantial and spacious mansion house' with barns, stables, a dovehouse, and

---

87 Bodl. MS. Dodsworth 143, f. 34v.; for rival claims, *Goldesborough Fam.* 103–6.

88 P.R.O., CP 25/2/196/13 Eliz. I Hil.; CP 25/2/196/18–19 Eliz. I Mich.; CP 25/2/197/30 Eliz. I East. For tenements alienated before 1599, O.R.O., D.Y. II/i/1, II/iii/1–2.

89 *Cat. Anct. D.* vi, p. 550.

90 P.R.O., CP 43/165, rot. 46; ibid. CP 25/2/588/1658/ East.; ibid. PROB 11/214, ff. 230–2.

91 B.L. Add. MS. 27535, f. 44; P.R.O., CP 25/2/340/17 Jas. I Hil.; CP 25/2/340/21 Jas. I Hil.; CP 25/2/473/10 Chas. I Hil.

92 P.R.O., PROB 11/214, ff. 230–2; ibid. CP 25/2/588/1656 East.; Bodl. MS. Top. Oxon. c 224, ff. 80–4; O.R.O., D.Y. XIV/i/1.

93 *Cal. Chart. R.* iv, p. 230.

94 Bodl. MS. Dodsworth 143, ff. 26, 28, 32v.–34, 36v.; *Cal. Inq. p.m.* ix, p. 184; xiii, pp. 31, 55–6.

95 *Feud. Aids*, iv. 194; cf. D. & C. Exeter, MSS. 4755; 4756, m. 3.

96 D. & C. Exeter, MS. 4756, m. 3; P.R.O., C 1/359, no. 19; ibid. C 142/24, no. 69; *L. & P. Hen. VIII*, i (2), p. 839, calling Joan a kinswoman and heir of John de Meaux.

97 P.R.O., CP 25/2/34/225; ibid. REQ 2/89/28; cf. *L. & P. Hen. VIII*, i (2), p. 839, implying that Standish was still owner in 1513.

98 P.R.O., CP 25/2/198/37 & 38 Eliz. I Mich.; cf. ibid. CP 40/1162, rot. 20, recording a Smallpage interest in 1555;

B.L. Add. MS. 27535, f. 44, still charging the 3s. quitrent to Haydock in 1609.

99 P.R.O., PROB 11/90, f. 250v.; PROB 11/128, f. 346v.; ibid. CP 25/2/340/15 Jas. I East.

1 O.R.O., D.Y. II/ii/1; Bodl. MS. Ch. Oxon. 4081; P.R.O., CP 25/2/473/10 Chas. I Mich.; cf. O.R.O., Acc. 2184, New Inn deeds; ibid. D.Y. XV/i/1–2, XV/ii/1–2, XV/iii/1–3.

2 P.R.O., PROB 11/905, f. 178 and v.; O.R.O., MSS. Wills Oxon. 140/3/17, 140/40/3/28; ibid. QSD L.22; Oxf. Jnl. Synopsis, 14 Dec. 1764; *Oxf. Jnl.* 9 Aug. 1800; M.I. in ch.

3 *Oxf. Jnl.* 9 Aug. 1800; O.R.O., incl. award; ibid. Mor. XIII/vii/1; P.R.O., RG 9/905, s.v. Kerwood's Yd.; ibid. PROB 11/1709, ff. 191v.–194.

4 *V.C.H. Oxon.* i. 414; D. & C. Exeter, MS. 640; P.R.O., JUST 1/700, m. 7.

5 Bodl. MS. Ch. Oxon. 4081; *Cal. Inq. p.m.* xiii, p. 55; *Cal. Pat.* 1350–4, 453; for Meux close, O.R.O., incl. award.

6 Bodl. MS. Dodsworth 143, f. 34; P.R.O., C 142/143, no. 51.

7 O.R.O., incl. award, s.v. Edw. Whitaker (Doiles).

8 *S. Midlands Arch.* xxii (1992), 56; inf. from B. G. Durham, Oxf. Arch. Unit.

9 O.R.O., incl. award and map.

10 Ibid.; P.R.O., CP 25/2/34/225; CP 25/2/196/13 Eliz. I Hil.

oxpens.[11] Though Jane Lissett may have lived there initially, by 1794 she occupied a house by the market place, and the manor house was let with the farm.[12] In 1861 the farmhouse was said to have been 'long since' converted into a pigeon house and later pulled down, and the site, then known as Kerwood's Yard, was occupied chiefly by agricultural labourers, some accommodated perhaps in converted farm buildings.[13] Most buildings were demolished in the late 19th century or early 20th, leaving a small, chiefly 18th-century stone-built range of two storeys, later gutted for use as a garage and outbuildings. The existing house, of timber and weatherboard and adjoining that range on the south, was built in the later 20th century. A malthouse to the north-west, built before 1876 and perhaps converted into a rifle range before 1909, was demolished before 1921.[14]

OTHER ESTATES. Land and a fishery in Weald granted to Osney abbey c. 1170 descended with the abbey's estate in Lew, and are treated below.[15] The Hospitallers held an estate in Weald and Burroway, attached to their preceptory at Clanfield, by 1279, when they owed 40s. a year and suit of court to the lord of Bampton Earls.[16] In 1575 the Crown granted the land in Burroway to speculators;[17] a house and two freehold yardlands in Weald which owed quit-rent to the Hospitallers in 1513 were owned in 1565 by Christopher Cheverell and his wife Isabel, who leased them,[18] but no further references have been found.

The Laundels family had land in Bampton by 1302,[19] and in the earlier 14th century a freehold and leasehold estate in Bampton, Weald, Lew, and elsewhere was built up probably by John Laundels (d. 1361), sheriff and escheator of Oxfordshire, and his son John, a commissioner of the peace.[20] Following Nicholas Laundels's death his lands passed to his relict Eleanor and her second husband John Hill of Burford and later of Bampton, who were in dispute with Laundels's trustees in 1421–2 and 1433.[21] The estate was acquired before 1455 by the Lovels of Minster Lovell, passing on Francis, Lord Lovel's forfeiture in 1485 to Jasper Tudor (d. s.p. 1495), duke of Bedford;[22] his lands reverted

to the Crown, which probably in 1514 granted a part, including land in Lew, to Thomas Howard (d. 1524), duke of Norfolk, but that estate has not been traced further.[23] Laundels or Landells farm (58 a.) in Weald, acquired by John Dudley (d. 1553), earl of Warwick, may have been the house and 54 a. which John Laundels held of Bampton Earls manor in 1361 for service of a rose, though its location suggests that it was taken originally from Exeter cathedral's rectory manor.[24] Following Dudley's forfeiture the Crown granted it in 1557 to Thomas Vavasour of Copmanthorpe (Yorks. W.R.) with 72 a. in Aston, and in the later 16th century and the 17th it changed hands frequently, passing by 1645, without the Aston land, to John Loder of Hatford (Berks.)[25] and later to the Dewe family of Bampton and their successors the Hawkinses, lessees of the parsonage estate. The farm was sold after Charles Hawkins's death in 1813, and was split up.[26] The homestead, which in the 18th century and early 19th lay on both sides of Landells Lane west of Bampton Manor, was presumably the site of Laundels' court mentioned in 1465,[27] associated perhaps with late 13th-century fortifications excavated on the lane's north side.[28] The buildings, of unknown date, were demolished after 1899.[29]

In 1687 Jesus College, Oxford, acquired from the Wood family of Oxford a freehold of c. 4¼ yardlands in Bampton and Weald, built up during the 17th century by John Palmer (d. 1650) and Bartholomew Coxeter (d. 1664), and by Coxeter's son-in-law John Gower (d. by 1684).[30] In the later 19th century and early 20th the college's estate was increased to c. 650 a. by the acquisition of, in particular, Backhouse, Castle, and Ham Court farms, formerly part of Bampton Earls manor, and of several cottages;[31] all except Ham Court farm and some of the cottages was sold in the later 20th century.[32]

College Farm, at the junction of Clanfield road and Weald Lane, was the house for the original college estate, and is a U-shaped building of limestone rubble with stone-slated roofs. It was apparently that held in the late 16th century with Roger Cook's 2 yardlands, and seems to have been inhabited successively by Palmer, Coxeter, and Gower.[33] In 1695 it was let with a kiln and malthouse to a Bampton mercer, reserving the

11 Oxf. Jnl. 9 Aug. 1800.
12 O.R.O., D.Y. XXXIII/i/1; ibid. MS. Wills Oxon. 140/3/28; Oxf. Jnl. 9 Aug. 1800; above, intro. (buildings).
13 O.R.O., Mor. XIII/vii/1; P.R.O., RG 9/905; O.S. Map 1/2,500, Oxon. XXXVII. 7 (1876 edn.), which, however, shows buildings essentially as in 1821: O.R.O., incl. award and map.
14 O.S. Map 1/2,500, Oxon. XXXVII. 7 (1876 and later edns.); O.R.O., Mor. XIII/ix/3, XIII/ix/10.
15 Below, econ. hist. (mills and fisheries); below, Lew, manor.
16 Bampton Hund. R. 17–18; Kts. Hospitallers in Eng. (Camd. Soc. [1st ser.], lxv), 26.
17 Cal. Pat. 1572–5, p. 411.
18 B.L. Add. Ch. 56460; P.R.O., REQ 2/193/33; cf. Bampton Hund. R. 18.
19 B.L. Add. Ch. 56458; P.R.O., E 179/161/10.
20 Cal. Inq. p.m. xi, p. 87; Cal. Pat. 1354–58, 296, 361; W. R. Williams, Parl. Hist. Oxon. (1899), 21.
21 P.R.O., C 1/7/54–57; B.L. Add. Ch. 56459; Cal. Pat. 1429–36, 485.
22 Linc. Dioc. Docs. (E.E.T.S. cxlix), 81–3; Cal. Pat. 1485–94, 64; 1557–8, 86; P.N. Oxon. (E.P.N.S.), ii. 365.

23 P.R.O., CP 40/1103, rot. 1 of deeds enrolled; ibid. STAC 2/29/190; cf. V.C.H. Oxon. xii. 60.
24 Cal. Pat. 1557–8, p. 86; Cal. Inq. p.m. xi, p. 87; below.
25 Jesus Coll. Mun., box 15, list 1, bdle. 1, no. 16; O.R.O., Stewart II/1–3; Cal. Pat. 1557–8, p. 86.
26 D. & C. Exeter, Ch. Comm. 72/91867, pp. 15–33; O.R.O., QSD L.22; Bodl. MS. d.d. Fitt c 4; C.O.S., par. reg. transcripts.
27 O.R.O., incl. award, s.v. Hawkins (no. 469), Geo. Richards (no. 512); B.L. Add. MS. 31323 III; D. & C. Exeter, MS. 4764; above, map on p. 18.
28 S. Midlands Arch. xvi. 89–90; above, intro.
29 O.S. Map 1/2,500, Oxon. XXXVII. 6 (1876 and later edns.); cf. B.L. Add. MS. 31323 III; below, plate 9, showing a thatched range west of Bampton Manor Ho.
30 Jesus Coll. Mun., box 15, lists 1–2.
31 Ibid. box 15, lists 4–5, 7, 11; ibid. shelf 3, 'Bk. of Farmers and Tenants', ff. 19–20.
32 Ibid. box 15, list 11 (College Fm. and Mill Green Cotts.); inf. from Dr. D. Rees, Jesus College, Oxford.
33 Jesus Coll. Mun., box 15, list 1, bdle. 1, nos. 6–9, 21, 24; ibid. list 2, conveyance 19 Oct. 1673, sale 13 May 1684.

great parlour, the dining room, the little room over the parlour, and use of the kitchen;[34] about that time it was rebuilt or entirely remodelled, re-using or retaining earlier features,[35] and by the late 18th century it was let to tenant farmers.[36] The north range, of two storeys, contained the parlour and hall, and the west wing the kitchen, with beyond it a broad passage entry from the road into the central courtyard. The east wing, attached only at its north-west corner, has a large ground-floor fireplace, and in the mid 19th century was used as a brewhouse.[37]

ECONOMIC HISTORY. AGRICULTURE.

In the mid 10th century Bampton formed part of a large unitary estate which cut across later field and township boundaries,[38] but by the 14th century and probably much earlier Bampton and Weald each had their own open fields. Demesne on Bampton Deanery manor in 1317 included 31 a. in Bampton's East field, and 248 a., some of it possibly inclosed, in Canons field further west;[39] from the later 14th century, however, Bampton's arable was divided chiefly between East (later Truelands, Gog, or Further) field, West (later Parson's Hedge or Lew Leaze) field, and Middle field. Arable in Hogs Acres, straddling the later Lew boundary, in 'Brokhurst', presumably Brockhurst or Brookfast furlong, later in Middle field, and in 'Linton', was separately itemized in 1397 and 1420.[40] A fourth field, Brookfast or Brookfurlong field, was taken from the southern part of East and Middle fields between 1737 and 1767.[41] A tenant in Weald held 8 a. in two fields in 1317,[42] and by the later 17th century Weald had six fields: Mill (later Wrights) field, mentioned in 1592; Ham, Bourton, and Haspwell (or Upwell) fields, mentioned in 1606; and Garsons and Dean fields,[43] the latter not always mentioned in terriers and perhaps taken from Bourton or Garsons fields.[44]

Both townships' meadows lay in the south along the Thames and its tributaries.[45] In 1086 those attached to Bampton manor yielded 65s., and 92 a., some presumably in Aston and Chimney, were recorded on Bampton Doilly and Bampton Deanery manors and on Ilbert de Lacy's estate.[46] Hay for winter feed at Witney was bought at Bampton in 1334–5,[47] and in 1609 Weald's Lammas meadows were estimated at 405 a. and Bampton's at 227 a.[48] Some remained lot meadows until inclosure,[49] though inclosed hams were held of Bampton Earls manor in the 13th century, and in the 14th the demesne included c. 60 a. of several meadow in Honeyham, Broadham, Derdesham, and elsewhere.[50] In the 16th and 17th centuries some several hams were rotated between different owners over two or more years.[51] The customary allotment of common meadow in 1691 was 5 a. per yardland (or 4½ a. on Bampton Deanery manor),[52] but there was much variation, and some more substantial farmers held large amounts of inclosed meadow,[53] availability of which was said in 1785 greatly to lessen the value of the common meadows.[54] Meadows and other lands flooded frequently, sometimes causing serious losses.[55]

Bampton's inhabitants presumably shared pasture rights in Aston's West moor from an early date, since by the 17th century it had been partitioned between the two townships.[56] In 1425 cattle (*grossa animalia*) were to be pastured 'in the moor', but horses or ploughbeasts (*averia*) in Rushey,[57] presumably near Rushey weir, and Bampton West moor remained a cow common in 1767. Then and in 1821 it covered c. 73 a.,[58] but it may formerly have included part of a large triangle of closes to the south-west: in 1609 permanent common pasture in Bampton reportedly totalled 498 a.,[59] and newly inclosed pasture grounds, some explicitly taken from the moor, were mentioned frequently from c. 1622.[60] Truelands closes to the north, recorded in 1627, may similarly have been taken from a formerly shared common,[61] though Brookfast (or Brockhurst) closes to the west, where Exeter cathedral had a pasture ground in 1439 and where piecemeal inclosure continued in the 17th century, came possibly from the arable.[62] In 1634 lessees of Bampton Deanery manor were accused of unlawful inclosure of commons and diversion of highways.[63] In Weald a band of regular inclo-

34 Jesus Coll. Mun., box 15, list 2, lease 5 Apr. 1695.
35 Cf. survey 1992 in C.O.S., SMR.
36 Jesus Coll. Mun., box 15, lists 2–3.
37 Ibid. list 3, survey 16 May 1873; ibid. undated valuation of fire-damage. The wing contains charred beams.
38 Above, intro. [boundaries].
39 D. & C. Exeter, MS. 2931; cf. B.L. Add. MS. 31323 III; below, this section.
40 P.R.O., C 136/95, no. 17; ibid. C 139/42, no. 86; Bodl. MS. Top. Oxon. c 224, ff. 80–4; B.L. Add. MS. 31323 III; ibid. Map C 7 e 16 (3), map between pp. 34–5, p. 60; D. & C. Exeter, MS. M 1.
41 Jesus Coll. Mun., box 15, list 2, terrier 30 Apr. 1737; B.L. Add. MS. 31323 III; ibid. Map C 7 e 16 (3), pp. 37, 60.
42 D. & C. Exeter, MS. 2931, s.v. *decima* (Weald).
43 B.L. Map C 7 e 16 (3), map between pp. 34–5; Bodl. MSS. d.d. Shrewsbury c 1/7 (13), c 2–4, *passim*; P.R.O., REQ 2/198/14, m. 2; O.R.O., MS. Wills Oxon. 193, ff. 231v.–232v.
44 e.g. Berks. R.O., D/EBr T25, mentioning lands in Bourton field 'in the Deane'.
45 B.L. Map C 7 e 16 (3), map betw. pp. 34–5; D. & C. Exeter, MS. M 1; O.R.O., MS. d.d. Par. Bampton a 2 (R).
46 V.C.H. Oxon. i. 400, 402, 405, 414.
47 Hants. R.O., Eccles. II 159346, m. 33d.
48 B.L. Add. MS. 27535, ff. 40v., 42.

49 B.L. Map C 7 e 16 (3), pp. 48–9, 68; D. & C. Exeter, Ch. Comm. 13/74363, pp. 5, 11; Jesus Coll. Mun., box 15, list 2, farm rep. 28 Feb. 1812.
50 *Bampton Hund. R.* 20; *Oseney Cart.* iv, p. 517; Giles, *Hist. Bampton*, 138; *Cal. Inq. p.m.* xvii, p. 339.
51 B.L. Map C 7 e 16 (3), p. 49; Jesus Coll. Mun., shelf 2, survey 1691, pp. 1–2.
52 Jesus Coll. Mun., shelf 2, survey 1691, p. 4.
53 B.L. Add. MS. 27535, ff. 37–42; ibid. Map C 7 e 16 (3), pp. 42, 48, 60; D. & C. Exeter, Ch. Comm. 13/74363, pp. 5, 11; O.R.O., Misc. Mar. I/146.
54 D. & C. Exeter, Ch. Comm. 13/74359.
55 e.g. D. & C. Exeter, MS. 5101; ibid. MS. 2933, p. 19; B.L. Map C 7 e 16 (3), p. 37.
56 B.L. Add. MS. 31323 III; O.R.O., Misc. WA I/1, f. 9.
57 D. & C. Exeter, MS. 4752.
58 B.L. Add. MS. 31323 III; O.R.O., incl. award, plan IV.
59 B.L. Add. MS. 27535, f. 42.
60 O.R.O., D.Y. II/iii/2, D.Y. XIV/i/1; Bodl. MS. d.d. Shrewsbury c 2/8 (13); cf. Berks. R.O., D/EBr T25; O.R.O., incl. award.
61 O.R.O., Stewart I/1; above, intro. [boundaries].
62 D. & C. Exeter, MS. 4756; O.R.O., Stewart I/1; ibid. incl. award, plan II.
63 D. & C. Exeter, MSS. 1996–7.

31

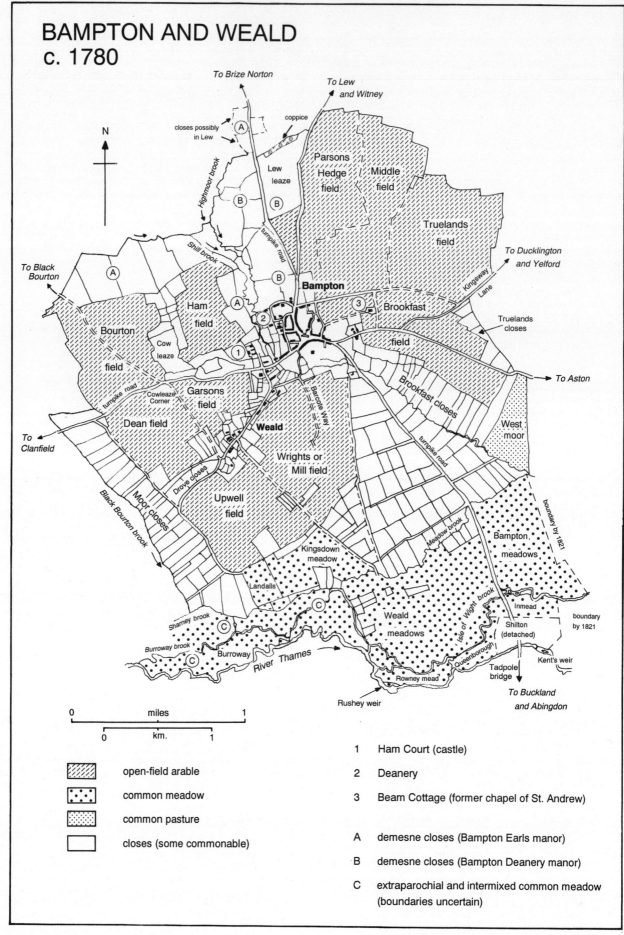

BAMPTON AND WEALD
c. 1780

N

To Brize Norton

To Lew
and Witney

closes possibly
in Lew

coppice

Highmoor brook

Lew
leaze

Parsons
Hedge
field

Middle
field

Truelands
field

To Black
Bourton

Shill brook

turnpike road

Bampton

To Ducklington
and Yelford

Kingsway
Lane

Brookfast

Truelands
closes

Ham
field

Bourton
field

Cow
leaze

field

To Aston

Brookfast closes

turnpike road

West
moor

turnpike road

Cowleaze
Corner

Garsons
field

Dean field

Weald

Wrights or
Mill field

Barcote Way

Meadow brook

Bampton
meadows

boundary by 1821

To
Clanfield

Moor closes

Drove closes

Upwell
field

Black Bourton brook

Kingsdown
meadow

Isle of Wight brook

Inmead

boundary
by 1821

Landalls

Weald
meadows

Shilton
(detached)

Kent's weir

Sharney brook

C

C

Queenborough

Burroway brook

C

Burroway

River Thames

Rowney mead

Tadpole
bridge

Rushey weir

To Buckland
and Abingdon

0   miles   1

0   km.   1

open-field arable

common meadow

common pasture

closes (some commonable)

1   Ham Court (castle)

2   Deanery

3   Beam Cottage (former chapel of St. Andrew)

A   demesne closes (Bampton Earls manor)

B   demesne closes (Bampton Deanery manor)

C   extraparochial and intermixed common meadow
     (boundaries uncertain)

sures called Moor closes along the parish's western edge may have been taken from another large common, and a wedge of inclosures to the east, called Drove closes, implies that Weald Lane formerly opened into it in a wide funnel-shape. If so the common had been inclosed apparently by 1618, and in the later 17th century and the 18th cottagers in Weald holding of Bampton Earls manor had cow commons in Cottage close (9 a.), one of the new closes.[64] Cow leaze, between Bourton and Ham fields, was inclosed pasture belonging partly to Aston Pogges manor by 1789.[65]

Additional pasture was available in the common fields and meadows and in some closes. In 1362 demesne meadow totalling 60 a. was commonable from when the hay was carried until 2 February, and a 'certain several pasture' from 29 September to 25 March, and in the 17th and 18th centuries some inclosed meadows were commonable from Lammas (1 August).[66] In 1789 sheep were allowed in the common meadows from All Saints (1 Nov.) to Old Lady Day (5 April) and in the open fields from harvest to seeding, and cows were pastured in the meadows from Old Lammas (12 August) to All Saints, though commons in Ham field were reserved for tenants of Ham Court. Weald's and perhaps Bampton's inhabitants enjoyed further common rights in Great Nipnam pasture in Black Bourton, and in meadows by the Thames belonging to Black Bourton, Alvescot, Brize Norton, and Shilton parishes.[67] The usual stint in 1609 was 12 beasts and 40 sheep per yardland in Bampton and 8 beasts and 40 sheep in Weald,[68] but by 1691 Weald's stint was 10 cows and 32 sheep, and in 1789 Bampton's was 8 cows and 20 sheep, perhaps because of inclosure of commons.[69] In 1812 sheep commons in Weald belonging to Jesus College's estate were of so little value that neither tenant stocked them.[70] Leys in the common fields and meadows were mentioned occasionally from the early 17th century.[71]

A wood called Boyvale, where Roger d'Oilly had housebote and haybote in 1279, may have lain outside the townships, though services on Bampton Deanery manor in 1317 included carting wood.[72] Up to 40 a. of woodland on Bampton Doilly manor was mentioned in 16th-century fines,[73] but except for a small coppice on the northern boundary there was no woodland in Bampton or Weald by the later 18th century,[74]

and timber mentioned in the 19th was presumably in hedgerows.[75]

Medieval yardlands on Bampton Earls manor seem to have comprised only 16 a., presumably excluding meadow,[76] though the size of Exeter cathedral's 3-ploughland demesne suggests an arable yardland on Bampton Deanery manor of nearer 27 a., held, as later, with 4½ a. of meadow.[77] Seventeenth-century yardlands varied greatly, but were usually reckoned to include c. 20–30 a. of open-field arable, and with meadow and inclosures, often a significant proportion, totalled usually between 30 and 40 a.[78] The field acres seem, however, to have been only between a half and three quarters of a statute acre.[79]

In 1086 the 27½-hide Bampton manor, including land in Aston, Lew, and elsewhere, had 6 ploughteams on the demesne, worked by 6 *servi*. Forty *villani*, 13 *bordarii*, and 17 *buri* had 16 ploughs, and were said to have had 26 in 1066. In all the manor rendered £82, making it the second richest royal estate in Oxfordshire, though the total included non-agricultural income and a £15 corn-rent; the rent was collected from other royal manors to which hundreds were annexed and was apparently associated with ancient demesne.[80] Bampton Deanery manor, partly in Chimney and Aston, had land for 6 ploughteams, but only 5 were recorded: 2 on the demesne, worked by 2 *servi*, and 3 held by 10 *villani* and 7 *bordarii*. Bampton Doilly manor, reportedly with land for 3 ploughteams, had 5½ teams in all, 2 of them on the demesne worked by 3 *servi* and 3½ held by 7 *villani* and 6 *bordarii*, and Ilbert de Lacy's estate, with land for 3 ploughteams, had 1 plough in demesne and half a plough held by 6 *villani* and 9 *bordarii*. All those estates had risen in value since 1066, Bampton Deanery from £4 to £6, Bampton Doilly from £2 to £4, and Ilbert's estate from £2 to £3.[81]

By 1279 there were 3 ploughlands in demesne on Bampton Earls manor, estimated in 1362 at 196 a. of arable, 60 a. of several meadow, and unspecified several pasture, all or part of it in Bampton and Lew.[82] The demesne may have been temporarily increased to 4 ploughlands before 1296, when 32 oxen were recorded along with 283 a. of arable, 132 a. of meadow, and 76 a. of pasture,[83] and in 1422 two thirds of the manor were said to have 4 ploughlands in demesne.[84] By

64 B.L. Map C 7 e 16 (3), map between pp. 34–5, p. 38; Berks. R.O., D/EBr T25; Bodl. MS. d.d. Shrewsbury c 2/8 (17); O.R.O., incl. award.
65 B.L. Map C 7 e 16 (3), map between pp. 34–5; O.R.O., MS. d.d. Par. Bampton a 2 (R).
66 B.L. Add. MS. 27535, ff. 40v., 42; Jesus Coll. Mun., shelf 2, survey 1795; Giles, *Hist. Bampton*, 138.
67 B.L. Map C 7 e 16 (3), pp. 37, 64; Ch. Ch. Arch., MS. Estates 63, f. 49; O.R.O., Shilton tithe award (1841); cf. O.S. Map 6", Oxon. XXXVII (1884 edn.).
68 B.L. Add. MS. 27535, ff. 37–42.
69 Jesus Coll. Mun., shelf 2, survey 1691, pp. 2–4; B.L. Map C 7 e 16 (3), pp. 37, 64; D. & C. Exeter, MS. 4544, pp. 4, 7.
70 Jesus Coll. Mun., box 15, list 2, farm rep. 28 Feb. 1812.
71 e.g. O.R.O., D.Y. II/iii/2, D.Y. XIX/iii/1; Bodl. MS. d.d. Shrewsbury c 2/8 (16).
72 D. & C. Exeter, MS. 2931; *Bampton Hund. R.* 28; cf.

below, Chimney, econ. hist.
73 e.g. P.R.O., CP 25/2/196/14 Eliz. I Hil.; cf. ibid. C 142/143, no. 51, mentioning a clearly fictional 500-a. wood.
74 B.L. Add. MS. 31323 III; D. & C. Exeter, MS. M 1.
75 *Oxf. Jnl.* 23 Dec. 1803; D. & C. Exeter, Ch. Comm. 13/74361a, survey 1811.
76 *Bampton Hund. R.* 18 n., 19–20, 26.
77 D. & C. Exeter, MS. 2931; below.
78 D. & C. Exeter, MS. 2934; B.L. Add. MS. 27535, ff. 37–43; Jesus Coll. Mun., shelf 2, survey 1691.
79 B.L. Map C 7 e 16 (3), p. 38; D. & C. Exeter, Ch. Comm. 13/74363.   80 *V.C.H. Oxon.* i. 374–5, 400.
81 Ibid. 402, 405, 414.
82 P.R.O., C 136/95, no. 17; C 139/42, no. 86; *Bampton Hund. R.* 17; Giles, *Hist. Bampton*, 138.
83 P.R.O., C 133/76, no. 2.
84 Ibid. C 138/58, no. 5.

1609 the demesne farm, then *c.* 462 a., included only 66½ a. of open-field arable compared with 322½ a. of inclosed arable, pasture, and meadow,[85] most of it in blocks of closes north of Weald's Bourton and Ham fields and around Ham Court;[86] some common rights had presumably been extinguished, since the farm had commons for only 4 yardlands.[87] In the 15th century and earlier the demesne was administered apparently through bailiffs and stewards, but in the later 16th century and the early 17th it was let sometimes with the house and sometimes separately to the earl's local agents or to local gentry, some of whom probably sublet it to resident farmers.[88] In 1660 both the house and the demesne were partitioned with the manor, and became indistinguishable from other tenanted farms.[89]

The d'Oillys' demesne comprised 3 ploughlands in 1279 and apparently in 1347–8, when its division between the two moieties was confirmed.[90] The demesne farms of both moities were let probably from the 15th century and certainly by the 16th.[91] Bampton Deanery demesne, also 3 ploughlands in 1279, was estimated in 1317 at 326½ a. of arable (including 47½ a. in Lew), and 51½ a. of several meadow in 'Hynemore' or Highmoor, in Broad mead (later in Haddon), and in Kingsdown by the Thames.[92] Though the arable was described as open-field land some lay in apparently consolidated blocks of 15–23 a., and by the 17th century and possibly the early 15th, when the lessee was required to maintain appurtenant closes,[93] the demesne included *c.* 200 a. of inclosures north of the manor house.[94] Both the demesne and the house were let from the late 14th century,[95] and though bailiffs were still appointed in the early 16th century there was none in 1634, when tenants complained of wastes committed by farmers of the manor and asked that one be reinstated.[96]

Except on Bampton Deanery manor, where 8 villeins each held yardlands, there had been much subdivision of tenant holdings by 1279.[97] On Bampton Doilly manor all 32 villein tenants held half yardlands, and on the Hospitallers' estate in Weald 3 held half yardlands and 2 held 5 a., perhaps a quarter-yardland. On Bampton Earls manor there were 7 villeins with a yardland, 4 with ¾-yardlands, and 17 with half a yardland, and 11 other tenants, including the miller and a smith, held houses with small amounts of land. Four cottagers, each with crofts, were recorded on Bampton Doilly manor, and 7 on Bampton Deanery manor, evidently a marked underestimate since in 1317 there were 37 cottagers holding 38½ cottages of the latter manor.[98] Freeholders, with tenements ranging from a few acres to 2½ yardlands, were recorded on all the chief estates except for Bampton Deanery, and in all *c.* 13½ yardlands were held freely compared with *c.* 45½ held by customary tenants.

Yardlanders on Bampton Deanery manor owed rents of 5*s.* 5*d.* including 20*d.* aid, and works valued at 10*s.* 2½*d.* in 1279 but 5*s.* 11¾*d.* in 1317, when they included heavy harvest works besides ploughing, harrowing, and carting.[99] In 1307 the tenants impleaded the farmer of the manor for attempting to increase services, claiming special status as tenants of ancient demesne.[1] Heriot was the best beast or 5*s.*, and villeins owed 2 gallons of beer or 2*d.* at every brewing, which in 1416–17 yielded 4*s.* in Bampton. Services on the manor were fully commuted by the early 15th century, when sale of works averaged 13*s.* 4*d.* for each of the eight Bampton yardlands.[2] On Bampton Earls manor yardlanders' rents in 1279 were similar but services were evidently lighter, and in 1296 included weeding, haymaking, and harvesting;[3] other payments in 1296 included aid, Peter's Pence, and churchscot (rendered in hens), and in 1362 hearthpenny was due at Pentecost.[4] Rents and services for half yardlands and smaller holdings in 1279 varied greatly, and on Bampton Earls manor 4 half-yardlanders owed rents only; tallage on the same manor was then charged proportionately at 13*d.* per yardland. Most freeholders in 1279 paid rents only, though several owed tallage and suit of court or hidage and scutage, and one acquitted his lord's obligations at the hundred court as part of his services.[5]

In 1306[6] Bampton and Weald were taxed on total movable wealth of £237 15*s.*, and in 1316 and 1327, when assessments included Haddon, on over £300. The number of contributors rose from *c.* 115 in 1306 to 143 in 1327, and the payment of £64 12*s.* 1*d.* for the whole parish in 1334, representing movables worth £969 1*s.* 3*d.*,[7] implies that the area's prosperity was increasing. Much of Bampton and Weald's assessed wealth may have been agricultural rather than commercial, however,[8] and neither average personalty (*c.* 43*s.* in 1327) nor assessed

---

[85] B.L. Add. MS. 27535, f. 37; the remaining 73 a. were common meadow.
[86] Bodl. MS. d.d. Shrewsbury c 1/7 (13); cf. B.L. Map C 7 e 16 (3), pp. 42 sqq., map between pp. 34–5; P.R.O., REQ 2/44/6.
[87] B.L. Add. MS. 27535, f. 37.
[88] Ibid.; above, manors (castle).
[89] Bodl. MS. d.d. Shrewsbury c 1/7 (13); B.L. Map C 7 e 16 (3), pp. 42 sqq.
[90] Bodl. MS. Dodsworth 143, ff. 32v.–33v.; *Bampton Hund. R.* 28.
[91] P.R.O., C 142/143, no. 51; ibid. REQ 2/89/28; above, manors (Bampton Doilly).
[92] *Bampton Hund. R.* 23; D. & C. Exeter, MS. 2931; cf. ibid Ch. Comm. 13/74363, p. 14.
[93] D. & C. Exeter, MSS. 6016/2/1–2.
[94] Ibid. MS. 2028; O.R.O., D.Y. VII/ii/1; ibid. incl.

award, plan V.
[95] Above, manors (Bampton Deanery).
[96] D. & C. Exeter, MSS. 1996–7, 5100–6; *Oxoniensia*, lvi. 116.
[97] Two paras. based on *Bampton Hund. R.* 17–20, 23–4, 28–9.
[98] D. & C. Exeter, MS. 2931; cf. P.R.O., C 139/42, no. 86. Figs. for 1317 exclude the vicarage hos.
[99] D. & C. Exeter, MS. 2931.
[1] *Abbrev. Plac.* (Rec. Com.), 300.
[2] D. & C. Exeter, MSS. 2931, 5100–5.
[3] P.R.O., C 133/76, no. 2.
[4] Ibid.; Giles, *Hist. Bampton*, 138.
[5] *Bampton Hund. R.* 28–9; cf. below, Aston and Cote, econ. hist.; Lew, econ. hist.; Shifford, econ. hist.
[6] Para. based on P.R.O., E 179/161/8–10; the 1306 list is damaged.
[7] *Historic Towns in Oxon.* ed. K. Rodwell, 201–2.
[8] Below, this section (trade and ind.).

wealth per acre was any higher in Bampton than in surrounding townships. Over half those assessed in 1316 paid on goods worth under 50s., and only 20 (15 per cent) on goods worth 80s. or more, among them the lord of Bampton Earls, with personalty of £13, one of the lords of Bampton Doilly, with £16 18s. 8d., and the lord of Aston Pogges, with £16 14s. 8d. The next wealthiest, taxed on over £8, were presumably freeholders, though between 1306 and 1327 there was little consistency in those paying the highest amounts, and few freeholding families mentioned in 1279 contributed to 14th-century subsidies or paid especially large sums.[9] Some low payments of under 16s. reflected in part the large number of cottagers, but there was no consistent correlation between wealth, size of holding, and legal status. Villein yardlanders on Bampton Deanery manor were taxed in 1316 on personalty ranging from 48s. (and possibly as little as 16s.) to over £7, and two cottagers were taxed on over 50s.[10]

Bampton seems to have escaped the worst effects of 14th-century plague,[11] and on Bampton Deanery manor some rents and services may have been increased in the 1380s.[12] By the early 15th century the population was evidently falling, however, and there were other signs of contraction. One cottage occupied in 1317 was derelict in 1397, when a new tenant was required to rebuild it, and from c. 1416 to c. 1422 at least 3 yardland holdings and 5 cottages were continuously unoccupied and 6 other cottages were held by one man.[13] Vacant cottages around the churchyard were absorbed then or later into the curtilages of the north and east vicarage houses.[14] In Weald, a croft and dovecot belonging to the Hospitallers in 1317 yielded nothing in 1416–17 because the croft was uncultivated and the dovecot destroyed,[15] and by the 1420s and 1430s some rents on Bampton Deanery manor were falling.[16] Division and amalgamation of holdings continued: a tenant of Bampton Earls manor held 1½ yardland in 1420,[17] and by the early 17th century holdings on Bampton Earls and Bampton Deanery manors ranged from ¼ yardland to 3 yardlands. There were then 13 cottages on the Deanery manor and c. 35 on Bampton Earls manor, at least 3 and possibly 5 of them built on the waste and carrying no common rights.[18] That

tendency may have continued during the 17th and 18th centuries as the population increased again: in 1700 there were 20 cottagers on the Talbots' moiety paying a total of 9s. 5d. a year, and in 1789 rent from cottages on the waste totalled 20s. for the whole manor.[19]

In 1296 the Talbots' demesne was sown with 70 a. of wheat, 22 a. of barley, 25 a. of dredge and oats, and 16 a. of beans and peas,[20] and the medieval name Linton suggests that flax was grown.[21] Wheat, barley, and beans, peas or vetches remained the chief crops, with oats mentioned occasionally.[22] Rarer crops in the 16th and 17th centuries included rye, maslin, hemp, and caraway,[23] and a testator in 1726 left 10 bu. of apples.[24] A piggery worth 100s. was mentioned frequently in the late 12th century and early 13th,[25] and sheep were kept in large numbers by 1187 when Bampton manor was understocked by 150;[26] over 200 sheep were recorded on Ham Court farm in 1592, when their dung was used as manure,[27] and the wealthy yeoman George Thompson (d. 1603) left 170.[28] Smaller flocks were recorded also. Cattle were kept in smaller numbers, and there was some dairying and cheese-making: the maltster Jethro Bunce left 10 cows and over 170 cheeses at his death in 1726,[29] though some farmers left arable produce worth more than their livestock.[30] Pigs, poultry, and bees were all kept in the 16th and 17th centuries, often but not exclusively by poorer inhabitants. A two-course rotation was followed in Bampton in 1296 when 133 a. (47 per cent) were sown out of 283 a. on the Talbots' demesne,[31] but a three-course rotation was noted in 1362 and 1661,[32] and in 1789 both Bampton and Weald followed a four-course rotation of (1) wheat (2) beans (3) barley or oats (4) fallow, which with occasional variations continued until inclosure. Weald's Ham field, as lighter land, continued on a separate three-course rotation in 1789.[33]

By the 16th century and probably much earlier Bampton was a relatively impoverished town of farmers and small traders, and may no longer have ranked as a significant market centre.[34] Only 56 persons paid a total of £5 0s. 6d. to the first subsidy of 1523–4, a figure lower than for any Oxfordshire market town except Charlbury, and the unfavourable contrast even with rela-

9   Rob. Gauwe (?), who paid the very high sum of 23s. 6d. in 1327, is unidentified and was perhaps entered in error.
10   Cf. D. & C. Exeter, MS. 2931.
11   Above, intro.
12   D. & C. Exeter, MS. 5100, s.v. Bampton, Aston and Chimney, noting increases by a late 14th-cent. farmer: cf. J. Blair, 'Bampton Deanery' (Bampton Research Paper 2, 1988), copy in C.O.S.
13   D. & C. Exeter, MSS. 2931, 4751 (s.v. 'Snowes'), 5100–5106.
14   Below, churches.
15   D. & C. Exeter, MS. 2931, s.v. decima (Weald); ibid. MS. 5100.
16   Ibid. MSS. 4752, 4755, 5100; cf. ibid. MS. 2931; Oxoniensia, lvi. 112.
17   P.R.O., C 139/42, no. 86.
18   D. & C. Exeter, MS. 2933, pp. 11–18; B.L. Add. MS. 27535, ff. 37–42.
19   Arundel Castle, MS. TP 288; B.L. Map C 7 e 16 (3), p. 36; cf. Longleat House (Wilts.), Coventry pps. CVI, ff. 35 and v., 42. Some of the cottages were in Lew.
20   P.R.O., C 133/76, no. 2.

21   Cal. Inq. p.m. xvii, p. 339; P.N. Oxon. (E.P.N.S.), ii. 457.
22   P.R.O., REQ 2/198/14; O.R.O., MSS. Wills Oxon., Bampton and Weald wills and inventories, on which rest of para. based.
23   e.g. P.R.O., REQ 2/198/14; O.R.O., MSS. Wills Oxon. 14/2/11, 131/5/29; Giles, Hist. Bampton, 143.
24   O.R.O., MS. Wills Oxon. 117/1/13.
25   e.g. Pipe R. 1176 (P.R.S. xxv), 29; 1242 (ed. H. L. Cannon), 49.
26   Ibid. 1187 (P.R.S. xxxvii), p. 67; cf. D. & C. Exeter, MS. 3550, ff. 52v.–53; ibid. MSS. 5100–5; Oxoniensia, lvi. 113.
27   P.R.O., REQ 2/198/14.
28   O.R.O., MS. Wills Oxon. 300/3/43; cf. ibid. 179, f. 330v.
29   Ibid. 117/1/13.
30   e.g. ibid. 7/2/21.
31   P.R.O., C 133/76, no. 2.
32   Giles, Hist. Bampton, 138, misdated 1365; Longleat House, Coventry pps. CVI, f. 66.
33   B.L. Map C 7 e 16 (3), p. 37; Jesus Coll. Mun., box 15, list 2, farm rep. 28 Feb. 1812; Young, Oxon. Agric. 122.
34   Below, this section (markets and fairs; trade and ind.).

tively poor towns like Eynsham was less marked but still evident in later 16th-century subsidies.[35] Most leading taxpayers seem to have been farmers or landowners rather than traders, among them Thomas Haydock, assessed on £8 in 1576, whose family acquired part of the Doilly manor.[36] Thomas Loskey (d. 1574), twice assessed on £10, was lessee of the Doilly demesne farm and of 1½ yardland under Exeter cathedral,[37] and others were farmers of apparently average wealth.[38] There seems not to have been a leading group of especially wealthy townsmen such as existed in Deddington,[39] though 17th-century probate inventories reveal the expected contrast between moderately prosperous yeomen and labourers and lesser husbandmen. Roughly half those for whom inventories survive left personalty of between £10 and £70, and a quarter left personalty of over £100,[40] among them Edward Wainwright (d. 1684) of Weald who left goods worth £653 mostly in money, bonds, and bills, but who in 1662 was taxed apparently on only one hearth.[41] Two thirds of those assessed in 1662 paid on between 2 and 4 hearths, and only 5 on more than 5 hearths, while 11 inhabitants in 1665 were exempted through poverty.[42]

Almost three quarters of the farms on Bampton Earls manor were leasehold by 1609, though copyholds were still granted in the early 17th century and some survived in 1700.[43] Not all early leases were at rack rent or for short terms, and though rackrenting and terms of 21 years or fewer became common from the later 17th century, in 1789 four leaseholds in Weald totalling c. 138 a. were held for lives at the old rents, and owed heriot and large entry fines.[44] On Bampton Deanery manor 1½ yardland of former customary land was leasehold by 1549,[45] but copyhold grants continued in the late 17th century;[46] in the 18th the copyhold nature of the estate was deliberately preserved by farmers of the manor, despite amalgamation of 17th-century holdings into large leasehold farms let at rack rent.[47] After 1812 Edward Whitaker granted the remaining copyholds to trustees, and against the cathedral chapter's will obtained separate inclosure allotments for each, even though they existed only as legal fictions and bore no relation to existing

farms.[48] Surviving copyholds were extinguished in 1868.[49]

Three leasehold farms of c. 193 a., 85 a., and 65 a. had been formed on Bampton Deanery manor by 1789.[50] College farm was then 160 a.,[51] and the Talbots' Ham Court farm 297 a., partly through amalgamations since 1700.[52] Land tax assessments suggest other farms of comparable size, most held by tenant farmers sometimes under several owners, though some smaller holdings survived until after inclosure.[53] The principal Bampton Deanery farm changed hands at least twice between 1775 and 1799, though the Talbots' Ham Court farm remained with the Sandelands family throughout the earlier 18th century and with the Sammons family from c. 1768.[54] Ebenezer Williams, of the Coventrys' Ham Court farm and formerly of Chimney, was one of several farmers noted in the later 18th century as especially wealthy.[55]

New crops, including turnips, clover, rye grass, and sainfoin, were introduced on the Talbots' manor before 1761.[56] The desirability of inclosure and consolidation was recognized from the 17th century,[57] but hostile tithe-owners and parsimonious landowners impeded it until 1812 when John Coventry revived the project, and an Act for inclosing Bampton, Weald, and Lew was obtained.[58] Outstanding problems over compensation for tithes and allocation of costs were overcome, and inclosure began in 1813; the award was made in 1821 and enrolled in 1827.[59] The earl of Shrewsbury and John Coventry received c. 8 a. and 24½ a. respectively for manorial rights, the earl receiving a further 466 a. in Bampton and Weald, and Coventry 463 a. including c. 225 a. for copyhold land. Another 72 a. were sold presumably to cover expenses. Exeter cathedral or its lessee Edward Whitaker received c. 210 a. for tithes, c. 293 a. for leasehold lands including the 'parsonage' or 'rectory' estate, and c. 230 a. for copyholds; Whitaker, as freeholder and lessee, received over 1,700 a. in all. Numerous other freeholders included John Roberts (185 a. including small leaseholds), Caroline Horde (c. 173 a. for Golofers or Knapps farm), Jesus College, Oxford (147 a. for College farm), Joseph Andrews (145 a.), and Charles Bourchier (45 a. attached to Bampton House and

35 P.R.O., E 179/161/173, 179; E 179/162/234, 320, 341; cf. *Historic Towns Oxon*. ed. K. Rodwell, 201–2, omitting figs. for Bampton Deanery; *V.C.H. Oxon*. xii. 132–3.

36 Above, manors.

37 O.R.O., MS. Wills Oxon. 185, ff. 280v.–282v.; P.R.O., C 142/143, no. 51; D. & C. Exeter, MS. 6015/3 (1), lease 13 June 3 Edw. VI.

38 Cf. O.R.O., MS. Wills Oxon. 10/4/21; ibid. 179, f. 319 and v.; 180, f. 144; 193, ff. 231v.–232v.

39 *V.C.H. Oxon*. xi. 102; cf. ibid. xii. 133.

40 O.R.O., MSS. Wills Oxon., Bampton and Weald inventories, *passim*.

41 Ibid. MS. Wills Oxon. 72/5/24; P.R.O., E 179/255/4, pt. i, f. 19; cf. Longleat House, Coventry pps. CVI, f. 87.

42 P.R.O., E 179/255/4, pt. i, ff. 19–20; *Hearth Tax Oxon*. 223.

43 B.L. Add. MS. 27535, f. 45; Bodl. MS. d.d. Shrewsbury c 1/6; Arundel Castle, MS. TP 288, no. 23.

44 B.L. Map C 7 e 16 (3), p. 40. For leases 1654–1852, Bodl. MSS. d.d. Shrewsbury c 1/7 (5), c 2–4, *passim*; Arundel Castle, MS. TP 19; ibid. TP 98, pp. 25–76; cf. Longleat House, Coventry pps. CVI, ff. 35 sqq.

45 D. & C. Exeter, MSS. 6015/3 (1); 2933, p. 11.

46 Ibid. MSS. 2933, 4775–4783.

47 Ibid. MSS. 2011–12, 2018, 2028, 2031, 2036; ibid. Ch. Comm. 13/74363.

48 Ibid. MSS. 2031, 6016/7 (bdles. 1–2); ibid. Ch. Comm. 13/74354–5, 80/134543–5.

49 D. & C. Exeter, Ch. Comm. 80/134547–8.

50 Ibid. 13/74363.

51 Jesus Coll. Mun., box 15, lists 2–3.

52 B.L. Map C 7 e 16 (3), p. 40–73; cf. Arundel Castle, MS. TP 288.

53 O.R.O., QSD L.22; ibid. incl. award.

54 D. & C. Exeter, MS. 6016/6; Arundel Castle, MS. TP 288, no. 1; Bodl. MS. d.d. Shrewsbury c 3/9 (23), c 4/10 (12); O.R.O., QSD L.22.

55 Oxf. Jnl. Synopsis, 17 Aug. 1771, 15 June 1775, 2 Mar. 1777, 6 Nov. 1782; O.R.O., QSD L.22.

56 Bodl. MS. d.d. Shrewsbury c 4/10 (5).

57 Longleat House, Coventry pps. CVI, ff. 57, 83; Arundel Castle, MS. TP 288, no. 1; B.L. Map C 7 e 16 (3), p. 37.

58 B.L. Map C 7 e 16 (3), p. 37; D. & C. Exeter, MS. 6016/7, bdle. 2; ibid. Ch. Comm. 13/74361a, survey 1811; Bampton Incl. Act, 52 Geo. III, c. 46 (Local and Personal, not printed).

59 D. & C. Exeter, MS. 6016/7, bdle. 2; Ch. Ch. Arch., MS. Estates 74, ff. 31, 34, 36; O.R.O., incl. award.

16½ a. for tithes), and there were many smaller allotments to both freeholders and lessees. The vicars received *c.* 4 a. for glebe and 616½ a. for tithes, mostly in large allotments near the Thames and near the Lew-Bampton boundary; the churchwardens received 10½ a., the trustees of the Bampton poor 19¾ a., and those of the National School 36¼ a., and 49 a. were awarded to trustees of a Swinbrook charity and 70 a. to those of an Abingdon almshouse.[60] Intermixed meadows south of Sharney brook were separately inclosed in 1851, and Shilton meadow was inclosed with Aston and Cote *c.* 1855.[61]

Most farms created by inclosure remained centred on existing homesteads, some of them in the centre of Bampton, though Coalpit Farm was built on the new Lew road soon after.[62] Not all were fully consolidated, and in the 1860s and 1870s scattered allotments on College and Ham Court farms made them expensive to work.[63] Inclosure failed to alleviate the immediate effects of depression: David Miller of College farm, a longstanding tenant whose lands were 'in a very superior state of cultivation', blamed his arrears in 1822 on the difficult times and heavy poor rates, and he subsequently received rent relief and help with essential repairs.[64] The labouring poor suffered serious unemployment by *c.* 1818 and still in the early 1830s,[65] and in 1835, following changes in the Poor Law, there were riots in Bampton and the surrounding area during which a violent attack was made on the wealthy farmer Jonathan Arnatt. Order was restored by Oxford police assisted by local farmers and gentry.[66]

In 1811 there were 132 families employed in agriculture, compared with 82 in trades, crafts, and manufacture, and 42 whose employment was unspecified. Twenty-four inhabitants in 1861, some also pursuing a trade, called themselves farmers, and over 350 agricultural labourers (including 12 shepherds) were recorded, by far the largest occupational group. There were then 16 farms over 100 a., employing 168 men, women, and children, and Deanery farm (with a homestead on Broad Street), Calais farm, the two Ham Court farms, and Mount Owen farm were each over 200 a.[67] Mixed farming continued, though some farms, notably College, Backhouse, and the two Ham Court farms, were over half devoted to arable in the later 19th century;[68] on College farm former

open-field land in the west of the parish was good root and barley land and was well suited for sheep, but wheat there was subject to blight, and former pasture in Moor close was fit for growing only oats and sheep-keep. On Ham Court farm crops scorched in dry seasons, and in 1864 its excellent state of cultivation, contrasting favourably with surrounding farms, was attributed to the tenant's skill.[69]

Wheat remained the chief crop, with barley ('perhaps the least productive' in 1848), oats, and peas, which grew well but were 'little cultivated'. Potatoes, apples, apricots, walnuts and pears were grown, and Jerusalem artichokes were 'astonishingly productive'.[70] Dairying continued, and beef cattle were also raised, among them Hereford oxen grazed by the tenant of the 'parsonage' farm in the early 19th century.[71] Sheep remained important and were kept by some small farmers: Thomas Spurrett, a Bampton publican and farmer of 48 a., had 36 in 1861, and in 1865 livestock on Mount Owen farm included 87 ewes and lambs, 50 cattle, and 30 pigs.[72]

Drainage remained difficult near the river and on the heavy clay in Weald.[73] Following the Thames Valley Drainage Acts of 1871 and 1874 parts of the Thames between Eynsham weir and Buscot were widened and deepened to improve arterial drainage and prevent flooding, though the Commissioners' occasional appropriation of small pieces of meadow to that end was not always welcomed by local farmers.[74] Inadequate drainage exacerbated the effects of depression in the 1870s and 1880s: a tenant of the 437-a. Deanery farm in 1876 blamed his failure largely on defective drains laid years earlier which could not cope with two excessively wet seasons, and his successor insisted that they be made good before accepting the lease. Other problems cited were foot-and-mouth disease, and scarcity of labour even at increased rates.[75] Another longstanding tenant gave up his farm soon after,[76] and though the tenant of Ham Court remained, exceptionally, fully solvent until 1884, he was then in difficulty and remained in arrears in 1888.[77]

Mixed farming continued in the 20th century, though by 1914 *c.* 56 per cent of Bampton and Weald was permanent pasture. Cattle (mostly dairy), pigs, and sheep were kept on an average scale for the region, though as elsewhere sheep

[60] Cf. *32nd Rep. Com. Char. pt. ii* [140], pp. 697–8, H.C. (1837–8), xxvi; *V.C.H. Berks.* iv. 450.

[61] O.R.O., Burroway incl. award; ibid. Aston and Cote incl. award; ibid. MS. Oxf. Dioc. c 457/1, Queenborough tithe award.

[62] Ibid. Bampton incl. award; P.R.O., HO 107/1731; O.S. Map 6", Oxon. XXXVII (1884 edn.).

[63] Jesus Coll. Mun., box 15, list 3, partics. of Coll. estate 16 May 1873; ibid. list 4, surv. of Ham Ct. farm 14 Nov. 1864.

[64] Ibid. box 15, list 3, Miller to Jesus Coll. 1 June 1822; valn. 14 Apr. 1823.

[65] O.R.O., MS. d.d. Par. Bampton c 8, ff. 51v., 73v., 137 and v.

[66] *Oxf. Jnl.* 23 May 1835; *Oxf. Herald,* 23 May 1835.

[67] P.R.O., RG 9/905; *Census,* 1811; cf. Bodl. G.A. Oxon. a 117, p. 66; Jesus Coll. Mun., box 15, list 4.

[68] Jesus Coll. Mun., box 15, list 3, partics. and valn. 16 May 1873; ibid. list 4, survey 14 Nov. 1864, schedule 1870; ibid. list 5, conveyance 26 Oct. 1865.

[69] Ibid. box 15, list 3, partics. and valn. 16 May 1873; ibid. list 4, survey 14 Nov. 1864.

[70] Giles, *Hist. Bampton,* 20–1; cf. O.R.O., Pocock I/6/1.

[71] W. Marshall, *Review of Reps. of Board of Agric.* (1815), 491; cf. D. & C. Exeter, Ch. Comm. 13/74361a (surv. of Parsonage estate 1811).

[72] *Oxf. Chron.* 9 Mar. 1861, 29 Apr. 1865; P.R.O., RG 9/905.

[73] Jesus Coll. Mun., box 15, list 3, Gerring to bursar 9 Feb. 1852; Giles, *Hist. Bampton,* 17; *Witney Express,* 19 Dec. 1872.

[74] Thames Valley Drainage Act, 1871, 34–5 Vic. c. 158 (Local and Personal); ibid. 1874, 37–8 Vic. c. 22 (Local and Personal); Jesus Coll. Mun., box 15, list 4, Lyford to College 27 Nov. 1885; ibid. list 7, Notice of Works under Thames Valley Drainage Acts, 28 Apr. 1885.

[75] Ch. Com. Rec., file 46184 (pt. 1/2), nos. 11381, 12250.

[76] Ibid. file 46184 (pt. 1/2), no. 13837; cf. P.R.O., HO 107/872.

[77] Jesus Coll. Mun., box 15, list 4, corresp. 1884–88.

farming apparently declined between 1909 and 1914. Wheat remained the chief crop, followed by barley, oats, mangolds, and small quantities of potatoes.[78]

MARKETS AND FAIRS. In 1086 Bampton had the only market explicitly noted in the county, rendering 50s. a year.[79] In 1187 it was said to have formerly rendered 70s., but a deduction of 25s. from the half-yearly farm of the manor was then being sought for losses caused by unauthorized markets.[80] In 1241 Henry III granted to Imbert Pugeys, then farming the royal manor, a weekly Wednesday market and an annual fair on the eve and feast of the Assumption (14–15 August), a grant transferred to William de Valence and his heirs in 1255.[81] Market tolls in 1296 totalled 40s. a year, but in 1362 were estimated together with pleas and perquisites of the manor and hundred courts at only 33s. 4d.[82] Since services on Chimney manor in 1317 included ferrying grain to Oxford, Bampton even then may not have provided a ready outlet, though communications between Chimney and Bampton were sometimes difficult,[83] and a Shifford man sold wheat at Bampton in 1334.[84] Robert Plot's description in 1677, repeated throughout the 18th century,[85] of an unparalleled trade in fellmongers' wares, brought from Witney, made into jackets, breeches, and leather linings at Bampton, and sold to buyers from Berkshire, Wiltshire, and Dorset, is unsubstantiated despite extensive evidence of leather working in the parish,[86] and if reliable may already have been outdated when it was written: in 1669 the market house was ruinous,[87] in 1673 the market was 'small' and apparently in decline, and by 1766 it had been discontinued 'for some years'.[88] Presumably its decline resulted partly from the competition of nearby towns with better communications, though falling population in the late medieval period, combined with loss of the royal and seigneurial patronage which had artificially accentuated the importance of the medieval town, may also have been significant.[89] Periodic attempts to resurrect the market met with little success: it was revived in 1766 for corn, cheese, butter, eggs, fish, poultry, and other provisions, in 1800, toll-free, for corn and cattle, and in 1840, following the building of the arcaded town hall for use as a market house, for cattle, being held thereafter on only the third Wednesday of each month.[90] Most farmers in the late 18th century and early 19th attended more accessible markets at Witney, Faringdon, Burford, and Oxford, and at Bampton in the 1840s there were only a few dealers mostly in eggs and butter, though 'large numbers' of pigs were sold.[91] In 1852 the market was almost in disuse, and though occasionally mentioned later as a monthly market for grain and stock it was finally discontinued in the early 1890s.[92]

The fair was still held on 15 August in 1592, when the tolls, as later, were let;[93] it was moved to 26 August (15 August old style) in 1756.[94] In 1793 it was primarily a 'good horse fair' and so continued, though toys were mentioned in 1819 and 1830 and cattle in 1852.[95] By the mid 19th century it lasted usually from 25 to 27 August, and included a pleasure fair described as 'a sort of carnival to all the neighbouring villages', well attended by children, servants, and others; in 1871 there were stalls, exhibitions, and shooting galleries.[96] The horse fair had all but disappeared by the mid 1930s, but the pleasure fair continued and in 1992 one still visited the town in August, though no longer on the traditional date.[97]

A 'fair or great market' for 'all sorts of cattle' was held on Whit Wednesday in 1753, but was not mentioned later.[98] An annual Michaelmas ox-roast, later a cattle and cheese fair also, was held by 1798 on the Wednesday before Old Michaelmas (10 October), suggesting that it predated the abandonment of the Julian calendar in 1752; it was last mentioned in 1804.[99] A new, toll-free horse and cattle fair, held annually on 26 March, was instituted in 1803 but was 'nearly obsolete' in 1847; a reference in 1848 to a former ox-roast on 24 March suggests that both fairs may have lapsed sufficiently long before as to become confused.[1]

TRADE AND INDUSTRY. The existence of a market in 1086 and its refoundation in the 13th century suggests commercial activity, and 17 buri on Bampton manor in 1086 may have been suburban smallholders of a type recorded in other 11th-century towns.[2] By the 14th century

78 Orr, *Oxon. Agric.*, statistical plates; cf. O.R.O., Pocock III/25/2; ibid. Adkin II/3; Bodl. G.A. Oxon. b 92 (41); ibid. G.A. Oxon. c 317/4, sale cats.
79 *V.C.H. Oxon.* i. 400; cf. ibid. iv. 9.
80 *Pipe R.* 1187 (P.R.S. xxxvii), 45; cf. ibid. 1182 (P.R.S. xxxi), 60.
81 *Cal. Chart. R.* 1226–57, 259, 449; *Cal. Pat.* 1247–58, 35.
82 P.R.O., C 133/76, no. 2; Giles, *Hist. Bampton*, 139.
83 Below, Chimney, intro.; econ. hist.
84 Bodl. MS. d.d. Harcourt c 126/8.
85 R. Plot, *Nat. Hist. Oxon.* (1677), pp. 279–80; cf. T. Cox, *Magna Britannia et Hibernia, Antiqua et Nova*, iv (1727), 413; S. Simpson, *Agreeable Historian* (1746), 778–9; G. Beaumont and H. Disney, *A New Tour thro' Eng.* [1768], 91.
86 Below, this section (trade and ind.).
87 Longleat House (Wilts.), Coventry pps. CVI, f. 87v.
88 R. Blome, *Britannia; Or, a Geographical Description of Eng.* (1673), 188; *Oxf. Jnl.* 8 Nov. 1766; cf. *Compleat Tradesman* (1684), omitting Bampton; O.R.O., P4/2/MS 1/5, f. 6.
89 Above, intro.; this section (agric.).
90 *Oxf. Jnl.* 8 Nov. 1766, 25 Oct. 1800; *Oxf. Chron.* 5, 10 Sept. 1840; 8, 15 May 1841; *Univ. Brit. Dir.* ii [1793], 252–3; Brewer, *Oxon.* [1819], 481; above, intro. (buildings).

91 B.L. Map C 7 e 16 (3), p. 36; Giles, *Hist. Bampton*, 21.
92 *Gardner's Dir. Oxon.* (1852); *P.O. Dir. Oxon.* (1854 and later edns.); *Kelly's Dir. Oxon.* (1891, 1895); cf. Reading Univ. Arch., OXF. 6/4/2; ibid. 6/1/3, p. 70.
93 P.R.O., REQ 2/198/14; B.L. Map C 7 e 16 (3), p. 36; Arundel Castle, MS. TP 100.
94 Oxf. Jnl. Synopsis, 9 Aug. 1756.
95 *Univ. Brit. Dir.* ii [1793], 252–3; *Pinnock's Hist. and Topog. Oxon.* (1819), 68; Pigot, *Lond. & Prov. Dir.* (1830); *Gardner's Dir. Oxon.* (1852); *Diary of J. S. Calvertt*, ed. C. Miller, 63, 149, 231.
96 Giles, *Hist. Bampton*, 59; *Gardner's Dir. Oxon.* (1852); *Oxf. Chron.* 2 Sept. 1854; *Oxf. Jnl.* 2 Sept. 1871; *Witney Express*, 31 Aug. 1871; *Oxf. Mail*, 25 Aug. 1972.
97 *Oxf. Mail*, 25 Aug. 1972; local inf.
98 *Oxf. Jnl.* 26 May 1753.
99 Ibid. 5 Oct. 1799, 6 Oct. 1804; L. W. Thwaites, 'Marketing of Agric. Produce in 18th-cent. Oxon.' (Birmingham Univ. Ph.D. thesis, 1981), 60.
1 *Oxf. Jnl.* 19 Feb. 1803; *P.O. Dir. Oxon.* (1847); Giles, *Hist. Bampton*, 59–60; cf. Arundel Castle, MS. TP 100.
2 J. Blair, *Intro. to Oxon. Domesday* (Alecto edn.), 4; above, this section (markets and fairs).

Bampton was not especially wealthy, however,[3] and medieval trade and industry is poorly documented. Salt-rights in Droitwich (Worcs.) were not explicitly mentioned after 1086,[4] though property there was still attached to the manor in the late 12th century[5] and salt tolls exacted at Shellingford fair (Berks.), associated presumably with salt sold on from Bampton, were mentioned in the early 13th.[6] In 1327 inhabitants taxed on c. £5-worth of goods included Edward Lespicer and Hugh 'le Tannare',[7] and cottagers contributing significant amounts to 14th-century subsidies[8] may have included craftsmen: a cottager surnamed le Napper was recorded in 1317.[9] Shops were mentioned in 1310 and 1420, and a draper in 1467.[10] Other recorded occupations fell within the usual range of rural trades: 14th-century occupational surnames included cooper, carpenter, and painter, a smithy was recorded in 1279,[11] and masons, carpenters, smiths, wheelwrights, coopers, tailors, cordwainers, and bakers were recorded in large numbers later.[12] Butchers were mentioned frequently from the early 16th century:[13] one in 1686 had a shop in Bampton and two stalls in Burford, and several 16th-century butchers had dealings with Witney tradesmen.[14]

Accounts of an unparalleled distributive trade in fellmongers' wares brought from Witney may have been exaggerated,[15] but there was extensive leather-working in the town. Fellmongers, curriers, leather dressers, collarmakers, and glovers were mentioned frequently in the 17th century and early 18th,[16] and in the early 19th 40 or 50 tan pits, thought to have been blocked c. 200 years earlier, were uncovered behind 'Mr. Robins's', probably Rosemary House on the west side of the market place.[17] An advertisement in 1799 for a house nearby commented on its suitability for a fellmonger and on the excellence of the water for dressing alum leather.[18] A currier in 1675 and a fellmonger in 1680 each made substantial bequests including gold rings and silver plate,[19] though they seem to have been exceptional; a fellmonger with goods worth £91 in 1721 apparently also brewed commercially, and no other fellmongers or leather workers for whom inventories survive left personalty of over

£40, a glover in 1677 leaving only £18-worth.[20] Simon Bassett (d. 1681), a fellmonger taxed on 5 hearths in 1665, issued a trade token in 1669, and seems also to have been a victualler.[21] Among those involved in manufacture a glover in 1662 left several horse hides and 'other small skins' worth £3 in his shop, and a leather dresser in 1720 left 52 dozen beaver skins worth £25 and 40 calf skins.[22] Fellmongers, collarmakers, leather dressers, and, later, saddlers and harnessmakers continued to be mentioned, though less frequently, in the 19th century and early 20th, among them a fellmonger prosecuted for nuisance in 1853,[23] but gloving seems virtually to have died out by the early 18th century. Benjamin Collingwood (d. 1749), son of a Bampton glover with premises on Bridge Street, called himself a leather dresser or tanner,[24] and by 1848 there was a single glove manufacturer who had to travel the country to find purchasers.[25]

The second largest occupational group in the late 16th century and the 17th was that involved in textile manufacture, reliant, presumably, upon Witney. A broadweaver whose goods in 1701 were valued at £60, including yarn and wool worth c. £39, was owed money by a Witney blanketeer, and several other weavers, clothworkers, woolwinders, and clothiers were recorded, most of them moderately prosperous with personalties ranging from c. £30 to £80.[26] A comb maker in 1696, exceptionally, made bequests totalling over £250.[27] Thereafter the local industry declined, though in 1781 a Bampton man became apprenticed to a Crawley fuller.[28] A Bampton weaver was on parish relief in 1793.[29]

Commercial brewing was evidently widespread c. 1667 when up to eight inhabitants were presented for breaching the assize of ale,[30] and maltsters recorded from the late 17th century included some who were relatively wealthy. Jethro Bunce (d. 1726), who probably built Grayshott House on High Street, called himself a maltster in his will and left goods worth over £200, though he was also a considerable dairy farmer.[31] A maltster in 1705 left personalty of over £100 mostly in book debts and money at interest, and in 1771 an inhabitant was robbed

3 Above, this section (agric.).
4 V.C.H. Oxon. i. 400.
5 V.C.H. Worcs. iii. 87; Pipe R. 1162 (P.R.S. v), 26; 1188 (P.R.S. xxxviii), 7.
6 J. Blair, A.-S. Oxon. 86; V.C.H. Berks. iv. 475.
7 P.R.O., E 179/161/9.
8 Above, this section (agric.).
9 D. & C. Exeter, MS. 2931.
10 P.R.O., CP 25/1/189/14, no. 36; ibid. C 139/42, no. 86; Cat. Anct. D. vi, p. 237.
11 Ibid. E 179/161/8–10; Bampton Hund. R. 20.
12 e.g. O.R.O., MSS. Wills Oxon., indexed in D. M. Barratt, Probate Recs. Oxon. 1516–1732 (British Rec. Soc. xciii–xciv).
13 Ibid.; Arundel Castle, MS. M 535; P.R.O., REQ 2/268/53.
14 O.R.O., MS. Wills Oxon. 175/2/13; Witney Ct. Bks. 126, 202, 208.
15 Above, this section (markets and fairs).
16 O.R.O., MSS. Wills Oxon., Bampton and Weald wills.
17 Giles, Hist. Bampton, 72; above, intro. (buildings).
18 Oxf. Jnl. 9 Mar. 1799.
19 P.R.O., PROB 11/349, f. 129 and v.; PROB 11/364, ff. 324v.–325.

20 O.R.O., MSS. Wills Oxon. 79/1/32, 163/3/41; cf. ibid. 7/2/28, 18/3/12, 125/1/19.
21 J. G. Milne, Cat. Oxon. 17th-cent. Tokens, pp. ix, 1, 31; cf. Longleat House, NMR 3315, s.a. 1667; ibid. Coventry pps. CVI, ff. 35v., 87v.; O.R.O., MS. Wills Oxon. 7/2/28.
22 O.R.O., MSS. Wills Oxon. 18/3/12, 125/1/19.
23 P.R.O., RG 9/905, RG 11/1514; O.R.O., MSS. Wills Oxon.; Oxf. Jnl. 27 Aug. 1853; Kelly's Dir. Oxon. (1883 and later edns.).
24 O.R.O., MSS. Wills Oxon. 121/5/2, 123/1/42; Bodl. MSS. d.d. Shrewsbury c 3/9 (2), c 2/8 (17).
25 Giles, Hist. Bampton, 72–3; cf. P.R.O., HO 107/872; ibid. RG 9/905.
26 O.R.O., MS. Wills Oxon. 174/2/47; ibid. Bampton and Weald wills and inventories, passim.
27 P.R.O., PROB 11/434, f. 185 and v.; cf. O.R.O., MS. Wills Oxon. 44/1/24.
28 O.R.O., D.Y. XXXVI/v/1; for mercers and drapers, below.
29 O.R.O., MS. d.d. Par. Bampton c 8, f. 5v.
30 Longleat House, NMR 3315, s.a. 1667 and passim; cf. P.R.O., E 179/255/4, pt. ii, f. 19.
31 O.R.O., MS. Wills Oxon. 117/1/13; above, intro. (buildings).

after being mistaken for the 'wealthy maltster' Joseph Shorey.[32] A malthouse on the corner of Samford Lane and Church View, built in the earlier 17th century, was demolished in the 1820s;[33] another, attached to nearby Sandford House (with which it was rebuilt in the 1830s) may have been that let to a Brize Norton farmer in 1716, and was demolished in the late 19th century.[34] A third, at College Farm, was mentioned from the mid 17th century and was perhaps associated with a later brewhouse in the south-east wing, though no trace of a kiln survives.[35] A malthouse on the north corner of Church Street and Church View, owned by Exeter cathedral, was let in 1789 to the tenant of the Talbot Inn[36] and in the earlier 19th century to members of the Bateman family, who were grocers, ironmongers and drapers as well as maltsters;[37] it was held in the 1850s and 1860s by the tenant of Deanery Farm on Broad Street and was demolished before 1903.[38] The Malt Shovel, north of Lavender Square, had a malthouse probably by the mid 18th century when it was owned by the maltster John Minchin, and passed later to John Ward, maltster, and to Ward's son-in-law Richard Hambidge, maltster and spirit merchant, before becoming a public house in the 1870s.[39] Some farms and presumably most inns had their own brewhouses,[40] though in the later 19th century and earlier 20th many public houses were acquired by large commercial breweries outside Bampton, notably Clinch and Co. of Witney.[41]

Other 17th-century shopkeepers issuing tradesmen's tokens included a tallow chandler and a mercer, and both trades were mentioned, with drapers, throughout the 17th century and the 18th.[42] A Burford chandler transferred his business to Bampton in 1764.[43] Mercers included John Willear (d. 1620) and his son Thomas (d. 1654), who bought part of Bampton Doilly manor and who owned a house on High Street;[44] William Nabbs, a mercer whose family bought another part of the manor, died at Bristol in 1690 leaving bequests of over £400, and probably had wide trade links.[45] Several general grocers' shops were recorded from the mid 18th century, though shopkeepers often pursued more than one trade. Edward Bateman, with a house and shop (later Eton Villas) on the corner of Broad Street and Church Street,[46] was a grocer, ironmonger, and carpenter in 1788,[47] and Thomas Bryan, a mercer, draper, and haberdasher living by the market place, sold trade licences and was an agent for the Phoenix Insurance Company.[48] Another grocer, draper, and dealer in spirits and liquors may have brewed commercially.[49] Other occupations catered for resident gentry and professionals, mostly local landowners and clergy, and reflect attempts to promote Bampton as a genteel country retreat.[50] Barbers were recorded from the late 17th century,[51] and by the 1760s there were two apothecaries and two or more clock- or watch-makers,[52] while in 1778 the stock of a bankrupt butcher, dealer and chapman included millinery, haberdashery, china, and hosiery.[53] From the early 19th century the solicitor James Rose, later in partnership with R. H. Bullen, son of a Bampton doctor, acted frequently in local transactions; the firm was succeeded by Bullen and Ravenor and later by Ravenor and Cuthbert,[54] who had offices at no. 9 High Street in 1923.[55] Holloways' printers, bookbinders, and booksellers was established by 1803, probably, as later, on the west side of the market place; they printed religious tracts and sale catalogues, the family serving also as insurance agents, stamp distributors and, for a time, postmasters.[56] The premises were acquired c. 1890 by the printer James Beard, formerly of Broad Street, who continued there until the early 20th century.[57]

Despite such businesses Bampton remained predominantly agricultural,[58] and in the 19th

32 O.R.O., MS. Wills Oxon. 121/3/11; Oxf. Jnl. Synopsis, 18 May 1771; cf. O.R.O., Mor. VIII/i/1.
33 Jesus Coll. Mun., box 15, list 1 (bdle. 1), including deeds from 1578; O.R.O., D.Y. VII/vi/9; Exeter Coll. Mun., M.II.1 B; below, plate 8.
34 Exeter Coll. Mun., M.II.1 B; O.R.O., D.Y. VII/vii/1, perhaps referring to Sandford Ho.; cf. ibid. D.Y. XVII/i/1 (Leighton Cottage); O.S. Map 1/2,500, Oxon. XXXVII. 6 (1876 and 1899 edns.).
35 Jesus Coll. Mun., box 15, list 1, bdle. 1, no. 24; ibid. list 2, lease 5 Apr. 1695; above, other estates.
36 D. & C. Exeter, Ch. Comm. 13/74363, p. 2; O.R.O., incl. award, no. 484; cf. Oxf. Jnl. Synopsis, 13 Jan. 1770, 6 Jan. 1779.
37 D. & C. Exeter, Ch. Comm. 13/74363a, no. 8/3; Univ. Brit. Dir. ii [1793], 252–3; Pigot, Lond. & Prov. Dir. (1830); Pigot, Nat. & Comm. Dir. (1842).
38 Bodl. G.A. Oxon. a 117, p. 66, no. 484; Ch. Com. Rec. L 7, p. 413; datestone on Belgrave Cottages.
39 O.R.O., D.Y. XXX/i/1; ibid. MS. d.d. Par. Bampton b 10, ff. 54v.–57; ibid. MS. Wills Oxon. 238/2/21; ibid. QSD L.22; P.R.O., HO 107/1731; ibid. RG 9/905; P.O. Dir. Oxon. (1877).
40 Arundel Castle, MS. TP 100; O.R.O., MS. Wills Oxon. 24/1/1; ibid. Crowdy I/51, lots 37, 52.
41 Courage Archive, Bristol, EK/E/4, pp. 5, 64, 84, 127, 147.
42 O.R.O., MSS. Wills Oxon., Bampton and Weald wills and inventories; Bodl. MS. Ch. Oxon. 2427; Milne, Cat. Oxon. 17th-cent. Tokens, pp. 1, 31.
43 Oxf. Jnl. Synopsis, 7 Apr. 1764; cf. O.R.O., MS. Wills Oxon. 140/3/28.

44 Bodl. MS. Ch. Oxon. 4081; O.R.O., MS. Wills Oxon. 70/1/62; P.R.O., PROB 11/237, f. 147 and v.
45 P.R.O., PROB 11/403, f. 89.
46 D. & C. Exeter, Ch. Comm. 13/74363, p. 2; ibid. 13/74363a, no. 8/8; O.R.O., incl. award, no. 479.
47 Oxf. Jnl. Synopsis, 17 Dec. 1788.
48 Ibid. 5 Nov. 1784, 29 Oct. 1785, 6 July 1786, 7 July, 8 Sept., 6 Oct., 13 Oct. 1787, 8 Aug. 1789; above, intro. (buildings).
49 Oxf. Jnl. Synopsis, 20 Aug. 1763, 13 July 1764, 26 July 1783.   50 Above, intro.
51 O.R.O., MSS. Wills Oxon. 45/4/1, 79/4/39, 130/4/24; ibid. Welch XCVII/i/2.
52 Oxf. Jnl. Synopsis, 3 Apr. 1756, 14 Mar. 1761, 27 Oct. 1762, 17 Sept. 1768, 8 June 1771, 17 Aug. 1776; Oxf. Jnl. 27 Oct. 1804, 10 Nov. 1804; Oxon. Clockmakers (Banbury Hist. Soc. iv), 144, 149.
53 Oxf. Jnl. Synopsis, 7 Aug. 1778.
54 Pigot, Lond. & Prov. Dir. (1830); Gardner's Dir. Oxon. (1852); Kelly's Dir. Oxon. (1903); C.O.S., par. reg. transcripts; cf. O.R.O., Mor. XIII/iii/1; ibid. Misc. Me I/2; ibid. Acc. 2184, Lamb inn deeds.
55 O.R.O., Adkin II/2.
56 C.O.S., OPA 4820, 4822; Oxf. Jnl. 10 Nov. 1804; P.O. Dir. Oxon. (1847 and later edns.); cf. Bodl. G. Pamph. 1776 (15); ibid. G.A. Oxon. 8° 636 (8); G.A. Oxon. a 117, p. 66; O.R.O., Pocock I/6/1.
57 P.R.O., RG 11/1514; C.O.S., OPA 4820; Kelly's Dir. Oxon. (1895 and later edns.); cf. Bodl. G.A. Oxon. b 6 (23); ibid. 11031 e 22.
58 Above, this section (agric.).

century only the building trade employed significant numbers: in 1861 there were c. 19 masons, several of them pursuing an additional trade, 15 carpenters, 6 plumbers, glaziers, or painters, and a builder with premises on Buckland Road, New Road, and at Weald.[59] Among prominent builders and masons, James Pettifer (d. 1842) built the town hall and Sandford House and worked at Ham Court, at the Talbot Inn, and in surrounding villages,[60] while Samuel Spencer (d. 1841) and Robert Plaster (d. 1877), one of a long-established family of carpenters and wheelwrights with premises on Bridge Street, built several houses in the town.[61] The aptly named Stone family included several masons, one of whom ran the Mason's Arms public house on Church View in the 1850s and 1860s,[62] and another mason was publican of the Horse Shoe, which had large yards adjoining.[63]

Other tradesmen in 1861 included over 20 cordwainers, cobblers, or shoemakers, and several tailors, drapers, bakers, grocers, smiths, and wheelwrights, many still pursuing more than one trade. There was one watchmaker, a tinman and brazier, a joiner and cabinet maker, and a hairdresser and toy dealer, and professionals included two veterinary surgeons and an inland revenue officer. Over 50 domestic servants, mostly women, were noted in 1861 in the homes of the more prosperous tradesmen and farmers and of the landed and professional classes, and several wives and daughters of labourers and lesser tradesmen supplemented family income by laundering, dressmaking, or bonnet and straw-hat making.[64] Two or more coal merchants recorded for much of the 19th century and early 20th relied at first on river transport and later on the railway.[65]

The principal shops remained concentrated on the market place, Cheapside, and High and Bridge Streets. Duttons' stores on Bridge Street, established reportedly in 1751 and certainly by 1793, was a general grocers and, at various times, tallow chandlers, chemists, and oil merchants, and continued until the 1980s.[66] Pembreys' drapery business, which expanded to occupy Lesta House and Strawberry Cottage on High Street and a nearby shop on Bushey Row, was established by 1861 when it employed 4 assistants and 3 apprentices, and continued into the later 20th century under the Smith and Busby

families.[67] Other long-lasting 19th- and 20th-century businesses included the Batemans' ironmongers and grocers on Broad Street, William Angell Smith's drapery and grocery business at Cheapside, George Joyner's bakers, grocers and confectioners west of the market place in a shop rebuilt by Joyner in 1871, and Eeles' grocers south of the market place, which continued in 1957[68] and was succeeded by a general stores. A cycle shop opened on High Street before 1911.[69] Prosperous tradesmen rebuilt or remodelled several shops and houses in the earlier 19th century,[70] and the butcher Henry Taylor (d. 1854), whose family continued as butchers in the 20th century, accumulated numerous tenements including the Doilly manor house site and the later Romany Inn on Bridge Street, then a butcher's shop and slaughter house.[71] Another butcher, farmer, and landowner, William Andrews (d. 1856), later called himself gentleman,[72] and the Duttons also acquired several houses.[73] Sunday opening may have been common before 1837, when local butchers and others unanimously agreed to abolish it.[74]

During the 20th century Bampton largely retained its range of retailers and tradesmen, remaining a comparatively self-contained community. By 1895 Duttons' stores provided banking services and there was a branch of Gillett and Co.'s (later Barclays) bank, which moved to the west side of the market place c. 1921 and to the south side in the 1970s, closing c. 1991.[75] In 1966 there were c. 20 shops along Bridge and High Streets and around the market place, stocking a wide range of provisions, and nearly half the employed inhabitants worked in Bampton; the low rate of vehicle ownership was thought to reflect a relatively high degree of self-containment compared with other Oxfordshire villages. Of those employed outside the town, 21 per cent worked in Witney and 10 per cent in Oxford.[76] Though some decline in local businesses was reported in the mid 1980s, shops in 1989 included a grocers and fruiterers, a butchers, a small supermarket, a newsagents, fabric and clothes shops, and a hardware store; there was a local thatcher, an upholsterer, and a small building firm, besides a G.P. and a dentist.[77] A small light-engineering works existed near Folly House in 1971, but Bampton's topog-

59 P.R.O., RG 9/905; Oxf. Chron. 4 Jan. 1862.
60 Exeter Coll. Mun., M.II.1 B; Arundel Castle, MS. TP 91, s.a. 1811–12; O.R.O., P2/2/MS 1/21, ff. 3–4; C.O.S., par. reg. transcripts; inscription on town hall.
61 B.L. Map C 7 e 16 (3), p. 59; Bodl. MSS. d.d. Shrewsbury c 4/10 (11), c 4/11 (2); above, intro. (buildings); cf. Oxf. Chron. 2 Aug. 1856.
62 P.R.O., RG 9/905; Jesus Coll. Mun., box 15, list 11; Gardner's Dir. Oxon. (1852); Cassey's Dir. Oxon. (1868).
63 Above, intro. (buildings).   64 P.R.O., RG 9/905.
65 Ibid. HO 107/872; Gardner's Dir. Oxon. (1852); Kelly's Dir. Oxon. (1883 and later edns.); above, intro.
66 O.R.O., incl. award, no. 899; Univ. Brit. Dir. ii [1793], 252–3; Kelly's Dir. Oxon. (1883 and later edns.); Witney Gaz. 13 Mar. 1980, advertisement.
67 P.R.O., RG 9/905; C.O.S., OPA 4829–31, 4833–4, 4845; Bodl. MS. Top. Oxon. c 484/1, no. 3755; Kelly's Dir. Oxon. (1883 and later edns.).
68 P.R.O., HO 107/872; ibid. RG 9/905; RG 11/1514; C.O.S., OPA 48·8, OPA 82/764; O.R.O., Crowdy I/51, town

plan; Bodl. MS. Top. Oxon. c 484/1, no. 4048; Gardner's Dir. Oxon. (1852); Kelly's Dir. Oxon. (1883 and later edns.); datestone inscribed G. J. 1871.
69 Kelly's Dir. Oxon. (1911 and later edns.); C.O.S., OPA 4845.
70 Above, intro. (buildings).
71 O.R.O., Mor. XIII/vi/1, XIII/vii/1–2, XIII/viii/1, XIII/ix/2; ibid. Misc. Me I/1; C.O.S., par. reg. transcripts, s.a. 1854; Kelly's Dir. Oxon. (1939).
72 O.R.O., Mor. XIII/i/2, XIII/ii/2, XIII/iii/1; ibid. MS. Wills Oxon. 274/1/35.
73 O.R.O., Adkin II/2; Jesus Coll. Mun., box 15, list 5, conveyance 11 Mar. 1880.
74 Oxf. Jnl. 13 May 1837.
75 Deeds in possession of Mr. and Mrs. Deacon, Poacher's Rest, Bampton; Kelly's Dir. Oxon. (1895 and later edns.); O.S. Map 1/2,500, SP 3003–3105 (1971 edn.).
76 M. W. Robinson, 'Bampton, Rep. on Survey and Plan' (TS. 1966): copy in C.O.S., SMR Bampton file.
77 Bampton, an Appraisal 1982–5; Bampton Dir. (1989): copies in C.O.S.

raphy and comparative isolation, combined with planning restrictions, discouraged any large-scale light industry.[78] Collett's motor repair garage at Cheapside was established *c.* 1903 when the first car to be run in Bampton was built there,[79] and garages partly on the former Lamb inn site in the market place and near the Talbot Inn on Bridge Street opened apparently by the mid 1940s. Collett's garage closed in the 1970s or 1980s, but that in the market place and another off Moonraker Lane remained open in 1990.[80]

MILLS AND FISHERIES. In 1086 there were 4 mills on Bampton manor rendering 25*s.* a year.[81] One was presumably the later Bampton mill north of Mill bridge, granted with the manor to William de Valence in 1248; it descended with the Coventrys' share after 1660, when, as later, it was a corn grist mill. In 1865 John Jones sold it to William Collett of Clanfield, whose trustees sold it to the Ecclesiastical Commissioners in 1888, and before 1899 it was demolished.[82] Probably it was the mill held in demesne in the late 13th century and early 15th[83] and later let with the demesne farm,[84] and in the 18th century and early 19th it was leased for lives.[85] A second mill on the manor, held with 5 a. in 1279 for 18*s.* 10*d.* rent, tallage, and services valued at 21*d.*, was presumably that let for 20*s.* a year in 1397 and 1420,[86] but later references to two mills seem to indicate only that the surviving Bampton mill was a double one.[87] A watermill and windmill reportedly attached to Bampton Doilly manor in 1572 are otherwise unrecorded.[88] In the 13th century millers were involved in disputes with Exeter cathedral over flooding caused by the high level of the mill pond. It was agreed that markers should be set to limit the pond's level, and that the dams or sluices should be removed for 3 weeks before and after the feast of St. John the Baptist (24 June) in return for half a quarter of wheat; they were to be removed for a day and a night if the markers became submerged.[89]

Several people named Fisher or *Piscator* were recorded in the early 14th century,[90] and fisher-

men were mentioned occasionally thereafter.[91] Fishmongers with premises in the town died in 1596 and 1626.[92] In 1086 the king received 20*s.* a year from fisheries in Bampton,[93] of which one was presumably at Rushey by the Thames, given to Osney abbey by the count of Boulogne *c.* 1170 with ½ yardland in Weald, and confirmed with its waters, weirs, and fisheries in the later 13th century.[94] In 1279 there were 3 weirs there, 2 held with ¼ yardland for 30*s.*, and one held with the other ¼ yardland for 13*s.* 4*d.* and service of providing a boat for 15 days before and after 24 June for those 'throwing down' the weir, presumably to lower the water level while the meadows were mown.[95] One or more of the weirs stood apparently on Isle of Wight brook, called the Black water or stream in 1650 and 1890; possibly they included the later Winney Wegs weir, removed before 1911, and a weir near the confluence of the brook and the Thames, removed before 1890.[96] By the early 16th century Rushey was let separately from the Weald tenements, which retained fishing rights in waters adjoining riverside meadows;[97] it was granted after the Dissolution to the bishopric of Oxford[98] but was sold *c.* 1577 and passed to various owners,[99] its 18th- and 19th-century lessees including the Rudge and later the Brooks and Winter families.[1] A stone pound lock, built in 1790, was in a 'frightful state' by 1857, 'stuffed up with bundles of straw to keep the water up to a certain height', and was rebuilt before 1898; the weir, 'old and broken' in 1871, was rebuilt in 1874, enlarged before 1888, and reconstructed in 1932. The house at Rushey was rebuilt *c.* 1896.[2]

A fishery owned by Exeter cathedral in 1086 and worth 52*s.* a year in 1279 was not mentioned later, and lay possibly in canalised streams near the Deanery where there were fishpools in 1317.[3] A fishery sold with Ham Court in 1865 may similarly have been in Shill brook or its tributaries, adjoining the farm's land.[4] Most other weirs and fisheries were probably in the network of tributaries north of the Thames, whose main stream lay mostly outside the parish.[5] Grants to

78 O.S. Map 1/2,500, SP 3003–3103 (1971 edn.); Robinson, 'Rep. on Survey and Plan'.

79 J. L. Hughes-Owens, *The Bampton We Have Lost*, 106: copy in C.O.S.; *Kelly's Dir. Oxon.* (1928 and later edns.); photos. in private possession, from originals held by Collett's daughter.

80 C.O.S., OPA 30055; *Country Life*, c (1946), 118; O.S. Map 1/2,500, SP 3003–3105 (1971 edn.).

81 *V.C.H. Oxon.* i. 400.

82 O.R.O., incl. award, no. 576; ibid. Tice I/v/6; Bodl. MS. d.d. Shrewsbury c 1/7 (13); D. & C. Exeter, Ch. Comm. 108/239654–8; *Cal. Pat.* 1258–66, 339; O.S. Map 1/2,500, Oxon. XXXVII. 6 (1876 and 1899 edns.).

83 P.R.O., C 133/76, no. 2; C 139/42, no. 86; C 138/58, no. 44; *Cal. Inq. p.m.* xvii, no. 918.

84 P.R.O., REQ 2/198/14, m. 2; B.L. Add. MS. 27535, f. 37.

85 O.R.O., Tice I/v/6; ibid. QSD L.22, mistakenly listing the tenant as owner-occupier.

86 P.R.O., C 136/95, no. 17; C 139/42, no. 86; *Bampton Hund. R.* 20.

87 e.g. Bodl. MS. d.d. Shrewsbury c 1/7 (13); B.L. Add. MS. 27535, f. 37; O.R.O., Tice I/v/4.

88 P.R.O., CP 25/2/196/14 Eliz. I Hil. For Windmill Hill furlong (site of later Windmill Ho.), O.R.O., incl. award; cf. Jesus Coll. Mun., box 15, list 2, farm rep. 28 Feb. 1812, calling Mill field Windmill field.

89 P.R.O., JUST 1/702A, m. 6d.

90 Ibid. E 179/161/8–10.

91 Ibid. REQ 2/268/53, m. 6; Oxf. Jnl. Synopsis, 22 June 1765.

92 O.R.O., MSS. Wills Oxon. 44/1/36, 299/1/5.

93 *V.C.H. Oxon.* i. 400.

94 *Oseney Cart.* iv, pp. 515–17.

95 Ibid. pp. 517–20; *Bampton Hund. R.* 18.

96 P.R.O., PROB 11/214, ff. 230–2; O.S. Map 1", sheet 13 (1830 edn.); F. S. Thacker, *Thames Highway* (1968), ii. 51, 64–6.

97 *Oseney Cart.* vi, pp. 232, 264; Ch. Ch. Arch., MS. Estates 60, f. 72.

98 *L. & P. Hen. VIII*, xvii, p. 490.

99 B.L. Add. Ch. 39971 (9); P.R.O., PROB 11/214, ff. 230–2; ibid. CP 25/2/198/39 & 40 Eliz. I Mich.; CP 25/2/864/6 Wm. and Mary Trin.; CP 25/2/865/13 Wm. and Mary Mich.

1 P.R.O., HO 107/1731; ibid. RG 9/905; Thacker, *Thames Highway*, ii. 62–3.

2 Oxf. Jnl. Synopsis, 15 Oct. 1790; Thacker, *Thames Highway*, ii. 62–5; *Thames Conservancy, 1857–1957* [*c.* 1957], 10, 16, 23, 55: copy in C.O.S.

3 *V.C.H. Oxon.* i. 402; *Bampton Hund. R.* 23; above, manors (Bampton Deanery). For a second fishery, below, Chimney, econ. hist.

4 Jesus Coll. Mun., box 15, list 4; cf. above, manors (castle).

5 O.S. Map 6", Oxon. XXXVII (1884 edn.).

Osney abbey by Geoffrey son of Robert of Bourton in the later 13th century included a weir between Rowney (near Rushey) and Derdesham, a fishery between 'Lutleneye' and 'le Muleam', and half a fishery (presumably half the stream) opposite Ralph Rushey's water between 'Shodforde' and Queenborough meadow. Grants to the abbey by the lord of Aston in 1275 included a fishery called Northlongwater, between Rowney and Queenborough, and two 'islands' in 'Newewerewater'.[6] A fishery later owned by Jesus College, Oxford, in a stream called 'Woodwire', apparently near Rowney and Dawsham, was acquired with a meadow called Osney ham close and was presumably part of the abbey's former possessions.[7] Three weirs attached to Bampton Doilly manor in 1279 may have been those from which Exeter cathedral owned the tithes in the 16th and 17th centuries;[8] fishing rights descended with both moieties of the manor from the 14th century but were mostly sold piecemeal in the 17th, and in 1800 the manor retained fishing rights only in a small private stream south of the manor house.[9] Fisheries in other tributaries were mentioned throughout the 16th and 17th centuries.[10]

Kent's or Rudge's weir by Tadpole bridge on the Thames, mentioned in 1746 and removed in 1869, belonged to the Throckmortons as lords of Buckland (formerly Berks.). Old Nans weir, a mile upstream from Rushey and also outside the parish, existed by 1784 and was removed c. 1868.[11] Walls weir, on Sharney brook, was shown on a map of 1830 but not later.[12]

LOCAL GOVERNMENT. MANOR COURTS.

From 1248 William de Valence, as lord of the manor and hundred of Bampton, claimed return of writs, assize of bread and ale, gallows, pillory, and tumbrel, and pleas of withernam, franchises allegedly held earlier by the counts of Boulogne but challenged by Edward I in 1285. Seventeenth-century lords had waifs, strays, and felons' goods throughout most of the ancient parish.[13] Courts baron were nominally held every three weeks and views of frankpledge twice

a year, in the 14th century and early 16th usually at Hock Day and Michaelmas,[14] but also at other times.[15] Following the division of Bampton Earls manor in 1660 courts baron and leet were held jointly by the lords of each moiety; the courts met in the later 17th century in April and in September or October, but by 1789 once a year only,[16] and though reportedly still held in 1842 they had lapsed by 1848.[17] A court house on the west side of the market place, apparently a first-storey chamber with rooms underneath and a garden behind which were let to tenants, was mentioned from 1609,[18] but in 1669 was in disrepair.[19] Possibly it was the 'parliament house' let to the parish in the 18th century, and in 1821 the building was held by trustees of the National school,[20] but it may have continued as a court house, and was perhaps the 'court-loft' mentioned as the site of courts leet in 1830.[21] Courts baron were said in 1842 to meet at the Talbot Inn,[22] and the court house was demolished in or before 1871 when the tenement was rebuilt.[23]

Tenants of the manor in Bampton, Weald, and Lew formed separate tithings. Business in the 16th and 17th centuries included enforcement of the assizes of bread and ale, suppression of nuisances, and agricultural affairs, notably scouring of watercourses, and copyholds were still granted in the later 17th century. Officers included a constable and tithingman for each tithing, a field warden for Bampton and another for Weald, two inspectors of carcasses, and in 1500 two aletasters;[24] the court appointed constables probably until 1842, though from the later 18th century they were increasingly answerable to the vestry.[25]

In 1270 the dean and chapter of Exeter secured the right to hold annual views of frankpledge for Bampton Deanery manor through William de Valence's bailiff for an annual payment of 3s., which in the 15th century came half from Bampton and Aston, and half from Chimney.[26] By the 15th century the cathedral's steward held the view,[27] though the payment to the Bampton court, charged from 1641 on lessees of Bampton Deanery manor,[28] continued in the 19th century.[29] In 1708

[6] *Oseney Cart.* iv, pp. 493–4, 520; cf. *Cal. Chart. R. 1226–57*, 235, 246.

[7] Jesus Coll. Mun., shelf 2, survey 1691, nos. 6, 13.

[8] D. & C. Exeter, MS. 640; ibid. MS. 6016/6, rental 1531–2; O.R.O., MS. Oxf. Archd. Oxon. c 31, f. 145; *Bampton Hund. R.* 28.

[9] Bodl. MS. Dodsworth 143, f. 34; P.R.O., CP 25/2/340/15 Jas. I East.; CP 25/2/473/10 Chas. I Mich.; CP 25/2/473/10 Chas. I Hil.; CP 25/2/588/1658 East.; *Oxf. Jnl.* 9 Aug. 1800.

[10] e.g. P.R.O., CP 25/2/792/2 Jas. II East.; CP 25/2/76/650; CP 25/2/196/3 Eliz. I Trin.; CP 25/2/863/3 Wm. and Mary Trin.

[11] Thacker, *Thames Highway*, ii. 51, 60–2, 66–7; R. Whitaker, *Plan of Proposed Canal from Kempsford to Abingdon* (1784): copy in Bodl. (E) C 17:13 (31).

[12] O.S. Map 1", sheet 13 (1830 edn.).

[13] *Bampton Hund. R.* 17; *Rot. Hund.* (Rec. Com.), ii. 30; Giles, *Hist. Bampton*, 130–2, Suppl. p. 2.

[14] *Bampton Hund. R.* 17–18, 20; Giles, *Hist. Bampton*, 138–9; Bodl. MS. d.d. Harcourt c 127/3, ct. 5 Oct. 21 Hen. VII.

[15] e.g. Arundel Castle, MS. M 535; cf. P.R.O., REQ 2/198/14, mentioning a hundred court in August.

[16] Longleat House (Wilts.), NMR 3315: ct. bk. 1667–73;

B.L. Map C 7 e 16 (3), p. 36.

[17] Pigot, *Royal Nat. & Comm. Dir.* (1842); Giles, *Hist. Bampton*, 53.

[18] O.R.O., incl. award, plan I (no. 500); B.L. Add. MS. 27535, f. 40v.; ibid. Map C 7 e 16 (3), p. 70; Arundel Castle, MS. TP 288, no. 18; ibid. MS. TP 104; Bodl. MS. d.d. Shrewsbury c 2/8 (23).

[19] Longleat House, Coventry pps. CVI, f. 87v.

[20] O.R.O., MSS. d.d. Par. Bampton b 10, f. 33v.; b 11, f. 160; b 12, f. 3v.; ibid. incl. award.

[21] Pigot, *Lond. & Prov. Dir.* (1830); cf. O.R.O., P4/2/MS 1/5, ff. 1–2.

[22] Pigot, *Royal Nat. & Comm. Dir.* (1842); the statement in Pigot, *Lond. & Prov. Dir.* (1830), that they met at the New Inn resulted probably from confusion with Bampton Deanery ct.

[23] Datestone on gable.

[24] Arundel Castle, MS. M 535; Longleat House, NMR 3285, 3315.

[25] Giles, *Hist. Bampton*, 53–4; below, this section (par. govt.).

[26] D. & C. Exeter, MSS. 643, 4751, 4770; *Bampton Hund. R.* 23.

[27] e.g. D. & C. Exeter, MS. 4758.

[28] Ibid. MSS. 1978, 4775; ibid. MS. 4030, p. 10.

[29] Ibid. MS. 6016/1/40.

the duke of Shrewsbury challenged the lessees' right to royalty, allegedly intending to prevent them from holding courts at all; the lessees replied, apparently correctly, that besides holding courts leet and baron and appointing fishers and fowlers they had always taken waifs and strays and enjoyed similar rights within their manor.[30]

Courts in the 14th, 15th, and early 16th centuries met irregularly two or three times a year, usually in October, when the annual view was held, and in April or May.[31] From the 17th century they were held jointly by the lessees of each moiety, but appear to have met only sporadically, and views were held sometimes in April.[32] A court leet was recorded in 1762, but from 1781 courts baron only, which from 1785 dealt solely with copyholds. The last known court was in 1860, and in 1868 surviving copyholds were surrendered out of court.[33] In the 19th century the courts met usually at the New Inn and occasionally in Bampton Manor House off Broad Street, but earlier venues are unknown.[34]

By 1396 there were three tithings for tenants in Bampton, Aston, and Chimney, and villein yardlanders in all three townships were required in 1317 to act as reeve if so elected by the court.[35] From probably 1270 and still in the early 16th century the court elected an aletaster for Bampton, and from the 15th century to the late 18th a constable for Bampton, Aston, and Clanfield.[36] Presentations in the 15th century and early 16th included failure to scour ditches, disputes over common rights, and fouling of public ways,[37] and in 1498 and 1503 Shifford's inhabitants were presented for not maintaining a watercourse adjoining the lordship.[38] In 1588 all disputes involving less than 40s. were reserved for the court on pain of a 40s. fine.[39]

Courts for Bampton Doilly manor were held by 1279, when they nominally met every three weeks; view of frankpledge was reserved to the Valences and their successors.[40] Courts were still held for the Goldsborough and possibly for the Meaux moiety in 1596, and lapsed presumably following the break-up of the manor in the early 17th century.[41] A constable and tithingman of Bampton Doilly were appointed at the hundred court in the 1670s and presumably earlier.[42]

Osney abbey's tenants in Weald attended the abbot's court at Black Bourton in the 14th century and still in the 16th.[43]

PARISH GOVERNMENT AND POOR RELIEF. Three wardens for Bampton church were recorded from the 16th century. In the 18th and probably earlier two were appointed by Bampton vestry, one, for Bampton, nominated by the vicar, the other, for Weald, Lew, and Lower Haddon, nominated by the parishioners. The third, for Aston, was presumably appointed separately by Aston's inhabitants.[44] Their income in the early 17th century may have included rent from parish lands and cottages then let on 21-year leases,[45] and in the 18th century they received rents from unspecified 'church lands', latterly through trustees;[46] at inclosure in 1821 they were awarded 10½ a. in Bampton, Weald, and Lew, including the 'poor house' on Weald Lane.[47] From 1768 to 1772 they refused to account to the vestry and were threatened with prosecution.[48] Following the division of the parish in 1857, the vestry appointed two churchwardens for Bampton Proper.[49] Sidesmen were recorded in the early 17th century.[50]

For poor-law and other civil purposes Bampton, Weald, and Lower Haddon were by the 18th century administered together through Bampton vestry. In the earlier 18th century the vestry seems to have met only sporadically, but by the late 18th and early 19th, as the burden of poor-law administration increased, there were up to 13 or 14 vestries a year, and spring and winter meetings remained frequent after 1834.[51] Meetings were usually in the vestry room in Bampton church,[52] judged small and damp in 1792 when it was to be enlarged and provided with a fireplace and better storage for muniments;[53] occasionally meetings were held in public houses or in the National school or vicarage house.[54] Though some meetings were poorly attended[55] minutes were often signed by 15 or more inhabitants including resident gentry and professionals, one or more of the vicars, and leading farmers, and actual attendance was sometimes higher: 55 inhabitants voted in a debate on poor-law administration in 1833.[56] From the later 18th century ad hoc committees were increasingly appointed to oversee poor relief, to audit accounts and administer charities, in 1832 to allocate clothing and tools for emigrants, and

30 D. & C. Exeter, MSS. 2005–8; cf. ibid. MS. 5016/6, survey 1650.
31 Ibid. MSS. 4751–73 (rolls from 1396).
32 Ibid. MSS. 4775–83; cf. O.R.O., D.Y. VII/v/4.
33 Bodl. MS. Ch. Oxon. 5275; D. & C. Exeter, Ch. Comm. 80/134543–5, 80/134547–8, 13/74354–7.
34 D. & C. Exeter, Ch. Comm. 13/74354.
35 Ibid. MSS. 2931, 4751.
36 Ibid. MSS. 643, 4751–83; ibid. Ch. Comm. 80/134543.   37 Ibid. MSS. 4751, 4766–8.
38 Ibid. MSS. 4769, 4772; cf. O.R.O., Misc. WA I/1, f. 99.
39 Bodl. MS. Rolls Oxon. 57.
40 Bampton Hund. R. 29; Arundel Castle, MS. M 535.
41 Cat. Anct. D. vi, p. 550; above, manors (Bampton Doilly).
42 Longleat House, NMR 3315, ct. 24 Sept. 1672 and passim.
43 Bodl. MSS. Ch. Oxon. 312–13, 333; Oseney Cart. vi, p. 240.
44 Protestation Rtns. and Tax Assess. 1–2, 6–8; Archdeacon's Ct. ii (O.R.S. xxiv), 134; C.O.S., par. reg. transcripts,

1538–1653; O.R.O., MS. d.d. Par. Bampton b 10, ff. 8v., 23, 55v.; ibid. MS. Oxf. Dioc. c 329, f. 10.
45 O.R.O., MS. d.d. Par. Bampton c 9, items a–b; they were not mentioned later, but cf. ibid. b 12, ff. 92v., 165.
46 Ibid. c 9, item c; b 10, ff. 47, 48v., 63v.; cf. ibid. ff. 3, 52v. For chwdns.' accts. 1814–16, ibid. c 12.
47 O.R.O., incl. award; below, this section.
48 O.R.O., MS. d.d. Par. Bampton b 10, f. 43v.
49 Ibid. c 8, ff. 186v., 191, 258; chwdns.' accts. 1869–1976, in custody of vicar and par. officers; below, churches.
50 O.R.O., MS. Wills Oxon. 54/3/9.
51 Ibid. MSS. d.d. Par. Bampton b 10, c 8 (vestry mins. 1730–1858), evidently omitting some early meetings: cf. ibid. MS. Oxf. Archd. Oxon. b 22, ff. 215v.–216.
52 e.g. ibid. MS. Oxf. Archd. Oxon. b 22, f. 215v.; ibid. MS. d.d. Par. Bampton c 8, passim; cf. Bodl. MS. Top. Oxon. b 220, f. 238v.; below, churches.
53 O.R.O., MS. d.d. Par. Bampton c 8, f. 1.
54 Ibid. b 10, f. 59; ibid. c 8, ff. 104, 115, 122v.
55 e.g. ibid. b 10, f. 68; ibid. c 8, ff. 31v., 117, 253.
56 Ibid. c 8, ff. 138v.–140; cf. ibid. f. 109.

from the 1850s to supervise the town hall;[57] from 1820, under the Vestries Act of 1819, a select vestry with c. 14–20 members was elected annually to deal with poor relief, though open meetings continued.[58] Most meetings seem to have been amicable, though in 1715 an inflated doctor's bill prompted abusive exchanges,[59] and occasionally the vestry was drawn into disputes involving the vicars or their curates. In 1822 ten members dissociated themselves from the impending prosecution of a vicar.[60]

In the 18th century the vestry nominated four surveyors of highways for Bampton and four for Weald, but only four seem to have been appointed in all, and following the General Highways Act of 1835 it was agreed to appoint one for each township. In the 1840s there was sometimes also a salaried assistant surveyor.[61] Inhabitants' obligations towards road repair, fixed periodically by the vestry, were then discharged partly in money and partly in carting duties.[62] Constables were appointed by the manor courts, but overseers and, later, farmers of the poor contributed to their charges from 1773, when three constables were noted, and on some earlier occasions.[63] In 1829 the vestry recommended 2 men to serve as constables for Bampton and Weald and another 6 to serve as tithingmen; in 1826 it ordered the constable of Weald to repair bridges in the meadows, and in 1833–4 it paid a tithingman's expenses.[64] Following the Parish Constables Act of 1842 it nominated usually 6 or 8 candidates to the magistrates.[65] Occasionally it addressed public order issues, in 1761 prosecuting a victualler for keeping a disorderly house, and in 1781 acting against those taking firewood from trees, hedges, and fences.[66] A salaried watchman was appointed in 1825 and again from 1827, when his duties included patrolling public houses, removing vagrants, preventing disorderly conduct around the church on Sundays, and reporting swearers and graffitors; a beadle, usually an old man acting as assistant, was also appointed and issued with a hat, coat, and staff. Despite later criticism of the watchman's efficiency the crime rate fell, and in 1835 and again in the 1840s two were appointed.[67] Minor officers included a sexton elected by the vestry, and a parish clerk appointed by the vicars, both offices tenable for life; from 1730 the sexton, until then responsible for collecting his

allowance of 4d. per yardland, received a salary from the poor rate, but the parish clerk was still paid partly in Easter offerings and other dues in the 1840s.[68]

Bampton and Weald (with Lower Haddon) each had a collector or overseer in 1642, appointed by the vestry perhaps then and certainly by the 18th century.[69] In the 17th century and earlier 18th they were responsible for Yelford, which contributed to the poor rate until c. 1758 but thereafter was administered separately.[70] In 1765 they were allowed 10s. 6d. for collecting their taxes, and in 1824 tried unsuccessfully to claim the balance of their accounts as salary; a salaried overseer receiving 6 gns. a year from the rate was appointed in 1762 and 1772.[71] Expenditure on the poor in the earlier 18th century was usually between £100 and £150, and in the later 18th c. £200, reaching £277 in 1770–1. From the 1790s it rose sharply and by 1803 was £1,074 or over 20s. per head of population, significantly above the national and county average.[72] Capitation rose to over 25s. by 1813 and, despite a fall in the next two years, to over 35s. by 1819. By 1825 it had fallen to c. 17s. (total expenditure £1,309), and in 1829, at c. 15s., was just below the county average, perhaps partly a result of administrative reforms.[73] Poor rates, 'not to be depended on' in 1789 and 'enormously high' in 1818,[74] prompted frequent complaints, usually on the grounds that they were unfairly assessed: a distress was levied on refusers in 1769 and frequent reassessments were attempted, including in 1814 when an inclosure commissioner was employed for a fee of 100 gns. raised from the rate. Complaints persisted, and in 1817 and 1819 the vestry again resolved to prosecute defaulters, though successive committees were established to investigate legitimate grievances.[75] In 1837 the Poor Law Commissioners ordered a new assessment, and in the 1840s, with payments still in arrears, it was decided to rate all resident tradesmen and labourers whether or not they belonged to the parish, partly so that poor inhabitants might be excused.[76]

A rented workhouse existed by 1718, when it housed only 2 adults and 3 children.[77] In the 1740s there were about a dozen inmates and in 1769 c. 21;[78] in 1763 a man and his family were to accept relief of 2s. 6d. a week or enter the workhouse.[79] The keeper's allowance per

57 Ibid. b 10, ff. 35v., 62, 67v.; ibid. c 8, ff. 4v., 6v., 7v., 16, 38v., 49, 50v., 59v., 133, 134v., 178, 217, 253v.

58 Ibid. c 8, ff. 67v.–68, 70v.–71, 76 and v., et seq.

59 O.R.O., MS. Oxf. Archd. Oxon. c 31, f. 137 and v.

60 Ibid. MSS. d.d. Par. Bampton b 10, ff. 27, 31, 32v.; c 8, ff. 44v.–45v., 77.

61 Ibid. b 10, ff. 11, 15; ibid. c 8, ff. 102, 154 and v., 168, 187, 192v.

62 e.g. ibid. c 8, ff. 165, 187v., 199v.

63 Ibid. b 10, f. 45v.; c 8, ff. 43v., 113; b 11, ff. 22v., 124v.; b 13, f. 1; above, this section (manor cts.).

64 Ibid. c 8, ff. 100v., 122; c 11, item d.

65 Ibid. c 8, ff. 175v., 176v., 181, 185v., 203, 209.

66 Ibid. b 10, ff. 26, 52.

67 Ibid. c 8, ff. 92v.–93, 109v.–111v., 116v., 118, 123, 149v.–153v., 169; P.O. Dir. Oxon. (1847); Giles, Hist. Bampton, 54.

68 O.R.O., MSS. d.d. Par. Bampton b 10, ff. 1, 29, 64; c 8, ff. 13, 73, 178–9; Giles, Hist. Bampton, 32.

69 Protestation Rtns. and Tax Assess. 6–7; O.R.O., MS. d.d. Par. Bampton b 10, ff. 8v., 73v.–80; for accts. from 1718, ibid. b 11–14.

70 O.R.O., QS/1708 Epiph./20; ibid. MSS. d.d. Par. Bampton b 11–13, passim; b 10, ff. 21v.–22.

71 Ibid. MSS. d.d. Par. Bampton b 10, ff. 28, 33, 43v.; c 8, f. 88.

72 Ibid. b 11–14; Poor Abstract, 1777, 1804, giving lower figs. than overseers' accts.; D. Eastwood, 'The Republic in the Village', Jnl. of Regional and Local Studies, xii, no. 1 (1992), 19–20; cf. Census, 1801.

73 Poor Abstract 1818; Poor Rate Returns, H.C. 556, p. 135 (1822), v; ibid. H.C. 334, p. 170 (1825), iv; ibid. H.C. 83, p. 157 (1830–1), xi; Eastwood, 'Republic in the Village', 24, 28; cf. Census, 1811–41.

74 D. & C. Exeter, MS. 4544, p. 8; ibid. Ch. Comm. 13/74361a, valuation 1818; cf. Jesus Coll. Mun., box 15, list 3, D. Miller to bursar 1 June 1822.

75 O.R.O., MSS. d.d. Par. Bampton b 10, ff. 35, 53, 65, 67v.; c 8, ff. 7v., 9v., 10, 38 and v., 42, 48v., 49v., 50v., 59 and v., 80 and v., 83, 104v., 129–30, 146.

76 Ibid. c 8, ff. 159v.–160v., 178, 200 and v.

77 Ibid. b 11, ff. 21 and v., 23, 49; b 10, f. 13v.–14.

78 Ibid. b 12, ff. 131v., 156v.–157v., 164; b 13, f. 1.

79 Ibid. b 10, f. 29v.; cf. ibid. f. 15v.

inmate, between 1*s*. 2*d*. and 1*s*. 4*d*. a week during 1759, was supplemented by occasional payments for fuel, medical bills, and in 1756 because of the dearness of provisions;[80] an inventory of workhouse goods was made in 1753, to be checked every six months.[81] A proposal in 1768 to build a new workhouse on Rosemary Lane to house and employ 60 or more inmates, the cost to be met from the poor rate, subscription, and from the charitable bequest of Mary Dewe (d. 1764), was evidently abandoned,[82] though a new workhouse was built or acquired *c*. 1772 and had accommodation for 30 in 1776.[83] In 1837 it was described as a house with two cottages and a garden adjoining, and was presumably the 'poor house' (later Lime Tree Cottages) on Weald Lane owned by the churchwardens in 1821, and known locally as Workhouse Yard.[84] Its relationship to a sacking factory reportedly established with money from Dewe's charity *c*. 1795, but which failed soon after, is unclear.[85] In 1793 the keeper was not fulfilling his obligations,[86] and in 1796 there were only *c*. 10–14 inmates, though 45, including children, were mentioned in 1803 and 23 in 1813.[87] Presumably it was the 'poor house' where prayers were said regularly in 1831, but from 1827 it was no longer mentioned in contracts for managing the poor, and in 1834 it was to be put into a proper state to receive them.[88]

From the 1770s to the early 19th century the poor were usually farmed, at first for between £150 and £200 a year depending on the duties contracted, but by 1806 for £650.[89] Salaried assistant overseers were appointed instead in 1812, 1817, and sometimes during the 1820s, but in other years farming continued for £1,400 or more.[90] From 1819 the vestry briefly operated the provisions of Gilbert's Act: the workhouse was refitted for the impotent poor, and a treasurer, visitor, and salaried guardian and governor were appointed.[91] Debate over management of the poor continued, and in 1829 it was finally decided to appoint an assistant overseer with a fixed salary.[92]

Regular out relief was received in the earlier 18th century usually by fewer than 20 people including children, though in 1769 fortnightly payments were being made to *c*. 23 adults (including 12 widows) and *c*. 6 children.[93] In

1720–1 the overseers provided four dozen poor badges, which the vestry ruled in 1780 should be worn as required by law.[94] By 1803 there were 64 adults and nearly 150 children under 14 on regular out relief (*c*. 20 per cent of the population), and 10 years later over 80 people probably excluding children;[95] a complex bread scale, dividing paupers into five classes whose varying allowances were related to bread prices, was introduced in 1821.[96] Relief frequently included clothing, given sometimes to young people entering service or being apprenticed:[97] between 1673 and 1845 the parish helped to apprentice nearly 100 children to masters inside and outside the parish, some paid for from charitable funds, though not all premiums were met in full and occasionally clothing only was provided.[98] In 1760 the vestry ruled that poor children should be bound out to farmers and others obliged by law to take them in such order as should be 'most equitable'.[99] Other regular payments included paupers' rents and funeral expenses, often with provision of ale.[1] Occasionally relief was given to destitute parishioners living elsewhere (including London),[2] and in 1826 the vestry authorized a loan to a resident Bampton man so that he could continue his dead father's business.[3]

Wool cards were occasionally provided in the 18th century, and in the 1730s and later some of those receiving extraordinary payments of 6*d*. or 1*s*. may have been roundsmen.[4] In 1803 those on out relief earned £25, with £15 spent on materials.[5] In 1741 the vestry agreed that non-settled labourers should not be employed during winter months, and by 1815, when a similar agreement was made,[6] employment of labourers was an acute and recurring problem. Various labour-rate schemes between the late 1810s and early 1830s aimed to ensure that ratepayers employed their share in proportion to their assessments, the amount paid out in wages being deducted from their rate; W. H. Chamberlin's Cropredy plan, which allowed for a free labour market, was briefly adopted in 1820,[7] but more usually ratepayers seem to have been allotted particular labourers.[8] Standard adult wages in 1818 were fixed at between 6*d*. and 2*s*. a day depending on the size of the labourer's family.[9] The schemes failed repeatedly after some in-

80 O.R.O., MS. d.d. Par. Bampton b 10, ff. 15 and v., 17, 22v., 23v., 29, 44v.
81 Ibid. f. 7.
82 Ibid. ff. 34v., 35v.; cf. O.R.O., incl. award.
83 O.R.O., MSS. d.d. Par. Bampton b 10, f. 42; b 13, ff. 34, 35v., mentioning the 'old workho.'; *Poor Abstract, 1777*.
84 O.R.O., MS. d.d. Par. Bampton c 8, f. 161v.; ibid. incl. award, no. 875; inf. from Maj. R. A. Colvile, Weald Manor. Cf. O.R.O., MS. d.d. Par. Bampton c 8, ff. 43v., 61, 75.
85 Below, charities.
86 O.R.O., MS. d.d. Par. Bampton c 8, f. 5.
87 Ibid. b 13, ff. 105, 112, 116v.; *Poor Abstract, 1804, 1818*; the 1813 fig. may exclude children.
88 O.R.O., MS. Oxf. Dioc. b 38, ff. 15–16; ibid. MS. d.d. Par. Bampton c 8, ff. 82, 109, 149v.
89 Ibid. MS. d.d. Par. Bampton b 10, ff. 44v., 46v., 50, 53v., 61v.–62, 66; c 8, ff. 4v.–5, 6v., 16, 43v.; b 14, f. 134v.
90 Ibid. c 8, ff. 32, 33v., 35, 46v., 71v.–72, 75, 82 and v., 85, 90, 96–9, 109, 113 and v.
91 Ibid. ff. 53 and v., 55–61.
92 Ibid. ff. 108v.–109, 120v.–121v., 124 and v., 126v., 131v., 140v., 146v.–147.
93 Ibid. b 11–13.

94 Ibid. b 10, f. 50v.; b 11, f. 49.
95 *Poor Abstract, 1804, 1818*; cf. Eastwood, 'Republic in the Village', 21.
96 O.R.O., MS. d.d. Par. Bampton b 15, 'List of Paupers and Bread Scale'; Eastwood, 'Republic in the Village', 24.
97 e.g. O.R.O., MSS. d.d. Par. Bampton b 10, ff. 7v.–8, 12, 14 and v.; b 11, f. 7v.
98 Ibid. b 11, ff. 7v., 23v.; ibid. b 15, indentures; below, charities. Most surviving indentures are pre-1750.
99 O.R.O., MS. d.d. Par. Bampton b 10, f. 24.
1 e.g. ibid. ff. 6, 7–8, 30v.; ibid. b 11, f. 38; b 13, f. 31.
2 Ibid. b 10, f. 20v.; ibid. c 8, f. 2v.
3 Ibid. c 8, f. 94.
4 Ibid. b 10, f. 8; b 12, ff. 40–3; b 13, ff. 21, 36v.
5 *Poor Abstract, 1804*.
6 O.R.O., MSS. d.d. Par. Bampton b 16, item f; c 8, f. 42v.
7 Ibid. c 8, ff. 59v.–60, 61; for pamphlet there cited, W. H. Chamberlin, *Plan for Employment of Labourers* [*c*. 1819]: copy in Bodl. G.A. Oxon. 8° 935.
8 O.R.O., MS. d.d. Par. Bampton c 8, ff. 51v.–52, 73v.–74, 78v.–79, 93v., 137.
9 Ibid. f. 51v.

habitants refused to employ their quota, and though ratepayers (including tradesmen) who accepted the system were encouraged to employ the remainder, in 1822 there were 80 labourers for whom the overseers could find no work.[10] In 1818 the surveyors were to employ some old and infirm; from 1826 relief was refused to labourers keeping pigs, dogs, donkeys, or poultry, which was said to breed dishonesty and discourage employment; from 1827 only the able-bodied and 'young lads' were found farm work, others being employed gravel-digging or on the roads;[11] and in 1833 the vestry proposed halving the number of labourers sent to smaller ratepayers, and distributing them among the remainder.[12] Public kitchens, where monthly accounts of parish payments to labourers were to be posted and which were presumably supported from rates, were mentioned in 1818,[13] and emigration was encouraged.[14]

Medical expenses were paid frequently throughout the 18th century and early 19th, sometimes for parishioners in hospitals or lunatic asylums in London and elsewhere.[15] In 1793 the overseers were to procure seawater for a patient on a doctor's recommendation.[16] In 1812 a local apothecary contracted to attend the poor, and from the 1820s contracts with local doctors were common, usually at £40 a year excluding midwifery and more serious cases.[17] The vacant school house was used during an epidemic of 'contagious fever' in 1769, and provision for smallpox victims was recorded throughout the 18th century;[18] in 1824 all those potentially chargeable to the parish were vaccinated.[19]

After 1834 Bampton formed part of Witney union.[20] The workhouse, at first a district workhouse for surrounding parishes, was sold in 1840 following several applications, and the proceeds were used to offset Bampton's contribution towards the union workhouse.[21] In the early 20th century a vicar asserted that poor relief in the parish remained utterly inadequate and established a Charity Committee to provide employment, set up soup kitchens, and lobby the Poor Law Guardians. Those abusing the system were blacklisted, though some inhabitants were claimed to be 'actually suffering from starvation'.[22]

The vestry continued after 1834 to nominate constables and assistant overseers, to appoint surveyors or waywardens, and to deal with rating, removals, and public health; by 1847 it appointed an assessor and collector of taxes and, presumably, the town criers mentioned then and still in 1899. In 1859 the surveyor was to serve notices on those fouling public streets, and in 1884 street cleaning was put out to tender.[23] By c. 1835 and again from 1867 the vestry operated some provisions of the Lighting and Watching Act of 1833, appointing a board of inspectors which in the 1840s met monthly in the town hall and to whom the watchmen and beadle were answerable; the Act's lighting provisions were briefly adopted in 1840, and in the early 1890s there was a lighting committee.[24] Vestry meetings continued in 1894 when Bampton became part of Witney rural district, and residual civil functions passed to a parish council, which in 1989 managed street lighting, the cemetery and playing fields, and allotments. In 1974 the parish became part of West Oxfordshire district.[25]

PUBLIC SERVICES. Street lighting with mineral spirit was introduced by the vestry in 1840, when 12 lamps were planned. The scheme, repeatedly curtailed or suspended because of the cost, was revived c. 1887 still using petroleum spirit, and continued until the early 20th century;[26] a private attempt in the 1860s to introduce gas lighting failed.[27] The Bampton, Aston, and District Gas and Water Co., later part of the Mid-Oxfordshire Gas and Water Co., established a gas works south of Aston road c. 1907. Water was supplied from a 125-foot bore-hole and a 40-foot water tower near the gas works.[28] Witney R.D.C. took over the water supply before 1939, and electricity, supplied by the Wessex Electric Co., was introduced c. 1934; street lighting was by gas from c. 1907 and electricity by 1939.[29] There was a sewage works on Buckland Road by the mid 1960s.[30]

The churchwardens paid for repair of a parish fire engine in 1813,[31] and in 1850 the vestry recommended procuring a new one and erecting

[10] Ibid. ff. 73v., 79v.–80, 85v.–86, 137; cf. above, econ. hist. (agric.).
[11] O.R.O., MS. d.d. Par. Bampton c 8, ff. 52, 93v., 94v., 100, 107v.
[12] Ibid. f. 137 and v.
[13] Ibid. f. 52.   [14] Above, intro.
[15] O.R.O., MSS. d.d. Par. Bampton b 10, ff. 15v., 20v., 23v., 26v., 28 and v., 51, 54v.–55, 56; c 8, f. 66.
[16] Ibid. c 8, f. 3v.
[17] Ibid. ff. 34, 61, 65v., 76, 86v., 90, 92, 95v., 108, 120v., 124, 126v., 131v., 140v., 146v.–147, 148, 149v.
[18] Ibid. b 10, ff. 35, 44v.; b 11, ff. 128 and v., 177v.; b 12, ff. 20v., 28v., 29v., 92v.; b 13, f. 28.
[19] Ibid. c 8, f. 84.
[20] O.R.O., RO 3251, pp. 201–3.
[21] Ibid. PLU 6/G/1A1/1, pp. 9, 130; ibid. MS. d.d. Par. Bampton c 8, ff. 159, 161v.–162, 167; Giles, Hist. Bampton, 101.
[22] 'Ch. Council Meetings ... 1917–23' (in custody of vicar and par. officers), ff. 79v. sqq.; Witney Gaz. 2 Feb. 1907.
[23] e.g. O.R.O., MS. d.d. Par. Bampton c 8, ff. 178, 189v., 200 and v., 213v., 220, 235v.–236, 240v., 255v.–256v., 260v.–261; ibid. c 12, item k, s.a. 1859, 1884; P.O. Dir. Oxon. (1847); Kelly's Dir. Oxon. (1899).
[24] O.R.O., MS. d.d. Par. Bampton c 8, ff. 156, 161, 163v., 166, 169; ibid. uncat. vestry mins. 1858–71, s.a. 1867; Giles, Hist. Bampton, 54; Kelly's Dir. Oxon. (1891 and later edns.); below, this section (public services).
[25] O.R.O., MS. d.d. Par. Bampton c 12, item k, passim; ibid. RO 3251, pp. 201–3; RO 3267; Bampton Dir. (1989), 2: copy in C.O.S.
[26] O.R.O., MSS. d.d. Par. Bampton c 8, ff. 169 and v., 221v.–222, 229–30, 258v.–259; c 12, item k, s.a. 1869–70, 1891; Oxf. Chron. 24 Jan., 3 Feb., 20 Nov., 11 Dec. 1852; Giles, Hist. Bampton, 53–4; Kelly's Dir. Oxon. (1887 and later edns.).
[27] Oxf. Chron. 5 Dec. 1863; P.O. Dir. Oxon. (1864, 1869); [E. G. Hunt], Music of a Merry Heart [1886], 191: copy in Bodl.
[28] Witney Gaz. 16 Feb. 1907; O.S. Map 1/2,500, Oxon. XXXVII. 7 (1921 edn.); Kelly's Dir. Oxon. (1907 and later edns.); Sale Cat., Valetta Lodge (1917): copy in Bodl. G.A. Oxon. c 317/4.
[29] O.R.O., MS. Oxf. Dioc. c 1713/1, faculty 1934; Kelly's Dir. Oxon. (1907 and later edns.); local inf.
[30] M. W. Robinson, 'Bampton, Rep. on Survey and Plan' (TS. 1966), p. 4: copy in C.O.S., SMR Bampton file; O.S. Map, 1/25,000, SP 20/30 (1977 edn.).
[31] J. L. Hughes-Owens, The Bampton We Have Lost, 115, citing subsequently lost receipt: copy in C.O.S.

three public pumps. The engine was again replaced *c.* 1880, and a motorised one was acquired *c.* 1929.[32] By 1877 it was housed under the arcaded town hall in a lockable engine house, and in 1891 it was managed by trustees;[33] church bells sounded the alarm until *c.* 1886 when a new bell, 'hardly more powerful than [a] dinner bell', was erected at the town hall.[34] By the late 1940s, when responsibility had passed to the county, the garage was too small for a standard engine,[35] and a new fire station was built *c.* 1971 on New Road.[36]

A police constable living in a private house was stationed in Bampton by 1861. A police station with a staff of two was mentioned from the 1890s, and in 1928 a new station was built on the northern edge of the town.[37]

CHURCHES. Bampton was the site of a late Anglo-Saxon minster whose extensive *parochia* seems to have included Clanfield, Alvescot, Black Bourton, Ducklington, Cokethorpe, Standlake, and Yelford. The churches of all those places were claimed as chapels in 1318, and most still buried at Bampton 'by ancient custom' in 1405 and in some cases until after the Reformation.[38] Despite gradual erosion of the church's jurisdiction the parish remained unusually large for Oxfordshire, with chapels at Shifford and, in the Middle Ages, at Lew, possibly at Lower Haddon and Chimney, and in Bampton itself.[39] Churches were built at Aston and at Lew in 1839 and 1841 respectively, and in 1857, under Order in Council of 1845, the parish was divided to form Bampton Proper, Bampton Lew, and Bampton Aston, the last including Chimney and Shifford.[40] Bampton Proper and Bampton Lew were united *c.* 1917,[41] and in 1976 both were merged with Bampton Aston and Clanfield to form a new benefice of Bampton-with-Clanfield, part of a group ministry with Lower Windrush.[42]

The parish church, parts of which are 11th-century or earlier, may have been preceded as a religious focus by a site east of the later town at the Beam. Burials near the medieval chapel of St. Andrew on the site of Beam Cottage are known only from the 11th century to the 13th, but the chapel's dedication, its location near an area of early settlement, and the name 'Beam'

(which predates 'Bampton' and implies an important local landmark, possibly a cross) suggest an early religious site, perhaps with a large, early medieval cemetery.[43] If so, a shift to the site of the later parish church occurred presumably with the establishment of the royal *tūn* between the 7th century and the mid 10th, by which time there was a small, endowed religious community apparently guarding the relics of St. Beornwald.[44] A pension of 13*s.* 4*d.* to Eynsham abbey, recorded from 1291 and paid after the Dissolution to the vicar of Eynsham, arose possibly from an agreement over tithes in Aston or Shifford, but may reflect early dependence on Eynsham minster: in the 17th century and still in the 19th it was associated with a sermon delivered in Bampton church by the vicar of Eynsham on the feast of the Assumption (15 August), presumably continuing a medieval practice.[45]

As at other significant minster sites there may formerly have been two adjacent churches, of which one dwindled to subsidiary status. The 'chapel of the Blessed Virgin' in which Roger d'Oilly and Exeter cathedral sealed an agreement in 1235 was perhaps the 'chapel or chantry' in Bampton churchyard controlled in 1395 by the owners of Bampton Doilly manor, a physical arrangement possibly reflected in the double dedication to St. Mary and St. John the Baptist recorded in 1317, though if the chapel originally belonged to the minster it is unclear how the d'Oillys obtained control of it.[46] Other early chapels in Bampton itself, forming part of an evidently planned ecclesiastical layout, included that west of the parish church in the Deanery, in origin perhaps an 11th-century double chapel, and a chantry chapel on Catte (later Queen) Street mentioned in 1402, the former and probably the latter on an east–west alignment with St. Andrew's chapel, the parish church, and the 'Lady well' west of the Deanery. Since freestanding purpose-built chantry chapels were rare, that on Catte Street, whose exact site is unknown, may have occupied an earlier, undocumented chapel.[47] Window glass in St. Andrew's chapel was mentioned in 1325, and extensive repairs in 1329 included work on the bells and bell-frame, repainting of an image (or statue) of St. Andrew, and rebuilding of a wall.[48] Repairs were carried out in 1421–2,[49] but no oblations were recorded later and the chapel had

32 O.R.O., MSS. d.d. Par. Bampton c 8, f. 212; c 12, item k, s.a. 1880; Hughes-Owens, *Bampton We Have Lost*, 117; *Oxf. Chron.* 5 Oct. 1850; cf. *Witney Express*, 9 Mar. 1871.
33 *P.O. Dir. Oxon.* (1877); *Kelly's Dir. Oxon.* (1883 and later edns.); O.R.O., MS. d.d. Par. Bampton c 12, item k, s.a. 1880.
34 [E. G. Hunt], *Music of a Merry Heart*, 287.
35 C.O.S., PRN 10609.
36 O.S. Map 1/2,500, SP 3003–3103 (1971 edn.); local inf.; cf. 'Bampton, Rep. on the Survey and Plan' (TS. 1966), p. 3.
37 P.R.O., RG 9/905, RG 11/1514; *Kelly's Dir. Oxon.* (1887 and later edns.); datestone on police ho. Police mentioned before establishment of a county constabulary in 1857 were presumably watchmen or constables: *Gardner's Dir. Oxon.* (1852); *The Times*, 7 Mar. 1855, p. 12.
38 D. & C. Exeter, MS. 648; ibid. MS. 2865, deposition of Hugh Folkes; above, Bampton, general intro. [boundaries]; below, Ducklington; Standlake; Yelford. Alvescot, Black Bourton, and Clanfield are reserved for treatment in a later volume.

39 Above, Bampton, general intro.; below, this section; Chimney; Lew; Lower Haddon; Shifford.
40 *Lond. Gaz.* 30 Dec. 1845, pp. 7351–5; O.R.O., MS. Oxf. Dioc. c 1711, presentation to Bampton Lew (1857); below, Aston and Cote, church; Lew, church.
41 O.R.O., MS. Oxf. Dioc. c 1713/1, Order in Council 19 May 1917.
42 Ibid. MS. Oxf. Dioc. c 1713/2, Order in Council 12 Apr. 1976; *Oxf. Dioc. Yr. Bk.* (1990), 87.
43 Above, intro.
44 Ibid.; J. Blair, 'Ecclesiastical Topography' (Bampton Research Paper 3, priv. print. 1990), 6–11: copy in C.O.S.
45 *V.C.H. Oxon.* xii. 103; for a similar pension arising from tithes in Black Bourton, below, this section.
46 Blair, 'Eccl. Topog.' 3–5; cf. below, this section [ch. archit.].
47 D. & C. Exeter, MS. 6016/a (for chantry chapel); Blair, 'Eccl. Topog.' 3, 5, 10–11; above, intro.; manors (Bampton Deanery).
48 D. & C. Exeter, MSS. 2788, m. 3; 2785, m. 1.
49 Ibid. MS. 5105.

been secularized by 1575, when 'the hermitage of Beane' was among lands granted to London speculators.[50]

The minster had lost its autonomy by the mid 11th century,[51] and in 1153 Bampton church was confirmed to Exeter cathedral chapter as two prebends; 60s. were to be added to the common fund if the church came 'into a better state', an allusion presumably to damage sustained during the siege of 1142.[52] Before the 1180s there seems to have been some reorganization, with the glebe, the house, and some tithes and offerings forming a 'prebend' or farm which became the later rectory manor. Two chaplaincies, portions, or prebends mentioned from c. 1190, and evidently in the gift of the farmer of the first 'prebend', presumably comprised the remaining tithes and offerings. The evidence suggests a small, embryonic secular college, but in 1220 the bishop of Lincoln confirmed the chapter's appropriation of the portion at their disposal and arranged for conversion of the two chaplaincies into three perpetual vicarages, together owing a pension of 15 marks (£10) to the chapter.[53] The arrangement took full effect in 1260–1, after which three portionary vicars were presented in the usual way.[54] Despite a claim by the king in 1286[55] the advowson remained with the dean and chapter of Exeter except during the Interregnum, when it was briefly acquired with the parsonage estate by Col. John Fielder, who seems not to have exercised it,[56] and in 1990 the dean and chapter retained joint patronage of the united benefice of Bampton-with-Clanfield.[57] A papal provision was made against the chapter's wishes in 1313, and the Crown unsuccessfully attempted to influence presentations in the late 15th century and in 1644.[58] Turns in the late 16th century and the 17th were granted to, among others, the bishop of Exeter, the earl of Clarendon, and gentry from Exeter or the Bampton area,[59] and in 1662 Charles II presented by lapse.[60]

The vicarage ordination did not specify the vicars' income, which later comprised a share of great and small tithes throughout the ancient parish and in Clanfield, and apparently half the oblations from the parish church and St. Andrew's chapel.[61] In the late 15th century the vicars also held at farm some appropriated tithes.[62] Tithes in Black Bourton were exchanged with Osney abbey in 1433 for tithes in Bampton, subject to a 15s. pension still payable to the abbey at the Dissolution, and vicars also paid the pension to Eynsham abbey.[63] The pension to Exeter cathedral, frequently in arrears in the later Middle Ages, was by the 17th century charged to lessees of the rectory manor.[64] A 'pension tithe' from lands in Standlake, worth 30s. a year in 1685 and presumably associated with a pension for burial rights owed in 1405,[65] was commuted to a fixed charge of £2 2s. 6d. before 1838, when it was irregularly received;[66] pensions from the vicar of Alvescot (13s. 4d.) and rector of Yelford (variously 5s. or 10s.), presumably also for parochial rights, had apparently lapsed by the early 19th century.[67] The vicarages were of equal value, and in the 17th century and probably earlier the vicars took the tithes of the various townships in rota;[68] by then some moduses had been established and tithes were sometimes leased, though others seem to have been collected in kind until the 19th century.[69] From the mid 13th century to the Dissolution the 3 portions together were valued at usually between c. £30 and £43 clear, placing all 3 vicars among the best-endowed in the county, wealthier than many rectors.[70] Total tithe income by 1615 was estimated at c. £240, and c. 1680 each portion was said to be worth £140,[71] though in 1677 a vicar's widow claimed that her husband had never received more than £50 a year net.[72] By 1799 the gross annual value of each portion averaged £324, and by 1845 over £515.[73]

At the inclosure of Bampton, Weald, and Lew the vicars each received c. 200 a. for tithes, and equal shares in an £85 corn rent from Lower Haddon to be re-assessed every 14 years. Vicarial tithe rents awarded from lands in Aston and Cote, Shifford, Chimney, Brighthampton, and Clanfield between 1839 and 1849 totalled over £1,000.[74] In 1857 the vicar of the new benefice of Bampton Proper received the glebe of the first

50   Ibid. MS. 4777, s.v. 'Armitage'; *Cal. Pat.* 1572–5, p. 411.
51   Above, manors (Bampton Deanery).
52   W. Holtzmann, *Papsturkunden in Eng.* ii (1935), p. 248; above, intro.
53   Blair, 'Medieval Clergy' (Bampton Research Paper 4, priv. print. 1991), 12–19: copy in C.O.S. For the chief evidence, *Reg. Antiquiss.* iii (L.R.S. xxix), p. 265; *Rot. Litt. Pat.* (Rec. Com.), 87; *Rot. Welles*, i (L.R.S. iii), 129; *Reg. Edm. Lacy*, ii (Cant. & York Soc. lxi), 339–41; above, manors (Bampton Deanery).
54   Blair, 'Medieval Clergy', 19; *Rot. Gravesend* (L.R.S. xx), 214, 224, 228.   55   *Abbrev. Plac.* (Rec. Com.), 278.
56   Mansfield Coll. Libr., S. Birch's 'Bk. of Prayers', 185–6; above, manors (Bampton Deanery).
57   *Oxf. Dioc. Yr. Bk.* (1990), 87.
58   Lincs. R.O., episc. reg. ii, f. 164v.; D. & C. Exeter, MSS. 3498 (32), 3499 (177); *Oxoniensia*, lvi (1991), 113–14.
59   e.g. O.A.S. *Rep.* (1914), 183, 192; O.R.O., MS. Oxf. Dioc. c 66, ff. 66–9, 72, 74–5.
60   O.R.O., MS. Oxf. Dioc. c 66, f. 73.
61   D. & C. Exeter, MS 2931, s.v. *decima* (detailing the chapter's share); P.R.O., C 2/Jas. I/H 33/34; O.R.O., MS. Oxf. Archd. Oxon. b 40, f. 44; cf. B.L. Add. Ch. 38921–2.
62   *Oxoniensia*, lvi. 118.
63   *Oseney Cart.* iv, pp. 496–8; *Valor Eccl.* (Rec. Com.), ii. 178; cf. above.

64   D. & C. Exeter, MSS. 1978, 1998; B.L. Add. Ch. 38925; Blair, 'Medieval Clergy', 23.
65   O.R.O., MS. Oxf. Archd. Oxon. b 40, f. 44; D. & C. Exeter, MS. 648.
66   'Bk. relating to Tythes' [c. 1838], in custody of vicar and par. officers; O.R.O., Standlake tithe award (1844); Giles, *Hist. Bampton*, 31.
67   *Valor Eccl.* (Rec. Com.), ii. 178; O.R.O., MS. Oxf. Archd. Oxon. b 40, f. 44; Giles, *Hist. Bampton*, 31, stating that Yelford still paid 20d. For Alvescot, cf. D. & C. Exeter, MS. 3672, p. 33.
68   *Valor Eccl.* (Rec. Com.), ii. 178; *Subsidy 1526*, 261; P.R.O., C 2/Jas. I/H 33/34; B.L. Add. Ch. 38921.
69   P.R.O., C 2/Jas. I/H 33/34; above, manors (Bampton Deanery).
70   *Rot. Gravesend* (L.R.S. xx), 214; Lunt, *Val. Norw.* 309; *Tax. Eccl.* (Rec. Com.), 32; *Inq. Non.* (Rec. Com.), 141; *Subsidy 1526*, 261 (probably before deduction of the chapter's pension); *Valor Eccl.* (Rec. Com.), ii. 178.
71   P.R.O., C 2/Jas. I/H 33/34; Bodl. MS. Tanner 32, ff. 158–159v.
72   O.R.O., MS. Oxf. Archd. Oxon. c 31, f. 139 and v.
73   Ibid. MSS. Oxf. Dioc. c 434, f. 138; c 746, ff. 115v.–116.
74   O.R.O., Bampton incl. award; ibid. tithe awards; Bampton Incl. Act, 52 Geo. III, c. 46 (Local and Personal, not printed), pp. 14–18.

and second (north and south) portions, tithe rent from Chimney, and much of the Haddon corn rent, yielding in all by 1866 a gross income of c. £600;[75] the corn rent was converted to a fixed rent charge of £91 in 1922, and the £10 pension to Exeter cathedral, charged solely to the vicar of Bampton Proper and latterly paid to the Ecclesiastical Commissioners, was commuted in 1931.[76]

No houses were provided under the vicarage ordination, suggesting that early 13th-century clergy may have lived in the Deanery, but by the late 13th century two and probably all three vicars had acquired houses respectively north, east, and south of the churchyard, rented from the cathedral chapter.[77] In 1288–9 William of Coleshill, vicar, agreed to pay the farmer 20s. a year for 'houses' opposite the farmer's (i.e. the Deanery) gate, evidently on or near the site of Cobb House north of the churchyard; the holding was later described as a 'court' or 'manse' built on the site of two earlier cottages, and during the 15th century or later the curtilage was extended eastwards by piecemeal incorporation of 4 adjoining tenements.[78] Rent for the house itself was paid in the early 15th century but not, apparently, by the 17th.[79] About 1500 there was a dovecot, presumably that later belonging to Wood House, in the newly-appropriated curtilage on the east,[80] and in 1685 the house included 6 ground-floor and 4 upper rooms, a study, and 2 lofts, with attached outhouses, rickyards, and commons.[81] In 1781 it needed substantial repairs,[82] and in 1799 it was mostly rebuilt by the vicar George Richards to designs by Daniel Harris of Oxford.[83] On the north-west a projecting, rubble-built wing with vaulted cellars is earlier, possibly the remains of a 17th-century kitchen.[84] After 1857 the house was assigned to Bampton Proper, and was sold after a new vicarage house was built to the north in 1958; that, too, was sold after 1976, the vicar of the united benefice living in Clanfield and later in a house off Broad Street.[85]

A house east of the churchyard,[86] on the site of later Kilmore House, was acquired in 1297 when the chapter's farmer let a plot to the vicar Richard de Beeston for 18d. a year. By the earlier 15th century the rent had been increased by 6d. but was frequently in arrears, and it was apparently no longer paid by the 17th.[87] The house's

curtilage was extended northwards or southwards presumably, like the north vicarage's, by incorporation of derelict cottages: a tenement adjoining the churchyard and the (east) vicar's house was mentioned in 1436, and in the 19th century quitrent was owed for land which had earlier belonged to an adjoining tenement.[88] From 1857 it briefly became the vicarage house for St. James's, Aston,[89] and was sold in 1866.[90] Descriptions of the house as *placea* or *cottagium* suggest that it was humbler than the north vicarage, though by 1685 it included 8 ground-floor and 5 upper rooms, a study, a closet, and 2 lofts, with outhouses including a barn, a granary with an annexed chamber, 2 stables and woodhouses, and a pigeon house.[91] The surviving, L-shaped house, remodelled in the 19th century probably after it ceased to be a vicarage, contains few datable features *in situ*, though the relative thinness of its walls suggests that it is post-medieval and possibly 17th-century. A reset, early 14th-century doorway in the porch and a 15th-century one in a garden wall are 19th-century insertions possibly from a different site.[92]

The south vicarage, later Churchgate House, was not recorded in medieval bailiffs' accounts, perhaps because it was held rent-free. In 1437 the dung heap of an incumbent of the south vicarage was allegedly fouling the gutter of a rectory manor tenement, suggesting that he lived near the churchyard, and in 1500 another south vicar left to his successors extensive household furnishings including hangings in the hall, and kitchen and brewhouse utensils.[93] South vicars occupied a forerunner of Churchgate House certainly by the early 16th century: a horn-and-scallop badge associated with Thomas Hoye, vicar 1500–23, was recorded there in the 17th century,[94] as were inscriptions to the vicars John and Henry Dotyn,[95] that to John Dotyn surviving reset in a garden wall. In 1685 the house was the largest of the three, containing 10 lower and 5 upper rooms besides a study, 3 closets, and 2 lofts; it seems to have been mostly rebuilt in the late 18th or early 19th century, though the west (rear) wing may be mid 16th-century and was perhaps rebuilt by one of the Dotyns.[96] A line of outbuildings on the north, remains of which formed the boundary with the churchyard in 1991, was ruinous by 1848.[97] From 1857 the

[75] *Lond. Gaz.* 30 Dec. 1845, p. 7354; Ch. Com. Rec. L 7, pp. 437–8.
[76] O.R.O., MS. d.d. Par. Bampton c 12, item h.
[77] Except where indicated, this and following two paras. based on Blair, 'Medieval Clergy', 26–9.
[78] Ibid.; cf. D. & C. Exeter, MS. 6016/7, bdle. 2, F. Whitaker to R. Barnes, 17 June 1812.
[79] D. & C. Exeter, MSS. 5100–5; cf. ibid. MSS. 4030, 2934.
[80] Ibid. MS. 3498 (34); Blair, 'Medieval Clergy', 28 n. The surviving dovecot is probably 16th-century.
[81] O.R.O., MS. Oxf. Archd. Oxon. b 40, f. 44; cf. ibid. MS. Oxf. Dioc. c 2202, no. 6. The respective vicarage hos. are identifiable partly from numbers of commons attached compared with later incl. allotments, and partly from archit. evidence.
[82] O.R.O., MS. Oxf. Archd. Oxon. b 22, ff. 207 and v., 209–13, 221 and v.
[83] Ibid. MSS. Oxf. Dioc. b 102; c 434, ff. 137v.–140; ibid. incl. award, s.v. G. Richards; Pevsner, *Oxon.* 432, wrongly stating that Harris rebuilt the S. vicarage ho.
[84] C.O.S., PRN 9924: survey 1984.

[85] O.S. Maps 1/2,500, Oxon. XXXVII. 6 (1876 and later edns.); SP 3003–3103 (1971 edn.); Bampton P.C.C. mins. 1949–67 (in custody of vicar and par. officers), s.a. 1958; *Oxf. Dioc. Yr. Bk.* (1976 and later edns.).
[86] Blair, 'Medieval Clergy', 28–9.
[87] D. & C. Exeter, MSS. 2934, 4030.
[88] Ibid. MS. 6016/7, bdle. 2, F. Whitaker to R. Barnes, 19 July 1812.
[89] Below, Aston, church.
[90] Ch. Com. Rec. L 7, pp. 361–3; cf. Giles, *Hist. Bampton*, 23.
[91] O.R.O., MSS. Oxf. Archd. Oxon. b 40, f. 44.
[92] Survey by J. Blair (1986).
[93] D. & C. Exeter, MS. 4751; *Some Oxon. Wills* (O.R.S. xxxix), 66.
[94] J. Aubrey, *Monumenta Britannica*, ed. J. Fowles, 581; Blair, 'Medieval Clergy', 27, App. C. col. 15.
[95] *Wood's Life*, ii (O.H.S. xxi), 20–1.
[96] O.R.O., MS. Oxf. Archd. Oxon. b 40, f. 44; survey by J. and S. Blair (1989). Pevsner, *Oxon.* 432, confuses it with the N. vicarage ho.
[97] Giles, *Hist. Bampton*, 23.

house was assigned to the vicar of Lew, and was sold c. 1917.[98]

Though some medieval vicars[99] were minor clergy from Exeter cathedral many were high-status academics mostly of West Country origin, attracted presumably by the proximity of Oxford, by the value of the benefices, and perhaps by Bampton's collegiate pretensions. Twenty-six (42 per cent) out of 62 vicars recorded between c. 1250 and 1550 were university graduates, and many from the 1390s were recruited from Oxford posts, among them three fellows of Exeter College, three fellows of Oriel, and a fellow of Balliol. Most resigned their fellowships on being presented to Bampton, and though some maintained links with Oxford, vicars seem usually to have resided and to have been closely involved in local society, many remaining at Bampton for life. At least four owned private houses there besides their vicarages, some were godfathers or wards to neighbours' children, and several made bequests to local gentry or farmers or to the poor.[1] Presumably they employed assistants: unbeneficed clergy were recorded frequently in Bampton throughout the Middle Ages, and in 1530 there were two curates of whom one had served for several years, though neither fulfilled his duties adequately. In 1516 a vicar made bequests to 3 parish clerks.[2]

Relations with the cathedral chapter were often strained, and between 1320 and 1322 the chapter had to recover by litigation huge debts incurred during a tithe dispute with Standlake. A late 15th-century farmer of the rectory manor described the vicars as litigious and 'not good payers'. About 1330 the vicars refused to accept responsibility for repair of the chancel and for provision of books and ornaments, the parishioners, according to the chapter, being customarily free from any obligation.[3] The distance from Exeter, a 5-day journey each way in 1306,[4] exacerbated such problems, and probably contributed to the vicars' tendency to view themselves in an independent, quasi-collegiate light: brasses of two 15th-century vicars show them wearing the almuce, a vestment reserved for canons and higher dignitaries, while the arrangement of stalls in the chancel seems to have been modelled on that of cathedral and other collegiate churches. The area around the church, surrounded by the vicarage houses, rectory manor house, and rectory-manor cottages, itself suggested a miniature cathedral close.[5]

A notable aspect of such pretensions was the continuing devotion to St. Beornwald,[6] perhaps a head of the Anglo-Saxon minster, whose relics were preserved at Bampton and whose cult survived until the Reformation and possibly beyond. His feast day (21 December)[7] was kept evidently in the early 12th century and still in the early 16th, and in 1406 the reliquary of the saint's head was repaired, partly at Exeter cathedral chapter's expense. Probably about that time a brass showing a vested ecclesiastic holding a crozier was made to embellish his shrine, remains of which survive in the north transept. An invocation to the saint in the 16th-century will of one vicar, and another's description of himself in 1521 as vicar of the parish church of St. Beornwald, suggest their participation, though the cult also had a popular basis: jurors in 1370-1 all claimed to have been present in Bampton church on Beornwald's feast day in 1349 to make offerings and to hear divine service in his honour, while a repentant Lollard reported men and women going barefoot c. 1481 to offer wax images and money at St. Beornwald's relics. Oblations from St. Beornwald's box were mentioned in 1497-8 and 1531-2, when they totalled £4 13s. 4d. It has been suggested that the burial in 1593 of one 'Barnold' may refer to the saint's relics, which had perhaps continued to be venerated by local Catholic sympathizers, and possibly at that time the brass was reset in the floor before the former shrine.[8]

Richard Crispin (south vicar 1523-c. 1530) was imprisoned for Catholic sympathies in 1547,[9] but outwardly most Bampton vicars seem to have accepted the Reformation. Two in the mid 16th century were married, one bought former chantry land in Lew, and in 1559 all three vicars subscribed to the Elizabethan settlement,[10] while the pluralist John Underhill, east vicar 1581-5 and later bishop of Oxford, was a protégé of the protestant earl of Leicester and of Sir Francis Walsingham.[11] Assertions that the Roman Catholic William Tresham (d. 1569) was vicar in Mary's reign were presumably mistaken, since all three vicarages are accounted for during that period.[12] Some 16th-century vicars may nevertheless have harboured Catholic sympathies: John Dyer (east vicar 1529-47), John Whyte (south vicar 1535-43), and Henry Dotyn (south vicar 1559-95) witnessed wills or acted as executors for the recusant More family of Lower Haddon, John Dotyn (south vicar 1543-59) made small bequests to a former nun of Syon (Mdx.), and the possible survival of the cult of St. Beornwald suggests their connivance.[13] John Howson (north vicar 1598-?1628), bishop of Oxford from 1619 and of Durham from 1628, who married a local woman in 1601, was noted 'to be very popish',[14] while John Prideaux (east vicar 1614-34), later bishop of Worcester, was

---

98 Below, Lew, church.
99 Blair, 'Medieval Clergy', 19-36, app. C; O.A.S. *Rep.* (1914), 183, 191-3.
1 Blair, 'Medieval Clergy', 21-2, 30-1, app. C.
2 Ibid. app. C, cols. 8, 17-18; *Subsidy 1526*, 261; *Visit. Dioc. Linc.* 49-50; cf. *Archdeacon's Ct.* (O.R.S. xxiii-xxiv), i. 16-17, ii, pp. xi, 229.   3 Blair, 'Medieval Clergy', 22-6.
4 D. & C. Exeter, MS. 2780, m. 2.
5 Blair, 'Medieval Clergy', 32-5.
6 *Oxoniensia*, xlix. 47-55; liv. 400-3, on which following para. based.
7 Given as 29 Jan. in 1370-1, evidently in error: *Oxoniensia*, liv. 401-3.   8 *Oxoniensia*, xlix. 54; liv. 401-2.
9 Emden, *O.U. Reg. 1501-40*, 155-6.

10 P.R.O., PROB 11/36, ff. 125v.-126; PROB 11/33, f. 89; Bodl. Top. Oxon. c 60, f. 208; O.A.S. *Rep.* (1914), 183, 189, 191, 193, 202.
11 O.A.S. *Rep.* (1914), 193; V. Green, *Commonwealth of Lincoln College*, 138-42; *D.N.B.*
12 *D.N.B.*; B. Willis, *Survey of the Cathedrals* (1742), iii. 405, 449, citing John Foxe, who did not, however, say that Tresham was vicar: *Acts and Mons.* ed. J. Pratt (4th edn.), vi. 566, 772. Cf. Blair, 'Medieval Clergy', App. C.
13 P.R.O., PROB 11/29, f. 89 and v.; PROB 11/44, ff. 115v.-116v.; PROB 11/45, f. 211v.; above, this section.
14 Bodl. MSS. Top. Oxon. c 118, f. 9; c 378, p. 258; C.O.S., Black Bourton par. reg. transcripts, s.a. 1601; O.A.S. *Rep.* (1914), 192-3; *D.N.B.*

theologically conservative.[15] During the Interregnum all three vicars were deprived, though two, including Prideaux's son-in-law William Hodges, were restored after the Act of Uniformity; their replacements included the Presbyterians John Osborne (east vicar 1648–62) and Samuel Birch (south vicar 1658–62), who remained active in Bampton until 1664 and in private complained of perceived laxity or pastoral neglect by his colleagues. Rous Clapton or Clopton, north vicar from 1647 and outlawed for debt in 1655, reportedly attempted to make the vicarage over to the rector of Witney to raise £120 for dilapidations, but was himself deprived c. 1654.[16]

Many 17th- and 18th-century vicars served long incumbencies, nearly half and possibly more had West Country origins, and all were university graduates, a quarter of them from Exeter College. Several held college fellowships, often resigning them before their presentation.[17] Their similar backgrounds were sometimes reflected in close family ties: a vicar in 1634 and another in 1668 resigned in favour of their respective sons-in-law[18] and between 1670 and 1715 the east vicarage twice passed from father to son, suggesting that as in the late Middle Ages vicars may sometimes have informally nominated their successors.[19] Not all resided permanently, some, like Prideaux, being noted pluralists,[20] at least two in the later 17th century residing chiefly at Exeter,[21] and two others residing at the Oxford colleges of which they were head,[22] but despite a withering attack by Bishop Fell on one vicar's accumulation of benefices[23] there is no evidence of neglect, and presumably their duties were undertaken by curates or by the other vicars. Several were buried at Bampton,[24] one in the early 17th century transcribed the parish registers,[25] and another in 1617 left books worth £4 in his house there.[26] Thomas Cooke, south vicar 1663–8 and archdeacon of Salop, entertained the antiquary Anthony Wood at Bampton in 1664.[27]

From the late 17th century several vicars held two Bampton portions simultaneously, but throughout the 18th century Bampton was never without the personal attention of at least one vicar. Most seem to have been conscientious and involved in local life, frequently signing vestry minutes and seeking leave of absence only through ill health,[28] and in 1747 one married a coheir of the lessee of Bampton Deanery manor.[29] The young John Conybeare, later bishop of Bristol, preached at Bampton in 1719 and 1721,[30] and in 1738 and later there were two Sunday services with two sermons (reduced in winter to one sermon for much of the 18th century), and prayers on Wednesdays, Fridays, Saturdays and specified feast days; children were catechized in Lent, and bishops of Oxford confirmed at Bampton frequently.[31] A choir was established by 1794.[32] Communicants at the monthly sacrament numbered 30–50 into the 19th century, rising to 60–80 at great festivals, and though the 'lower class' were said to be slack in attendance, by 1831 the average congregation was c. 700 (c. 30 per cent of the population).[33] Until the 1750s the vicars divided their duties by 3-monthly stints, but during the later 18th century served every third week; c. 1800 they again resolved to serve for quarters, though discord arose in 1817 when a vicar insisted on conducting the service out of turn.[34]

Curates, employed as required, were often highly qualified and sometimes served for long periods,[35] though relations were occasionally strained. Charles Hawtrey (d. 1796), east vicar for nearly forty years and a double portionist for ten, was publicly attacked for his puritanical policies by his colleagues' curate Thomas Middleton, the non-resident vicar of Clanfield, prompting a vestry resolution in Middleton's favour signed by 33 inhabitants,[36] and in the 1780s a curate of Hawtrey's neglected his duties and was briefly imprisoned for assault.[37] Samuel Johnson, north vicar 1780–84, whose 'wild ... and unbecoming' manner of reading caused hilarity and fuelled fears that Dissent would prosper, seems to have resided despite parish-

15 O.R.O., MS. Oxf. Dioc. c 66, ff. 65, 70; *D.N.B.*

16 *L.J.* ix. 13; *Walker Revised*, ed. A. G. Matthews, 296–7; *Calamy Revised*, ed. A. G. Matthews, 56–7, 374; *Der Pietismus in Gestalten und Wirkungen*, ed. H. Bornkamm et al. (Arbeiten zur Geschichte des Pietismus, xiv), 343–54; O.R.O., MS. Oxf. Dioc. c 66, ff. 70–2, 74, 77; D. & C. Exeter, MS. 4030, p. 10; below, nonconf.

17 Oldfield, 'Clerus Oxf. Dioc.', anachronistically calling the N., E., and S. vicarages Bampton Lew, Aston, and Proper; O.R.O., Cal. Oxf. presentation deeds, ser. 1, ff. 65–79; ser. 2, ff. 9–11; cf. *Alum. Oxon. 1500–1714, 1715–1886*; *Alum. Cantab.* ed. J. and J. A. Venn.

18 John Prideaux and Thos. Cooke: O.R.O., MS. Oxf. Dioc. c 66, ff. 70, 76; ibid. par. reg. transcripts, 22 June 1634; *Wood's Life*, ii. 20; *D.N.B.* s.v. Prideaux.

19 O.R.O., MSS. Oxf. Dioc. c 66, f. 77; c 266, (reverse nos.) f. 32; *Reg. Exeter Coll.* (O.H.S. xxvii), 101, s.v. Hodges; *Alum. Oxon. 1500–1714*, iv. 1386, s.v. Snell; cf. Blair, 'Medieval Clergy', 20–1.

20 *V.C.H. Oxon.* xii. 32, 408; cf. *Reg. Exeter Coll.* (O.H.S. xxvii), 101, s.v. Hodges; P.R.O., PROB 11/352, ff. 340 and v.

21 Bodl. MS. Tanner 32, ff. 158–159v.; O.R.O., MS. d.d. Par. Bampton c 9, copy of will of Edw. Cotton 1674; cf. *Alum. Oxon. 1500–1714*, i. 333; iv. 1386.

22 Bodl. MS. Tanner 32, ff. 158–159v.; O.R.O., MSS. Oxf. Dioc. d 558, ff. 33–6; d 564, ff. 29–31; cf. *D.N.B.* s.v. A. Bury; *V.C.H. Oxon.* iii. 106, s.v. H. Barton.

23 Bodl. MS. Tanner 32, ff. 158–159v.

24 C.O.S., par. reg. transcripts.

25 Rob. Joye: O.R.O., MS. d.d. Par. Bampton c 1, s.a. 1614 and *passim*; cf. ibid. MSS. Wills Oxon. 11/3/37, 11/3/49, 11/4/2, 30/1/26, 300/3/43; P.R.O., PROB 11/114, f. 96.

26 O.R.O., MS. Wills Oxon. 78/1/31.

27 *Alum. Oxon. 1500–1714*, i. 322; *Wood's Life*, ii (O.H.S. xxi), 20–1, 153.

28 O.R.O. MS. d.d. Par. Bampton b 10, c 8, *passim*; *Secker's Corresp.* 191, 217–18, 237, 256; cf. *Secker's Visit.* 12–14; O.R.O., MSS. Oxf. Dioc. d 555, f. 29; d 558, ff. 33–6; d 564, ff. 29–31.

29 O.R.O., par. reg. transcripts, 7 Oct. 1747.

30 Bodl. MS. Eng. th. e 49, ff. 79–99v.; *D.N.B.*

31 O.R.O., MSS. Oxf. Dioc. d 558, ff. 33–6; d 564, ff. 29–31; d 572, ff. 21–2; c 655, ff. 101–2; *Secker's Visit.* 13; *Secker's Corresp.* pp. xxv, 150.

32 O.R.O., MS. d.d. Par. Bampton c 8, f.6.

33 O.R.O., MSS. Oxf. Dioc. d 561, ff. 37–40; d 564, ff. 29–31; d 566, ff. 17–18; d 572, ff. 21–2; b 36, ff. 15–16; *Secker's Visit.* 13.

34 O.R.O., MSS. Oxf. Dioc. c 654, ff. 42v., 53v., 95v.; c 655, ff. 101–2; c 662, f. 153 and v.; ibid. MS. d.d. Par. Bampton c 8, ff. 44v.–45v.; *Secker's Corresp.* 192–3.

35 Oldfield, 'Clerus Oxf. Dioc.'; *Alum. Oxon. 1500–1714, 1715–1886*; *Secker's Corresp.* 191–2.

36 *Oxon. Local Hist.* ii, no. 4 (1986), 120–5.

37 O.R.O., MS. Oxf. Dioc. c 654, ff. 87, 90–101, 162–4; ibid. MS. Oxf. Archd. Oxon. b 22, ff. 217–20.

ioners' demands that he substitute a curate.[38] Hugh Owen (east vicar 1797–1828), a well known antiquary, resided chiefly at Shrewsbury but took an active interest in Bampton's affairs, his portion being served by successive curates accommodated in the vicarage house.[39]

Owen's contemporary George Richards (north vicar 1796–1824), a former fellow of Oriel College, later vicar of St. Martin-in-the-Fields, London, and a minor poet, resided from c. 1798, and briefly served Owen's cure also.[40] 'Universally beloved and respected',[41] he rebuilt the north vicarage house and was instrumental in establishment of a National school, repairs to the church,[42] and provision of an organ, reportedly intending to introduce monthly sung services 'as in cathedrals'. The last innovation prompted controversy c. 1814 and was opposed by Richards's colleague Thomas Burrow (south vicar 1799–1837), who allegedly abandoned the afternoon sermon in retaliation and rescheduled weekly prayers to accommodate his field sports.[43] The organ prompted further controversy in 1850, when its resiting and other changes led to anonymous charges of Puseyism.[44] Burrow's successor Dacres Adams (d. 1871), who became first vicar of Bampton Proper and 'bequeathed ... a rich legacy of good feeling towards the church', also resided, as did J. R. Winstanley (east vicar 1828–43), but other vicars lived elsewhere.[45] From 1846 the north vicar's curate was J. A. Giles, author, editor, translator, and historian of the parish, who though 'richly cultivated' and well meaning was judged eccentric and 'quite unfit for his office'. In 1854 he was forced by the bishop to withdraw a book on the New Testament published at his private printing press at the vicarage house,[46] and in 1855 he was briefly imprisoned for concealing a clandestine marriage by falsifying the parish register.[47]

In 1854 division of duties between the three vicars was said to unsettle parishioners and was partly blamed for low attendance,[48] but from 1857, when the parish was divided, there was evidently improvement. Church attendance during the later 19th century, 'very good' in 1875, was said repeatedly to be steady or increasing, though in 1872 only 50 out of c. 300 adults habitually absent were thought to be dissenters, and in 1866 the vicar complained of indifference. Many inhabitants in the 1870s and 1880s worshipped interchangeably at church, chapel, or not at all, and 'would probably be at a loss how to describe themselves'. 'Working men' boycotted the church during the strikes of the early 1870s, but by 1875 they were returning, and provision of adequate free sittings for the poor boosted attendance particularly in the evenings, though rented pews continued to cause friction in 1896.[49] All the 19th- and early 20th-century vicars of Bampton Proper resided, some, like their predecessors, moving from West Country benefices and most staying for incumbencies of 10 or 20 years, though none in the earlier 20th century stayed for life.[50]

The church of *ST. MARY THE VIRGIN*, so called by 1742,[51] was said in 1292 to be dedicated to St. John the Baptist, in 1317 to St. Mary and St. John the Baptist, in 1335 to St. John the Baptist and St. Beornwald, and in 1370 and 1521 to St. Beornwald.[52] It is chiefly of limestone rubble with stone-slated roofs, and is of notable size and quality, comprising chancel with north vestry and south porch, central tower with stone spire, north and south transepts with eastern chapels, a chapel on the west side of the south transept, and a four-bay aisled nave with west and south porches.[53] Remains of an earlier church or chapel may underlie the north transept,[54] but the oldest standing fabric is the eastern end of an early nave built of coursed rubble laid partly in herringbone courses, later incorporated into the base of the tower; contemporary with or later than that work is the late 11th- or early 12th-century chancel arch, with chip-carved decoration. A tower 'built in olden times of wondrous form and with extraordinary skill and ingenuity' was mentioned in the 12th century, and excavations against the external west wall of the present nave revealed the footing of a structure with a projecting stair-base, probably remains of an early Norman west tower.[55]

In the late 12th century the church was made cruciform by the addition of transepts, a central tower, and a new chancel; its size was then exceptional by normal parochial standards, reflecting its quasi-collegiate status. The north transept is misaligned in relation to the rest of the church, and excavations against the external east wall of its eastern chapel revealed a footing likely to predate the late 12th-century work; the chapel, which contained St. Beornwald's shrine,

38 O.R.O., MS. Oxf. Dioc. c 654, ff. 80–1; Oxf. Jnl. Synopsis, 8 Mar. 1784.
39 O.R.O., MSS. Oxf. Dioc. d 566, f. 17–18; c 327, ff. 199, 248; d 705, f. 22; b 6, ff. 109–110v., 113–114v.; c 662, 8–9v., 151–2; *D.N.B.*
40 O.R.O., MSS. Oxf. Dioc. c 655, ff. 62–3; c 662, ff. 151–4; *D.N.B.*
41 *Gent. Mag.* N.S. vii. 662–3.
42 Above and below, this section; below, educ.
43 O.R.O., MS. Oxf. Dioc. c 662, ff. 7–11, 13–14, 112–13, 151–4; cf. ibid. MS. d.d. Par. Bampton c 8, ff. 44v.–45v.
44 *Oxf. Chron.* 23 Mar., 6 Apr., 4 May, 11 May, 18 May, 29 June, 19 Oct. 1850.
45 O.R.O. MS. d.d. Par. c 8, s.a. 1801–58; ibid. MSS. Oxf. Dioc. b 35, f. 19; c 332, pp. 53–4; [E. G. Hunt], *Music of a Merry Heart*, 190; *Wilb. Visit.* 10–11.
46 O.R.O., CPZ 1, no. 22; ibid. CPZ 1, Brief for Prosecution 1855, p. 3; *Wilb. Visit.* 10; *D.N.B.*; cf. Magd. Coll. Mun., MS. 800 (i), flyleaf.
47 O.R.O., CPZ 1, *passim*; *The Times*, 7 Mar., 7 June 1855.
48 *Wilb. Visit.* 10–11.

49 O.R.O., MSS. Oxf. Dioc. c 332, pp. 53–4; c 338, ff. 31–2; c 341, ff. 50–1; c 344, ff. 35–6; c 347, ff. 33–4; c 350, ff. 30–1; c 353, ff. 29–30; c 356, ff. 29–30; c 359, ff. 27–8; c 362, ff. 29–30; ibid. MS. d.d. Par. Bampton c 12, item k, s.a. 1896.
50 O.R.O., MS. Oxf. Dioc. c 1712, presentations; *Kelly's Dir. Oxon.* (1883 and later edns.).
51 J. Ecton, *Thesaurus Rerum Ecclesiasticarum* (1742), 477–8; *Oxf. Dioc. Yr. Bk.* (1990), 87. This and the following four paragraphs were written by J. Blair.
52 J. Blair, 'Ecclesiastical Topography' (Bampton Research Paper 3, priv. print. 1990), 4: copy in C.O.S.
53 Illust. before late 19th-cent. alterations in Bodl. MSS. Top. Oxon. a 64, no. 2; a 65, nos. 56–60, 65; c 522, f. 21; ibid. MS. Don. b 14, f. 113; O.R.O., MS. Oxf. Dioc. c 1712 (plans and elevations); Skelton, *Antiq. Oxon.*, Bampton Hundred, plate 6; below, plates 1, 8. Cf. *Jnl. Brit. Arch. Assoc.* N.S. xxii (1916), 1–12, 113–22, figs. 1–43; Pevsner, *Oxon.* 429–31; O.A.S. *Rep.* (1871), 33–40.
54 Below.
55 *Gesta Stephani*, ed. K. R. Potter and R. H. C. Davis (2nd edn. 1976), 138–9; excavation by J. Blair (1990).

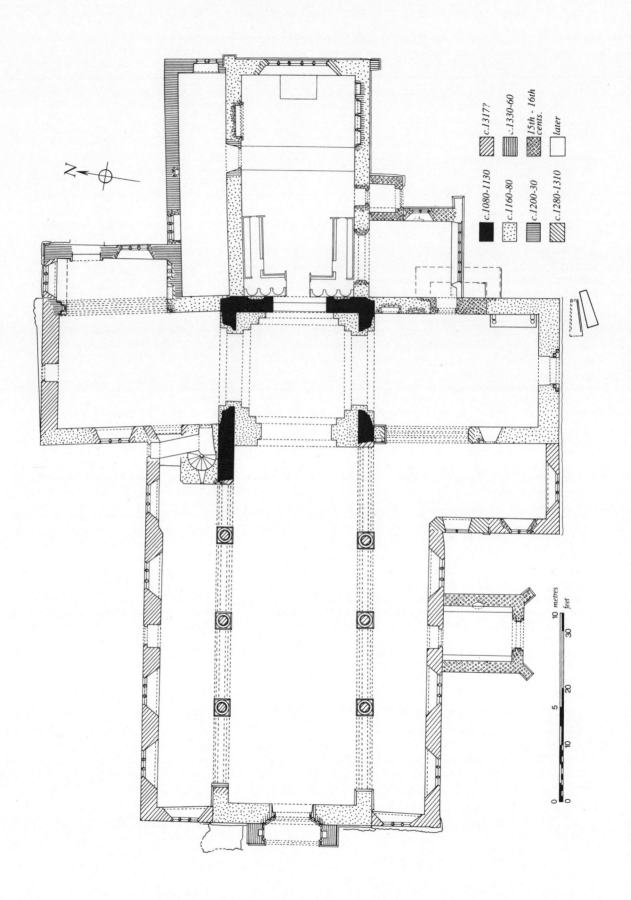

may therefore perpetuate some earlier structure whose alignment is respected by that of the transept.[56] The south transept has on its east side a large, round-headed arch, now blocked, which formerly opened into a shallow, rectangular altar-recess identified by excavation;[57] the transept's south doorway has elaborate Romanesque decoration, and in the early 19th century retained its door with original ironwork.[58] The tower, supported on four pointed arches of plain square orders, contains an internal blind arcade (later concealed by the ringing-chamber floor) of paired round-headed recesses with scalloped capitals; on the north side one of the recesses pierces the wall to overlook the north transept, and is entered from the stair-turret by a passage in the thickness of the wall, an arrangement which suggests a gallery overlooking St. Beornwald's shrine. The position of the stair-turret within the body of the church precludes a 12th-century north aisle, but a south aisle of that date is suggested both by the west respond of the existing arcade, and by the many fragments of chevron-moulded voussoirs re-used in the wall above it.

The long, narrow vestry, added c. 1200, retains an original doorway, still with its door and ironwork, into the chancel, and an original east window. In the early 13th century the north transept's east chapel was remodelled with a broad arch towards the transept, and a gabled recess, probably to be identified as St. Beornwald's shrine, in its east wall;[59] the piscina and sedilia in the chancel are of similar date. In the mid 13th century the tower was heightened and the spire added. At the base of the spire are corner shafts bearing standing figures, identified as St. Andrew on the north-west, St. John the Baptist on the south-west, perhaps St. Beornwald on the north-east, and St. Peter on the south-east, an apparently unique feature which may reflect the figure-sculpture of Wells cathedral; the figure of St. Andrew was renewed in the late 19th century[60] and that of St. John the Baptist in 1991.

Between c. 1290 and 1320 the whole church apart from the chancel, vestry, and crossing was remodelled, beginning with the addition of the south-western chapel, and including the total rebuilding of the nave. Work of that period is characterized by triplets of cusped lancet windows with cusped rere-arches, a distinctive feature which occurs (perhaps under Bampton's influence) in several local churches, and derives ultimately from the Somerset area; an indul-

gence granted in 1317 to all who contributed to the 'construction and repair' of Bampton church presumably refers to that rebuilding.[61] Then or soon afterwards the north transept chapel was again remodelled, and the shrine-niche provided with a richly decorated canopy.[62] The west porch was added in the mid to late 14th century, and a set of image-niches in the south transept, later concealed by the organ, in the 15th.[63]

The chancel was remodelled in 1497–9, all or part of the work to designs of the mason Thomas Martyn and the carpenter David Owretayn.[64] New work included square-headed Perpendicular windows and a low-pitched timber roof, since destroyed. The chancel south porch, probably contemporary, mostly survives, as does a tall and elaborate Easter sepulchre on the north side of the altar. A clerestory was added to the nave and transepts about the same time.[65]

The south porch of the nave was added probably in the earlier 16th century. At a similar date the altar-recess east of the south transept was replaced by a much larger mortuary chapel built probably by the More family of Lower Haddon, entered from the transept through a door in the blocking of the Romanesque arch, and with a large opening to the chancel on the north. John More (d. 1542) instructed his executors to provide window glass and altar furnishings, and bequeathed a cow to the churchwardens towards the chapel's upkeep.[66] In 1669, as the Haddon aisle, the chapel was sold by the non-resident lord of Haddon to Thomas Horde (d. 1715), who remodelled it c. 1702, probably reducing it in size, and provided for repair of its glass and maintenance of family tombs.[67] Its east window was blocked for a monument c. 1671.

Women's and men's doors were mentioned in the 17th century.[68] Private box- and other pews in the north aisle and elsewhere by the later 17th century were the occasion of a fracas in the church in 1674,[69] and by the early 18th century there were private galleries in the north and probably south aisles, and a public one at the west end; in the 19th century the galleries provided 260 sittings but effectively cut off the transepts, and services were conducted within the nave only.[70] In 1792 the vestry was refitted,[71] and in 1841 an additional north doorway was inserted.[72]

Between 1867 and 1870 the architect Ewan Christian supervised a major restoration financed by mortgage and subscription.[73] The chancel and nave walls were lowered and new roofs of steeper pitch provided, destroying the nave clerestory;

56 Excavation by J. Blair (1989); for shrine, below.
57 Excavation by J. Blair (1989).
58 Bodl. MS. Top. Oxon. a 65, no. 59.
59 *Oxoniensia*, xlix. 50–4, mistakenly attributing those features to the 14th cent.
60 [E. G. Hunt], *Music of a Merry Heart*, 196–7.
61 Lincs. R.O., episc. reg. iii (Dalderby), f. 372.
62 *Oxoniensia*, xlix. 51.
63 Bodl. MS. Top. Oxon. a 65, no. 60; *Jnl. Brit. Arch. Assoc.* N.S. xxii (1916), fig. 21.
64 D. & C. Exeter, MS. 5106; ibid. MS. 3754, ff. 131, 134.
65 For lost features, Skelton, *Antiq. Oxon.*, Bampton Hundred, pl. 6; Bodl. MSS. Top. Oxon. a 64, no. 2; a 65, nos. 65–6; plan and elevation of 1858 in ch.
66 P.R.O., PROB 11/29, f. 89 and v.

67 Ibid. PROB 11/551, f. 253; O.R.O., D.Y. XI/i/3; mutilated date on parapet, interpreted as 1702 in Pevsner, *Oxon.* 431, but as 1709 in O.R.O., MS. Oxf. Dioc. c 1712, letter of 1894.
68 O.R.O., MSS. Wills Oxon. 30/3/42, 75/4/20.
69 Ibid. MS. Oxf. Archd. Oxon. c 120, ff. 17v.–20; cf. ibid. c 1, f. 5v.; ibid. MSS. Oxf. Dioc. c 104, ff. 6, 7, 11, 12; c 454, f. 46.
70 Ibid. MS. Oxf. Dioc. c 104, ff. 8, 13; Giles, *Hist. Bampton*, 24; plan and elevation of 1858 in ch.
71 Above, local govt. (par. govt.).
72 O.R.O., MS. Oxf. Archd. Oxon. c 36, f. 39v.; plan of 1858 in ch.; Bodl. MSS. Top. Oxon. a 65, no. 66; c 522, f. 21.
73 O.R.O., MS. Oxf. Dioc. c 1712; ibid. d 797, ff. 127v.–131.

15th-century fenestration in the south side of the chancel was replaced, and the east window enlarged; the archway between the Horde chapel and the chancel was rebuilt in different form on the old jambs, and the sedilia were remodelled; the roofs of the vestry and chancel south porch were renewed and the new north door blocked; and flooring was renewed and a new ceiling provided under the ringers' chamber. Pews were replaced over several years by open benches and the galleries were removed,[74] and then or *c.* 1859[75] the south-west chapel was reroofed, new windows inserted into the north and south ends of the transepts, and a new window and door into the north side of the vestry. The top of the spire was rebuilt in 1872 following lightning damage.[76] The Horde chapel, 'ruinous' in 1786 and used as a store by the 19th century, was converted into a new vestry in 1894, and the north transept chapel was refitted for daily services in 1908 by relatives of Philip Southby of Bampton House.[77] Heating was installed under the vestry by 1894 and in 1891 money was being raised towards lighting the church apparently with oil lamps; electric lighting was installed in 1934.[78]

Early 16th-century stalls with misericord seats along the west wall of the chancel, and benches along the north and south walls, all much restored, perhaps replaced those said to be 'defective' *c.* 1520.[79] Six stalls survived in 1858 but only four in 1867.[80] Carved on one bench-end and on one of the misericords is a hunting horn hanging from a scallop shell between the initials TH, and on another misericord the monogram JS: probably they refer to the vicars Thomas Hoye (1500–23) and John Southwode (1506–24), suggesting that one of the lost stalls bore the initials of their colleague.[81] The other bench-end bears the arms of the see of Exeter. The font base is 14th-century, with blind tracery panels; the 19th-century bowl, 'new' in 1847, replaced a square, 12th-century bowl with round-headed blind arcading.[82] Though briefly moved to the south-west chapel *c.* 1813 the font was returned to the nave before 1867,[83] and in 1992 stood in the south aisle. A late 14th- or early 15th-century stone reredos showing Christ between the apostles, against the east wall of the north transept by the early 19th century, was placed in the chancel under the east window *c.* 1875.[84] The pulpit, lectern, and reading desk,

against the central north column of the nave for much of the 19th century, were renewed *c.* 1870 and moved to the east end; the large stone and marble pulpit then introduced was replaced in 1959 by one of oak, given in memory of Col. A. M. Colvile (d. 1952) of Weald Manor.[85] The organ, by John Gray of London and paid for by subscription, was installed in a gallery at the east end of the nave, displacing the pulpit, in 1812, after plans to replace instrumentalists with a barrel organ were abandoned;[86] it was moved to the south transept's west chapel in 1850 (when it may have acquired its present neo-Gothic case), and to the east wall of the transept probably *c.* 1870, when it was rebuilt and enlarged.[87] It was restored in 1992.[88] A pair of mid 18th-century mahogany chairs in Gothic style, of unknown provenance, were sold in 1981.[89]

Heraldic glass recorded in the earlier 18th century included arms of the More family, perhaps in the Horde chapel, and of Exeter College. Surviving stained glass is 19th- and early 20th-century, and includes windows given in memory of Edward Whitaker (d. 1825), Dacres Adams (d. 1871), and members of the Southby family, who donated the great east window *c.* 1872.[90]

A weathered, early 14th-century effigy of a woman, formerly in the churchyard,[91] and a late 14th-century effigy of a knight with a helm under his head bearing the Talbot crest, lie loose in the south and north transepts respectively; also in the south transept are a medieval stone coffin and two cross-slabs. In the north transept's east chapel, before the shrine-niche (where it was found buried *c.* 1960), is the indent of an early 15th-century brass showing an ecclesiastic holding a crozier, perhaps a representation of St. Beornwald which may have adorned his shrine.[92] Memorials to several vicars include wall monuments to Thomas Cooke (d. 1669) and Stephen Philips (d. 1684) in the Horde chapel, and in the chancel marble slabs to Thomas Snell the elder and younger (d. 1717 and 1758), and floor brasses to Thomas Plymyswode (d. 1417) and Robert Holcot (d. 1500), not *in situ*.[93] Also in the Horde chapel are the 17th and early 18th-century grave slabs, placed vertically against the wall in 1894,[94] of several of the Horde family, and an elaborate wall monument to Barbara Horde (d. 1671) and Thomas (d. 1715); a brass to Frances Horde (d. 1633) is in the chancel. A large monument to George Thompson (d. 1603),

74 O.R.O., MS. Oxf. Dioc. c 341, ff. 50–1; c 344, ff. 35–6; cf. *Witney Express*, 19, 26 Aug. 1869.
75 *Oxf. Chron.* 16 Aug. 1859.
76 *Witney Express*, 23 May, 13 June, 3 Oct. 1872; [Hunt], *Music of a Merry Heart*, 195–8.
77 O.R.O., MS. Oxf. Archd. Oxon. c 50, f. 41; faculties in ibid. MS. Oxf. Dioc. c 1712; plaques in ch.
78 Bodl. G.A. Oxon. c 317/4, advertisement for bazaar 1891, cutting *re* new vestry 17 Nov. 1894; O.R.O., MS. Oxf. Dioc. c 1713/1, faculty 1934; cf. ibid. c 1712, plan of 1867; *Jnl. Brit. Arch. Assoc.* N.S. xxii (1916), figs.
79 *Visit. Dioc. Linc.* i. 131.
80 Plan of 1858 in ch.; O.R.O., MS. Oxf. Dioc. c 1712, plans of 1867; cf. *Oxf. Chron.* 18 Aug. 1859.
81 Blair, 'Medieval Clergy', 27, 33–4.
82 O.R.O., MS. Oxf. Archd. Oxon. c 36, f. 48; Bodl. MS. Top. Oxon. a 65, no. 56.
83 Bodl. MS. Don. c 90, pp. 370–1; O.R.O., MS. Oxf. Dioc. c 1712, plans of 1867.

84 Bodl. MS. Don. c 90, p. 370; O.R.O., MS. Oxf. Dioc. c 341, ff. 50–1.
85 *Jnl. Brit. Arch. Assoc.* N.S. xxii, fig. 26; Bodl. MS. Don. c 90, p. 370; O.R.O., MS. Oxf. Dioc. c 1712, docs. *re* restoration; ibid. c 1713/1, faculty 1959.
86 O.R.O., MS. d.d. Par. Bampton c 8, ff. 28–29v., 32v., 35v.–37, 172; for Gray, Pigot, *Lond. & Prov. Dir.* (1823–4), 188.
87 *Oxf. Chron.* 23 Mar., 4 May 1850; O.R.O., MS. Oxf. Dioc. c 1712, plans of 1867 and 1894; ibid. c 338, ff. 31–2; plan of 1858 in ch.
88 *Bampton Beam*, vol. 8, no.2 (1993), 4: copy in C.O.S.
89 O.R.O., MS. Oxf. Dioc. c 1713/2, faculty 1981.
90 *Par. Colln.* i. 20; inscriptions in ch.
91 Bodl. MS. Top. Oxon. d 218, f. 42; O.R.O. MS. d.d. Par. Bampton c 12, item k, s.a. 1908.
92 *Oxoniensia*, xlix. 52–4; above, this section.
93 Cf. Bodl. MS. Don. c 90, p. 370; ibid. MS. Top. Oxon. a 65, no. 65.
94 O.R.O., MS. Oxf. Dioc. c 1712, faculty.

comprising tomb chest, effigy, and pedimented canopy, lies against the south transept's east wall. Lost monuments include an inscribed marble grave slab probably to the vicar Thomas Hoye (d. 1532);[95] no sign remains of a family vault in the north transept for which Richard Coxeter (d. 1740) obtained permission in 1721.[96]

A 'new' clock and chimes were installed in 1733–4 by John Reynolds of Hagbourne (Berks.), presumably replacing an earlier mechanism. A new hand and dial were fitted in 1752, and repairs were carried out by Hunt (probably Thomas Hunt) of Burford in 1785.[97] In 1848 the chimes played an 'ancient carol' at certain hours, but the clock was by then notoriously unreliable.[98] The carillon was replaced by Gillett and Johnston of Croydon in 1907 and was reconstructed in 1962 by John Smith and sons of Derby, who also replaced the clock mechanism.[99]

The Lady bell of Bampton was evidently of some repute in the mid 16th century,[1] and in 1629 the bells appear to have been recast and their number increased to six. Five bells of that date survive, of which three are attributed to Nathaniel Bolter. A replacement bell by Mears and Stainbank was hung in 1865 and two more were added in 1906, making a ring of eight; a new frame was installed in 1903, replacing one of 1608 perhaps by Matthew Chancelor of Berkshire. The saunce is of 1626, by James Keene of Woodstock.[2] The plate includes a silver chalice of 1595, a pair of silver patens of 1618, a silver tankard flagon of 1720, bought partly with money bequeathed by Mary Croft (d. 1719), and a silver table-spoon of 1765; 20th-century plate includes a chalice and paten given in memory of E. G. Hunt, vicar 1872–95.[3] The registers begin in 1538.[4]

The churchyard was closed for burials in 1889. A new cemetery for Witney union was consecrated the following year, on former glebe north of Landells Lane bought by the Witney board of guardians as rural sanitary authority. It was extended in 1947.[5]

NONCONFORMITY. Some vicars in the mid 16th century were associated with the recusant

Mores of Lower Haddon,[6] but no recusants were noted in Bampton in the earlier 17th century, only two or three in the late 17th century and early 18th, when they included a shoemaker and a labourer, and none in 1738.[7] Up to 8 papists, mostly tradesmen, were noted throughout the parish in the later 18th century, but there were none by the early 19th.[8] An oratory at Ham Court in the upper part of the former gatehouse, dedicated to the Virgin and served by a priest from Buckland (then Berks.), was established by Bertram Arthur Talbot in 1856, shortly before his death; it was closed the following year, and the fittings were removed to Oxford and later to Witney.[9]

In 1676 c. 45 undifferentiated nonconformists were noted in the whole parish.[10] The Presbyterian Samuel Birch, intruded into the south vicarage in 1658, instituted a lectureship, and held conventicles attended by friends from Witney, Alvescot, and Aston as well as Bampton; following his ejection he rented the south vicarage house for two years before being removed to Shilton in 1664.[11] A few Presbyterians were reported in the parish in the later 18th century, but none later.[12] Quaker families fined regularly in the later 17th century, and who attended a meeting at Alvescot, included at least four and probably more from Bampton and Weald. Though some were 'very poor', others included the relatively prosperous comb-maker John Hill, and Edward Bettres or Bettrice, perhaps related to the prominent Oxford Quaker Richard Bettrice.[13] Only two Quaker families were reported in the parish in 1738,[14] and in 1761 the Quaker wife of a Bampton blacksmith and possibly her brother were converted to Anglicanism. There were no Quakers by 1768.[15]

From the later 17th century members of four or five Bampton families, chiefly prosperous farmers and tradesmen, attended the Baptist meeting at Cote,[16] ministers for which seem to have lived in Bampton in the 1770s and c. 1798–1810.[17] A small stone-and-slated chapel with c. 100 sittings, served from Cote, was built south of High Street c. 1778.[18] Prominent members in the 19th century included the prosperous Duttons and Holloways,[19] and although sung

95 *Par. Colln.* i. 19, reading Thos. Kavi, presumably for Hoye.
96 O.R.O., MS. Oxf. Dioc. c 104, f. 8.
97 Ibid. MS. d.d. Par. Bampton b 10, ff. 2, 6, 58v.; *Oxon. Clockmakers* (Banbury Hist. Soc. iv), 29, 136; for Hunt, *Univ. Brit. Dir.* ii [1793], 412.
98 Giles, *Hist. Bampton*, 26; O.R.O., CPZ 1, no. 12.
99 'Terrier and Inventory, 1982', in custody of vicar and par. officers; *Oxon. Clockmakers* (Banbury Hist. Soc. iv), 29.
1 *Acts and Mons. of John Foxe*, ed. J. Pratt (4th edn. 1877), vi. 566.   2 *Ch. Bells Oxon.* 28–9.
3 B.L. Add. Ch. 38936; Evans, *Ch. Plate*, 10–11.
4 O.R.O., MSS. d.d. Par. Bampton c 1–7, b 1–7, d 1.
5 Ibid. MS. d.d. Par. Bampton c 12, item k, 26 Apr. 1889; ibid. MS. Oxf. Dioc. c 1712, consecration etc. 1890; ibid. c 1713/1, faculty 1947.
6 Above, churches.
7 *Protestation Rtns. and Tax. Assess.* 6–7; *Compton Census*, ed. Whiteman, 422; *Bp. Fell and Nonconf.* 5, 37, 51; *Oxoniensia*, xiii. 80; *Secker's Visit.* 12.
8 O.R.O., MSS. Oxf. Dioc. d 558, f. 33; d 561, f. 37; d 564, f. 29; d 566, f. 17; d 570, f. 21; c 327, p. 134; *Rtn. Papists 1767*, ii (Cath. Rec. Soc. occas. publ. no. 2), 114.
9 Stapleton, *Cath. Miss.* 172–3; *Oxf. Chron.* 21 June 1856; cf. *Complete Peerage*, xi. 710 sqq.
10 *Compton Census*, ed. Whiteman, 417 n., 422.

11 Mansfield Coll. Libr., S. Birch's 'Bk. of Prayers', pp. 183 sqq.; *Calamy Revised*, ed. A. G. Matthews, 56–7; *Der Pietismus in Gestalten und Wirkungen*, ed. H. Bornkamm, F. Heyer, and A. Schindler, 350–2; cf. *Hearth Tax Oxon.* 222, listing him under Bampton in 1665 apparently in error.
12 O.R.O., MSS. Oxf. Dioc. d 558, ff. 33–6; d 564, ff. 29–31; c 327, p. 134.
13 Ibid. BOQM 1/ii/1–3; ibid. MS. Wills Oxon. 35/1/40; P.R.O., PROB 11/434, f. 185 and v.; *Bp. Fell and Nonconf.* pp. xxiv, 5, 50; *V.C.H. Oxon.* iv. 415.
14 *Secker's Visit.* 13.
15 O.R.O., MSS. Oxf. Dioc. c 654, ff. 32–3; d 558, ff. 33–6.
16 Regent's Park Coll., Cote Ch. Bk. 1647–1882; *Bp. Fell and Nonconf.* 5, 51; B. Williams, *Memorials of the Fam. of Williams* (1844), 33–4; below, Aston and Cote, nonconf.
17 Baptist Union Corpn. file 1367/2, lease 9 May 1780; ibid. file 1367/4, lease 28 Apr. 1778; O.R.O., QSD L.22, s.v. Stennett; J. Stanley, *Church in the Hop Garden* [c. 1936], 170.
18 Baptist Union Corpn. file 1367/4, lease and release 1778; *Ch. and Chapel, 1851*, no. 24; cf. *Kelly's Dir. Oxon.* (1891).
19 O.R.O., MS. Oxf. Dioc. c 644, f. 185; Baptist Union Corpn. files 1367/1–4; Stanley, *Hop Garden*, 144–5, 169–70, 188–91.

services in Bampton church were claimed in 1814 to have virtually closed the meeting house,[20] attendance in 1850–1 averaged 80.[21] During the earlier 20th century numbers declined: by 1944 there was a Sunday school of only 12, and in the early 1950s morning services were discontinued. Membership rose slightly thereafter, and in 1971 the congregation was c. 20, but by 1991 the chapel, still dependent on Cote, was disused.[22] A Particular Baptist chapel on Buckland road, opened in 1861 with c. 90 sittings, had no connection with Cote.[23] It remained a chapel in 1950, but by 1955 was a private house.[24]

Three Methodist meeting houses were registered in Weald between 1826 and 1834, one of them a former stable, the others houses near the mill and on Cheyne Lane. In 1851 a cottage in Weald 'formerly for poor persons', presumably the former poor house on Weald Lane, was returned as a Wesleyan chapel with 60 sittings and had an average attendance of 20–25 for morning and evening services, though only 3–5 inhabitants were claimed as members of the Witney and Faringdon circuit.[25] Membership remained low or non-existent,[26] and although a mission room seating 100 was reported in 1891, the same year Bampton's 'spiritual destitution' prompted calls for establishment of a chapel. The Earlys of Witney donated £200, and in 1892 a stone-and-slated chapel in Gothic style, seating 130, was built on the north side of Bridge Street.[27] Membership doubled to over 30 by 1900 but fell to 16 by 1911, rising to 22 in the 1930s,[28] and the chapel remained open in 1992.

A Salvation Army meeting at Bampton in 1887, organized by Herbert Booth and c. 12 others who came from Witney on tricycles, was attended by c. 300–400 people.[29] No later references have been found.

EDUCATION. Robert Veysey of Chimney, by will proved 1635, left £200 to endow a free school at Bampton, and another £100 to erect a stone building 'with ashlar work'.[30] Nothing had been done by 1650 when John Palmer, one of the trustees, left a further £100 providing that Veysey's will was performed, but by 1653, when the first master was appointed, a single-storeyed

ashlar schoolhouse with attics and pitched stone-slated roofs had been built on former parish land on Church View.[31] Henry Coxeter (d. 1654) bequeathed £10 and Richard Dewe (d. 1684) £50,[32] and in 1695 three closes near later Calais Farm, estimated at c. 12 a., were bought and vested in trustees.[33] A cottage and garden west of the schoolhouse were bought with voluntary contributions in 1783 for an incoming master.[34] In 1784 Mary Frederick (d. 1785), Elizabeth Snell (d. 1788), and Susannah Frederick (d. 1798) purchased annuities yielding £16 a year to augment the master's salary, on condition that he should teach English and arithmetic free to 10 boys chosen by them or their trustees; Susannah also invested £100 left by her aunt Mary Croft (d. 1719) to teach 12 poor boys and girls of Bampton to read the bible, which legacy Mary's executors had evidently neglected. Since the school took only boys, the Croft income, £5 8s. in 1824, was shared between the master and a schoolmistress, who taught the girls elsewhere; the girls and their endowment were transferred to the National school in 1812, and the boys in 1824, the master's share having been unclaimed and allowed to accrue since 1817.[35] In the early 19th century dividends from £300 bequeathed by Susannah towards Bampton Sunday schools were divided between the same master and mistress with a small amount used for books, but passed in 1824 to the National school.[36] In 1750 the master's total income exceeded £20;[37] by the early 19th century it included c. £50 rent and c. £17 from the Frederick endowments, the Croft income being then received by an undermaster, but by the 1860s it was only c. £36.[38]

The first master, William Jackson, was a 'noted grammarian' formerly of Charlbury school.[39] A successor in the later 17th century was a pauper student of Queen's College, Oxford.[40] By the early 18th century the school seems to have been less exclusively concerned with classics teaching than some local grammar schools: both the Croft and Frederick endowments stipulated elementary education, and although in 1732 all boys 'fit to be taught Latin' were to be admitted for fees of 2s. 6d. entrance and 1s. a quarter and the master was to be qualified to teach Greek, he was also to teach English for fees of 5s. entrance and 5s. a quarter. Pupils were to be catechized

[20] O.R.O., MS. Oxf. Dioc. c 662, ff. 8–9v.
[21] Ch. and Chapel, 1851, no. 24.
[22] Regent's Park Coll., Cote Ch. Bk. 1882–1972, passim; Baptist Union Dir. (1990–1); inf. from pastor.
[23] Oxf. Chron. 18 May 1861; O.S. Map 1/2,500, Oxon. XXXVII. 7 (1876 and later edns.); Kelly's Dir. Oxon. (1891).
[24] Gospel Standard (1950); O.R.O., electoral regs. (1955), s.v. D. L. Green; O.S. Map 1/2,500, SP 3003–3103 (1971 edn.).
[25] O.R.O., MS. Oxf. Dioc. c 645, ff. 66, 225, 237; ibid. Witney and Faringdon Meth. Circuit I/1b; Ch. and Chapel, 1851, no. 471.
[26] O.R.O., Witney and Faringdon Meth. Circuit I/1b–e.
[27] Ibid. I/4b, pp. 54–5; Kelly's Dir. Oxon. (1891 and 1895 edns.); O.S. Map 1/2,500, Oxon. XXXVII. 7 (1876 and 1899 edns.). Pevsner, Oxon. 431 misdates it.
[28] O.R.O., Witney and Faringdon Meth. Circuit I/1f–i.
[29] Oxf. Chron. 30 Apr. 1887.
[30] P.R.O., PROB 11/169, f. 61 and v.; V.C.H. Oxon. i. 462.
[31] P.R.O., PROB 11/214, ff. 230–2; Giles, Hist. Bampton, pp. 145–6, 150–1; below, plate 8; cf. O.R.O., MS. d.d. Par. Bampton c 9, item b, lease 1 Jan. 10 Chas. I.

[32] P.R.O., PROB 11/234, f. 217; O.R.O., MS. Wills Oxon. 18/4/38.
[33] B.L. Add. Ch. 38932; 10th Rep. Com. Char. 341. At inclosure they comprised 9 a.
[34] 10th Rep. Com. Char. 341; O.R.O., MS. d.d. Par. Bampton c 12, letter 18 Oct. 1897; ibid. incl. award, plan I. It was demolished in the early 20th cent.: O.S. Map 1/2,500, Oxon. XXXVII. 6 (1876 and later edns.).
[35] 10th Rep. Com. Char. 342–4; O.R.O., D.Y. XXXII/i/1; B.L. Add. Ch. 38936; below. The Frederick endowments were not always received: O.R.O., MS. Oxf. Dioc. b 6, ff. 103–4; ibid. MS. d.d. Par. Bampton c 8, ff. 118v., 215, 217; Giles, Hist. Bampton. 98.
[36] P.R.O., PROB 11/1308, ff. 83–5; 10th Rep. Com. Char. 345; below.
[37] Secker's Corresp. 193; cf. Secker's Visit. 13; O.R.O., MS. d.d. Par. Bampton c 12, item b, lease 1756.
[38] 10th Rep. Com. Char. 342, 344–5; Schs. Inquiry [3966-XI], pp. 213–14, H.C. (1867–8), xxviii (10).
[39] V.C.H. Oxon. i. 462.
[40] Par. Colln. i. 17–18; Alum. Oxon. 1500–1714, s.v. Leonard Fell.

and attend church on Wednesdays, Fridays, and saints' days.[41] From 1732 to 1782 the master was Thomas Middleton, non-resident vicar of Clanfield, who in 1750 was accused of making a sinecure of the post and who in 1756, following his temporary ejection, attempted to retain the school closes;[42] there were no pupils in 1768 or 1771, and the master in 1774, apparently Middleton, taught in his own house.[43] On Middleton's death the school was re-established in the schoolhouse and fees were raised to 5s. a quarter,[44] but in the early 19th century it was again neglected, no classics being taught and English teaching being left to an undermaster. Ten boys were taught free, the rest paying fees 'on the master's terms'.[45]

Thirty pupils were recorded in 1815, but after new fees of 21s. entrance and 21s. a quarter were introduced in 1819 the average intake fell to 6, and on the master's resignation in 1822 it proved difficult to find a successor. Income was too little for repairs, the buildings were inadequate, and before the transfer of the Croft scholars to the National school, grammar school boys and those learning to read had to be taught in one room.[46] The school, closed repeatedly during the earlier 19th century,[47] had only one pupil in 1852 when it was 'not in accord with the wants of Bampton',[48] though in 1864 there were 13 day boys mostly under the age of 12, and 11 boarders, chiefly farmers' sons, paying between £20 and £25 a year and accommodated in the schoolhouse. Subjects included Latin, Greek, English, and arithmetic, and pupils were entered for public schools; the master was then a layman.[49] Funding remained difficult and the school had again closed by 1898 when, under a Charity Commission Scheme, its income was to provide exhibitions in educational institutions for children from within the ancient parish; its land and stock then comprised the schoolhouse and garden, c. 8 a., and c. £457 consols, together producing c. £32 a year.[50] The Scheme was renewed by the Board of Education in 1906, the schoolhouse being used thenceforth for classes, lectures, and meetings, and from 1964 as a public library.[51]

A private school was reportedly held in the court loft or court house in the earlier 18th century.[52] In 1808 three small schools funded by voluntary payments taught reading, arithmetic, and needlework, and there was a Sunday school for each sex, c. 150 children in all being taught. Younger children in the 1830s still relied on 2 or 3 private schools as there was no public infant

BAMPTON NATIONAL SCHOOL c. 1840

school.[53] A National school run on the Bell system was established in 1812 in a purpose-built, free-standing stone-and-slated schoolhouse at the top of Bridge Street, with support from the vicar George Richards.[54] Subjects included spelling, reading, and religious instruction; some boys learned arithmetic and writing, and some girls learned writing, needlework, and knitting. Church attendance was compulsory.[55] The cost was met chiefly from arrears from the parish's Shilton estate, rent from which was diverted permanently to the school. Income in 1815 comprised £36 from the estate, £20 from pence, and £10 from fees of 10 other children,[56] and in 1819 the master received £40 a year and the mistress £20.[57] In 1824 the Charity Commissioners confirmed diversion of the Shilton estate income and approved the transfer to the school of Mary Croft's legacy (£5 8s. a year), of Mary Dewe's manufactory charity (£20 a year), and of Susannah Frederick's Sunday school bequest (£9 a year), providing pupils received religious instruction on Sundays; even so salaries in 1848 were a 'miserable pittance'.[58]

Attendance rose from 65 boys and 75 girls in 1812 to 81 boys and 92 girls in 1815, and nearly 200 children attended an anniversary meeting in 1855.[59] The earl of Shrewsbury provided a site

[41] Giles, Hist. Bampton, 160–1; cf. M. A. Fleming, Witney Grammar Sch. 6, 13; Par. Colln. i. 17.
[42] O.R.O., MS. d.d. Par. Bampton c 12, legal opinion 7 Dec. 1756; Secker's Corresp. 9, 193.
[43] O.R.O., MS. d.d. Par. Bampton b 10, f. 34v.; ibid. MSS. Oxf. Dioc. c 654, ff. 42–43v.; d 561, f. 37; d 564, f. 29; Giles, Hist. Bampton, 159.
[44] Oxf. Jnl. Synopsis, 7 July 1783; Giles, Hist. Bampton, 159.   [45] 10th Rep. Com. Char. 342.
[46] Ibid.; O.R.O., MS. Oxf. Dioc. c 433, f. 22.
[47] 10th Rep. Com. Char. 342; Educ. Enq. Abstract, H.C. 62, p. 739 (1835), xlii; Digest Schs. and Chars. for Educ. [435], p. 89, H.C. (1843), xviii; Giles, Hist. Bampton, 91.
[48] Gardner's Dir. Oxon. (1852).
[49] Schs. Inquiry [3966-XI], pp. 213–14, H.C. (1867–8), xxviii (10).

[50] O.R.O., MS. d.d. Par. Bampton c 12, copy of Scheme.
[51] Board of Educ. Scheme 8 Oct. 1906; inf. from Major R. A. Colvile, Weald Manor. Kelly's Dir. Oxon. (1911) wrongly states that the school was reopened in 1906.
[52] O.R.O., P4/2/MS 1/5, ff. 1–2.
[53] Ibid. MSS. Oxf. Dioc. d 707, f. 14; b 39, f. 27.
[54] Ibid. c 433, f. 13; c 662, f. 8; ibid. incl. award; illust. in Bodl. MSS. Top. Oxon. b 220, f. 244; d 218, f. 48.
[55] O.R.O., MS. Oxf. Dioc. c 433 ff. 13 and v., 16–17, 19–21v.
[56] Ibid.; 10th Rep. Com. Char. 345, 347; Giles, Hist. Bampton, 99; below, charities.
[57] Educ. of Poor, H.C. 224, p. 718 (1819), ix (2).
[58] 10th Rep. Com. Char. 344–5, 347; Giles, Hist. Bampton, 99.
[59] O.R.O., MSS. Oxf. Dioc. c 433, ff. 13v., 17; c 662, ff. 48–9; Oxf. Chron. 21 July 1855.

for a larger school on Church View before 1860, and building, financed by subscription, began in 1863; the new school was opened in 1864.[60] The building, of local stone with Bath stone dressings and stone-slated roofs, was designed in Gothic style by William Wilkinson of Oxford, with accommodation for 156 children in two rooms;[61] its forerunner was demolished before 1876.[62]

The school was again short of accommodation by 1871, when 172 children attended on the day of the government inspection.[63] A voluntary rate was sought to avoid imposition of a school board,[64] and in 1873 an infant school was opened in the newly enlarged National school building.[65] By 1910 there were 124 juniors and 71 infants. Reports in the late 19th century were mixed, though scholarships were won regularly to Witney, Bampton, and Burford grammar schools.[66]

By 1927 the upper forms had become the senior school for the surrounding villages. New buildings were added on the west in 1947, and the school acquired controlled status in 1949; in 1959 there were 294 pupils. In 1960 the senior department became a Secondary Modern with 140 on the register, but in 1965, when the roll was 96, all the pupils were transferred to Wood Green Comprehensive in Witney, and the Bampton school closed. A new Church of England primary school built on the town's northern edge in 1961 had 260 children in 1970, when buildings at the back of the former National school, then a youth centre, were used as an annexe. The roll was 142 in 1993.[67]

A young ladies' needlework school was mentioned in 1782,[68] and from the late 18th century there were several private boarding schools with pupils drawn chiefly from outside the parish. An academy for young gentlemen mentioned in 1790[69] was followed by John Beechey's Mansion House Academy, established reportedly c. 1815 and moved in the 1820s to Weald Manor; in 1841 it had 17 boys aged from 9 to 14, but closed in the later 1850s.[70] G. H. Drewe's St. Mary's College, opened in Weald Manor in 1859 and similarly modelled on public schools, had over 50 boys in 1861 aged from 5 to 18, but closed c. 1863.[71] A third gentlemen's boarding school, Thomas Leforestier's Classical and Commercial Academy, was established by 1841 apparently in the Grange on High Street and closed c. 1864;[72] a boys' boarding school on Lavender Square, reportedly closed in 1880, is otherwise unrecorded.[73] A ladies' boarding school later in Prospect House on Broad Street, established by 1830 and with 11 pupils in 1841,[74] was taken over c. 1863 by Sarah and Rebecca Pembrey and moved before 1871 to the Elms on Broad Street, where before 1876 schoolrooms and extra accommodation (later South Elms) were added. It moved before 1903 to Valetta (later Ampney) Lodge on High Street and closed by 1915.[75] A ladies' boarding school on High Street, apparently in Lime Tree House, was recorded from the late 1840s to 1868.[76] John Bryant ran a small day- and, for a time, boarding school on Weald Lane by 1861, which moved later to the market place and continued in the early 20th century.[77] J. A. Giles, curate 1846–55, prepared private pupils for Oxford university and the army.[78]

CHARITIES FOR THE POOR.[79] George Thompson, by will proved 1604,[80] gave an annual rent charge of £6 for the poor of Bampton, Weald, and Lew. In the early 19th century it was distributed yearly in money, and the dole continued in 1854.[81] Leonard Wilmot (d. 1608) of Clanfield gave in his lifetime a rent charge of £2 for the poor of Bampton, Weald, Lew, and Aston and Cote;[82] in the late 18th century and early 19th the churchwardens retained it, but in 1848 it provided blankets lent to the poor in winter. Julian Walter of Appleton (formerly Berks.), by will proved 1660,[83] left a house and lands, the rent to be distributed to the poor of Bampton in bread with 8s. reserved for an annual dinner for the churchwardens and overseers. The rent was £42 in 1848.

Following an enquiry in 1680 into misuse of Bampton charities,[84] c. 12 a. were bought c. 1687

60 Jesus Coll. Mun., box 15, list 7, letter from W. Dyke 16 Mar. 1860; *The Builder*, xxi (1863), 485; *Oxf. Chron.* 21 Mar. 1863, 28 May 1864; misdated in Pevsner, *Oxon.* 432. A datestone of 1871 evidently refers only to acquisition of the freehold: O.R.O., Crowdy I/51, lot 53.
61 *The Builder*, xxi. 485.
62 O.S. Map 1/2,500, Oxon. XXXVII. 7 (1876).
63 *Returns relating to Elementary Educ.* H.C. 201, p. 324 (1871), lv.
64 *Oxf. Chron.* 28 June 1873.
65 Ibid. 28 June, 12 July 1873; O.R.O., T/SL/68 ii; ibid. Crowdy I/51, town plan. O.S. Map 1/2,500, Oxon. XXXVII. 7 (1876 edn.) fails to show additions to the bldg.
66 O.R.O., T/SL/68 i–iii; ibid. T/SA/30.
67 Ibid. T/SL/68 iii–iv; Oxon. C.C. Educ. Dept., Ducker Davis survey; O.S. Map 1/2,500, SP 3003–3103 (1971 edn.); inf. from L.E.A.
68 Oxf. Jnl. Synopsis, 21 Sept. 1782.
69 Ibid. 12 July 1790.
70 P.R.O., HO 107/872; Bodl. MS. Top. Oxon. d 218, f. 38v.; Pigot, *Lond. & Prov. Dir.* (1830); *Oxf. Jnl.* 8 Jan. 1831; *Oxf. Chron.* 7 July 1855; cf. O.R.O., incl. award, s.v. Chas. Tunstall.
71 Bodl. G.A. Oxon. c 22 (2); P.R.O., RG 9/905; *Dutton, Allen & Co.'s Dir. Oxon.* (1863); *Oxf. Chron.* 5 Sept. 1863; cf. O.R.O., Crowdy I/51, lot 20.
72 P.R.O., HO 107/872; HO 107/1731; ibid. RG

9/905; *Gardner's Dir. Oxon.* (1852); *P.O. Dir. Oxon.* (1864).
73 *Witney Express*, 26 Feb. 1880.
74 Run by the Trafford fam.: Pigot, *Lond. & Prov. Dir.* (1830); *Billing's Dir. Oxon.* (1854); P.R.O., HO 107/872.
75 P.R.O., RG 9/905, RG 10/1451; *Dutton, Allen & Co.'s Dir. Oxon.* (1863); *Kelly's Dir. Oxon.* (1887 and later edns.); O.S. Map 1/2,500, Oxon. XXXVII. 7 (1876 edn.); cf. *Oxf. Times*, 4 Sept. 1992.
76 Eliz. Steede's: *P.O. Dir. Oxon.* (1847); *Cassey & Co.'s Dir. Oxon.* (1868); P.R.O., HO 107/1731; ibid. RG 9/905; RG 10/1451.
77 P.R.O., RG 9/905; RG 11/1514; *P.O. Dir. Oxon.* (1864); *Kelly's Dir. Oxon.* (1883 and later edns.); J. L. Hughes-Owens, *Bampton We Have Lost*, 92: copy in C.O.S.
78 O.R.O., CPZ 1, letter to bp. 26 Oct. 1854; *D.N.B.*; above, church.
79 Based, except where stated, on *10th Rep. Com. Char.* 345–56; Giles, *Hist. Bampton*, 88–102, 155–60.
80 O.R.O., MS. Wills Oxon. 191, f. 415.
81 *Oxf. Chron.* 23 Dec. 1854.
82 Not mentioned in his will: P.R.O., PROB 11/112, ff. 102v.–103v. Cf. below, Aston and Cote, charities; Lew, charities.
83 Berks. R.O., MS. Wills Berks. 137/74.
84 O.R.O., MS. d.d. Par. Bampton c 9, item e; printed in Giles, *Hist. Bampton*, 151–5.

using the bequests of John Palmer (£100 to the poor of Bampton and Weald by will proved 1650),[85] John Butt (£20 to the poor of Bampton by will proved 1610),[86] John Tull (£5 to the poor of Bampton by will proved 1615),[87] Robert Veysey of Chimney (£10 to 12 poor widows of Bampton and Weald by will proved 1666),[88] and Henry Clanfield (date and amount unknown). Before 1801 the rent was divided into 33 parts, 25 representing Palmer's bequest and 8 the rest. Income in 1801 was £27; c. 2 a. was sold at inclosure, and in 1848 income was £15 of which £3 14s. went to the town bread fund, the rest, after land tax, being added to the vicars' fund for supplying coal to the poor in winter.

Sir William Coventry, by will proved 1686, left £100 towards apprenticing poor children, at least 17 of whom were indentured within 3 years.[89] The bequest was not mentioned later and was presumably either lost or amalgamated with other apprenticing charities. In 1706 an estate at Shilton (formerly Berks.) was bought with bequests of Richard Coxeter (£10 for apprenticing to masters outside the parish, by will proved 1683), Dorothy Loder (£300 to set the poor to work, by will proved 1702),[90] and reportedly of the vicar Edward Cotton (£25 from a bequest of £50 by will proved 1676).[91] Income was £36 in the early 19th century, but following criticisms of apprenticing policy it was diverted before 1815 to the National school.[92] Thomas Horde, by will proved 1716, left £10 each to Bampton and Weald for apprenticing 2 boys or girls, but though the gift was applied in the earlier 18th century it was lost by the 19th. A £10 rent charge left by Horde on lands in Aston and Cote for the poorest of Bampton and Weald seems never to have been paid.[93]

In 1726 c. 10 a. were bought with bequests of William Osborn, vicar (£100 for apprenticing by will proved 1646),[94] Edward Cotton, vicar (£50 to poor churchgoing householders, by will proved 1676),[95] Tobias Sadler (£50 for bread by will proved 1676),[96] Richard Blagrave (d. 1675, £10 for bread by oral testimony),[97] Thomas Hall (£5 for bread by will proved 1693) and his wife Anne (£5 for bread),[98] Ann Coxeter (£10 for bread to poor widows, by will proved 1695),[99] Robert Jeeves of Lew (£5 to poor labourers by will proved 1703),[1] Robert Cripps (£5 for poor widowers by will proved 1705),[2] and John Hol-

loway (d. 1720, £100 for bread by will); another £60 from unspecified bread charities probably included Michael Fawdrey's bequest of 50s. in 1726.[3] Three-eighths of the income were used for apprenticing under Osborn's and Cotton's bequests, a quarter for bread under Holloway's bequest, and the rest for bread or otherwise. Of c. £22 income in 1848 c. £14 went to the bread fund, c. £5 to an accumulating apprentice fund, and c. £3 was distributed in half crowns.

Mary Dewe (d. 1764) left £200 by will to employ the poor of Bampton 'in some manufactory'.[4] The interest was diverted to a proposed new workhouse in 1768 and towards medical expenses in 1784, and an attempt to establish a sacking factory was reportedly made c. 1795.[5] In 1815 South Sea annuities belonging to the charity were sold for c. £264, which was combined with c. £47 from a 'manufactory account' presumably representing the sacking cloth venture, and with accrued dividends of £253 presumably from another charity. The interest from £500 remaining after expenses was diverted to the National school. Susannah Frederick's bequest of £200 by will proved 1798,[6] the interest to be distributed in clothing, was received by 1824 after a delay, and before 1839[7] both that and the Dewe legacy were invested with an organist's subscription fund totalling c. £600, the income being distributed proportionately to the poor in linen, to the National school, and to the organist.

Joseph Carter of Bristol, by will proved 1769, left £50, the interest to be paid to the unrelieved poor. Much of the bequest was lost c. 1837, and in 1844 capital and interest totalled only c. £30.[8] Edward Church (d. 1771) left an estate at Weald worth £14 a year to benefit poor widows, but his heir-at-law recovered it; James Leverett of Witney, by will proved 1783,[9] left £50 for bread, which was never received. Elizabeth Snell, by will proved 1788,[10] left £200 which in 1824 produced c. £8, though more was then distributed in kind. Thomas Dewe (d. by 1862) of Longworth (formerly Berks.) left £300, the interest to buy blankets, sheets, or clothing for the poor of Weald.[11] In 1801 total charitable income was c. £180, and in 1824 there were 100 loaves distributed weekly; many charities were mismanaged or neglected, and repeated attempts were made to overhaul their administration.[12]

A Scheme of 1888 combined Bampton's,

85 P.R.O., PROB 11/214, ff. 230–2.
86 O.R.O., MS. Wills Oxon. 54/3/9.
87 P.R.O., PROB 11/126, f. 251 and v.
88 Ibid. PROB 11/322, f. 363v.
89 Ibid. PROB 11/384, f. 14v.; O.R.O., MS. d.d. Par. Bampton b 15, item d.
90 P.R.O., PROB 11/372, f. 18v.; PROB 11/464, f. 153.
91 10th Rep. Com. Char. 345, wrongly stating that the bequest was for apprenticing; cf. O.R.O., MS. d.d. Par. Bampton c 9, copies of will; Giles, Hist. Bampton, 152–3; below.
92 Above, educ.
93 P.R.O., PROB 11/551, ff. 252–3; O.R.O., MSS. d.d. Par. Bampton b 11, f. 23v.; b 15, indentures.
94 P.R.O., PROB 11/196, f. 276v.
95 Copies in O.R.O., MS. d.d. Par. Bampton c 9.
96 P.R.O., PROB 11/351, f. 327.
97 Giles, Hist. Bampton, 152, 154.
98 Ibid. 89; O.R.O., MS. Wills Oxon. 34/4/23.
99 O.R.O., MS. Wills Oxon. 121/1/26.

1 Ibid. 38/2/25; cf. below, Lew, charities.
2 O.R.O., MS. Wills Oxon. 121/3/11.
3 Ibid. 128/1/7. Lost bequests by Henry (£20) and Bartholomew Coxeter (£30), by wills proved 1654 and 1664, were perhaps also used to purchase some of the estates described: P.R.O., PROB 11/234, f. 217; PROB 11/314, f. 333v.
4 O.R.O., MS. d.d. Par. Bampton c 9, extract from will; C.O.S., par. reg. transcripts.
5 O.R.O., MS. d.d. Par. Bampton b 10, ff. 34v., 54v.; ibid. MS. Oxf. Dioc. c 327, p. 199; Char. Don. 966–7; 10th Rep. Com. Char. 347; above, local govt. (par. govt.).
6 P.R.O., PROB 11/1308, f. 83.
7 O.R.O., MS. d.d. Par. Bampton c 8, f. 165v.
8 Giles, Hist. Bampton, 98.
9 Copy in Bodl. G.A. Oxon. 8° 364.
10 P.R.O., PROB 11/1161, ff. 325v.–327.
11 O.R.O., MS. d.d. Par. Bampton c 12, extract from will.
12 Ibid. b 10, ff. 36, 38v.–40v., 54, 61; c 8, ff. 2v., 118v.–119v., 212 and v.; Giles, Hist. Bampton, 88, 155–60.

Lew's, Aston's, and Brighthampton's charities, two organists' funds, and church lands totalling c. 12 a. as the Bampton Consolidated Charities. Under Schemes of 1906 and 1911 the Shilton estate and Mary Dewe bequest became the Bampton Educational Charity, and the church lands and organists' funds the Bampton Proper Ecclesiastical Charity. Total income of the Con-

solidated Charities in 1969 was c. £369, of which c. £155 were expended in general charitable relief in Bampton and Weald. Under a Scheme of 1972 the eleemosynary charities were reconstituted as the Bampton Welfare Trust, some income from which was used for educational purposes in 1993.[13]

ASTON AND COTE

ASTON AND COTE township (2,997 a.) adjoined the parish boundary on the north and south.[14] Parts of its eastern and south-eastern boundaries were described in 10th- and 11th-century grants of adjacent estates at Ducklington, Shifford, and Chimney; its western boundary with Bampton and Weald, discussed above, was established probably after the mid 10th century, and followed furlongs and divisions of common pasture and meadow.[15]

Abingdon Lane, an ancient route running south-eastwards through Yelford and Brighthampton to the Thames crossing at Newbridge, cut across the township's northern tip.[16] A branch leading southwards towards the Thames crossing at Shifford ran down the eastern boundary from an early date: its northern stretch, which branched eastwards into Shifford and continued to Brighthampton, was suppressed in 1629 because of flooding,[17] and the southern stretch, called 'the way' in a description of Shifford's boundaries in 1005, was abandoned apparently between 1625 and 1767.[18] Cote Lane presumably also originated as a route to the river crossings at Shifford or Duxford, and in the 18th and 19th centuries continued through Shifford to Newbridge.[19] Kingsway Lane north-west of Aston village, part of the pre-inclosure road from Ducklington and Claywell to Bampton, may have been important in the early Middle Ages, and it has been suggested that its western end formed part of an inferred minor Roman road through Bampton from a crossing of the river Windrush at Gill Mill; an intersecting track running southwards to Aston village through Stone Bridge furlong may have been part of a 'way' which ran south or south-westwards across a stone bridge in the 10th century.[20]

The Brighthampton road, formerly a bridle-way, was confirmed as the principal route eastwards in the early 17th century,[21] and by the late 18th roads or lanes linking Aston with Bampton, Brighthampton, and Chimney largely followed their later courses.[22] The earlier tracks

north of the village were suppressed at inclosure c. 1853, when a new 30-ft. road from Aston to Ducklington and Witney was laid out across the former common and open fields; the Aston section of Abingdon Lane was confirmed, and Cote Lane was extended northwards to meet it. The road towards Chimney was confirmed as a 20-ft. carriageway, with a tow path leading westwards to Isle of Wight and Tadpole bridges alongside the newly straightened Great brook.[23]

An Aston man was transporting wood and fuel to Oxford by boat in the early 17th century,[24] and in 1808 coal for domestic use was transported by river from Cassington wharf.[25] There were carriers from Aston and Cote to Oxford and Witney in the 1840s, when both hamlets received letters through Bampton. Aston's post office, by 1841 probably already on its later site on the south side of the square, became a money order and telegraph office before 1915,[26] and remained open in 1992.

Cropmarks suggesting prehistoric settlement have been noted south of Aston, east of Cote Lane, and in the south-east near the Shifford boundary.[27] An irregular enclosure on the Thames floodplain south of Great brook may be a Neolithic causewayed camp,[28] and there have been isolated Neolithic and Bronze-Age finds north of Aston High Street and near the north end of Cote Lane. Iron-Age pottery and a brooch were found south of Cote House.[29] A probable settlement site straddling the modern Brighthampton road east of Cote may have been reorganized in the Roman period, and it has been suggested that a large, double-ditched enclosure on the township's eastern edge south of Brighthampton road may be a Roman fort, though it does not lie on any known Roman roads.[30] Two coins of Trajan and Hadrian were discovered in Cote in the 19th century.[31] South of Great brook two square enclosures contained within Bronze-Age ring ditches are probably of Roman or post-Roman date.[32]

13 O.R.C.C., Kimber files; inf. from Major R. A. Colvile, Weald Manor.   14 Above, Bampton, general intro.
15 Above, Bampton and Weald, intro.; below, Chimney, intro.; Shifford, intro.; Ducklington, intro.
16 Jefferys, Oxon. Map (1767); below, Lew, intro.; Standlake, intro.
17 Bodl. MS. Top. Oxon. c 118, f. 7 and v.
18 Grundy, Saxon Oxon. 54; Jefferys, Oxon. Map (1767); below, Shifford, intro.; plate 39.
19 B.L. Add. MS. 31323 HHH; O.S. Map 1", sheet 13 (1830 edn.).
20 B.L. Add. MS. 31323 HHH; above, Bampton and Weald, intro.
21 Bodl. MS. Top. Oxon. c 118, f. 7 and v.; the road there described bypassed Aston village, crossing the com-

mon to join Yelford or Abingdon Lane.
22 B.L. Add. MS. 31323 HHH; Jefferys, Oxon. Map (1767).
23 O.R.O., incl. award; above, map on p. 6.
24 P.R.O., C 2/Jas. I/U 1/56, answer of Wm. Minchin.
25 Bodl. MS. Ch. Oxon. 5273; for a wharf near Tadpole bridge, above, Bampton and Weald, intro.
26 P.O. Dir. Oxon. (1847 and later edns.); Kelly's Dir. Oxon. (1883 and later edns.); O.R.O., tithe award (1841), f. 71 (no. 1531).
27 D. Benson and D. Miles, Upper Thames Valley, 39–41.
28 Ibid. 39; C.B.A. Group 9, Newsletter, iii (1973), 34.
29 C.O.S., PRN 4479–80, 5585, 12677; V.C.H. Oxon. i. 262.
30 Benson and Miles, Upper Thames Valley, 40–1; C.O.S., PRN 8655, 11571.   31 V.C.H. Oxon. i. 335.
32 S. Midlands Arch. xxii (1992), 56–7, 61.

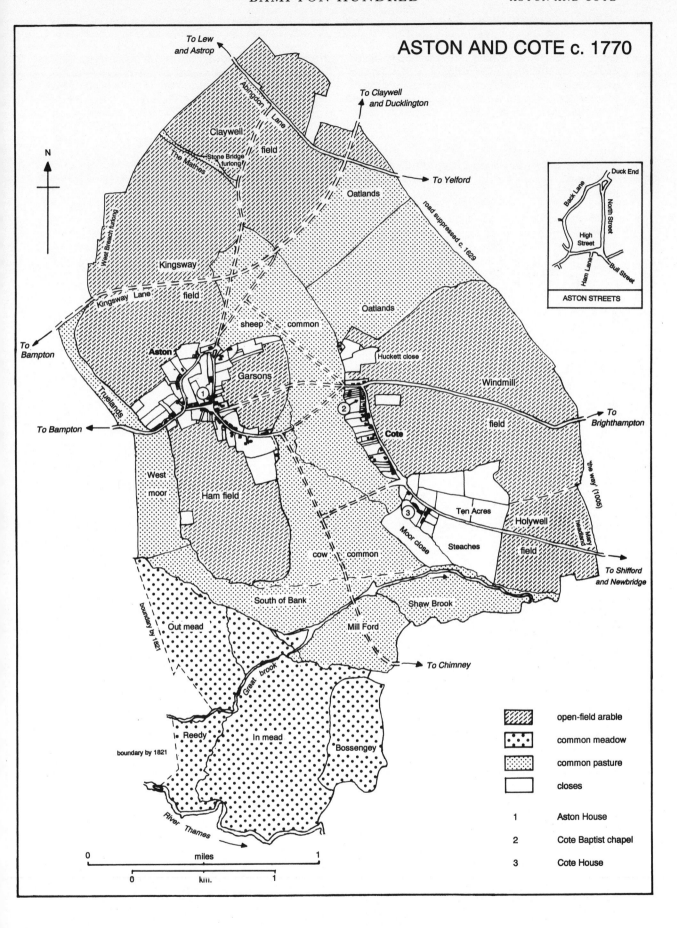

ASTON AND COTE c. 1770

To Lew
and Astrop

To Claywell
and Ducklington

Claywell
field

Stone Bridge
furlong

The Mathes

Oatlands

To Yelford

road suppressed c. 1629

N

West Breach furlong

Kingsway
field

Kingsway Lane

sheep common

Aston

Garsons

Oatlands

Huckett close

Windmill
field

To Bampton

Truelands

To Bampton

Cote

To Brighthampton

West
moor

Ham field

cow common

Moor close

Ten Acres

Steaches

'the way' (1005)

Mary headland

Holywell
field

To Shifford
and Newbridge

South of Bank

Shaw Brook

Mill Ford

To Chimney

boundary by 1821

Out mead

Great brook

Reedy

In mead

Bossengey

boundary by 1821

River Thames

Duck End

Back Lane

North Street

High
Street

Ham Lane

Bull Street

ASTON STREETS

0   miles   1

0   km.   1

open-field arable

common meadow

common pasture

closes

1   Aston House

2   Cote Baptist chapel

3   Cote House

Cropmarks suggesting Anglo-Saxon sunken huts have been noted on the gravel terraces east of Cote, near areas of probable earlier settlement.[33] All lie within the later open fields, perhaps supporting indications that the medieval fields and township boundaries were established after the mid 10th century.[34] Aston (i.e. Bampton's east *tūn*), on a gravel terrace south of Kingsway Lane, existed in some form by 958 when the 'boundary of the people of Aston' was mentioned,[35] and in 984 King Aethelred granted 2 *cassati* there to his 'minister' Aelfwine.[36] Cote, a straggling line of cottages and farmsteads along Cote Lane, was recorded by name only from 1203[37] but probably existed much earlier; in the mid 13th century manorial organization and land tenure there were no different from elsewhere in the township.[38]

Neither Aston nor Cote was separately entered in Domesday Book. In 1279 *c.* 59 of the tenants listed probably resided[39] and at least another 11 seem to have been omitted,[40] implying over 70 households of which 15 or more were in Cote.[41] That some holdings had apparently been recently divided[42] may indicate rising population, and Aston and Cote remained by far the most populous, though not the wealthiest, of Bampton's outlying townships. Over 63 inhabitants were taxed in 1306, 76 in 1316, and 78 in 1327, and in 1377 poll tax was paid by 156 inhabitants over 14, suggesting that 14th-century depopulation had been less marked than in some Oxfordshire parishes.[43] As elsewhere in the parish there may have been contraction during the 15th century,[44] but 113 male inhabitants were listed in 1642,[45] implying an adult population of *c.* 226; 68 houses were assessed for hearth tax in 1662, possibly an underassessment.[46] Between a fifth and a third of the population probably then lived at Cote, where 75 adults were noted in 1676.[47] Several holdings had been divided between two or more tenants by *c.* 1668, and in 1657 a poor Aston man obtained permission to build a cottage on the waste, though in the late 17th century and early 18th the death rate seems temporarily to have exceeded the birth rate:[48] periods of unusually high mortality were 1693–4,

caused perhaps by an outbreak of 'contagious disease',[49] 1700, 1711, and 1728, in which year there was smallpox in Bampton,[50] and the 1760s. From the mid 18th century baptisms usually outnumbered burials, and by 1801 the population was 628 accommodated in 115 houses; in 1841 it was 727, of whom 204 lived at Cote. After reaching a peak of 908 in 1871 it declined, with intermissions, to 531 in 1931. By 1951 it had risen to 678, partly because of boundary changes, and from the 1960s it rose steadily to 1,221 in 1991.[51]

Aston's topography may in part have been conditioned by a rectilinear arrangement of fields and roads also discernible around Bampton, and possibly of Roman or earlier origin.[52] Though High Street runs from east to west several roads and lanes are aligned north-west to south-east or north-east to south-west, among them the road towards Bampton, Cote road, a small lane branching north-west from the intersection of High Street and Back Lane, and Bull Street,[53] so called by 1841 from the public house near its southern end.[54] North Street (formerly Duckend) Farm, north of the gravel terrace,[55] originated perhaps as part of a separate 'end', and is connected with the main village by North Street and by the sinuous Back Lane, which together embrace an area of pasture closes. Aston cross, where High Street, North Street, and Bull Street converge in an open triangular space later called the square, was mentioned in the 16th century as a meeting place of the Sixteens, elected officers responsible for agricultural regulation.[56] Only the base seems to have survived in 1848,[57] but a cross was marked on the Ordnance Survey map of 1876 and a new war memorial cross was erected on the site shortly after the First World War.[58]

In the 18th century houses extended along the full length of High and Bull Streets, and there were isolated cottages and farmsteads along North Street and Back Lane. Since a tenement recorded from the Middle Ages lay at Bull Street's extreme south-east end, presumably the lane had been settled from an early date.[59] The surname 'at well', recorded in the 13th century

33 Benson and Miles, *Upper Thames Valley*, 40–1.
34 Above, Bampton and Weald, intro.
35 *on easthaema gemaere*: Grundy, *Saxon Oxon.* 30; cf. *P.N. Oxon.* (E.P.N.S.), ii. 449.
36 *Early Chart. of Thames Valley*, ed. M. Gelling, no. 282 (*aet Eastun*).
37 *Cur. Reg. R.* iii. 77; *P.N. Oxon.* (E.P.N.S.), ii. 302.
38 Below, econ. hist.
39 *Bampton Hund. R.* 21–3. The figure omits the abbot of Eynsham, the freeholders Robert le Caus and Robert of Yelford, and Emma Lovel who probably lived in East Weald: *Eynsham Cart.* ii, pp. 12, 14.
40 Below, econ. hist.
41 *Bampton Hund. R.* 21, 23; *Eynsham Cart.* ii, pp. 12, 14–15; Giles, *Hist. Bampton*, 135–6; D. & C. Exeter, MS. 4753; ibid. Ch. Comm. 13/74363a.
42 *Bampton Hund. R.* 21.
43 P.R.O., E 179/161/8–10; E 179/161/42; below, econ. hist. Part of the 1306 list is missing.
44 Below, econ. hist.
45 *Protestation Rtns. and Tax Assess.* 8.
46 P.R.O., E 179/255/4, pt. i, f. 18; cf. O.R.O., Misc. WA I/1, ff. 5–6v., listing *c.* 84 occupiers of land (some non-resident), and several cottages, possibly sublet.
47 *Compton Census*, ed. Whiteman, 417; O.R.O., Misc. WA I/1, ff. 5–6v., naming 17 occupiers of land in Cote and 67 in Aston.

48 O.R.O., Misc. WA I/1, ff. 5–6v.; Giles, *Hist. Bampton*, Suppl. p. 3; C.O.S., Bampton par. reg. transcripts. Aston inhabitants were not consistently distinguished in Bampton regs. before the mid 18th century; Shifford's early regs., recording Cote burials, are lost.
49 O.R.O., MS. Wills Oxon. 73/2/32.
50 Ibid. MS. d.d. Par. Bampton b 11, ff. 175–194v.
51 C.O.S., Bampton par. reg. transcripts; *Census*, 1801–1991, wrongly counting 343 Aston inhabitants under Lew in 1981.
52 Above, Bampton and Weald, intro.
53 Jefferys, *Oxon. Map* (1767); O.S. Map 6″, Oxon. XXXVII (1884 edn.).
54 P.R.O., HO 107/872; below, this section.
55 O.S. Map 1/2,500, Oxon. XXXVII. 8 (1876 edn.); Geol. Surv. Map 1/50,000, solid and drift, sheet 236 (1982 edn.).
56 O.R.O., Misc. WA I/1, f. 1v.; below, local govt.
57 Giles, *Hist. Bampton*, facing p. 73; cf. O.R.O., Acc. 2184, Red Lion deeds, 1–2 Oct. 1839, mentioning the 'market cross'.
58 O.S. Map 1/2,500, Oxon. XXXVII. 8 (1876 edn.); *Kelly's Dir. Oxon.* (1924); below, plate 11.
59 Jefferys, *Oxon. Map* (1767); B.L. Add. MS. 31323 HHH; O.R.O., tithe award and map (1841), showing an Exeter cathedral tenement near Lower Fm.; cf. D. & C. Exeter, MSS. 2931, 4544; below, manors.

and referring possibly to a medieval holy well near the township's eastern edge, suggests that medieval settlement in Cote extended at least as far as the site of Cote House and possibly to the Shifford boundary,[60] though by the 18th century Cote House marked the southernmost limit of expansion.[61] Cottages south of Bull Street and near North Street Farm, and a farmhouse west of later Cote Lodge Farm, all on the edge of the common, were established by the mid 18th century,[62] but there were no other outlying farmsteads before inclosure.

Thatched Cottage on North Street incorporates in its central bay a late 16th- or early 17th-century one-roomed cottage whose walls may originally have been timber-framed, suggesting that, as in Bampton, timber construction may have been common in the medieval period. The cottage, which included attics and a gable chimney stack, had been rewalled in stone by the time a two-storeyed addition was made on the south perhaps in the 18th century. Most surviving buildings are of limestone rubble with stone-slated roofs, though thatch may formerly have been common,[63] and some houses in the later 19th century, among them Newhouse Farm, were built of local Aston brick.[64] Several 17th- or early 18th-century farmhouses survive in both hamlets, among them Cote Farmhouse and Cote Cottage and, in Aston, North Street Farm, Westerleigh, West End Cottage, the Elms (facing Aston square), and cottages on Back Lane; West End Farm, on a site near the southern end of Back Lane occupied probably from the Middle Ages, incorporates a late 16th- or early 17th-century house of one storey with attics and a cross passage, whose southern end was truncated when two west-facing houses were built onto a side lane before 1773.[65] The most notable building in Aston, besides the church, is Aston House at the south end of North Street, erected for the Baptist minister on the site of an earlier cottage c. 1744.[66] The symmetrical main block incorporates a 5-bayed front of two storeys and attics, faced with red brick and with ashlar dressings and a segmental pediment over the central doorway; the interior retains some original panelling and other fittings. A service wing at the rear was extended in the 19th century. On Cote Lane Milton Lodge was rebuilt c. 1720 probably by members of the prosperous Wil-

liams family[67] and has a symmetrical 5-bayed entrance front with a shell hood; fittings include panelled dados and an original staircase with turned balusters.[68] Cote House and the 18th-century Baptist chapel at the northern end of Cote Lane are described below.[69] In 1848 Aston was judged 'humble and primeval-looking' and its architecture mediocre,[70] though inclosure, delayed until c. 1853, was said in 1856 to be improving its appearance, with new houses being built and others altered.[71] Newhouse and Cote Lodge Farms, the latter on the newly established road leading north from Cote hamlet, were built before 1876, and labourers' cottages on Cote road during the same period,[72] though in 1890 the vicar commented on the poor condition of the township's cottages.[73] Also rebuilt in the 19th century were the post office and nearby Red Lion public house on Aston square, and farmsteads on Back Lane, North Street, and in Cote. New institutional buildings in Aston included the church (1838) and adjacent National school (1856) on Cote road, the later-demolished vicarage house (c. 1858) south of High Street, and the Baptist chapel and British school (1845) on North Street. Westfield House, on Aston's western edge, was built as a private school c. 1913, and a Baptist Hall was built on Cote road in 1929 and was replaced in 1980 by a larger Fellowship Centre.[74]

New drains were being laid in 1856, which it was hoped would transform the 'damp and dirty street towards Cote' into a 'clean and healthy locality'.[75] Contaminated wells in Cote may have caused a diphtheria epidemic in 1893,[76] but despite the establishment c. 1907 of the Bampton, Aston and District Gas and Water Co. the water supply was chiefly from wells until the Second World War,[77] and in 1938 the parish council voted against being supplied with water and electricity by the Rural District Council.[78] Electricity was introduced before 1949,[79] gas before 1939,[80] and mains drainage c. 1967.[81]

There was little expansion of either hamlet until the 1960s, when large numbers of houses were built along Cote road, off Bull Street, and, following the demolition of the vicarage house, south of High Street. In 1965 a total of 57 new houses was expected within two years,[82] and limited expansion continued in the 1970s and 1980s. Old people's accommodation was built

60 *Bampton Hund. R.* 23; D. & C. Exeter, MS. 2931; below, this section.
61 Jefferys, *Oxon. Map* (1767).
62 Ibid.; O.R.O., tithe map (1841).
63 e.g. Ch. Com. Rec. L 7, pp. 415, 425 (nos. 18, 92, 94–5, 97).
64 Local inf.; cf. below, econ. hist.
65 B.L. Add. MS. 31323 HHH; the tenement belonged to Exeter cathedral apparently from the Middle Ages.
66 Baptist Union Corpn. file 1367/2, deeds 1742–4; below, nonconf.; illust. in J. Stanley, *Church in the Hop Garden* [c. 1936], facing p. 166.
67 Datestone inscribed IWM 1720; O.R.O., tithe award (1841), ff. 85–7, no. 3142; below, econ. hist.; cf. Pevsner, *Oxon.* 338, suggesting c. 1750.
68 D.o.E., *Revised Hist. Bldgs. List: Aston Bampton and Shifford* (1988), 3: copy in C.O.S.
69 Below, manors; nonconf.
70 Giles, *Hist. Bampton*, 73.
71 *Oxf. Chron.* 8 Nov. 1856.

72 O.R.O., tithe map (1857); O.S. Map 1/2,500, Oxon. XXXVII. 8 (1876 edn.); cf. P.R.O., RG 9/905; RG 11/1514.
73 O.R.O., MS. Oxf. Dioc. c 356, ff. 31–2.
74 Below, church; nonconf.; educ.
75 *Oxf. Chron.* 8 Nov. 1856.
76 Mins. of Aston Sch. Managers and Trustees 1871–1940 (in custody of vicar and par. officers), s.a. 1893.
77 *Aston and Cote, a Village Guide* (1989): copy in C.O.S.; above, Bampton and Weald, local govt. (public services).
78 Aston P.C.C. Mins. 1920–39 (in custody of vicar and par. officers), 8 Feb. 1938.
79 O.R.O., MS. Oxf. Dioc. c 1710, faculty for electric light.
80 *Kelly's Dir. Oxon.* (1939).
81 Mins. of Aston Sch. Managers 1964–85 (in custody of vicar and par. officers), p. 3.
82 Ibid.; O.S. Maps 6", SP 30 SW (1960 edn.); 1/2,500, SP 3402–3502, 3403–3503 (1972 edn.).

north of the Baptist Hall on Cote road in 1975,[83] and a new village hall, replacing an ex-army hut acquired originally by the British Legion, *c.* 1985.[84] In Cote there was some infilling from the 1960s, but most of the eastern side of Cote Lane remained unbuilt in 1995.

A disorderly alehouse in Aston was suppressed at the inhabitants' request in 1700.[85] In the mid 18th century there were 3 or 4 licensed ale-houses, among them the Red Lion, probably then, as later, on the south side of Aston square, and the Ball or Bull, not necessarily the later Bull on Bull Street.[86] From 1784 until the early 19th century the Red Lion only was recorded in Aston, and the Star, opened *c.* 1802 at the junction of High Street and Ham Lane, closed *c.* 1860 after the vicar acquired the site.[87] The later Bull existed by 1841, was rebuilt in 1865 probably by James Gibbons of Eynsham Brewery,[88] and closed *c.* 1992; the Red Lion remained open in 1995. In Cote the unidentified Black Horse was licensed from 1779 to 1801,[89] and a beerhouse recorded from 1869 closed after 1939.[90]

An Aston coal club established in 1859 was funded by subscription and from the township's share of the Bampton charities, and in the 1870s had over 100 members.[91] A Bampton-Aston blanket club established in 1850 continued in 1872, and was probably also financed wholly or partly from charitable income.[92] A library and reading room opened in 1860[93] was not mentioned later. A cricket club existed by 1869,[94] and in the 1870s and the early 20th century a 3-day annual fête in Aston included a pleasure fair in the square.[95]

Holywell field, on the south-eastern edge of the township, was so called by 1432. The 13th-century surname 'at well', and a 15th-century reference to open-field land lying 'towards the holy well' (*versus le holywelle*),[96] suggest that the spring from which it was named continued as a religious site throughout the later Middle Ages. If, like Bampton's Lady well, it was associated with the Virgin,[97] it may have lain near the later Mary headland on the Aston-Shifford boundary, close to the intersection of 'the way' mentioned in 1005 and of the modern Cote–Shifford road;[98] alternatively it may have been further north near Cote House, where Lady close (so called from

the 17th century) was taken possibly from Holywell field *c.* 1662.[99] No later references have been found, and the well's site had been lost perhaps by the 17th century.

In the 16th century inhabitants laying out a meadow in Aston were entitled to bread and a gallon of ale from those with rights there, and complex meadow customs persisted until inclosure.[1]

MANORS AND OTHER ESTATES. In the Anglo-Saxon period Aston and Cote formed part of Bampton manor. A part (later 4 yard-lands) belonged from the 10th century to Bampton minster's estate, later Bampton Deanery manor, and from the 12th to the 17th century 7 or 8 yardlands were attached to Shifford manor.[2] In 1238 Henry III granted £15-worth of land to Imbert Pugeys, increased to £30-worth in 1239[3] and known later as the manor of *ASTON BAMPTON, ASTON POGGES,* or *ASTON BOUGES.* Though chiefly in Aston and Cote it later included land in Weald, perhaps part of the original grant, or perhaps associated with ½ yardland acquired before 1275 from John Paulinus, son of the king's buyer, or with 40 a. acquired before 1279 from Miles of Hastings, lord of Yelford.[4] The manor was held of Bampton manor for a sword or 1*s.* 6*d.*, still paid annually in the 19th century.[5]

Imbert died probably by 1269 and was succeeded by his son Robert (d. probably by 1327), whose coheirs were his granddaughters Gilles, wife of John de Moleyns, Joan, wife of Bartholomew Galian, and Alice, wife of William de Langley.[6] Under an earlier settlement a third passed in dower to Alice, relict of Robert's son Thomas, who married Richard de Waleden and was living in 1353.[7] The other two thirds and the reversion were quitclaimed by the other coheirs to Joan and Bartholomew in 1328,[8] and by Thomas Galian and others to Gilles and John de Moleyns in 1353; a third of the two thirds was secured as dower by Elizabeth, relict of Robert Pugeys's son Peter, and her husband Nicholas del Spense, and in the 1330s William Golafre (d. 1358) acquired a life interest in the various portions and reversions.[9] In 1357 Moleyns was outlawed and his lands seized, but

83 *Witney Gaz.* 18 Nov. 1976.
84 Ibid. 26 Aug. 1976; local inf.
85 O.R.O., Cal. Q.S. iii, p. 363.
86 Ibid. QSD V/1–2; ibid. Acc. 2184, Red Lion deeds.
87 Ibid. QSD V/2–4; ibid. tithe award (1857), f. 7; letter 1 Oct. 1929 *re* acquisition of land for vic. ho. (copy in possession of Mr. P. E. Luckett, New Shifford Fm.); P.R.O., RG 9/905.
88 O.R.O., tithe award (1841), f. 84; ibid. Mor. XVIII/vi/2; datestone I.G.(?) 1865.
89 O.R.O., QSD V/2–4.
90 Courage Archive, Bristol, EK/E/4, p. 89; *P.O. Dir. Oxon.* (1869, 1877); *Kelly's Dir. Oxon.* (1883 and later edns.).
91 *Oxf. Jnl.* 4 June 1859; *Witney Express,* 5 Jan. 1871; *Home Visitor for Aston, Cogges and Ducklington* (June 1879), p. 2: copy in Bodl. Per. Oxon. 8° 578.
92 *Witney Express,* 5 Dec., 19 Dec. 1872; cf. Giles, *Hist. Bampton,* 92.
93 *Oxf. Chron.* 15 Dec. 1860.
94 *Witney Express,* 29 July 1869; *Home Visitor for Aston, Cogges and Ducklington* (June 1879), p. 2.
95 *Witney Express,* 18 July 1872; photo. *c.* 1910 in private

possession.
96 D. & C. Exeter, MSS. 2931, 4755; *Bampton Hund. R.* 23.
97 Above, Bampton and Weald, intro.
98 B.L. Add. MS. 31323 HHH; O.R.O., tithe map (1841), giving 'Merry headland'; above [roads].
99 O.R.O., tithe award and map (1841); P.R.O., C 78/2018.
1 O.R.O., Misc. WA I/1, f. 2; below, econ. hist.
2 *Bampton Hund. R.* 22–3; above, Bampton and Weald, manors; below, Shifford, manor.
3 *Cal. Chart. R.* 1226–57, 235–6, 246.
4 *Bampton Hund. R.* 21; *Rot. Hund.* (Rec. Com.), ii. 30; below, this section (Golofers).
5 *Cal. Chart. R.* 1226–57, 235, 246; Giles, *Hist. Bampton,* 107.
6 P.R.O., E 179/161/9, s.v. Bampton, listing Galian in 1327; *V.C.H. Bucks.* iii. 305; *Bampton Hund. R.* 21.
7 P.R.O., CP 25/1/189/14, no. 104; CP 25/1/190/18, no. 29; *Cal. Close,* 1349–54, 603.
8 P.R.O., CP 25/1/189/17, no. 13.
9 Ibid. CP 25/1/190/20, no. 68; CP 25/1/190/18, no. 29; *Cal. Close,* 1349–54, 603, 606; *V.C.H. Bucks.* iii. 305 n.; below, this section (Golofers).

in 1361 following his death Gilles recovered all but the two dower portions, and on her death in 1367 the apparently reunited manor passed to her son Sir William de Moleyns (d. 1381).[10]

Before 1378 all or part of the manor was settled on William's son Richard (d. 1384), whose son William (d. 1425) succeeded probably in 1399;[11] in 1417 he leased the manor for their lives to William and Elizabeth Wyot, with provision for his wife Margery.[12] The reversion passed to his son William, who died seised in 1429 leaving an infant daughter, Eleanor.[13] She married Sir Robert Hungerford, later Lord Hungerford and Lord Moleyns, who was attainted in 1461 and executed in 1464, and in 1472 Eleanor settled the manor on herself and her second husband Sir Oliver Maningham, with remainder to their executors for seven years and to her granddaughter Mary, later *suo jure* Baroness Botreaux.[14] Eleanor died after 1487[15] and Oliver in 1499, and on or before Mary's death c. 1533 the manor passed to her son George Hastings, earl of Huntingdon, who with his son Francis sold it in 1537 to Roland (later Sir Roland) Hill, a London mercer.[16]

In 1553 Hill sold the manor to Alan Horde of the Middle Temple.[17] Horde died in 1554 leaving it in dower to his relict Dorothy, who in 1566 held it with her second husband Sir Laurence Taylor of Diddington (Hunts.).[18] On her death in 1577 the manor passed under an earlier settlement to her son Alan Horde (d. 1603) of Ewell (Surrey) and Hoards Park (Salop.), who in 1583 granted a 2,000-year lease to his brother Thomas;[19] two thirds were later seized by the Crown following Thomas's non-payment of fines for recusancy,[20] but on his death c. 1607 outstanding debts were pardoned and the reunited manor passed successively to his nephews Alan (d. 1609) and Thomas Horde (d. 1662), later Sir Thomas.[21] In 1657 Thomas settled the manor on his son Thomas,[22] later M.P. for Oxfordshire, who in 1685 was briefly imprisoned in Oxford castle for suspected complicity in

Monmouth's rebellion and who in 1709 granted an annual rent charge of £24 from the manor for the benefit of poor prisoners there.[23] The manor passed on Thomas's death in 1715 to his son Alan, sheriff of Oxfordshire in 1724,[24] and apparently before 1721 to Thomas's grandson Giles Palmer (d. 1734) of Compton Scorpion in Ilmington (Warws.), who took the surname of Horde.[25] From him it passed to Thomas Horde (d. 1785) of Cote and later of Lower Swell (Glos.), sheriff of Oxfordshire in 1747 and 1753, and to Thomas's granddaughter Caroline Horde (d. 1836), who bequeathed it to the Revd. Henry Hippisley (d. 1838);[26] it then passed to Henry's son Henry, of Lambourn Place (Berks.), and to Captain (later Col.) William Henry Hippisley, whose trustees sold the estate (1,191 a. in Aston and Cote) with the manorial quitrents in 1920, most farms being bought by their tenants.[27] The 'lordship' was sold twice in the early 1980s, but with no land or exercisable rights.[28]

Henry III granted a messuage and building plot to Imbert Pugeys in 1238,[29] and there was a manor house presumably by 1279 when land was in demesne.[30] Robert Pugeys witnessed a document at Lew in 1303,[31] but no later medieval owners or lessees are known to have resided and in 1418 the manorial dovecot was ruinous.[32] The medieval buildings stood probably on the site of Cote House, the manor house by the 17th century:[33] a reset medieval window head survives in the house's east wall, and fragments possibly of a medieval moat or fishpond to the west. The surviving house,[34] of coursed limestone rubble with ashlar dressings and gabled stone-slated roofs, comprises a hall range with end wings projecting northwards, and a low, 20th-century service range to the east, and is two-storeyed with attics; in 1665 it was taxed on 11 hearths.[35] The east wing, of the mid 16th century, was built presumably for one of the Hordes, though none are known to have lived there before the 17th century. It is low-ceilinged and gabled, with large windows which are inappropriate for its

[10] *Complete Peerage*, ix. 39; *Cal. Close*, 1360–4, 192; 1364–8, 405–6. A partial restoration of Moleyns's lands to Sir Wm. in 1359 excluded Aston: *Cal. Close*, 1354–60, 564.

[11] *Cal. Pat.* 1377–81, 251; *Cal. Fine R.* 1391–99, 230, 237; *Complete Peerage*, ix. 41.

[12] *Cal. Close*, 1413–19, 437, 442.

[13] P.R.O., C 139/17, no. 29; C 139/45, no. 38. For Wm.'s relict's dower, ibid. SC 6/761, no. 3.

[14] *Complete Peerage*, ix. 41–3; vi. 618–22; *Cal. Close*, 1454–61, 451–2; Hist. MSS. Com. 78, *Hastings*, i, p. 303.

[15] P.R.O., SC 2/155/9; cf. *Complete Peerage*, vi. 621, wrongly suggesting that Eleanor d. 1476.

[16] *Complete Peerage*, vi. 621–4; *Topographer and Genealogist*, ii (1853), 517–19. Mary had possession of all or part by 1497, and George by June 1532: *Dom. Incl.* i. 369–70; Hist. MSS. Com. 78, *Hastings*, i, pp. 309–10.

[17] Bodl. MS. Top. Oxon. b 169, f. 25; *Topog. and Geneal.* i. 36, 39; ii. 519, calling him citizen and mercer of London.

[18] P.R.O., PROB 11/37, ff. 53v.–54; ibid. REQ 2/21/29.

[19] O.R.O., Misc. Mar. I/19, I/146; P.R.O., C 142/304, no. 28; *V.C.H. Surrey*, iii. 282.

[20] *Recusant Roll*, 1592–3 (Catholic Rec. Soc. xviii), 254; 1593–4 (Catholic Rec. Soc. lvii), 123.

[21] O.R.O., Misc. Mar. I/20, I/146; *Chanc. Pat. R.* 3–5 *Jas. I* (L. & I. Soc. 98), ff. 327, 333; P.R.O., C 142/323, no. 58; for genealogy, *Topog. and Geneal.* i (1846), 36.

[22] P.R.O., C 3/448/71.

[23] W. R. Williams, *Parl. Hist. Oxon.* (1899), 65, citing an earlier deed; Bodl. MS. Top. Oxon. c 290, ff. 44–5; *Wood's*

Life, iii. 145. A tradition that one of the Hordes was imprisoned for refusing James I or Charles I entry to the manor ho. is without foundation.

[24] P.R.O., PROB 11/551, ff. 249–61; O.R.O., Misc. Mar. I/42–3; C. Peters, *Lord Lieutenants Oxon.* 146–7.

[25] P.R.O., PROB 11/551, f. 251v.; Bodl. MSS. Ch. Oxon. 2429, 3560–1, 3801–3; *V.C.H. Warws.* v. 100.

[26] Bodl. MSS. Ch. Oxon. 3805–6; O.R.O., MS. Oxf. Dioc. c 2165, no. 5 (cert. of title 1839); Peters, *Lord Lieutenants Oxon.* 148, 151.

[27] O.R.O., MS. Oxf. Dioc. c 2165, no. 5; *Kelly's Dir. Oxon.* (1883 and later edns.); *Sale Cat.* (1920): copy in Bodl. G.A. Oxon. b 92*/1.

[28] *Sunday Telegraph*, 22 Sept. 1982; corresp. with V.C.H. and O.R.O.

[29] *Close R.* 1237–42, 102, locating the plot (like the rest of the land) in 'Bampton'.

[30] *Bampton Hund. R.* 21.

[31] Exeter Coll. Mun., M.II.1.

[32] Below, econ. hist. A house, dovecot, and fishpond held with part of the manor in 1358, below, this section (Golofers).

[33] Giles, *Hist. Bampton*, Suppl. pp. 8–9; P.R.O., PROB 11/551, f. 250v.; O.R.O., tithe awards.

[34] Below, plate 14; cf. Bodl. MS. Top. Oxon. c 6, p. 41; *Country Life*, xv (1904), 567–9; xcix (1946), 1176–9; Pevsner, *Oxon.* 558; *Sale Cat., Aston and Cote Estate* (1920): copy in Bodl. G.A. Oxon. b 92*/1; Giles, *Hist. Bampton*, 84–5.

[35] *Hearth Tax Oxon.* 210.

use as a kitchen or service area, and originated perhaps as a free-standing house or as a parlour wing for an earlier hall. The hall range and west wing were built probably for Thomas Horde (d. c. 1607) after 1583 or for Sir Thomas Horde (d. 1662), who at first let the house with part of the demesne, but who resided from c. 1630.[36] The main entrance was then by a cross passage at the hall's east end, implying that the east wing was to be used as service rooms, and there was a stair turret at the end of the passage. Scars on the turret's east side suggest that the new south front may formerly have extended further eastwards. About 1700 a new main entrance was made in the centre of the north front, presumably for Thomas Horde (d. 1715), and the principal rooms were refurbished.

After Thomas Horde (d. 1785) moved to Lower Swell (Glos.) in the early 1760s[37] the house was let to tenant farmers,[38] and c. 1843 Henry Hippisley removed some of the furnishings to his new house at Lambourn Place (Berks.);[39] surviving interior decoration includes some 17th-century panelling, an early 17th-century open-well staircase in the west wing, and early 17th-century fireplaces with moulded stone surrounds in the west wing and hall. The building ceased to be a farmhouse after 1922, and was renovated several times during the 20th century. Its unhealthy position, surrounded by low-lying land liable to flooding, was commented on in 1627, and in 1670 prompted Thomas Horde to inclose some of the land adjoining; the grounds then included an orchard lying next to Cote moor.[40] A formal courtyard was laid out in front of the house perhaps c. 1704, the date of scrolled wrought-iron gates bearing Thomas Horde's initials, and a garden canal was made to the north-west perhaps re-using part of an earlier moat or fishpond.

The submanor of GOLOFERS or GUL-LIVERS originated in William Golafre's acquisition before 1339 of a life interest in two thirds of two thirds of Aston manor, which on his death in 1358 included a chief house, dovecot and fishpond (worth nothing), 15 tenant yardlands and over 200 a. of demesne, and pleas and perquisites of the court.[41] In 1359 the estate was given to John Laundels in custody, and from 1361 was reunited with Aston Pogges,[42] though in the 16th century it was often still mentioned as a separate manor.[43] In 1608 Golofer's or Gulliver's farm (4–5 yardlands), mostly or wholly in Bampton and Weald, was let to Sir Laurence Tanfield, chief baron of the Exchequer,[44] and was consistently called a farm thereafter;[45] it remained part of Aston manor in 1870 but was sold separately from the main estate presumably in the early 20th century.[46] The house for the farm, called a 'capital messuage' in 1765 but not necessarily the site of Golafre's house,[47] was that in Weald later called Knapps Farm, south of Bridge Street.[48] It comprises a long range of limestone rubble, aligned east–west and not quite parallel to the street, and in 1662 was taxed on 2 hearths.[49] The thatched eastern end, now one storey with an attic, retains 3 bays of a soot-encrusted, formerly open timber roof and evidence of timber framing,[50] but the building is not of high status and may be no earlier than the late 16th century. The house appears to have been enlarged westwards in two stages; interior fittings are of the 18th century and earlier 19th, though the structure is probably earlier.

An estate of 3 yardlands in Aston or Cote and 4 in Lew, perhaps connected with 6 *cassati* at Aston, Lew, and Brighthampton granted to Aelfwine the king's *scriptor* in 984,[51] was held in 1066 by Alwin and in 1086 by Aretius the king's minister; before 1198 it passed to Robert the forester of Liddington through his wife Denise. The land in Aston was held by the serjeanty or service of providing for 40 days a man equipped with helmet, lance, and body armour or (later) with bows and arrows, and that in Lew by serjeanty of carrying a falcon before the king or of mewing or guarding a lanner falcon.[52] Claims to the Aston lands in 1203 and 1232 by Avinia, wife of Henry of Abingdon, evidently failed,[53] and from Robert, possibly the Robert of Yelford who held it in 1236, the estate passed to presumably another Robert of Yelford (d. 1293), and to his son (d. 1328) and grandson, also called Robert. Before 1367 the youngest Robert granted the Aston land and one yardland in Lew to Edmund of Yelford for life.[54] Two or more yardlands in Aston and Cote and 1½ in Lew were held with Yelford Walwyn manor in 1546 but had apparently become detached by the mid 17th century, and the estate has not been traced further.[55]

Richard Cosin (d. 1596), a prominent civil lawyer, accumulated 5½ yardlands in Aston and Cote in the late 16th century, held reportedly of

36 O.R.O., Misc. Mar. I/22–3; Berks. R.O., D/ELl T33A; *Acts of P.C.* 1627–8, 109–10.
37 Bodl. MS. Ch. Oxon. 2429; O.R.O., Welch XVIII/1–2; *V.C.H. Glos.* vi. 167.
38 Below, econ. hist.
39 Giles, *Hist. Bampton*, 84–5; *V.C.H. Berks.* iv. 252.
40 P.R.O., C 78/2018; *Acts of P.C.* 1627–8, 109–10.
41 P.R.O., CP 25/1/190/18, no. 29; ibid. C 135/139, no. 13; above, this section (Aston Pogges).
42 *Cal. Fine R.* 1356–68, 90; above.
43 e.g. *L. & P. Hen. VIII*, v, p. 582; *Topographer and Genealogist*, ii. 517–19; P.R.O., REQ 2/21/29; O.R.O., Misc. Mar. I/19–20; below, local govt.
44 Bodl. MS. Ch. Oxon. 2424; O.R.O., Misc. Mar. I/23.
45 P.R.O., PROB 11/551, f. 250v.; O.R.O., Welch XVIII/1; ibid. QSD L.22.
46 O.R.O., Crowdy I/51, town plan; *Sale Cat., Knapps*

fm. (1941): copy in ibid. Adkin II/3.
47 O.R.O., Welch XVIII/1; Golafre may have held the man. ho. in Cote.
48 O.R.O., Bampton incl. award, no. 888; ibid. QSD. L. 22; Jesus Coll. Mun., box 15, list 2, cottage lease 7 Aug. 1772, mentioning lane adjoining Gullivers.
49 P.R.O., E 179/255/4, pt. i, f. 19.
50 *S. Midlands Arch.* xxii (1992), 57 sqq., 62.
51 *Early Chart. of Thames Valley*, ed. M. Gelling, no. 282.
52 *V.C.H. Oxon.* i. 387, 423; *Bk. of Fees*, i. 11, 251, 589; ii. 830; *Cur. Reg. R.* iii. 77; *Bampton Hund. R.* 22, 24.
53 *Cur. Reg. R.* iii. 77; iv. 47, 54; xiv, p. 494; xv, p. 53.
54 *Bk. of Fees*, i. 589; *Cal. Inq. p.m.* iii, p. 65; vii, p. 113; Giles, *Hist. Bampton*, 139–40; *Cal. Pat.* 1367–70, 9.
55 P.R.O., C 142/75, no. 42; B.L. Add. Ch. 38961; O.R.O., Misc. WA I/1, ff. 5–6v. Part may have been acquired by Ric. Cosin: below.

the Crown for knight service.[56] Part, including a share in a mansion house in Cote, passed to his half-brother Roger Medhopp (d. 1605) of Aston and later of Cote, who in 1585 had bought 3½ yardlands and a house there from William Pates of Cheltenham.[57] From Roger the estate passed to his son Henry (d. 1647) and grandson Thomas (d. 1674), taxed on 5 hearths in 1662.[58] Thereafter piecemeal sales reduced the estate, and neither it nor the family were mentioned after the later 17th century.[59] Another part of Cosin's estate (1⅙ yardland) was acquired apparently from his cousin Ann Waterhouse by Sir Laurence Tanfield (d. 1625), whose grandson Sir Lucius Cary conveyed it to Thomas Horde in 1630.[60]

The name Aston Riche or Rithe was recorded intermittently from the late 14th century, but no landholders called Riche have been traced, and by the late 15th century some or all of the land was attached to a freehold formerly belonging to the Laundels family of Bampton.[61]

ECONOMIC HISTORY. Aston and Cote shared a field system apparently by 1239, when demesne granted with the manor included 55 a. in North field, 64 a. in South field, and 24 a. in East field.[62] A holding in 1432 was fairly evenly divided between North (later Claywell) field in the north-west, Kingsway field north of Aston hamlet, Windmill field east of Cote, and Holywell field in the south-east.[63] The smaller Garsons or Gastons, which lay east of Aston hamlet and whose name suggests an intake from common pasture, was mentioned in 1417,[64] and Ham field, south of Aston, from the 17th century.[65] Nearly all of the fields lay on the river gravels.[66]

Extensive meadows adjoined the Thames and its tributaries.[67] Demesne meadow in 1238 and 1239 included 25½ a. in North mead, eight hams, and three 'islands', of which some, notably Rowney and Queenborough, lay in Bampton or Weald and descended later with Golofers farm.[68] Aston Inmead, presumably also former demesne, lay in the south by the river.[69] By the 17th century and probably the mid 16th Inmead, Outmead, and Bossengey near the Chimney

boundary, together c. 450 a., were common lot meadows and so remained until inclosure,[70] and in the 19th century and presumably earlier some inhabitants had additional rights in Shilton's neighbouring lot meadow.[71] There was little several meadow other than in small closes in the hamlets, though by the 17th century and probably from the Middle Ages the Sixteens disposed of a few small, scattered hams mostly assigned to town officers, and there were isolated strips of meadow in the common fields.[72]

In the 19th century and presumably earlier the lot meadows were divided into 13 (perhaps formerly 16) 'layings out', each comprising 4 'sets' of varying quality. There were 16 named lots, originally one for each ploughland, though by the 17th century some lots were shared by up to 10 tenants and many inhabitants held shares in more than one lot. Each tenant kept a piece of wood inscribed with a mark representing his lot, used in the draw at a time fixed by the Sixteens and grass stewards; the first draw bestowed rights in the first set of the laying out, and the second in the second set, though in the 18th and 19th centuries informal exchanges were common.[73] The standard allotment per yardland seems to have been 7–8 a., though in the 17th century Bampton Deanery tenants had less, and in the 18th century there was much variation.[74] In 1593 tenants with mowing but not feeding rights were to remove their hay by Lammas eve (31 July), or leave it for the inhabitants' cattle.[75]

Demesne in 1238–9 included a third of an ox pasture called 'Hamm', a third of a cow pasture called Roughmead, and a third of a pasture for 200 sheep.[76] In the 17th century and the 19th the 'large and rich commons' exceeded 850 a., mostly occupying a swathe of alluvium running between the hamlets from the meadows to the north-east boundary.[77] In 1657 and later the central common was divided into a sheep common (c. 130 a.) on the north, called Sheep Marsh or Aston common, and a cow common (including Chimney Lake and Cote moor or common) on the south.[78] Other commons mentioned from the 17th century included Aston mead and Oatlands (c. 227 a.), perhaps partly former arable, Shaw Brook and Mill Ford (c. 152 a.) south of Great brook, Long hams (4 a.), and West

56 P.R.O., C 142/270, no. 104; ibid. PROB 11/90, f. 424 and v.; D.N.B., giving date of death as 1597.
57 P.R.O., PROB 11/90, ff. 423–8; PROB 11/107, ff. 282–3; ibid. REQ 2/253/13; O.R.O., Mor. XIV/i/1; cf. ibid. Misc. Mar. I/12–15.
58 P.R.O., PROB 11/107, ff. 282–3; ibid. E 179/255/4, pt. i, f. 18; O.R.O., MSS. Wills Oxon. 44/3/23, 45/2/1.
59 O.R.O., Misc. Mar. I/27; Bodl. MSS. Ch. Oxon. 3775, 3783; cf. O.R.O., Misc. Mar. I/32, 37.
60 P.R.O., C 142/270, no. 104; ibid. C 60/451, no. 25; O.R.O., Misc. Mar. I/21; ibid. Mor. XIV/i/1; Berks. R.O., D/ELl T33A.
61 P.R.O., C 140/19, no. 20; Eynsham Cart. ii, p. 147; Cal. Pat. 1557–8, 86; above, Bampton and Weald, other estates; cf. P.N. Oxon. (E.P.N.S.), ii. 302.
62 Cal. Chart. R. 1226–57, p. 246.
63 D. & C. Exeter, MS. 4755; cf. O.R.O., tithe award (1841).
64 D. & C. Exeter, MSS. 5100–1, s.v. venditio garbarum; cf. English Place Name Elements (E.P.N.S.), i. 191; Bampton Hund. R. 21 (Maud de la Garstone).
65 O.R.O., Mor. XIV/i/1.
66 Ibid. tithe award (1841); Geol. Surv. Map 1/50,000, solid and drift, sheet 236 (1982 edn.).
67 O.R.O., tithe award (1841).
68 Cal. Chart. R. 1226–57, pp. 235, 246; O.R.O., Misc. Mar. I/146; above, manors (Golofers).
69 O.R.O., tithe award and map (1841); D. & C. Exeter, MS. M 1.
70 O.R.O., tithe award (1841); Cal. Pat. 1557–8, 86; Giles, Hist. Bampton, Suppl. pp. 3, 7; Archaeologia, xxxv. 471.
71 O.R.O., Shilton tithe award (1841).
72 Ibid. Misc. WA I/1, f. 7; ibid. tithe award (1841); for the Sixteens, below, local govt.
73 O.R.O., Misc. WA I/1, ff. 3v.–4; Giles, Hist. Bampton, 78–80.
74 'Bk. relating to Tythes' [1838] (in custody of vicar and par. officers of Bampton); Berks. R.O., D/EWe E3, pp. 11–21 [of 2nd pagination]; D. & C. Exeter, MSS. 2934, 6016/6; ibid. Ch. Comm. 13/74363.
75 O.R.O., Misc. WA I/1, f. 2.
76 Cal. Chart. R. 1226–57, pp. 235, 246.
77 Giles, Hist. Bampton, Suppl. pp. 3, 11; O.R.O., tithe award (1841), f. 90; above, Bampton, general intro.
78 Giles, Hist. Bampton, 75, Suppl. p. 11; B.L. Add. MS. 31323 HHH.

moor (*c.* 61 a.), partitioned between Aston and Bampton by the 17th century and presumably shared earlier.[79] Truelands (21 a.) further north, probably also partitioned at an early date[80] and possibly reduced by medieval assarting,[81] was mentioned in the 15th century;[82] in 1740 it was reserved for sheep, but in 1841 it was common meadow.[83] A few leys, providing additional grassland, were listed in 1657.[84] In the 17th century Cote moor, Shaw Brook, and Mill Ford were hained from 1 March to 3 May, and West moor and Aston mead from 25 March until broken by order, usually in April. Inmead and Outmead were commonable for cattle and sheep from 1 August to 25 March.[85] The stint per yardland, traditionally 12 cattle (or 6 horses) and 40 sheep but regulated annually by the Sixteens, varied from 8 cows and 16 sheep in 1779 and 1848 to the full allowance in 1754; in 1657 there were reckoned to be 818 cow and 2,560 sheep commons in all, some held with cottages or without land, and more were actually being stocked.[86]

In 1497 Mary, Lady Hastings and Botreaux, demolished a tenant's house in Cote and converted its 20-a. holding to pasture,[87] and in the 1660s Thomas Horde attempted to promote a general inclosure of the township with the aim of improving the land for cattle and sheep, converting low-lying arable to pasture or meadow, and reducing flooding. Under an agreement of 1662 financial aid was promised to tenants who inclosed, and provision was made for exchanges, abatement of commons, and arbitration; Horde subsequently inclosed *c.* 120 a. near Cote House, taken mostly from Holywell field and Cote moor, and abated 240 sheep commons, but despite consensus that inclosure was in the general interest few tenants or freeholders inclosed more than 2 or 3 a., and no further inclosure was recorded until the 1850s.[88] Flooding of meadows in particular, mentioned in the 15th century,[89] remained a problem, and drainage channels dug to protect them in 1668 were paid for by a levy on all landholders.[90]

A half yardland in 1432 included 11¼ a. of arable,[91] but yardlands in 1668 were reckoned apparently at 30 a., and the theoretical division of the township into 64 yardlands suggests a statute measure of *c.* 26 a. excluding meadow.[92]

Most recorded yardlands contained up to 32 a. of arable,[93] though in the 17th and 18th centuries some on Bampton Deanery and the former Shifford manor included 20 a. or less.[94]

Aston and Cote were not entered separately in Domesday Book.[95] Forty-four villeins in 1279 held yardlands, 5 held half yardlands, another 6 shared yardlands presumably following recent divisions, and one held 2 yardlands. Of those, 44, mostly yardlanders, held of Aston manor, and the rest of Bampton Deanery manor (4 yardlanders) and Eynsham abbey's Shifford manor.[96] No cottagers were mentioned, though one was recorded at different times on each of the manors,[97] and in 1328 there were 3 cottagers and 5 otherwise unrecorded villeins on Robert of Yelford's estate.[98] Eight and a half freehold yardlands were recorded, 3 kept in demesne by Robert of Yelford and 2 by Eynsham abbey; 2 others were held of the abbey, and 1½ was sublet by its lay owner. On Aston manor 2 ploughlands were in demesne, and since some land attached to the manor lay in Bampton and Weald the township probably then, as later, totalled 64 yardlands.[99] In the early 14th century lay taxpayers' average personalty was generally lower than in Bampton's other outlying townships; individual payments in 1316 ranged from 9*d.* on goods worth 12*s.* to 15*s.* 9*d.* on goods worth over £12, apparently from the villein tenant of 2 yardlands, and Aston manor's demesne was taxed on goods worth over £5. Most villein yardlanders seem to have been taxed on between *c.* 48*s.* and 80*s.*,[1] and one cottager on Bampton Deanery manor was taxed apparently on 40*s.*[2]

Labour services in 1279 seem, like rents, to have been heaviest on Bampton Deanery manor, on which, as in Bampton, they were valued at 10*s.* 2½*d.* for a yardlander. On Eynsham abbey's manor rents per yardland in Aston were 4*s.* and services were valued at under 5*s.*, and in Cote 2 tenants of Aston manor and all 4 abbey tenants held for rents only.[3] Services on Bampton Deanery manor in 1317 remained broadly similar to those on the manor in Bampton, though aid was reportedly charged at 5*s.* per yardland.[4] On Eynsham abbey's manor *c.* 1360 most yardlanders owed 2 days' harrowing, 1 day's ploughing, 1 day's weeding, 6 days' mowing and hay-lifting, 3 days' carting, and 3 bedrips, besides 5*s.* rent,

79 O.R.O., Misc. WA I/1, ff. 7v., 9, 139v.; ibid. tithe award (1841); Giles, *Hist. Bampton*, Suppl. p. 11, reading Outlands.

80 Above, Bampton and Weald, intro. [boundaries].

81 e.g. O.R.O., tithe map (1841), showing Westbreach furlong to the north.

82 Bodl. MS. d.d. Harcourt c 126/14, ct. 12 Oct. 2 Hen. IV; *Eynsham Cart.* ii, p. lxxxi.

83 O.R.O., Misc. WA I/1, f. 33; ibid. tithe award (1841), f. 90; cf. ibid. Misc. BRA XIV/ii/1.

84 Giles, *Hist. Bampton*, Suppl. pp. 3, 7.

85 O.R.O., Misc. WA I/1, ff. 7v., 24v., 28v., 40v., 54.

86 Ibid. ff. 5–6v. and *passim*; Giles, *Hist. Bampton*, 77.

87 *Dom. of Incl.* ed. I. S. Leadam, i. 369–70.

88 Giles, *Hist. Bampton*, Suppl. pp. 7–11, implying that Moor close was inclosed by 1657; P.R.O., C 78/2018; D. & C. Exeter, MSS. 1983, 2033–4; below, this section.

89 D. & C. Exeter, MS. 5104, s.v. *venditio feni*.

90 O.R.O., Misc. WA I/1, ff. 78, 119; cf. ibid. ff. 8, 99; *Oxf. Jnl.* 25 Jan. 1834 (incl. meeting, nos. 6–7).

91 D. & C. Exeter, MS. 4755.

92 O.R.O., Misc. WA I/1, [f. v], f. 6v.; ibid. tithe award

(1841); cf. O.S. *Area Bk.* (1877).

93 e.g. Bodl. MSS. Ch. Oxon. 3561–2, 3792, 4301; *Gent. Mag.* N.S. xxxii. 592; *Cal. Pat.* 1557–8, 86; *Archaeologia*, xxxiii. 270–1.

94 D. & C. Exeter, MSS. 2934, 6016/6; Berks. R.O., D/EWe E3, pp. 11–21 [of 2nd pagination].

95 For Domesday estates including land in Aston, above Bampton and Weald, econ. hist. (agric.).

96 *Bampton Hund. R.* 21–3. Rob. of Haddon's and Emma Lovel's entries seem to belong elsewhere: cf. *Eynsham Cart.* ii, pp. 12, 14, s.v. East Weald; *Rot. Hund.* (Rec. Com.), ii. 30.

97 *Cal. Chart. R.* 1226–57, 235, 246; *Eynsham Cart.* ii, p. 12; D. & C. Exeter, MS. 2931.

98 Giles, *Hist. Bampton*, 135–6, misdated to 1329.

99 Ibid. Suppl. p. 1; *Bampton Hund. R.* 21–3; above, manors (Golofers).

1 P.R.O., E 179/161/8–10; cf. *Bampton Hund. R.* 21–3.

2 John Aumfray: cf. D. & C. Exeter, MS. 2931.

3 *Bampton Hund. R.* 21–3.

4 D. & C. Exeter, MS. 2931; cf. above, Bampton and Weald, econ. hist. (agric.).

2 capons at Christmas, and aid, heriot, and toll of beer; the 2-yardland holding, from which ½ yardland had become detached and which was not explicitly called villein land, owed similar services besides 11s. rent, 9d. fishsilver, and the task of discharging the abbot's obligations to the hundred and county courts.[5] One abbey tenant had by then compounded his services for 12s. rent, and services and aid were fully commuted c. 1385–6, earlier than on the same manor in Shifford;[6] on Bampton Deanery manor services were commuted by 1416–17.[7] Tenants of Aston Pogges manor were said in 1378 to be in open revolt, refusing services, taking oaths of resistance, and holding daily assemblies, and the justices were empowered to imprison those indicted.[8] Though the revolt was presumably crushed all or part of the demesne was let by 1440–2 and possibly by 1417–18, when the manorial dovecot was ruinous.[9]

Assized rents continued to rise in the late 14th century but were falling by the early 15th on Eynsham abbey's manor.[10] Entry fines too fell sharply,[11] and individual rent reductions were recorded on both ecclesiastical manors, perhaps reflecting long-term difficulties.[12] Until the earlier 15th century or later holdings seem to have remained fairly stable,[13] but by the 17th century farms of ½ or ¼ yardland and of 2 yardlands or more were common, some larger ones incorporating freehold, copyhold, and leasehold under more than one owner. There were then c. 25 cottages, some held and presumably sublet by tenants of larger holdings.[14]

In the 16th and 17th centuries Aston and Cote's prosperity and social structure seems to have been broadly similar to that of neighbouring townships,[15] despite an unusual preponderance of houses (over 70 per cent) taxed in the mid 17th century on one hearth only.[16] As elsewhere in the parish there were some moderately prosperous yeomen. Between 1678 and 1728 five of the Williamses, a family reputedly of Welsh immigrants settled in Cote by the 15th century, left personalty valued at over £100, and two of them personalty of over £300,[17] while Mark Brickland (d. 1680), tenant of 2 yardlands under the Hordes, and Tompson Hanks (d.

1680), a freeholder and tenant of 2½ yardlands under Exeter cathedral, were sometimes called gentlemen. Brickland left personalty worth £528 including a lease (£200), money owed him (£150), and plate (£18),[18] and other notable farmers included members of the Newman, Young, Ricketts, Sparrowhawk, Frime, and Bartlett families. By contrast 6 inhabitants were exonerated from hearth tax in 1665 through poverty, among them a cottager who, excluding his lease, left personalty worth only £12, and in 1604 an Aston inhabitant left goods worth £6.[19]

Farming was mixed, the chief crops being wheat, barley, and pulse, beans, or peas, though oats, maslin, rye, sainfoin, and hops were also mentioned.[20] Cattle, some for dairying, and sheep were recorded frequently, usually in small numbers, though Henry Medhopp (d. 1647) had 11 milch beasts and 160 sheep, and a Cote farmer in 1714 had 178 sheep. Humphrey Linsey (d. 1728) of Cote, whose personalty was valued at over £300 including leases, left sheep and wool together worth £75 and cattle worth £18, besides £61-worth of corn and hay. Cheese was mentioned frequently, and poultry, pigs, and bees were kept.[21] A 3-course rotation was followed perhaps in 1358[22] and certainly in the mid 17th century,[23] but in 1678 a 4-course system was adopted, Garsons being grouped with Claywell field, and the Ham with Holywell field. In 1742 the sequence was (1) wheat or barley, (2) beans or peas, (3) barley, (4) fallow, but the order of rotation and combination of fields were altered frequently during the 18th century, and in 1769 it was decided to combine Claywell and Holywell fields and to re-adopt a 3-course rotation, with the Ham and Garsons cropped separately.[24] The fields were again reordered in 1770 and a 4-course system persisted in 1848, when Windmill and Holywell fields apparently formed a single Cote field.[25]

Most tenements formerly belonging to Shifford manor were converted to freehold by Edward Yate (d. 1645) or his son Sir John (d. c. 1658),[26] though four, totalling 2¾ yardlands, remained lifehold in 1748.[27] On Aston manor a few farms were held at rack rent by the 1660s, and 99-year lifehold leases renewable for large

5 *Eynsham Cart.* ii, pp. 11–15; *Bampton Hund. R.* 22; cf. Giles, *Hist. Bampton*, 135–6.
6 *Eynsham Cart.* ii, p. 11; B.L. Harl. Rolls L.1, L.2.
7 D. & C. Exeter, MS. 5100.
8 *Cal. Pat.* 1377–81, p. 251.
9 P.R.O., SC 6/761, no. 3; D. & C. Exeter, MS. 5101, s.v. *venditio agnorum.*
10 Bodl. MSS. d.d. Harcourt c 128/3–4; B.L. Harl. Rolls K.41, L.1, L.3–7; cf. D. & C. Exeter, MS. 5100, s.v. *venditio operum.*
11 e.g. B.L. Harl. Roll L.8, s.v. Stevens's; cf. *Eynsham Cart.* ii, p. 11.
12 e.g. B.L. Harl. Roll G.2; D. & C. Exeter, MS. 4753, ct. 10 Dec. 6 Hen. VI; cf. above, Bampton and Weald, econ. hist. (agric.); below, Chimney, econ. hist.; Shifford, econ. hist.
13 *Bampton Hund. R.* 21–3; *Eynsham Cart.* ii, pp. 11–12; Bodl. MSS. d.d. Harcourt c 126/14–16; B.L. Harl. Rolls L.8–9; D. & C. Exeter, MSS. 2931, 4751–73.
14 O.R.O., Misc. WA I/1, ff. 5–6v.; cf. Giles, *Hist. Bampton*, Suppl. p. 3.
15 P.R.O., E 179/161/172, E 179/162/234, E 179/162/320, E 179/162/341; O.R.O., MSS. Wills Oxon., Aston and Cote wills and inventories; *Hearth Tax Oxon.* 210–11.

16 P.R.O., E 179/255/4, pt. i, f. 18.
17 O.R.O., MSS. Wills Oxon. 73/2/32, 74/1/14, 88/3/6, 300/6/49, 300/6/53; cf. ibid. Misc. WA I/1, ff. 5, 6v.; B. Williams, *Mems. of the Fam. of Williams* (priv. print. 1849).
18 O.R.O., MSS. Wills Oxon. 7/2/2, 34/1/25; ibid. Misc. WA I/1, ff. 2v., 5v.–6; Giles, *Hist. Bampton*, Suppl. p. 10.
19 *Hearth Tax Oxon.* 211; O.R.O., MSS. Wills Oxon. 2/1/27, 4/1/10.
20 For rarer crops, O.R.O., MSS. Wills Oxon. 11/4/9, 30/1/26, 34/1/25; *Gent. Mag* N.S. xxxii. 593.
21 O.R.O., MSS. Wills Oxon. 44/3/23, 133/4/41, 169/5/11; ibid. Aston and Cote wills and inventories, *passim*; *Gent. Mag.* N.S. xxxii. 592–4.
22 P.R.O., C 135/139, no. 13, describing Wm. Golafre's demesne, possibly in Bampton: above, manors (Golofers).
23 *Gent. Mag.* N.S. xxxii. 594.
24 O.R.O., Misc. WA I/1, ff. 36v., 42, 61v., 64, 103v.
25 Ibid. f. 65v.; ibid. tithe award (1841); Giles, *Hist. Bampton*, 75; D. & C. Exeter, MS. 6016/7, bdle. 1, sketch map 1844.
26 Giles, *Hist. Bampton*, Suppl. pp. 1, 4–5, naming Sir John; the implied date of c. 1637 suggests Edward.
27 Berks. R.O., D/EWe E3, pp. 11–21 [of 2nd pagination]; cf. O.R.O., Misc WA I/1, ff. 5–6v.

entry fines gradually superseded copyhold during the late 17th century and early 18th; they remained common in the 1770s, when most tenants still owed suit of court and payments in lieu of heriot and poultry.[28] Some larger leasehold farms emerged during the later 18th century, notably 5½ yardlands kept in demesne with Cote House for much of the 17th century and earlier 18th, but let with the house to the Townsend family probably from the 1760s.[29] In 1841 the farm comprised c. 230 a. including over 100 a. of old inclosure, but only three other farms then exceeded 100 a., and many remained under 30 a., a reflection chiefly of the continuance of open-field agriculture.[30] Though some farms incorporated freeholds most larger ones were still amalgamations under various owners, and there were no substantial owner-occupiers.[31]

Plans possibly to inclose Aston and Cote with Bampton[32] were abandoned, and a proposal in 1834, supported by tenants and initially by Caroline Horde, met with hostility from most proprietors.[33] An Act was finally obtained in 1852, and inclosure commenced the following year; the award was sealed in 1855.[34] Henry Hippisley received 1,715 a. (including 86 a. leased for lives and 16 a. of old inclosure), besides 66 a. awarded for manorial rights and immediately sold. Exeter cathedral received 176½ a., mostly held by copyholders in trust but actually leased at rack rent.[35] Awards were made to over 50 freeholders, only 16 of them resident; many allotments comprised only a few acres, often in lieu of mowing or common rights, and few exceeded 40 a., though William Prior of Aston received c. 72 a., and Benjamin Williams of Hillingdon (Mdx.) 158 a. in Cote. By 1857 the later farm pattern was established: there were then eight farms over 100 a., and by 1861 there were ten, including five over 200 a. and one (Cote House farm) of c. 450 a. All were predominantly leasehold, five being held of Aston manor. Most remained centred on farmsteads in Aston and along Cote Lane, though Newhouse Farm (with 270 a. in 1861) and Cote Lodge Farm (174 a. in 1881) were both built after 1857.[36]

In 1861 over 260 inhabitants, 68 per cent of those whose occupations were recorded, were called agricultural labourers, and the chief farms and smallholdings employed c. 180 men, women, and boys. Others dependent on agriculture included 10 shepherds and 3 dairymaids, a pig dealer (and grocer), 2 cattle dealers, a seedsman, and a fruiterer. Some smallholders with farms under 30 a. remained, among them a dairywoman with 25 a. and 2 farmers and poulterers with 11 a. and 7 a., but few were recorded as farmers in the 1870s.[37] Prominent farming families included the Townsends, tenants of Duckend (or North Street) farm in 1742 and still in 1939, the Lucketts, who held several farms in the 19th century and early 20th, the Bakers, tenants of Lower farm in Aston and of the Williams family's freehold in Cote, and from 1855 the Gilletts of Cote House farm.[38] Though a few farms were predominantly arable or pastoral, farming generally remained mixed.[39] Cote House farm produced cider in the 1840s,[40] and in 1855 its stock included wheat, barley, beans, tartar oats, and hay, besides dairy cattle, sheep, and pigs.[41] On Aston's mixed Manor farm in 1882–3 there were c. 150 sheep, 40 cattle, and 66 pigs, and feed included swedes, mangolds, and turnips as well as oats, bran, beans, tail barley, and wheat.[42] Charles Gillett of Cote House farm, a noted breeder of Oxford Down rams, won prizes at the Royal Agricultural Show in 1862, and it was later claimed that another Gillett had bred the 'original' flock of Oxford Downs at Cote;[43] though the family played a significant rôle the breed was, however, well established before the Gilletts settled in the township.[44]

In 1872 a meeting of the agricultural workers' union in Aston was well attended, and in 1890 the vicar cited low wages among the chief impediments to his ministry.[45] Agricultural depression during the 1870s presumably affected Aston and Cote as it did neighbouring townships, and the tenant of Newhouse farm, vacated after 1877, may have been a victim; in 1881 nearly 130 labourers were still employed on the chief farms, however, 53 of them by the Gilletts, and many established farmers survived in the 1890s or later.[46] Farms remained remarkably stable: in 1920 the acreages of Newhouse, North, Duckend, Kingsway, Cote Lodge, and Cote House farms differed little from those in 1857, and all survived in 1939, when there were 10

28 Giles, *Hist. Bampton*, Suppl. p. 1; O.R.O., Misc. WA I/1, ff. 5–6v.; ibid. Misc. Mar. I/40, 43, 45, 53; Bodl. MSS. Ch. Oxon. 2429, 2637, 3547, 3555–7, 3560–2, 3777–82, 3785–90, 3792, 3794–8, 3801–3, 3805–6, 4300–1, 4303–5.
29 P.R.O., C 78/2018; ibid. PROB 11/551, f. 251; O.R.O., Misc. Mar. I/30; ibid. Welch XVIII/1; ibid. QSD L.12; above, manors (Aston Pogges).
30 O.R.O., tithe award (1841), ff. 50–6 and *passim*.
31 Ibid.; cf. ibid. QSD L.12.
32 D. & C. Exeter, MS. 6016/7, bdle. 2, G. Richards to R. Barnes, 19 Nov. 1811, possibly referring only to Aston manor lands in Bampton and Weald.
33 *Oxf. Jnl.* 25 Jan. 1834; D. & C. Exeter, MS. 6016/7, bdle. 1, notes re proposed incl. May 1834; ibid. bdle. 3, Draft Bill for inclosing lands in Aston and Cote (1834).
34 Incl. Act, 16 & 17 Vic. c. 3; O.R.O., incl. award; *Oxf. Chron.* 24 Jan. 1852, 5 Nov. 1853, 18 Feb. 1854.
35 Cf. above, Bampton and Weald, econ. hist. (agric.).
36 O.R.O., altered tithe apportionment (1857); P.R.O., RG 9/905, RG 11/1514; above, intro.
37 P.R.O., RG 9/905; RG 11/1514; cf. *P.O. Dir. Oxon.* (1864 and later edns.); *Kelly's Dir. Oxon.* (1883

and later edns.).
38 O.R.O., tithe award (1841); altered tithe apportionment (1857); P.R.O., RG 9/905, RG 11/1514; *Kelly's Dir. Oxon.* (1883 and later edns.); inf. from Mrs. Powell (née Townsend), North Street Fm.
39 O.R.O., altered tithe apportionment (1857); P.R.O., RG 9/905.
40 Giles, *Hist. Bampton*, 21.
41 *Oxf. Chron.* 5 May, 20 Oct. 1855; for other fms., ibid. 1 Nov. 1851, 25 Sept. 1852, 2 Oct. 1852, 26 Nov. 1853, 11 Mar. 1854.
42 Reading Univ. Arch., OXF. 6/1/3, 6/4/2.
43 *Oxf. Chron.* 28 July 1860, 28 June 1862; *Jnl. R. Agric. Soc.* xx. 309; *Sale Cat., Freehold and Accom. Land at Cote* (1922): copy in possession of Mr. P. E. Luckett, New Shifford Fm.
44 *Jnl. Hist. Geog.* ix. 187; *Jnl. R. Agric. Soc.* xv. 230, xx. 309; *V.C.H. Oxon.* xii. 110.
45 *Witney Express*, 13 June 1872; O.R.O., MS. Oxf. Dioc. c 356, f. 32.
46 *P.O. Dir. Oxon.* (1864 and later edns.); *Kelly's Dir. Oxon.* (1883 and later edns.); P.R.O., RG 11/1514.

chief farms including 5 of over 150 a.[47] The overall proportion of arable, *c.* 70 per cent in 1877, fell to *c.* 44 per cent by 1914, when the chief crops remained wheat, barley, and oats, with some swedes, turnips, and mangolds. Cattle were still kept in relatively high numbers for the area, though sheep remained less numerous than further west and numbers were declining; most farms retained cattle sheds and piggeries in 1920.[48]

Occupational surnames in the 13th century and early 14th included smith, carpenter, and nailer,[49] and the usual rural tradesmen were recorded from the 16th century, notably smiths, wheelwrights, carpenters, and tailors, most though not all in Aston.[50] Few were wealthy, though a blacksmith in 1681 left personalty worth *c.* £177 including over £100 in debts, and a tailor in 1711 *c.* £176 including a lease worth £154.[51] A butcher in Aston was mentioned in 1595,[52] and bakers and a chandler in the later 18th century.[53] In 1601 an Aston narrow-weaver impleaded a Witney man for debt,[54] in 1637 there was a dyer with personalty worth *c.* £5, and in 1676 another weaver;[55] a glover with personalty of *c.* £5 died *c.* 1670 and a cordwainer was mentioned in 1706,[56] but there is no other evidence of textile manufacture or leather working.

Sir Thomas Horde (d. 1662) built a malthouse in 1657, presumably near Cote House. The following year he sold 92 qr. of malt for £122, but by 1659 he was making a loss.[57] A Cote maltster was mentioned in 1725,[58] but no malthouse was recorded there later. A malthouse in Aston, leased in 1656 when it was sold by Thomas Medhopp with other property, may have been that later owned by James Williams (d. 1728), whose personalty of nearly £390 included malt worth £113;[59] Mark Brickland (d. 1680) left 46 qr., and other 17th-century testators left small quantities.[60] An apparently short-lived starch and hair-powder manufactory was set up in Aston by Joseph Williams in 1787, with a warehouse in London,[61] and in 1801 another family member ran a nursery at Aston for fruit- and forest-trees and flowering shrubs.[62]

In 1811 only 17 families out of 136 were

supported by non-agricultural occupations, and the proportion remained similar throughout the 19th century. In 1881 tradesmen in Aston included a few wheelwrights and carpenters, 2 stone masons, 2 blacksmiths, 3 shoe- or boot-makers, a tailoress, several grocers and general dealers (often combined with other trades), 3 butchers, and 3 bakers.[63] Throughout the 19th century and earlier 20th several members of the Long family were carpenters and wheelwrights as well as postmasters and undertakers,[64] and ran a 'celebrated' wagon and cart works adjoining Ham Lane which employed *c.* 15 men; the last wagon was made in 1913, though the works, with their own sawpit, continued for repairs long after and retained some of their fittings in 1989.[65] Members of the Kimber family were black-smiths in 1847 and still *c.* 1950, and there were other long-lived family businesses.[66] In 1939 there was a blacksmith and wheelwright, a gro-cer, butcher, and baker, and at Cote a hurdle-maker and saddler.[67] In 1991 Aston retained a general store, post office, and motor repair gar-age near the square, but there were no shops in Cote. A laundry off Back Lane, run until *c.* 1920 by a training school for domestic servants, con-tinued commercially until *c.* 1972, employing labourers' wives and daughters in the earlier 20th century; the building was occupied later by a clockmaker, and in 1980 by several small businesses including metal-polishing, wood-craft, and upholstery firms.[68]

A brick kiln was built after inclosure beside the Aston–Witney road, on land north-west of North Street Farm formerly part of Kingsway field. In 1857 it was held under the Hippisleys by Richard Eustace of Kingsway farm, who from the 1870s to the early 1890s called himself a brickmaker and in 1881 employed 2 men there.[69] The works closed apparently in the early 20th century, and by 1920 the site was a cottage and smallholding; remaining buildings had been de-molished by 1971, though traces of the adjoining claypit remained.[70]

Hugh the miller held a yardland in Aston in villeinage in 1239,[71] but no mill is known despite the names Windmill field, recorded in 1432, and Mill (or Milk) Ford and brook, so called by the 17th century perhaps from Bampton mill up-

[47] O.R.O., altered tithe apportionment (1857); *Sale Cat., Aston and Cote Estate* (1920): copy in Bodl. G.A. Oxon. b 92*/1 (2); *Kelly's Dir. Oxon.* (1939).

[48] O.S. *Area Bk.* (1877); Orr, *Oxon. Agric.,* statistical plates; *Sale Cat., Aston and Cote Estate* (1920); cf. Reading Univ. Arch., OXF. 1/1/1 (labour accts. 1909–21).

[49] *Cal. Chart. R.* 1226–57, pp. 235, 246; P.R.O., E 179/161/10.

[50] O.R.O., MSS. Wills Oxon., Aston and Cote wills and inventories; ibid. Misc. Mar. I/34–6, 38, 52; Bodl. MSS. Ch. Oxon. 3784, 3791.

[51] O.R.O., MSS. Wills Oxon. 62/1/21, 78/4/2.

[52] *Witney Ct. Bks.* 142.

[53] O.R.O., MSS. Wills Oxon. 57/4/42, 142/3/34; ibid. Misc. BRA XIV/iv/7.   [54] *Witney Ct. Bks.* 173.

[55] O.R.O., MSS. Wills Oxon. 83/1/5, 169/3/7, 14/2/14.

[56] Ibid. 66/4/2; ibid. Misc. BRA XIV/ii/7.

[57] *Gent. Mag.* N.S. xxxii. 592.

[58] O.R.O., Misc. Mar. I/44.

[59] Ibid. Misc. Mar. I/27; ibid. MS. Wills Oxon. 74/1/14; cf. ibid. Misc. Mar. I/32.

[60] O.R.O., MS. Wills Oxon. 7/2/2; ibid. Aston and Cote inventories, *passim*; cf. Bodl. MS. Top. Oxon. e 632, f. 15.

[61] *Oxf. Jnl.* 14 July, 3 Nov. 1787.

[62] Ibid. 7 Nov. 1801.

[63] *Census,* 1811; P.R.O., RG 11/1514.

[64] O.R.O., tithe award 1841, ff. 11, 71; *P.O. Dir. Oxon.* (1847 and later edns.); *Kelly's Dir. Oxon.* (1883 and later edns.); *Witney Gaz.* 12 July 1979.

[65] C.O.S., PRN 1638; *Oxf. Jnl.* 22 Aug. 1863; *Witney Gaz.* 12 July 1979; *Aston and Cote Village Guide* (1989): copy in C.O.S.

[66] *P.O. Dir. Oxon.* (1847 and later edns.); *Kelly's Dir. Oxon.* (1883 and later edns.); C.O.S., PRN 529.

[67] *Kelly's Dir. Oxon.* (1939); cf. C.O.S., PRN 2318, 2406.

[68] *Oxf. Mail,* 19 Jan. 1977; *Witney Gaz.* 12 July 1979, 9 Oct. 1980; below, educ.

[69] O.R.O., incl. maps; ibid. altered tithe apportionment (1857); P.R.O., RG 11/1514; O.S. Map 1/2,500, Oxon. XXXVII. 8 (1876 edn.); *P.O. Dir. Oxon.* (1877); *Kelly's Dir. Oxon.* (1883 and later edns.).

[70] *Kelly's Dir. Oxon.* (1895 and later edns.); *Sale Cat., Aston and Cote Estate* (1920), lot 11; O.S. Maps 1/2,500, Oxon. XXXVII. 8 (1899 and 1921 edns.); ibid. SP 3403–3503 (1971 edn.).

[71] *Cal. Chart. R.* 1226–57, 246.

stream.[72] Fishermen were recorded from the Middle Ages,[73] and in 1657 streams north of the Thames contained a 'good store' of fish;[74] the Thames itself lay outside the township.[75] By the 16th century some fisheries were held with particular freeholds, leaseholds, and, apparently, lots in the common meadow; others were common waters in which tenants in 1657 claimed uncontrolled rights against Thomas Horde as lord of the manor.[76] By 1670 it was accepted that none might fish, hunt, or hawk within the lordship without Horde's licence, in token of which he scoured all common waters at his own cost; some waters, however, remained 'free' to the freeholders, the lord, and his tenants,[77] and in 1704 a freehold tenement carried the right to fish, dig gravel and mortar, and cut thorns 'as other freeholders of Aston do'.[78]

Coxes weir, apparently near Shaw Brook, was bought by Horde in 1657.[79] A customary right of the lord of Bampton hundred to fish once a year in Aston's common water, confirmed in 1593,[80] was not recorded afterwards.

LOCAL GOVERNMENT. The lord of Aston Pogges claimed courts baron and views of frankpledge in 1279, though then and later tenants attended the lord of Bampton's hundred court once a year after Michaelmas, and in the 17th century chose a constable, tithingman, and herdsman there. A tithingman for 'Aston hundred', presumably representing the freeholders, was also appointed by the Bampton court, where he made his presentations.[81] A dispute over royalty c. 1660 was settled reportedly in the lord of Aston's favour, but in the later 17th century the Bampton court retained some jurisdiction and habitually fined Aston inhabitants for failure to scour watercourses.[82] The Aston court seems by the later 15th century to have dealt solely or primarily with copyholds, though in the early 16th century tenants received no copies of the grants made, which created confusion later.[83] Courts baron were still held in 1764 and, reportedly, in 1852 at Cote House,[84] but presumably lapsed at inclosure. Separate courts were held for the submanor of Golofers in the 14th century and were mentioned in the 16th, probably in error, after it was reunited with Aston manor.[85]

Tenants in Aston and Cote of Bampton Deanery manor attended that manor's court as a separate tithing. In the 14th century and still in the early 16th they had their own aletaster, and in the late 18th and probably the 15th shared a constable with the manor's tenants in Bampton and Clanfield.[86] Tenants of Shifford manor attended the Shifford court until 1612 when the lord sold their holdings.[87]

Agricultural regulation was by 1593 the responsibility of the Sixteens, a body of 16 inhabitants (one for each of the 16 ploughlands into which the township was theoretically divided) who were elected annually at Aston cross on Lady Eve by all the householders, any not attending being fined 4d.[88] The Sixteens' independence has been cited as evidence for a free village community at Aston and Cote in the Middle Ages and traced to Anglo-Saxon antecedents,[89] but there is no indication that the township's early manorial organization was different from elsewhere in the parish, and the system probably resulted, as claimed in the 17th century,[90] from the township's division between several lordships and freeholds, combined, perhaps, with laxity on the part of non-resident lords. In 1657 Thomas Horde (d. 1715) attempted to annexe the Sixteens' rights and responsibilities to his manor court, electing rival officers, extracting covenants from copyholders that they would not recognize the Sixteens' authority, and seizing the meadows under their control. A compromise preserved the Sixteens' rights while accepting that they acted with the lord's consent, and that officers, once elected, should be sworn at the manor court.[91] The Sixteens continued until the inclosure of Aston and Cote in 1855, meeting latterly in a public house.[92]

In the 16th century and later the Sixteens allotted shares in meadows, instituted and enforced field orders through imposition of fines, and had power to distrain; by the early 18th century and still in the mid 19th they provided town bulls.[93] Ordinarily they met at Aston cross on the Tuesday of Easter week, the Wednesday of Rogation week, the Wednesday of Whitsun week, and on Lammas Eve, with a quorum of nine, but could be summoned to the cross between meetings if field orders were broken. They remained accountable to the inhabitants and their officers, who after a warning could impound their goods and fine them.[94] Major decisions such as re-ordering the fields appar-

72 D. & C. Exeter, MS. 4755; O.R.O., Misc. WA I/1, ff. 7v., 9, 126; Longleat House, NMR 3315, ct. 9 Apr. 1672, mentioning mill ditch.
73 P.R.O., E 179/161/9; O.R.O., Misc. Mar. I/18; Bodl. MS. Ch. Oxon. 3777; Cal. Chart. R. 1226–57, 246.
74 Giles, Hist. Bampton, Suppl. p. 4.
75 O.S. Map 6", Oxon. XXXVII (1884 edn.).
76 Giles, Hist. Bampton, Suppl. pp. 4, 6–7; O.R.O., Misc. WA I/1, f. 125v.; cf. ibid. Misc. Mar. I/13–15, 18.
77 O.R.O., Misc. WA I/1, f. 126; cf. S. A. and H. S. Moore, Hist. and Law of Fisheries (1903), 49, 51.
78 Bodl. MS. Ch. Oxon. 5269.
79 Ibid. 3774; cf. O.R.O., Misc. WA I/1, ff. 120–1.
80 O.R.O., Misc. WA I/1, f. 2.
81 Bampton Hund. R. 21; Giles, Hist. Bampton, Suppl. p. 2; Arundel Castle, MS. M 535; Longleat House (Wilts.), NMR 3315, passim.
82 Longleat House, Coventry pps. CVI, f. 95; ibid. NMR 3315; cf. Giles, Hist. Bampton, Suppl. p. 11.

83 P.R.O., SC 2/155/9; ibid. REQ 2/21/29; Giles, Hist. Bampton, 140; below, this section.
84 Oxf. Jnl. Synopsis, 13 June 1764; Gardner's Dir. Oxon. (1852).
85 P.R.O., C 135/139, no. 13; ibid. REQ 2/21/29.
86 D. & C. Exeter, MSS. 4751–83; ibid. Ch. Comm. 80/134543; above, Bampton and Weald, local govt. (manor courts).
87 Below, Shifford, manor, local govt.
88 O.R.O., Misc. WA I/1, ff. 1v.–2v., printed in Archaeologia, xxxv. 472–4; Giles, Hist. Bampton, 77–8.
89 Archaeologia, xxxiii. 269–78; Arch. Jnl. xliv. 405; cf. F. W. Maitland, Collected Papers, ed. H. A. L. Fisher, ii. 337–65.   90 Giles, Hist. Bampton, Suppl. p. 2.
91 Ibid. Suppl. pp. 1–7, 9; O.R.O., Misc. WA I/1, [ff. ii–iv], f. 7.
92 Giles, Hist. Bampton, 77–8; Archaeologia, xxxiii. 278.
93 O.R.O., Misc. WA I/1, passim; Giles, Hist. Bampton, 78–80, Suppl. p. 2.
94 O.R.O., Misc. WA I/1, ff. 1v.–2v.

ently needed the inhabitants' agreement.[95] Officers were elected annually, some by the lord's tenants among the Sixteens, others by the 'hundred tenants', presumably freeholders or tenants of other manors. In the late 16th century and the 18th the officers included 3 grass stewards, a hayward, a cowherd, and 2 water haywards.[96] All those offices carried small hams in the meadows; other hams allotted by the Sixteens, but possibly no longer attached to particular offices by the 17th century, included warden's, smith's, wonter's (or mole-catcher's), and brander's.[97] By the earlier 19th century there were 4 grass stewards and a cowherd, still with their own hams.[98] Constables, appointed at the Bampton court possibly until 1842, reportedly continued in the early 1850s when there was said to be one for Aston and one for Cote.[99]

Aston paid church rates to Bampton until the 19th century,[1] and by the 16th seems to have appointed a warden for Bampton church.[2] Cote appointed a chapelwarden for Shifford probably in the 15th century and still in the late 19th.[3] Two churchwardens for the newly-built Aston church were appointed presumably from 1839, and were so called by 1850.[4] As a new ecclesiastical district Aston, like Lew, retained responsibility for repairs to Bampton church for 20 years, though in 1855 Aston's ratepayers objected to the rate set, claiming that they were being charged for more general expenditure.[5]

For poor-law and other civil purposes Aston and Cote were administered together.[6] A surveyor of highways was chosen by the inhabitants and the Sixteens in the 17th century,[7] and a collector was noted in 1642; overseers, probably two, were mentioned occasionally thereafter. In the late 17th century the overseers received rent from some or all of the 'town lands', possibly sold before 1841 when the 'parish' owned only four cottages in the hamlets;[8] those too had apparently been sold by 1857,[9] though at inclosure in 1855 the churchwardens and overseers received 10 a. as a poor allotment, subject to annual rent charges of £17.[10] A vestry, presumably replacing an earlier assembly, met in the 1850s up to 4 times a year, at first in the Star inn or Red Lion and from 1855 in the vestry room in Aston church; it appointed two

surveyors of highways and from 1856 two poor-allotment wardens, and nominated usually 4 overseers to the magistrates. Its only other recorded business was making church, highway, and poor rates, and in 1849 it authorized a fund towards emigration costs.[11] An armed watchman and sometimes a beadle were separately appointed under the Lighting and Watching Act in the 1840s and 1850s, and in 1842 tithingmen were to assist them on Saturday nights.[12] After 1894 the vestry's residual functions passed to a parish council, which continued in 1991.[13]

Poor law expenditure in 1775–6 was £130, falling by 1784 to possibly c. £57; in 1785 the poor were reportedly farmed for £115.[14] By 1803 expenditure was £477, c. 15s. per head of population, and by 1813 it had doubled to £940, c. 30s. per head. Despite a temporary fall it rose after 1815 to c. 39s. per head, falling gradually in the mid 1820s to c. 18s., but rising again by 1832 to 30s., a total expenditure of £1,084.[15] Throughout that period the poor rate, said c. 1828 to have been formerly very low, was frequently higher than in any of Bampton's hamlets except Chimney, and c. 1818 one farm let for £115 a year was charged over £60.[16] In 1803 there were 50 adults and 55 children on regular relief, c. 16 per cent of the population, and 57 people on occasional relief, though only 2s. 4d. was spent on materials to employ them; from 1813 to 1815 there were c. 49 people on regular and c. 11 on occasional relief.[17] No overseers' accounts are known.[18]

From 1834 Aston and Cote belonged to Witney union, and from 1894 to Witney rural district. In 1974 they became part of West Oxfordshire district.[19]

CHURCH. A church was built in Aston in 1838 on land given by Henry Hippisley, the cost met from subscriptions and from funds invested by C. L. Kerby, vicar of Bampton, and his predecessor George Richards, who reportedly initiated the scheme. In 1839 it was consecrated as a chapel of ease with its own burial ground,[20] and in 1857, under Order in Council of 1845, it became the parish church for Bampton Aston, serving Aston, Cote, and the parochial chapelry of Shifford. In 1976 it became part of the united

95 e.g. ibid. ff. 36v., 64, 65v., 103v.
96 Ibid. ff. 1v., 119v.; Giles, *Hist. Bampton*, Suppl. pp. 2–4.
97 Giles, *Hist. Bampton*, Suppl. pp. 3, 7; O.R.O., Misc. WA I/1, f. 7.
98 Giles, *Hist. Bampton*, 77–8; *Archaeologia*, xxxiii. 277; O.R.O., tithe award (1841), ff. 7, 14, 50.
99 *Lascelles & Co.'s Dir. Oxon.* (1853); *Billing's Dir. Oxon.* (1854); above, this section.
1 D. & C. Exeter, MS. 6016/8, notes *re* division of par. c. 1845.
2 Above, Bampton and Weald, local govt. (par. govt.).
3 Below, Shifford, church.
4 O.R.O., MS. d.d. Par. Aston e 2, *passim*; below, church
5 O.R.O., MS. d.d. Par. Bampton c 8, ff. 244v.–246v.; *Oxf. Chron.* 14 July 1855; cf. Lew Church Bk. 1842–88 (in custody of vicar and par. officers), s.a. 1856.
6 D. & C. Exeter, MS. 6016/8, notes *re* division of par. c. 1845.   7 O.R.O., Misc. WA I/1, ff. 119v., 121.
8 Ibid. ff. 9v., 16v.–17; ibid. tithe award (1841), f. 75; *Protestation Rtns. and Tax Assess.* 8; for town hams, above, this section.

9 O.R.O., tithe award (1857), ff. 4, 6, 12 (nos. 4, 31, 59, 139).
10 Ibid. incl. award.
11 Ibid. MS. d.d. Par. Bampton Aston e 2 (vestry mins. 1849–56).
12 Minutes of Aston Watch Cttee. 1841–56, photocopy in possession of Mr. G. Sparrowhawk, Aston.
13 Local inf.
14 *Poor Abstract, 1787, 1804*; Bodl. MS. Top. Oxon. e 632, f. 12, implying a slightly lower average for 1783–5.
15 *Poor Abstract, 1804, 1818*; *Poor Rate Returns*, H.C. 556, p. 135 (1822), v; ibid. H.C. 334, p. 170 (1825), iv; ibid. H.C. 83, p. 157 (1830–1), xi; ibid. H.C. 444, p. 153 (1835), xlvii; cf. *Census*, 1801–41.
16 Bodl. MS. Top. Oxon. e 632, f. 12; D. & C. Exeter, Ch. Comm. 13/74361a, valn. May 1818.
17 *Poor Abstract, 1804, 1818*.
18 For extracts 1780–5, Bodl. MS. Top. Oxon. e 632, f. 12.
19 O.R.O., RO 3251, pp. 201–3; RO 3267.
20 Ibid. MSS. Oxf. Dioc. c 436, pp. 416–28; c 2165, no. 5; *Oxf. Chron.* 4 Aug. 1838; cf. Ch. Ch. Arch., MS. Estates 74, ff. 117–18; Giles, *Hist. Bampton*, 74, wrongly giving date of consecration as 1840.

benefice of Bampton with Clanfield. The advowson was vested in 1857 in the dean and chapter of Exeter, who remained joint patrons of the united benefice in 1990.[21] The endowment comprised tithe rents from Aston and Cote, Shifford, and Brighthampton, and one eighth of a Haddon corn rent formerly assigned to the vicars of Bampton; income in 1866 was reportedly c. £800 a year, but in 1899 gross income was only c. £560 and net income c. £400.[22]

Bampton's east vicarage house was at first assigned to the new living, but c. 1858 a new vicarage house was built in Aston south of High Street on land acquired from the Hippisleys, some of whose tithe rents were waived in return; the cost was met by mortgage and by temporary diversion of £60 from the Haddon corn rent.[23] The house, a large two-storeyed building of stone and slate with hoodmoulds over some of the windows, continued as a vicarage until 1963 and was demolished c. 1968;[24] the east vicarage house in Bampton was sold in 1866.[25]

Until 1857 the church was served by vicars of Bampton or their curates. There was a single morning or afternoon service, and the number of communicants was 'small'.[26] Thereafter Ralph Barnes (d. 1884), non-resident east vicar of Bampton, became sole vicar of Bampton Aston, installing curates who lived in the new vicarage house. George Sandham Griffith, curate 1858–74, who mostly served the parish alone and was for a time curate of Yelford also, complained that he had inadequate time for catechizing or for holding as many services as desired: throughout the later 19th century there were usually two Sunday services at Aston, the second held alternately in the afternoon or evening to allow time for a service at Shifford. Among his chief difficulties was long-established Baptist Dissent, though of an estimated half to two-thirds of the population who were habitual non-attenders only 50 per cent were thought to be Baptists. Other problems were the indifference and, in 1866, outright hostility of the absentee lord Henry Hippisley, though Griffith's disciplinarian and rather puritanical approach possibly did little to promote local harmony. In 1863 he quarrelled with his assistant at Shifford, whom the bishop accused of fomenting opposition to Griffith, and in 1866 the churchwardens refused to act following disagreements over a local charity.[27] Under A. T. C. Cowie (1884–1900), the first resident vicar, church attendance increased, and in the 1890s remained steady despite falling population; improvements were made to the church, and in 1890 Cowie claimed that his chief problem was past neglect, combined with non-resident landlords, poor housing, and low wages.[28] Vicars resided until the early 1960s, after which the benefice was held in plurality with Bampton Proper, and most vicars remained at Aston for ten years or more.[29]

The church of *ST. JAMES*,[30] designed by Thomas Greenshields of Oxford[31] in plain 13th-century style, is of stone with a concrete-tiled roof; it comprises chancel, nave with north and south transepts, and a west tower to which a steeple was added in 1860, the cost met partly from a bequest of William Monk (d. 1848).[32] Restorations were carried out reportedly by Joseph Clarke in 1862,[33] and by H. G. W. Drinkwater between 1885 and 1889, when the chancel was remodelled and refitted, a new altar, lectern, and seating were provided, and the octagonal stone font, given by the Revd. John Nelson in 1839, was moved to a 'more suitable' position. Plans to enlarge the chancel and add a new south vestry seem to have been abandoned.[34] The original Stonesfield- slated roofs, of poor quality, were replaced in 1962.[35] A 'new' organ bought in 1870 was replaced in 1896; that was electrified in 1949,[36] and stood in 1992 at the angle of the chancel and north transept, the latter used then, as in 1848,[37] as a vestry. The hexagonal oak pulpit and other fittings are 19th-century. Commemorative stained glass in the east window was given in 1948, when the altar was lowered and a reredos removed; more commemorative glass was given in 1955, and new windows with coloured medallions were inserted in 1969. Electric lighting was introduced in 1949.[38] The ring of 6 bells, acquired partly from Monk's bequest, is of 1883, by J. Taylor of Loughborough, and the plate includes 4 pieces of silver donated by Henry Hippisley in 1839.[39] The churchyard was extended northwards in 1939.[40]

[21] O.R.O., MS. Oxf. Dioc. c 1710, presentations; ibid. c 1713/2, Order in Council 1976; *Lond. Gaz.* 30 Dec. 1845, p. 7354; *Oxf. Dioc. Yr. Bk.* (1990), 87.

[22] *Lond. Gaz.* 30 Dec. 1845, pp. 7353–4 (misprinting tithe rents from Aston and Cote, cf. O.R.O., MS. Oxf. Dioc. c 746, ff. 115v.–116); Ch. Com. Rec. L 7, p. 439; O.R.O. MS. d.d. Par. Bampton c 10, item b; above, Bampton and Weald, churches.

[23] *Lond. Gaz.* 30 Dec. 1845, p. 7354; O.S. Map 1/2,500, Oxon. XXXVII. 8 (1876 edn.); letter of 1929 in possession of Mr. P. E. Luckett, New Shifford Fm., reciting deed of 28 Aug. 1858.

[24] *Voices, the Newsletter for Aston, Cote, Shifford and Chimney,* nos. 2–3: copy in C.O.S.; Aston P.C.C. mins. 1951–69 (in custody of vicar and par. officers), s.a. 1963; inf. from Suzanne Kelsey, Bampton.

[25] Above, Bampton and Weald, churches.

[26] *Wilb. Visit.* 10–12.

[27] O.R.O., MSS. Oxf. Dioc. c 332, pp. 57–9; c 335, ff. 27–8; c 338, ff. 33–7; c 341, ff. 46–7; c 344, ff. 31–2; c 347, ff. 29–30; c 350, ff. 34–5; *Wilb. Letter Bks.* p. 395.

[28] O.R.O., MSS. Oxf. Dioc. c 353, ff. 31–2; c 356, ff. 31–2; c 362, ff. 31–2; c 365, ff. 31–2.

[29] O.R.O., MS. Oxf. Dioc. c 1710, presentations; *Oxf. Dioc. Cal. and Clergy List* [later *Yr. Bk.*] (1900 and later edns.).

[30] *Ch. and Chapel, 1851,* no. 17; *Oxf. Dioc. Yr. Bk.* (1990), 87.

[31] *Gent. Mag.* N.S. xii. 640–1; Pevsner, *Oxon.* 426; illust. in Bodl. MSS. Top. Oxon. c 522, f. 21v.; c 852, f. 65; d 218, f. 30.

[32] *Oxf. Chron.* 26 May 1860; Giles, *Hist. Bampton,* 74; cf. plan in O.R.O., MS. Oxf. Dioc. c 436, p. 417.

[33] Pevsner, *Oxon.* 426.

[34] O.R.O., MS. Oxf. Dioc. c 353, f. 32; ibid. c 1710, faculty 1885; Bodl. G.A. Oxon. c 317/4, advertisement for reopening 1889; for the font, Giles, *Hist. Bampton,* 74.

[35] O.R.O., MS. Oxf. Dioc. c 1710, faculty 1962, with report of 1957.

[36] Ibid. faculty 1949; ibid. c 365, ff. 31–2; *Witney Express,* 13 Oct. 1870.

[37] Giles, *Hist. Bampton,* 73.

[38] O.R.O., MS. Oxf. Dioc. c 1710, faculties.

[39] *Ch. Bells Oxon.* i, p. 20; Evans, *Ch. Plate Oxon.* 11.

[40] O.R.O., MS. Oxf. Dioc. c 1710, consecration 1939.

NONCONFORMITY. A Cote will in 1561 contained Roman Catholic formulae,[41] and recusants in the late 16th century and early 17th included the non-resident lord Thomas Horde (d. *c.* 1607) and members of the Allen family.[42] Elizabeth Cary (d. 1639), Viscountess Falkland, a convert to Catholicism, was living at Cote House as lessee in 1627,[43] and a daughter of Thomas Horde (d. 1715), himself staunchly anti-Catholic, was also converted, but no other papists are known.[44]

At least one Quaker was reported in 1682,[45] but from the later 17th century the most numerous dissenting body was Anabaptist. Of *c.* 19 listed in Bampton parish in 1682 half or more, including members of the wealthy Williams and Brickland families, came probably from Aston or Cote,[46] the distance of which from the parish church presumably contributed to the rise of Dissent, and seven nonconformists noted at Cote in 1676 may also have been Baptists.[47] Then and for long afterwards they were associated with the congregation at Longworth (formerly Berks.), which became independent *c.* 1656 and which the Cote meeting eventually superseded.[48] Joseph Collett (d. 1741), who reputedly made a baptistry in the garden of his father's house at Cote and as a teenager *c.* 1700 attracted large congregations there, became first minister of Cote and Longworth in 1703; a chapel built on land given by John Williams, apparently on the site of the later building, was registered for meetings in 1704.[49] The chapelyard was used for burials probably from the chapel's foundation, and the chapel was registered for marriages in 1839.[50] By the early 19th century ministers were supported from trusts and bequests, not all from local people,[51] and in 1780 Aston House on North Street, built by a local Baptist *c.* 1744 for use as a manse, was acquired outright,[52] though not all ministers lived there.[53] The house was sold in 1958, and in 1960 a new manse was built on Cote Road; that was sold in 1980, and in 1992 the minister lived in a private house.[54]

Under Joseph Stennett (minister 1742–69), one of an eminent Baptist family, and Thomas Dunscombe (1772–97), numbers increased: 19 Baptist families were reported in the parish in 1768, and under Dunscombe membership rose from 85 in 1772, of whom 15 were of the Williams family, to over 100.[55] The dereliction of Shifford chapel from 1772 to 1784 presumably contributed to the increase.[56] Members were drawn from a wide area of west Oxfordshire and north Berkshire, and despite the vicars' assertion in 1738 that many were 'mean and illiterate', both the education and social standing of early ministers, many of whom may have had private means, and the support of families such as the Williamses and, later, of gentry such as the Atkinses of Kingston Lisle (in Sparsholt, then Berks.), ensured that the congregation remained 'unusually well-to-do'.[57] In the later 18th century and the 19th the circuit was widened with the establishment of chapels at Bampton, Standlake, Ducklington, Buckland, and Faringdon,[58] and at Aston in the early 19th century services held reportedly in the barn of a Cote deacon enjoyed a 'good congregation'.[59] Houses in Aston were registered for meetings in 1820 and 1824,[60] and in 1845 a plain stone chapel in Gothic style, served from Cote and with sittings for *c.* 160, was built north of Aston House; a gallery was added in 1858.[61] From the late 18th century Conformists repeatedly expressed concern at the threat of Dissent,[62] though relations may not always have been hostile: Dunscombe was apparently involved with Bampton vestry and workhouse and may have acted as a trustee for the Bampton curate Thomas Middleton (d. 1782),[63] and in 1811 the Cote meeting resolved to admit paedobaptists and become a 'mixed' communion.[64]

Average morning attendance at Cote by 1850–1 was 200 and at Aston 130, and during the pastorate of Benjamin Arthur (1856–82), responsible for a major restoration of Cote chapel, membership of the Cote meeting reached *c.* 195

41 Ibid. MS. Wills Oxon. 184, f. 16v.
42 *Recusant Roll 1593–4* (Cath. Rec. Soc. lvii), 123; *1594–5* (Cath. Rec. Soc. lxi), 71; H. E. Salter, 'Oxon. Recusants', O.A.S. *Rep.* (1924), 35, 37, 40, 46.
43 *Acts of P.C.* 1627–8, 109–10; *Complete Peerage*, v. 239–40; cf. O.R.O., Misc. Mar. I/22.
44 P.R.O., PROB 11/551, f. 250v.; Berks. R.O., D/E1 Z5/1; Stapleton, *Cath. Miss.* 173.
45 *Bp. Fell and Nonconf.* 5.
46 Ibid. 5, 51; cf. O.R.O., Misc. WA I/1, ff. 5–6v.; ibid. MS. Wills Oxon. 163/2/55.
47 *Compton Census*, ed. Whiteman, 422.
48 Regent's Park Coll., Oxf., Cote Ch. Bks. 1647–1882, 1882–1972; ibid. Longworth Ch. Bk. 1652–1708; J. Stanley, *Church in the Hop Garden* [*c.* 1936], 55 sqq.; E. A. Payne, *Baptists of Berks.* (1951), 31, 45, 68; H. Eden, 'Cote Baptist Church' (TS. *c.* 1957), 6–7: copy in C.O.S.
49 Regent's Park Coll., cert. of registration 1704; Stanley, *Hop Garden*, 109 sqq.; B. Williams, *Memorials of the Family of Williams* (priv. print. 1849), 12–13, 21–2, 33–4, 36; for deeds from 1705, Baptist Union Corpn. file 1367/1. Collett was evidently non-resident in 1738: *Secker's Visit.* 32.
50 Monuments in chapelyd., partly listed in R.C.H.M. *Inv. Nonconf. Chapels in Central Eng.* ed. C. Stell (1986), 168; Giles, *Hist. Bampton*, 175–6; *Lond. Gaz.* 9 Apr. 1839, p. 763.
51 P.R.O., PROB 11/1215, f. 242 and v.; O.R.O., MS. Wills Oxon. 159/3/4; Regent's Park Coll., Cote Ch. Bk. 1647–1882, list of chars. (n.d. but after 1830); *Brief Acct. of*

Trusts created by A. Atkins (1803): copy in Baptist Union Corpn. file 1367/3; J. Ivimey, *Hist. Eng. Baptists*, iv. 551–4; *V.C.H. Berks.* iv. 319.
52 Baptist Union Corpn. files 1367/2–3, deeds 1742–1830; cf. Stanley, *Hop Garden*, 146; above, intro.
53 Above, Bampton and Weald, nonconf.
54 Regent's Park Coll., Cote Ch. Bk. 1882–1972, s.a. 1957–61; inf. from pastor.
55 O.R.O., MS. Oxf. Dioc. d 558, f. 33; Regent's Park Coll., Cote Ch. Bk. 1647–1882; cf. Stanley, *Hop Garden*, 120–65.
56 O.R.O., MS. Oxf. Dioc. c 327, p. 134; below, Shifford, church.
57 Regent's Park College, Cote Ch. Bks., *passim*; Stanley, *Hop Garden*, 117, 133–4, 186–7; *Secker's Visit.* 13.
58 Stanley, *Hop Garden*, 135–42, 171, 191, 209; Payne, *Baptists of Berks.* 86; above, Bampton and Weald; below, Ducklington; Standlake.
59 Stanley, *Hop Garden*, 197; J. Hinton, *Hist. Sketch of Assoc. Churches* (1821), 8: copy in Bodl. 11135 e. 90 (11).
60 O.R.O., MSS. Oxf. Dioc. c 644, f. 216; c 645, f. 38.
61 *Ch. and Chapel, 1851*, no. 18; H. Eden, 'Cote Baptist Church' (TS. *c.* 1957), 14; datestone.
62 e.g. O.R.O., MSS. Oxf. Dioc. c 327, p. 134; c 654, ff. 80–1; c 662, ff. 8–9v., 13–14.
63 Ibid. MS. Wills Oxon. 142/4/15; ibid. MS. d.d. Par. Bampton b 10, ff. 59, 62; Oxf. Jnl Synopsis, 30 Nov. 1782.
64 Regent's Park Coll., Cote Ch. Bk. 1647–1882, s.a. 1811.

with congregations of up to 400.[65] In 1859 Arthur introduced open-air baptism, the first of which, for 10 candidates, was attended by several hundred.[66] Thereafter the small stipend and rigours of serving a large rural circuit made it difficult to keep adequate pastors for long.[67]

During the 20th century there were some long vacancies and affairs were often managed almost entirely by the deacons, several of whom came then, as earlier, from outside the parish. By 1959 there were women deacons, despite earlier objections. Meetings were sometimes chaired by mediators from Regent's Park College, Oxford, and in the 1960s occasional help was received from New Road Baptist church in Oxford and from U.S.A.A.F. chaplains from Brize Norton. By 1906 Cote chapel had 60 resident members and 32 non-resident members, the decline being attributed in 1908 to the 'New Theology'; membership in 1935 was 52, rising to 104 in 1971 but falling to c. 85 (excluding children) by 1990. The chapel remained open in 1992. At Aston the Sunday school had 50 children in 1944, the largest figure in the circuit, and in 1971 the congregation was c. 22, but the chapel was closed in 1981 and became a private house.[68] A church hall with a capacity of c. 250, built on Cote road in Aston in 1929, was replaced in 1980 by a Baptist Fellowship Centre on the same site, and thereafter most meetings were held there.[69]

The existing Cote chapel,[70] a large single-cell building of limestone rubble with a gabled stone-slated roof and a projecting north vestry, seems to have been built by Stennett in 1756, soon after the chapelyard was enlarged;[71] a gallery was reportedly added the following year.[72] In the late 1850s all but the outer shell was rebuilt under Benjamin Arthur: the earlier double gable was replaced by a single flat-topped gable concealing the roof valley, the chapel was refloored and the vestries enlarged, new pews (including a table pew over the central baptistry) were installed and new galleries added, and a new pulpit at the west end replaced an 18th-century one on the south.[73] An organ, by Henry Jones of London, was installed in 1867. Electric light was introduced in 1948, and a major renovation was carried out in 1955, when stables

adjoining the road, apparently those built in 1757, were converted to other uses; they survived in 1992.[74]

A Methodist minister from Faringdon (then Berks.) preached occasionally at Cote in the later 1850s, but complained of indifference.[75] In 1866 Primitive Methodists were meeting in a cottage in Aston or Cote, and camp meetings were held at Cote and 'near Bampton' throughout the 1860s, apparently without success.[76]

EDUCATION. By deeds of 1709 and 1713 ratified under his will Thomas Horde (d. 1715) charged lands in Aston manor with £6 a year to teach 20 poor children of Aston and Cote to read the Bible.[77] Though the bequest was recorded throughout the 18th century,[78] two elementary day schools recorded in 1808 and together teaching 50 children were unendowed, and then as in 1824 the bequest was received presumably by the Sunday school.[79]

By 1835 the bequest was paid to a National school which had 30 pupils paying pence.[80] In 1868 the school's annual income totalled c. £42, including, besides the Horde charity, c. £3 from unspecified Bampton charities and £5 from the unidentified Betton's charity, received from the Ironmongers' Company. It then received no government grant, and lack of support from most landowners meant that it was running at a deficit.[81] Its original site is unknown,[82] but in 1856 a new National schoolroom and house, designed in 13th-century style by James Castle of Oxford, were built east of the church on land allotted to the vicar and churchwardens at inclosure, the cost met by the vicars, by subscription, and by a government grant.[83] By 1866 accommodation had been increased from 72 to 95, and by 1868 there were 42 boys and 56 girls on the roll from Aston, Cote, Chimney, and Shifford. Many parents saw little advantage, however, and attendance was usually lower. About 17 children were employed in farm and other work almost continuously, and 24 temporarily paid for by the curate were removed as soon as he withdrew support.[84]

A dissenting school opened in 1827 and with 50 pupils in 1835 was presumably the British

65 Regent's Park Coll., Cote Ch. Bk. 1882–1972; *Ch. and Chapel, 1851*, nos. 18, 122; *Oxf. Chron.* 17 Sept. 1859; Stanley, *Hop Garden*, 204–10, 222.
66 *Oxf. Jnl.* 11 June 1859.
67 Regent's Park Coll., Cote Ch. Bk. 1882–1972, *passim*; Stanley, *Hop Garden*, 211–38; Eden, 'Cote Baptist Ch.' (TS. c. 1957), 10–12.
68 Regent's Park Coll., Cote Ch. Bk. 1882–1972, *passim*; *Baptist Union Dir.* (1990–1); inf. from pastor.
69 Regent's Park Coll., Cote Ch. Bk. 1882–1972, s.a. 1928–30; Eden, 'Cote Baptist Church' (TS. c. 1957), 11; inf. from pastor.
70 Below, plate 13; cf. *Inv. Nonconf. Chapels*, ed. Stell, 167–9; Stanley, *Hop Garden*, facing pp. 134, 182 (conjectural), 198, 214, 230; Pevsner, *Oxon.* 557.
71 Baptist Union Corpn. file 1367/1, endorsement on conveyance 10 Dec. 1755. A mortgage of 1739/40 cited in *Inv. Nonconf. Chapels*, ed. Stell, 168, relates not to the chapel but to Aston Ho.: Baptist Union Corpn. file 1367/2. The assertion in Pevsner, *Oxon.* 557 n. that alterations were made c. 1750 lacks evidence.
72 Stanley, *Hop Garden*, 123.
73 *Inv. Nonconf. Chapels*, ed. Stell, 167–8; Stanley, *Hop Garden*, 205–8; *Oxf. Chron.* 17 Sept. 1859.
74 H. Eden, 'Cote Baptist Church' (TS. c. 1957), 13–14; Baptist Union Corpn. file 1367/1, endorsement on conveyance 10 Dec. 1755.
75 O.R.O., P 115/J/1, 30 Oct. 1856 and *passim*.
76 Ibid. MS. Oxf. Dioc. c 332, p. 58; *Oxf. Chron.* 2 June 1860, 6 June 1863; *Witney Express*, 19 May 1870.
77 Giles, *Hist. Bampton*, 94–5; P.R.O., PROB 11/551, f. 254v.
78 *Acct. of Char. Schs. in Gt. Britain and Ireland* (1713), 19; *Secker's Visit.* 13; *Univ. Brit. Dir.* ii [1793], 252–3.
79 O.R.O., MS. Oxf. Dioc. d 707, f. 148; *10th Rep. Com. Char.* 354.
80 *Educ. Enq. Abstract*, H.C. 62, p. 739 (1835), xlii.
81 *Rep. Com. Children and Women in Agric.* [4202-I], p. 346, H.C. (1868–9), xiii.
82 Not shown on O.R.O., tithe map (1841).
83 O.R.O., incl. award; *Oxf. Chron.* 2 Aug. 1856; *Rep. of Educ. Cttee. of Council 1858–9*, H.C. 2510, p. 625 (1859 Sess. I), xxi (2); datestone.
84 *Oxf. Chron.* 2 Aug. 1856; *Returns relating to Pars.* H.C. 114, pp. 344–5, (1867–8), liii; *Rep. Com. Children and Women in Agric.* [4202-I], p. 346, H.C. (1868–9), xiii.

school established in Aston House by Richard Pryce, minister of Cote 1819–40, which moved first to a barn in Aston owned by a Baptist deacon, and in 1845 to the newly built Baptist chapel and schoolroom on North Street.[85] In 1871 the National and British schools together provided accommodation for 152 children, and 168 attended on inspection day, but since the British school was also used for worship the inspector ruled that the National school must increase its accommodation to 160, intimating that a school board, an unlimited compulsory rate, and increased fees might be unavoidable.[86] In response the National school's trustees appointed a certificated master and mistress, agreed new fees of between 2d. and 6d. a week, raised a voluntary rate to which Shifford and Chimney initially refused to contribute, and established a committee to look into efficiency and fund-raising.[87] Accommodation in the National school came under additional pressure after Shifford and Chimney were merged with Aston and Cote into one school district c. 1872, and in 1874 a new infant room increased accommodation to 165, the cost met chiefly from voluntary subscriptions including £50 each from Henry Hippisley and Col. Edward Harcourt.[88] The British school, which like the National suffered from inadequate financial support,[89] closed in 1874, when an expected influx of pupils to the National school was counterbalanced by falling population; average attendance in 1875–6 was only 76, and in 1879 some children were withdrawn to an evidently short-lived dame school in the former British schoolroom.[90] Following the British school's closure two nonconformists were usually invited onto the National school's board, a practice reinstated in 1899 after several years' lapse.[91]

During the later 1870s the National school was usually judged satisfactory, though individual subjects were criticized and there were threats to reduce the government grant. Income in 1874–5 included a grant of c. £60, reduced to £48 the following year, voluntary contributions (c. £64), school pence (£26), and charitable endowments (£14), and in 1881 the Ironmongers' Company withdrew Betton's charity since the school had a balance in hand. Fees, formerly related to parents' means, were re-placed in 1878 by flat rates of 1d. for those under 7 years and 2d. for those older, and voluntary rates were raised occasionally.[92] Average attendance during the 1880s rose from 97 to 136,[93] and in 1894 another new infant room was added, the cost met by voluntary donations; thereafter attendance fell with population, though in 1900 the infant mistress had more children than she could manage.[94] Reports continued to be satisfactory,[95] and in 1926 the school became a junior school for children under 11, the seniors going to Bampton. Though average attendance fell to 50 by 1939 and in 1962 there were only 58 on the roll, the school was then a 'robust community'.[96] Extensions were built in the 1950s and c. 1973, and in 1993, when further extensions were planned, the roll was 111.[97]

A second dissenting school, with 20–30 pupils in 1808, was perhaps connected with a boarding school reportedly opened in Aston House by a relative of Joseph Stennett, minister of Cote 1798–1810.[98] Another, supported from parental contributions, had 18 pupils in 1835, but was not mentioned later.[99] A private day school opened in 1826, supported from voluntary contributions and pence, continued in 1835,[1] and a private day and night school, run, according to the curate, by 'a dwarf of bad character', was mentioned in the 1860s but had closed by 1872.[2] A school training young girls for domestic service was established in Aston in 1888 with 5 or 6 pupils, and in 1913, with c. 70 girls aged from 12 to 16, moved to newly-built premises (later St. Joseph's) on Bampton Road. That school taught standard academic subjects as well as domestic skills, and received a government grant; additional income included profits from its commercial laundry business, run from the original building off Back Lane.[3] The school closed between 1920 and 1924,[4] and St. Joseph's was used as an orphanage and, in the late 1930s, as a home for Spanish Civil War refugees.[5] In 1992, as Westfield House, it was occupied by a private nursery school.

CHARITIES FOR THE POOR. Leonard Wilmot's charity[6] included 13s. 4d. a year to the poor of Aston and Cote, received in the late 17th century and, irregularly, in the early 19th.[7] In

---

85 *Educ. Enq. Abstract* (1835), p. 739; J. Stanley, *Church in the Hop Garden* [c. 1936], 197; *Ch. and Chapel, 1851*, no. 18.

86 *Returns relating to Elem. Educ.* H.C. 201, p. 324 (1871), lv; *Oxf. Jnl.* 25 Feb. 1871.

87 O.R.O., MS. Oxf. Dioc. c 338, f. 35; Mins. of Aston Sch. Managers and Trustees 1871–1940 (in custody of vicar and par. officers of Bampton), pp. 4–44.

88 Mins. of Aston Sch. Managers, pp. 47–62; *Oxf. Chron.* 4 Oct. 1873; *Return of Public Elem. Schs. 1875–6* [C. 1882], pp. 212–13, H.C. (1877), lxvii.

89 *Rep. Com. Children and Women in Agric.* p. 346.

90 O.R.O., MS. Oxf. Dioc. c 338, f. 33v.; Mins. of Aston Sch. Managers, 7 Oct. 1874, 5 June 1876, Apr. 1879; *Return of Public Elem. Schs. 1875–6*, pp. 212–13.

91 Mins. of Aston Sch. Managers, 8 June 1899 and inserted letter.

92 Mins. of Aston Sch. Managers; *Return of Public Elem. Schs. 1875–6*, pp. 212–13

93 *Rep. of Educ. Cttee. of Council, 1879–80* [C. 2562-I], p. 675, H.C. (1880), xxii; *1882–3* [C. 3706- I], pp. 717–9, H.C. (1883), xxv; *Public Elem. Schs. Return*, H.C. 403, pp. 212–17 (1890), lvi.

94 Mins. of Aston Sch. Managers, s.a. 1893–4, 1900; *Return of Non-Provided Schs.* H.C. 178, p. 18 (1906), lxxxviii.

95 Mins. of Aston Sch. Managers, *passim.*

96 O.R.O., T/S Misc./19 (5), 27 Nov. 1962; inf. from L.E.A.

97 Mins. of Aston Sch. Managers 1964–85 (in custody of vicar and par. officers); Oxon. C.C. Educ. Dept., Ducker Davis survey.

98 O.R.O., MS. Oxf. Dioc. d 707, f. 148; Stanley, *Hop Garden*, 170.

99 *Educ. Enq. Abstract* (1835), p. 739.   1 Ibid.

2 O.R.O., MSS. Oxf. Dioc. c 332, pp. 57–9; c 335, f. 27v.; c 338, f. 33v.

3 Bodl. G.A. Oxon. c 317/4, *27th Annual Rep.* [1915] and newspaper reprints; P.R.O., RG 12/1175, no. 18; above, econ. hist.

4 *Kelly's Dir. Oxon.* (1920 and later edns.).

5 *Oxf. Times*, 1 Aug. 1986.

6 Above, Bampton and Weald, charities.

7 O.R.O., Misc. WA I/1, f. 9v.; *Char. Don.* 966–7; *10th Rep. Com. Char.* 355.

the later 17th century annual distributions were made from bequests by Thomas Cox (33s. 4d. to the poor of Cote by will proved 1614), John Palmer (£50 to the poor of Aston and Cote by will proved 1650), and John Moulden of Cote (£5 to the poor of Aston and Cote, date unknown), but by the late 18th century all were lost.[8] A bequest of £5 by Robert Dale of Cote, by will proved 1659, had not been received by 1680 when his wife's executor was ordered to give it up, and that, too, was lost by 1787.[9] The outcome of a claim in the late 17th century to a share in Sir William Coventry's apprenticing charity, itself later lost,[10] is unknown.

By deeds of 1709 and 1713 Thomas Horde (d. 1715) charged 5½ yardlands in Aston and Cote with £10 a year to provide 10 woollen coats and 10 pairs of stockings for men, and 10 canvas shifts and 10 pairs of stockings for women, recipients to be elected by the Sixteens and the lord of the manor. Arrears of that and other charges on the lands were repaid c. 1731 after a Chancery suit, and part (£109) was invested.[11] Only £8 was received for clothing 'for many

years', but in the early 19th century more was paid than required.[12] Bequests by Horde of £10 each to Aston and Cote for apprenticing 2 boys and girls were lost.[13]

Thomas Fox of Aston, by deed of 1721 and will proved 1731, left a 10s. rent charge distributed in the early 19th century to poor widows; payment was refused from c. 1811.[14] William Monk of Aston, by will dated 1848, left £30 at interest for poor widows and £50 at interest to provide coal.[15]

In 1888[16] the only Aston eleemosynary charity was Horde's,[17] incorporated that year into the Bampton Consolidated Charities. In 1969 c. £31 was distributed in Aston and Cote, which also shared in the consolidated educational charity, and in 1972 Horde's charity, still providing £10 a year, was incorporated into the Bampton Welfare Trust. Poor allotments totalling c. 9 a., awarded at inclosure, yielded insufficient income to allow distributions to the poor in 1965; under a Scheme of 1970 income from the balance of c. £200 was to benefit poor persons in Aston Bampton and Shifford.[18]

CHIMNEY

AN estate at Chimney, identical with the later township (668 a.), existed probably by the 950s and certainly by 1069, when its boundaries followed the Thames on the east and south, and streams on the west and north. A small deviation from the Thames, near Duxford, presumably represented the river's earlier course.[19] The name Chimney, meaning 'Ceomma's island', reflects its low-lying position surrounded by watercourses, and in the Middle Ages and later much of the township flooded frequently.[20]

The road northwards to Aston followed its later course by 1767 and was confirmed in 1855,[21] though then and earlier the township was sometimes cut off by floods for several weeks.[22] A track leading southwards to Duxford, where there was a river crossing by the 11th century, was presumably early, but must often have been impassable and was not always shown on early maps.[23] In 1317 demesne produce was carried to Oxford by river,[24] and in the 16th and 17th centuries several testators owned boats;[25] in the early 19th century harvest produce was

transported in punts along side streams from the Thames, and in 1896 free lock passes were issued to inhabitants travelling to Shifford chapel along Shifford lock cut, constructed 1896–8.[26] A ferry from Chimney was claimed in 1261 to have sunk with loss of life;[27] the Duxford ferry, outside the township in Berkshire, was marked on a map of 1767 and continued into the 20th century.[28]

Little evidence has been noted of early occupation,[29] though 2nd-century Roman pottery was found west of Chimney Farm, and a 3rd- or 4th-century coin east of the existing hamlet.[30] Part of an exceptionally large late Anglo-Saxon burial ground, in use from the mid 10th century and established presumably from Bampton minster, was excavated immediately west of Chimney Farm: in all it covered probably over 2,400 square metres, and the inferred number of burials (1,500–2,000) suggests that it served a wide area. No excavated burials were later than the mid 11th century, and presumably the cemetery was abandoned in favour of that at Bampton after the church passed to Exeter cathedral.[31] No

8 P.R.O., PROB 11/124, f. 381 and v.; PROB 11/214, ff. 230–2; Char. Don. 966–7; Giles, Hist. Bampton, 89; 10th Rep. Com. Char. 355.
9 P.R.O., PROB 11/288, ff. 242v.–243; Giles, Hist. Bampton, 152, 154; Char. Don. 966–7.
10 O.R.O., Misc. WA I/1, f. 9v.; above, Bampton and Weald, charities.
11 P.R.O., PROB 11/551, ff. 254v.–255, revoking a deed of 1707; Giles, Hist. Bampton, 94–6; 6th Rep. Com. Char. H.C. 12, p. 406 (1822), ix (2). Cf. above, manors (Aston Pogges); educ.
12 10th Rep. Com. Char. 354.
13 Ibid.; P.R.O., PROB 11/551, f. 252v.
14 O.R.O., MS. Wills Oxon. 128/1/41; 10th Rep. Com. Char. 355; cf. Char. Don. 966–7, stating £50 by deed.
15 Giles, Hist. Bampton, 100.
16 Para. based on O.R.C.C., Kimber files.
17 Recorded as £24 a year, apparently through confusion with a different rent charge: above, manors (Aston Pogges). A second charity was for church repairs: Giles, Hist. Bampton, 101.
18 O.R.C.C., Kimber files; O.R.O., incl. award.

19 Grundy, Saxon. Oxon. 12–14; O.S. Map 6", Oxon. XXXVIII (1883 edn.); above, Bampton and Weald, manors (Bampton Deanery).
20 P.N. Oxon. (E.P.N.S.), ii. 302; below, econ. hist.
21 Jefferys, Oxon. Map (1767); above, Aston and Cote, intro.
22 D. & C. Exeter, MSS. 2018–19; Oxf. Jnl. Synopsis, 24 Oct. 1778; Giles, Hist. Bampton, 87.
23 P.N. Berks. (E.P.N.S.), ii. 392; O.S. Map 1", sheet 13 (1830 edn.); cf. Jefferys, Oxon. Map (1767).
24 Below, econ. hist.
25 e.g. O.R.O., MS. Wills Oxon. 184, f. 116v.; ibid. 43/1/20, 127/1/6, 297/1/12.
26 F. S. Thacker, Thames Highway (1968 edn.), ii. 73–4.
27 P.R.O., JUST 1/701, m. 23.
28 Jefferys, Oxon. Map (1767); D. & C. Exeter, MS. M 1; Thacker, Thames Highway, ii. 72.
29 D. Benson and D. Miles, The Upper Thames Valley, 39–40; Oxoniensia, liv. 50, 53; C.O.S., PRN 1613, 8179, 8203.
30 Oxoniensia, xxix/xxx. 190; ibid. liv. 48, 53.
31 Ibid. liv. 45–56; cf. above, Bampton and Weald, intro.; manors (Bampton Deanery); church.

evidence was found for a pagan cemetery, despite 19th-century reports of burials with 'swords and armour'.[32]

Chimney was not separately noted in Domesday Book, though some of the 17 tenants (excluding *servi*) listed on Bampton Deanery manor may have lived there.[33] By the late 13th century and early 14th there were *c.* 18 peasant households including 2 cottages,[34] and the population may have been increasing: 16 landholders

houses were recorded in 1801 when the population was 25, and six, including four labourers' cottages, from the 1820s to early 1840s. From 46 in 1821 the population fell to 36 in 1841 and to 24 ten years later, remaining under 30 until 1911 when it reached 33; in 1931, the last year for which separate figures are available, it was 24.[41]

The medieval hamlet occupied the southern edge of a narrow gravel island in the alluvium.[42]

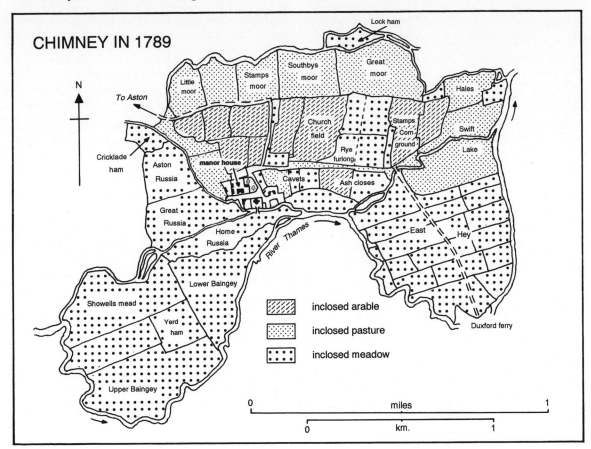

CHIMNEY IN 1789

inclosed arable

inclosed pasture

inclosed meadow

were taxed in 1306, 19 in 1316, and 25 in 1327, though in the last year especially some may have been entered under Chimney in error.[35] As in Shifford the impact of 14th-century plague may have been relatively limited, but by the early 15th century the population was clearly falling[36] and seems never to have recovered fully: 4 inhabitants were taxed in 1524 and 7 in 1542-3, and in 1642 only 14 male inhabitants were listed, suggesting an adult population of *c.* 28.[37] In 1634 the lessee of the manor claimed that there had been no more than 7 inhabitants, presumably meaning households, within living memory,[38] and 7 houses were taxed in 1662.[39] By 1775 there were only three farms and by 1841 two;[40] three

Finds immediately west of Chimney Farm included scattered pottery of the 12th to 15th centuries and at least two undated hearths,[43] and rectilinear earthworks noted east of the surviving hamlet include house platforms, croft boundary ditches, and hollow ways.[44] Decayed peasant houses were mentioned frequently in the 15th century,[45] and by the early 17th some closes east of the surviving hamlet were pasture.[46] By 1789 settlement was concentrated chiefly around the 17th-century manor house, then a farmstead, south-west of modern Chimney Farm, with a few agricultural buildings east of Lower Farm; there were then three farms, all including adjacent tofts and homesteads.[47]

32 *Oxoniensia*, liv. 45-7, 54.
33 *V.C.H. Oxon.* i. 402; below, manor.
34 *Bampton Hund. R.* 76-7; D. & C. Exeter, MS. 2931.
35 P.R.O., E 179/161/8-10; below, econ. hist.
36 Below, econ. hist.; no poll tax return for 1377 has been found.
37 P.R.O., E 179/161/172, E 179/162/234; *Protestation Rtns. and Tax Assess.* 9, repeating one name.
38 D. & C. Exeter, MS. 1998.
39 P.R.O., E 179/255/4, pt. i, f. 27.   40 Below, econ. hist.

41 *Census*, 1801-1931; P.R.O., HO 107/872; O.R.O., tithe award. After 1931 Chimney was returned with Aston.
42 Geol. Surv. Map 1/50,000, solid and drift, sheet 236 (1982 edn.).
43 *Oxoniensia*, xvii/xviii. 223; ibid. liv. 49, 53.
44 C.O.S., PRN 951.
45 D. & C. Exeter, MSS. 4751-70; below, econ. hist.
46 D. & C. Exeter, MS. 4775; cf. O.R.O., tithe award.
47 D. & C. Exeter, MS. M 1; ibid. MS. 2032; O.R.O., tithe award.

Most of those buildings were demolished in the 19th century and early 20th, leaving Lower Farm, which is of late 17th-century origin. Chimney Farm Cottages were built apparently in the early 19th century, and Chimney Farm, further south on part of the demolished manor house's orchard, in the late 19th, replacing a short-lived farmhouse further west. The Little House, north-east of Chimney Farm Cottages, is of the early 20th century.[48]

Timber construction may have been common in the Middle Ages, but surviving houses in 1866 were of stone (presumably limestone rubble) with tiled or stone-slated roofs, and only a few agricultural buildings were thatched.[49] Chimney Farm Cottages incorporate earlier stone-mullioned windows with hoodmoulds, perhaps from the manor house. Both Chimney Farm and the Little House are of brick.

A 'tavern' in a villein's house was mentioned in 1261.[50] A probably Royalist garrison reported in March 1645[51] was billeted presumably in the manor house.

MANOR. Chimney formed part of Bampton manor until granted to Bampton minster in the mid 10th century, and remained part of Bampton Deanery manor thereafter.[52] A lease of most of the township, with a share in manorial rights, was acquired in 1617 by Robert Veysey (d. 1635) of Taynton,[53] one of a local family which had an interest by 1603, and who had allegedly 'raised himself from nothing' through 'usury and crafty bargaining'.[54] He settled it on his nephew Robert Veysey (d. 1666) of Queen's College, Oxford, and later of Chimney, who bought it from the parliamentary commissioners c. 1650 and secured renewal of the lease in 1662.[55] The younger Robert was succeeded by his second wife Christian[56] and, before 1691, by another Robert Veysey, evidently not his son; that Robert died in 1700 leaving an infant son also called Robert.[57] From 1718 or earlier lessees held in trust for John Veysey of Chimney, living in 1733,[58] but by 1751 and probably from 1740 the estate, then 627 a., was held through

trustees by George Baskerville (d. 1777) of London.[59] He left it to Abraham Atkins (d. 1792) of Clapham (Mdx.) and Kingston Lisle in Sparsholt (Berks.),[60] who in 1786 vested a part (266 a.) in trustees for the support of Baptist ministers.[61] The rest (376 a.) passed to his nephew Edwin Martin (d. 1799), who took the additional surname Atkins, and to Edwin's son Atkins Edwin Martin Atkins, whose trustees recovered the remaining part of the Chimney estate in 1844.[62] Manorial rights became separated in 1838,[63] and in 1921 the Ecclesiastical Commissioners sold the estate to their tenant, C. J. Bartless.[64]

A probably stone-built manor house, south-west of modern Chimney Farm, was erected by Robert Veysey (d. 1635), presumably in the 1620s when he returned to Chimney from Taynton.[65] In 1635 it included a hall and parlour, both with rooms above, an upper and lower kitchen, an upper and lower study, and various service rooms, with more upper rooms at the 'parlour stair head' and 'on the entry', and a cockloft over the hall.[66] It was taxed on 8 hearths in the 1660s,[67] and in 1789 comprised an east–west range with end wings projecting southwards.[68] It remained the Veyseys' principal residence, and in the later 18th century George Baskerville reserved part for his own use, dividing his time between there and London; the rest was let to a tenant farmer,[69] and though Abraham Atkins reserved Baskerville's part for a relative in his will[70] no later owners of Chimney lived there. The house was demolished between 1830 and 1846.[71]

ECONOMIC HISTORY. Chimney's small open fields seem to have lain in a band across the middle of the township, on a gravel and clay terrace which still provided the only arable in the 19th century.[72] Church field, north-east of the hamlet, East or Great field (perhaps identical with Church field), and West field were apparently still open fields in 1681, but were probably much reduced and had been inclosed by 1789. Arable and pasture closes to the east

48 D. & C. Exeter, MS. M 1; ibid. Ch. Comm. 13/74363a; O.R.O., tithe map; O.S. Map 1", sheet 13 (1830 edn.); ibid. 1/2,500, Oxon. XXXVII. 16 (1876 and later edns.). For the man. ho., below, manor.
49 Ch. Com. Rec. L 7, pp. 357–9; cf. O.R.O., tithe award.
50 P.R.O., JUST 1/701, m. 23 and v. (ref. from J. Blair); cf. Bampton Hund. R. 76.
51 Bodl. MS. Top. Oxon. c 378, p. 409.
52 Above, Bampton and Weald, manors.
53 O.R.O., D.Y. VII/i/1; 1½ yardland was held with the Bampton moiety of the manor: D. & C. Exeter, MS. 4030, p. 11.
54 D. & C. Exeter, MS. 2000; B.L. Add. Ch. 38959; Bodl. MS. Top. Oxon. c 378, p. 272; cf. O.R.O., MS. Wills Oxon. 180, f. 39v.; ibid. 155/4/7; P.R.O., PROB 11/169, f. 59. A claim in Oxon. Visit. (Harl. Soc. v), 256–7 that Rob. was related to John Veysey, bp. of Exeter, is unsubstantiated: cf. D.N.B.
55 Bodl. MSS. d.d. Harcourt c 109/28–32; D. & C. Exeter, MS. 1982; ibid. MS. 4030, p. 10; Oxon. Visit. (Harl. Soc. v), 256–7.
56 P.R.O., PROB 11/322, f. 363v.; D. & C. Exeter, MS. 2001; Oxon. Visit. 256–7; cf. O.R.O., D.Y. VII/v/5; D. & C. Exeter, MSS. 6016/1/4–11.
57 O.R.O., D.Y. VII/vi/5; D. & C. Exeter, MSS. 6016/1/12–14; cf. Bodl. MS. d.d. Harcourt c 110/17.
58 D. & C. Exeter, MS. 4783; O.R.O., D.Y. VII/vi/7; cf.

ibid. MS. Wills Oxon. 87/6/13.
59 D. & C. Exeter, MSS. 6016/1/25–35; ibid. MSS. 1987–8, 2014.
60 P.R.O., PROB 11/1037, ff. 87–9.
61 V.C.H. Berks. iv. 319; Brief Acct. of Trusts created by A. Atkins (1803): copy in Baptist Union Corpn. file 1367/3; D. & C. Exeter, Ch. Comm. 14/74389.
62 P.R.O., PROB 11/1215, ff. 231v.–246; D. & C. Exeter, MSS. 6016/1/36–8; ibid. MS. 6016/9; ibid. Ch. Comm. 14/74386, 74389–93; Burke, Land. Gent. (1871), 34; V.C.H. Berks. iv. 315.
63 Above, Bampton and Weald, manors (Bampton Deanery).
64 Ch. Com. Rec. 38451.
65 D. & C. Exeter, MS. 1998; Bodl. MSS. d.d. Harcourt c 109/28–30; for stonework possibly from the house, above, intro.
66 B.L. Add. Ch. 38960.
67 Hearth Tax Oxon. 227; P.R.O., E 179/255/4, pt. i, f. 27.
68 D. & C. Exeter, MS. M 1.
69 Ibid. MSS. 1987, 1989, 2013–5, 2019–20; ibid. MS. 6016/6, letter from G. Frederick 22 Sept. 1768.
70 P.R.O., PROB 11/1215, f. 242v.
71 O.S. Map 1", sheet 13 (1830 edn.); O.R.O., tithe award and map; Giles, Hist. Bampton, 87.
72 O.R.O., tithe award and map; Geol. Surv. Map 1/50,000, solid and drift, sheet 236 (1982 edn.).

and west, recorded in the 17th century and including Corn ground, Long Acres, and Rye furlong, had presumably been taken from the fields earlier.[73] Yardlands in 1650 varied in size but were usually reckoned at *c*. 24 a., though the division of the township into 12 yardlands suggests a statute measure of up to 50 a. including meadow.[74]

Part of a common pasture at 'Sewalesweare', presumably near Showells mead in the south-west, was illegally appropriated by a tenant in 1429,[75] and was not mentioned later. The moor, which stretched across the north of the township adjoining Aston's and Shifford's commons,[76] was common pasture presumably from the Middle Ages: a tenant had 24 sheep and 2 colts there in 1611, and a 2-yardland holding in 1626 included 4 beast commons in the moor and horse commons in Horse leaze, perhaps a sub-division of the moor.[77] All or most of it seems to have been inclosed by the lessee of the manor during the 1630s, apparently without the lord's knowledge or permission, and by 1665 several tenants had no common rights at all and others had rights only in the highways, though holdings included numerous closes both in the moor and elsewhere.[78] Surviving common rights in 1665 were valued usually at *c*. 5*s*. per yardland.[79]

In the 18th century and presumably earlier Chimney's southern part and some areas further north were meadow.[80] All or part of Easthey, later the township's entire south-east corner within a loop of the Thames,[81] was by 1279 let to the tenants in common; the rent, recorded as 16*d*. presumably per yardland, rose by stages to a total of 66*s*. 8*d*. in 1317, still paid in 1420–1.[82] By the mid 17th century and probably much earlier Easthey had been divided into small closes held by various tenants.[83] Baingey, within another loop of the Thames in the south-west, was still partly common meadow in the mid 17th century, when some tenants held yards of meadow there proportionate to their holdings.[84] Most other meadows were then held severally as small hams and closes, and by 1789 Baingey, too, had been partitioned among the remaining tenants.[85] Although of excellent quality the meadows flooded frequently, which left a watery, putrefying scum after the waters had subsided, and greatly lessened their value.[86] Scouring of watercourses was mentioned frequently in 15th-century court rolls,[87] and lessees of the manor in the

1760s and 1770s, pressing for allowances, claimed that despite attempted improvements the problem had worsened, for which they blamed penning of the Thames for navigation by 'a lawless set of bargemen'.[88] In wet summers all but '3 or 4 fields that lie high near the homes' was sometimes flooded, ruining arable crops also.[89]

A wood called Cawatys or Cawete, mentioned in 1442 when the tenants were to ditch and hedge it, presumably included the later Cavet and perhaps Ash closes east of the hamlet, which together totalled *c*. 20 a.[90] In the Middle Ages the wood was apparently kept in demesne, and was perhaps that from which both Chimney and Bampton tenants in 1588 were to have timber for repairs at the lord's discretion.[91] It may have been reduced by 1504 when there were closes adjoining it, and the following year the homage was fined for cutting three small trees there without licence.[92] By the early 17th century the area was mostly pasture closes, and in 1619–20 Robert Veysey claimed that there was little wood in the township, which prompted tenants to plant quickset thorn hedges and fruit and other trees around their houses both for 'harbouring their cattle' and for fuel and timber.[93] In the 1630s and 1650s, however, lessees of the manor were accused of wastes including wrongful felling of trees,[94] and a tenant's holding in 1665 included 80 trees in Little Cabett (½ a.).[95] In 1789 the only trees were alongside some of the streams and in hedgerows between closes, presumably the source of timber sold from the estate in 1811.[96]

Chimney was not separately surveyed in 1086.[97] In 1279 there were 12 yardlands divided among 16 villein tenants, one holding 1½ yardland, 5 holding 1 yardland, 2 holding ¾ yardland, and 8 holding ½ yardland, and in 1317 there were also two cottages, one held for rent and the other for rent and services. Yardlanders owed similar harrowing, mowing, and harvest services as on the same manor in Bampton, but no ploughing or fallowing and less carting of wood; every two yardlanders were to supply a boat and two men for one day to ferry grain to Oxford, and at harvest all the tenants together were to find six carts to transport produce from the demesne. In 1279 the services were valued at 4*s*. 9¼*d*. per yardland compared with 10*s*. 2½*d*. in Bampton. Tenants of smaller holdings owed

73   D. & C. Exeter, MSS. 2934, 4775, 4780; ibid. MS. 2933, pp. 6–8; ibid. MS. M 1; ibid. Ch. Comm. 13/74363, pp. 31–5.
74   D. & C. Exeter, MS. 2933, p. 9; cf. O.S. *Area Bk.* (1877); below, this section.
75   D. & C. Exeter, MS. 4754.
76   Ibid. MS. M 1; O.R.O., tithe award and map.
77   O.R.O., MS. Wills Oxon. 297/1/12; D. & C. Exeter, MS. 4775.
78   D. & C. Exeter, MSS. 1996–7, 2934, 4776; ibid. MS. M 1; Bodl. MS. Ch. Oxon. 4491.
79   D. & C. Exeter, MS. 2934.
80   Ibid. MS. M 1; ibid. MS. 1993; ibid. Ch. Comm. 13/74363, pp. 30–5.
81   Ibid. MS. M 1; O.R.O., tithe award and map.
82   *Bampton Hund. R.* 77; D. & C. Exeter, MS. 2931, s.v. piscaria de Chimen'; ibid. MSS. 5100–4.
83   D. & C. Exeter, MSS. 2934, 4776; ibid. MS. M 1.
84   Ibid. MSS. 2934, 4775.
85   D. & C. Exeter, MSS. 2933–4, 4775–6; ibid. MS. M 1;

ibid. Ch. Comm. 13/74363.
86   Ibid. Ch. Comm. 13/74361a, valn. 1818; cf. P.R.O., C 2/Jas. I/U 1/56; ibid. E 134/1656–7/Hil. 20.
87   D. & C. Exeter, MSS. 4751–73.
88   Ibid. MSS. 1993, 2009–11, 2018.
89   Ibid. MS. 4544, p. 23; cf. ibid. MS. 2933, p. 9; ibid. MS. 6016/6, G. Frederick to D. & C. 22 Sept. 1768.
90   D. & C. Exeter, MS. 4757; ibid. Ch. Comm. 13/74363a.
91   Bodl. MS. Rolls Oxon. 57.
92   D. & C. Exeter, MS. 4773.
93   Ibid. MSS. 4775–6; P.R.O., C 2/Jas. I/U 1/56.
94   P.R.O., E 134/1656–7/Hil. 20, mm. 1–2; D. & C. Exeter, MSS. 1996–7, 3499 (166).
95   D. & C. Exeter, MS. 2934.
96   Ibid. MS. M 1; ibid. Ch. Comm. 13/74361a, survey of Parsonage estate 1811.
97   For Exeter cathedral's manor, including Chimney, above, Bampton and Weald, econ. hist. (agric.).

the same services as yardlanders but with a proportionate reduction in ferrying and carting. Rents were charged proportionately at 5s. 8d. a yardland including 20d. aid, slightly heavier than in Bampton, and all except cottagers owed hearthpenny.[98] Land granted in villeinage in 1262 for 21s. 1d. a year[99] cannot be identified later. Harrowing and hay-lifting services were apparently sometimes commuted by 1317, presumably because of the distance from the demesne, which probably explains differences in rents and services generally between Chimney and Bampton. All services were commuted before 1416–17, when sale of works from the 12 yardlands and one cottage yielded 93s. 11½d.[1]

Assessed wealth rose from c. £60 in 1306 to over £96 in 1327, though some substantial taxpayers seem not to have been manorial tenants and, since there were no freeholds, were perhaps entered under Chimney in error. Average personalty was nevertheless relatively high compared with Bampton's other outlying townships, with some large payments from villeins. The wealthiest taxpayer in 1316, assessed on goods worth £8, held a yardland with a share in a fishery, and the tenant of 1½ yardland was taxed on £6, though one tenant of ¾ yardland paid on only 20s. The lowest contributors in 1316, each assessed on 12s., were a cottager and possibly a half-yardlander, though some individual assessments varied widely in different years.[2]

Rent increases in the late 14th century suggest that the effects of the Black Death were limited,[3] but by the early 15th century holdings were becoming concentrated among fewer tenants, notably members of the Sely family, some holdings were remaining vacant, and rents were falling.[4] In 1437 a tenant was presented to the manor court for removing doors, a lead cistern, and other fittings from a presumably vacant house of which he was tenant,[5] and in 1427 a vacated croft was let to all the tenants in common.[6] In 1438 a yardlander left the lordship 'on account of poverty', and his goods were seized.[7] Though depopulation evidently halted, Chimney seems never to have recovered fully,[8] and none of the surnames mentioned from the 13th century to the 15th survived into the 16th and 17th.

Several inhabitants in the 16th and 17th centuries were moderately successful yeomen by local standards, and some held lands elsewhere.[9]

Sixteenth-century taxpayers, including members of the Veysey, Minchin, and Farr families which all remained prominent in the 17th century, paid frequently on between £3 and £5-worth of goods, and in 1561 a tenant taxed possibly on £4 in 1523–4 left goods worth c. £77.[10] Three tenants in the 17th and early 18th century left over £200 and four more left over £100, while William Farr (d. 1623) and Thomas Stampe (d. 1694) were called gentlemen.[11] Only one inhabitant was taxed on less than three hearths in 1662, though one was discharged through poverty in 1665, and two widows in the late 16th century and early 17th left less than £10.[12]

Repairs to a tenant's sheephouse and cowhouse were required in 1490,[13] and in the 17th century livestock often accounted for most of an individual's wealth.[14] Most testators owned some cattle, several made cheese, and herds of 10 and 24 were recorded in 1594 and 1718.[15] Not all testators left sheep, perhaps because pastures were too low and wet, though a tenant in 1605 had 59 worth £18 besides 11 cows and a calf worth £20, and William Farr had 30 in 1623.[16] Pigs and poultry, including ducks and, in the 15th century, geese,[17] were also kept. Wheat, beans, pulses, and barley were all grown, hemp was mentioned in 1611,[18] and several farmers made malt, though hay was often the most valuable crop: a tenant in 1605 left 30 loads worth £20, and in 1719 another's was valued at £56 compared with wheat, beans, and barley worth c. £66.[19]

Tenants in the earlier 17th century still held by copy, granted for two lives and a widow's estate. Farms then ranged from ¼ yardland to 2 yardlands, and there was a cottager whose house was being built or rebuilt c. 1615.[20] Manorial customs, including housebote, hedgebote, and firebote, were confirmed in 1588, but litigation arose between Robert Veysey (d. 1635) and a tenant in the 1620s,[21] and in 1657 Veysey's successor was accused of destroying copyholds in Chimney. One farm of ½ yardland and another of ¾ yardland, from which lands had reportedly been detached, were then let at rack rent, and seven surviving copyholds were held by relatives of the Veyseys who apparently sublet them also at rack rent.[22] The practice evidently continued,[23] and though copyhold and leasehold lands were still distinguished in the 18th century, in practice the whole estate was then let.

98 D. & C. Exeter, MS. 2931; *Bampton Hund. R.* 76–7.
99 D. & C. Exeter, MS. 736.
1 Ibid. MS. 2931, substituting *vel dabit* for *et valet*; ibid. MS. 5100.
2 P.R.O., E 179/161/8–10; cf. *Bampton Hund. R.* 76–7; D. & C. Exeter, MS. 2931.
3 D. & C. Exeter, MSS. 5100–5, s.v. *vendatio operum*; ibid. MS. 3550, ff. 52v.–53; cf. above, intro.
4 D. & C. Exeter MSS. 4751–4773 (ct. rolls 1396–1505); cf. ibid. MS. 2931.
5 Ibid. MS. 4751, s.a. 16 Hen. VI.
6 Ibid. MS. 4753.
7 Ibid. MS. 4751.
8 Above, intro.
9 e.g. O.R.O., MS. Wills Oxon. 43/1/20; P.R.O., PROB 11/145, f. 387 and v.; PROB 11/250, ff. 356v.–357; PROB 11/357, ff. 108v.–109.
10 P.R.O., E 179/161/172; E 179/162/234, 320, 341; O.R.O., MS. Wills Oxon. 184, f. 21 and v.
11 O.R.O., MSS. Wills Oxon. 43/3/19, 43/4/47, 122/1/22,

127/1/6, 163/3/21, 174/2/32, 297/1/12.
12 Ibid. 120/1/13; ibid. 185, f. 460; P.R.O., E 179/255/4, pt. i, f. 27; *Hearth Tax Oxon.* 227.
13 D. & C. Exeter, MS. 4768.
14 Para. based on O.R.O., MSS. Wills Oxon., Chimney wills and inventories.
15 O.R.O., MSS. Wills Oxon. 3/3/30, 122/1/22.
16 Ibid. 43/3/19, 127/1/6; cf. P.R.O., C 2/Jas. I/U 1/56, answer of Wm. Minchin.
17 D. & C. Exeter, MS. 4761.
18 O.R.O., MS. Wills Oxon. 297/1/12.
19 Ibid. 43/3/19, 122/1/22.
20 D. & C. Exeter, MSS. 2933–4, 4775–6; P.R.O., PROB 11/132, f. 242 and v.
21 Bodl. MS. Rolls Oxon. 57; P.R.O., C 2/Jas. I/B 14/60.
22 P.R.O., E 134/1656–7/Hil. 20; D. & C. Exeter, MS. 2933, pp. 5–9; ibid. MS. 2934; cf. *Protestation Rtns. and Tax Assess.* 9; P.R.O., E 179/255/4, pt. i, f. 27.
23 D. & C. Exeter, MS. 4780.

There were by then only 3 farms, one (218 a.) centred on the manor house, another (245 a.) centred on Lower Farm, and a third (95 a.) centred on a later-demolished homestead south of the manor house. As in the 17th century a few small hams, totalling 96 a. in 1789, were held by outsiders.[24] By 1841 the estate had been consolidated into two farms of c. 358 a. and 239 a., centred still on Lower Farm and on the manor house, and later on the predecessor of modern Chimney Farm.[25]

Continued flooding and the impossibility of improving the land led in the mid 18th century to repeated disputes over renewal fines between Exeter cathedral and lessees of the manor, and in 1775 and 1776 two tenants, one of 20 years' standing, quit rather than accept a 10 per cent rent increase.[26] In 1866 it was hoped that an embankment recently built by the tenants would improve matters,[27] and the Thames Valley Drainage schemes of the later 19th century were said in 1914 to have had some effect generally, though seasonal flooding on low ground continued, notably in meadows south of Shifford Lock cut.[28] The area of arable was increased slightly during the earlier 19th century from c. 85 a. (13 per cent) to c. 143 a. (22 per cent), chiefly through conversion of closes in the former moor and east and south of Church field, and by 1877 arable totalled 205 a. (32 per cent);[29] Chimney remained chiefly pastoral, however, and in 1914 dairy farming predominated, sheep being kept in very small numbers compared with further west. Wheat was the chief crop, followed by barley, oats, swedes and turnips, and mangolds.[30] The estate was run as a single farm from the early 20th century.[31]

One of two fisheries owned by Exeter cathedral in 1086, together worth 33s. a year, was presumably in Chimney, where in 1279 the chapter had 3 weirs and a fishery in the Thames worth 20s.[32] One was perhaps the 'Sewalesweare' mentioned in 1429, presumably near Showells mead;[33] a later weir near there, said to have survived in 1821, did not, however, belong to the Chimney estate.[34] Later weirs at Duxford and Tenfoot bridge also lay outside the lordship in Berkshire,[35] and the sites of the other medieval weirs are unknown. By 1317 fishing rights were leased

to 10 tenants for 33s. 8d. a year, individual payments (unrelated to the size of their other holdings) varying from 1s. to 10s. 2d.;[36] four Chimney tenants and a co-defendant probably from Shifford were named before the justices in eyre for fishing with kiddles in 1285, and in 1429 seven tenants were fined by the manor court for taking pickerel contrary to Statute.[37] Rent for the fishery was still recorded in the earlier 15th century, when a Chimney tenant owed 12d. fish tithe from 2 'locks',[38] and in the 16th and 17th centuries fishing rights in the Thames and its backstreams continued to be let piecemeal to tenants and sometimes, with small hams, to outsiders.[39] Two copyholds in the 1650s and 1660s included fishpools, one of them at Lock ham adjoining the township's northern boundary.[40] By the later 18th century all the fishing rights, together with the 'fishing hams' by the western boundary and birding of the water meadows, were held by Richard Kent, presumably one of the family associated with Tadpole and Duxford weirs;[41] the hams and fishery remained in the family in 1847[42] but were not mentioned later.

LOCAL GOVERNMENT. Chimney's inhabitants attended Bampton Deanery manor court as a separate tithing, probably from the late 13th century and certainly by the 14th. In 1437 and still in 1781 the court elected a constable for Chimney, and in the early 17th century two or three grass stewards;[43] earlier it presumably elected a hayward, since Hayward's Lane was mentioned in 1450.[44] In 1641 the tithing was fined for not maintaining a pair of stocks.[45]

The township appointed a chapelwarden for Shifford probably in the 15th century and still in the late 19th.[46] Only one overseer for Chimney and Shifford was mentioned in 1642,[47] but in 1666 both townships may have had their own,[48] and in the later 18th century Chimney administered its own poor relief. Despite its small population large sums were spent, £17 in 1775–6 and about the same between 1783 and 1785; £36 (c. 27s. per head) were spent in 1803, when 1 adult and 4 children received out relief. By 1813 capitation was c. 52s., and by 1817 £3 7s., the highest in the area; 6 or 7 people,

24 Ibid. MSS. 1987–93; ibid. Ch. Comm. 13/74363, pp. 30–5; ibid. Ch. Comm. 13/74363a.

25 P.R.O., HO 107/872; O.R.O., tithe award; above, intro.

26 D. & C. Exeter, MSS. 1989–90, 2009–12, 2017–20; ibid. MS. 6016/6, G. Frederick to D. & C. 22 Sept. 1768.

27 Ch. Com. Rec. L 7, p. 443.

28 O.S. Maps 1/2,500, Oxon. XXXVII. 16, XXXVIII. 13 (1899 edn.); Orr, Oxon. Agric. 46.

29 D. & C. Exeter, Ch. Comm. 13/74363, p. 35; ibid. 13/74363a, nos. 39–51; O.R.O., tithe award; O.S. Area Bk. (1877).

30 Orr, Oxon. Agric. statistical plates.

31 Kelly's Dir. Oxon. (1883 and later edns.).

32 V.C.H. Oxon. i. 402; Bampton Hund. R. 76.

33 D. & C. Exeter, MS. 4754; cf. O.R.O., tithe award and map.

34 F. S. Thacker, Thames Highway (1968 edn.), ii. 67–9.

35 O.S. Map 6", Oxon. XXXVII–XXXVIII (1883–4 edns.); D. & C. Exeter, MS. M 1; ibid. MS. 4544, p. 22. For the weirs, Thacker, Thames Highway, ii. 69–72.

36 D. & C. Exeter, MS. 2931; Bampton Hund. R. 77 n. mistakenly gives the total as £2 13s. 8d.

37 D. & C. Exeter, MS. 4754; P.R.O., JUST 1/705, m. 22 (ref. from J. Blair).

38 D. & C. Exeter, MSS. 5100–4; cf. ibid. MSS. 4751, 4754.

39 Ibid. MSS. 4772, 2934; O.R.O., MSS. Wills Oxon. 43/1/20, 43/3/19; P.R.O., E 134/1656–7/Hil. 20, m. 3 and d.

40 D. & C. Exeter, MSS. 2933, p. 7; 2934, s.v. Veysey, Farr.

41 Ibid. MS. 1992; ibid. Ch. Comm. 13/74363a, no. 47; Thacker, Thames Highway, ii. 66–7, 72.

42 O.R.O., tithe award.

43 D. & C. Exeter, MSS. 4751–83; ibid. Ch. Comm. 80/134543; above, Bampton and Weald, local govt. (manor cts.).

44 D. & C. Exeter, MS. 4759.

45 Ibid. MS. 4776; cf. O.R.O., Cal. Q.S. ix, p. 53.

46 Below, Shifford, church.

47 Protestation Rtns. and Tax Assess. 1.

48 P.R.O., PROB 11/322, f. 363v.

perhaps including children, were receiving regular relief between 1813 and 1815, and another 7 or 8 occasional relief. In the 1820s capitation was never less than £1 4s. and by 1832 was over £2, a total expenditure of £87;[49] poor rates in 1835 totalled c. £70.[50]

From 1834 Chimney belonged to Witney union, and from 1894 to Witney rural district. In 1974 it became part of West Oxfordshire district.[51]

CHURCH. A chapel of St. James was mentioned in 1575, when it was sold as a 'cottage'.[52] No earlier references have been found, and there is no evidence to link the chapel to Chimney's Anglo-Saxon burial ground.[53] In the 1630s Robert Veysey (d. 1635) was accused of profaning the chapel, suggesting that it still served some ecclesiastical function, and in 1657 a 50-year-old deponent remembered hearing the epistles, gospels, and Lord's Prayer read there; another recalled it being used as a school, however, and in 1634 Veysey asserted that it had been used for c. 70 years as a church house for Whitsun ales, claiming further to have rebuilt it in the early 1620s after Chimney's inhabitants refused to meet the cost.[54] In the late 1650s it was reportedly used for impounding cattle, and was demolished perhaps in 1758 and certainly

by 1789.[55] Its site, said in 1657 to be 'near' the Veyseys' manor house, is unidentified; the remains of 'Chapel Barn', west of modern Chimney Farm, are not identifiably medieval.[56]

NONCONFORMITY. A will in 1572 contained Roman Catholic invocations,[57] but no recusants were noted later. Tenants in the later 18th century and the 19th, notably members of the Williams, Pinnock, and probably Peck families, were prominent members of the Baptist meeting at Cote,[58] and Abraham Atkins (d. 1792), non-resident lessee of Chimney under Exeter cathedral, established trusts in support of several Baptist congregations including Cote.[59]

EDUCATION. In 1657 a man recalled going to school in the former chapel at Chimney c. 1600,[60] but no later references have been found. Children in the 19th century attended Aston school.[61]

CHARITIES FOR THE POOR. A bequest by Robert Veysey (d. 1666) to the poor of Chimney and Shifford was lost by 1787, when Chimney had no recorded charities.[62]

LOWER HADDON

IN the 14th century Lower or Little Haddon, later c. 457 a.,[63] was taxed with Marsh Haddon in Brize Norton parish as a single township.[64] From the 13th century and probably from the 11th the two were tenurially distinct, however, the later estate boundary coinciding with that of the parish, and possibly there were two separate foci from an early date.[65] The name, meaning 'uncultivated hill slope', suggests relatively late colonization; no evidence of early occupation has been noted on either site, and neither was mentioned before the early 13th century.[66] The prefixes 'Marsh' and 'Little' were recorded in the late 13th century and early 14th, though Little Haddon seems then to have been the more populous.[67] The name

Lower Haddon became established in the later 19th century.[68]

In 1279 only 5 tenants were recorded at Lower Haddon besides the lord, presumably indicating c. 6 houses; 4 inhabitants were noted at Marsh Haddon, and in 1306 there were 13 taxpayers in the two settlements.[69] The population was probably little altered in 1331 when rents at Lower Haddon exceeded those recorded in 1279;[70] only 10 persons over 14 paid poll tax in 1377, however,[71] which, assuming the return was for both estates, suggests serious depopulation, far greater than in most of Bampton's hamlets. Only three houses were recorded on Little Haddon manor in 1496[72] and in the mid 17th century, when they were assessed on 7, 4, and 3 hearths,[73]

49 *Poor Abstract, 1804, 1818*; *Poor Rate Returns*, H.C. 556, p. 135 (1822), v; ibid. H.C. 334, p. 170 (1825), iv; ibid. H.C. 83, p. 157 (1830–1), xi; ibid. H.C. 444, p. 153 (1835), xlvii; cf. *Census*, 1801–41.
50 D. & C. Exeter, Ch. Comm. 13/74364.
51 O.R.O., RO 3251, pp. 201–3; RO 3267.
52 P.R.O., C 66/1125, m. 23. 53 Above, intro.
54 *Cal. S.P. Dom.* 1635–6, 113; P.R.O., E 134/1656–7/Hil. 20, m. 3 and d.; D. & C. Exeter, MS. 1998.
55 P.R.O., E 134/1656–7/Hil. 20, m. 2; Bodl. MS. Top. Oxon. d 218, f. 41; D. & C. Exeter, MS. 4544; ibid. MS. M 1.
56 P.R.O., E 134/1656–7/Hil. 20, mm. 2d.–4; *Oxoniensia*, liv. 48, 50.
57 O.R.O., MS. Wills Oxon. 185, ff. 127v.–128.
58 'Cote Baptist Ch. Recs.' (TS. in C.O.S.), *passim*; B. Williams, *Memorials of the Family of Williams* (priv. print. 1849), 37; Baptist Union Corpn. file 1367/2, trust renewal 1830; cf. D. & C. Exeter, MS. 2032.
59 P.R.O., PROB 11/1215, f. 242 and v.; *V.C.H. Berks.* iv. 319; *Brief Acct. of Trusts created by A. Atkins* (1803): copy in Baptist Union Corpn. file 1367/3; above, manor.

60 P.R.O., E 134/1656–7/Hil. 20, m. 3.
61 Above, Aston and Cote, educ.
62 *Char. Don.* 968–9; below, Shifford, charities.
63 O.R.O., Bampton incl. award; for boundaries, above, Bampton, general intro.; Bampton and Weald, intro.
64 P.R.O., E 179/161/10; cf. *Bampton Hund. R.* 24, 26–7; *Sel. Coroners' Rolls* (Selden Soc. ix), p. 93.
65 *Bampton Hund. R.* 24, 26–7; *V.C.H. Oxon.* i. 415, 423–4; O.R.O., Bampton incl. award, plan V. Brize Norton is reserved for treatment in a later volume.
66 *P.N. Oxon.* (E.P.N.S.), ii. 307.
67 *Bampton Hund. R.* 24, 26–7; *Cal. Pat.* 1330–4, pp. 88, 115.
68 O.S. Map 6", Oxon. XXXVII (1884 edn.); cf. Jefferys, *Oxon. Map* (1767), showing Bampton Haddon.
69 *Bampton Hund. R.* 24, 26–7; P.R.O., E 179/161/10; cf. ibid. E 179/161/8–9.
70 Below, econ. hist. 71 P.R.O., E 179/161/42.
72 *Cal. Inq. p.m. Hen. VII*, i, p. 535.
73 P.R.O., E 179/255/4, pt. i, f. 19; *Hearth Tax Oxon.* 223; cf. *Protestation Rtns. and Tax Assess.* 7; B.L. Add. Ch. 38921, calling Lower Haddon a 'lone house or farm' in 1639.

and from the later 18th century there were only two,[74] one of them the former manor house, later Lower Haddon Farm, described below.[75] The other, *c.* 150 yd. to the north-east, was that called

built across Lower Haddon's northern part *c.* 1873; the line was closed in 1962.[79] Brize Norton military airbase, which occupies Lower Haddon's western part, was opened in 1937

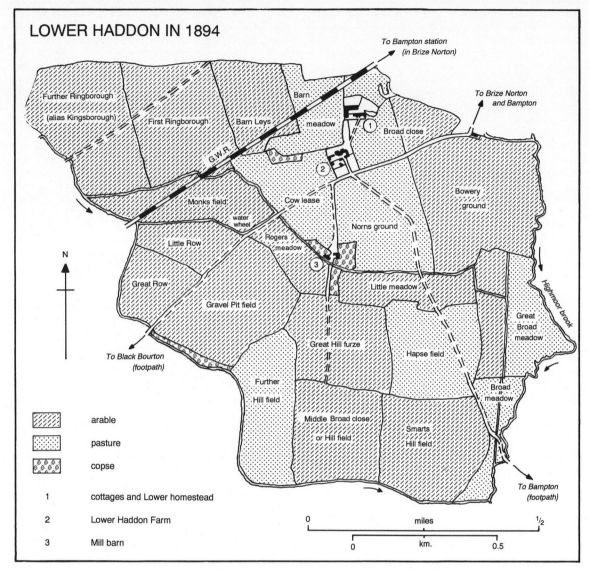

LOWER HADDON IN 1894

To Bampton station (in Brize Norton)

To Brize Norton and Bampton

Further Ringborough
(alias Kingsborough)
First Ringborough
Barn Leys
Barn
meadow
Broad close
G.W.R.
Monks field
water wheel
Cow lease
Bowery ground
Norns ground
Rogers meadow
Little Row
Great Row
Gravel Pit field
Little meadow
Great Broad meadow
Hapse field
Great Hill furze
Further Hill field
Broad meadow
Middle Broad close or Hill field
Smarts Hill field
Highmoor brook

To Black Bourton (footpath)

To Bampton (footpath)

N

arable

pasture

copse

1   cottages and Lower homestead

2   Lower Haddon Farm

3   Mill barn

0   miles   ½

0   km.   0.5

the 'Lower House', recorded from the early 17th century when it was temporarily occupied by a relative of the lord and was described as a mansion house.[76] It was later occupied by tenant farmers and *c.* 1800 was converted into a cowhouse and agricultural buildings;[77] labourers' cottages on the site in the later 19th century were demolished in the 20th reportedly following a fire, though agricultural buildings remained in 1992. Other cottages were built on the approach from the Bampton–Brize Norton road before 1894.[78]

Part of the East Gloucestershire railway was

and extended in the 1950s, its perimeter fence coming within a few hundred yards of the farmhouse. Proposals *c.* 1957 to extend the main runway across the Bampton–Brize Norton road were rejected.[80]

MANOR. In 1279 *c.* 2 carucates in Lower Haddon, later *LITTLE HADDON* manor, were held of William de Valence by John of Haddon for rent and tallage totalling 29*s.* 11*d.*, perhaps following a recent grant since the holding was not mentioned in Henry III's bestowal of Bamp-

74 Blenheim Mun., shelf J 4, box 19, conveyance 1782; cf. ibid. conveyance 1724; O.R.O., QSD E.1, pp. 95–6; ibid. D.Y. V/i/4; D.Y. XI/i/1–2.

75 Below, manor.

76 B.L. Add. Ch. 38918; O.R.O., D.Y. VI/i/1–2; D.Y. VI/i/ 7; ibid. Bampton incl. award, plan V.

77 Blenheim Mun., shelf J 4, box 19, conveyances 1782, 1803; ibid. box 20, release 1844; *Hearth Tax Oxon.* 223.

78 *Sale Cat.* (1894): copy (with plan) in Bodl. G.A. Oxon. b 90 (12); P.R.O., RG 11/1514, s.v. Weald; inf. from Mr. J. R. Bosley, Lower Haddon Fm.

79 Above, Bampton and Weald, intro.; O.S. Map 6", Oxon. XXXVII (1884 edn.).

80 *Rec. of Witney* (Witney and District Hist. and Arch. Soc. Newsletter), no. 5 (Dec. 1978), p. 8: copy in C.O.S.; *Oxf. Times*, 1 Feb. 1957; inf. from Mr. J. R. Bosley.

ton manor on William in 1248.[81] Before 1324 Aymer de Valence regranted the estate, later 10 yardlands,[82] to the same or another John in fee simple, to be held of Bampton manor for quit-rent of 29s. 11d.;[83] the sum was still owed in the 18th century, though in 1496 and later the manor was said to be held for knight service as ½ or ¹⁄₁₀ knight's fee.[84]

John granted the estate to John Laurence de la More, who before 1331 gave it to his son Thomas (later Sir Thomas) de la More or at More, knight of the shire in 1340, 1343, and 1351.[85] It passed probably to Thomas's son Thomas (d. c. 1393), a royal justice, to that Thomas's son Thomas (d. by 1424), to the youngest Thomas's brother Robert More (fl. 1445), and to Robert's son John More (d. 1493);[86] thereafter it passed to John's relict Ellen (d. 1495) and grandson John (d. 1542), to that John's son Thomas (d. 1561), to Thomas's son William (d. 1608), and to William's cousin John More, to whom William's relict Hester gave up a life interest.[87] In 1608 John conveyed a moiety to his relative Bartholomew Peisley, who had already acquired an interest and was then living at Haddon, but the following year the moiety was sold back.[88] John More later mortgaged the estate, and in 1625 sold it to Sir Edward Yate (d. 1645), Bt., of Buckland (formerly Berks.), apparently to clear his debts;[89] it descended with Buckland until the late 18th century, passing through marriage in 1690 to the Throckmortons of Coughton (Warws.).[90]

In 1793 trustees appointed by Sir Robert Throckmorton (d. 1791) sold it to a firm of Chipping Norton bankers, who in 1803 sold it to Edward Whitaker of Bampton. Whitaker heavily mortgaged the estate and died in 1825, leaving it in trust, but by a Chancery order of 1834 full ownership was vested in the surviving mortgagee, Rear Admiral Robert Jackson, who had sued the trustees and beneficiaries under Whitaker's will for non-payment of the interest and capital.[91] In 1842 Jackson sold the estate to George Churchill (d. 1857), duke of Marlborough, who vested it in trustees;[92] though it was still called a manor in 1845 manorial rights were not mentioned later and had probably lapsed, and thereafter the estate was usually described as a

farm. Following an abortive sale in 1894 it was sold by the Blenheim estate to the tenant, R. C. Nisbet, between 1920 and 1924.[93]

There was a manor house presumably in 1279, when John of Haddon held 6 yardlands in demesne, and certainly by 1331, when Thomas de la More was licensed to have an oratory in his house there,[94] though until the 16th century not all lords may have resided.[95] Probably the house stood on the site of Lower Haddon Farm, whose west wing contains on the ground floor a richly moulded and beamed ceiling of the late 16th century or early 17th, and which was presumably the house or 'capital messuage' with a grange mentioned frequently between 1581 and 1625.[96] After the Mores sold the manor the house was let to farmers, and was taxed on probably 7 hearths in 1662 and 1665;[97] in the 18th century a central chimney was inserted, and the large room with the beamed ceiling was divided into two rooms and a passage, presumably following the demolition of an earlier parlour wing on the west. A much-altered eastern cross wing, now containing an entrance hall, staircase, and kitchen, was later enlarged by the piecemeal addition of a parallel range along its east side, and in the early 19th century the old and new wings were both given a new south front. The older parts of the house seem to have been entirely refaced and refenestrated later in the century.

ECONOMIC HISTORY. Lower Haddon may have had its own fields in 1279 when holdings were measured in yardlands,[98] but by the 17th century and probably much earlier the township had been fully inclosed, perhaps following 14th- and 15th-century depopulation.[99] Apse wood, recorded in 1331 and presumably including later Hapse field (c. 24 a.) in the south-east, had been cleared probably by 1496 when no woodland was mentioned,[1] and in the 17th century was evidently inclosed meadow and pasture.[2] Around 30 a. of woodland mentioned in early 17th-century fines lay apparently in small coppices in the north-east and elsewhere,[3] and throughout the 19th century there was c. 3 a. of wood and coppice.[4]

[81] *Bampton Hund. R.* 26–7; *Close R.* 1247–51, 133; cf. D. & C. Exeter, MS. 736; *Oxon. Eyre, 1241* (O.R.S. lvi), no. 506.
[82] *Cal. Inq. p. m. Hen. VII,* i, p. 535.
[83] *Cal. Pat.* 1330–4, 88, giving the service as 29s.; cf., however, P.R.O., C 139/42, no. 86; B.L. Add. MS. 27535, f. 44 (29s. 11½d.); Arundel Castle, MS. TP 288.
[84] O.R.O., QSD E.1, p. 97; P.R.O., C 142/66, no. 60; *Cal. Inq. p.m. Hen. VII,* i, p. 535.
[85] *Cal. Pat.* 1330–4, 88, 115; *Chron. Reigns Edw. I and II* (Rolls Ser.), ii, p. lxiii; Lincs. R.O., episc. regs. v, f. 167v.; vii, f. 164v.
[86] *Cal. Close* 1392–6, 141; *Cal. Inq. p.m. Hen. VII,* i, p. 399; Balliol Coll. Arch., A.19.50; Magd. Coll. Mun., Standlake 7A, 14–15, 18, 23A; Bodl. MSS. d.d. Harcourt c 68/18–44, witness lists.
[87] *Cal. Inq. p.m. Hen. VII,* i, pp. 399, 534–5; P.R.O., PROB 11/29, ff. 89 and v.; PROB 11/44, ff. 115v.–116v.; PROB 11/113, ff. 101v.–102; O.R.O., D.Y. V/i/1–3.
[88] O.R.O., D.Y. V/i/1–6; D.Y. VI/i/1; ibid. Misc. Bod. VIII/i/1; B.L. Add. Ch. 38915–6.
[89] O.R.O., D.Y. VI/i/2, 4, 6, 8; B.L. Add. Ch. 38918–9; cf. O.A.S. *Rep.* (1871), 37 n.
[90] e.g. B.L. Add. Ch. 38521; O.R.O., D.Y. VI/i/7; D.Y.

XI/i/3; Blenheim Mun., shelf J 4, box 20, settlement 23 Apr. 1724; cf. G.E.C. *Baronetage,* i. 205–6; ii. 197–8.
[91] Blenheim Mun., shelf J 4, box 19.
[92] Ibid. box 20.
[93] *Sale Cat.* 3 July 1894: copy in Bodl. G.A. Oxon. b 90 (12); *Kelly's Dir. Oxon.* (1920 and 1924 edns.).
[94] *Bampton Hund. R.* 26–7; Lincs. R.O., episc. regs. v, ff. 164v., 167v.; vii, f. 164v.
[95] Below, Northmoor, manors.
[96] *Acts of P.C.* 1581–2, 290; 1587–8, 72; O.R.O., D.Y. V/i/1–3; B.L. Add. Ch. 38915, 38918.
[97] *Hearth Tax Oxon.* 223; P.R.O., E179/255/4, pt. i, f. 19; Blenheim Mun., shelf J 4, box 19, settlement 10 Aug. 1782.
[98] *Bampton Hund. R.* 24, 26–7.
[99] B.L. Add. Ch. 38918; O.R.O., Bampton incl. award, plan V; above, intro.
[1] *Cal. Pat.* 1330–4, 88, 115; *Cal. Inq. p.m. Hen. VII,* i, p. 535; O.R.O., Bampton incl. award.
[2] B.L. Add. Ch. 38918.
[3] Ibid.; O.R.O., D.Y. V/i/2; D.Y. XI/i/2; cf. O.R.O., Bampton incl. award.
[4] O.R.O., Bampton incl. award; Blenheim Mun., shelf J 4, box 20, release 9 Dec. 1844; Bodl. G.A. Oxon. b 90 (12).

In 1086 Haddon was surveyed presumably with Bampton. In 1279 there were 6 yardlands in demesne, and 3 freehold and 2 villein tenants each held ½ yardland; of the freehold tenements one owed 2s. and was sublet for 2s. 6d., though the others each owed 1d. only. The villeins each owed 20d. rent, besides unusually heavy labour services valued at 10s. 4d.[5] In the earlier 14th century the township was taxed separately from Bampton only in 1306,[6] when 13 inhabitants of Marsh and Lower Haddon paid a total of 25s. 8d.; excepting John of Haddon's payment of 7s., presumably for the demesne, contributions ranged from 9d. on goods worth 22s. 6d. to 3s. on goods worth 90s. A taxpayer assessed on c. 50s. was probably a freeholder, and another assessed on 60s. may have been a villein;[7] average personalty was slightly lower than in Bampton's other outlying townships.

Rents in 1331 totalled 31s. 11½d.,[8] more than the total for rents and services in 1279, but Haddon seems to have suffered serious depopulation during the 14th century; by the later 15th, when there were only 3 houses, it had perhaps already been inclosed.[9] The Mores may by then have exploited much of the township directly, and in the 16th century they were taxed on lands valued at up to £80 a year. Some land was presumably let to the remaining inhabitants, and from c. 1625 the manor house and farm were let also.[10] In the mid 17th century and early 18th there were 3 chief farms held at rack rent, and some land was let to outsiders, including c. 95 a. held by Bampton and Black Bourton butchers in 1736.[11] By the 1770s the whole of Lower Haddon was let with land elsewhere as a farm of c. 500 a., for much of the 19th century to the Gilletts,[12] and in the 1920s it was sold as a single farm.[13]

Despite early inclosure, farming remained mixed. John More had over 200 sheep in 1540, pastured apparently in Lew,[14] and dairying and cheesemaking were recorded in the 17th and 18th centuries; some land was arable in 1625, and a tenant in 1710 had crops worth £100 besides dairy cattle, pigs, and 20 sheep.[15] In 1844 Haddon farm was 62 per cent arable and by 1894 over 70 per cent, though it was capable of supporting a good head of stock, notably sheep, and included piggeries and a sheepwash.[16] A shepherd was recorded in 1881.[17]

A broadweaver was mentioned in 1705.[18] A waterwheel on a small stream in the north-west and a 'mill house' (apparently only a barn or shed) some distance away were marked on a map of 1894,[19] but no other references have been found.

LOCAL GOVERNMENT. In 1279 the lord of Little Haddon and presumably his tenants owed suit to Bampton Earls manor.[20] A separate court baron may have been instituted in the early 14th century when Haddon manor was regranted in fee,[21] but in 1500 the tithingman attended the Bampton view of frankpledge, at which his successors were still appointed in the later 17th century.[22] For poor-law and other civil purposes Haddon was administered with Bampton and Weald through Bampton vestry, treated above.[23]

CHURCH. No documentary evidence has been found for a parochial chapel at Lower Haddon, though a large, reportedly cruciform stone barn c. 360 yd. south of Lower Haddon Farm, demolished c. 1956 when its site was taken into Brize Norton airfield, featured lancet windows and crosses on the gables, and in the early 20th century was locally believed to have been a former chapel.[24] If so the absence of 16th-century documentation, in contrast with Bampton's other chapels, would suggest that it had been secularized before the Reformation, perhaps following late medieval depopulation;[25] the building was not marked on early 19th-century maps, however, and may simply have been a field barn built soon after Bampton's inclosure.[26]

NONCONFORMITY. The Mores were noted recusants into the 17th century. Mass, attended by family members and servants, was said regularly in their manor house in 1581; in the same year Phillippe Pollard of Lower Haddon confessed to having sheltered the Jesuit Edmund Campion in her house there, and in 1587 William More's goods were temporarily siezed after he was accused of harbouring seminary priests.[27] His daughter Ann Vaughan and son-in-law Thomas Tempest were fined also.[28] Later lords, though recusant, were non-resident,[29] and no further nonconformity is recorded.

5 *Bampton Hund. R.* 26–7.   6 P.R.O., E 179/161/10.
7 Cf. *Bampton Hund. R.* 24, 26–7.
8 *Cal. Pat.* 1330–4, 88, 115.
9 *Cal. Inq. p.m. Hen. VII,* i, p. 535; above, intro.
10 P.R.O., E 179/162/234, E 179/162/320, E 179/162/341; above, manor.
11 O.R.O., QSD E.1, pp. 94–7; ibid. D.Y. VI/ii/1; P.R.O., E 179/255/4, pt. i, f. 19; *Hearth Tax Oxon.* 223.
12 Blenheim Mun., shelf J 4, box 19, settlement 10 Aug. 1782; ibid. box 20, release 9 Dec. 1844; P.R.O., RG 9/905; *Oxf. Jnl.* 14 Aug. 1773; *Kelly's Dir. Oxon.* (1883 and later edns.).
13 Above, manor.   14 Below, Lew, econ. hist.
15 B.L. Add. Ch. 38918; O.R.O., MSS. Wills Oxon. 61/3/17, 174/3/8.
16 Blenheim Mun., shelf J 4, box 20, release 9 Dec. 1844; Bodl. G.A. Oxon. b 90 (12).
17 P.R.O., RG 11/1514.
18 O.R.O., Cal. Q.S. i, p. 124b.
19 Bodl. G.A. Oxon. b 90 (12).
20 *Bampton Hund. R.* 26.   21 *Cal. Pat.* 1330–4, 88.

22 Arundel Castle, MS. M 535; Longleat House (Wilts.), NMR 3315, ct. 4 Oct. 1668.
23 Above, Bampton and Weald, local govt. (par. govt.).
24 W. J. Monk, *A Ramble in Oxon.* [c. 1925], 43, 56: copy in Bodl. G.A. Oxon. 8° 1041; O.S. Map 6", Oxon. XXXVII (1884 edn.), s.v. Mill Barn; local inf.
25 Above, intro.; cf. above, Chimney, church; below, Lew, churches.
26 O.R.O., Bampton incl. award, plan VI; ibid. MS. d.d. Par. Bampton a 2 (R); cf. A. Bryant, *Oxon. Map* (1824); Blenheim Mun., shelf J4, box 20, release of Haddon estate 1844, neither confirming a cruciform plan.
27 *Acts of P.C.* 1581–2, 290; 1587–8, 72–3, 100; Stapleton, *Cath. Miss.* 2, 175.
28 *Recusant Roll, 1593–4* (Cath. Rec. Soc. lvii), 127; Stapleton, *Cath. Miss.* 2; cf. P.R.O., PROB 11/113, ff. 101v.–102.
29 G.E.C. *Baronetage,* i. 205–6, ii. 198; *Secker's Visit.* 12; above, manor. The assertion in *Kelly's Dir. Oxon.* (1939) that the Throckmorton plot against Elizabeth I was laid at Lower Haddon is false.

LEW

LEW (1,642 a.) adjoined the parish boundary on the west, north, and north-east, Aston's fields in the south-east, Bampton's fields in the south, and Highmoor brook in the south-west. All those boundaries, mostly established before the later 18th century, are discussed above.[30]

Abingdon Lane, an ancient route leading south-eastwards towards Thames crossings at Shifford and Newbridge, ran along the township's northern edge, and until inclosure *c.* 1821 continued across Lew heath into Aston;[31] probably it was the 'old way' mentioned in 969.[32] A stone causeway excavated on Elm Bank ditch north of Hill View, evidently the stone 'bridge' or 'ford' mentioned in 10th-century charters, suggests an east–west route perhaps from Ducklington to Lew and thence to Bampton, which presumably intersected Abingdon Lane,[33] and a 'highway' running north-eastwards from Abingdon Lane into Ducklington, probably south of Barley Park wood, was mentioned in 1318.[34] Another 10th-century 'way' ran probably north-eastwards along Lew's south-western boundary, and continued presumably across the later open fields, connecting perhaps with the surviving back lane on which Manor Farm stands, or with a roughly parallel green lane which survived until inclosure.[35] The Witney–Bampton road through Lew village, presumably also ancient, formerly met the Brize Norton road just north of Bampton; it was superseded as the chief route in 1771 by a turnpike running west of Lew barrow from a tollgate on Lew's northern boundary, which met the Brize Norton road near another tollgate at Venn bridge.[36] That road was abandoned at inclosure, when the turnpike was rerouted through Lew village and a new section to the Brize Norton road was built across former open fields; the road was disturnpiked in 1874.[37] Also at inclosure Abingdon Lane was replaced by a new road to Yelford which left the Witney road just north of Lew village, and a road southwards to Bampton was established across former open fields via later Mount Owen Farm.[38] No carriers are known, but there was a receiving office by the 1850s, at first in Church (formerly Post Office) Farmhouse, and by 1921 in later Post Office Cottage north of the church. It closed between 1939 and 1971.[39]

Cropmarks, including Bronze-Age ring-ditches, have been noted chiefly in the south-west of the township near the Bampton boundary.[40] A prominent round-barrow west of the later hamlet is undated but probably early Anglo-Saxon,[41] and a settlement named from it existed presumably in 984 when Aethelred granted land 'at the barrow' (*aet Hlaewe*) to his 'minister' Aelfwine.[42] Three *villani* and 3 *bordarii* were recorded on two small estates in Lew in 1086, but much of the later township was included in the royal manor of Bampton and was not separately described.[43]

Up to 33 of the tenants and freeholders listed in 1279 may have resided, and since others may have been omitted[44] there were probably between 30 and 40 households. At least 27 inhabitants were taxed in 1306, 30 in 1316, and 38 in 1327, but in 1377 poll tax was paid by only 25 inhabitants over 14,[45] suggesting that the effects of 14th-century plague had been catastrophic. The township may have suffered further from the 15th-century depopulation evident elsewhere in the parish,[46] and no more than 14 inhabitants contributed to 16th-century subsidies;[47] only 34 male inhabitants were listed in 1642, and 22 houses were assessed for hearth tax in 1662, half of them on only one or two hearths.[48] High numbers of burials were recorded in 1728–30, during the 1760s, and in 1790, but from the 1750s baptisms usually outnumbered burials[49] and by 1801 there were 222 inhabitants and 36 houses. The population rose to 266, accommodated in 46 houses, by 1821, but fell steadily thereafter to only 92 in 1901, when 6 out of 34 surviving houses were vacant. Despite a slight increase to 116 in 1921 it continued to fall during the 20th century, and in 1991 was 59.[50]

The base and part of the shaft of an apparently

30   Above, Bampton, general intro.; Bampton and Weald, intro.; Aston and Cote, intro.
31   O.R.O., MS. d.d. Par. Bampton a 2 (R); Jefferys, *Oxon. Map* (1767); O.S. Map 1/2,500, Oxon. XXXI. 15 (1876 edn.); below, Shifford, intro.; Standlake, intro.
32   Grundy, *Saxon Oxon.* 80; *Oxoniensia*, lvii. 344; cf. J. Blair, *A.-S. Oxon.* 131.
33   *Oxoniensia*, lvii. 342–8.
34   D. & C. Exeter, MS. 2865; below, Ducklington, intro.
35   O.R.O., MS. d.d. Par. Bampton a 2 (R); above, Bampton and Weald, intro. [boundaries].
36   Jefferys, *Oxon. Map* (1767); Davis, *Oxon Map* (1797); Witney–Clanfield Turnpike Act, 11 Geo. III, c. 73: copy in Bodl. L. Eng. B 53 c. Highways 5 (2).
37   O.R.O., Bampton, Weald, and Lew incl. award; Turnpike Act, 37 & 38 Vic. c. 95; *Return of Roads Disturnpiked*, H.C. 353, p. 7 (1878), lxvi; above, map on p. 6.
38   O.R.O., incl. award; above, map on p. 6.
39   *Lascelle's Dir. Oxon.* (1853); *P.O. Dir. Oxon.* (1864 and later edns.); *Kelly's Dir. Oxon.* (1883 and later edns.); O.S. Maps 1/2,500, Oxon. XXXI. 15 (1880 and later edns.); SP 3206–3306 (1972 edn.); *Sale Cat., Lew Estate* (1914): copy in C.O.S.

40   D. Benson and D. Miles, *The Upper Thames Valley*, 36–7; *Oxoniensia*, xxiv. 100; C.O.S., PRN 3208, 3211, 3306, 12185.
41   J. Blair, *A.-S. Oxon.* 45–6; below, plate 17; cf. B.L. Add. MS. 38776, f. 45; C.O.S., PRN 2577, wrongly suggesting that it is the remains of a motte and bailey castle.
42   *Early Chart. of Thames Valley*, ed. M. Gelling, no. 282; *P.N. Oxon.* (E.P.N.S.), ii. 327.
43   *V.C.H. Oxon.* i. 411, 423; below, manor.
44   *Bampton Hund. R.* 24–6; below, econ. hist.
45   P.R.O., E 179/161/8–10; ibid. E 179/161/42. The 1306 list is damaged.
46   Above, Bampton and Weald, econ. hist.; Chimney, econ. hist.; below, Shifford, econ. hist.
47   P.R.O., E 179/161/173; E 179/162/234; E 179/162/320; E 179/162/341.
48   Ibid. E 179/255/4, pt. i, f. 21; *Protestation Rtns. and Tax Assess.* 7.
49   C.O.S., Bampton par. reg. transcripts; Lew's inhabitants were not consistently distinguished earlier.
50   *Census*, 1801–1991, wrongly counting 343 Aston inhabitants under Lew in 1981.

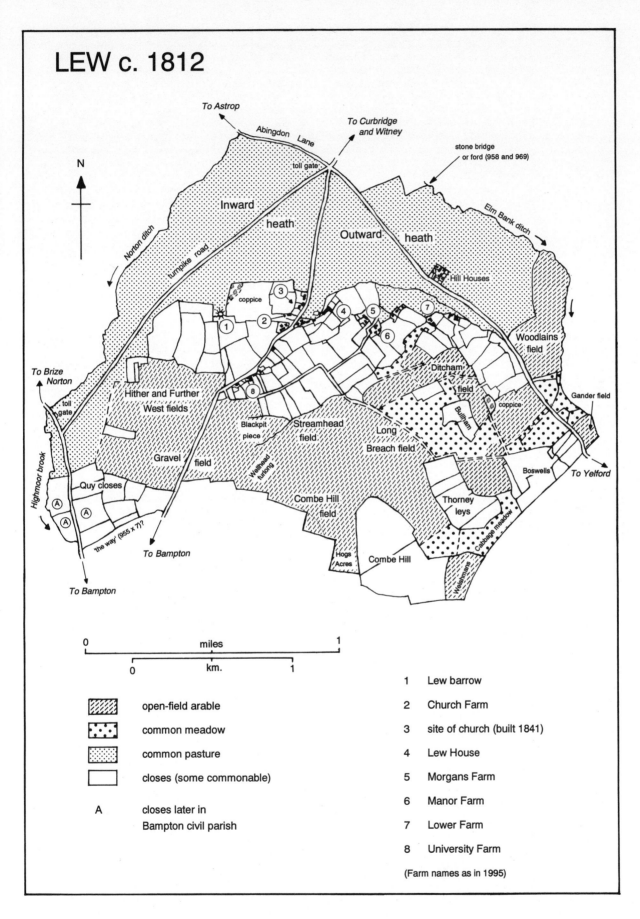

LEW c. 1812

To Astrop

To Curbridge
and Witney

Abingdon   Lane

stone bridge
or ford (958 and 969)

toll gate

N

Inward   heath

Outward   heath

Elm Bank ditch

Norton ditch

turnpike road

Hill Houses

coppice

Woodlains
field

To Brize
Norton

Ditcham
field

Gander field

coppice

toll
gate

Bullpen

Hither and Further

West fields

Blackpit
piece

Streamhead
field

Long

Breach field

Boswells

To Yelford

Highmoor brook

Gravel   field

Wellhead turlong

Thorney
leys

Cabbage meadow

Quy closes

Combe Hill
field

Welshmans

"the way" (955 x 7)?

To Bampton

Hogs
Acres

Combe Hill

To Bampton

0	miles	1

0	km.	1

▨ open-field arable

⣿ common meadow

⣀ common pasture

☐ closes (some commonable)

Ⓐ closes later in
Bampton civil parish

1   Lew barrow

2   Church Farm

3   site of church (built 1841)

4   Lew House

5   Morgans Farm

6   Manor Farm

7   Lower Farm

8   University Farm

(Farm names as in 1995)

late medieval cross survive east of the Witney–Bampton road near the modern church,[51] on the edge of what may formerly have been a small, triangular green:[52] the surname 'at green' was recorded in the 13th and 14th centuries,[53] and cottages set back from the road still line its probable eastern edge along what is now an approach to Lew House. Early settlement may not have been clearly nucleated, however. Freehold tenements c. ½ km. south of the hamlet on the modern Bampton road, including University Farm and neighbouring cottages, were established by the 17th century and possibly much earlier,[54] and the medieval surname 'at well' may indicate settlement south of University Farm along the putative 10th-century route across the later open fields, though known cropmarks are not medieval.[55] The site of Manor Farm was occupied by the late 16th century and possibly from the Middle Ages,[56] and by the 18th century there were farmhouses along the southern edge of the heath, some attached to the chief Bampton manor and presumably long established.[57] Of those, Lower Farm includes a datestone inscribed RIM 1675, perhaps for Robert Jeeves (or Geeves) (d. 1703) and his wife Margery,[58] and a neighbouring farmhouse formerly attached to the same manor was demolished in the late 19th century.[59] Cottages built 'on the waste' before 1700, perhaps including two said to have no common rights in 1609, were presumably those on Lew heath at Hill View or Hill Houses, shown on a map of 1767,[60] and in the 19th century the site seems to have included up to 8 or 9 separate labourers' dwellings.[61] Those remaining were cleared in the 20th century, and the existing house was newly built.[62]

A few farmhouses and cottages of 17th- and 18th-century origin, some of them fairly substantial, reflect Lew's status as a small agricultural community with some moderately prosperous yeoman farmers.[63] Most are of limestone rubble with stone-slated roofs, though Thatched Cottage near University Farm retains its thatch; both thatch (for agricultural buildings) and slate were mentioned in the 18th century.[64] The most notable

building is Lew House, so called by 1909,[65] on the east side of the putative green, a large L-shaped building of several periods owned in the late 18th century and earlier 19th by the Arnatts, then the chief farming family in the township;[66] it passed later to a succession of farmers and landowners, among them H. B. Arnaud, who sublet it, and from the 1930s the Radclyffe family.[67] Two ranges of 17th-century origin survive at the house's north-east corner, of which one, formerly the main range, contains late 17th-century panelling. The other, a cross wing which incorporates the present main entrance, has been much altered but was probably at the parlour end. No trace survives of an early service wing. In 1786 an additional block with a dressed stone gable, perhaps housing a kitchen, was built alongside the cross wing probably by Jonathan Arnatt (d. 1799) and his wife Elizabeth,[68] and in 1909 the house was extensively remodelled by the architect John Belcher:[69] a porch was added to the entrance front, and some fenestration and interior decoration were renewed, possibly including some panelling in the 17th-century range. The long, irregular service wing, incorporating former outbuildings, has an attached range of thatched kennels.

In the 19th and 20th centuries Lew, with its falling population, experienced little new building, and the only additions of note were the church, built in 1841, and the Congregational chapel (later a school) near University Farm, built c. 1840.[70] Mount Owen Farm, just within the township boundary in the south-east and named reportedly after a vicar of Bampton, was built in the 1830s after inclosure.[71] A single pair of council houses was built opposite University Farm before 1960, and isolated houses were built on the more easterly Bampton road, but otherwise 20th-century development was confined to restoration and extension of some older houses.[72] Water was supplied by Witney R.D.C. by 1939, and electricity was available by the late 1950s.[73]

A fire in 1714 destroyed several houses, causing losses valued at over £160.[74] A public house

51 O.S. Map 1/2,500, SP 3206–3306 (1972 edn.); Oxoniensia, xxxviii. 307; C.O.S., PRN 2573, 2577. It was not marked on O.S. maps before 1921, but cf. Bodl. MS. Top. Oxon. d 218, f. 150.
52 O.R.O., MS. d.d. Par. Bampton a 2 (R); O.S. Map 1/2,500, SP 3206–3306 (1972 edn.).
53 Bampton Hund. R. 25; P.R.O., E 179/161/8–9.
54 Oxf. Univ. Arch., SEP/Q/9; below, manor; econ. hist.
55 Below, this section; cf. Benson and Miles, Upper Thames Valley, 37. Furlong names S. of Univ. Fm. included Blackpits: O.R.O., MS. d.d. Par. Bampton a 2 (R).
56 Ch. Ch. Arch., Lew A 1–4; P.R.O., C 2/Jas. I/O 4/6; ibid. REQ 2/413/90; below, manor.
57 Jefferys, Oxon. Map (1767); O.R.O., incl. award.
58 Cf. O.R.O., MS. Wills Oxon. 38/2/25; C.O.S., par. reg. transcripts, s.v. Jeeves.
59 B.L. Add. MS. C 7 e 16 (3), pp. 35, 72; O.S. Map 1/2,500, Oxon. XXXI. 15 (1880 and later edns.).
60 Arundel Castle, MS. TP 288; B.L. Add. MS. 27535, f. 43; Jefferys, Oxon. Map (1767).
61 O.R.O., incl. award, plan VI; P.R.O., HO 107/872; ibid. RG 11/1514; Ch. Ch. Arch., MS. Estates 74, ff. 189–90.
62 O.S. Map 1/2,500, Oxon. XXXI. 15 (1899 and 1921 edns.); ibid. 6", SP 30 NW. (1960 edn.).
63 Below, manor; econ. hist.; cf. D.o.E. Revised Hist.

Bldgs. List, Lew (1989), 126–8: copy in C.O.S.
64 Oxf. Univ. Arch., SEP/Q/25, f. 1v. and flyleaf; Ch. Ch. Arch., MS. Estates 74, f. 12.
65 Academy Archit. xxxvi (1909), 52; O.S. Map 1/2,500, Oxon. XXXI. 15 (1921 edn.). The name formerly attached to Manor Fm. to the NE., and in 1899 this ho. was Lew Fm.: ibid. (1880 and later edns.).
66 O.R.O., Bampton incl. award, no. 192; ibid. QSD L.180; below, econ. hist.
67 P.R.O., HO 107/872; ibid. RG 11/1514; P.O. Dir. Oxon. (1877); Kelly's Dir. Oxon. (1883 and later edns.); inf. from Capt. C. R. Radclyffe.
68 Datestone, JAE(?) 1786; C.O.S., Bampton par. reg. transcripts. The inscription WWA 1777 in a garden wall refers probably to Arnatt's son Wm. Wright Arnatt: O.R.O., Cal. Q.S., p. 96.
69 Academy Archit. xxxvi (1909), 52; below plate 16.
70 Below, church; nonconf.; educ.
71 O.S. Map 1", sheet XIII (1830 edn.); P.R.O., HO 107/872, s.v. Bampton; Giles, Hist. Bampton, 44.
72 O.S. Map 6", SP 30 NW. (1960 edn.); ibid. 1/25,000, SP 20/30 (1977 edn.); below, manor.
73 Kelly's Dir. Oxon. (1939); Sale Cat., University Fm. (1959), p. 2: copy in C.O.S.
74 O.R.O., QSR Mich. 1714, nos. 5–6.

licensed by 1754 was presumably the later Chequers, so called by 1773 and sold in 1800 with an associated blacksmith's shop,[75] but not mentioned later.

The surname 'at well' was recorded in the 13th and 14th centuries,[76] but no medieval holy wells are known. Wellhead furlong, recorded in 1746, adjoined the township's southern boundary south of University Farm, and a spring nearby was noted in 1884;[77] both lay close to the putative early medieval route across the later open fields.[78]

MANOR AND OTHER ESTATES. Until the 19th century much of Lew belonged to the royal manor of Bampton and to its successor Bampton Earls.[79] A separate estate in Lew and Weald, built up by Osney abbey during the 12th and 13th centuries, was called *LEW* manor in 1542 and 1546, but in fact formed a member of the abbey's manor or bailiwick of Black Bourton.[80] Geoffrey Gibewyn gave six yardlands to the abbey *c.* 1225, perhaps the 1½ hides held by Hugh de Bolbec of Walter Giffard in 1086,[81] but by 1279 two yardlands had become detached, perhaps in connexion with a fine of 1198 or following a dispute with the Belet family in 1227.[82] A rent charge of 24s. from Bampton manor, part of a prebend of 60s. formerly held by Peverel the priest and granted to the abbey by the Empress Maud in 1141, was exchanged *c.* 1170 by Matthew, count of Boulogne, for ½ yardland in Weald and a fishery at Rushey on the river Thames, and during the 13th century there were further small grants of meadows, common rights, and fisheries.[83]

In 1542 most of the estate passed with the abbey's other lands to the new cathedral of Christ and St. Mary at Osney, and in 1546 to its successor, Christ Church.[84] Two of the yardlands in Lew, then held in socage, became detached and were acquired before 1633 by the Wenmans of Caswell manor in Witney,[85] who rented the other 2 yardlands, which were closely intermingled, from Christ Church.[86] The combined leasehold and freehold estate, 156 a.

after inclosure, passed from Sir Francis Wenman (d. 1640) to his relict Ann and son Sir Francis (d. 1680), Bt., to Francis's son Sir Richard (d. 1690), Viscount Wenman from 1686, and to Richard's relict Catherine (d. 1742), who married James Bertie (d. 1699), earl of Abingdon, and, later, Francis Wroughton (d. 1733) of Eastcott (Wilts.). It then passed to Catherine's grandson Philip (d. 1760), Viscount Wenman, and his trustees, later descending with Thame Park to Sophia Wykeham[87] who sold it in 1824. The freehold part (*c.* 74½ a.) was bought by Thomas Denton, purchaser of the Coventrys' share of Bampton Earls manor, with which it was sold after 1859 to John Jones of Worcester; Jones sold his entire Lew estate (302 a.) in 1863 to Christ Church, which in 1871 added the earl of Shrewsbury's land (*c.* 73 a.) and made further small purchases later.[88] Christ Church sold most of its Lew estate in 1985;[89] its remaining Weald tenement, on the site of Weald Manor Farm, was sold with 5 a. in 1877.[90]

Osney abbey maintained no demesne farm or manor house at Lew, and by the 17th century the joint leasehold and freehold estate was centred on the later Manor Farm, formerly Lew House or the Manor House,[91] which then as earlier was let to tenant farmers.[92] There may formerly have been two houses on the site, one each for the leasehold and freehold farms,[93] but until inclosure the curtilages remained confused and in 1818 the southern (then leasehold) part contained only dilapidated farm buildings, used from *c.* 1824 as a homestead for nearby Morgan's Farm.[94] The existing house on the northern (then freehold) part, a 'substantial farmhouse' in 1824, was presumably that called a mansion house in 1633, and said to be 'well slated' in 1738;[95] a small 17th-century range survives at its south-west corner, and was extended on the north-east in the 18th century. The existing service wing, which runs north-west from the 17th-century range, seems to have been added in the 19th century[96] but has been partly rebuilt, and before 1848 additions were made south-east of the main range perhaps for Denton, who occupied the house in the

[75] Ibid. QSD V/1–3; Oxf. Jnl. Synopsis, 5 Mar., 17 Sept. 1768; *Oxf. Jnl.* 3 May 1800.

[76] *Bampton Hund. R.* 26 (*ad fontem*); P.R.O., E 179/161/8–10.

[77] Oxf. Univ. Arch., SEP/Q/5; O.R.O., MS. d.d. Par. Bampton a 2 (R); O.S. Map 6", Oxon. XXXI (1884 edn.).

[78] Above, this section.

[79] Above, Bampton and Weald, manors.

[80] *L. & P. Hen. VIII,* xvii, p. 490; xxi (2), p. 334; *Oseney Cart.* vi, pp. 203–4; Bodl. MSS. Ch. Oxon. 312–13, 333.

[81] *Oseney Cart.* iv, pp. 500–1; *V.C.H. Oxon.* i. 411.

[82] *Bampton Hund. R.* 25; *Feet of Fines 9 Ric. I* (P.R.S. xxiii), no. 132; *Cur. Reg. R.* xiii, p. 27.

[83] *Oseney Cart.* iv, pp. 63–4, 349, 493–4, 498–9, 515–20; *Bampton Hund. R.* 18; above, Bampton and Weald, econ. hist. (mills and fisheries).

[84] *L. & P. Hen. VIII,* xvii, p. 490; xxi (2), p. 334; *V.C.H. Oxon.* ii. 29, 31–2.

[85] P.R.O., C 142/66, no. 60; C 142/133, no. 90; C 142/311, no. 111; Ch. Ch. Arch., MS. Estates 74, f. 4; cf. *Oseney Cart.* vi, pp. 232, 264. The Wenmans held other land in Lew by 1534: O.R.O., MS. Wills Oxon. 181, f. 17v.

[86] Ch. Ch. Arch., Lew A 1–36; ibid. MS. Estates 74, ff. 1 sqq.

[87] Ibid. Lew A 6–36; *Complete Peerage,* xii (2), 492–4; *V.C.H. Oxon.* vii. 177.

[88] Ch. Ch. Arch., MS. Estates 74, ff. 86–94v., 97–8, 134–41, 144–5, 148–162v.; above, Bampton and Weald, manors (Bampton Earls); cf. O.R.O., Bampton incl. award. For the leasehold (81 a.), Ch. Ch. Arch., MS. Estates 74, ff. 95 sqq.; Bodl. C 17 b. 24 (60).

[89] Inf. from the assistant treasurer, Christ Church.

[90] Ch. Ch. Arch., MS. Estates 60, ff. 72 sqq., 104; O.R.O., Bampton incl. award, no. 584.

[91] O.R.O., Bampton incl. award, plan VI, nos. 203–4; O.S. Map 1/2,500, Oxon. XXXI. 15 (1880 and later edns.); ibid. 1/25,000, SP 20/30 (1977 edn.). Not to be confused with the later Lew House (for which above, intro.), or with Lower Fm., called Manor Fm. in 1880 through its connexion with the Coventrys.

[92] Ch. Ch. Arch., Lew A 1–47; P.R.O., C 2/Jas. I/O 4/6; below, econ. hist.

[93] e.g. Ch. Ch. Arch., MS. Estates 74, ff. 12, 15; but cf. ibid. ff. 6, 11.

[94] Ibid. ff. 4, 6, 16 and v., 31, 65–8, 75–6, 95 sqq.; Ch. Ch. Arch., Maps Lew 3.

[95] Ch. Ch. Arch., MS. Estates 74, ff. 4, 11, 94.

[96] O.R.O., Bampton incl. award, plan VI; ibid. MS. d.d. Par. Bampton a 2 (R).

1840s.[97] In the later 19th century the house was let with Lower (then Manor) farm;[98] in the later 20th it fell derelict, and was extensively remodelled *c.* 1985[99] when former farm buildings round a courtyard to the south-west were converted for domestic use.

An estate held in 1086 by Aretius the king's minister, and lands owned in the later Middle Ages by the Laundels family, are treated above.[1] A freehold of 5½ yardlands, held in 1651 by Francis Wenman (d. 1680), Bt., descended with his other Lew estate to Philip, Viscount Wenman, who in 1747 sold it to Oxford university, the owner until 1959.[2] Until 1769 it was let as two farms and included two houses and homesteads, of which one, near Church and Lew House Cottages, was given in exchange to Jonathan Arnatt at inclosure in 1821, when it was occupied by labourers. The other, later University Farm, is of 17th-century origin and was remodelled shortly before 1746, when the kitchen cross-wing was probably added. By 1767 it was in disrepair and was used as a poorhouse, and in 1809 it was labourers' accommodation;[3] in the earlier 19th century it again became the farmhouse for the university estate, then *c.* 200 a., and was repaired and extended south-westwards.[4] The university bought adjacent tenements and closes to the east and south in 1895 from S. A. Saunder and Frances Stubbs, whose grandfather Samuel Saunder had bought them from the Jeeves family of Lew in 1824 and 1831.[5]

ECONOMIC HISTORY. Lew's fields were mentioned in 1298, when a holding of 2 a. was unevenly divided among three named furlongs.[6] A 90-a. estate in the early 18th century was unevenly divided among Upper field, Lower field, Woodlains, and Blackpit piece,[7] and in the later 18th century there were seven fields covering the township's southern part, cropped on a four-course rotation: on the west, Hither west and Further west fields; in the centre, Stream (or Streamhead) and Combe Hill (or Wellhead) fields; and on the east, Gander, Woodlains, and Roughlains fields,[8] the last perhaps identical with the Thorney Leaze and Bullham fields mentioned in 1789.[9] The fields were regrouped

before 1809 when the quarters were Further west and Long Breach fields, Home west and Whitehill fields, Gravel and Streamhead fields, and Combe Hill and Woodlains fields, not all of them adjoining, and Bullham and Ditcham fields were mentioned also.[10] Meadows, two of which were held severally for rent in 1279,[11] lay chiefly in the east, and in the 18th century included Cabbage, Park, and Woodlains meads, and Bull hook, where Christ Church had 6 a. severally every 12 years.[12] By then there were also meadow closes further west.[13]

Inhabitants enjoyed extensive common and furze-cutting rights on Lew heath, some 400–500 a. covering the township's northern part.[14] By the 18th century and possibly in 1318, when Lew Home heath was mentioned,[15] it was divided into an inner cow common on the north-west and an outer sheep common on the north-east, each estimated at *c.* 200 a. In 1609 the stint was 12 beasts and 60 sheep per yardland, and in 1746 it was 8 cows on the inner heath and 50 sheep and 2 cows or 1 horse on the outer;[16] for part of the year, in the 16th century apparently between 1 August and 25 March, sheep and cattle were depastured on both commons indiscriminately, and in 1809 the outer common's value for cows was said to be greatly lessened because of their intermixture with sheep.[17] In 1318 Aymer de Valence, as owner of the waste, challenged Exeter cathedral's right to commons in Lew Home heath, then divided into east and west parts, but later accepted that the cathedral's demesne carried common rights though its tenants were excluded. Commons in the heath were let with the cathedral's demesne in 1430, though the dispute evidently recurred later in the century.[18] In 1540 Lew's inhabitants impleaded John More of Lower Haddon for depasturing over 200 sheep on the common, and before 1625 his successors sold 250 sheep commons there, presumably those owned chiefly by outsiders *c.* 1798.[19] Combe Hill near Lew's southern boundary, a 73-a. (later 60-a.) Lammas ground of poor pasture and furze which in the early 14th century may have been open-field arable, was partitioned between the lords of Bampton and Aston in 1678, and in the 18th century claims to common rights there by Bampton's inhabitants were overturned.[20] Park mead and presumably other

97 Giles, *Hist. Bampton*, illust. facing p. 87; P.R.O., HO 107/872.
98 Ch. Ch. Arch., MS. Estates 74, ff. 134–5, 138 and v.; ibid. Lew B 3–4. 99 Local inf.
1 Above, Bampton and Weald, other estates; Aston and Cote, manors [other estates].
2 Oxf. Univ. Arch., SEP/Q/9, SEP/Q/13; *Sale Cat., Univ. Fm.* (1959), relating its sale by Nuffield College: copy in C.O.S.; above.
3 Oxf. Univ. Arch., SEP/Q/4–6, 19, 25, 30, 32; cf. O.R.O., Bampton incl. award.
4 Oxf. Univ. Arch., WP α/42/2; O.R.O., incl. award; P.R.O., HO 107/872; RG 9/905.
5 Oxf. Univ. Arch., SEP/Q/39, 45, 49, 52; ibid. USOL/51/5; for earlier deeds, ibid. SEP/Q/15–18, 20–4, 27–8, 31, 33–5.
6 B.L. Add. Ch. 67114; cf. D. & C. Exeter, MSS. 2931, 4751, 4756.
7 Ch. Ch. Arch., MS. Estates 74, f. 14; cf. ibid. f. 4.
8 Oxf. Univ. Arch., SEP/Q/4–5, 25; cf. O.R.O., MS. d.d. Par. Bampton a 2 (R); ibid. Bampton incl. award, plan VI.
9 B.L. Map C 7 e 16 (3), pp. 35, 64, 72.

10 Oxf. Univ. Arch., SEP/Q/30; O.R.O., incl. award, plan VI and schedule. 11 *Bampton Hund. R.* 25–6.
12 O.R.O., MS. d.d. Par. Bampton a 2 (R); Ch. Ch. Arch., MS. Estates 74, ff. 12, 14–15 (saying every 5 years); Oxf. Univ. Arch., SEP/Q/13, SEP/Q/25. 13 Below.
14 B.L. Add. MS. 27535, f. 43; Oxf. Univ. Arch., SEP/Q/25, ff. 6v.–7; O.R.O., MS. d.d. Par. Bampton a 2 (R); cf. ibid. P4/2/MS 1/5, ff. 2–3.
15 D. & C. Exeter, MS. 644.
16 B.L. Add. MS. 27535, f. 42v.–43; Oxf. Univ. Arch., SEP/Q/5, p. 3 (giving stint for 3¼ yardlands: cf. ibid. SEP/Q/13); ibid. SEP/Q/25, f. 6v.
17 Oxf. Univ. Arch., SEP/Q/25, f. 6v.; ibid. SEP/Q/30; P.R.O., STAC 2/29/190.
18 D. & C. Exeter, MSS. 644, 6016/2/1; *Oxoniensia*, lvi. 112–13.
19 P.R.O., STAC 2/29/190; B.L. Add. Ch. 38918; Oxf. Univ. Arch., SEP/Q/26.
20 Bodl. MS. d.d. Shrewsbury c 2/8 (1); B.L. Map C 7 e 16 (3), pp. 35, 48–9; Oxf. Univ. Arch., SEP/Q/25, f. 6v.; D. & C. Exeter, MS. 2931, mentioning an arable furlong in 'le Comb'.

meadows were commonable from 1 August in 1767.[21]

By the 17th or 18th century a band of small irregular closes, some taken presumably from the heath and many of them probably medieval in origin, stretched across the middle of the township.[22] A tenant illegally inclosed some common land *c.* 1668, and in the 1760s a small piece of heathland adjoining Pound close, north-west of the hamlet, was inclosed with the lord's permission.[23] Quy closes in the south-west, perhaps arable in 1317 when Quyhay furlong was mentioned,[24] were inclosed presumably before 1420 when the Talbots' demesne included pasture in 'Overquyhey' and in 'Thorneylese', the latter one of another group of closes in the south-east.[25] Medieval assart-ing is suggested by the furlong names Pease-, Long-, and Shortbreach, the last two in the south-east, and perhaps also by the names of Roughlains and Woodlains fields, which abutted the heath and included the worst arable land.[26] No medieval woodland was recorded, though in the 18th century there was valuable hedgerow oak and elm between the closes and open fields: Christ Church's estate included some 500–600 trees *c.* 1729, and over 200 oaks, elms, and ashes in 1833.[27] Two small coppices existed *c.* 1812, but Ditcham wood and a smaller plantation further west are 19th-century.[28]

In 1086 much of Lew lay within the royal manor of Bampton.[29] Hugh de Bolbec's 1½-hide estate had one ploughteam worked presumably by the single bordar recorded, and on Aretius's 7-yardland estate in Lew and in Aston and Cote 3 *villani* and 2 bordars shared one ploughteam and, since no *servi* were mentioned, perhaps worked a second recorded on the demesne, which was later in Aston and Cote. Both estates had risen in value since 1066, Bolbec's from 10*s.* to 20*s.*, and Aretius's from 20*s.* to 35*s.*[30] By 1279[31] there were 17 villeins holding of the former royal manor, 4 with yardlands (each reckoned at *c.* 16 a. presumably excluding meadow), 10 with half yardlands, one with ¼ yardland, and 2 sharing a presumably recently-divided yardland. Rents and services varied, but were broadly similar to those in Bampton and Weald on the same manor. No other villeins were mentioned in 1279, but one was recorded on a freehold yardland of the Belet family in 1227, and two on Robert of Yelford's estate in

1328.[32] Fifteen free tenants in 1279 occupied holdings ranging from a house and half yardland shared between three sisters to 4 yardlands; some owed tallage, suit of court, or hidage and scutage, and Osney abbey's free tenant of 2 yardlands discharged the abbot's obligations at the hundred court, for which he seems to have received a 4*s.* rent-allowance.[33] There was much subletting, one freeholder holding land under 8 owners and himself leasing a small parcel to another inhabitant.[34]

Early 14th-century subsidies suggest that Lew was one of Bampton's more prosperous hamlets, assessed wealth rising from *c.* £84 in 1306 to over £135 in 1327, and the number of taxpayers from 27 to 38. Roughly half were assessed on between 16*s.* and 50*s.*-worth of goods, and none on less than 11*s.* 8*d.* The highest contributors in 1316 were assessed on over £9 and £12 respec-tively, and those in 1327 on £10 and £19; presumably they were freeholders, though assessed wealth of villein families varied greatly, and some who had held in villeinage in 1279 and 1294 were among the highest taxpayers.[35]

The township's losses in 14th-century plagues[36] were perhaps exacerbated by the 15th-century depopulation evident elsewhere in the parish.[37] Reduced population led to amalgamation of holdings, and by 1609 the Bampton Earls land was held as 5 farms of between 1 and 3 yard-lands.[38] Several moderately prosperous yeoman families were recorded throughout the 16th and 17th centuries, among them the Startups or Bartletts, the Shaws, Moulders, and Wises, and later the Jeeveses and Collingwoods, though the Saunders family, which paid large amounts in 16th-century subsidies, was not mentioned later.[39] William Wise (d. 1687) left goods worth over £200, including a study of books.[40] Some leading farmers were freeholders, though several held of Bampton Earls manor, and a farmer who in 1686 left goods worth over £137 was tenant under at least 4 landowners.[41] Over half the contributors to the 1662 hearth tax paid on 2 or 3 hearths or more,[42] and some taxed on fewer may have been cottagers: 3 cottagers were re-corded in 1609, and their numbers may have increased during the 17th and 18th centuries as population rose.[43]

Farms on Bampton Earls manor remained copyhold in 1609, and at least one in 1789 was let for lives at the old quitrent, though it was

21 Oxf. Univ. Arch., SEP/Q/25, f. 8.
22 O.R.O., MS. d.d. Par. Bampton a 2 (R); Ch. Ch. Arch., MS. Estates 74, ff. 4, 11, 14–15; Oxf. Univ. Arch., SEP/Q/4–5, SEP/Q/25.
23 Longleat House, NMR 3315, ct. 4 Oct. 1668; Oxf. Univ. Arch., SEP/Q/25, f. 1v.
24 D. & C. Exeter, MS. 2931.
25 P.R.O., C 139/42, no. 86; ibid. REQ 2/44/6; O.R.O., Bampton incl. award.
26 Ch. Ch. Arch., MS. Estates 74, f. 4; Oxf. Univ. Arch., SEP/Q/4; SEP/Q/25, f. 6v.; O.R.O., MS. d.d. Par. Bampton a 2 (R).
27 Ch. Ch. Arch., MS. Estates 74, ff. 6, 11, 16, 106v.
28 O.R.O., MS. d.d. Par. Bampton a 2 (R); ibid. incl. award, plan VI; O.S. Map 6", Oxon. XXXI (1884 edn.).
29 Above, Bampton and Weald, manors; this article, manor.
30 *V.C.H. Oxon.* i. 411, 423; for Aretius's demesne, cf. Giles, *Hist. Bampton,* 135.

31 *Bampton Hund. R.* 24–6.
32 *Curia Regis R.* xiii, pp. 85–6; Giles, *Hist. Bampton,* 136; above, Aston and Cote, manors [other estates].
33 *Bampton Hund. R.* 25; *Oseney Cart.* vi, pp. 203–4, 232, 248.
34 *Bampton Hund. R.* 25–6, s.v. Mic. Belet.
35 Ibid. 24–6; P.R.O., E 179/161/4, 8–10.
36 Above, intro.
37 Above, Bampton and Weald, intro.; Chimney, intro.; below, Shifford, intro.
38 B.L. Add. MS. 27535, ff. 42v.–43.
39 P.R.O., E 179/161/173; E 179/162/234, 320, 341; E 179/255/4, pt. i, f. 21; O.R.O., MSS. Wills Oxon., Lew wills and inventories.
40 O.R.O., MS. Wills Oxon. 73/2/6.
41 Ibid. 38/2/25, 78/3/21, 80/1/35; B.L. Add. MS. 27535, ff. 42v.–43; Oxf. Univ. Arch., SEP/Q/15–43.
42 P.R.O., E 179/255/4, pt. i, f. 21.
43 B.L. Add. MS. 27535, f. 43; ibid. Map C 7 e 16 (3), p. 36; above, intro.

then sublet presumably at rack rent.[44] There were c. 7 large leasehold farms in 1789, 4 on Bampton Earls manor, another held under 3 non-resident freeholders, and the Oxford university and Wenman estates, both over 100 a., and most large farmers occupied additional small parcels under other owners.[45] The sole large owner-occupier, Jonathan Arnatt of Lew House, before 1785 added University farm to his extensive freehold and leasehold estate, and by the later 18th century held c. 35 per cent of taxable land in the township.[46] Few holdings included more than 20 a. of open-field arable, but many farms were held with significant acreages of inclosed meadow and pasture: Oxford university's estate in 1767 included 83 a. of inclosures compared with 111 a. in the open fields, though such a preponderance was unusual.[47] Four people paying less than 10s. land tax in 1785 were apparently cottagers.[48]

Agriculture was mixed from the Middle Ages, with perhaps a slight bias towards pastoral farming. A villein yardlander in 1227 held 20 sheep of his lady for 10s. a year paid instead of aid,[49] and in 1534 the Witney wool merchant and stapler Richard Wenman left sheep and cattle in Lew and at Weald.[50] Several 17th-century testators left flocks of up to 100, and some others left smaller flocks;[51] on Oxford university's estate in the 1790s Berkshire breeds predominated, larger types being thought impractical.[52] Cattle, pigs, and poultry were also mentioned frequently, and bees occasionally.[53] In 1789 Lew's extensive commons were favourably contrasted with the poor-quality arable, though the value of the commons was lessened by a tendency to sheep rot, and the stiff clay was said to produce excellent wheat and beans and reasonable oats and barley. The usual course was then (1) wheat, (2) beans, (3) oats and barley, and (4) fallow, though in the 1790s Jonathan Arnatt achieved good results on some of the poorest land by sowing clover after beans, allowing cattle and sheep to feed on it during the fallow year. The land was nevertheless deemed unsuitable for turnips without cheap lime, whose use was recommended both to improve lighter land and to allow more sheep to be raised.[54] Some poorer inhabitants in the later 18th century supplemented their income by poaching in nearby woodland.[55]

Inclosure, advocated in the later 18th century, was not achieved until 1812–21 under the Act for Bampton and Weald.[56] John Coventry and the earl of Shrewsbury, joint lords of Bampton Earls, respectively received c. 345 a. and 73 a. in the township; Jonathan Arnatt the younger received 207 a. for his freehold, Sophia Wykeham 81½ a. for her leasehold under Christ Church and 74½ a. for her freehold, Oxford university 200 a., and George Richards, a vicar of Bampton, 180 a. for later Morgan's farm, held in his own right.[57] Most farms continued to be run from existing homesteads. By 1861 there were 5 farms, all but one of 200 a. or more, and one, probably the former Arnatt estate, of 400 a.; in all they employed c. 68 men, women, and children, and 65 labourers, one living in a shed, were recorded, along with 3 carters, 2 shepherds, and 2 cattle dealers.[58]

The benefits of inclosure were not immediate. In 1816 it was doubted whether the tenant of Christ Church's farm could continue without rent abatement, and in 1824 a sale catalogue acknowledged that the farm had not improved, claiming nonetheless that it would quickly repay investment, notably for drainage, and suggesting that if converted to grass it would make an excellent dairy farm. Though the farm remained mixed, by 1833 it was 'well managed' despite the cold wet soil.[59] Before 1824 much of the former heath was converted to arable and so remained, though in 1826 a proprietor complained that it had not yet been brought into proper cultivation,[60] and on individual farms the proportion of arable often remained slightly lower than in Bampton and Weald. On Christ Church's farm in 1824 and on Manor (later Lower) farm in 1864 it was under 40 per cent, though Morgan's farm was 74 per cent arable in 1879 and good corn-growing land was reported.[61]

Drainage remained poor. In 1863 heavy clay soil on Manor (Lower) farm made the arable 'uncertain' and expensive to cultivate and the grassland 'poor', though some arable on Christ Church's farm was drained at the tenant's expense before 1861, and before 1870 the Talbots' farm was partially drained by the Lands Improvement Co.[62] Presumably such problems exacerbated the effects of agricultural depression in the 1870s: the longstanding tenant of Lower and Manor farms was bankrupted in 1878, and of 5 chief farmers in 1861 only one remained in 1881.[63] In 1872 labourers demanding increased wages were reportedly evicted by a Lew farmer.[64]

The bias towards pastoral farming continued to 1914, when 73 per cent of the township was

44 B.L. Add. MS. 27535, ff. 42v.–43, 45; ibid. Map C 7 e 16 (3), pp. 72–3.
45 O.R.O., QSD L.180; cf. Oxf. Univ. Arch., SEP/Q/19, SEP/Q/25; Ch. Ch. Arch., MS. Estates 74, ff. 11, 15–16v.; above, manor [other estates].
46 O.R.O., QSD L.180; Oxf. Univ. Arch., SEP/Q/25, f. 1v.; SEP/Q/30.
47 Oxf. Univ. Arch., SEP/Q/25; cf. B.L. Add. MS. 27535, ff. 42v.–43; Ch. Ch. Arch., MS. Estates 74, ff. 4, 12, 16.
48 O.R.O., QSD L.180; cf. Oxf. Univ. Arch., SEP/Q/26.
49 Cur. Reg. R. xiii, pp. 85–6.
50 O.R.O., MS. Wills Oxon. 181, f. 17v.
51 Ibid. 6/2/3, 45/4/2, 80/1/35; ibid. Lew wills and inventories, passim.
52 Oxf. Univ. Arch., SEP/Q/25, f. 7v.
53 O.R.O., MSS. Wills Oxon., Lew wills and inventories.
54 B.L. Map C 7 e 16 (3), p. 37; Oxf. Univ. Arch.,

SEP/Q/25, ff. 6v.–7v.
55 O.R.O., QSR East. 1775, Epiph. 1782, Epiph. 1783.
56 Oxf. Univ. Arch., SEP/Q/25, f. 7v.; Ch. Ch. Arch., MS. Estates 74, f. 17; above, Bampton and Weald, econ. hist. (agric.).
57 O.R.O., Bampton incl. award; above, Bampton and Weald, econ. hist. (agric.).
58 P.R.O., RG 9/905; above, intro.
59 Ch. Ch. Arch., MS. Estates 74, ff. 59, 94, 106 and v.
60 Ibid. ff. 92v.–94, 99–100, 102–3; Bodl. C 17 b.24 (60); O.R.O., Crowdy I/51, lot 32.
61 Ch. Ch. Arch., MS. Estates 74, ff. 94, 134–5; ibid. Lew B 2; Bodl. C 17 b.24 (60).
62 Ch. Ch. Arch., MS. Estates 74, ff. 132–5, 148–9.
63 Ibid. ff. 178–84; ibid. Lew B 2–3; P.R.O., RG 9/905; RG 11/1514.
64 Agric. Trade Unionism in Oxon. (O.R.S. xlviii), 12.

under permanent pasture. Sheep were still kept, though in smaller numbers than in 1909, perhaps reflecting a shift towards dairy farming. Wheat remained the chief crop, followed by barley (20 per cent), oats (11 per cent), and a few swedes and mangolds.[65] Four chief farms remained in 1939, of which Church, University, and Manor farms were over 150 a. In 1959 University farm (216 a.) was a well-managed mixed and dairy farm with a good herd of Ayrshire cattle, though drainage on some land was still thought inadequate.[66]

Rural trades in Lew were recorded infrequently. John the cooper, perhaps formerly of Marsh Haddon, was mentioned in 1327, and the surname Iremonger or le Ferur in the late 13th and early 14th century, when it was evidently hereditary.[67] Weavers, masons, and a tailor with land in Curbridge were recorded in the 17th century,[68] and a cordwainer and a carpenter in the 18th.[69] A 'coal pit' mentioned in 1607 was probably the site of charcoal burning rather than of mineral extraction, and lay perhaps in the township's southern part near later Coalpit Farm, built after inclosure and so named by 1851.[70] A maltster was recorded in 1723, and the Chequers public house had a malthouse and bakehouse in 1768 and a smithy in 1800.[71] Only three families had non-agricultural occupations in 1811, and four in 1831;[72] non-agricultural inhabitants in 1861 were a grocer and postmaster, a toll-collector, and a retired wine-merchant living at Manor Farm (then called Lew House).[73] University Farm opened as a guesthouse c. 1959, and in 1992 was an hotel and restaurant; the post office, still the only shop in 1939, had closed by 1989.[74]

Windmill headland, on high ground near the township's southern boundary, was recorded in 1746,[75] but no mills are known.

LOCAL GOVERNMENT. From the 13th century to the early 19th tenants of Bampton Earls manor attended that manor's Bampton court, which in the 17th century and probably later appointed a constable, tithingman, and herdsman. Tithingmen for 'Lew hundred', presumably representing freeholders and tenants of other manors, were also elected at the annual view at

Bampton, where they made their presentations.[76] Osney abbey's tenants attended the abbot's court at Black Bourton by the 14th century and until the Dissolution.[77]

After Lew church was built in 1841 the chapelry appointed usually two chapelwardens, called churchwardens from 1857 and supported from rates.[78] There was one warden in 1990.[79] The township levied its own highway rate by the early 19th century, and presumably appointed a surveyor as in the 1850s.[80]

The township's stocks and whipping post were in good repair in 1688.[81] A collector or overseer was recorded in 1642, and in 1767 a dilapidated farmhouse owned by Oxford university, apparently University Farm, was used as a poorhouse.[82] In 1775–6 £42 was spent on relief, between 1783 and 1785 an average of £35, and in 1803 £225, just under 20s. per head of population.[83] Expenditure rose by 1813 to c. 37s. per head, fell in 1815 to 25s., but by 1818 had risen to 48s.; in the 1820s it was much lower, falling by 1828 to c. 16s. per head (total expenditure £200), though by 1832 capitation was again over 20s.[84] In 1803 regular out relief went to 16 adults and 31 children, c. 20 per cent of the population, and occasional relief to 25 others; 21–26 people, perhaps including children, were helped regularly between 1813 and 1815, and 13–18 occasionally.[85]

After 1834 Lew became part of Witney union, and from 1894 of Witney rural district. In 1974 it became part of West Oxfordshire district.[86]

CHURCHES. A 'free chapel' in the patronage of the Belet family and endowed with tithes from their lands existed by 1224, when Exeter cathedral unsuccessfully challenged the arrangement.[87] Before 1303 the chapel acquired some glebe, said to be 15 a. in 1399.[88] The advowson passed in the 14th century to a succession of owners, including members of the Talbot and Laundels families and, in 1399, Thomas Dyer, a vicar of Bampton, who as patron was to offer 1 lb. of wax before the image of the Blessed Virgin at Lew on the feast of the Assumption.[89] No appointments are known, though Robert of Cokethorpe, chaplain, involved in the suit of 1224,[90] perhaps served the chapel. In 1549,

[65] Orr, *Oxon. Agric.* 45 and statistical plates; cf. *Sale Cat., Lew Estate* (1914): copy on microfilm in C.O.S.
[66] *Kelly's Dir. Oxon.* (1939); *Sale Cat., University fm.* (1959): copy in C.O.S.
[67] P.R.O., E 179/161/8–10; *Bampton Hund. R.* 24, 26; cf. R. McKinley, *Surnames Oxon.* (Eng. Surnames Ser. iii), 125–6.
[68] O.R.O., MSS. Wills Oxon. 11/3/40, 172/4/45; *Witney Ct. Bks.* 168, 174, 196; Blenheim Mun., B/M/148, p. 561.
[69] Oxf. Univ. Arch., SEP/Q/21; Arundel Castle, MS. TP 98, pp. 75–6.
[70] *Witney Ct. Bks.* 196 and n.; P.R.O., HO 107/1731.
[71] Bodl. MS. d.d. Shrewsbury c 3/9 (8); Oxf. Jnl. Synopsis, 17 Sept. 1768; *Oxf. Jnl.* 3 May 1800.
[72] *Census,* 1811–31.
[73] P.R.O., RG 9/905; cf. above, manor.
[74] *Kelly's Dir. Oxon.* (1883 and later edns.); inf. from Mr. M. J. Rouse, Univ. Fm.
[75] Oxf. Univ. Arch., SEP/Q/5, p. 2; O.R.O., MS. d.d. Par. Bampton a 2 (R).
[76] Arundel Castle, MS. M 535; Longleat House (Wilts.),

NMR 3315, *passim*; *Bampton Hund. R.* 24 n.
[77] Bodl. MSS. Ch. Oxon. 312–13, 333; P.R.O., REQ 2/413/90; *Oseney Cart.* vi, p. 240.
[78] O.R.O., MS. Oxf. Dioc. c 746, f. 14v.; Lew Church Bk. 1842–88, in custody of vicar and par. officers of Bampton.
[79] *Oxf. Dioc. Yr. Bk.* (1990), 87.
[80] D. & C. Exeter, MS. 6016/8, notes re division of parish c. 1845; Lew Church Bk. 1842–88.
[81] *Oxon. Justices in 17th Cent.* (O.R.S. xvi), 85.
[82] *Protestation Rtns. and Tax Assess.* 2, 7; Oxf. Univ. Arch., SEP/Q/25.   [83] *Poor Abstract, 1804.*
[84] Ibid. *1818; Poor Rate Returns,* H.C. 556, p. 135 (1822), v; ibid. H.C. 334, p. 170 (1825), iv; ibid. H.C. 83, p. 157 (1830–1), xi; ibid. H.C. 444, p. 153 (1835), xlvii; *Census,* 1801–41.
[85] *Poor Abstract, 1804, 1818.*
[86] O.R.O., RO 3251, pp. 201–3; RO 3267.
[87] *Cur. Reg. R.* xi, pp. 534–5.
[88] Exeter Coll. Mun., M.II.1.
[89] Ibid.
[90] *Cur. Reg. R.* xi, pp. 534–5.

following suppression of chantries, the chapel was sold as the chantry- or free chapel of Lew 'founded' by Thomas Dyer, with 7 a. of open-field arable and corn tithes from 7 yardlands and 7 a., together yielding 6s. 8d. a year; in 1575 it was bought by London speculators as a 'cottage or tenement' formerly given for maintenance of a light.[91] Chapel orchard, adjoining Witney road, was mentioned in the later 18th century,[92] but the chapel's location is otherwise unknown.

The later church, built by subscription in 1841 on land donated by Jonathan Arnatt, was consecrated in 1842 as a chapel of ease with its own burial ground. In 1857 it became, under Order in Council of 1845, the parish church for Bampton Lew, conterminous with Lew township, and the advowson was vested in the dean and chapter of Exeter;[93] the church was licensed for marriages c. 1858. The benefice was united by Order in Council of 1917 with Bampton Proper, from 1976 part of the united benefice of Bampton with Clanfield.[94] The endowment comprised c. 216 a. formerly attached to Bampton's east vicarage, tithe rents in Clanfield worth c. £90 a year, and the south vicarage house in Bampton;[95] net income fell from c. £300 in 1866 to £200 in 1917, and both the small endowment and the house's distance from the church were repeatedly cited by vicars as their chief impediments, making it difficult to find incumbents.[96] After 1917 the vicarage house was sold, and vicars of the joint benefice lived in the house at Bampton formerly assigned to Bampton Proper.[97]

Until 1857 the church was served from Bampton, and in 1854 the number of communicants was 'small'.[98] Thereafter all Bampton Lew's vicars resided and seem to have been active in parish life, serving the cure alone. Henry Joy (1869–80) and Joseph Jackson (1887–1917) raised funds for church repairs and for new schools, difficult in a parish with few inhabitants and resident landowners, and in 1894 Jackson intervened on behalf of parishioners seeking a rent reduction. There were two Sunday services and a monthly sacrament. Average attendance in 1869 was 75–100, with about a dozen habitual absentees who were thought in 1872 to be

dissenters; communicants numbered usually between 10 and 15, and children were catechized or otherwise instructed regularly.[99]

The small, stone-built church of *HOLY TRINITY*,[1] designed by William Wilkinson[2] in 13th-century style, comprises chancel, nave with south porch and north vestry, and, over the porch, an octagonal turret apparently modelled on that of Cogges church. In 1851 there were 100 free and 60 other sittings.[3] Subsidence necessitated underpinning and buttressing in the 1870s and in 1896, and in 1920–1 a restoration by N. W. Harrison included underpinning, re-roofing, and redraining. The pews were then rebuilt without their doors, and the pulpit was lowered. In 1963 the bell turret was reroofed with copper.[4] Stained glass includes a window to the memory of F. E. Lott, vicar 1857–69; the bell, by Thomas Mears of London, is dated 1841, and the plate includes a silver chalice, a pair of patens, and a flagon, given in 1841 by Thomas Denton.[5] A lych-gate was added in 1892.[6]

NONCONFORMITY. In the early 17th century two members of the Wise family were fined for recusancy.[7] In the later 17th century three or four inhabitants who attended a Quaker meeting at Alvescot included the prosperous farmer William Wise, and Joseph Briscoe (d. 1715) of Lew left land at Alvescot to benefit poor Quakers attending the Witney and Alvescot meetings.[8]

Two Lew inhabitants belonged to the Congregational church at Witney in 1835 and another 4 by 1840,[9] when a small stone chapel with reportedly 160 sittings, said to have been planned before Lew church was contemplated, was built near University Farm on the initiative of the Witney minister Robert Tozer.[10] The Witney church belonged to the Association of Baptist Congregational Churches, and there was evidently co-operation with the Baptist chapel at Cote: one of the Lew members was baptized there in 1839, and in 1856 trustees of Lew Congregational chapel included the minister of Cote.[11] Average attendance in 1850–1 was 33, but only 14 were present on Census Sunday, and

91 Bodl. MS. Top. Oxon. c 60, f. 208; P.R.O., C 66/1125, m. 23.

92 O.R.O., P4/2/MS 1/5, f. 4, asserting, without evidence, that vicars of Bampton officiated in the chapel during the Interregnum.

93 *Oxf. Chron.* 29 May 1841; *Lond. Gaz.* 30 Dec. 1845, pp. 7353–4; O.R.O., MSS. Oxf. Dioc. c 746, ff. 12–17; c 1711, presentations; Lew church bk. 1842–88 (in custody of vicar and par. officers), s.a. 1857.

94 O.R.O., MSS. Oxf. Dioc. c 1713/1, Order in Council 1917; c 1713/2, Order in Council 1976.

95 *Lond. Gaz.* 30 Dec. 1845, pp. 7353–4; O.S. Map 1/2,500, Oxon. XXXVII. 6 (1876 and later edns.); cf. O.R.O., Bampton incl. award, s.v. Thos. Burrows.

96 Ch. Com. Rec. L 7, pp. 438–9; O.R.O., MS. Oxf. Dioc. c 1713/1, corresp. and docs. *re* union 1917; ibid. c 335, ff. 25–6; c 341, ff. 48–9; c 344, ff. 33–4; c 356, ff. 33–4; c 362, ff. 33–4.

97 O.R.O., MS. Oxf. Dioc. c 1713/1, Order in Council 1917; above, Bampton and Weald, churches.

98 *Wilb. Visit.* 10–12.

99 O.R.O., MSS. Oxf. Dioc. c 332, pp. 54–6; c 335, ff. 25–6; c 338, ff. 29–30; c 341, ff. 48–9; c 344, ff. 33–4; c 347, ff. 31–2; c 350, ff. 32–3; c 356, ff. 33–4; c 359, ff. 31–2; c 362,

ff. 33–4; c 365, ff. 33–4; Ch. Ch. Arch., MS. Estates 74, ff. 147 and v., 169–70, 173–5, 189–95.

1 *Ch. and Chapel, 1851*, no. 264, giving wrong erection date; *Oxf. Dioc. Yr. Bk.* (1990), 87.

2 *Oxf. Chron.* 29 May 1841.

3 *Ch. and Chapel, 1851*, no. 264; below, plate 15; cf. Pevsner, *Oxon.* 682–3.

4 O.R.O., MSS. Oxf. Dioc. c 338, f. 30; c 341, ff. 48–9; c 1713/1, faculties; ibid. MS. d.d. Par. Bampton c 10, item c; Ch. Ch. Arch., MS. Estates 74, ff. 194–5.

5 O.R.O., MS. Oxf. Dioc. c 344, ff. 33–4; *Ch. Bells Oxon.* ii, p. 202; Evans, *Ch. Plate Oxon.* 12.

6 Date on gate.

7 H. E. Salter, 'Oxon. Recusants', O.A.S. *Rep.* (1924), 19–20, 40, 46, 53.

8 *Bp. Fell and Nonconf.* 5, 50–1; O.R.O., BOQM 1/ii/3; ibid. MS. Wills Oxon. 8/4/34.

9 O.R.O., WCC I/1, pp. 101, 117.

10 *Ch. and Chapel, 1851*, no. 265; W. H. Summers, *Hist. Berks., S. Bucks., and S. Oxon. Congregational Churches* (1905), 273; Giles, *Hist. Bampton*, 87, stating that it was not completed until after Lew church was finished in 1841.

11 O.R.O., WCC I/1, p. 117; *Oxf. Chron.* 8 Mar. 1856; Summers, *Hist. Congregational Chs.* 272.

during the 1860s and 1870s Dissent in Lew declined steadily. From 1856 to 1858 and again by 1875 the chapel was let to the parish on weekdays for use as a school, and in 1878 only one dissenter was reported.[12]

EDUCATION. An interdenominational day school was opened in 1856 in the Congregational chapel, which was leased for a nominal rent.[13] From 1858 to 1865 the school was moved to a nearby cottage, but following disputes over rent it was moved back to the chapel before 1875.[14] It was at first run by the master and mistress of a Sunday school,[15] and in 1866 was a dame school supported from voluntary contributions, school pence, and 16s. 3d. a year paid to the vicar from the Bampton charities.[16] Landowners' subscriptions rose from £11 in 1874 to c. £16 following appeals by the vicar.[17] Between 14 and 20 'very young' children of both sexes were attending in 1866 and were catechized by the vicar; by 1871, when 30 children attended on inspection day, there were 43 on the day school register and 53 on the Sunday school register.[18]

Despite repeated attempts to raise funds for a purpose-built schoolroom[19] the school continued in the chapel, which could accommodate 64 in 1880.[20] Improvements in 1876, including the renting of playgrounds at the rear and provision of separate offices for boys and girls, averted the threat of a school board, and thereafter the school received a government grant.[21] A headmistress appointed in 1876 continued until 1907, and though children in the 1870s and 1880s were reportedly of low standard for their age, in 1886 the school was efficient.[22]

Only c. 25 children were on the register in 1876 and 1899, when several were only 3 years old.

Abnormal amounts of illness between 1896 and 1900 lowered attendance, and in the early 20th century constantly shifting population made continuity difficult; in 1901 the inspection was attended by only 13 children of whom some had already attended 4 different schools. In 1903 the school avoided closure only after being transferred to the County Council, and cramped accommodation and rapid turnover of staff and pupils repeatedly hampered improvement. The seniors were transferred to Bampton in 1926, leaving only 11 children at Lew, and in 1927 the school closed.[23]

A night school for men, held twice a week by the two day-school teachers in 1869 and 1872, had ceased by 1878.[24]

CHARITIES FOR THE POOR. Lew's share of George Thompson's and Leonard Wilmot's charities[25] was represented in the late 18th century and early 19th by 'dole money' of £1 0s. 8d., paid irregularly from Bampton churchwardens' account and distributed in bread. In 1819 seven years' arrears were distributed in cheap coal, and in 1824 the Charity Commissioners ruled that regular payment should be made from Bampton's charity account.[26] Robert Jeeves, by will proved 1703, left £5 to benefit poor labourers of Lew,[27] and Thomas Horde, by will proved 1716, left £10 for apprenticing two boys or girls,[28] but though the Horde bequest was applied in the earlier 18th century[29] both charities were lost by the early 19th.

Under a Scheme of 1888 Lew's charities became part of Bampton Consolidated Charities, which in 1969 distributed c. £6 in Lew. In 1972 they became part of the Bampton Welfare Trust.[30]

SHIFFORD

AN estate at Shifford, conterminous with the later township (775 a.), existed by 1005. From 'summer ford' at the estate's south-eastern corner the boundary ran westwards along the river Thames and along a stream forming Chimney's north-east boundary, before turning north and then east along 'the way'; it then than ran southwards to the Thames along a meandering stream canalized c. 1850 at the inclosure of Standlake and Brighthampton. Cynlaf's stone, a

landmark on 'the way', may have marked a kink in the western boundary west of New Cottages, where a possible relict roadline intersects, and Kentwin's tree, also on 'the way', perhaps marked Shifford's north-west corner. The southern part of the western boundary was evidently adjusted later, presumably after the truncation or suppression of 'the way', and in the 19th century followed field boundaries. Small deviations from the Thames, notably near

12 *Ch. and Chapel, 1851*, no. 265; O.R.O., MSS. Oxf. Dioc. c 332, pp. 54–6; c 335, ff. 25–6; c 338, f. 29v.; c 341, ff. 48–9; c 344, ff. 33–4; below, educ.
13 *Oxf. Chron.* 8 Mar. 1856; above, nonconf.
14 *Oxf. Jnl.* 29 Sept. 1866; O.R.O., MSS. Oxf. Dioc. c 341, ff. 48–9; c 344, ff. 33v.–34. *Dutton's Dir. Oxon.* (1863) wrongly stated that it was still in the chapel.
15 *Oxf. Chron.* 8 Mar. 1856; cf. *Wilb. Visit.* 11.
16 O.R.O., MSS. Oxf. Dioc. c 332, ff. 54–6; c 338, ff. 29–30.
17 Ch. Ch. Arch., MS. Estates 74, ff. 173–5, 177; *Public Elem. Schs. Return*, H.C. 403, p. 212 (1890), lvi; *Return of Schs. 1893* [C. 7529], pp. 494–5, H.C. (1894), lxv.
18 O.R.O., MSS. Oxf. Dioc. c 332, ff. 54–6; c 338, ff. 29–30; *Returns relating to Elem. Educ.* H.C. 201, p. 324 (1871), lv.
19 *Oxf. Jnl.* 29 Sept. 1866; O.R.O., MS. Oxf. Dioc. c 341, ff. 48–9; Ch. Ch. Arch., MS. Estates 74, ff. 147 and v., 191–193v.

20 O.S. Map 1/2,500, Oxon. XXXI. 15 (1899 and later edns.); *Rep. of Educ. Cttee. of Council (1879–80)* [C. 2562-I], p. 675, H.C. (1880), xxii.
21 O.R.O., MS. Oxf. Dioc. c 344, ff. 33v.–34; ibid. T/SL/33 i; Oxf. Univ. Arch., SEP/Q/46–7.
22 O.R.O., T/SL/33 i–ii.
23 Ibid. T/SL/33 ii. The bldg. became part of University Fm.: *Sale Cat.* (1959), copy in C.O.S.
24 O.R.O., MSS. Oxf. Dioc. c 335, ff. 25–6; c 338, ff. 29–30; c 344, ff. 33–4.
25 Above, Bampton and Weald, charities.
26 *Char. Don.* 968–9; *10th Rep. Com. Char.* 354.
27 O.R.O., MS. Wills Oxon. 38/2/25.
28 P.R.O., PROB 11/551, f. 253.
29 O.R.O., MS. d.d. Par. Bampton b 11, indenture 29 Nov. 1736.
30 O.R.C.C., Kimber files; above, Bampton and Weald, charities.

Great brook, presumably represent the river's earlier course.[31]

Cropmarks in the south-west suggest trackways associated with Romano-British settlement, extending westwards towards Cote and eastwards towards Standlake.[32] Later roads focused

14th century or early 15th, and in 1629 the northern continuation of 'the way' was suppressed because of frequent flooding, together with a branch road to Brighthampton which crossed Shifford's northern edge near Shifford Marsh, Claxhurst, and Stoneham hook. The

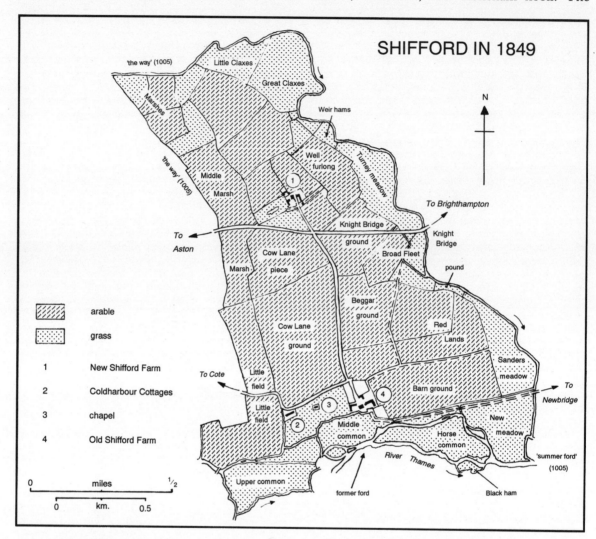

SHIFFORD IN 1849

arable

grass

1 New Shifford Farm

2 Coldharbour Cottages

3 chapel

4 Old Shifford Farm

on the ford from which Shifford ('sheep ford') is named,[33] discernible in 1992 south of Old Shifford Farm, and recorded in 958 as 'stone bridge', a term probably denoting a paved causeway.[34] Both Cote Lane and 'the way' along the township's western boundary, the latter perhaps identical with the 'royal way' adjoining North field c. 1360,[35] originated presumably as routes to that crossing and thence into Berkshire, and further north 'the way' continued along Aston's eastern boundary to meet Abingdon Lane, an ancient route leading north-westwards towards Brize Norton. The ford's importance was presumably diminished by the building of Newbridge (in Northmoor parish) in the late

part of 'the way' bordering Shifford had disappeared by the later 18th century.[36] The Aston–Brighthampton road, crossing Shifford's eastern boundary brook at Knight Bridge and running across the former open fields, was a bridleway until 1629 when it became the chief carriage route, and since Knight Bridge was recorded in the 13th century was presumably of early origin.[37] A ferry across the Thames to Longworth, held with a cottage for rent and service, was noted from the mid 13th century to the mid 15th; a testator in 1593 owned a boat,[38] and in the mid 18th century some farm produce was transported by water.[39]

Undated cropmarks have been noted on the

[31] Grundy, *Saxon Oxon.* 54, which misidentifies 'summer ford'; O.R.O., tithe map; cf. *Early Chart. of Thames Valley*, ed. M. Gelling, p. 139

[32] *Oxoniensia*, lx. 97–8, 172; *S. Midlands Arch.* xix (1989), 47; below.

[33] *P.N. Oxon.* (E.P.N.S.), ii. 327.

[34] *P.N. Berks.* (E.P.N.S.), iii. 706–7; *Oxoniensia*, lvii. 348.

[35] *Eynsham Cart.* ii, p. 4.

[36] Bodl. MS. Top. Oxon. c 118, f. 7 and v.; Jefferys,

Oxon. Map (1767); above, Aston and Cote, intro.; Lew, intro.; below, Standlake, intro.; below, plate 39.

[37] Bodl. MS. Top. Oxon. c 118, f. 7 and v.; for Knight Bridge, ibid. MS. d.d. Harcourt c 296, tithe award schedule; O.R.O., tithe map; ibid. Standlake tithe map; *P.N. Oxon.* (E.P.N.S.), ii. 328.

[38] *Eynsham Cart.* i, p. 11; ii, pp. lxvii, 10, 186–9; O.R.O., MS. Wills Oxon. 189, f. 31.

[39] Bodl. MSS. d.d. Harcourt c 133/3, p. 57; c 136/2, p. 2.

township's western edge north of Coldharbour
Cottages, north-west of New Shifford Farm, and
south-east of Old Shifford Farm.[40] Excavations
in the south-east near Brighthampton cut
revealed a small Iron-Age and Romano-British
settlement occupied from the 1st century B.C. to
the 1st or early 2nd century A.D., supported chiefly
from animal husbandry; immediately to the north
was a settlement occupied from the late 3rd century to the late 4th, but apparently unconnected
with the first. Finds on the later site indicated
mixed but still predominantly pastoral farming,
and traces were found of large rectilinear fields
enclosed within ditches.[41] No evidence was
found of later occupation.

A late Anglo-Saxon spearhead, *seax*, and
prick-spur were dredged from the Thames near
Shifford in 1914.[42] There was a settlement at or
near the ford presumably by 1005 when the vill or
township (*villa*) was granted to Eynsham abbey,
and 13 tenants, each presumably representing a
household, were recorded in 1086.[43] By 1279
there were 23 tenants including 13 cottagers, and
the apparently recent division of some holdings
suggests increasing population; 11 landholders
excluding the abbot of Eynsham were taxed in
1306, 14 in 1316, and 15 in 1327.[44] Though there
was evidently depopulation later in the century,
Shifford seems to have suffered less than many
Oxfordshire parishes: 18 tenants were listed *c.*
1360 when only one cottage holding remained
vacant, and in 1377 there were 50 persons over
14 liable for poll tax.[45]

Fifteenth-century contraction may have
affected the population more seriously, perhaps
chiefly at the expense of cottagers and smallholders,[46] though in the 16th and 17th centuries
Shifford remained almost as populous as Lew:
12 inhabitants were taxed in 1542–4,[47] and in the
later 17th century there seem to have been 15–23
houses including 4–5 cottages, and an adult
population of at least 50–60.[48] A survey of 1755
listed 7 farmhouses and 7 cottages,[49] but inclosure of the township by the Harcourts soon after
left only two farmhouses, one (Old Shifford
Farm) near the site of the former village, the
other (New Shifford Farm) built *c.* ¾ mile to the
north in the former open fields *c.* 1758.[50] Other
houses mentioned in 19th-century censuses were
agricultural labourers' cottages.[51] In all, the town-

ship contained 7 houses occupied by 8 families
in 1801, 9 in 1831 and 1841, 8 in the 1860s and
1870s, and 10 in 1881, the population rising
during the same period from 38 to 70. During
the 1880s it fell sharply to 31 as a result of
agricultural depression, and in 1891 there were
5 vacant houses; by 1901 it was 40 accommodated
in 9 houses, but fell to 22 by 1921. There were 39
inhabitants by 1931, and 27 in 1951, the last year
for which separate figures are available.[52]

Though Shifford chapel was rebuilt in the 19th
century its medieval predecessor, documented
from the early 13th, seems to have occupied the
same site.[53] A much-damaged limestone col-
umn-base found north of Old Shifford Farm,
the corners hacked off giving it an octagonal
appearance, was evidently not *in situ* and may
not be medieval.[54] House platforms, with what
may be former drainage ditches running between
them, survive south of the chapel on the edge of
the narrow gravel terrace, and extend south of a
boundary ditch into what in the 17th and 18th
centuries was common pasture;[55] a villein's
house immediately east of the chapel was
mentioned *c.* 1360,[56] and in the 15th century
buildings associated with Eynsham abbey's
stone-built manorial farmstead faced or adjoined
the chapelyard.[57] A large depression south of the
chapel may be remains of a former green, but
has evidently been altered and deepened by
gravel digging; from there a deep hollow way
runs south-westwards towards former common
pasture and open-field land. Old Shifford Farm
to the east, built in the late 17th century, is
described below;[58] Coldharbour Cottages west
of the chapel, gutted by fire and left derelict in
1974, were built apparently in the early 19th
century,[59] and New Shifford Cottages before 1876.
South Farm, by the Aston–Brighthampton road,
was built *c.* 1960 and New Cottages before
1976.[60] Electricity was supplied to Old Shifford
c. 1948, and to New Shifford *c.* 1961; there was
no mains water, drainage or gas in 1993.[61]

A tradition, current by 1677, that King Alfred
held a *witan* at Shifford arose from a reference
to 'Sifford' or 'Sevorde' in the probably 12th-
century poem known as 'The Proverbs of
Alfred'.[62] That the poem referred to an actual
assembly is unlikely, and the identification with
Shifford is impossible on linguistic and historical

40 D. Benson and D. Miles, *The Upper Thames Valley,
an Arch. Surv. of the River Gravels*, 40–1; C.O.S., PRN 1597,
8668–74, 11572.
41 *S. Midlands Arch.* xix (1989), 47; xx (1990), 85–8;
Oxoniensia, lx. 93–175; C.O.S., PRN 8229–32; cf. ibid. PRN
1036, 3081.   42 *V.C.H. Oxon.* i. 369, 372.
43 Ibid. 403; *Eynsham Cart.* i, p. 21.
44 *Bampton Hund. R.* 65–6; P.R.O., E 179/161/8–10.
45 *Eynsham Cart.* ii, pp. 7–13; P.R.O., E 179/161/42;
below, econ. hist.
46 Below, econ. hist.
47 P.R.O., E 179/162/234.
48 Ibid. E 179/255/4, pt. i, f. 23; *Hearth Tax Oxon.* 232;
Protestation Rtns. and Tax Assess. 9; *Compton Census*, ed.
Whiteman, 417, 422; Bodl. MSS. d.d. Harcourt c 110/1, c
110/21, c 127/17; cf. ibid. c 296, survey *c.* 1602. Par. regs.
survive from the 1780s.
49 Bodl. MS. d.d. Harcourt c 112/5; cf. ibid. c 296,
partics. of estate of Peter Standley [*c.* 1750], listing 4
farmhouses and 6 cottages.
50 Below, econ. hist.; for New Shifford Fm., Bodl. MS.
d.d. Harcourt c 136/2, pp. 80–2; dated beam in barn.

51 P.R.O., HO 107/872; ibid. RG 11/1514; O.R.O., tithe
map; Bodl. MS. d.d. Harcourt c 296, tithe award schedule.
52 *Census*, 1801–1951; below, econ. hist. Thereafter
Shifford was returned with Aston.
53 Below, church.
54 Inf. from R. A. Chambers and J. Blair; drawing in
C.O.S., SMR (unnumbered in 1995).
55 Cf. C.O.S., PRN 1080, 4589; ibid. SMR air photos.,
SP 3602/B, SP 3701/B–C; below, econ. hist.
56 *Eynsham Cart.* ii, p. 7.
57 Below, manor.   58 Ibid.
59 Jefferys, *Oxon. Map* (1767); Davis, *Oxon. Map* (1797);
O.R.O., tithe map; inf. from Mrs. Carter, Old Shifford Fm.
60 O.S. Maps 1/2,500, Oxon. XXXVIII. 9 (1876 and
later edns.); 6", SP 30 SE (1960 edn.) and sheet 42/30
(provisional edn. *c.* 1960); 1/2,5000, SP 20/30 (1976 edn.).
61 Inf. from Mrs. Carter, Old Shifford Fm.
62 Plot, *Nat. Hist. Oxon.* (1677), p. 22; J. Spelman, *Life of
Alfred the Great* (1709), 125–6; Giles, *Hist. Bampton*, 86,
125–6; cf. *Proverbs of Alfred*, ed. W. W. Skeat (1907); H. P.
South, *Proverbs of Alfred in the Light of the Maidstone MS.*
(1931).

grounds:[63] Oxford and the region dependent on it were not directly controlled by Wessex until 911,[64] and significant assemblies would in any case have presumably met at Bampton. The names Court close (for the area around the chapel) and Kingsway field, cited in support of the tradition in the 19th century,[65] refer respectively to the site of Eynsham abbey's manorial farmstead, and to a lane leading through Aston apparently to the royal *tūn* at Bampton.[66]

MANOR. Before 975 King Edgar granted *SHIFFORD* to Brihtnoth, the ealdorman killed at the battle of Maldon in 991. The estate later passed to Leofwine and to his kinsman Aethelmar, who granted it to Eynsham abbey at its refoundation in 1005.[67] After the Conquest the abbey's Oxfordshire lands passed temporarily to the bishops of Dorchester and later of Lincoln, but were restored probably before 1086, when Shifford was assessed at 3 hides, and thereafter the abbey retained the manor until the Dissolution.[68] During the 12th and 13th centuries land elsewhere became attached to the manor. Roger d'Oilly gave 2 yardlands in Aston before 1142, and his son Roger another yardland before 1180;[69] 6 yardlands in Aston and 4 in East Weald (later Claywell) in Ducklington, held probably by Theodoric the goldsmith in 1086, were given before 1190 by Ralph de Chesney,[70] and there were further small grants in Aston, Cote, and East Weald during the 13th century.[71] Meals owed by the abbey on St. Bartholomew's day (24 August) to neighbouring lords' tenants in Aston, apparently as quitrent for lands or meadows outside the township attached to Shifford manor, were commuted or compounded for in the mid 13th century.[72]

In 1539 the Crown granted the manor to Sir George Darcy, and it passed with other of Eynsham abbey's lands to Sir Edward North in 1543 and to Edward Stanley (d. 1572), earl of Derby, in 1545.[73] By 1586 all or part, including the demesne farm, was held for a term of years by the earl's grandson, Edward Stanley of Eynsham, in whose name courts were held in 1597 and 1599;[74] the freehold seems, however, to have descended to Edward's cousin Ferdinando Stanley (d. 1594), later earl of Derby, and to

Ferdinando's brother William, earl of Derby, who in 1600 sold the manor to Joseph Mayne of Creslow (Bucks.).[75]

In 1610 Mayne sold the manor to the royal justice Sir David Williams (d. 1613) and to Edward Yate of Buckland (then Berks.), who in 1612 partitioned it, Williams receiving the lands in Shifford with the manorial rights, and Yate those in Ducklington, Aston, Cote, and Standlake,[76] which became attached to Buckland. Much of the land in Aston and Cote, 8½ or 9 yardlands in the mid 17th century, had been sold by 1748, and at inclosure in 1855 the lord of Buckland received only c. 1 a. for mowing rights.[77] Williams settled Shifford in 1613 on his second son Thomas, who mortgaged it and in 1623, with his brother Sir Henry, sold a long leasehold to Robert Veysey (d. 1635) of Taynton and later of Chimney; the same year Thomas and Henry sold the reversion to Veysey's nephews Robert Veysey (d. 1666) of Queen's College, Oxford, and his brother William.[78] In 1630 the elder Robert, who in 1625 had recovered the lease of the demesne farm, settled the manor on himself for life with reversion to the younger Robert and his wife Anne, and in 1634 he surrendered his interest.[79] By 1675 the manor was held by Robert and Anne Veysey's surviving son Sunnybank, who in 1697 sold it to Josiah Bacon, a London merchant, to discharge his debts.[80]

Bacon died in 1703 leaving the manor in trust for his uncle's great-grandson Josiah Bacon, a minor; he died before 1717 when it was settled on his sister Elizabeth (d. 1726) and her husband Thomas Slaughter, who took the name Bacon.[81] Thomas died in 1736, when under Elizabeth's will her lands passed to her half-brothers George, John, and Peter Standley; George died in 1737 leaving his share to Peter, who received Shifford in a partition of family estates in 1742, and sold it in 1755 to Simon Harcourt (d. 1777), Earl Harcourt.[82] Thereafter Shifford descended with Nuneham Courtenay, passing in 1891 to Aubrey Harcourt, who in 1898 sold it to H. L. Cripps.[83] A proposed sale in 1906 was abandoned, and following Cripps's death c. 1916 the land was sold to the tenants of Old and New Shifford farms and manorial rights lapsed.[84]

A freehold yardland in Shifford manor, sold in 1482,[85] became divided but was later reabsorbed.

63 Cf. Skeat, op. cit. 53; South, op. cit. 25 sqq.
64 *A.-S. Chron.* ed. D. Whitelock, 62.
65 Bodl. MS. Top. Oxon. e 633, f. 4; ibid. d 218, ff. 207v., 214; *Kelly's Dir. Oxon.* (1895 and later edns.).
66 Below, manor; above, Bampton and Weald, intro.
67 *Eynsham Cart.* i, pp. 20 n., 21; *D.N.B.* s.v. Brihtnoth.
68 *V.C.H. Oxon.* i. 403; xii. 104; *Valor Eccl.* ii. 208.
69 Above, Bampton and Weald, manors (Bampton Doilly).
70 Below, Ducklington, manors (Claywell). Two of the Aston yardlands were freely held of the abbey for 3*s.* quitrent, still accounted for in the 15th century: B.L. Harl. Rolls K. 41, L. 1, L. 7.
71 *Eynsham Cart.* i, pp. 177, 185; ii, pp. lxv–lxvii; *Bampton Hund. R.* 21–3.
72 *Eynsham Cart.* i, pp. 196, 203, 206, 279–80; for later payments, ibid. ii, pp. lxvi, 15.
73 *L. & P. Hen. VIII*, xiv (1), p. 417; xviii (1), pp. 446, 540; xx (2), p. 540; *V.C.H. Oxon.* xii. 120.
74 Bodl. MSS. d.d. Harcourt c 113/10, c 127/12; *V.C.H. Oxon.* xii. 120.

75 Bodl. MSS. d.d. Harcourt c 109/1–3, c 109/5, c 113/10–11; P.R.O., CP 25/2/198/40 Eliz. I Hil.; *Complete Peerage*, iv. 212–14.
76 Bodl. MSS. d.d. Harcourt c 109/6–8, 10, 12; c 127/14; cf. ibid. c 109/5 (endorsement), c 109/33.
77 Giles, *Hist. Bampton*, Suppl. p. 1; O.R.O., Misc. WA I/1, ff. 5–6v.; ibid. Aston and Cote incl. award, s.v. Throckmorton; Berks. R.O., D/EWe E3, pp. 11–21 [of repeated pagination near end]; cf. *V.C.H. Berks.* iv. 455.
78 Bodl. MSS. d.d. Harcourt, c 109/11, c 109/13–14, c 109/19–23.
79 Ibid. c 109/25–7, c 109/29–32; cf. ibid. c 109/28.
80 Ibid. c 110/1–2, 10, 13, 15–22; c 111/1, 3, 5, 7–8.
81 Ibid. c 111/9–13, 15, 17; c 112/4
82 Ibid. c 111/14, 16–17; c 112/1–5.
83 *V.C.H. Oxon.* v. 242; conveyance 30 Apr. 1898 (copy in possession of Mr. P. E. Luckett, New Shifford Fm.).
84 Ch. Ch. Arch., MS. Estates 80, ff. 167–9; *Kelly's Dir. Oxon.* (1915 and later edns.); docs. in possession of Mr. P. E. Luckett.
85 O.R.O., Warner II/i/1; cf. below, econ. hist.

Thomas Williams bought a third in 1618,[86] and in 1686 Bishop Fell devised another third to Christ Church, Oxford, which in 1906 sold its land (19 a.) to H. L. Cripps.[87] The remaining third was presumably that sold to Earl Harcourt in 1757.[88]

Eynsham abbey maintained a home farm at Shifford throughout the Middle Ages and probably by 1086, when one ploughland was in demesne;[89] occasional visits by the abbot and other officers were recorded in the 14th and 15th centuries.[90] Some or all of the buildings seem to have been near the chapel: a wall next to the churchyard and a gate 'towards' it were mentioned in the 14th century,[91] and in the late 16th and early 17th remains of the demesne farm included a dovecot in Court close, reportedly the close in which the chapel stands.[92] About 1360 the 'court' with its buildings was valued at 6s. 8d. a year.[93] Repairs recorded in later bailiffs' accounts were mostly of agricultural buildings, though a cookhouse or kitchen (coquina) was repaired or rebuilt in 1363 and the hall and grange in 1397–8, when 5 cartloads of stone were brought for buttresses. The dovecot was mentioned from 1434.[94] The house was excluded from the farm of the manor in 1434[95] and may have been derelict by 1470, when the site of the manor was leased with the adjacent close and dovecot for only 2s. a year;[96] a 'capital messuage' held with Court close and with former demesne land in the late 16th century and the 17th,[97] presumably the 'manor house' briefly occupied by Sunnybank Veysey in the 1680s,[98] was not necessarily on the same site, and may have been a predecessor of Old Shifford Farm, the only farmhouse in the former hamlet to survive inclosure in the 1750s.[99] That house's late 17th-century south range, built possibly for Veysey, retains a contemporary staircase with turned balusters and a moulded handrail; a parallel north range was added in the 19th century. Farm buildings to the east include a timber-framed granary.

ECONOMIC HISTORY. Shifford had its own open fields until the mid 18th century, when it was inclosed by the Harcourts and reorganized as two farms. In the 14th century the demesne was divided fairly evenly between North field, including the area around New Shifford Farm, East field in the south-east, and an unnamed field in the south-west; the arable was differently grouped for cropping, however, two groups of furlongs in the east and west fields following four-course rotations, and North field and a probably adjoining furlong, which together contained the poorest land and had perhaps been brought into cultivation more recently, following a three-course rotation.[1] By the early 17th century the fields had been reordered, and lay apparently in three broad swathes running roughly south-west to north-east: a holding in 1608 contained 13 a. in Beggar field in the south-east, 17 a. in Middle field, which included the site of New Shifford Farm and the later Broad Fleet, and 17 a. in West or Windmill (later Marsh) field.[2] The fields were apparently unchanged in 1706,[3] though Great Common field (470 a.) and Little Common field (46 a.) were recorded c. 1755.[4] A lease in 1759[5] mentioned Beggar and Marsh fields, Little field in the south-west, and Knight Bridge field on the east, perhaps reflecting a division into quarters, but most strips were described only by reference to furlongs, and by then New Shifford Farm had been built[6] and inclosure and consolidation were probably under way. Payments by the Harcourts for ditching, hedging, grubbing, and road-making were made in the later 1750s,[7] and by 1788 Old and New Shifford farms were fully inclosed, Christ Church's land being consolidated in a small group of closes on the east.[8] Yardlands were reckoned at 40 a. c. 1360 and at 'above' 35 a. in the early 17th century, when ⅓ yardland comprised 15 a. excluding meadow.[9]

Meadows, estimated in 1086 at 50 a., lay mostly in the east along the boundary stream.[10] Demesne meadow and pasture c. 1360 included Claxhurst (35 a.) in the north-east, Shifford mead and 'Russhehammes', both described as pasture, and Addehurst, Chattoksham, and Langhurst in Standlake parish,[11] the last farmed from c. 1377 and sold with the Aston and Ducklington part of the estate in 1612.[12] Twelve Acres, variously used as meadow and pasture, was divided into 12 parcels of which 6 belonged to the demesne in rotation and 6 to the tenants of one free and one unfree yardland.[13] Though

86 Bodl. MS. d.d. Harcourt c 113/8; for earlier deeds, ibid. c 113/1–7.
87 Ch. Ch. Arch., MS. Estates 80, ff. 41v., 167–73.
88 Bodl. MSS. d.d. Harcourt c 113/15–30.
89 V.C.H. Oxon. i. 403.
90 Bodl. MSS. d.d. Harcourt c 128/2, c 128/4; B.L. Harl. Roll L. 2.
91 Bodl. MS. d.d. Harcourt c 128/1; B.L. Harl. Roll L. 2.
92 Bodl. MSS. d.d. Harcourt c 109/5, c 113/10; ibid. c 296, survey c. 1602; inf. from Mr. P. E. Luckett, New Shifford Fm. The name, still recorded in 1803, does not appear on 19th-cent. maps.
93 Eynsham Cart. ii, p. 2.
94 Bodl. MSS. d.d. Harcourt c 128/1–2, 4–5; B.L. Harl. Rolls L. 2, L. 6–7.   95 Below, econ. hist.
96 B.L. Harl. Roll G. 2; cf. Giles, Hist. Bampton, 141.
97 Bodl. MS. d.d. Harcourt c 296, survey ?1602 (marked '162' on dorse); ibid. c 113/10, c 109/27, c 127/13, describing it as in disrepair in 1604.
98 Ibid. c 110/17, c 110/21–2, c 111/7–8; he was non-resident in the 1670s and by 1697.
99 Above, intro.; below, econ. hist.; cf., however, Bodl.

MSS. d.d. Harcourt c 110/21–2, mentioning another 'Shifford Farmhouse'.
1 Eynsham Cart. ii, pp. 2–4; cf. O.R.O., tithe map; Bodl. MS. d.d. Harcourt d 30 (tithe award schedule); ibid. b 40 (R). Furlongs in North field included 'le Brech'.
2 Bodl. MS. d.d. Harcourt c 113/13.
3 Ch. Ch. Arch., Treasury bks. lv. b. 30, ff. 82–6.
4 Bodl. MS. d.d. Harcourt c 296, partics. of estate of Peter Standley.
5 Ibid., lease 24 Dec. 1759.
6 Above, intro.
7 Bodl. MSS. d.d. Harcourt c 133/3, p. 27; c 136/3; c 296, abstract of Shifford accts. 2 Jan. 1757.
8 Ibid. c 296, partics. of Shifford fms. 1788; ibid. d 29; ibid. b 40 (R).
9 Eynsham Cart. ii, p. 7; Bodl. MSS. d.d. Harcourt c 113/1–2, c 113/15; ibid. c 296, survey ?1602.
10 O.R.O., tithe map; Bodl. MSS. d.d. Harcourt d 30, b 40 (R); V.C.H. Oxon. i. 403.
11 Eynsham Cart. ii, pp. 4–5; below, Standlake, econ. hist.
12 Bodl. MSS. d.d. Harcourt c 109/10, c 128/4–6.
13 Eynsham Cart. ii, p. 5 and n.

a holding in 1706 still carried rights in the common meadows,[14] by then most meadow seems to have been hams held in severalty: Weirhams and Nineknolls descended with particular farms by the 16th century,[15] and in 1759 Christ Church's ⅓ yardland included c. 2 a. in New meadow (mentioned in 1586), Withy ham, Thurney (or Turney) mead, and Flexlake, with leys in East mead and in Sandleys or Sanders mead.[16]

Common pasture, 2 furlongs by 1 furlong in 1086,[17] adjoined the Thames and Chimney moor in the south, on land said in the early 17th century to be rich and suitable for meadow.[18] Pasture at Summerford in the township's south-east corner was confirmed to Eynsham abbey in the 1150s,[19] and cow common or lease, apparently in the south-west, was mentioned in 1332 and c. 1360. All or part of cow lease was then in demesne, but by 1363 it was let to the tenants for 3s. (later 3s. 4d.) a year, and seems later to have been commonable with other pastures.[20] In 1566 and 1759 there were cow, sheep, and horse commons,[21] the last lying apparently south-east of the village between two streams of the Thames.[22] Langhurst and other demesne meadows, pastures, and fallows were commonable in the mid 14th century from 1 August until 25 March, and in the 17th century occasional orders in the manor court regulated grazing in the fields;[23] the stint per yardland was then usually c. 40 sheep, 8 or 9 cows, and 3 horses, though in some years it was more,[24] and the most frequently recorded transgression was pasturing animals in the wrong common.[25] The township intercommoned in the 14th century with Standlake, Brighthampton, and Hardwick from 1 August to 10 November, and with Aston and Cote, Yelford, and apparently Chimney from 29 September to 10 November,[26] but no later references have been found. A few holdings included pasture closes by the 16th century.[27]

A withy bed (virgulus) called 'Wodehey' was mentioned in 1459, when a tenant was fined for folding animals there and destroying young trees.[28] Elms worth £200 in the early 17th century[29] may have been in hedgerows along the edges of the fields, and no woods were recorded later. Fourteenth-century tenants paid for pannage, not necessarily within the township,[30] and in 1608 pigs were excluded from the commons between 25 March and 29 September.[31]

In 1086 eight villani and five bordarii had 5 ploughteams, the number for which there was said to be land, and since no servi were recorded perhaps worked another on the demesne. The estate's value had risen from £4 in 1066 to £5.[32] There were still 8 villein yardlands in 1279, held for 4s. 8½d. rent and works valued at 10s., though one was divided between two tenants; another 13 tenants held a total of 8 cottages, 4 houses, and 31½ a. for varied rents and services, the largest holding comprising 5½ a. with a fishery, and 5 cottages being apparently landless.[33] A ninth yardland was held freely by the 1220s for 10s. a year and service of discharging the lord's and township's suit to the hundred and county courts; the tenant owed heriot and cornbote, and in 1331 claimed unsuccessfully that he did not owe homage or suit to the abbot's court.[34] The service was transferred c. 1426 to a holding let to the abbey's bailiff.[35]

Average personalty in 1306 and 1327 was higher than in Bampton's other hamlets, though in 1306 the total included payments for the demesne. The total value of movables assessed rose from £45 17s. 6d. in 1306 to £65 in 1327. The wealthiest tenant in 1306, assessed on 110s., was a villein yardlander; other yardlanders were taxed on between 42s. 6d. and 80s., the two half-yardlanders on 45s. and 52s. 6d., and the free yardlander on 50s. The lowest payment was from a cottager assessed on 20s., and the overall pattern remained similar in 1327.[36]

Six villein yardlands and the two half yardlands survived c. 1360,[37] when all but one were held by the same families as in 1279. The eighth yardland, granted to a Chimney tenant in 1332,[38] had been fragmented, allowing some cottagers, all descendants of 13th-century tenants, to accumulate holdings of ¼ or ½ yardland or more. Some other cottage holdings had been combined, perhaps following the Black Death, though 5 tenants still had 5 a. or less. Yardlanders' rents were still 4s. 8½d., including Peter's Pence,[39] 9d. fishsilver, and cornbote, but excluding aid, pannage, small payments in kind, and 1d. or a gallon of ale at every brewing. Their services, disputed in 1337,[40] included works at the winter and Lenten sowings and at Christmas, and heavy harvest works. Rents and services for smaller holdings varied considerably c. 1360, but seem generally to have been lighter than in 1279. Aid, totalling usually between 46s.

14 Ch. Ch. Arch., Treasury bks. lv. b. 30, ff. 82–6.
15 Bodl. MSS. d.d. Harcourt c 127/8, 12, 16.
16 Ibid. c 296, lease 24 Dec. 1759; ibid. c 113/12.
17 V.C.H. Oxon. i. 403.
18 O.R.O., tithe map; Bodl. MS. d.d. Harcourt d 30; ibid. c 296, survey c. 1602.
19 Eynsham Cart. i, pp. 87–8; above, intro.
20 Bodl. MSS. d.d. Harcourt c 126/6, c 126/14 (ct. 8 July 23 Ric. II), c 128/2; ibid. c 127/8, f. 14; B.L. Harl. Rolls L. 2–4; Eynsham Cart. ii, p. 5.
21 Bodl. MSS. d.d. Harcourt c 127/8, f. 14; c 296, lease 24 Dec. 1759.
22 O.R.O., tithe map; Bodl. MS. d.d. Harcourt d 30 (schedule); ibid. b 40 (R).
23 Eynsham Cart. ii, p. 6; Bodl. MS. d.d. Harcourt c 127/13.
24 Bodl. MSS. d.d. Harcourt c 113/9, c 113/13, c 127/8; ibid. c 296, terrier of Ellins's estate, survey c. 1602; Ch. Ch. Arch., Treasury bks. lv. b. 30, ff. 82–6.
25 e.g. Bodl. MSS. d.d. Harcourt c 126/6, c 126/14, c

127/8, c 127/13.
26 Eynsham Cart. ii, p. 6.
27 e.g. Bodl. MSS. d.d. Harcourt c 110/21–2, c 113/10, c 127/8.
28 B.L. Harl. Roll L. 13.
29 Bodl. MS. d.d. Harcourt c 296, survey c. 1602.
30 Ibid. c 126/14, c 128/3; Eynsham Cart. ii, p. 7.
31 Bodl. MS. d.d. Harcourt c 127/13.
32 V.C.H. Oxon. i. 403.
33 Bampton Hund. R. 65–6.
34 Ibid. 65 and n.; Bodl. MS. d.d. Harcourt c 126/3.
35 P.R.O., SC 6/961/14; B.L. Harl. Rolls L. 6, L. 10.
36 P.R.O., E 179/161/8–10; cf. Bampton Hund. R. 65–6; Eynsham Cart. ii, pp. 7–10.
37 Eynsham Cart. ii, pp. 7–10, 12–13, on which rest of para. based.
38 Bodl. MS. d.d. Harcourt c 126/6.
39 Cf. Eynsham Cart. i, pp. 47, 67; ii, p. lxii.
40 Bodl. MS. d.d. Harcourt c 126/11.

1.　BAMPTON: the church from the north-west in 1821

2.　BAMPTON: Ham Court from the east in 1821

3.   BAMPTON: the market place and town hall *c.* 1900, looking east

4.   BAMPTON: the horse fair in 1904, looking south-west along Bridge Street

5. BAMPTON: High Street *c.* 1903, looking east

6. BAMPTON: Broad Street from the north *c.* 1915, showing the Elms on the left

7.   BAMPTON: the Deanery from the south-east *c.* 1890

8.   BAMPTON: the grammar school and nearby malthouse from the south-east in 1821

9.   BAMPTON: Bampton Manor House from the south-east *c.* 1900

10.   BAMPTON: Weald Manor from the south-east in 1978

11. ASTON: the square and war memorial *c.* 1920, looking east

12. ASTON: Longs' cartworks and wheelwright's shop in the mid 20th century

13. COTE: the Baptist chapel from the south-east in the early 20th century

14. COTE: Cote House from the north in the early 20th century

15. LEW: the church from the south-east *c.* 1900

16. LEW: design for the remodelling of Lew House by John Belcher *c.* 1909

17. LEW: Lew barrow

18. SHIFFORD: the deserted village seen from the chapel c. 1887

19. DUCKLINGTON: the church, school, and pond *c.* 1890

20. DUCKLINGTON: the planting of an oak to celebrate the coronation
of Edward VII and Alexandra in 1902

The Nativity in the north-east angle

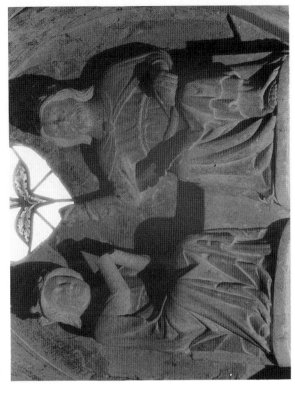

The Coronation of the Virgin in the east window

21. DUCKLINGTON CHURCH NORTH AISLE

22. COKETHORPE: Cokethorpe House from the south-east *c.* 1895

23. COKETHORPE: the chapel from the south-west in 1824

24. NORTHMOOR: the vicar's cottages opposite the church in 1873

25. COKETHORPE: Fish House in 1901

26. NORTHMOOR: Manor Farm from the south-west in 1964, before restoration

27. NORTHMOOR: Rectory Farm from the north in 1826

28. NORTHMOOR: Newbridge and the Rose Revived public house *c.* 1890

29. NORTHMOOR: Bablock Hythe *c.* 1880, looking west

30. STANDLAKE: the church from the south-east in 1821

31. STANDLAKE: the north end of the village from the air, showing the probable moated sites of the Mauduit (north) and Giffard manor houses and associated ditches

32. STANDLAKE: Gaunt House from the south-west in 1901

33. STANDLAKE: Gaunt Mill in 1979

34. STANDLAKE: the Green *c.* 1900, looking south-westwards along High Street

35. STANDLAKE: the village band outside the Golden Balls public house, Brighthampton, *c.* 1907

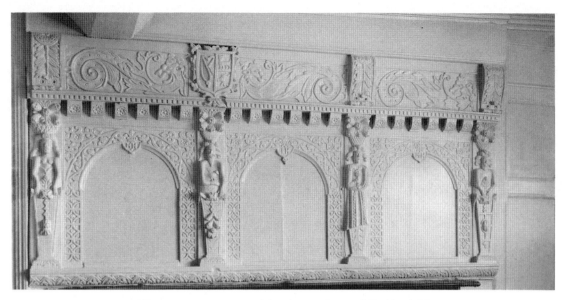

36. YELFORD: overmantel in the parlour of Yelford Manor

37. YELFORD: Yelford Manor and the church from the north-east in 1825

38. YELFORD: Yelford Manor from the west in the 1990s

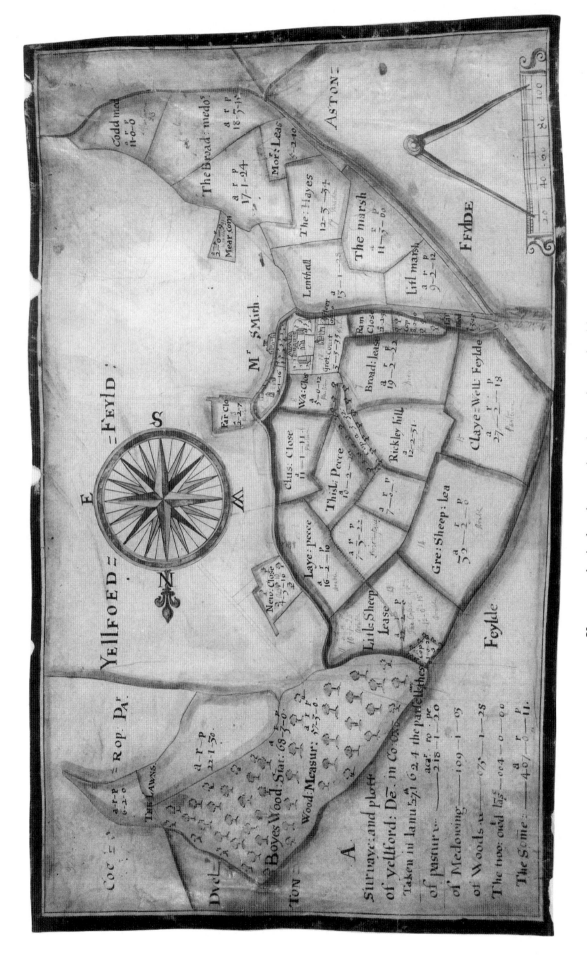

39. YELFORD: the inclosed estate in 1625, on internal evidence
a clumsy copy of an authentic map, with mid 19th-century pencil additions

and 50s., was replaced with a fixed rent by 1380–1,[41] but some labour services were still demanded in the early 15th century despite partial commutation on a few holdings.[42] Presumably all labour services were abandoned soon afterwards when the manor and demesne began to be farmed.[43]

Relative economic stability in the 14th century may have been followed by contraction in the early 15th. Arrears rose from c. £9 in 1391–2 to over £22 in 1407–8, and individual rent reductions were negotiated frequently.[44] Assize rents generally, which rose slowly during the 14th century, seem to have been reduced c. 1422–3, and by the 1450s total rent from tenants at will and by indenture was lower still.[45] Entry fines, 100s. or more in the mid 14th century, also fell sharply,[46] though by 1497–8 when free and customary rents totalled over £12, perhaps partly from former demesne, there may have been some recovery.[47] Several holdings were divided, amalgamated, or abandoned,[48] and the process continued in the 16th century apparently at the expense of the smallest holdings: by the early 17th century there were 13 copyhold tenants, of whom 2 held amalgamations of 1½ yardland with various closes and meadows, 4 held yardlands, 5 held half yardlands, and one held ¼ yardland, while another held a house and close.[49] None of the family names prominent from the late 13th century to the early 15th survived in the 16th and 17th.

The demesne, 2 ploughlands in 1279 and taxed on goods worth over £13 in 1306, may have been reduced to one ploughland by c. 1360, when it included 161 a. of open-field arable and 99 a. of meadow and pasture.[50] In 1397–8 c. 114 a. were sown, but in 1404–5 only 97 a.[51] Small parcels of land were occasionally leased at will, and in the early 15th century meadows and pastures were sometimes 'sold' for the year,[52] but otherwise the demesne was still managed directly through the reeve or bailiff, misleadingly called 'farmer' in 1379 and 1391.[53] Permanently employed labourers usually included a ploughman and one or two drovers, and additional labour was hired at harvest time to complement that of customary tenants, who in 1398 harvested only 23 a.[54] Demesne farming seems to have been chiefly arable: c. 12 to 14 oxen and 2 or 3 horses were usually recorded, besides capons, geese,

and hens which mostly went to Eynsham as customary renders, and no sheep were mentioned. The most usual course c. 1360 was (1) barley, (2) pulse or peas, (3) wheat, and (4) fallow,[55] and in 1397–8, a typical year, c. 43¼ a. on the demesne were sown with wheat, 34¾ a. with dredge, 21 a. with pulse, and 15¼ a. with oats. Some produce was consumed within the manor, some dredge being malted and brewed, but varying quantities were sold and significant amounts of wheat and dredge went to the abbey's grange.[56]

By 1427 part of the demesne seems to have been farmed by tenants for annual renders of 6 qr. of barley and 6 qr. of wheat, still accounted for in the 1440s,[57] and from 1434 the whole manor, including rents, perquisites, and agricultural buildings but excluding the house, the ferry, wards and escheats, and Langhurst meadow, was farmed for £11 6s. 8d. a year to the former bailiff.[58] By 1458 rents and perquisites were again administered directly, but the demesne, including the 'site' of the manor, continued to be let in parcels, much of it to the Stokes family.[59] By the late 16th century 1½ yardland of former demesne was held with a chief house and various tenements and closes by the Ford family, the remaining land having apparently been absorbed into other holdings.[60]

Tenant husbandry by the late 16th century was mixed but predominantly arable.[61] The chief crops remained wheat and barley followed by pulses and vetches, and oats and dill were mentioned in 1681.[62] Flocks of 60 sheep or more were mentioned in the late 14th century and mid 15th,[63] and in 1601 four tenants were fined for wrongly depasturing flocks of between 14 and 30;[64] one of the culprits left none at his death in 1611, however,[65] and sheep were mentioned in only a few 17th-century probate inventories. Flocks of 63 in 1681 and of 41 in 1702 were exceptional, and both were owned by especially wealthy mixed farmers who kept other livestock.[66] Dairying and cheesemaking were recorded in the 17th century and early 18th, several testators kept a few pigs, and poultry and bees were mentioned occasionally.

Some moderately prosperous yeomen were recorded in the 16th and 17th centuries, and a few leading families, notably the Farrs, Harrises, Darbys, and Gilletts, and later the Keenes and

41 Ibid. c 128/3–4, c 126/7–11; B.L. Harl. Roll K. 41.
42 P.R.O., SC 6/961/13; cf. B.L. Harl. Rolls L. 2–4.
43 Below; cf. P.R.O., SC 6/961/15; B.L. Harl. Roll G. 2.
44 B.L. Harl. Rolls L. 1, L. 5–6; P.R.O., SC 6/961/13–14.
45 Eynsham Cart. ii, pp. 12–14; Bodl. MSS. d.d. Harcourt c 128/1; B.L. Harl. Rolls K. 41, L. 1, L. 5, G. 2; P.R.O., SC 6/961/13–15.
46 Eynsham Cart. ii, p. 7; Bodl. MSS. d.d. Harcourt c 126/5, c 126/14.
47 Bodl. MS. d.d. Harcourt c 128/6.
48 e.g. Rolfs: B.L. Harl. Roll. L. 10; Bodl. MS. d.d. Harcourt c 126/14, ct. 21 July 21 Ric. II; Bampton Hund. R. 65. Cf. Bodl. MSS. d.d. Harcourt c 126/1–15, c 127/1–12, c 128/1–7; B.L. Harl. Rolls K. 41, L. 1–17.
49 Bodl. MS. d.d. Harcourt c 296, survey c. 1602.
50 P.R.O., E 179/161/10; Bampton Hund. R. 65; Eynsham Cart. ii, pp. 2–6.
51 B.L. Harl. Rolls L. 2, L. 4.
52 Eynsham Cart. ii, p. 9; B.L. Harl. Rolls L. 2–6.
53 e.g. Bodl. MSS. d.d. Harcourt c 128/1–4; B.L. Harl.

Rolls K. 41, L. 1–6; P.R.O., SC 6/961/13–14; Eynsham Cart. ii, pp. 10–11; cf. below, local govt.
54 B.L. Harl. Roll L. 2.
55 Eynsham Cart. ii, pp. 2–3.
56 B.L. Harl. Rolls L. 2–4.
57 Ibid. L. 10; P.R.O., SC 6/961/14; SC 6/961/20.
58 B.L. Harl. Rolls L. 7, L. 10; Bodl. MS. d.d. Harcourt c 128/5.
59 P.R.O., SC 6/961/15; B.L. Harl. Roll G. 2; Giles, Hist. Bampton, 141.
60 Bodl. MS. d.d. Harcourt c 113/10; ibid. c 296, survey c. 1602; above, manor.
61 Para. based on O.R.O., MSS. Wills Oxon., Shifford wills and inventories.
62 O.R.O., MS. Wills Oxon. 169/1/31.
63 Bodl. MS. d.d. Harcourt c 126/14; B.L. Harl. Roll L. 13.
64 Bodl. MS. d.d. Harcourt c 127/12, ct. 15 Oct. 43 Eliz. I.
65 O.R.O., MS. Wills Oxon. 25/3/35.
66 Ibid. 169/1/31, 53/2/3.

Bannisters, survived for several generations.[67] Most 16th- and 17th-century testators left goods valued at between £20 and £80, and nearly all inhabitants in 1662 were taxed on 2 hearths, only William Keene (3 hearths) and Thomas Sperrinke (4 hearths) being taxed on more, and 3 others, probably cottagers, on one only.[68] Until the 18th century there was little further consolidation of holdings: in 1699 there were 4 or more cottagers, and most copyhold tenants still held a yardland or less,[69] the chief exception being an amalgamation of 3¾ yardlands, 60 a. of meadow, and various closes, composed partly of former demesne and held in 1688 by John Pearce (d. 1702) and Henry Harris. Christopher Keene (d. 1681), who left goods worth nearly £300 and lived in a house with at least 8 rooms, was perhaps an earlier tenant.[70] Copyholds persisted in 1707, but by the mid 18th century Shifford contained 4–6 farms, some of them evidently quite large, held at rack rent, and half a dozen cottages.[71]

From 1755 the Harcourts administered the estate directly, and from c. 1760 let it as two farms of c. 435 a. and 338 a. centred on Old and New Shifford Farms.[72] Both tenants seem to have failed before 1769,[73] but from c. 1770 to 1890 the farms remained with the Williams family and their relatives the Wallises.[74] Improvements carried out by the Harcourts in the 1750s included ditching and drainage, notably through installation of floodgates at the 'Clexes' (formerly Claxhurst) in the northeast, and farming remained mixed, with sheep again important: 500 were mentioned in 1757, and in 1758–9 receipts from four years' wool exceeded £230. Pigs, horses, and horned cattle were also reared. The chief crops remained wheat and barley, with beans, peas, vetches, oats, and, by then, turnips and clover; some stock and produce went to the Harcourts' estates at Cokethorpe and Nuneham, but most was sold piecemeal to local buyers, and in 1755 some pulse was carted to Burford presumably for sale.[75] Tenants practised similar husbandry, including dairying, in the early 19th century, though in the later 1840s after tithe commutation there may have been a shift towards arable farming, the proportion of pasture and meadow falling from c. 45 per cent on both farms to 37 per cent at New and to 28 per cent at Old Shifford.[76] By 1871 the proportion of

pasture and meadow was even smaller, though both farms were described as sheep and dairy farms: Old Shifford Farm included piggeries, and Oxford Down sheep were mentioned in 1860. Steam power was used on the arable by the 1870s.[77] Drainage remained difficult, and in 1829 flooding caused serious losses.[78]

Difficulties during the agricultural depression of the 1870s and 1880s,[79] following which the whole estate was again administered directly from 1890 until its sale in 1898,[80] perhaps contributed to a renewed emphasis on pastoral farming. Livestock in 1893 included 72 cattle, 7 hogs, and, though none was mentioned in 1890, 712 sheep; 106 a. were under wheat, 91 a. under barley, 53 a. under beans and tares, and 42 a. under black oats, and winter feed and other crops included mangolds, swedes, turnips, vetches, rye grass, and maize.[81] By 1906 the two farms, run as one with a bailiff at Old Shifford, were 64 per cent pasture, supporting over 100 cattle and a flock of Hampshire Down sheep of 'exceptional quality and size', which in 1904 won prizes at the World's Fair exhibition at St. Louis (Missouri). Horses were bred also.[82] The bias towards pastoral farming continued in 1914 despite a sharp reduction in the number of sheep,[83] but during the 20th century arable farming revived: in 1991 the chief crop was winter wheat, and only a few beef cattle were pastured near the river.[84]

There was a clothworker in Shifford in the early 1650s,[85] but no other trades were recorded. A windmill worth 20s. a year existed by the early 14th century, when Eynsham abbey's tenants in Shifford, Aston, Cote, and Claywell owed suit; in 1331 those from Shifford and Cote were freed from grinding corn there in return for 3 qr. of toll corn a year. The mill was derelict in 1332 when a former miller's son took a 20-year lease and agreed to rebuild it at his own cost using the lord's timber, but no later references have been found, and by c. 1360 it had evidently been demolished.[86] A mill mentioned in 1459 and sold c. 1460 lay outside the parish.[87]

Two weirs in the Thames mentioned in 1005 were either near Great brook, or near a smaller side channel which formerly left and rejoined the Thames south-east of the hamlet.[88] In 1086 the manor rendered 250 eels.[89] In 1279 Eynsham abbey had a weir and free fishery in the Thames worth 13s. 4d., and a cottager shared another

[67] P.R.O., E 179/161/172–3; E 179/162/234; E 179/162/341; E 179/255/4, pt. i, f. 23; Bodl. MS. d.d. Harcourt c 127/18; ibid. c 296, survey c. 1602; O.R.O., MSS. Wills Oxon.; *Protestation Rtns. and Tax Assess.* 9.

[68] P.R.O., E 179/255/4, pt. i, f. 23; O.R.O., MSS. Wills Oxon., Shifford inventories.

[69] Bodl. MS. d.d. Harcourt c 127/17; cf. ibid. c 110/21–2, c 127/18, listing a 2-yardland holding.

[70] Ibid. c 110/22; O.R.O., MSS. Wills Oxon. 53/2/3, 169/1/31.

[71] Bodl. MSS. d.d. Harcourt c 127/18, c 112/5; ibid. c 296, partics. of estate of P. Standley.

[72] Ibid. c 133/3, c 136/2, c 137/2; ibid. c 296, partics. 1788.

[73] Bodl. MSS. d.d. Harcourt c 137/2, p. 21; c 144/1, p. 17; Oxf. Jnl. Synopsis, 27 May 1769.

[74] Bodl. MSS. d.d. Harcourt c 144/1, c 153/1, e 30–1; B. Williams, *Mems. of Williams Fam.* (priv. print. 1849), 17–18.

[75] Bodl. MSS. d.d. Harcourt c 133/3, c 134/4, c 134/7, c 135/3, c 136/2; ibid. c 296, abstract of accts.

[76] Ibid. d 29–30; ibid. c 296, surveys 1788 and 1803, tithe

award 1849, lease 31 Aug. 1860; Williams, *Mems. of Williams Fam.* 17–18.

[77] Bodl. MS. d.d. Harcourt c 266, pp. 63–7; *Oxf. Chron.* 4 Aug. 1860.   [78] Bodl. MS. d.d. Harcourt e 5.

[79] Ibid. b 25–6, b 42.

[80] Ibid. e 23, e 30–1; above, manor.

[81] Bodl. MS. d.d. Harcourt e 23.

[82] *Sale Cat., Shifford Manor Estate* (1906): copy on microfilm in C.O.S.

[83] Orr, *Oxon. Agric.* 45–6, and statistical plates.

[84] Inf. from Mr. P. E. Luckett, New Shifford Fm.

[85] P.R.O., PROB 11/262, f. 413 and v.

[86] Bodl. MSS. d.d. Harcourt c 126/3, c 126/6; *Eynsham Cart.* ii, p. 2.

[87] P.R.O., SC 6/961/15; B.L. Harl. Roll G. 2; cf. *Eynsham Cart.* ii, pp. li–lii.

[88] Grundy, *Saxon Oxon.* 54–5, assuming the latter; O.S. Map 6", Oxon. XXXVIII (1883 edn.).

[89] *V.C.H. Oxon.* i. 403.

fishery for rent and services; two other tenants had fisheries with their holdings *c.* 1360, and then as in *c.* 1338 tenants collectively paid 6*d.* a year for common fishing in 'Hammeslake' and 'Estelake'.[90] The lord's fishery, still distinguished in the 16th century,[91] seems usually to have been leased, and was not accounted for with the demesne in the 14th and 15th centuries. Illegal fishing was periodically reported in the manor court: 8 tenants were fined in 1336 for fishing with contrivances (*ingeniis*) other than shove-nets, and in 1615 a Witney man was fined for fishing in the common waters. In 1525 it was agreed that no tenant should fish the common waters except on Fridays.[92] Fishing rights in backstreams as well as in the Thames were still leased piecemeal in the 17th century,[93] but by the mid 18th were held by a Standlake fisher-man, and from the 1760s were let with Old Shifford farm.[94] In 1766 the Harcourts' rights over the whole width of the Thames opposite Black ham, where the river had evidently altered its course, were upheld against landowners on the Berkshire side, though Shifford weir, further upstream above Great brook, remained outside the lordship.[95]

LOCAL GOVERNMENT. Courts for Shifford manor were held by 1269, when pleas and perquisites totalled 6*s.* 8*d.*[96] Perquisites from East Weald (Claywell) in Ducklington were recorded separately, suggesting a separate session and possibly court, but by the early 14th century the homages of Shifford, Aston, and East Weald (which evidently included the manor's tenants in Cote) all attended the Shifford court.[97] In the 14th century and earlier 15th the court met up to four times a year, but by the early 16th apparently only twice, usually in March or April and October, and from the later 16th it met at other times also.[98] View of frankpledge was reserved for the hundred court, where Shifford's tithingman presented in 1500 and paid 3*s.* cert-money apparently for the half year, a sum which tenants complained in 1505 had been illegally raised to 8*s.* for the two annual views at Bampton.[99] Edward North held a view

at Shifford in 1544, and in the 17th century the manor was sold with its court leet and view of frankpledge,[1] but in the 1670s the Bampton court retained some jurisdiction and habitually fined Shifford's inhabitants for failure to scour watercourses.[2]

Medieval courts settled pleas of debt and other petty disputes besides granting copyholds, ex-acting childwite and fines for agricultural misdemeanours, and issuing licences for marriage and, occasionally, for going outside the manor.[3] Reeves and apparently rent collectors were elected throughout the 14th century.[4] Officers in the late 15th century and early 16th included a hayward, 2 water bailiffs, and in 1506 2 super-visors of fields, fisheries, and waters, and in 1616 there were 2 grass stewards.[5] Constables, men-tioned from 1642 to the 1750s, were appointed by the Bampton court.[6] Copyhold grants contin-ued throughout the 17th century, and courts baron, with courts of survey, were held in 1699 and 1707; no later courts are known, and although the manor was sold with its courts and perquis-ites in 1755 they presumably lapsed following Shifford's inclosure soon after.[7]

In the 19th century and probably by the late 15th Shifford had 4 church- or chapelwardens, appointed by Shifford, Chimney, Cote, and Brighthampton,[8] though only 2 wardens were mentioned in 1530.[9] After the division of Bamp-ton parish in 1857 Shifford 'vestry', so called by 1859 and attended by representatives of those townships, continued to appoint usually 4 wardens, but from the 1880s sometimes only 2 or three.[10] There was one warden in 1990.[11] In 1817 there was a 'parish' clerk, whose income the chapelwardens agreed to increase following intervention by a vicar of Bampton.[12]

Shifford may have shared an overseer with Chimney in the earlier 17th century but had its own probably by 1666,[13] and in 1759 may have had two.[14] Only a single weekly allowance was being paid *c.* 1755, and total parish expenditure rarely exceeded £4.[15] In 1775–6 £3 17*s.* was spent on poor relief, between 1783 and 1785 an average of £3 6*s.*, but in 1803 £21. By 1814 the total was £34, and in 1820 £66, or 30*s.* per head; from 1821 expenditure ranged usually between

90 *Bampton Hund. R.* 65–6; *Eynsham Cart.* ii, pp. 9–10; Bodl. MS. d.d. Harcourt c 128/1.
91 *Eynsham Cart.* ii, p. 9; B.L. Harl. Roll L. 16.
92 Bodl. MSS. d.d. Harcourt c 126/9, c 127/16; B.L. Harl. Roll L. 17.
93 Bodl. MSS. d.d. Harcourt c 127/17–18.
94 Ibid. c 296, deposition of Ric. Townsend of Standlake [1766]; ibid. c 133/3, c 137/2, c 144/1, b 10.
95 Ibid. c 296, W. Lenthall to Harcourt, 11 Feb. 1766; O.R.O., tithe map; O.S. Map 6", Oxon. XXXVIII (1883 edn.); F. S. Thacker, *Thames Highway* (1968), ii. 67, 72–4.
96 *Eynsham Cart.* i, pp. 10–11.
97 Ibid.; Bodl. MSS. d.d. Harcourt c 126/2–4, c 126/14, c 127/1.
98 For ct. rolls 1318–1707, Bodl. MSS. d.d. Harcourt c 126/1–16, c 127/1–18; B.L. Harl. Rolls L. 8–9, 11–17; P.R.O., SC 2/197/62–3.
99 Arundel Castle, MS. M 535; Bodl. MS. d.d. Harcourt c 127/3, cts. 5 Oct., 28 Apr. 21 Hen. VII; cf. ibid. c 128/6. For earlier discharge of suit to the hundred ct. by a tenant, above, econ. hist.
1 Bodl. MSS. d.d. Harcourt c 109/2, 6, 13; c 127/6.
2 Longleat House (Wilts.), NMR 3315, *passim*; below, this section.
3 e.g. Bodl. MSS. d.d. Harcourt c 126/1–16.

4 Ibid. c 126/4, c 126/7, c 126/14 (cts. 5 Nov. 1 Hen. IV, 12 July 3 Hen. IV); cf. *Eynsham Cart.* ii, pp. 10–11.
5 Bodl. MSS. d.d. Harcourt c 126/16; c 127/3–4, 16; B.L. Harl. Rolls L. 16–17.
6 Longleat House, NMR 3315, cts. 2 Apr. 1667, 29 Sept. 1669; Bodl. MS. d.d. Harcourt c 133/3, p. 17; *Protestation Rtns. and Tax Assess.* 9.
7 Bodl. MSS. d.d. Harcourt c 127/12–18, c 112/5; above, econ. hist.
8 D. & C. Exeter, MS. 6016/8, notes *re* division of par. *c.* 1845; *Eynsham Cart.* ii, p. lxvii; cf. *Protestation Rtns. and Tax Assess.* 1, 8–9; O.R.O., MS. Oxf. Dioc. c 24, f. 373; ibid. MS. Oxf. Archd. Oxon. c 99.
9 *Visit. Dioc. Linc.* ii. 52.
10 Shifford Vestry/P.C.C. Mins. 1859–1976, in custody of vicar and par. officers of Bampton; O.R.O., MS. d.d. Par. Bampton Aston d 1.
11 *Oxf. Dioc. Yr. Bk.* (1990), 87.
12 O.R.O., MS. Oxf. Dioc. d 577, ff. 80–1.
13 *Protestation Rtns. and Tax Assess.* 1; P.R.O., PROB 11/322, f. 363v.
14 Bodl. MS. d.d. Harcourt c 136/2, p. 17.
15 Ibid. c 133/3, p. 17; c 134/4, p. 17; c 134/7, p. 17; c 135/3, p. 17; c 136/2, p. 17.

£38 and £45, rising in 1831 to £68 or c. 29s. per head.[16] In 1803 there were 2 adults and 4 children on regular out relief and 5 people on occasional relief; from 1813 to 1815 two or three people received relief regularly and the same number occasionally.[17]

After 1834 Shifford belonged to Witney union, and from 1894 to Witney rural district. In 1974 it became part of West Oxfordshire district.[18]

CHURCH. A chapel existed c. 1230 when Eynsham abbey, as lord, agreed to give the vicars of Bampton 2 lb. of wax a year for lighting it on St. Laurence's feast day.[19] It had no endowment and remained subject to Bampton until 1857, when under Order in Council of 1845 it was incorporated into Bampton Aston parish,[20] from 1976 part of the united benefice of Bampton with Clanfield.[21] The chapelry in 1405 and still in the 19th century included Shifford, Cote, Chimney, and that part of Brighthampton within Bampton parish.[22] In the late 15th century inhabitants of Shifford and Chimney successfully petitioned the dean of Exeter to allow burial at Shifford, though in the 16th and 17th centuries testators sometimes specified burial at the mother church.[23] The chapel had baptismal rights by the 18th century and probably from the Middle Ages.[24]

In the early 15th century the chapel was served by a chaplain from Bampton once a week.[25] Then and throughout the 14th century the abbot of Eynsham was obliged to accommodate him in the manor house on the nights of Christmas, Easter, and St. Laurence's day, providing ale, light, and oats, and supplying 2 candles at vespers on the vigil of St. Laurence.[26] In 1499 the abbey allowed a cottage in Cote to be used by the chapelwardens for church ales, though in 1504 and 1506 it was in disrepair.[27] In 1510 the homage of Shifford agreed that no-one should fish with *cooppis* for nine months except for the benefit of Shifford chapel,[28] and several 16th and 17th-century testators made bequests towards the chapel's upkeep,[29] among them members of

the Veysey family of Chimney, some of whom were buried there.[30]

Few medieval chaplains are known,[31] though 16th-century curates and clerks witnessing Shifford or Chimney wills may have served the chapel.[32] Edward Joye (curate c. 1634), a graduate of St. John's College, Cambridge, and probably related to the Bampton vicar Robert Joye (d. 1614), was a schoolmaster in Bampton,[33] and William Standard, an intruded vicar of Bampton probably ejected c. 1662, may have been curate in 1664.[34] In the late 17th century and early 18th Thomas Horde (d. 1715) of Cote worshipped and received the sacrament regularly at Shifford;[35] by then the weekly duty, one morning service with prayers and a sermon 'when the weather and floods permit',[36] was evidently undertaken by vicars of Bampton or their substitutes, who arranged for replacements from Oxford as necessary. From the 1730s the cure was served without licence for £20 a year by Thomas Middleton, the non-resident vicar of Clanfield, who by 1738 employed his Clanfield curate to do the duty every third Sunday and was criticized by the bishop for consequent disruption of services in his own parish. In 1750 the Bampton vicar William Reynolds substituted his own resident curate, citing local demands for an additional Sunday service and alleging that Middleton's farming activities and numerous benefices prevented him from fulfilling his duties adequately; thereafter Middleton served Shifford only occasionally, but was still claiming arrears against Reynolds' widow in 1752.[37]

From c. 1772 to 1784 the chapel was derelict and there were no services, and following its reopening the chancel remained for some years in such disrepair that the sacrament could not be administered, parishioners and the chief landowners being unwilling to meet the cost of renovation.[38] By 1787 repairs were complete, but there continued to be only one Sunday service and sermon, with the sacrament administered three times a year to 18–20 communicants in 1790, and by 1808 four times a year to 20 or 30.

[16] *Poor Abstract, 1804, 1818*; *Poor Rate Returns*, H.C. 556, p. 135 (1822), v; ibid. H.C. 334, p. 170 (1825), iv; ibid. H.C. 83, p. 157 (1830–1), xi; ibid. H.C. 444, p. 153 (1835), xlvii; cf. *Census*, 1801–41.

[17] *Poor Abstract, 1804, 1818.*

[18] O.R.O., RO 3251, pp. 201–3; RO 3267.

[19] D. & C. Exeter, MS. 3672, p. 8; for dedication to St. Laurence, below.

[20] D. & C. Exeter, MSS. 648, 2865; *Ch. and Chapel, 1851*, no. 381; *Lond. Gaz.* 30 Dec. 1845, p. 7354.

[21] O.R.O., MS. Oxf. Dioc. c 1713/2, Order in Council 12 Apr. 1976.

[22] D. & C. Exeter, MS. 648; O.R.O., MS. Oxf. Dioc. d 571, f. 75; ibid. MS. Oxf. Archd. Oxon. b 26, f. 270.

[23] *Oxoniensia*, lvi. 112–13; O.R.O., MSS. Wills Oxon. 180, ff. 114v.–115; 184, ff. 16v., 21 and v., 116v.; 185, ff. 201v.–202, 460; 3/2/55, 3/3/28, 5/5/1, 22/1/13, 25/1/29, 43/1/20, 126/1/2; P.R.O., PROB 11/288, ff. 242v.–243; C.O.S., par. reg. transcripts.

[24] C.O.S., par. reg. transcripts; for marriages, O.R.O., MS. Oxf. Dioc. c 658, f. 167.

[25] B.L. Harl. Roll L. 3, s.v. *expense forinsece.*

[26] *Eynsham Cart.* ii, p. 6; Bodl. MS. d.d. Harcourt c 128/1; B.L. Harl. Rolls L. 3–4.

[27] *Eynsham Cart.* ii, p. lxvii; Bodl. MS. d.d. Harcourt c 127/3, ct. 5 Oct. 20 Hen. VII; ibid. c 127/4.

[28] *Eynsham Cart.* ii, p. lxvii.

[29] e.g. O.R.O., MSS. Wills Oxon. 11/1/32, 25/1/68, 39/1/63, 43/4/47, 127/1/6; ibid. 184, f. 16v.; P.R.O., PROB 11/132, f. 242 and v.; PROB 11/107, ff. 282–3.

[30] O.R.O., MS. Wills Oxon. 68/3/23; P.R.O., PROB 11/169, f. 59; PROB 11/252, f. 293.

[31] For a possible example, J. Blair, 'Medieval Clergy' (Bampton Research Paper 4, priv. print. 1991), app. C, col. 17: copy in C.O.S.

[32] Geof. Slyngar (c. 1556–9), Rob. Duccurth (1552), John Burnet (c. 1597–1602): O.R.O., MSS. Wills Oxon. 180, ff. 108v.–109; 184, f. 116v.; 186, f. 73 and v.; ibid. 11/1/32; 11/1/70; 39/1/63; O.A.S. *Rep.* (1913), 157; ibid. (1914), 189, 201; C.O.S., Standlake par. reg. transcripts, s.a. 1600.

[33] O.R.O., MS. Oxf. Dioc. e 9, ff. 182–3; ibid. MSS. Wills Oxon. 68/3/23, 131/5/29; Bodl. MS. Top. Oxon. c 118, f. 9; C.O.S., Bampton par. reg. transcripts, s.a. 1614.

[34] *Der Pietismus in Gestalten und Wirkungen*, ed. H. Bornkamm et al. (Arbeiten zur Geschichte des Pietismus, xiv), 349; O.R.O., MS. Oxf. Archd. Oxon. c 131, f. 18; cf. ibid. Cal. Oxf. presentation deeds, ser. 1.

[35] *Par. Colln.* iii. 253–4.

[36] O.R.O., MS. Oxf. Dioc. b 15, f. 98; cf. ibid. d 558, f. 35; *Secker's Visit.* 13.

[37] *Secker's Corresp.* 9, 191–4, 216–17.

[38] O.R.O., MS. Oxf. Archd. Oxon. c 99, ff. 27–42; ibid. MSS. Oxf. Dioc. d 564, ff. 29–31; c 327, p. 134; below, this section.

Average attendance in 1851 was 50 for the weekly service. During the earlier 19th century the chapel continued to be served in rota by the vicars or their curates and occasionally by outsiders;[39] it briefly had its own curate c. 1863, but from 1857 was served usually by the curate and later by the vicar of Aston, who conducted a morning or afternoon service with a sermon to fit in with his Aston duty.[40] In 1896 there were 2 services a month but in the 1960s only one, and in 1991 there were monthly evening prayers and a monthly communion.[41]

was in disrepair in 1770, and by 1772 the 'greatest part' of the chapel was ruinous, the rest being 'in a very bad condition and not fit to stand'. Rebuilding began c. 1781 and the chapel was serviceable by 1784, though the chancel remained 'much dilapidated by the long ruin of the church' until c. 1787, confirming that the chapel was rebuilt on the same site probably incorporating parts of the medieval fabric.[47] In the early 19th century it was of stone and slate and comprised a gabled, evidently aisleless nave with a plain south porch, and a lower, gabled

SHIFFORD CHAPEL c. 1850

The chapel of *ST. MARY*, so called by 1891[42] but dedicated in the Middle Ages to St. Laurence,[43] is of 1861–2. Nothing remains of its medieval predecessor except a rehung, possibly 13th-century bell, and the base of an apparently medieval cross in the churchyard.[44] Window glass needed repair in 1510, and in the early 18th century a south window contained figures reportedly of the Virgin, St. James, and St. Anthony;[45] a testator in 1605 requested burial in the south aisle near his seat, and made bequests towards building two pillars or buttresses against the chapel's north wall.[46] The chancel of the 'ancient', presumably medieval, building

chancel with a round-headed south door and a large, pointed east window, possibly of 14th-century origin. In the west gable of the nave were two small circular openings with, below, a central, possibly round-headed window. All other fenestration was modern, including two Venetian windows in the nave south wall flanking the central porch.[48] The chancel arch, said in the later 19th century to have been 'Saxon',[49] was presumably rounded. There was a gallery by the mid 19th century, when the chapel, said to be 'hardly distinguishable from the cottages', had 109 sittings, only 31 of them free.[50]

In 1861 it was decided to rebuild rather than

39 O.R.O., MSS. Oxf. Dioc. d 571, ff. 75–6; d 705, f. 22; b 38, ff. 15–16; ibid. MS. Oxf. Archd. Oxon. b 26, f. 272; *Ch. and Chapel, 1851*, no. 381, misleadingly implying two services: cf. *Wilb. Visit.* 12.
40 *Wilb. Letter Bks.*, p. 395; O.R.O., MSS. Oxf. Dioc. c 332, p. 58; c 335, f. 27v.; c 338, f. 33v.; c 341, f. 46v.; c 353, f. 31.
41 O.R.O., MSS. Oxf. Dioc. c 362, ff. 31–2; c 1710, corresp. *re* faculty 1964; notice in ch. 1991.
42 *Census*, 1891; *Oxf. Dioc. Yr. Bk.* (1990), 87; cf. Bodl. MS. Dep. d 78, f. 66, claiming dedication 'to the mother of St. Paul', presumably in error.
43 D. & C. Exeter, MS. 3672, p. 8; *Cal. Papal Reg.* i. 544, referring probably to St. Laurence martyr rather than St. Laurence abp.: cf. *Oxf. Dict. of Saints* (2nd edn.), s.v. St. Laurence.

44 *Ch. Bells Oxon.* iv, p. 370; *Oxoniensia*, xxxviii. 308; cf. *Par. Colln.* iii. 368.
45 *Eynsham Cart.* ii, p. lxvii; *Par. Colln.* iii. 254–5.
46 P.R.O., PROB 11/107, ff. 282–3.
47 O.R.O., MS. Oxf. Archd. Oxon. c 99, ff. 26–42; ibid. MS. Oxf. Dioc. c 327, p. 134; Giles, *Hist. Bampton*, 86 n.; Bodl. MS. Dep. d 78, f. 66; cf. Jefferys, *Oxon. Map* (1767).
48 B.L. Add. MS. 36356, f. 156b, showing the roof of a N. aisle apparently in error; Bodl. MS. Top. Oxon. b 90, no. 82; O.R.O., MS. Oxf. Archd. Oxon. c 42, ff. 235v., 239v.–240; Giles, *Hist. Bampton*, facing p. 84. Bodl. MS. Top. Oxon. a 68, no. 457, labelled Shifford, depicts a different ch.
49 Bodl. MS. Top. Oxon. d 218, f. 211v.
50 Ibid. c 104, ff. 274–5; ibid. MS. Dep. d 78, f. 66.

repair the chapel, the cost being met by mortgage, subscriptions, and other donations, and work was completed early in 1862.[51] The building,[52] designed in Gothic style by Joseph Clarke and built on its predecessor's foundations,[53] is of stone with Stonesfield-slated roofs, and comprises a small chancel with a vestry on the north, and a nave with south porch and west bellcóte; it is lit by plain lancets and by a small quadripartite circular east window. New glass with coloured medallions, and stained glass in the circular east window, was inserted in 1971.[54] The larger bell, similar to products of the Burford foundry, is of 1685 and is inscribed 'H. Allen', probably a chapelwarden;[55] the font and pulpit are modern. Electric heating replaced a coke stove in 1964, but lighting was partly from candles until 1976.[56]

Reset against the inside west wall of the nave are a grave slab to Thomas Brown (d. 1799) and his wife Mary, and a black slate tablet to Susan Blithe (d. 1645), related by marriage to the Veyseys of Chimney.[57] Several 18th-century monuments survive in the churchyard, among them a large tomb-chest to Robert Darby (d. 1772) of Cote and his wife Mary (d. 1801).[58] The plate includes a silver chalice given by Robert Veysey (d. 1666) and repaired by his relict Christian in 1688–9, and a silver paten given in 1706 by Thomas Horde (d. 1715); a silver chalice and paten of 1855 were given by the widow of W. M. Birch, vicar of Bampton Aston 1900–12.[59] Registers survive from 1783, earlier ones having

apparently been irreparably damaged while the chapel was derelict.[60] The churchyard was closed for burials c. 1969.[61]

NONCONFORMITY. The Williamses and their successors the Wallises, tenants at Old and New Shifford from the later 18th century to the late 19th, were prominent members of the Baptist meeting at Cote,[62] to which William Williams (d. 1830) made bequests.[63] No other nonconformity is known.

EDUCATION. A Sunday school supported by voluntary contributions, established in 1832 and with usually 11 or 12 pupils, continued in 1854 but had evidently lapsed by the 1860s.[64] By then children attended Aston National school.[65]

CHARITIES FOR THE POOR. Robert Veysey, by will proved 1666, left £10 for a yearly dole to 8 poor of Shifford and Chimney.[66] William Farr of Brighthampton, by will proved 1691, left £5 at interest to the poor of Shifford,[67] and Thomas Horde, by will proved 1716, gave a £6 rent charge and £10 for apprenticing 2 boys or girls.[68] All were lost by 1787.[69] A bequest by E. W. Harcourt (d. 1891) to Shifford chapelry was divided in 1892 between Old and New Shifford (£12), Chimney (£2), and Brighthampton (£11).[70]

DUCKLINGTON

DUCKLINGTON lies on the west bank of the river Windrush immediately south of Witney and 5 miles north-east of Bampton.[71] It was a predominantly rural parish until the later 20th century when, as Witney spread southwards, Ducklington village acquired suburban features. In 1876 the ancient parish, which included Hardwick township, comprised 2,261 a. of which 1,941 a. lay in Ducklington township and 671 a. in Hardwick.[72] After transfers to and from the parish in 1886 under the Divided Parishes Acts Ducklington was reduced to 1,934 a. and Hardwick, by then a civil parish, to 442 a., the

principal change being the transfer from Hardwick to Standlake of a large detached portion (241 a.) lying between Yelford and Cokethorpe Park.[73] In 1932 Ducklington was enlarged to 3,075 a. by the addition of most of Cogges (1,082 a.) and parts of Curbridge and Shilton; at the same time Ducklington lost 39 a. on the north to Witney and 202 a. on the south to the newly created parish of Hardwick-with-Yelford. The latter comprised 1,624 a., made up of most of the former Hardwick parish (440 a.), the whole of Yelford (336 a.), and 848 a. of Ducklington and Standlake, including the whole of

[51] *Oxf. Chron.* 9 Feb., 29 June, 6 July 1861; Bodl. MSS. Top. Oxon. c 104, ff. 274–80; c 103, ff. 42–3; O.R.O., MSS. Oxf. Dioc. d 795, ff. 142v.–143; d 796, f. 43.
[52] Bodl. MS. Top. Oxon. c 852, f. 74, mislabelled 'Yelford'; ibid. c 522, f. 22; Pevsner, *Oxon.* 754, which misdates it.   [53] Ch. Com. Rec. L 7, p. 439.
[54] O.R.O., MS. Oxf. Dioc. c 1710, faculty 1971.
[55] *Ch. Bells Oxon.* iv, p. 371.
[56] O.R.O., MS. Oxf. Dioc. c 1710, faculty 1964; local inf.
[57] Cf. *Par. Colln.* iii. 254–5; Bodl. MS. d.d. Harcourt c 109/29.
[58] For inscriptions, Giles, *Hist. Bampton,* 174–5.
[59] Evans, *Ch. Plate Oxon.* 11–12.
[60] O.R.O., MSS. d.d. Par. Shifford, e 1–3, b 1; ibid. MS. Oxf. Dioc. c 658, ff. 167–8; cf. ibid. c 596, containing some transcripts from 1721.   [61] Local inf.
[62] B. Williams, *Memorials of the Fam. of Williams* (priv. print. 1849), 18–19, 35, 37; 'Cote Baptist Ch. Recs.' (TS. in C.O.S.); Baptist Union Corpn. file 1367/1, trust renewals 1830, 1867; above, econ. hist.
[63] Regent's Park Coll., Oxf., Cote Ch. Bk. 1647–1882, list of chars. (n.d. but after 1830); 'Cote Baptist Ch. Recs.' s.a 1830.

[64] *Educ. Enq. Abstract,* H.C. 62, p. 739 (1835), xlii; *Ch. and Chapel, 1851,* no. 381; *Wilb. Visit.* 11; O.R.O., MSS. Oxf. Dioc. c 332, p. 58; c 335, ff. 27v.–28.
[65] Above, Aston and Cote, educ.
[66] P.R.O., PROB 11/322, f. 363v.
[67] Ibid. PROB 11/403, f. 184v.
[68] Ibid. PROB 11/551, ff. 252v.–253.
[69] *Char. Don.* 970–1.
[70] Shifford vestry and P.C.C. mins. 1859–1976 (in custody of vicar and par. officers), 16 May 1892.
[71] This article was completed in 1995. The principal maps used were O.R.O., tithe maps of Duckl. (1838), Standlake (1839), and Hardwick (1852); ibid., incl. maps of Duckl. (1839) and Standlake (1853); O.S. Map 1", sheets 13 (1830 edn.), 45 (1833 edn.); ibid. 1/25,000, SP 20/30 (1978 edn.); ibid. 6", Oxon. XXXI, XXXII, XXXVII, XXXVIII (1883–4 and later edns.). For Duckl. and Hardwick villages, ibid. 1/2,500, Oxon. XXXI. 12, XXXII. 13 (1876 and later edns.).
[72] O.S. *Area Bk.* (1877).
[73] *Census,* 1891; O.S. Maps 6", Oxon. XXXI, XXXII, XXXVII, XXXVIII (1900 edn.).

Cokethorpe Park.[74] In 1967 Ducklington was reduced to 1,940 a. (785 ha.) by the transfer of 459 ha. east of the river Windrush to South Leigh. In 1985 a minor boundary change on the north enlarged Ducklington to 791 ha. Hardwick-with-Yelford remained unchanged at 657 ha.[75] This article treats the history of the ancient parish, and also of that part of Cokethorpe which until 1932 belonged to Standlake.

The 19th-century boundaries of Ducklington parish (excluding Hardwick) were largely those of an estate granted in 958 by King Edgar to his 'minister' Earnulf from land which belonged earlier to the large royal estate centred on Bampton. The grant was of 14 hides at Ducklington, together with the 'old church at East Lea' and its 40 a., and also *Byrnan lea*, presumably the site of the later Barley Park.[76] The east boundary of the estate, as of the 19th-century parish, followed the river Windrush southwards from Ducklington village,[77] its deviation from one branch of the river to another presumably reflecting the apportionment of valuable river meadows between various estates. On Standlake brook ¾ mile east of Hardwick the boundary reached another branch of the Windrush, since dried up,[78] where it turned sharply upstream towards and probably past Hardwick. At an 'old ford' the estate boundary left the Windrush to follow a stream one furlong south of a church. The stream was presumably the small watercourse on the boundary of Cokethorpe Park just south of Cokethorpe chapel, which was evidently the 'old church of East Lea'. The surviving channelled watercourse may earlier have meandered along the edge of the gravel terrace to the north end of Berryham plantation where a ford, the site of a Romano-British causeway,[79] may have been the 'old ford' of 958.

Beyond Cokethorpe chapel the Anglo-Saxon boundary continued along the stream, then uphill through a *haga* (? game enclosure) to a *burh* (? camp) ditch. The last was probably on the south-western edge of Home wood, where a notably straight perimeter ditch respects a rectangular moated earthwork of unknown date;[80] even if the earthwork postdates the charter the perimeter ditch itself may mark the site of the *burh* ditch, since there was much early settlement in the fields immediately adjacent.[81] The *haga* was probably a wooded enclosure, perhaps a royal park: although divided by the boundary of 958 it seems to have retained or recovered its integrity, since later a large area west of Cokethorpe

chapel, including woodland north of the boundary of 958, and assarted woodland (the Breaches) south of that boundary, became part of Standlake manor and parish.[82] The transfer of its northern part from the Ducklington estate presumably occurred before parish boundaries were firmly established, perhaps before 1066.

The Saxon estate boundary seems to have continued along the south-western edge of Home wood and the southern edge of Boys wood. The 'old rode' of 958 may have been where the perimeter ditch of Home wood turns sharply westwards, 'Scot's hollow' the declivity occupied by the Long Train, and 'Wenburh's bridge' where the stream on the edge of Boys wood turns south to Yelford. From the south-west corner of Boys wood the boundaries of Saxon estate and later parish once more coincided, running south-westwards past Claywell down a ditch which in 958 led to the boundary of the 'men of Aston'. The zig-zag parish boundary north-west of its junction with Aston near Claywell farm survives from the estate boundary of 958, which in that section evidently picked its way round arable strips before reaching 'the brook of Aegel's spring', now Elm Bank ditch on Ducklington's west boundary. The west and north boundaries of the Saxon estate and later parish followed Elm Bank ditch to a 'stone ford', identified west of Coursehill Farm where Ducklington's boundary meets those of Lew and Curbridge;[83] the 'fugel' (bird) slade was probably the narrow valley where the parish boundary turns sharply north-east, passing to Colwell brook, so named in 958, which formed the parish boundary as far as Emma's bridge in the north-east.[84] Thence the estate and parish boundaries followed a watercourse (*hastinges lace*), which was evidently straightened in later times,[85] to rejoin the Windrush near Ducklington village.

After the removal from Ducklington of the suggested early park the southern parish boundary with Standlake followed the north-west edge of Boys wood. Its medieval line south-eastwards through the later Cokethorpe Park is uncertain: assarted closes mostly on the west side of the park, including the site of Cokethorpe House, were in Standlake, but the chapel and much of the east side of the later park remained in Ducklington.[86] Because Cokethorpe chapel served Hardwick that township also became part of Ducklington, despite prolonged insistence by Bampton parish on certain parochial rights.[87]

The boundaries within Cokethorpe Park were simplified at or before the inclosure of Ducklington in 1839 when a straight line running north

74 *Census*, 1931; O.S. Map 1/25,000, SP 42/30 (1949 edn.).
75 *Census*, 1971, 1991; West Oxon. (Parishes) Order, 1985.
76 P. H. Sawyer, *A.-S. Chart.* no. 678; *Cart. Sax.* ed. Birch, no. 1036; *Early Chart. of Thames Valley*, ed. M. Gelling, pp. 131–2; *P.N. Oxon.* ii. 486; Grundy, *Saxon Oxon.* 28–33; J. Blair, *A.-S. Oxon.*, 131.
77 Witney charters of 969 and 1044 help to interpret this and northern sections of the boundary: Sawyer, *A.-S. Chart.* nos. 771, 1001; *P.N. Oxon.* ii. 489–90; Grundy, *Saxon Oxon.* 76–85.
78 For its course near Standlake brook, T. G. Allen and M. A. Robinson, *Mingies Ditch*, 8.
79 C.O.S., PRN 14077, 14100; *S. Midlands Arch.* xix. 48–50.
80 C.O.S., PRN 3982, 3955 where it is suggested that the earthwork, which existed in 1767 (Jefferys, *Oxon. Map*), was

dug to supply the adjacent icehouse. Its protrusion into open-field arable makes that less likely.
81 Below, Yelford, intro.
82 Below, Standlake, econ. hist. (agric.); O.R.O., Standlake incl. map B.
83 J. Blair and A. Millard, 'An Anglo-Saxon Landmark Rediscovered', *Oxoniensia*, lvii. 342–7.
84 Cf. ibid. 343, indicating a different line on the evidence of the Witney charter of 1044 which clearly contains serious omissions: Grundy, *Saxon Oxon.* 32 (points 27–30), 79–80 (points 22–8), 82–3 (points 3–5).
85 Perhaps in connexion with irrigation of the Moors: below, econ. hist.
86 e.g. Bodl. MS. d.d. Harcourt c 13/2; B.N.C. Mun., Room B ser., 534, terrier 11 Feb. 1761, terrier and map 1 Oct. 1765.
87 Below, church.

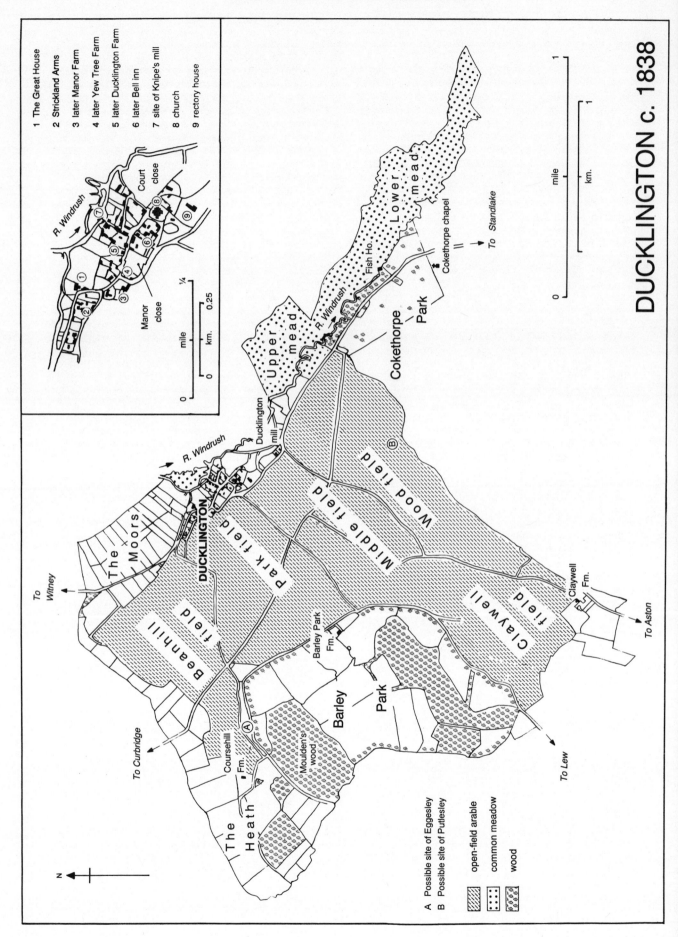

DUCKLINGTON c. 1838

1 The Great House
2 Strickland Arms
3 later Manor Farm
4 later Yew Tree Farm
5 later Ducklington Farm
6 later Bell inn
7 site of Knipe's mill
8 church
9 rectory house

Court close

Manor close

R. Windrush

mile
km.   0.25
0

A Possible site of Eggesley
B Possible site of Putlesley

open-field arable
common meadow
wood

To Witney

The Moors

DUCKLINGTON

R. Windrush

Ducklington mill

Upper mead

Lower mead

Fish Ho.

R. Windrush

Cokethorpe Park

Cokethorpe chapel

To Standlake

Park field

Middle field

Wood field

Beanhill field

Claywell field

Claywell Fm.

To Aston

Coursehill Fm.

Moulden's wood

Barley Park Fm.

Barley Park

The Heath

To Curbridge

To Lew

N

mile
km.
0

from Cokethorpe House became the boundary between Standlake on the west and Ducklington, and a straight line running east from the house and north of the chapel divided Ducklington from Hardwick.[88] Hardwick's boundaries elsewhere were largely undefined until inclosure, since its fields were intermixed with those of Standlake and came to include some of Yelford's open fields.[89] Certainly the township was bounded on the east by the Windrush and on part of the west by the inclosed Breaches, and included Hardwick field, and Hardwick common where the inhabitants had their principal holdings.[90] When Hardwick was inclosed and its tithes apportioned in 1852–3 its boundaries were redefined to include c. 425 a. around the village and a large detached area near Yelford.[91] Those boundaries were mostly obliterated after the changes of 1886 and the creation of Hardwick-with-Yelford parish in 1932.[92]

In the peripheral river valleys the land is low-lying (c. 75 m.) but a ridge of higher ground extends from Coursehill Farm in the north-west to Cokethorpe Park in the south-east, its highest point being 96 m. near the centre of the parish. Alluvium overlies flood plain gravel in the river valleys, and gravel extends westwards from the river Windrush beneath the villages of Ducklington and Hardwick, into Cokethorpe Park, including the sites of chapel and house, and, further south, across much of the former Hardwick field towards the Breaches. There are islands of deposited gravel on higher ground, notably around Barley Park Farm and Home Farm, Cokethorpe. The rest of the parish lies on Oxford Clay.[93]

Several Anglo-Saxon settlement names within the later parish incorporate *lea(h)*,[94] their location suggesting that much of the higher ground was wooded. Large stretches of woodland survive,[95] partly perhaps because of medieval and later imparkment. Barley Park in the north-west of the parish was created or enlarged in the mid 13th century, and was an enclosed deer park of some 375 a. in the 16th century and possibly later.[96] The creation of Cokethorpe Park (c. 310 a.) in the 18th century increased the wooded area, although its principal woodland lay in Standlake parish.[97] Before the inclosure of Ducklington's open fields in 1839 the alluvium in the valleys was largely reserved for meadow and pasture, the arable fields stretching westwards from the village to Barley Park and southwards between the park and Boys wood to Claywell.[98]

The principal road through the parish was the north–south route from Witney through the village, past Hardwick, to Standlake and a crossing of the river Thames at Newbridge: it formed part of the London–Gloucester road.[99] A bypass west of Ducklington village was built in 1974–5. A road from Hardwick across Hardwick common to Standlake was laid out at the inclosure of Standlake in 1853;[1] its heavy usage for gravel transport led to the provision of a bypass south of Hardwick in 1974–5. Minor roads[2] linking Ducklington to Curbridge and Aston were altered and confirmed at the inclosure of Ducklington in 1839. The Aston road earlier followed a more easterly line down the valley to Claywell. The lane from Hardwick to Yelford was realigned further south at the inclosure of Standlake. Before 1839 a road called Broadway branching from the Ducklington–Standlake road west of Ducklington mill ran north-westwards to the junction of the Curbridge road and the track to Coursehill Farm. That track probably survives from an early road, in part called Greenway, running from the 'stone ford' of 958 on Ducklington's west boundary past Coursehill Farm, near the site of a deserted medieval settlement, Eggesley.[3] Another east–west route, confirmed in part as Lew footway in 1839, ran westward past Barley Park Farm to Lew. Further south a probably more substantial road known as Lew way, confirmed in part in 1839, crossed from Lew into Ducklington south-west of Barley Park wood, following the ancient park pale north-eastwards; from it there may have been a branch eastwards to meet the former Claywell–Ducklington road on the high ground north of Boys wood, whence a lane, partly surviving, crossed the open fields to Ducklington mill. That suggested route may have been the 'highway' running eastwards from 'Barley ditch' across Ducklington to the Windrush which was alleged in 1318 to be Bampton's north-east boundary: although the road was probably never an ancient boundary it conveniently divided Ducklington from Cokethorpe and Hardwick, over which Bampton church had stronger claims.[4]

In the mid 19th century there was a regular carrying service to Witney, Oxford, and Abingdon.[5] The nearest railway station was at Faringdon (Berks.) from 1840, until Witney and South Leigh stations were opened in 1861.[6] Ducklington had a short-lived post office in 1861; another was opened in 1888, attached at first to a grocer's shop in the house later Church Farm, and by the early 20th century established in the Square.[7]

[88] O.R.O., incl. map.
[89] Below, Yelford, intro.
[90] O.R.O., Standlake incl. map B; below, econ. hist.
[91] Ibid., Hardwick tithe award and map; O.S. Map 6", Oxon. XXXII, XXXVIII (1883 edn.).
[92] e.g. O.S. Map 1/25,000, SP 42/30 (1949 edn.).
[93] Geol. Surv. Map 1", solid and drift, sheet 236 (1947 edn.).
[94] Below, this section.
[95] Below, econ. hist.
[96] Ibid.   [97] Below, manors (Cokethorpe).
[98] Below, econ. hist. For surviving ridge and furrow, M. Aston and T. Rowley, Landscape Arch. fig. 37.
[99] e.g. Leyland, Itin. ed. Toulmin Smith, v. 73; Wood's City of Oxf. ii (O.H.S. xvii), 499.
[1] O.R.O., Standlake incl. award.

[2] Except where stated the rest of this para. is based on Jefferys, Oxon. Map (1767); Davis, Oxon. Map (1797); O.S. Map 1", sheets 13 (1830 edn.), 45 (1833 edn.); O.R.O., Duckl. and Standlake incl. awards and maps (1839, 1853).
[3] Below, this section.
[4] D. & C. Exeter, MS. 2865; below, church.
[5] P.O. Dir. Oxon. (1847 and later edns.).
[6] E. T. Macdermot and C. R. Clinker, Hist. G.W.R. i. 53–4; V.C.H. Oxon. xii. 239.
[7] P.R.O., RG 9/906; RG 12/1176; Bodl. MS. Top. Oxon. b 78, ff. 73–5; Kelly's Dir. Oxon. (1887 and later edns.); O.S. Map 1/2,500, XXXI.12 (1899 edn.); O.R.O., District Valuation surv. and map (c. 1912), plots 1726, 1740. For photos., C.O.S., OPA 1994/93/3; M. Harris, Village Christmases, 59.

There are indications of Bronze Age occupation west of Ducklington village and south of Cokethorpe Park.[8] South-east of Hardwick was a small middle Iron-Age settlement, protected by a circular double ditch; it was largely pastoral and perhaps occupied only seasonally.[9] A small late Iron-Age settlement was found on the line of Hardwick's bypass,[10] and there are cropmark indications of other probable prehistoric sites, notably just west of Ducklington, north of Boys wood, and west of Hardwick.[11] A Romano-British settlement including slated and tiled structures was found on the line of the bypass south-west of Ducklington; it was occupied between the 2nd and 4th centuries.[12] Of similar date was an apparently linear settlement beside a Roman or Romanized road which, partly on a wooden causeway, crossed branches of the river Windrush between Gill Mill (now in South Leigh) and Berryham plantation north-west of Hardwick.[13] The settlement straddled the later parish boundary, extending on both sides of Standlake brook. Votive reliefs found on and near the site may indicate a temple.[14] South-west of the Windrush crossing the Roman road presumably passed close to Cokethorpe chapel.[15]

Two graves, probably 7th-century, one clearly Christian with notably rich goods, were found in 1860 in Wormwood close, north of Church Street in Ducklington.[16] The graves were probably in a large burial ground, since many skeletons were reportedly found in a garden on the east, now attached to Windrush Cottage.[17] Isolated 7th-century graves with rich goods were found south-east of Ducklington near Red Lodge,[18] and on the south-east boundary of Cokethorpe Park.[19] The Ducklington finds, together with those in a large burial ground just outside the later parish boundary towards Yelford,[20] suggest substantial, and fairly prosperous, Anglo-Saxon presence in the area by the 7th century.

By then Ducklington (? Ducel's *tūn*)[21] may have been settled, and in 958 was evidently a nucleated village, possibly with a church.[22] The large estate centred on Ducklington contained several other settlements and a very early church. The 'old church of East Lea', though standing in or near the probably minor Saxon settlement of Cokethorpe (? Cocca's *throp*),[23] continued to be regarded as the church of East Lea rather than of Cokethorpe until the early 13th century.[24] East Lea may not have been a single settlement but a larger area, perhaps so named because it was a clearing on the east of the belt of woodland which partly survives as Home and Boys woods; in the early 13th century woodland there, belonging to Standlake manor, was referred to as the 'wood of East Lea'.[25] Cokethorpe chapel's antiquity and its location in a small hamlet suggest that its origins may have been associated with the conversion of a pagan area rather than the service of an established Christian community; the chapel's proximity to a reputed holy well, its location on or near a Roman or earlier road, and its probable original dedication to St. Michael support the possibility that it replaced an existing shrine.[26]

Other Anglo-Saxon settlements within the ancient parish seem to have been associated with woodland clearance. Eggesley in the north-west and Putlesley or Puttesley probably near the centre of the parish were small hamlets in the early Middle Ages, their names perhaps combining personal names with *lea*.[27] There may also have been early settlement at *Byrnan lea* (? Beorna's *lea*, later Barley) in the west, mentioned in 958.[28] Claywell was a hamlet in the south-west of the parish, surviving as Claywell Farm.[29] In 1086 it was Welde and later Weald, denoting woodland or cleared woodland, and was frequently East Weald in distinction to Weald in Bampton;[30] the form Clayweld, in use by the 15th century,[31] corrupted to Claywell. Hardwick in the south-east of the parish was not part of the Ducklington estate of 958.[32] Its name (*heordewic*), combining 'herd' with an element usually denoting a small farm,[33] suggests that it was in origin a subsidiary pastoral settlement, perhaps of Brighthampton (in Standlake) with which it was later linked tenurially.[34]

In 1086 there were *c*. 50 recorded tenants on the manors of Ducklington, Claywell, and Hardwick[35] and in 1279 over 75 named tenants on those manors, not necessarily all resident.[36] In 1306 there were 66 taxpayers in Ducklington and its hamlets, and in 1327 a similar number (57 in Ducklington and Claywell, probably fewer than 20 in Hardwick).[37] After mid 14th-century plagues the population may have been greatly reduced: in 1377 only 103 persons over 14 were assessed for poll tax, a figure which probably

8 C.O.S., PRN 3948, 5527.
9 Ibid. 8311; T. G. Allen and M. A. Robinson, *Mingies Ditch* (1993), *passim*.
10 C.O.S., PRN 9732; *Oxoniensia*, xli. 21–35.
11 e.g. C.O.S., PRN 3952, 3990, 5470–1, 5881, 8210–11.
12 Ibid. 5991; *Oxoniensia*, xl. 171–200.
13 C.O.S., PRN 11636, 14077, 14100.
14 M. Henig and others, *Roman Sculpture from the Cotswold Region*, nos. 36, 124.
15 A line north of the chapel shown in Oxf. Arch. Unit, Gill Mill Farm Assessment 1988, fig. 1 (copy in C.O.S., PRN 11636) may be that of an avenue laid out in the early 18th cent.: below, manors (Cokethorpe).
16 C.O.S., PRN 1543; *Proc. Soc. Antiq.* 2nd ser., i. 100; *Oxoniensia*, xxxvi. 110.
17 Bodl. MS. Top. Oxon. b 78, f. 30. For identification of the site, from tenants' names in ibid., cf. O.R.O. District Valuation surv. and map (*c*. 1912), plots 1624, 1704.
18 C.O.S., PRN 11280; *Oxoniensia*, xl. 189–98.
19 C.O.S., PRN 1542; *Proc. Soc. Antq.* [1st ser.], iv. 93, 217.
20 Below, Yelford, intro.

21 *P.N. Oxon.* (E.P.N.S.), ii. 317.
22 Ibid. 486, where the estate boundaries begin and end 'at Ducklington'; below, church.
23 *P.N. Oxon.* (E.P.N.S.), ii. 324.
24 Below, church.
25 *Cal. Pat.* 1334–8, 23, confirming an undated early 13th-century grant.
26 *Hearne's Colln.* xi (O.H.S. lxii), 67; above, this section; below, church [Cokethorpe].
27 Below, this section.
28 *P.N. Oxon.* (E.P.N.S.), ii. 317.
29 Above, this section.
30 *P.N. Oxon.* (E.P.N.S.), ii. 317–18.
31 *Eynsham Cart.* ii, p. xix.
32 Above, this section.
33 *P.N. Oxon.* (E.P.N.S.), ii. 324, 471.
34 Below, manors.
35 *V.C.H. Oxon.* i. 405, 414, 423, 425: the figure assumes that Hardwick may be part of Wadard's Brighthampton estate.
36 *Bampton Hund. R.* 59–64.
37 P.R.O., E 179/161/9, 10.

excluded Hardwick,[38] and in the later Middle Ages several minor settlements were deserted. In 1523–4 only 11 in Ducklington and 5 in Hardwick paid subsidy, and the highest numbers assessed for 16th-century subsidies were 20 and 8 respectively in 1542–4;[39] a few other Ducklington parishioners continued to live in Cokethorpe, discussed below.

From the later 16th century baptisms consistently outnumbered burials, a rise in the period 1600–40 from roughly 9 baptisms and 4 burials a year to 13 and 7 respectively indicating rapid population growth.[40] In 1641 the Protestation oath was sworn by 150 men and women in Ducklington, 73 in Hardwick.[41] The 51 houses assessed for hearth tax in Ducklington in 1662 included one in Claywell and some in Cokethorpe, while in Hardwick fewer than a dozen houses and 25 hearths were assessed.[42] In the 1690s, the 1730s, and the 1790s there were roughly 13 baptisms and 9 burials a year, and in 1801 there were 101 families in 82 houses, and the population was 442, including 121 in Hardwick.[43] Numbers increased steadily to a peak in 1871 of 629 (including 149 in Hardwick), falling to 540 in 1891 and 486 (97 in Hardwick) in 1931.[44] Thereafter the population of the newly created Hardwick-with-Yelford was fairly stable, falling to 85 in 1961 and rising to 112 in 1991.[45] Ducklington's population of 549 in 1951 and 740 in 1961 included the villages of Cogges and South Leigh. The transformation of Ducklington village into a dormitory suburb, chiefly from the 1960s, was evident in 1971 when, with reduced boundaries comparable to those of 1931, the parish had a population of 1,274 in 405 households, a rise from 104 households in 1931. Growth slowed thereafter, and in 1991 the population was 1,437.[46]

At Eggesley in 1279 there were 9 tenants of Ducklington manor, each with a house and half yardland.[47] Some are identifiable among Ducklington taxpayers in the early 14th century,[48] but no later reference to the hamlet is known. Its probable site was between Coursehill Farm and Moulden's wood (called Edgeley coppice in the 17th century and later),[49] where two adjacent fields, one called Edgerley ground in 1839,[50] retain signs of house platforms and have yielded early medieval pottery.[51] At least one ancient road seems to have served the settlement.[52]

There may have been a related but distinct settlement at Coursehill: men 'of Coursehill' were recorded c. 1200 and in the early 14th century,[53] and a holding there belonged to Eynsham abbey in 1335.[54] By the later 15th century the same holding, evidently deserted, was 'a meadow below Ducklington'.[55]

At Putlesley in 1279 there were 3 tenants of Ducklington manor, and Eynsham abbey held a yardland there in demesne.[56] Tenants may be identified among early 14th-century Ducklington taxpayers, and a decayed holding once Robert Puttesley's was mentioned in 1430.[57] The hamlet's name may have been preserved in Pitchless hill, applied in the early 19th century to the high ground north-west of Boys wood;[58] a possible settlement site there has been suggested, on the gravel immediately north-west of Home Farm, which lacks the ridge and furrow covering most of Pitchless hill.[59]

Claywell was a much more substantial settlement whose desertion in the later Middle Ages, though apparently gradual, may have begun with a serious onslaught of plague, since Yelford, a mile to the south-east, was largely abandoned in the same period.[60] In 1086 there were 10 tenants on Theoderic's Claywell manor, some probably at Aston; in addition there were presumably several Claywell tenants of Ducklington manor.[61] In 1279 there were 9 such tenants, and 6 or 7 others holding of Theoderic's successor, the abbot of Eynsham.[62] In 1306 and 1316 there were c. 14 and 17 taxpayers at Claywell, and an apparently similar number in 1327 when Claywell was assessed with Ducklington.[63] In c. 1360 Eynsham abbey retained 6 Claywell holdings whose rents were sharply reduced between 1403[64] and the 1420s, when much was in hand.[65] Whether the late 14th-century tenants lived at Claywell is uncertain, but it may be significant that 'fishsilver', apparently payable by all the abbey's Claywell tenants, was more than 25 years in arrears by 1407.[66] In 1430 Ducklington manor's holdings at Claywell were let at only half their earlier rent because of decays and shortage of tenants.[67] Later in the 15th century the abbey's estate was let at will to one tenant;[68] he may have sublet to several others, but from the 16th century the estate, usually described as Claywell farm, seems to have been a single holding.[69] Ducklington manor's land in

---

38 Ibid. E 179/161/42.
39 Ibid. E 179/161/172; E 179/162/223–4.
40 C.O.S., par. reg. transcripts.
41 *Protestation Rtns. and Tax Assess.* 22–4. The figure for Hardwick may include a few Yelford inhabitants.
42 P.R.O., E 179/255/4; E 179/164/504, containing a largely illegible entry for Hardwick and Yelford.
43 C.O.S., par. reg. transcripts; *Census*, 1801.
44 *Census*, 1821–1931.
45 Ibid. 1951–91. The high figure of 183 in 1971 includes boarders at Cokethorpe School.
46 *Census*, 1951–91.   47 *Bampton Hund. R.* 62.
48 P.R.O., E 179/161/8–10.
49 Bodl. MS. Ch. Oxon. c 43, no. 4320; O.R.O., incl. award, s.v. Leake, Chas.
50 O.R.O., incl. award and map, plot 171.
51 C.O.S., PRN 3953.   52 Above, this section.
53 *Eynsham Cart.* i, pp. 160–1; *Cal. Close, 1327–30*, 377; P.R.O., E 179/161/9, s.v. Duckl.
54 Bodl. MSS. d.d. Harcourt c 126/9, 11; c 128/1–4.
55 e.g. P.R.O., SC 6/961/15; B.L. Harl. Roll G. 2.

56 *Bampton Hund. R.* 60, 62.
57 P.R.O., E 179/161/8; ibid. E 142/84, no. 6.
58 O.R.O., Duckl. tithe map, plot. 262.
59 C.O.S., PRN 3954; Aston and Rowley, *Landscape Arch.* fig. 37.
60 Below, Yelford intro.
61 *V.C.H. Oxon.* i. 423; below, manors.
62 *Bampton Hund. R.* 61–2. To the abbey tenants should probably be added Emma Lovel, recorded under Aston: ibid. 22; cf. *Eynsham Cart.* ii, pp. 12, 14.
63 P.R.O., E 179/161/8–9. An incomplete assessment for 1306 is identifiable as Claywell from surviving names: ibid. E 179/161/10, m. 21d.
64 *Eynsham Cart.* ii, pp. 12, 14; Bodl. MS. d.d. Harcourt c 128/1–4; B.L. Harl. Rolls K. 41, L. 1, L. 3.
65 P.R.O., SC 6/961/14; B.L. Harl. Roll L. 6.
66 P.R.O., SC 6/961/13.
67 Ibid. E 142/84, no. 6.
68 Ibid. SC 6/961/15; B.L. Harl. Rolls L. 7, L. 10, G. 2; Bodl. MS. d.d. Harcourt c 128/6.
69 e.g. P.R.O., C 1/1284/8; Bodl. MS. d.d. Harcourt c 109/6.

Claywell was presumably worked from Ducklington.

Claywell lay at the foot of a narrow valley two miles south of Ducklington, to which it was linked directly by the Lew–Ducklington road, rerouted further west at inclosure.[70] Another road, mentioned in 1306, ran from Claywell through or beside Yelford's open fields towards a wood, unidentified, called Weldehamho.[71] Claywell may have had a chapel, since the post-medieval tenants of Claywell Farm paid rent to Ducklington church, allegedly for a former churchyard.[72] The descent of Claywell Farm suggests that it occupies land formerly part of Eynsham abbey's estate, possibly a manorial site.[73] Two closes south and south-east of the house, however, belonged before inclosure in 1839 to Walter Strickland of Cokethorpe, who had acquired much of the land attached to Ducklington manor;[74] they may have contained medieval tenements of that manor. Earthworks indicating former buildings are particularly marked in a close west of the house.[75] That close and the site of the farm buildings south of the house were Upper and Lower Paddock in 1839, and the alleged churchyard was said to be in 'the Paddock'.[76] A ditch east of the farm buildings marks the line of the former Lew–Ducklington road.[77]

Cokethorpe, which had only three or four recorded houses in 1279,[78] remained a small hamlet until reduced in the 18th century to an isolated chapel in the newly created park around Cokethorpe House.[79] No early open fields were recorded,[80] and no clear boundaries of Cokethorpe are discernible. There were 2 taxpayers in the hamlet in 1523–4 and 6 in 1543–4.[81] At least 4 houses there belonged to Ducklington manor in the early 16th century,[82] and several shops paying rents to the manor were said to have closed in the 1530s when pilgrimages to St. Mary's shrine in Cokethorpe were suppressed.[83] A few other houses in Cokethorpe belonged at that time to other estates,[84] but no house was mentioned in the Standlake part until one of gentry status was built on the site of Cokethorpe House in the later 16th century. In 1641 the Protestation oath was sworn by 12 men and women in the Ducklington part of Cokethorpe, and presumably there were a few residents in the Standlake part, notably at Cokethorpe House, whose owner Elizabeth Stonehouse apparently did not take the oath but was assessed

for tax there in that year.[85] In 1662 at least four Cokethorpe houses were assessed for hearth tax in Ducklington and the 14-hearth Cokethorpe House and at least one other in Standlake.[86]

Although some houses seem to have been removed when Sir Simon, later Viscount, Harcourt took over Cokethorpe House c. 1710 others survived near the chapel and road until the park was extended some time after his death in 1727.[87] No local wills of Cokethorpe inhabitants survive after the 1720s, and by the 1760s the chapel stood isolated in the park.[88] Peripheral lodges were added later and Cokethorpe Park's 19th-century population, still divided between Standlake and Ducklington parishes, was usually more than 25. On census day in 1851, when the owner's family and guests numbered 5, there were 12 living-in servants and c. 25 other residents in lodges and cottages in the park; in 1881, when the family was absent, there were still over 20 residents in the house and park.[89]

Visible remains of the former hamlet are few, although possible house sites have been noted just within the park south of the chapel; in 1601 Hardwick's open fields in that area abutted 'Cokethorpe town's end'.[90] Earthworks immediately east of the chapel and evidently within the former churchyard mark the site of a building of unknown date and function.[91] A waterlogged hollow further east may be the site of a holy well remembered in the early 18th century.[92] A rectangular enclosure revealed by cropmarks c. 120 m. north of the chapel may be prehistoric.[93]

Ducklington village lies in the north-east corner of the parish on the Standlake–Witney road and very close to the river Windrush. Its early nucleus was presumably near the church, and it is likely that Church Street, leading towards Witney, was the site of early houses; by the early 11th century there was a mill on the Windrush at the end of the lane leading north from the Square.[94] The medieval manor house, demolished before 1430, probably stood north of the church in the field, once Court close, partly occupied by the modern graveyard. A later manor house, built in the 17th century and demolished in the 18th, stood on the south side of Church Street on a site which until modern times was a paddock called Manor close.[95] The Old Rectory, in large grounds south of the church, incorporates medieval timbers and is presumably on the site of the medieval rectory house.[96] A high cross, presumably medieval,

70 Above, this section.
71 New Coll. Arch., 13968.
72 Below, church.
73 Below, manors.
74 O.R.O., incl. award and map, plots 219–20.
75 C.O.S., PRN 954.
76 O.R.O., incl. award and map, plots 215–16; ibid. MS. d.d. Par. Duckl. b 9.
77 O.R.O., incl. award and map, plot 221.
78 *Bampton Hund. R.* 62. The house of Clement of Cokethorpe, held of Standlake manor, should perhaps be included: ibid. 70.
79 For the house and park, below, manors.
80 Below, econ. hist.
81 P.R.O., E 179/161/172; E 179/162/233–4.
82 *L. & P. Hen. VIII*, viii, p. 47.
83 P.R.O., SC 6/Hen. VIII/7248; below, church.
84 e.g. P.R.O., C 142/307, no. 64; B.N.C. Mun.,

Cokethorpe deeds *passim*.
85 *Protestation Rtns. and Tax Assess.* 22, 26–7.
86 P.R.O., E 179/255/4, pt. i, f.23, where Mr. Stonner (Stonehouse) and Jas. Mountain were of Cokethorpe; ibid. f. 31, where Cokethorpe houses are at the end of the assessment.
87 Below, manors (Cokethorpe).
88 Jefferys, *Oxon. Map* (1767).
89 P.R.O., HO 107/1731; ibid. RG 11/1514–15. Figures exclude the Fish House and Park or Home Farm (outside the park), but include the lodges.
90 C.O.S., PRN 957; O.R.O., MS. Oxf. Archd. Oxon. b 40, f. 119.
91 Field survey plan in possession of Dr. W. J. Blair, The Queens College, Oxford.
92 *Hearne's Colln.* xi (O.H.S. lxxii), 67.
93 C.O.S., PRN 13513.   94 Below, econ. hist. (mills).
95 Below, manors.   96 Below, church.

survived in the 17th century near a place or lane called Trumpenys,[97] probably a corruption of the Ducklington surname Turnpenny; it was perhaps in the Square.

By the earlier 19th century the main built area was around Church Street and the Square but also stretched north-eastwards along Witney Road almost to its junction with Curbridge Road; older houses survive throughout that area. Further along the Witney road a separate group of cottages, of which the earliest may be of the late 17th century, was called Little Ducklington by the early 19th century;[98] Chalcroft common, separating the cottages from the main village, was later sometimes called the green and in 1995 included a childrens' recreation area.[99] By the early 19th century another distinct group of cottages stood on the Standlake road south-east of the village at Ducklington mill, the latter probably the New mill of 1279.[1]

Within the village the distribution and orientation of surviving older buildings suggests that the main Standlake–Witney road in earlier times ran along Church Street, perhaps entering the village on a line east of the Old Rectory: no older houses face on to the section of Standlake Road running north-west from the Old Rectory, and its south-west side abutted the open fields; it was presumably a back lane until becoming the preferred through route. One effect of its increased importance was to define, at the point where the road to Aston left the village, a triangular green, which thereafter perhaps shifted the focus of the village. With its large pond (called Pitch pond in 1831)[2] overlooked by a distinguished church, it was seen to typify the 'breadth of rurality' for which Ducklington was noted.[3] The National school of 1857 was built to face the green; until the 1990s an oak tree planted in 1902 to mark the coronation of Edward VII stood at its centre;[4] and it was chosen as the site of the village war memorial.

The older buildings in the village are almost all of coursed or uncoursed limestone rubble, and many of the 17th-century cottages are single-storeyed with attics, thatched, sometimes gabled, and built on a 2- or 3-unit plan presumably typical of a village which in the 1660s was composed largely of houses taxed on one or two hearths.[5] Examples of such houses are the early 17th-century Windrush Cottage, which retains ovolo-moulded wood-mullioned windows, Church Farm, possibly of the late 16th century, with stone-mullioned windows and a through passage, the Bell inn and the Strickland Arms, both much altered but 17th-century in origin, and several cottages on Witney Road (nos. 27, 29, and 31). Similar thatched houses, but of two

storeys, are the late 17th-century Old Bakehouse and two houses at Little Ducklington (nos. 61 and 63 Witney Road). Most of the 17th-century houses have stop-chamfered beams and chamfered bressumers; several have projecting bread ovens, and there are winder stairs at Church Farm and no. 29 Witney Road. Many older houses in the village were stone-slated, although in modern times many have been reroofed with concrete tiles. Larger 17th-century farmhouses included Manor Farm,[6] Lynden House in Church Street, dated 1661, and Ducklington Farm in Church Street, where a garden wall has a datestone of 1682 with the initials IMV, perhaps for Martin and Ursula Johnson.[7] Lynden House, of two storeys with attics, retains chamfered beams and has a gabled central stair turret; Ducklington Farm, though also retaining some 17th-century features, was refaced and extended at the rear in the early 19th century. Both houses have been almost entirely refenestrated in the 20th century, in common with many of the other older houses in the village.

Several houses have 18th-century extensions, but there are no larger houses of that period. The principal 18th-century house, the Great House, near no. 14 Witney Road, was demolished c. 1840.[8] Two 19th-century houses of some pretension are the Manor House and Yew Tree Farm. The former, called Ducklington House until renamed in the late 19th century, is an early 19th-century remodelling and extension of a probably 18th-century farmhouse. It was built for Thomas Lee (d. 1863), a solicitor and local landowner.[9] The house was vacant for many years before its purchase in 1886 by Gerard Waefelaer, a retired sea captain, who until his death in 1912 fulfilled the rôle of resident squire with 'liberality'.[10] Yew Tree Farm was rebuilt as a gentleman's residence, probably in the 1860s, by J. S. Beaumont: it has a symmetrical 5-bayed front in the Italianate style, with a central porch supported on Tuscan columns; the land fronting the house on the opposite side of Standlake Road was planted as a park.[11] Outside the village large farmhouses built after inclosure in 1839 were Coursehill Farm and Home Farm, Cokethorpe, and Barley Park Farm was rebuilt.[12]

Institutional buildings, besides the school, were the Baptist chapel of 1868,[13] a parish room, established in the former tithe barn c. 1930 and much rebuilt as a village hall in 1975,[14] and a new school of 1962.[15] Since the Second World War, and particularly from the 1970s, large numbers of houses have been built, some on large estates south and west of the Standlake–Witney road, others lining that road, and many in former farmyards and gardens in the village.

97 O.R.O., Peake II/v/1; Bodl. MS. Ch. Oxon. a 31, no. 702.
98 O.R.O., incl. award and map.
99 Ibid.; M. Harris, *A Kind of Magic*, passim.
1   O.R.O., incl. award and map; below, econ. hist. (mills).
2   O.R.O., MS. d.d. Par. Duckl. b 9, terrier.
3   O.A.S. *Rep.* (1871), 3; above, plate 19.
4   Bodl. MS. Top. Oxon. b 78, ff. 264–5; above, plate 20.
5   P.R.O., E 179/255/4.
6   Below, other estates.
7   Cf. O.R.O., MS. Wills Oxon. 168/4/19: admin. of 1716.
8   Below, other estates.
9   Bodl. MS. Top. Oxon. b 78, ff. 86–7; O.R.O., incl.

award and map, plot 22; P.R.O., HO 107/1731. For the Lees, C.O.S., par. reg. transcripts, *passim*.
10 Bodl. MS. Top. Oxon. b 78, ff. 71, 83, 225, 231; deeds of 1886 at the Manor House; *Witney Express*, 17 Dec. 1885; Magd. Coll. Mun., MS. 799 (vi), s.a. 1912. For a description of the house in 1921, Bodl. G.A. Oxon. c 224 (10).
11 Bodl. MS. Top. Oxon. b 78, ff. 252–4.
12 Ibid. ff. 30v., 86–7; below, econ. hist.
13 Below, nonconf.
14 M. Harris, *A Kind of Magic*, 168; *Witney Gaz.* 7 Aug. 1975.
15 Below, educ.

Many old houses and barns have been converted or rebuilt. In the 1960s a large sewage plant was established in the north of the parish.

The hamlet of Hardwick lies in the south-east of the parish on the bank of the river Windrush, connected by minor lanes with the Standlake–Witney road. Its houses line a single street which in the 19th century, when called High Street,[16] ran south from the mill to the common. South of the hamlet, in early inclosures lining the western edge of the common, were a few cottages and Manor Farm.[17] A manorial park, mentioned in the early 17th century when its fences were the responsibility of Hardwick tenants,[18] was perhaps one of the closes adjacent to the hamlet. From the later 19th century some older houses and several farm buildings were demolished, and the bypass of 1974–5 isolated Manor Farm from the hamlet.[19] The surviving older houses are of coursed limestone rubble, some with stone slate roofs. Several have brick arched windows inserted during later 19th-century restoration. The larger houses are Hardwick Mill[20] and Manor Farm, the latter a much altered house of the 18th century, with a taller early 19th-century extension.

The Strickland Arms in Ducklington was established under that name by 1839, and the Bell seems to have been opened slightly later, certainly by 1846.[21] In the mid 18th century there were sometimes three, but usually two, licensed houses in Ducklington, the Ball and the Chequers. The Chequers seems to have closed in the 1770s but the Ball survived into the 19th century and was perhaps the later Strickland Arms.[22] A short-lived alehouse in Little Ducklington was mentioned in 1864.[23] In Hardwick a victualler was licensed in 1753 but no alehouse was mentioned thereafter until the 1840s when the Angel was opened in a house owned by Thomas Lee, acquired in 1860 by Walter Strickland; it survived into the 1960s.[24]

An 'Easter custom', which included the charitable distribution of pies but was evidently also the occasion for traditional festivity, died out in the 19th century.[25] Whitsun celebrations in Ducklington in the early 19th century included a maypole, and villagers were involved in the annual Whitsun hunt in Wychwood forest. The morris tradition in Ducklington died out in the later 19th century.[26] Celebration of the village feast on St. Bartholomew's day (24 Aug.) included, in the late 19th century, the setting up of stalls, and a small fair continued to be held in the early 20th century.[27] Most formal village entertainment in the 19th century was associated with the church and school, or was provided by the owners of Cokethorpe Park.[28] There were the usual sporting clubs, cricket being particularly encouraged by the rector; Ducklington and Cokethorpe had separate clubs.[29] A Penny Bank established c. 1872 and a parish library, started by the rector in 1873, survived through the century. A reading room was established in a cottage in the 1880s.[30] When the parish room opened c. 1930 a Reading Room club associated with it was largely a social club which co-ordinated the use of the room for village activities.[31]

In 1398 a riotous assembly met at Cokethorpe and marched on Bampton.[32] Ducklington suffered more prolonged disruption in the 1640s when its location on the strategically important route over Newbridge brought it into daily contact with troops of both factions.[33] Cokethorpe Park as the principal residence of Simon Harcourt, Viscount Harcourt, was for several years after his loss of office in 1714 a gathering place for some of the chief *literati* of the day.[34]

Ducklington's natives included the prominent early 14th-century mayor of Oxford, John of Ducklington,[35] and the broadcaster Mollie Harris (d. 1995), known for her performance as Martha Woodford in the B.B.C. radio series 'The Archers'.

MANORS. The 14-hide estate at Ducklington which King Edgar granted to his 'minister' Earnulf in 958 seems to have been reduced in size before 1086, when only 11 hides were recorded on two Ducklington estates. The shortfall was partly accounted for by the creation of a 2½-hide estate at Claywell, although probably only 1 hide of that had been part of the Saxon estate at Ducklington; possibly the transfer to Standlake of a large area in the south of the estate had already taken place.[36]

In 1086 Robert d'Oilly held 4 hides in Ducklington in chief. He was probably also the Robert who was tenant there of 7 hides of the fee of William FitzOsbern, earl of Hereford, whose

16 e.g. P.R.O., RG 9/906.
17 Cf. O.R.O., Hardwick tithe award and map; ibid. Standlake incl. award and map.
18 e.g. St. John's Coll. Mun. XI.10 (205–6); XI.11, p. 46.
19 Cf. O.S. Maps 1/2500, Oxon. XXXII. 13 (1876 and later edns.); ibid. SP 3605–6.
20 Below, econ. hist. (mills).
21 Cf. O.R.O., tithe award and map, plots 9–10, 61; *Hunt's Oxf. Dir.* (1846); *P.O. Dir. Oxon.* (1847); *Billing's Dir. Oxon.* (1854); P.R.O., HO 107/1731. For deeds of the Bell site 1785–1894, O.R.O., B 5/12/D/1–14.
22 O.R.O., QSD V/1–4. Cf. Bodl. MS. Top. Oxon. b 78, f. 178v.
23 *P.O. Dir. Oxon.* (1864).
24 Ibid. QSD V/1; ibid. tithe award and map 202, plot 4019; *Hunt's Oxf. Dir.* (1846); *Wilb. Letter Bks.*, p. 152; St. John's Coll. Mun., EST. I. A.15, pp. 400 sqq.; ibid. EST. I. A.16, pp. 73–8; M. Bee, 'Clinch & Co., Brewers', *Oxon. Local Hist.* ii (3), 85; Courage Arch., Bristol: Clinch & Co. reg. of title deeds, p. 133. The Angel was the house now

'Joylaw'.
25 Bodl. MS. Top. Oxon. b 78, ff. 63, 211v.; below, charities.
26 K. Chandler, 'Morris Dancing at Ducklington' (priv. print): copy in C.O.S.
27 e.g. *Witney Express*, 2 Sept. 1880; M. Harris, *A Kind of Magic*, 155–6.
28 e.g. Bodl. MS. Top. Oxon. b 78, f. 81; *Witney Express*, 23 Feb. 1871; *Oxf. Times*, 18 Jan. 1896.
29 *Witney Express*, 5 Aug. 1869, 30 June 1870, 1 Aug. 1872.
30 Magd. Coll. Mun., MS. 799 (i–vi): par. mags. *passim*.
31 O.R.O., MSS. d.d. Par. Duckl. e 5, f. 1.
32 *Oxon. Sessions of the Peace* (O.R.S. liii), 43.
33 Bodl. MS. Top. Oxon. c 378, *passim*.
34 *Harcourt Papers*, ed. E. W. Harcourt, iii, *passim*; *D.N.B.*
35 Bodl. MS. Top. Oxon. b 78, f. 22; *V.C.H. Oxon.* iv. 38, 374, and *passim*.
36 Above, intro.; below, this section.

lands had passed to the Crown in 1075 after the rebellion of William's son Roger.[37] Robert d'Oilly died *c.* 1093 and *DUCKLINGTON* manor descended with his barony of Hook Norton.[38] Henry d'Oilly, lord in 1230, died without issue in 1232; his heir, after the dower of his relict Maud (d. 1261), wife of William de Cauntelo, was a nephew Thomas de Newburgh, earl of Warwick (d. 1242). Thomas's sister and heir Margaret, countess of Warwick, was recorded as overlord of 2 knights' fees in Ducklington in 1242–3.[39] The reversion escheated to the Crown on her death without issue in 1253, but was regranted to her husband John de Plessis who entered on the manor on Maud de Cauntelo's death.[40] John died in 1263 and Ducklington descended from father to son in the Plessis family, being held by four successive Hughs.[41] John de Plessis, brother and heir of Hugh (d. 1349), died without issue in or before 1354. The barony of Plessis, which had been created in 1297, passed to John's sister Eleanor Lenvesey,[42] but Ducklington seems to have descended separately: a Hugh de Plessis (d. 1363) and a John de Plessis (fl. 1372) were recorded as overlords[43] but thereafter the heirs of the former undertenants held in chief.

The Roger who was recorded as Robert d'Oilly's tenant at Ducklington in 1086 was probably Roger de Chesney, since Ducklington and Roger's other Domesday estates at Heyford and Wicken (Northants.) were all later held by the Chesneys.[44] Hugh de Chesney (fl. 1163), probably Roger's eldest son, was succeeded before 1166 by Ralph de Chesney 'of Ducklington', who was amerced for forest offences in 1176.[45] Ralph died *c.* 1195 and Ducklington passed to his daughter Lucy and her husband Guy de Dive.[46] Guy died in 1218 leaving a minor son William who before 1224 married Margaret, daughter of his guardian John of Bassingbourn, and died in 1261.[47] His son John died fighting against the king at Evesham in 1265.[48] Osbert Giffard was granted the forfeited lands and the wardship of the heir, but Ducklington was granted for life to John's relict Sibyl, a decision disputed by Giffard in 1268 on the ground that Ducklington was the most valuable part of the

Dive estates.[49] Sibyl and her second husband Richard of Carbrook retained the manor into the 1290s.[50] In 1292 free warren in Ducklington was granted to John de Dive, son of Sibyl's son Henry (d. 1277), but he was not formally granted seisin until of age in 1295.[51]

John died in 1310 and was followed by his son Henry (d. 1326 or 1327).[52] Henry's relict Martha, assigned dower in two thirds of the manor in 1327,[53] was still in possession in 1343 when a settlement of the manor was made by Henry's son John.[54] After John's unrecorded death *c.* 1350[55] the manor seems to have descended in two parts until reunited in the hands of the Lovel family in the mid 15th century.

One part, held with the advowson and acquiring the name of *DUCKLINGTON BRETON*, derived from the dower in one third of the manor held by John de Dive's relict Joan, who married William Breton. Breton was a landholder in Ducklington in 1361,[56] and Joan was still alive in 1386.[57] Presumably she conveyed Ducklington to John, Lord Lovel who at his death in 1408 held a Ducklington manor, allegedly of Gilbert, Lord Talbot, perhaps because of suit owed to Bampton hundred court.[58] Lovel's son John died in 1414 holding the reversion of Ducklington Breton after the life interest of his mother Maud, who died in 1423 holding, by the same service as John, Lord Lovel (d. 1408), what was evidently about a third of the earlier Ducklington manor.[59] She was succeeded by her grandson William Lovel, Lord Lovel and Holand (d. 1455), who held Ducklington as 1 knight's fee in 1428.[60]

The other two thirds of Ducklington passed from John de Dive (d. *c.* 1350) to his son Henry (d. *c.* 1360),[61] who during his lifetime let, and later seems to have granted, the reversion to Roger Mortimer (d. 1360), earl of March.[62] The life interest of Henry's relict Elizabeth, who married Edward Twyford, was established despite several challenges, notably in 1372 when the manor was mistakenly taken into the king's hands and regranted to Edmund Mortimer, earl of March.[63] In 1377 Edmund agreed to pay an annuity to Elizabeth Parles, presumably the former Elizabeth Twyford, in return for her life

37 *V.C.H. Oxon.* i. 388, 414, 425.
38 Sanders, *Eng. Baronies*, 54.
39 *Close R.* 1227–30, 388; *Bk. of Fees*, ii. 823; *Complete Peerage*, xii (2), 366.
40 Sanders, *Eng. Baronies*, 54; cf. *Cal. Pat.* 1258–66, 184–5; *Close R.* 1261–4, 178.
41 *Cal. Inq. p.m.* i, p. 168; iii, p. 41; viii, p. 70; ix, p. 183.
42 *Complete Peerage*, x. 551.
43 *Cal. Inq. p.m.* xi, pp. 469–70; xiii, p. 161; *Cal. Close*, 1364–8, 2–3.
44 *V.C.H. Oxon.* i. 414, 425. For the Chesneys, *Eynsham Cart.* i, pp. 411–23.
45 *Eynsham Cart.* i, pp. 412–13; *Red Bk. Exch.* 305; *Pipe R.* 1176 (P.R.S. xxv), 31.
46 *Eynsham Cart.* i, pp. 85–6, 89–91, 159–61, 193–4.
47 *Ex. e Rot. Fin.* i. 19, 115–16; ii. 364. For a dispute between John of Bassingbourn and the overlord, Henry d'Oilly, *Close R.* 1227–31, 388.
48 *Cal. Inq. Misc.* i, p. 261. For John's inq. (of 1272), *Cal. Inq. p.m.* i, p. 262.
49 *Close R.* 1264–8, 130; *Cal. Pat.* 1258–66, 541; *Abbrev. Plac.* (Rec. Com.), 167; cf. *V.C.H. Oxon.* xi. 92; Farrer, *Honors and Knights' Fees*, iii. 63.
50 *Bampton Hund. R.* 59–62; *Cal. Inq. p.m.* iii, p. 96.

51 *Cal. Chart. R.* 1257–1300, 415; *Cal. Close*, 1288–96, 415; *Cal. Inq. p.m.* ii, p. 139; cf. *Cal. Pat.* 1292–1301, 141; *Reg. Sutton*, viii (L.R.S. lxxvi), 189.
52 *Cal. Inq. p.m.* v, p. 145; vii, p. 10; *Cal. Mem. R.* 1326–7, p. 364.
53 *Cal. Close*, 1327–30, 377; P.R.O., C 135/8, no. 5.
54 P.R.O., CP 25/1/190/19, no. 2; CP 25(1)/287/41, no. 29; B.L. Add. MS. 6041, ff. 43v.–44v.
55 He was recorded as lord in 1346 and 1349: *Feud. Aids* iv. 182; *Cal. Inq. p.m.* ix, p. 183. For an uncorroborated statement that he died in 1343, O.A.S. *Rep.* (1871), 9.
56 *Cal. Inq. p.m.* xi, pp. 86–7.
57 *V.C.H. Oxon.* xi. 92.
58 P.R.O., C 137/66, no. 29.
59 Ibid. C 138/8, no. 30; C 139/6, no. 51.
60 *Feud. Aids*, iv. 194–5.
61 The date of Henry's death, without issue, is given as 1362 in Baker, *Northants.* ii. 254, but he may have been dead by 1360: *Cal. Inq. p.m.* xii, pp. 161–2.
62 B.L. Add. MS. 6041, ff. 43v.–44v.; *Cal. Inq. p.m.* xiii, pp. 161–2; xv, p. 383.
63 Cf. B.L. Add. MS. 6041, ff. 43v.–44v.; *Cal. Inq. p.m.* xiii, pp. 161–2; xv, p. 383; *Cal. Fine R.* 1369–77, 178; *Cal. Pat.* 1374–7, 110.

interest in Ducklington,[64] but before his death in 1381 he had granted his reversionary interest for life to a retainer, Sir John, later Lord Lovel (d. 1408).[65] Ducklington was not recorded among the possessions of Roger Mortimer (d. 1398), earl of March, but in 1415 Roger's son Edmund, earl of March, settled the manor in trust.[66] Before his death in 1425 Edmund granted an annuity of £10 from the manor to William Cottesmore, who was recorded as lord of ½ fee at Ducklington in 1428.[67] During the minority of Edmund Mortimer's nephew and heir Richard Plantagenet, duke of York, the fee was in royal hands.[68] In 1449 Richard reunited the manor by granting his portion of Ducklington to the lord of the other portion, William Lovel, Lord Lovel.[69] Ducklington's later inclusion in the possessions of the earldom of March claimed by the Crown against the coheirs of Edward IV was presumably an error.[70]

Shortly before his death in 1455 William Lovel settled the reunited manor, still nominally held of the Talbots for hundredal service at Bampton, on trustees;[71] it passed to his son John (d. 1465) and John's relict Joan (d. 1466), both of whom held from Roger Beaufitz, presumably associated with John Talbot (d. 1473) earl of Shrewsbury, a minor.[72] Their son Francis, until 1477 a minor in the wardship of Richard Neville, earl of Warwick, and others,[73] died at or after the battle of Stoke in 1487.[74] As an opponent of Henry VII he had been attainted in 1485, and in 1486 Ducklington was granted from the forfeited estates to Thomas Lovel, possibly a kinsman, son of Sir Ralph Lovel of Barton Bendish (Norf.). Thomas, chancellor of the Exchequer under Henry VII and Henry VIII, died without issue in 1524 having bequeathed the manor to his nephew Francis Lovel, but because the grant of 1486 had been in tail male Ducklington reverted to the Crown.[75]

In 1525 the king granted it to Sir Thomas More, after whose attainder and execution in 1535 it was regranted to the courtier Sir Henry Norreys. The following year Norreys was attainted and executed for alleged intimacy with Anne Boleyn.[76] Ducklington was then retained by the Crown and administered by a bailiff.[77] In 1545 it was bought by speculators, Sir Richard Long and Christopher Edmonds,[78] who sold it in or before 1547 to Sir John Williams of Rycote, treasurer of the Court of Augmentations.[79] By 1552 Williams had sold it to Sir John Brome of Holton,[80] who died in 1558 holding Ducklington in chief.[81] His son Sir Christopher Brome (d. 1589), in financial difficulties, disposed of much of the manor, including Barley Park,[82] and in 1591 Sir Christopher's son George sold the rest to Walter Jones of Chastleton and his son Henry.[83] In 1603 they sold Ducklington manor to the owners of Barley Park, William Bayley and his wife Elizabeth.[84] The manor descended in the Bayley family from father to son, William (d. 1613) being succeeded by Richard (d. 1644) and William (d. 1688).[85] In 1685 William sold the advowson and mortgaged the manor, and in 1687 the mortgagee, Richard Stevens, acquired a 1,000-year lease without provision for redemption.[86] William Bayley's son William (d. 1716) retained an interest, however, and when Barley Park was sold in the 1690s Bayley was associated with Stevens's executor in the sale of at least part of it, Moulden's wood.[87] They may have disposed of most of the manorial estate: in 1697 Bayley, by then of Yelford, sold two Ducklington farms,[88] and when in 1712 he and an unidentified Col. Chivers (perhaps connected with Stevens) sold the manor to Simon Harcourt, Lord Harcourt, the only land besides the manorhouse grounds was a 3-yardland estate let for years at rack rent.[89] The manor descended with Harcourt's Cokethorpe Park estate.[90] Manorial rights were recorded into the 20th century.[91]

The medieval manor house, described in some detail in 1328 when it was divided for dower,[92] was set in a garden which extended to the river Windrush. By 1430, however, there was only a precinct which 'once contained' a manor house.[93] Its probable site was Court close, recorded from the 16th century, a large field between the church and the river.[94]

From the later Middle Ages Ducklington's lords were non-resident until in the early 17th century William Bayley (d. 1613) rebuilt a house

---

64 B.L. Add. MS. 6041, ff. 43v.–44v.; P.R.O., CP 25 (1)/190/22, no. 75. An inq. on Eliz., wife of Henry de Dive, does not mention her marriages: Cal. Inq. p.m. xv, p. 383.

65 Cal. Inq. p.m. xv, p. 219.

66 Ibid. xvii, pp. 453–4; P.R.O., CP 25(1)/291/63, no. 31; ibid. C 139/18, no. 19.

67 Cf. P.R.O., E 142/84/6; Feud. Aids iv. 194–5.

68 e.g. Cal. Fine R. 1422–30, 202; P.R.O., E 142/84/6.

69 Ibid. CP 25(1)/191/28, no. 31.

70 Cat. Anct. D. iv. A 7551; L. & P. Hen. VIII, Addenda 1509–47, p. 75.   71 P.R.O., C 139/158, no. 28.

72 Ibid. C 140/13, no. 27; ibid. C 140/19, no. 20. Cf. Liber de Antiquis Legibus (Camd. Soc. xxxiv), pp. ccxxvii–ccxxix.

73 e.g. presentation to rectory in 1467: Bodl. MS. Top. Oxon. c 55, f. 153.

74 Complete Peerage, viii. 223–5.

75 Cal. Pat. 1485–94, 25; Testamenta Vetusta, ed. N. H. Nicolas, ii. 640; D.N.B.

76 L. & P. Hen. VIII, viii, p. 47; x, p. 364; D.N.B.

77 e.g. P.R.O., SC 6/Hen. VIII/6066, 7247–50.

78 L. & P. Hen. VIII, xx (2), p. 117; P.R.O., E 318/15/725.

79 Cf. Fringford descent: V.C.H. Oxon. vi. 127; P.R.O., CP 40/1139, mm. 5, 7d. Long was dead by July 1547: Cal. Pat. 1547–8, 184.

80 Presentations to the living of Duckl. were made by Williams in 1550 and by Brome in Nov. 1552: Bodl. MS. Top. Oxon. b 78, ff. 147v.–148v.; P.R.O., REQ 2/210/99.

81 P.R.O., C 142/119, no. 140.

82 Ibid. C 142/221, no. 106; below.

83 P.R.O., C 66/1369, mm. 37–8. For the Bromes, Oxon. Visit. 229–30; J. M. French, Milton in Chancery, 167; V.C.H. Oxon. v. 125–6. For the Joneses, Oxon. Visit. 1634, 17.

84 P.R.O., CP 25/2/339/1 Jas. I Mich.

85 Ibid. PROB 11/121, ff. 341v.–344; Macray, Index of Duckl. Par. Regs. 55. For the Bayleys, Oxon. Visit. 1634, 3; Bodl. MS. Ch. Oxon. a 30, no. 666; ibid. MS. Top. Oxon. b 78, ff. 26–7, 212v. (which contains inaccuracies); ibid. Gooch MSS., G 2–5.

86 Below, church; Bodl. MS. Ch. Oxon. a 30, no. 666.

87 Bodl. MS. Ch. Oxon. c 43, no. 4320; below, other estates.

88 Bodl. MS. Top. Oxon. d 46, f. 30.

89 P.R.O., CP 25/2/957/11 Anne Mich.; Bodl. MS. d.d. Harcourt b 5, ff. 2v.–4.

90 Below, this section.

91 Kelly's Dir. Oxon. (1899 and later edns.).

92 Cal. Close, 1327–30, 377–8.

93 P.R.O., E 142/84/6, m. 5.

94 O.R.O., SL/9/02/3D/07; ibid., incl. map, plot 73.

bought from Robert Foster, whose holding had been granted away from the manor on a 2,000-year lease in 1587.[95] The house retained the name Foster's in the 1680s,[96] but was evidently the Ducklington manor house granted to Harcourt in 1712.[97] In 1722 he let it for lives to an associate, Samuel Scott, and his wife Elizabeth,[98] but after Scott's death in 1727 the manor house was in hand.[99] It was repaired in 1723, but lessees in the 1740s paid rents so low that decay seems indicated.[1] The manor house was pulled down c. 1754.[2] The 'close where the manor house stood'[3] was probably that called in 1838 Manor close, south-east of the surviving Yew Tree House:[4] the Bayleys' house is known to have abutted a furlong called Lillands, which lay immediately south-west of Manor close on the site of the modern Feilden Close.[5] A house on the Witney road, demolished c. 1840 and reputedly the 'old manor house', was the chief house of a substantial estate but not a manor house.[6]

Claywell lay within the Ducklington estate granted by King Edgar in 958.[7] Part of Claywell probably belonged to one of the Ducklington estates mentioned in 1086, since 8 yardlands there belonged to Richard of Carbrook in 1279.[8] That land descended with Ducklington manor later; quitrents paid to the manor in 1716 for an estate formerly Lord's were probably for Claywell,[9] and part of the site of the former village was later attached to Ducklington manorial holdings.[10]

Some of Claywell, however, was probably separated from the Ducklington estate before the Conquest: in 1086 Theodoric the goldsmith, who had been in the service of Edward the Confessor, held 2½ hides in 'Welde' (Claywell), which had been held freely by his wife.[11] Theodoric was succeeded by Walter de Cauz,[12] who in 1179 granted the estate, as 1 hide in Claywell and 1½ hide in Aston, to the tenant Ralph de Chesney, lord of Ducklington, reserving a rent of 15s. a year.[13] Before 1185 Ralph granted the Claywell hide and the Aston land to Eynsham abbey, which was to pay the same rent to Walter.[14] The abbey acquired at least 2 more yardlands from later lords of Ducklington, Guy and William de Dive,[15] and its Claywell estate

in 1279 comprised perhaps 7 yardlands, with a further yardland in Putlesley.[16] In the mid 13th century the abbey was released from the 15s. rent by an heir to the estates of Walter de Cauz, Cecily de Cumberwell.[17]

Eynsham abbey retained *EAST WEALD*, later *CLAYWELL*, manor until the Dissolution, administering it in the later Middle Ages, when it was perhaps reduced to a single farm, with Shifford manor (in Bampton).[18] It passed with Shifford to Sir George Darcey in 1539, to Sir Edward North in 1543, to the Stanleys, earls of Derby, in 1545, and was purchased in 1600 by Joseph Mayne of Creslow (Bucks.).[19] From 1544 Claywell was sublet by Sir Edward North to Leonard Yate of Witney, clothier,[20] and Yates of Witney were still suitors of Shifford court for land in Claywell, not necessarily the farm estate, in the 1570s.[21] In 1610 Claywell farm, reckoned as 5 yardlands, was held, on a long lease of unknown date, by Thomas North,[22] but in that year Joseph Mayne sold the freehold, along with his Shifford estate, to Sir David Williams and Edward Yate of Buckland (formerly Berks.).[23] In 1612 Williams and Yate completed a partition whereby Claywell passed to Yate, whose son Sir John was holding it when sequestrated for recusancy in 1654.[24] After his death c. 1658 it was held by his son Sir Charles (d. 1680) and grandson Sir John (d. 1690). Sir John's sister and heir, Mary Throckmorton, and Apollonia Yate, eldest daughter of Sir John (d. c. 1658), who was granted a reversionary interest in Claywell in 1658, were still holding Yate estates (perhaps including Claywell) in 1717.[25] Before 1731, however, Claywell passed to William Townesend, from whom it was bought by the Revd. Samuel Adams, who in that year made a settlement.[26] Adams (d. 1751), rector of Alvescot, bequeathed Claywell, after the life interests of his wife Susannah and niece Elizabeth Adams to a nephew, the Revd. Knightley Adams (d. 1769), who did not, however, hold Claywell at his death.[27] By 1785 the owner of Claywell was John Woolridge, and from c. 1818 until the 1840s it was owned and farmed by the Townsends of Cote;[28] by 1847 it was farmed by James Wood-

95   P.R.O., PROB 11/121, ff. 341v.–344; below, econ. hist.
96   Bodl. MS. Top. Oxon. b 78, ff. 26–7.
97   e.g. Bodl. MS. d.d. Harcourt b 5, ff. 2v.–4.
98   Ibid. ff. 77v., 79v.; ibid. c 13/2–4. For Scott, ibid. c 9/5–7.
99   O.R.O., MS. Wills Oxon. 151/2/2; Bodl. MS. d.d. Harcourt b 8, pp. 15–18.
1   Bodl. MSS. d.d. Harcourt b 5, f. 79v.; c 263, rental c. 1737, valuation c. 1747.
2   Ibid. c 25/1–3: lease of 1757, referring to the manor house 'lately taken down'; cf. ibid. c 263, rentals of 1753 (with later amendments) and 1757.
3   e.g. Bodl. MSS. d.d. Harcourt c 134/1, p. 18; c 134/2, p. 18.
4   O.R.O., incl. map, plot 5.
5   Ibid. Peake II/ix/1. For Lillands, ibid. tithe award 138, incl. award.
6   Below, other estates.
7   Above, intro. [boundaries].
8   V.C.H. Oxon. i. 414, 425; Bampton Hund. R. 61–2.
9   Bodl. MS. d.d. Harcourt b 5, ff. 3v.–4; for the Lords, below, this section.
10   Above, intro. [Claywell].
11   V.C.H. Oxon. i. 387, 423.
12   Eynsham Cart. i, p. 130; ii, p. lxv.
13   Ibid. i, pp. 88, 129–30, 402.
14   Ibid. 82–3.

15   Ibid. 159–61, 184–5, 193–4.
16   Bampton Hund. R. 61–2. Emma Lovel's holding, entered under Aston (ibid. 22), seems to have been in Claywell: cf. Eynsham Cart. ii, pp. 12, 14.
17   Eynsham Cart. i, pp. 207–8, but cf., for its apparent survival, ibid. 88; Cal. Pat. 1266–72, 475.
18   Above, intro.
19   Bodl. MS. d.d. Harcourt c 109/1–3; above, Bampton: Shifford, manor.
20   P.R.O., C 1/1284/8.
21   Bodl. MS. d.d. Harcourt c 127/8, ff. 22v., 30v., 31v.
22   Ibid. c 109/6: the name may be a scribal error for Thomas Lord, who was of Claywell at his death in 1631: C.O.S., par. reg. transcripts.
23   Bodl. MS. d.d. Harcourt c 109/6; P.R.O., CP 25/2/339/8 Jas. I Hil.
24   Bodl. MS. d.d. Harcourt c 109/10; ibid. MS. Top. Oxon. b 78, f. 29.
25   G. E. C. Baronetage, i. 205; Berks. R.O., D/EX 358/1; Guildhall Libr., MS. 17199.
26   Berks. R.O., D/EX 358/23/2.
27   P.R.O., PROB 11/786, ff. 137–138v.; PROB 11/953, ff. 42v.–43v.
28   O.R.O., land tax assess.; ibid. incl. award; ibid. MS. d.d. Par. Duckl. b 7: payments from Claywell.

bridge, who had married a Townsend, and it remained in his family until the 1890s.[29]

In 1544 Leonard Yate's tenancy of Claywell was disputed by Thomas Ford, the occupier.[30] The Lord family farmed Claywell for much of the 17th century,[31] the Leveridges in the early 18th, and the Foxes in the late 18th.[32] Claywell Farm, standing among the earthworks of the deserted settlement, may occupy the site of Eynsham abbey's early manor house. Presumably it was the house on which, in 1662, Christopher Lord was assessed on 5 hearths.[33] The surviving building is L-shaped and stone-slated, its symmetrical dressed-stone south front rebuilt or added in 1842 by the Townsends,[34] its coursed rubble rear range probably 18th-century. A farm cottage to the north, built before 1839,[35] was largely remodelled c. 1990.

In 1086 Hardwick presumably belonged to one of the two estates recorded under Brighthampton, and probably to the 1½ hide which Wadard held of Odo, bishop of Bayeux, and which was forfeited to the Crown on Odo's fall.[36] In 1131 Henry I granted land worth £10 from the royal manor of Bampton to the newly founded priory of St. Gervase and St. Protase attached to the cathedral of Sées (Orne); the land was said to be in Brighthampton, but then and later evidently included Hardwick,[37] which continued to be claimed as ancient demesne.[38] The £10 worth of land was accounted for annually in the Exchequer,[39] and in 1199 the estate was included in a papal confirmation of the priory's possessions.[40] It was enlarged at various times, but in 1242–3 was still recorded as £10 worth of land in Hardwick.[41] In or before 1245 the priory granted its estate in Brighthampton, Hardwick, and Yelford to Walter de Grey, archbishop of York, who gave it to his nephew Walter, son of Robert de Grey.[42] The estate, previously held in free alms, was assessed at ¹⁄₂₀th of a knight's fee; in 1295 it was said to be held freely, but the knight service was confirmed in 1304 and later.[43]

After the death of the younger Walter de Grey in 1268[44] HARDWICK manor descended with the Greys' adjacent estates in Cogges and Standlake from father to son to Bartholomew,

Lord Grey (d. 1375).[45] Bartholomew's brother and heir Robert, Lord Grey (d. 1388) was succeeded by his second wife Elizabeth (later Clinton, later Russell), who held in dower until her death in 1423.[46] The manor then passed to the coheirs of Joan Deincourt (d. 1408), daughter of Robert de Grey (d. 1388): they were Alice, wife of William Lovel, Lord Lovel, and Margaret, wife of Sir Ralph Cromwell.[47] Margaret died without issue in 1454,[48] and when Alice, as Lady Sudeley, died in 1474 her heir was her grandson Francis, Lord Lovel.[49]

On Lovel's attainder after the battle of Bosworth Field the forfeited manor was granted by Henry VII in 1486 to his uncle Jasper, duke of Bedford.[50] On Jasper's death without legitimate issue in 1495[51] it reverted to the Crown and was regranted in 1514 to Thomas Howard, duke of Norfolk.[52] Thomas's son and heir Thomas sold it back to the Crown in 1540.[53] In 1544 part of it, centred on Yelford, was granted to Alexander Unton and passed later to Wadham College, Oxford.[54] The rest was granted in 1554 as ¹⁄₄₀th of a knight's fee to John Herle, esquire of the Stable.[55] Herle sold a few holdings in Hardwick in 1569,[56] but the main estate, as the manor of *HARDWICK AND BRIGHTHAMPTON*, was sold in 1571 to St. John's College, Oxford, which retained it thereafter.[57]

The manor contained a court and curtilage in 1295, but in 1312 the manor house was reported to be 'not built' and in 1423 only the site of a manor was valued.[58] The site may have been Court close in Hardwick, belonging to St. John's College and let with the mill in the 16th and 17th centuries.[59] Court close was not named among the lands (apparently unchanged) included in the mill estate in the 19th century, but may have been one of the adjacent closes, by then partly occupied by farm buildings.[60] Manor Farm, another St. John's holding, acquired that name in the 20th century, and was earlier College Farm.[61]

All the area covered by the surviving Cokethorpe Park, including the chapel, lay within the bounds of the large Ducklington estate granted by King Edgar in 958.[62] Some of

29 P.R.O., HO 107/1731; *P.O. Dir. Oxon.* (1847 and later edns.); *Kelly's Dir. Oxon.* (1883 and later edns.); *Rtn. of Owners of Land* [C 1097], p. 22, H.C. (1874), lxxii.
30 P.R.O., C 1/1284/8.
31 Bodl. MS. Top. Oxon. b 78, f. 212; O.R.O., MSS. Wills Oxon. 41/4/16, 298/5/50; W. D. Macray, 'Index of Duckl. Par. Regs.', O.A.S. *Rep.* (1880), s.v. Lord.
32 Berks. R.O., D/EX 358/23/2; O.R.O., MS. Wills Oxon. 83/2/30; ibid. land tax assess.
33 P.R.O., E 179/255/4.
34 Datestones on gables, with initials RT and WT, recorded wrongly in D.o.E., *Revised Hist. Bldg. List* (1988).
35 O.R.O., incl. award and map.
36 *V.C.H. Oxon.* i. 405, 426.
37 *Reg. Regum Anglo-Norm.* ii, nos. 1698, 1711; C. H. Haskins, *Norman Institutions*, 300–3; *Rot. Litt. Claus.* (Rec. Com.), ii. 149.
38 e.g. P.R.O., JUST 1/713, m. 1v.; *Bampton Hund. R.* 63.
39 e.g. *Pipe R.* 1161 (P.R.S. iv), 26; ibid. 1230 (P.R.S. N.S. iv), 245.
40 *Letters of Innocent III*, ed. C. R. and M. G. Cheney, p. 22.
41 *Oxon. Fines*, pp. 12, 89; *Bk. of Fees*, ii. 832.
42 *Cal. Chart. R. 1226–57*, 285; cf. *Oxon. Fines*, pp. 131–2.
43 *Cal. Chart. R. 1226–57*, 285; Bodl. MS. Rawl. B 103, f. 224; *Cal. Inq. p.m.* iii, p. 183; *Cal. Close, 1302–7*, 203;

Feud. Aids, iv. 174.
44 *Ex. e Rot. Fin.* (Rec. Com.), ii. 464–5.
45 Below, Standlake, manors.
46 *Cal. Inq. p.m.* xvi, p. 222; *Cal. Close, 1385–9*, 544; *Complete Peerage*, vi. 149–50; P.R.O., C 139/12, no. 15.
47 P.R.O., C 139/12, no. 15; *Complete Peerage*, iv. 124–7; vi. 150.
48 P.R.O., C 139/159, no. 34; *Complete Peerage*, iv. 127–8.
49 P.R.O., C 140/47, no. 64; *Complete Peerage*, viii. 222–3; xii (1), 421.
50 *Cal. Pat. 1485–94*, 64; *Complete Peerage*, viii. 225.
51 *Complete Peerage*, ii. 73.
52 *L. & P. Hen. VIII*, i (2), pp. 1170–1; xv, pp. 218–19.
53 Ibid. xv, pp. 218–19, 470.
54 Ibid. xix (2), p. 471; below, Yelford, manors.
55 *Cal. Pat. 1554–5*, 313; 1555–7, 130.
56 Below, other estates.
57 W. H. Stevenson and H. E. Salter, *Early Hist. St. John's Coll.* (O.H.S. N.S. i), 156, 275.
58 P.R.O., C 133/72, no. 6; C 134/29, no. 11; C 139/12, no. 36.
59 e.g. St. John's Coll. Mun., XI.10 (152); XI.15, p. 123.
60 O.R.O., Hardwick tithe award and map, plots 4008–9.
61 St. John's Coll. Mun., XVII.68A.
62 *Cart. Sax.* ed. Birch, no. 1036; above, intro.

it descended with that estate and became part of Ducklington manor, but by the 13th century much of the west side of the area, including the site of the later Cokethorpe House but not the chapel, was attached to Standlake manor and belonged to Standlake parish.[63] In 1279 Clement of Cokethorpe's freehold house held of the Giffard portion of Standlake manor may have been in Cokethorpe. Three other holdings certainly in Cokethorpe at that date were all attached to Ducklington manor.[64] One of them, a freehold tenement of Robert of Yelford, was presumably among the 3 houses and 2½ yardlands in Cokethorpe held by Edmund Walwyn at his death in 1439, since elsewhere the Walwyns succeeded to the Yelford family's estates.[65] Edmund's estate was said to be held of William Lovel's Hardwick manor, although it seems more likely to have been held of Ducklington manor, also held by the Lovels.[66] On the death of Joan Lovel in 1466 she was said to be holding Ducklington manor and also COKETHORPE manor, perhaps referring to the Walwyn estate; it was worth only £2 13s. 4d., and was reportedly held by Joan in socage from Sir Richard Reyser.[67] That name was perhaps an error for Thomas Raysaker, Ducklington's rector, whose precursor as rector in 1444 was taking the revenues of Edmund Walwyn's estate.[68] The Walwyn property in Cokethorpe has not been identified later, nor any other reference found to the Lovels' reputed Cokethorpe manor. Ducklington manor retained at least 4 tenements in Cokethorpe in the early 16th century,[69] and estates in Hardwick, Yelford, and Sutton (in Stanton Harcourt) at various times claimed appurtenancies there.[70] The bulk of the later park, however, descended with Standlake manor.

In 1555 the reversion of some former Standlake demesne, including many closes and meadows later associated with Cokethorpe and by then known usually as Golofers manor, was acquired by Francis Fettiplace from Cuthbert Temple.[71] Fettiplace (d. 1558) also held another part of Standlake, once belonging to the Giffards and later the Fienneses: in 1573 his daughter Cecily and her husband Edward East of Bledlow (Bucks.) settled the manor of GOLOFERS or GIFFARDS alias STANDLAKE FIENNES on themselves and their heirs.[72] The Easts, noted recusants, were resident at Cokethorpe by 1577; their only daughter Dorothy (d. 1588) married Thomas Fitzherbert, later, in exile, a leading Jesuit.[73] The Easts were still concerned in the manor in 1606, but in 1610 Fitzherbert's son Edward and his wife Bridget sold it to Sir David Williams.[74]

Williams, a justice of King's Bench, died in 1613, having settled the estate on his second son Thomas.[75] Thomas (d. 1636) was resident at Cokethorpe until at least 1623.[76] His son David was married at Cokethorpe in 1634 to Elizabeth Carew, whose family, headed by Sir Matthew Carew, seem to have been resident, perhaps as lessees, from 1625 or earlier.[77] In 1635 David Williams sold the manor to Elizabeth Stonehouse of Radley (formerly Berks.) and her third son William.[78] The Stonehouse family lived at Cokethorpe for most of the 17th century. At his death in 1660 William Stonehouse was succeeded by his eldest son William;[79] Nicholas Bowell (d. 1688), who was also living at Cokethorpe in 1673, had married the elder William's relict Elizabeth.[80] In 1696 William Stonehouse conveyed the manor, by then sometimes also called COKETHORPE manor,[81] to William Jennens, who in that year granted it to trustees on his marriage to Mary Wiseman. After Jennens's death in 1708 an Act was obtained to clear incumbrances on the estate, and by 1710 it had been acquired by Sir Simon Harcourt, one of the trustees of 1696.[82]

Sir Simon, appointed Lord Keeper in 1710 and Lord Chancellor in 1713, created Baron Harcourt in 1711 and Viscount Harcourt in 1721, added Ducklington manor to the estate in 1712; Cokethorpe was his principal residence.[83] After his death in 1727 his third wife Elizabeth (d. 1748) retained a life interest, but she gave Simon's grandson and heir Simon, created Earl Harcourt in 1749, possession of the house and park; in 1737 he was formally leasing from her the farmland.[84] In the early 1750s Earl Harcourt extended the Cokethorpe estate, notably by buying Barley Park, but from 1755 was planning a new seat at Nuneham Courtenay.[85]

In 1766 he sold the Cokethorpe estate to

63 Above, intro.
64 *Bampton Hund. R.* 62, 70.
65 P.R.O., C 139/113, no. 14; below, Yelford, manors.
66 For similar confusion over the Walwyns and Lovels cf. below, Yelford, manors.
67 P.R.O., C 140/19, no. 20.
68 Ibid. C 139/113, no. 14; Bodl. G.A. Oxon. 8° 469 (6): list of rectors.
69 e.g. *L. & P. Hen. VIII*, viii, p. 47.
70 e.g. ibid. xix (1), p. 618; xx (2), p. 117; *Cal. Pat. 1550–3*, 248; *1566–9*, p. 339.
71 *Cal. Pat. 1554–5*, 138–9; below, Standlake, manors.
72 Magd. Coll. Mun., Standlake deeds 625; *Cal. Pat. 1572–5*, p. 64; P.R.O., CP 25/2/196/15 & 16 Eliz. I Mich.
73 P.R.O., E 179/162/345; Bodl. MS. Top. Oxon. b 78, f. 294; *V.C.H. Bucks.* ii. 249; *Visit. Bucks.* (Harl. Soc. lviii), 163; below, nonconf.
74 P.R.O., CP 25/2/339/4 Jas. I East.; CP 25/2/339/8 Jas. I East.
75 Bodl. MS. Top. Oxon. b 78, ff. 297–300; P.R.O., C 142/346, no. 80; *D.N.B.*
76 Bodl. MS. Top. Oxon. b 78, ff. 297–300; ibid. MS. d.d. Harcourt c 109/20–1.

77 Bodl. MS. Top. Oxon. b 78, ff. 297–300; C.O.S., Duckl. par. reg. transcripts, marriages 1634, burials 1633 (s.v. Carew); ibid., Standlake par. reg. transcripts, baptisms 1625–35 (s.v. Carey, *recte* Carew). For Sir Matthew, W. A. Shaw, *Knights of Eng.* ii. 114.
78 P.R.O., CP 43/213, rot. 27; ibid. CP 25/2/473/11 Chas. I Trin., Hil.; Bodl. MS. Top. Oxon. c 378, pp. 273, 276. For the Stonehouse family, *V.C.H. Berks.* iv. 412; *Visit. Berks.* ii (Harl. Soc. lvii), 217.
79 P.R.O., PROB 11/302, f. 118v.
80 R. Blome, *Britannia* (1673), 45; *Wood's Life*, iii (O.H.S. xxvi), 242–3; P.R.O., PROB 11/391, f. 78v.
81 e.g. Magd. Coll. Mun. 141/5: mortgage of 1678.
82 P.R.O., CP 25/2/865/8 Wm. III Trin.; *Act re Inheritance of William Jennens*, 8 Anne, c. 10 (Priv. Act); Bodl. MSS. d.d. Harcourt c 13/2–4; c 49/10; c 262 (R): undated roll, *c.* 1711.
83 *D.N.B.*; *Complete Peerage*, vi. 298–301; *Harcourt Papers*, ed. E. W. Harcourt, iii. 34, 49, 56, and *passim*.
84 Bodl. MSS. d.d. Harcourt c 267, survs. of *c.* 1727 and later; ibid. c 263, survs. of 1727 and later; ibid. c 300, lease of 1737.
85 *V.C.H. Oxon.* v. 237.

Maximilian Western,[86] son of Maximilian Western (d. 1764), a director of the East India Company.[87] Western resided at Cokethorpe until his death in 1801, having been predeceased by his son Maximilian (d. 1795).[88] His heirs, after the life interest of his relict Elizabeth (d. 1804),[89] were his daughters Elizabeth, wife of Francis Sackville Lloyd (later Lloyd Wheate) of Glympton Park,[90] and Frances, who in 1803 married Walter Strickland of Boynton (Yorks.).[91] After Lloyd Wheate's death in 1812 the Strick-

demar Cottrell-Dormer (d. 1906), grandson of Charles Cottrell-Dormer of Rousham (d. 1874) and Frances, eldest daughter of Walter Strickland (d. 1839). Cokethorpe was occupied for much of the late 19th century and early 20th by C. A. Cottrell-Dormer's younger brother, John (later John Upton).[94] In 1908 the estate was sold to Capt. P. H. G. Feilden who was resident from 1911 until his death in 1944. He was succeeded by his son Major-General (later Sir) Randle Guy Feilden. In 1957 the house and part of the park

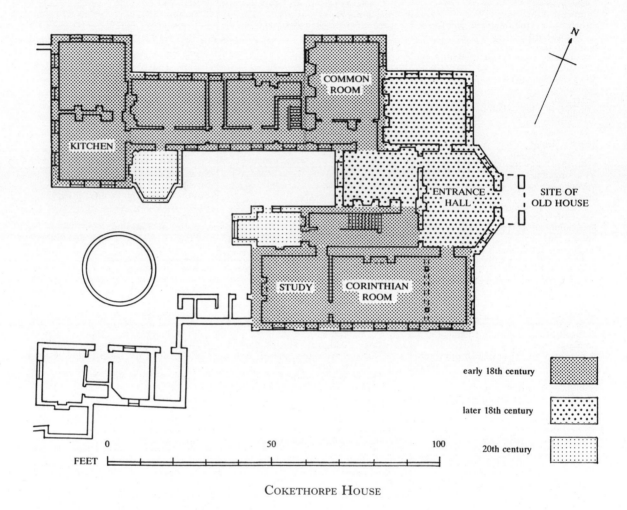

COKETHORPE HOUSE

lands seem to have become sole owners. By 1817 they were resident at Cokethorpe, which after the death of Maximilian Western had been let, notably to Capt. Edward Shirley.[92] Walter Strickland died in 1839 and was succeeded by his son Walter, who in 1844 married Catherine Thornhill; Walter died in 1870 and Catherine in 1892.[93] The estate then passed to Clement Al-

were let to Francis Brown, who opened Cokethorpe School. In 1966 the school trustees bought the freehold.[95]

There was probably no gentleman's house at Cokethorpe until the Easts settled there in the 1570s. In 1611, when held by Sir David Williams, the estate included a close 'whereon the house now standeth and is to be builded'.[96] The

[86] P.R.O., CP 25/2/1388/8 Geo. III Mich.; Bodl. MS. d.d. Harcourt c 300, pps. re sale of Cokethorpe. A purchase date of 1765, mentioned in e.g. Western's will (P.R.O., PROB 11/1353, ff. 80–1) is incorrect.

[87] Gent. Mag. (1764), p. 198; P.R.O., PROB 11/898, ff. 67–69v.; Burke, Peerage (1878), pp. 1254–5 (containing some inaccuracies).

[88] P.R.O., PROB 11/1353, ff. 80–1; C.O.S., Standlake par. reg. transcripts, burials, 10 July 1795, 17 Jan. 1801.

[89] C.O.S., Standlake par. reg. transcripts, burials 3 May 1804.

[90] O.R.O., FC VIII/11.

[91] For the Stricklands, Burke, Land. Gent. (1871), ii. 1332.

[92] O.R.O., land tax assess.; Bodl. MS. Top. Oxon. b 78, ff. 305–6.

[93] Witney Gaz. 6 Feb. 1892: obituary.

[94] Kelly's Dir. Oxon. (1899 and later edns.); Burke, Land. Gent. (1952); Bodl. MS. Top. Oxon. b 78, ff. 267, 303.

[95] Inf. from Cokethorpe School; Witney Gaz. 21 Jan. 1911. For the Feildens, Burke, Land. Gent. (1952); Who's Who (1950 and later edns.).

[96] Bodl. MS. Top. Oxon. b 78, ff. 297–300.

intended new building was perhaps complete by 1613 when Sir David Williams bequeathed plate which was to remain at Cokethorpe 'as heirlooms'.[97] For a time, when occupied by Williams's son Thomas, the house seems to have been called Williams Lodge.[98] Probably it was the building which, until the later 18th century, occupied the site of the east front and part of the forecourt of the surviving Cokethorpe House.[99] Simon, Lord Harcourt (d. 1727), seems to have begun his extensions to that earlier house on the north:[1] to the projecting block (incorporating the staff common room in 1995) which possibly pre-dates the Harcourts[2] he added on the west a five-bayed range and end pavilion. The range contained some high-status rooms until (probably in the early 20th century) it became the kitchen block. The surviving south front was built c. 1720, as an extension of the earlier house, to the designs of Dr. George Clarke of Oxford.[3] Its centrepiece is a 3-bayed panelled room, later called the Queen Anne room (though post-dating her death)[4] or the Corinthian room, referring to the heavy pilasters which punctuate the oak panelling; when the east front was rebuilt the room was extended eastwards by one bay to incorporate an existing small room, the earlier wall being replaced by panelled Corinthian piers. In the early 18th century the Corinthian room was evidently the chief reception room, while the panelled headmaster's study on the west was the state bedroom. Above the Corinthian room was a 3-bayed library, completed in 1721,[5] stripped out and turned into bedrooms probably in the mid 19th century.

The earlier, 17th-century, house was demolished and replaced by the existing east front and central canted entrance bay[6] soon after Cokethorpe was purchased by Maximilian Western in 1766. The roof balustrades and some of the attics seem to have been the work of Walter Strickland in the 1820s,[7] although attics on the south were allegedly added in 1844, presumably on the marriage of Walter Strickland (d. 1870).[8] For several years following their purchase of the house in 1908 the Feildens extensively renovated the interior in 18th-century style, altering or replacing panelling, and adding fireplaces.[9] All the sash windows on the principal

fronts date from that period. The stables and service buildings which form the western court were built at various times from the early 18th century;[10] the circular building in the centre was probably a game larder.

By the 1620s the grounds of Cokethorpe House extended well to the east of the house,[11] but the creation and landscaping of the surviving park seems to have been the work of the Harcourts in the earlier 18th century. There was reference c. 1711 to three demolished houses in Cokethorpe, including Mountain's, which had stood near the road some 80 m. north-east of the chapel,[12] and in 1712 the north side of the churchyard was annexed to allow an avenue or vista to be laid out from the east front of the house towards the road.[13] Much of the east side of the later park, however, seems to have remained in closes, many of them arable, and some of the hamlet survived. Between the chapel and road was 'Peck's house', the farmhouse for the estate's principal farm, which seems to have continued in use for many years.[14] Another, unlocated, house (Hart's), with a substantial attached estate in the Ducklington part of Cokethorpe, also survived into the 1720s.[15] The park was extended by Simon, later Earl, Harcourt some time after he took over Cokethorpe in 1727. By 1745 he had acquired Hart's estate, which was kept in hand,[16] and by then the estate's farmland was much reduced and probably no longer worked from the farmhouse near the chapel.[17] Harcourt had added to the park on the west by acquiring the Lawns, between Home and Boys woods, formerly held by the lords of Yelford;[18] the Long Train, a wood at the west end of the Lawns, was probably planted to mark a new park boundary.[19] By 1766 when Harcourt sold the park it had reached its full extent and was estimated variously at between 280 a. and 310 a., including Home wood and the Lawns;[20] it extended east to the river and was well wooded throughout, with no significant buildings except Cokethorpe House, the isolated chapel, and the Water House (later Fish House) on the river Windrush.[21]

Fish House[22] was evidently designed as an eye-catcher, but its primary function was to pump water to the house and estate. It was built in

97 Ibid.
98 e.g. Bodl. MS. d.d. Harcourt c 109/12–13.
99 Partly shown on plans for an extension c. 1720: Worcester Coll. Libr., YD 3, nos. 177–84.
1 The following owes much to an account by D. Sturdy in *The Peacock* (Cokethorpe Sch. mag.), xxv (1986), 5–11: copy in C.O.S. For a plan of the house in 1944, N.M.R. Many refs. to building work in early 18th-century accts. cannot safely be assigned to Cokethorpe: Bodl. MS. d.d. Harcourt b 5–6.
2 The early 18th-century-style panelling in the common room, although apparently not authentic, respects a window on the west, blocked c. 1715.
3 Worcester Coll. Libr. YD 3, nos. 177–84; H. M. Colvin, *Cat. of Archit. Drawings in Worcester Coll.*, pp. 28–9; ibid. *Biog. Dict. Brit. Archit. 1600–1840*, 216–17.
4 The tradition, recorded e.g. in J. P. Neale, *Views of Seats* (1820), iii [s.v. Cokethorpe], that the queen gave the panelling for the room where she dined with Lord Harcourt perhaps refers to another room.
5 *The Peacock*, xxv (1986), 10–11.
6 Above, plate 22.
7 Cf. Neale, *Views* (1820), iii; ibid. (1824), i.

8 C.O.S., PRN 11202, notes by J. Cartland, apparently based on Cokethorpe acct. bks. in his possession.
9 *Witney Gaz.* 21 Jan. 1911; dates on chimneypieces.
10 *Harcourt Papers*, ii. 123; Bodl. MS. d.d. Harcourt b 5, f. 102.
11 B.N.C. Mun., plan of a Cokethorpe estate c. 1629.
12 Ibid.; ibid. Room B. ser., 534, terriers 1761, 1765; Bodl. MS. d.d. Harcourt c 262 (R). Cf. O.R.O., Standlake incl. map B, pecked outline north of Cokethorpe chapel.
13 Bodl. MS. d.d. Harcourt c 14/1.
14 Ibid.; below, econ. hist.
15 Cf. Bodl. MSS. d.d. Harcourt b 5, f. 3v.; b 8, p. 17: quitrents 1716, 1727.
16 Ibid. c 133/1, p. 6; c 263, surv. 1753.
17 Below, econ. hist.
18 Below, Yelford, manors (Yelford Walwyn); Bodl. MSS. d.d. Harcourt c 133/1, p. 5: land tax payment; c 300, pps. re sale of Cokethorpe, 1766.
19 Bodl. MS. d.d. Harcourt c 300, pps. re sale of Cokethorpe (ref. to 'pieces above the wood new planted').
20 Ibid. c 300, pps. re sale of Cokethorpe; cf. O.S. Map 1/2,500, Oxon. XXXII. 13, XXXVIII. 1 (1876 edn.).
21 Jefferys, *Oxon. Map* (1767).
22 Above, plate 25.

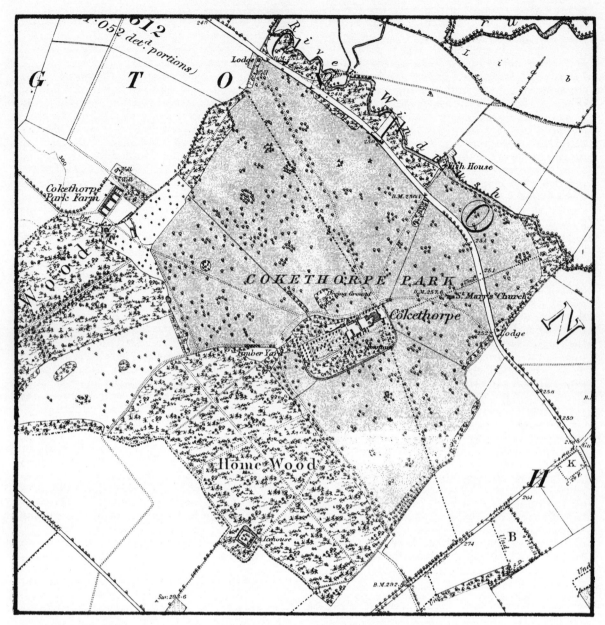

COKETHORPE PARK IN 1876

1723–4, replacing an earlier 'fish house' of un-known date and purpose.[23] It comprised a gothicized tower, incorporating re-used frag-ments of carved masonry; it housed a watermill and a dwelling house, perhaps for a fisherman. The undershot water-wheel was linked to pump-ing equipment, and the survival of grinding stones indicates a dual function.[24] The house abutting the tower dates from the mid 19th century.

Walter Strickland (d. 1839) laid out gardens at Cokethorpe House 'on an improved principle', perhaps those surrounding the house which by 1839 were divided from the park by a ha-ha; by 1876 they included formal gardens, a wilderness,

and a fountain.[25] Strickland also built the sur-viving lodges where the Ducklington–Standlake road entered and left the park; that on the north was Coachman's Lodge in 1831.[26] By the 1870s there was no sign of an avenue or vista passing the north side of the chapel; the surviving avenue from the house to the north lodge, aligned on the steeple of Witney church, was seriously decayed, suggesting that it had been part of the 18th-century design; there were indications of a possible vista towards Fish House. The trees in the body of the park were chiefly deciduous, but evergreens, perhaps 19th-century additions, had been planted extensively in Fish House plantation and other peripheral belts, and in the

[23] Bodl. MS. d.d. Harcourt b 5, ff. 77, 91v., 94v.; datestone on bldg.
[24] C.O.S., PRN 4375, which includes plans but misdates the building's 'conversion' to a pump house.

[25] Neale, *Views* (1820), iii; O.S. Map. 1/2,500, Oxon. XXXIII. 13 (1876 edn.).
[26] Neale, *Views* (1820), iii; O.R.O., MS. d.d. Par. Duckl. b 9.

garden south of the house.[27] The north avenue was restored before 1921,[28] but elsewhere in the park many trees were lost in the 20th century, particularly through elm disease in the 1970s.

OTHER ESTATES. Barley Park formed part of Ducklington manor until sold by the Bromes in the 1580s to Thomas Yate, who in 1586 sold it to the queen's physician Walter Bayley (d. 1592).[29] Park and manor were reunited when Bayley's son William (d. 1613) bought the manor, and they descended together until the later 17th century.[30] In 1693 part of the park, Edgeley coppice later Moulden's wood (then 58 a.), was sold from the manor to Edward Moulden, a Witney ironmonger.[31] Probably in the same year the main part of Barley Park was sold to the Revd. Edward Alston.[32] Alston's estate seems to have passed soon afterwards to Thomas Brereton (d. 1699) of East Marden (Suss.), between whose daughters, Mary (d. 1701) and Frances (d. 1727), it was divided. Frances, who inherited her sister's share, married first the Revd. Edward Onley of Cottesmore (Rut.) and later, before 1717, Paul Collins,[33] who survived her but was dead by 1746.[34] The estate descended under Frances Collins's will to her nephew Thomas William Brereton and his son Thomas. They sold it c. 1754 to Simon, Earl Harcourt.[35]

The Barley Park estate held by the Collinses and their successors evidently excluded not only Moulden's wood but other parts of the park for which, in 1716, the families of Carter and Barker were paying freehold quitrents to Ducklington manor.[36] William Barker, yeoman (d. 1691), was 'of Barley' and Barkers were resident in Ducklington until the 1720s.[37] The Carters were perhaps associated with Claywell, since they also held of Ducklington manor an estate held earlier by the Lords,[38] and another connexion between the park and Claywell is suggested by the name Dr. Adams's wood (possibly the same as Carter's copse), presumably referring to Samuel Adams (d. 1751), lord of Claywell.[39] The Barley Park estate acquired by Simon, Earl Harcourt, from the Breretons comprised only 148 a. around Barley Park Farm, including the main wood, the closes along its eastern edge, and a few on the north: the west side, the southern tip, and much of the north part of the former park belonged to other estates.[40] During the 1750s, however, Harcourt acquired Carter's estate (sometimes called Littleton's) and smaller estates which seem to have included parts of the former park; he also acquired half (some 22 a.) of Moulden's wood.[41] All descended thereafter with the Cokethorpe estate. The other part of Moulden's wood retained the name Edgeley coppice in the 18th century, suggesting that it had been sold off soon after its acquisition by Edward Moulden in 1693; it was owned in the late 18th century and early 19th by the Leake family,[42] and was acquired at inclosure in 1839 by Walter Strickland of Cokethorpe in an exchange with Charles Leake. Strickland by then owned almost all the former Barley Park.[43] In 1919 Barley Park farm, and Coursehill farm which included part of the former park, were sold.[44]

In the 16th century Barley Park contained a ranger's lodge and probably another house.[45] The royal bailiff Thomas Lawley at his death in 1549 was 'of Barley Park', as was Richard Hickes, gent., c. 1590.[46] William Bayley (d. 1613) was also so described, but he and later Bayleys seem to have lived in Ducklington manor house.[47] The house ground in the park was mentioned in 1661.[48] Both William Barker and Edward Alston may have lived in the park in the 1690s and c. 1718 Barley Park was described as the seat of Paul Collins;[49] for a short time the house may have been called Ducklington Place.[50] By the mid 18th century it was probably a working farmhouse.[51] Much was spent on repair or rebuilding when it became part of the Cokethorpe estate.[52] The surviving Barley Park Farm seems to date from a rebuilding by Walter

[27] O.S. Map 1/2,500, Oxon. XXXII. 13, XXXVIII. 1 (1876 edn.)

[28] Ibid. XXXII. 13 (1921 edn.).

[29] Bodl. MS. Dep d 72, f. 23; ibid. MS. Ch. Oxon. a 66, no. 2620; ibid. MS. Top. Oxon. b 78, ff. 202–3; P.R.O., PROB 11/79, f. 179v. For the creation and development of the park, below, econ. hist.

[30] Bodl. MS. Ch. Oxon. a 30, no. 666: abstract of title 1599–1693; above, manors.

[31] O.R.O., Misc. Mar. I/120; Bodl. MS. Ch. Oxon. c 43, no. 4320; Berks. R.O., D/ER 5526.

[32] O.R.O., MS. Oxf. Dioc. c 104, f. 69; Par. Colln. 128; Foster, Alumni.

[33] Par. Colln. 128, giving an inaccurate descent; Bodl. MS. d.d. Harcourt b 5, ff. 3v.–4, quitrents, 1716; ibid. c 263, rental, 1722; P.R.O., CP 25/2/1049/3 Geo. I Trin.; ibid., PROB 11/453, f. 15v.–16v.; PROB 11/463, f. 129v.–131v.; PROB 11/619, ff. 309v.–313. For the Breretons, V.C.H. Suss. iv. 168.

[34] P.R.O., PROB 11/619, ff. 309v.–313, particularly marginal note re admin. in 1746.

[35] Cf. P.R.O., CP 43/673, rot. 291; ibid. CP 43/689, rot. 267; Bodl. MS. d.d. Harcourt c 133/2: ref. to 'Barley Park in hand from Lady Day 1754'.

[36] Bodl. MS. d.d. Harcourt b 5, ff. 3v.–4.

[37] O.R.O., MSS. Wills Oxon. 7/5/13, 8/3/17, 9/1/6, 116/2/19; C.O.S., par. reg. transcripts.

[38] Bodl. MS. d.d. Harcourt b 5, ff. 3v.–4; above, manors (Claywell).

[39] Bodl. MS. d.d. Harcourt c 300, pps. re sale of Cokethorpe; O.R.O., Duckl. tithe award and map, plot 201; above, manors (Claywell).

[40] Bodl. MS. d.d. Harcourt c 300, valuation (1751) of Barley Park in pps. re sale of Cokethorpe estate; cf. O.R.O., Duckl. tithe award and map, plots 187 sqq.

[41] Bodl. MSS. d.d. Harcourt c 300, pps. re sale of Cokethorpe; c 263, rental 1753, where a Littleton pays quitrent for Lord's estate; c 134/2, p. 15 and passim.

[42] O.R.O., land tax assess. 1785–1831, where the Leakes' share of Moulden's wood was called Edgeley coppice.

[43] O.R.O., Duckl. incl. award.

[44] Sale Cat. Duckl. and Hardwick (1919): copy in C.O.S.; Kelly's Dir. Oxon. (1920). For an attempted sale in 1912, Bodl. MS. Top. Oxon. b 78, ff. 267–75.

[45] P.R.O., E 315/273, f. 49; Bodl. MS. Ch. Oxon. a 66, no. 2620.

[46] O.R.O., MS. Wills Oxon. 179, f. 308; Acts of P.C. 1590–1, 241.

[47] Oxon. Visit. 3; above, manors.

[48] Bodl. MS. Ch. Oxon. a 30, no. 666.

[49] O.R.O., MS. Wills Oxon. 7/5/13; ibid. MS. Oxf. Dioc. c 104, f. 69; Par. Colln. ii. 128.

[50] e.g. Oxon. map (1777) by E. Bowen, reprinted as Royal Eng. Atlas (1871), no. 29.

[51] e.g. Bodl. MS. Top. Oxon. b 78, f. 28; ibid. MS. d.d. Harcourt c 144/1: 1765 rental; Oxf. Jnl. Synopsis, 1 Feb. 1783.

[52] Bodl. MS. d.d. Harcourt c 133/2, pp. 40–1, 53.

Strickland c. 1840, but in a field to the south-west is a large banked enclosure, perhaps the site of an earlier house.[53]

A large freehold and leasehold estate in Ducklington was accumulated by the Harris family.[54] Richard Harris (d. 1545) was the highest tax-payer in Ducklington in 1542–3;[55] his son Thomas (d. 1565) added to his estate,[56] and his grandson Bartholomew (d. 1632) acquired the largest (6 yardlands) of the 2,000-year leasehold estates created when the manorial estate was dispersed in 1587.[57] When Bartholomew's son Thomas predeceased him in 1626 the family's holding, thought to be held in chief by knight service as part of Ducklington manor, included two houses, 3½ yardlands of customary land, 2½ yardlands of former demesne, and various closes, notably Court close, the possible site of the medieval manor house. The family also held another house and 1½ yardland, its tenure unknown but probably the freehold bought in 1557 from the Tailor family.[58]

The estate seems to have passed to Bartholomew Harris (d. 1705) and Thomas Harris (d. 1728), whose leasehold and freehold holdings of Ducklington manor passed in the mid 18th century to the Davis family.[59] They had been acquired by either Anthony Davis, who was buried in Ducklington in 1746, or by his son Capt. George Davis (d. 1765), then resident.[60] In 1762, however, apparently because of mortgage difficulties elsewhere, Davis surrendered his Ducklington estate to Simon, Earl Harcourt, to whom the rack rent of the farmland, occupied by Thomas Stone, was paid until 1769. In that year Davis's son George (d. 1814) regained possession.[61] He continued to let most of it as a single large farm,[62] but resided in Ducklington before moving in 1785 to Benson.[63] In 1772 he enlarged the estate by acquiring another of Ducklington manor's ancient leaseholds, a house and 3 yardlands long held by the Colliers, and in 1787 he sold the whole to John Nalder of Northmoor (d. 1797).[64] Nalder's son Noble Kent Nalder (d. 1830) sold the estate in 1829 to Walter Strickland of Cokethorpe Park,[65] and it descended thereafter with the Cokethorpe estate.

The chief farm on the former Nalder estate was worked from the surviving Manor Farm, probably the principal working farmhouse of the estate from the time of the Harrises;[66] the farm-house acquired with Collier's estate had been turned into cottages by 1820.[67] Manor Farm is a large stone and stone-slated house, of 2 storeys with attics; the main range, of the later 17th century with gable chimneys, was extended west, beyond the kitchen stack, in the 18th century and an outshut with service rooms added in the 19th century. The Davises and Nalders resided in another house which, although probably acquired with the Harris estate, was evidently greatly enlarged or rebuilt. At inclosure in 1839 it was a vacant building called the Great House, owned by Walter Strickland, and standing north of the surviving no. 14 Witney Road; soon afterwards the Stricklands demolished it and used the materials to build an outlying farmhouse. In the later 19th century, mistakenly identified as the 'old manor house' of Ducklington, it was remembered as a house of some 13 bedrooms, with an ornate interior and an entrance surmounted by carved heads and an inscription containing the name Davis.[68] It was presumably the gentleman's residence in Ducklington which in 1766, during the minority of the younger George Davis, was offered to let; it was described as recently finished, with 7 bedrooms and 7 garrets, set in lawns and flower gardens with a summer house and 'serpentine canal'.[69] No. 14 Witney Road, alleged to have been the kitchen end of the Great House, dates from the 17th century or earlier, and contained an ancient oak door which in the 1980s was removed to Rectory Cottage, Yelford.[70]

Wadham College, Oxford, acquired an estate in Hardwick which derived from the division of the manor in the mid 16th century. The part centred on Yelford, granted away in 1544, lay in fields which came to be regarded as in Hardwick;[71] the owner of that estate, William Edwards, in 1570 added two holdings in Hardwick proper which had been granted from the manor in 1569 to Peter Ranckell of Witney.[72]

53 C.O.S., PRN 3847.
54 For the Harrises cf. *Index of Duckl. Par. Regs.*; O.R.O., MSS. Wills Oxon. 179, f. 131; 184, f. 173; 31/1/30; P.R.O., C 142/436, no. 44; Bodl. MS. Top. Oxon. b 78, f. 24.
55 P.R.O., E 179/162/234, m. 18d.
56 Bodl. MS. d.d. Dew c 3/1; B.L. Add. Ch. 57174.
57 O.R.O., SL/9/02/3D/07; cf. Bodl. MS. d.d. Harcourt b 5, ff. 2v.–4, leasehold quitrents, 1716. For the dispersal of the manorial estate, below, econ. hist.
58 P.R.O., C 142/436, no. 44; Bodl. MS. d.d. Dew c 3/1. Harrises holding 3½ yardlands and a mill in the 16th century seems to be of another family: cf. O.R.O., MSS. Wills Oxon. 187, f. 376; 190, f. 311; P.R.O., C 3/408/165; ibid. C 5/625/62.
59 Bodl. MS. d.d. Harcourt c 133/2: surv. of 1754–5, listing quitrents of Thos. Harris 'now Mr. Davis'.
60 Ibid. b 4/1, f. 41; c 300, copy of Chancery judgement (1759) in Cholsey bdle.; O.R.O., MS. Wills Oxon. 79/1/84; *Oxf. Jnl.* 13 July 1765.
61 *Harcourt Papers*, ed. E. W. Harcourt, iii. 100; Bodl. MSS. d.d. Harcourt c 138/6; c 141/1; c 145/1; c 147/1; c 300, copy of Chancery judgement.
62 Bodl. MS. Ch. Oxon. c 81, nos. 5290–1.
63 *Oxf. Jnl.* 27 June 1785; O.R.O., Ta. VIII/i/6.
64 O.R.O., SL/9/02/3D/01-2; ibid. land tax assess. 1785–

1831. In 1716 the estate, identified by its quit rent of 31s., was held by John Collier: Bodl. MS. d.d. Harcourt b 5, ff. 2v.–4.
65 O.R.O., SL/9/02/3D/06-08; ibid. land tax assess; Bodl. MS. Top. Oxon. b 78, ff. 86–7. For the Nalders, C.O.S., Northmoor par. reg. transcripts.
66 O.R.O., land tax assess. 1831, estate owned by Strickland, tenant Thos. Goffe; ibid. MS. d.d. Par. Duckl. b 9, s.a. 1834; ibid. Duckl. tithe award and map, plot 1. Another large Strickland farmhouse, the later Church Farm, was not a former Nalder property, having belonged until c. 1828 to John Chapman: ibid. plot 25; ibid. land tax assess. 1825–31.
67 Ibid. SL/9/02/3D/07. Its site (ibid. Duckl. tithe map, plots 37–9) may be identified from ibid. SL/9/3D/02; Bodl. MS. Ch. Oxon c 81, no. 5291.
68 O.R.O., Duckl. tithe map, plot 40; Bodl. MSS. Top. Oxon. d 271, f. 21; b 78, ff. 30v., 86–7, where the materials are stated variously to have been used at Barley Park Farm and Coursehill Farm.
69 *Oxf. Jnl.* 22 March 1766.
70 Bodl. MS. Top. Oxon. b 78, f. 86; M. Harris, *Where the Windrush Flows*, 117.
71 Below, Yelford, manors.
72 St. John's Coll. Mun., XVII.5; Wadham Coll. Mun., 86/3–4; P.R.O., C 66/1069, m. 9.

After the Edwards family's estate in Yelford and Hardwick passed to Wadham College in 1636 the Hardwick part, separately let, was usually described as a house, 1½ yardland, and 3 berry-dells (former demesne) and in 1772 comprised an estimated 52 a.[73] After inclosure in 1853 Wadham College's Hardwick estate comprised c. 75 a., enlarged by purchase in 1864 to c. 98 a.[74] Most of the farmland was sold in 1968 and the village property in 1975.[75]

ECONOMIC HISTORY. Ducklington's open fields covered much of the central part of the township.[76] Before inclosure in 1839 the furlongs were grouped in five fields, with Beanhill field in the north, Park field between the village and Barley Park, Middle field parallel to it on the south-east, and Wood field ranged along the north side of Cokethorpe Park; in the south-west, between Boys Wood and Barley Park, was Claywell field.[77] The medieval fields were probably similarly widespread, the demesne arable in 1328 lying in furlongs which, where identifiable, were in the later Claywell, Middle, and Beanhill fields.[78] An unidentified *Aldefelde* containing 25½ a. of demesne granted to Eynsham abbey c. 1200 was probably on the west side of the parish where the abbey's holdings were concentrated.[79] Edgerley field, mentioned in the 17th century when it was mostly in closes,[80] referred to an area in the north-west near the deserted hamlet of Eggesley.[81]

In 1086 both parts of Ducklington manor had permanent pasture (1 furlong by 1 furlong).[82] Later the chief area of common grazing was the heathland at Coursehill, which seems to have been inclosed in the 17th century.[83] The manorial meadow in 1086 was estimated at 60 a.[84] In the early 19th century the common meadow (194 a.) lay chiefly along the river Windrush;[85] some, notably Gooseham, lay near the village,[86] but the larger stretches, Upper and Lower mead, lay south of Ducklington mill. Smaller meadows such as Seal ham, which contained demesne in 1328, also lay in that area.[87] Ducklington men held meadow strips in Wagg's ham near Hardwick and in Yelford mead near Yelford, both of which were intercommoned with other manors; both were surveyed with Ducklington's fields in

1839 but remained uninclosed until Hardwick's fields were treated in 1853.[88] In 1601 some parishioners held meadow strips west of Barley Park, 'staked out from Lew mead' but apparently tithable to Ducklington.[89] Other early meadows, perhaps not commonable, included one at Coursehill.[90]

Much of the common meadow was apportioned by lot:[91] in 1601 the glebe meadow was mostly described as fixed pieces, but the same pieces c. 1689 lay in Upper, Lower, and Yelford meads 'according as the meadow runs'.[92] Some Ducklington yardlands included 3 or 4 acres of lot meadow, presumably the 'yard meads' mentioned in connexion with several other Ducklington holdings.[93] The Moors, c. 66 a. north of the village, was possibly common meadow before its inclosure in or before the 17th century: it comprises long, narrow closes lying across a central watercourse, perhaps indicating artificially 'floated' meadows. Moor closes, created before 1670,[94] were attached to various Ducklington holdings which, when first granted as manorial leaseholds in 1587, had common rights but no meadow in severalty. Many of the closes were of 3 a. or 6 a., suggesting that the partition observed the traditional meadow quotas of Ducklington's yardlands.[95]

In 1086 both parts of Ducklington manor had woodland 3 furlongs by 2 furlongs.[96] Since the later Boys and Home woods may already have been transferred to Standlake manor,[97] Ducklington's woodland may have been in the Barley Park area. It was presumably the 'wood towards Bampton' held by Guy de Dive, lord of Ducklington, c. 1200.[98] By the 1240s William de Dive had an inclosed wood or park there with assarts and uninclosed woodland to the south where manorial tenants had grazing rights. An attempt to inclose or impark the 'foreign' or uninclosed wood was opposed by Eynsham abbey, and Dive agreed to desist unless the abbot gave leave;[99] the foreign wood remained uninclosed in 1328.[1] The manorial park was mentioned regularly from the 13th century,[2] usually carrying a low value since only underwood and pannage were included.[3]

Barley Park was so called by the 15th century, and poaching there by Oxford scholars was recorded in 1506.[4] By the early 16th century the lords of Ducklington paid £1 6s. 8d. a year to

73 Wadham Coll. Mun., 86/29, 50, 123–4; ibid. 35/27–8.
74 O.R.O., Standlake incl. award; Wadham Coll. Mun., 86/46E, 64–7.
75 Wadham Coll. Mun., 86/85–6, 92, 95.
76 e.g. Davis, *Oxon. Map* (1797).
77 The pre-inclosure fields may be located only approximately from O.R.O., incl. award. Cf. map on p. 129 and, for observed ridge and furrow, M. Aston and T. Rowley, *Landscape Arch.* 135.
78 *Cal. Close, 1327–30,* 377.
79 *Eynsham Cart.* i, pp. 159–61, 193–4; *Cal. Close, 1327–30,* 372. For Eynsham's estate, above, manors (Claywell).
80 O.R.O., Welch LXVIII/3, 5.
81 Above, intro.
82 *V.C.H. Oxon.* i. 414, 425.
83 Below, this section.
84 *V.C.H. Oxon.* i. 414, 425.
85 O.R.O., MS. d.d. Par. Duckl. b 9.
86 Ibid. incl. award and map, plot 265.
87 *Cal. Close, 1327–30,* 377; O.R.O., incl. award, private roads (Seal Ham road).

88 O.R.O., incl. award and map; cf. Standlake incl. map B.
89 Ibid. MS. Oxf. Archd. Oxon. b 40, f. 119.
90 e.g. P.R.O., SC 6/961/15.
91 e.g. O.R.O., Peake II/iv/1, relating to Upper and Lower meads.
92 O.R.O., MS. Oxf. Archd. Oxon. b 40, ff. 118–19.
93 e.g. ibid. Peake XX/x/1–2; cf. ibid. II/iv/1, where 3¼ yardlands seems to have 13 a. of meadow.
94 Longleat Ho., NMR 3315, s.a. 1670.
95 O.R.O., Misc. Cox I/15; ibid. Peake II/iv/1–2; ibid. Welch LXVIII/1–5; ibid. incl. award; Bodl. MS. Ch. Oxon. c 81, no. 5291; O.S. Map 1/2,500, Oxon. XXXI. 12 (1876 edn.); ibid. *Area Bk.* (1877).
96 *V.C.H. Oxon.* i. 414, 425.   97 Above, intro.
98 *Eynsham Cart.* i, pp. 160–1.
99 Ibid. i, pp. 184–5, 193–4; P.R.O., JUST 1/699, m. 22v.
1 *Cal. Close, 1327–30,* 377–8.
2 e.g. *Cal. Pat. 1258–66,* 541; *Bampton Hund. R.* 541.
3 P.R.O., C 132/41, no. 5; C 134/21, no. 2; C 139/6, no. 51; *Cal. Close, 1327–30,* 377–8.
4 e.g. *Cal. Pat. 1485–94,* 25; *Reg. Magd. Coll.* N.S. i. 44.

the lords of Bampton for land taken into the park, presumably the *c.* 25 a. of park said to be in or near the park but 'in Bampton' in the 17th century.[5] Its location is uncertain, but part of Edgeley coppice (later Moulden's wood) was described in 1839 as lying in Ducklington or Lew and Bampton.[6] The wood seems to have been brought within the park pale, as were, presumably, the medieval uninclosed wood and grazing ground in the south, where the pale evidently abutted directly on the arable of Claywell and Middle fields.[7] From the 1520s Thomas Lawley (d. 1549), parker to successive lords of Ducklington, restored and restocked the park: the work included quicksetting 1,000 perches of deer fence and repairing the park lodge.[8] When sold by the Crown in 1545 the park was 'fully replenished with the king's deer' and contained *c.* 120 a. of woodland, divided into several coppices, mostly 'oaken spires' and maple of between 10 and 36 years' growth.[9] In 1601 the park was reckoned to contain *c.* 330 a., of which 110 a. were woodland;[10] at its fullest extent the park comprised nearer 375 a.[11]

In the 17th century former demesne pastures at Great Coursehill were planted, becoming later Great Heath plantation (*c.* 17 a.).[12] In the 1690s Edgeley coppice (Moulden's wood) was separated from Barley Park where, in the the 18th century, additional plantations were made.[13] Davis's coppice, north of Moulden's wood, was presumably planted in the mid 18th century by one of the Davises, prominent Ducklington residents.[14] In Cokethorpe Park the Harcourts planted coppices and peripheral belts in the mid 18th century,[15] and in the 1750s acquired Barley Park and parts of Moulden's wood and Coursehill plantation;[16] at or before inclosure in 1839 the Stricklands of Cokethorpe acquired all the woodland in the parish.[17]

In the 1760s most of the woodland was cut on a 10-year cycle.[18] Oak and elm predominated and were sold regularly from the Cokethorpe estate in the 19th century.[19] At inclosure and in the 1870s there were *c.* 160 a. of woodland in Ducklington;[20] the Standlake part of Cokethorpe Park contained another 70 a. of woodland, excluding Boys wood (73 a.) which the Stricklands held on lease from the lords of Yelford.[21] The Cokethorpe estate kept the woods in hand throughout the 19th century, but in 1919 sold those in the north-west of the parish with the

surrounding farmland.[22] The woodland area was reduced in the 20th century, notably by the removal of Great Heath plantation and the southern tip of Barley Park wood.[23]

Hardwick's open fields were intermixed from an early date with those of Brighthampton, Yelford, and Standlake. When the shared fields were inclosed in 1853 the *c.* 450 a. of open-field holdings deemed to be in Hardwick[24] included arable in Brighthampton's West field and Standlake's South field. The greatest concentration, however, was in Hardwick field, which occupied perhaps 190 a. south of Cokethorpe Park between the hamlet and Breach Farm. Hardwick field was divided into Wood (earlier Long Hedge) and Church fields in the north-west and north-east, and Hale and Dry (or Costall Bush) fields in the south-west and south-east.[25] Many Hardwick holdings lay in Yelford field, since from the 16th century or earlier the uninclosed part of Yelford parish had been treated, except for tithe, as an integral part of Hardwick's fields.[26]

In 1086 Wadard's Brighthampton estate, later probably part of Hardwick manor, included 16 a. of meadow.[27] Later Hardwick's common meadows lay chiefly on the river Windrush in Rough meadow, Up meadow, and Underdown, some of them lot meadows shared with Standlake, and there were also meadow holdings in Yelford meadow and the Marshes (adjoining Shifford boundary stream).[28] No pasture was mentioned in 1086 but until inclosure Hardwick had a large common (over 120 a.) south of the hamlet, sometimes called Hardwick Great Moor.[29] In the shared fields the inhabitants of Hardwick, Brighthampton, Standlake, and Yelford had common rights over most of the fallow and stubble; many of the meadows were commonable after Lammas.[30] In the mid 16th century Hardwick men complained of exclusion from their traditional Lammas grazing for sheep on Standlake Down and for cattle in Volnhurst: both belonged to Standlake but were intercommoned.[31] Hardwick men apparently had no rights on Standlake common, and likewise Hardwick common was exclusive to their cattle.[32] In the 16th and 17th centuries stints for a yardland were usually 10 draught cattle, 4 horses, 6 pigs, and 50 cattle; none were allowed more than 2 geese.[33] By the later 18th century

5   P.R.O., SC 6/Hen. VIII/6066, 7247; ibid. C 142/333, no. 24; B.L. Add. MS. 27535, f. 44; Bodl. MS. Ch. Oxon. a 30, no. 666; O.R.O., Duckl. tithe award.
6   O.R.O., incl. award, s.v. Leake, Chas.
7   Ibid. incl. award and map.
8   *L. & P. Hen. VIII, Addenda,* i, p. 148; P.R.O., SC 6/Hen. VIII/6066, 7247–50; E 315/273, f. 49.
9   Ibid. E 318/15/725.
10   O.R.O., MS. Oxf. Archd. Oxon. b 40, f. 119.
11   Cf. O.R.O., incl. award; O.S. Map 1/2,500, Oxon. XXXI.16 (1876 edn.); O.S. *Area Bk.* (1877).
12   O.R.O., Peake II/iv/1, II/v/1, II/vi/1.
13   Above, other estates.
14   O.R.O., incl. map. For the Davises, above, other estates.
15   Above, manors (Cokethorpe).
16   Above, other estates; Bodl. MS. d.d. Harcourt c 300, pps. *re* sale of Cokethorpe.
17   O.R.O., incl. award and map.
18   Bodl. MS. d.d. Harcourt c 300, pps. *re* sale of Cokethorpe.
19   e.g. *Oxf. Jnl.* 10 Jan. 1801, 10 Dec. 1803, 27 Apr. 1805;

Witney Express, 16 Mar. 1871.
20   Cf. O.R.O., incl. map; O.S. *Area Bk.* (1877).
21   O.S. *Area Bk.* (1877).; O.R.O., Standlake tithe award. For Boys wood, below, Standlake, econ. hist. (agric.).
22   *Sale Cat. Duckl. and Hardwick* (1919): copy in C.O.S.
23   O.S. Map 1/25,000, SP 20/30 (1978 edn.).
24   Excluding a few old inclosures declared allotable.
25   O.R.O., Standlake incl. award and maps. For earlier names, Wadham Coll. Mun., 86/123–4.
26   Below, Yelford, intro.
27   *V.C.H. Oxon.* i. 405.
28   O.R.O., Standlake incl. award and maps; St. John's Coll. Mun., XVII.45. For the shared meadows, below, Standlake, econ. hist. (agric.).
29   O.R.O., Standlake incl. award, map B.
30   Magd. Coll. Mun., D-Y 447.
31   P.R.O., E 321/11/25.
32   Magd. Coll. Mun., D-Y 447.
33   e.g. P.R.O., SC 2/197/43; St. John's Coll. Mun., XI.9–10, *passim*; XVII.14.

cow commons seem to have been reduced to 8 per yardland.[34]

Cokethorpe seems to have had no separate fields, and most holdings there, attached to Ducklington or Standlake manors,[35] comprised closes or woodland in the area of the later park. By the later 16th century 1½ yardland in the Ducklington part of Cokethorpe was made up entirely of arable and grass closes, most of them apparently in the north-eastern part of the later park.[36] Common rights attached to Cokethorpe holdings in the 16th century were presumably excercised in Hardwick or Ducklington.[37]

In 1086 the two parts of Ducklington manor together contained land for 10 ploughs, but 12 were in use, 5 on the demesne worked by 9 serfs and 7 held by tenants (13 villeins and 11 bordars). The value of the manor had risen from £10 at the Conquest to £13.[38] Additions to the demesne (*inhechinges*, possibly temporary hitchings) were mentioned in the 1170s.[39] In 1272 the demesne comprised 4 ploughlands, meadow and pasture worth £6, the park and its wood, and a dovecot and fishpond.[40] In 1295 and the early 14th century there were 3 ploughlands in demesne, estimated at 230 a. and 250 a. and conventionally valued at 4*d.* an acre; in 1328, however, *c.* 167 a. of demesne arable, probably two-thirds of the whole, was worth only 1½ *d.* (or 2*d.* if an assumed third was valueless fallow). Demesne meadow, variously 30 a. and 50 a., was worth 2*s.* an acre, and there was unspecified several pasture.[41] In 1372 the demesne arable was undiminished, since two-thirds of the manor contained 180 a.[42] In 1423 a third of the manor had 97 a. of demesne arable and 10 a. of meadow, but in 1430 demesne farming seems to have ceased on the other part of the manor: the site of a former manor house and all or most of the demesne was divided among several tenants.[43]

In 1272 there were 25 villein yardlands worth £20 a year on Ducklington manor, and freehold rents of over £13.[44] In 1279 the manor comprised over 40 yardlands, including land at Claywell, Putlesley, Eggesley, and Cokethorpe. Some 19½ yardlands were held by 23 freeholders and 19 single yardlands and 4 half yardlands were held by villeins; 43 a. were held by 5 cotters, and 18 a. of 'foreland' (possibly assarted land, worth 6*d.* an acre) was let to villeins.[45] On Eynsham abbey's Claywell manor, which included a demesne yardland at Putlesley, there were 4 villein yardlanders, and 3 or 4 half-yardlanders

who each held an additional 5 a.[46] Thus the fields of Ducklington contained some 50 yardlands, excluding 3 ploughlands of demesne and the glebe. In 1601 Ducklington was reckoned to contain 60¾ yardlands, including 2 yardlands of glebe.[47] A yardland containing only 20 a. seems to be implied in 1279,[48] but later yardlands were larger: the glebe in 1601 comprised some 54 field acres, and in 1771 an estate which in 1587 was 1½ yardland comprised 66 field acres (46 statute acres).[49]

Later surveys of Ducklington manorial holdings differed widely in detail but show a general fall in the combined value of rents and services between 1279 and the mid 14th century. Labour services in the early 14th century included 12 days' work at the hay harvest, probably 6 days' reaping and carrying corn, 1 day carrying wood, and some winter ploughing.[50] Overall manorial values were maintained into the later 14th century,[51] suggesting that disruption through plague was not prolonged. By the 1420s, however, values were seriously reduced; on the Lovels' third of the manor yardlands were yielding rents of only 5*s.* each, and on the other part rents were frequently reduced from the probably standard 12*s.* a yardland because of decay or lack of tenants. Holdings were usually of 1¼ yardland or less, and then demesne arable was divided between two tenants, the grassland between six.[52] By the 1480s the manor had risen in value to over £46[53] and in the early 16th century yielded over £40 gross, including £26 from copyholders and £14 13*s.* 4*d.* from Barley Park.[54]

In 1086 Wadard's Brighthampton estate had land for 1 plough, which was in demesne worked by 1 *servus*, 1 villein, and 5 bordars.[55] In 1279 the demesne, centred on Hardwick, still comprised 1 ploughland, which in 1295 included 100 a. worth 4*d.* an acre; there were 15 a. of demesne meadow and several pasture worth 10*s.* a year.[56] In 1312 the demesne arable was said to be only 60 a. worth 2*d.* an acre, but a proportionate reduction in reported grassland and tenant holdings suggests that only two thirds of the manor was included.[57] In 1279 the tenant land in the Hardwick part of the manor comprised 2½ yardlands held by 3 freeholders,[58] 5 yardlands held by 8 villeins, and 11 a. held by 3 cottars.[59] The standard rent for a villein yardland was 6*s.* 7*d.*, with services valued at 4*s.* 2½*d.*: in 1295 services included 27 days' work between Michaelmas and mid summer, with additional weeding, mowing, haymaking, and carrying, and boon works in the

34 St. John's Coll. Mun., XVII.45.
35 Above, manors (Cokethorpe).
36 Cf. Bodl. MS. Ch. Oxon. c 24, no. 3629; ibid. MS. d.d. Harcourt c 13/2–4.
37 B.N.C. Mun., Cokethorpe 1–9.
38 *V.C.H. Oxon.* i. 414, 425.
39 *Oseney Cart.* iv, p. 524.
40 P.R.O., C 132/41, no. 5.
41 *Bampton Hund. R.* 59; P.R.O., C 134/21, no. 2; C 135/1, no. 27; *Cal. Close,* 1327–30, 377–8.
42 P.R.O., C 135/228, no. 8.
43 Ibid. C 139/6, no. 51; ibid. E 142/84, no. 6.
44 Ibid. C 132/41, no. 5.
45 *Bampton Hund. R.* 59–62
46 Ibid. 61–2. Emma Lovel, recorded under Aston, should probably be included: ibid. 22; cf. *Eynsham Cart.* ii, pp. 12, 14.
47 O.R.O., MS. Oxf. Archd. Oxon. b 40, f. 119.

48 *Bampton Hund. R.* 12, 62, s.v. Baston.
49 O.R.O., MS. Oxf. Archd. Oxon. b 40, f. 119; ibid. Peake II/iii/1; II/iv/1, details of 'old estate'.
50 *Bampton Hund. R.* 59–62; P.R.O., C 134/21, no. 2; C 135/1, no. 27.
51 P.R.O., C 135/1, no. 27; C 135/228, no. 8.
52 Ibid. C 139/6, no. 51; ibid. E 142/84, no. 6.
53 *Cal. Pat.* 1485–94, 25.
54 Cf. P.R.O., SC 6/Hen. VIII/6066, 7247–50; ibid. E 318/15/725.
55 *V.C.H. Oxon.* i. 405.
56 *Bampton Hund. R.* 63; P.R.O., C 133/72, no. 6.
57 P.R.O., C 134/29, no. 11.
58 *Bampton Hund. R.* 63: one ½ yardland may have been in Yelford.
59 *Bampton Hund. R.* 63–4: Beard mill, included as a Hardwick cottar holding, lay in Standlake: below, Standlake, econ. hist. (mills).

corn harvest. Tenants also paid aid and churchscot.[60] Later manorial surveys do not distinguish between Hardwick and Brighthampton tenants.[61] In 1423 the manor contained 15 houses, 2 cottages, and 18 yardlands, mostly valued at 5s. a yardland; there seems to have been a small quantity of residual demesne.[62]

Before the mid 16th century Hardwick's demesne, reputedly 7 yardlands, was divided among the tenants in pieces called berrydells (presumably bury doles) of 4½ a.; some tenants had meadow pieces, perhaps also former demesne.[63] After the partition of the manor in the mid 16th century the holdings centred on Hardwick passed to St. John's College, except for two which had been sold from the manor in 1569 and passed later to Wadham College;[64] freeholders paid quitrents to St. John's, many of them presumably for land in Brighthampton. In the later 16th century the 7 Hardwick copyholds of St. John's comprised some 4 yardlands with a few other acres and berrydells, and the later Wadham holding comprised 2 yardlands.[65] Hardwick in 1601 was reckoned to contain c. 10 yardlands.[66] The Hardwick yardland was reputedly 35 customary acres, but most seem to have been smaller.[67]

By the early 14th century Ducklington's demesne arable, although dispersed widely over the fields, lay in blocks of up to 25 a. in some furlongs.[68] By then there may have been a three-yearly rotation of crops, since a claim to half the tithes of a piece of land in Claywell was also expressed as a right to tithe of the first harvest after the fallow.[69] In 1372 a third of the demesne arable lay fallow and in common.[70] Crop rotation in Hardwick's fields probably followed that in the partly intermixed fields of Standlake.[71]

The average value of moveables taxed in Ducklington and Claywell in the early 14th century varied from c. 47s. 6d. in 1316 to c. 36s. in 1327; in Hardwick in 1306 the average value was c. 36s., and the rise when Hardwick was later assessed with Brighthampton and Yelford suggests that the wealthier tenants of the joint manor lived in those other settlements.[72] In Ducklington in 1316 the highest contributors, two members of the Dive family, manorial lords, together paid over £1 on goods worth £16 13s. 4d.; 15 paid less than 2s. and only four above 4s. In Claywell the range of payments was narrower, between 18d. and 7s., with only three below 2s.

and 11 between 2s. and 4s. Hardwick's chief contributor in 1306 was Joan de Grey, lady of the manor, who paid 5s. of the total 19s. 1d.; 15 others paid between 4d. and 18d. on goods worth between 10s. and 45s.[73] From 1334 Ducklington's standard assessment was £5 15s. 3d., little more than half that of nearby Standlake, suggesting that it was not prosperous; by contrast Hardwick with its members (presumably Brighthampton and Yelford) was assessed at £7 5s.[74]

In 1523–4 Ducklington's total subsidy of only 17s. 4d. was paid by 11 contributors; Hardwick's 5s. 6d. was paid by 5 contributors and Cokethorpe's 2s. by two. There were no wealthy men, the highest assessment being on only £7 worth of goods.[75] In 1543–4 the 35 contributors in the three settlements paid a total £2 10s. 6d.; Robert Bullock of Cokethorpe paid on goods worth £14 and in Ducklington Richard Harris, whose family later owned one of the largest farms, paid on £12 worth.[76] In later 16th-century subsidies[77] a small group paid on goods worth between £3 and £10, the wealthiest being the Harrises, Thomas Wilshire, a miller, James Foster, whose house later became the Bayleys' manor house, and in Hardwick the Bullock and Edwards families.[78]

In 1587 Sir Christopher Brome broke up Ducklington manor by granting the copyholds and demesne, together some 47 yardlands, on 2,000-year leases for substantial initial payments and low fixed rents.[79] Twenty leaseholds were created,[80] the few known purchase prices ranging from £30 for a house and 1½ yardlands to £94 for a house and 3¾ yardlands.[81] Most leases seem to have been taken up by the existing copyholders. The largest comprised 6 yardlands, including 2½ yardlands of demesne;[82] at least 4 other leases were of 3 yardlands or more. Later the long-leasehold tenure caused legal uncertainty:[83] in 1627 one leasehold estate was thought to be held in chief[84] and intermittently the leaseholds were valued, as 'chattel leases', with a testator's personalty.[85] After an Act of 1881 the tenure was treated as freehold.[86]

Each yardland in 1587, including those on the demesne, was granted with one share in the manor's common pasture, which was notionally to be divided into 47¼ parts, presumably representing the yardlands with surviving shares.[87] The discrepancy between that figure and the reputed 60¾ yardlands in Ducklington in 1601[88]

60 *Bampton Hund. R.* 63–4; P.R.O., C 133/72, no. 6.
61 P.R.O., C 133/72, no. 6; C 134/29, no. 11.
62 Ibid. C 139/12, no. 36.
63 St. John's Coll. Mun., XVII.14.
64 Above, other estates.
65 Cf. St. John's Coll. Mun., XVII.5, 14, 16; Wadham Coll. Mun., 86/3.
66 O.R.O., MS. Oxf. Archd. Oxon. b 40, f. 119.
67 St. John's Coll. Mun., XVII.14.
68 *Cal. Close,* 1327–30, 377–8.
69 D. & C. Exeter, MS. 2931.
70 P.R.O., C 135/228, no. 8.
71 Below, Standlake, econ. hist. (agric.).
72 P.R.O., E 179/161/8–10.
73 Ibid.
74 Glasscock, *Subsidy 1334,* 237.
75 P.R.O., E 179/161/172–3.
76 Ibid. E 179/162/223, 234.
77 e.g. ibid. E 179/162/320, 321, 341, 345, 398.

78 For Wilshire's mill, below econ. hist. (mills); for the Bayleys, above, manors.
79 For comparable ventures, *Agric. Hist. Eng. and Wales,* iv, ed. J. Thirsk, 486. For the extent of the estate, below.
80 P.R.O., C 142/333, no. 23, naming the original lessees.
81 The chief refs. to original leases are O.R.O., SL/9/02/3D/01,07; ibid. Peake II/i/1, II/iii/1, II/v/1, II/vii/1, II/x/2; Bodl. MSS. Ch. Oxon. a 30, no. 668; c 24, nos. 3629–30; P.R.O., C 3/408/165.
82 For the Harris holding, above, other estates.
83 Cf. A. W. B. Simpson, *Hist. Land Law,* 234.
84 P.R.O., C 142/436, no. 44.
85 e.g. O.R.O., MSS. Wills Oxon. 86/4/46, 87/5/5, 156/3/25.
86 Conveyancing and Law of Property Act, 44 & 45 Vic. c 41, s. 65; cf. Bodl. G.A. Oxon. b 90 (23), conditions of sale.
87 e.g. O.R.O., Peake II/i/1, for a tortuous definition of lessees' common rights.
88 O.R.O., MS. Oxf. Archd. Oxon. b 40, f. 119.

may be accounted for partly by the yardlands in Claywell manor.[89] Perhaps common rights attached to freehold yardlands were excluded from the notional division; certainly the total of quitrents from some 26 yardlands in 1587, compared with the total from all leaseholds in 1716,[90] suggests that all or most of the 47¼ yardlands were former copyhold and demesne. Some ancient freehold quitrents recorded in 1716[91] were for inclosed holdings in Barley Park and elsewhere which may have had no common rights; others, however, were for open-field holdings, notably 6d. paid by Nicholas Wansell, which was for 4 yardlands which had certainly included common rights.[92]

The creation of leaseholds may have been followed rapidly by a partition and inclosure of common pasture, as well as of the Moors mentioned above. In 1587 all the new leaseholds had shares in the common pasture at Coursehill in the north-west of the parish.[93] Great Coursehill included a piece of several pasture, partly wooded and probably former demesne, which was commonable by all manorial tenants between Lammas and Lady Day; by 1615, however, it had been newly ditched and divided off from the rest of Coursehill and by 1705 was evidently an inclosed coppice (the later Great Heath plantation) offering no common rights.[94] Its owners, the Ballows, had by then also acquired in severalty Little Coursehill (c. 10 a.), identifiable as Heath close in the extreme north-west corner of the parish.[95] A close called New close in 1619 may be identified as part of the later Oxfar close north of Coursehill Farm.[96] Immediately west in 1619 was part of Ducklington Cow Leys, presumably common pasture but by the later 17th century an inclosed piece of glebe.[97] Other early closes held in severalty in the Coursehill area were first mentioned in the 17th century,[98] and closes further east may date from the same period.[99] By the early 19th century there was no common pasture, and the entire northern fringe of the parish comprised pasture closes.[1]

The acquisition of leaseholds in 1587 presumably confirmed the position of the small group of wealthier farmers. In 1610 the resident lord was assessed on land worth £14, 5 farmers on goods worth between £3 and £6, and 4 on lands worth £1; in Hardwick William Edwards, owner of the later Wadham estate, paid on land worth £4 and 2 men on land worth £1.[2] The range of

payments in 1628 was very similar.[3] In 1662, when 51 householders in Ducklington and Claywell paid tax on 132 hearths, as many as 40 paid on 3 hearths or less. The larger houses were the rectory (12 hearths), the manor house (8), and the Harris family's house (7), and there were a few substantial farmhouses in the village, in the Ducklington part of Cokethorpe, and at Claywell.[4]

Several farmers, mostly yeomen, left personalty worth over £200 at their deaths. The more valuable inventories included those of farmers in Claywell and Cokethorpe as well as Ducklington, and of members of the Green family of Ducklington blacksmiths.[5] Thomas Saunders of Cokethorpe (d. 1614) and Thomas Barker of Ducklington (d. 1706), both active farmers, made very large cash bequests, the latter's approaching £1,000.[6] Besides manorial lords such as the Bayleys and Stonehouses several testators, including the Johnsons in Ducklington, were styled gentlemen, owned small estates elsewhere, and made substantial bequests.[7]

Mixed farming was general on farms both large and small. The owner of one of the larger 16th-century flocks (160) also kept cows, bullocks, and oxen; one of the principal early 17th-century farmers grew wheat, barley, maslin, pulse, and hay, and had 120 sheep, a dairy herd worth £45, 12 pigs, and 8 horses.[8] Flocks of c. 250 sheep were recorded at Claywell in 1663 and Ducklington in 1706.[9] The tenant of the large Farm estate at Cokethorpe in the early 18th century grew much wheat and barley, but also kept many sheep and cattle.[10] Some testators had small quantities of flax and hemp, or stocks of bees.[11] Malt and malting equipment were recorded regularly, and at Hardwick in 1680 there was a maltster.[12] Other specialists, besides the wealthy blacksmiths, included several shoemakers, wheelwrights, and weavers, a glover, a tanner, and a fellmonger, the last also selling drapery and hosiery.[13] Thomas Edgerley of Hardwick (d. 1620), called yeoman but also a carrier or 'far carter',[14] had teams of horses and trading contacts in London, Burford, and elsewhere; his son Thomas moved to Oxford and was appointed London carrier to the university.[15]

By 1716 Ducklington manor had 22 leaseholders and 10 freeholders; most estates were evidently unaltered from 1587, and at least 7 were held by the families of original lessees.[16] The number of farms in Ducklington hardly changed between 1601, when 2 yardlands of glebe scattered in the

89 Bodl. MS. d.d. Harcourt c 109/6.
90 Ibid. b 5, f. 3v.   91 Ibid. ff. 3v.–4.
92 Cf. ibid. MS. Top. Oxon. d 46, f. 30; Magd. Coll. Mun., Misc. 413.
93 e.g. O.R.O., Peake II/i/1, II/iv/1.
94 Ibid. II/iv/1, II/v/1, II/vi/1.
95 Ibid. II/iv/1–2; O.R.O., Duckl. tithe map, plot 160.
96 Cf. ibid. Peake II/iv/1, II/vii/1, ibid. Duckl. tithe map, plot 152.
97 Cf. Ibid. Peake II/vii/1; ibid. tithe map, plot 153; ibid. MS. Oxf. Archd. Oxon. b 40, f. 118, ref. to 'several ground' of 4 a. with Hen. Ballow on the north (sic).
98 Bodl. MS. Top. Oxon. d 46, f. 30; P.R.O., C 142/436, no. 44; O.R.O., tithe map, plots 167, 172.
99 Bodl. MS. Top. Oxon. c 81, no. 5291; O.R.O., Peake II/iv/2; ibid. tithe map, plots 142, 144.
1 O.R.O., incl. award and map.
2 P.R.O., E 179/163/435.   3 Ibid. E 179/164/476.
4 Ibid. E 179/255/4. No return for Hardwick has been found.

5 O.R.O., MSS. Wills Oxon. 27/2/29, 41/4/16, 83/2/30, 116/2/19, 138/3/17, 166/2/18, 297/5/21. For values inflated by chattel leases, ibid. 8/2/21, 86/4/46, 87/5/5, 137/2/4, 156/3/25.
6 P.R.O., PROB 11/123, f. 290v.; O.R.O., MS. Wills Oxon. 116/2/19.
7 O.R.O., MSS. Wills Oxon. 53/3/8, 137/1/52, 137/2/4, 207, f. 25v.; P.R.O., PROB 11/457, f. 233 and v.
8 O.R.O., MSS. Wills Oxon. 183, f. 391; 297/5/21.
9 Ibid. 41/4/16, 116/2/19.
10 Ibid. 138/3/17.
11 Ibid. 60/2/32, 86/2/15, 148/3/12.
12 Ibid. 37/4/7, 34/1/32.
13 Ibid. 81/1/21.
14 Witney Ct. Bks. 167, 176.
15 O.R.O., MS. Wills Oxon. 164/4/8: inventory dated 1625; Reg. Univ. Oxf. ii (1), ed. A. Clark (O.H.S. x), 316, 405.
16 Cf. Bodl. MS. d.d. Harcourt b 5, ff. 3v.–4; P.R.O., C 142/333, no. 23.

open fields abutted the lands of 17 owners, and 1771, when an estate of comparable size abutted the lands of 16 owners.[17]

In the early 18th century most of the farmland attached to the Cokethorpe estate was let: former demesne meadows in Standlake (some 40 a.) were divided among several tenants,[18] and a 3-yardland holding in Ducklington was let separately until the 1750s when it was included in the lease of Barley Park farm;[19] most of the farmland, however, formed the Farm estate, worked from a house (probably Peck's) in the Ducklington part of Cokethorpe.[20] In 1714 the Farm included c. 20 a. of closes in Ducklington, most on the east side of the later park, c. 132 a. in Standlake, chiefly closes around the later Breach Farm and in the later park, and a little open-field land and lot meadow in Ducklington, Hardwick, and Standlake.[21] Leases of the Farm were recorded until the late 1730s,[22] but by the 1750s much was in hand, having probably been taken into the park. The farmhouse near the chapel was removed, the residual farmland presumably being worked from Breach Farm, where there were buildings by 1767.[23]

Hardwick's farms in the 18th century were small: the three principal holdings of St. John's College were all under 50 a., Wadham College's estate was c. 52 a., and the Hardwick part of Cokethorpe's Farm estate was probably smaller.[24] The Mountains, however, lessees of the Wadham estate and undertenants of the St. John's copyhold centred on the later Manor Farm,[25] may have worked the holdings as a single farm.

Some of Ducklington's holdings remained intact from the 16th century until inclosure,[26] but the formation of larger farms began in the later 18th century. The former Harris estate, owned by the Davises and probably worked from the later Manor Farm,[27] remained one of the largest farms: in 1782 its 320 estimated acres included 236 a. of open-field arable and 80 a. of closes, mostly grass.[28] When Barley Park became part of the Cokethorpe estate in the 1750s it contained an established farm of c. 148 a., which was enlarged before 1755 by purchase of adjacent holdings.[29] Closes north of the park, acquired by the Cokethorpe estate in 1752 and at first let separately,[30] seem to have been merged in the 400-acre Barley Park farm by the 1780s.[31] Other farms of over 100 a.[32] included Claywell farm,

much of it old inclosure, the later Yew Tree farm, and a farm, chiefly the Locktons' ancient leasehold, probably worked from a farmhouse at the east end of Back Lane.[33] The Druce family built up and let a farm of c. 105 a., the core of the later Ducklington farm. By 1819 Walter Strickland of Cokethorpe held some 600 a. in the parish, keeping 140 a. of woods and park in hand; Barley Park farm was let with c. 210 a., and 250 a. were let to Samuel Druce and John Nalder, who owned other Ducklington farms. Nalder's own farm, the later Manor farm, was the largest outside the Cokethorpe estate; Strickland bought it before inclosure, along with many smaller Ducklington holdings.[34]

Mixed farming continued even on farms with much inclosed grassland. On the Cokethorpe estate in the earlier 18th century many of the closes later imparked were used for cereals.[35] Adherence to 'the old dull beaten road' was blamed for the poor husbandry on the estate in the 1730s.[36] Later the parish's extensive inclosed pastures encouraged some specialisation: soon after the Harcourts acquired Barley Park they had a flock of 800 sheep there.[37] In 1801 it was reported that of Ducklington's estimated 1,980 a. only 514 a. (26 per cent) was arable and as much as 1,310 a. (66 per cent) permanent grass; Hardwick's 473 a. were fairly evenly divided, with 259 a. (55 per cent) arable.[38] If the figures for Ducklington were reliable much was converted to tillage before 1819 when 956 a. of arable and only 801 a. of grass were reported. By the 1830s Ducklington was reckoned to comprise 1,898 a., with 1,000 a. of arable, 880 a. of it in the open fields; there were 600 a. of pasture closes, 194 a. of common meadow, and over 100 a. of woodland. The arable, assuming a four-course rotation of crops, was valued at £4 an acre if the crops were turnips, barley, beans, and wheat, and c. £3 if the course included a fallow year. The common meadow and inclosed pasture was valued at £2 an acre, the woodland at £1.[39]

Inclosure, planned from 1819 but several times deferred,[40] was completed for Ducklington township in 1839; at the same time tithes were commuted.[41] The award treated an area of 1,882 a., allotting c. 1,057 a. of open-field land; some 12 a. in detached, intercommoned meadows (Wagg's ham and Yelford mead) were left

[17] O.R.O., MS. Oxf. Archd. Oxon. b 40, f. 119; ibid. Peake II/iv/2.
[18] Bodl. MS. d.d. Harcourt b 8, pp. 14–18; c 267, passim.
[19] Ibid. b 5, f. 3, s.v. Bedwell's; c 134/1, p. 18; c 144/1, p. 14.
[20] Ibid. c 300, lease of 1724 citing earlier lease; ibid. c 13/2–4. For Peck, ibid. c 262 (R); above, manors (Cokethorpe).
[21] Cf. Bodl. MSS. d.d. Harcourt c 300, lease of 1724; c 13/2–4, for acreages.
[22] Ibid. c 300, lease of 1724; b 8, pp. 15–18; c 263, rental c. 1737 and passim.
[23] Ibid. c 263, rentals 1747 and later; Jefferys, Oxon. Map (1767).
[24] St. John's College Mun., XVII.45; Wadham Coll. Mun., 86/124; O.R.O., land tax assess. 1785–1831.
[25] e.g. Wadham Coll. Mun., 86/53–9; St. John's Coll. Mun., XVII.45.
[26] Cf. Bodl. MSS. d.d. Harcourt b 8, p. 17: quitrents 1727; c 133/2, p. 12: quitrents 1754; O.R.O., land tax assess. 1785–1831; ibid. Duckl. tithe award and incl. award.
[27] Above, other estates.
[28] Bodl. MS. Ch. Oxon. c 81, no. 5291.
[29] Bodl. MSS. d.d. Harcourt c 300, pps. re sale of Cokethorpe; c 134/1, p. 18. For the earlier farm, ibid. MS. Top. Oxon. b 78, f. 28.
[30] Bodl. MSS. d.d. Harcourt c 300, corresp. 1751–2 re Ballows in pps. re sale of Cokethorpe; c 263, accts. 1753, 1757. For the closes, O.R.O., Peake II/ii–viii, passim.
[31] O.R.O., land tax assess. 1785–7; Oxf. Jnl. Synopsis, 1 Feb. 1783.
[32] The rest of this para. is based on O.R.O., land tax assess. 1785–1831; ibid. MS. d.d. Par. Duckl. b 9: tithe pps. 1819 sqq.; ibid. Duckl. tithe and incl. awards and maps.
[33] O.R.O., incl. award s.v. Pinkney and incl. map, plot 72.
[34] Ibid. incl. award s.v. Strickland. For Nalder, above, other estates.
[35] Bodl. MS. d.d. Harcourt b 5, ff. 45, 57v. sqq., 94v.
[36] Ibid. b 34.
[37] Ibid. c 133/2, pp. 54–5.
[38] P.R.O., HO 67/18.
[39] O.R.O., MS. d.d. Par. Duckl. b 9.
[40] Bodl. MS. Top. Oxon. b 78, ff. 117, 167–8.
[41] O.R.O., Duckl. tithe and incl. awards and maps.

uninclosed until Hardwick's inclosure in 1853.[42] The principal allottees, the Stricklands of Cokethorpe, after exchanges received over 600 a., bringing their total holding in the township to *c.* 1,035 a., including an in-hand estate of 275 a. which comprised the Ducklington part of Cokethorpe Park and most of the outlying woodland. Only 13 others had any stake in the open fields, some with a few acres, and only the Revd. J. H. Pinkney, a non-resident landlord, received over 100 a. for an estate combining two leaseholds which had survived largely intact from 1587.[43]

When Hardwick was inclosed in 1853 *c.* 585 a. of the township's 670 a. were allotted; the relatively few old inclosures were in and near the hamlet, around the later Manor Farm, and at Yelford.[44] The chief allotments, excluding the Yelford part of Hardwick, were to St. John's College (*c.* 158 a.),[45] to Walter Strickland of Cokethorpe (143 a.), and to Wadham College for its Hardwick farm (75 a.). Strickland had evidently enlarged his Hardwick holdings by buying up land shortly before inclosure, acquiring as much as 105 a. of freehold.[46] He was also lessee of St. John's College's Hardwick mill estate. Thomas Lee, a Ducklington solicitor related to the Alders, tenants of St. John's from the early 17th century,[47] received 27 a. for freehold; he also held the former Alder copyhold and a St. John's leasehold, making a post-inclosure farm of *c.* 100 a.

In Ducklington after inclosure the Cokethorpe estate's farmland was divided between Manor and Barley Park farms (both over 200 a.), Coursehill farm (144 a.), its farmhouse apparently under construction in 1839,[48] and a farm of 175 a. worked temporarily from a village farmhouse, probably the later Church Farm.[49] The fields of the last lay in a block north-west of Cokethorpe Park where, before 1851, Walter Strickland built Cokethorpe Park (later Home) Farm to serve his in-hand estate.[50] He continued to let Manor, Barley, and Coursehill farms, which in 1851 together comprised *c.* 650 a. and employed 28 labourers; Home farm, then and later, was usually managed by a bailiff.[51] Various rearrangements in the 1880s, including a temporary union of Home and Barley farms, were probably in response to the agricultural depression.[52] Barley and Coursehill were still large tenant farms in the late 19th century,[53] but

Manor farm, occupied by the Wilsdens from the 1840s until the 1930s, was reduced to only 110 a. when sold to Edwin Wilsden in 1919.[54] In that year most of the outlying parts of the Cokethorpe estate, first offered for sale in 1912, were sold: with their woodland Barley Park farm comprised over 350 a. and Coursehill 380 a.[55]

The chief Ducklington farms outside the Cokethorpe estate, all between 100 and 150 a. in 1839, were Claywell farm, the later Ducklington and Yew Tree farms worked from the village, and the unnamed farm owned by Pinkney, with farm buildings both at the later Windrush Farm and the east end of Back Lane.[56] By 1861 Claywell farm comprised 130 a.; in 1881 it was much larger, probably briefly, comprising 380 a. and employing 14 labourers, but by 1900 was reduced to its former size.[57] Ducklington farm, *c.* 160 a. in 1861 and *c.* 200 a. in the early 20th century, was acquired in 1862 by the Strainges, who farmed it from the house in Church Street for over a century before building a new farmhouse near Coursehill in the 1990s.[58] The later Yew Tree farm, 155 a. in 1861, was bought soon afterwards by J. S. Beaumont,[59] who in 1865 also bought the former Pinkney farm (132 a.);[60] Beaumont let some of his land but in 1871 was farming 225 a. from Yew Tree Farm and employing 13 labourers.[61] The Holtoms, millers and farmers at Ducklington mill, enlarged their farming interest in the later 19th century and by 1881 farmed 125 a.;[62] in the 1890s they bought most of Beaumont's estate centred on Yew Tree Farm,[63] but not Windrush Farm which continued as a separate small farm.[64] In the 20th century the outlying farms, particularly Home, Barley Park, and Coursehill took over most of the farmland in the parish. Of farms based in the village only Ducklington farm was over 150 a. by 1939; Yew Tree farm comprised only 124 a. in 1953.[65] The last working farmhouse, Ducklington Farm, continued in use until the 1980s.

In Hardwick the chief post-inclosure farms were College, later Manor farm, and three worked from farmhouses in the hamlet. The Mountains, farming between 130 and 150 a. at Manor farm,[66] held land from both St. John's and Wadham colleges; Wadham enlarged its estate to 98 a. by purchase in the 1860s.[67] The Lee estate at inclosure and into the 1860s was held by Charles Florey, who farmed some 120 a.

[42] Cf. ibid.; ibid. Standlake incl. award and map B; below, map on p. 172.
[43] For its earlier history, O.R.O., Peake II/i/1, II/ii/1, II/x, *passim*.
[44] O.R.O., Standlake incl. award.
[45] Including Lee's copyhold, which was held of the college.
[46] Cf. O.R.O. land tax assess. 1820–1831, when Strickland's holding seems to have been relatively small, and there were many small proprietors.
[47] St. John's Coll. Mun., XI.10–20, *passim*.
[48] O.R.O., Duckl. incl. and tithe awards and maps, plot 155.
[49] Ibid. plot 25.
[50] P.R.O., HO 107/1731.
[51] Ibid.; P.R.O., RG 9/906; RG 10/1452.
[52] Ibid. RG 11/1515; *Kelly's Dir. Oxon.* (1883).
[53] P.R.O., RG 12/1176; *Kelly's Dir. Oxon* (1891 and later edns.)
[54] C.O.S., par. reg. transcripts; *Sale Cat., Cokethorpe Estate* (1919): copy in C.O.S.
[55] Bodl. G.A. Oxon. b 90 (23); *Sale Cat., Cokethorpe Estate* (1919).

[56] O.R.O., Duckl. tithe award and map.
[57] P.R.O., RG 9/906; RG 11/1515; Bodl. G.A. Oxon. b 90 (25).
[58] P.R.O., RG 9/906; Bodl. G.A. Oxon. c 317/8: *Sale Cat.* (1861); ibid. MS. Top. Oxon. b 78, f. 236; O.R.O., MS. Oxf. Dioc. b 9, tithe receipts 1900–26; O.R.O., Welch LIII/1–12; ibid. District Valuation Surv. *c.* 1910; *P.O. Dir. Oxon.* (1864 and later edns.); local information.
[59] P.R.O., RG 9/906; *P.O. Dir. Oxon.* (1864 and later edns.); cf. O.R.O., Peake II/xiii/4.
[60] Cf. C.O.S., *Sale Cat., Duckl.* (1861); Bodl. MS. Top. Oxon. b 78, ff. 252–4, showing Beaumont's later estate.
[61] P.R.O., RG 10/1452.
[62] Ibid.; ibid. RG 11/1515.
[63] Bodl. MS. Top. Oxon. b 78, ff. 252–4. For the mill estate, ibid. f. 242.
[64] Ibid. ff. 252–4; O.R.O., District Valuation Surv. *c.* 1910; *Kelly's Dir. Oxon.* (1939).
[65] *Kelly's Dir. Oxon.* (1939); C.O.S., *Sale Cat.* (1953).
[66] e.g. P.R.O., HO 107/1731; RG 9/906; RG 10/1452.
[67] Wadham Coll. Mun., 86/60–8.

from a house on the south side of High Street.[68] Much of Strickland's large holding was held with Hardwick mill by Alfred Hickman, who in 1851 was farming 210 a.; later Mill farm, too, was held by the Mountain family.[69] Hardwick farm, some 70 a. of Strickland's land worked from a house on the north side of High Street and held by the Cosiers throughout the later 19th century, was sold from the Cokethorpe estate in 1919.[70] The agricultural depression seriously affected Hardwick in the 1880s, notably bankrupting the Mountains.[71] St. John's College bought many small cottages and united some of its holdings in a farm of c. 170 a. centred on Manor Farm, let to Robert Eagle, who was also Wadham's lessee.[72] Manor farm, later held by the Florey family, remained the principal farm in the 20th century.[73]

After inclosure most Ducklington farms were between 60 and 75 per cent arable, the extremes being Barley Park farm (only 45 per cent) and Ducklington farm (88 per cent).[74] By the 1870s, however, less than 60 per cent of the farmland was arable and by 1914 nearly three-quarters was permanent pasture.[75] In the later 19th century the chief crops were wheat, barley, beans, turnips, and vetches.[76] In 1914 half the arable area was under wheat and barley, and other main crops were oats (11 per cent), and turnips and mangolds (each 5 per cent). In the mid 19th century sheep and cattle from Strickland's Home farm were praised.[77] Sheep, dairy, and stock farming became predominant in the parish, but sheep numbers halved to only 38 per 100 a. in the early 20th century; by then pig numbers (9 per 100 a.) were high for the region.[78] Farms remained mixed, ranging from largely cereal farms such as Ducklington farm (70 per cent arable in 1888) and Manor farm (90 per cent arable in 1919) to Claywell farm (only 10 per cent arable in 1900) and the large dairy and stock-raising farms at Coursehill and Barley Park (43 and 20 per cent arable in 1919).[79] Later specialisation included pig farming at Coursehill and Claywell in the 1930s.[80]

Gravel pits and claypits in the parish were mentioned in 1601, and fuller's earth near Claywell was also exploited at that date.[81] In the 1760s a gravel pit in Hardwick was so enlarged that it was undermining the road.[82] In the early 19th century there was a brick kiln on the clays in the west of the parish.[83] Large-scale commercial gravel extraction, begun in the later 20th century, has chiefly affected the south-east of the parish around Hardwick.[84]

By the 19th century most inhabitants were employed in agriculture and related trades: 64 of the 104 families in Ducklington and Hardwick in 1831 were supported directly by agriculture,[85] which was reported in 1834 to provide full employment only in the summer. A labourers' income, even when supplemented by relief, was below 10s. a week; cottage rents were from £2 10s. a year, and allotments were let to 19 families.[86] In the 1860s some boys were employed on farms throughout the year, and women mostly in the summer.[87] In Ducklington in 1851, besides the usual range of craftsmen and shopkeepers, there were 3 sawyers and 2 woodmen, 3 fishermen, and, reflecting the influence of the Cokethorpe estate, several gamekeepers, gardeners, butlers, and other specialist servants. In Hardwick, except for such servants, the population was almost entirely engaged in agriculture.[88] In 1861 Ducklington's shopkeepers included 2 shoemakers, 2 bakers, a tailor, a wheeler, and a grocer. By 1881 there were 2 grocers in Ducklington and 1 in Hardwick. There was a small brewery in Ducklington, opened by the innkeeper of the Strickland Arms c. 1866 and closed by 1891.[89] In the later 19th century the agricultural trades included cattle and corn dealers and Ducklington mill became an important employer.[90]

Witney, particularly its textile industry, had long influenced Ducklington's economy, providing apprenticeships and other employment and encouraging fulling in Ducklington's mills.[91] In the 19th century, however, although the blanket factories reputedly drew employees from nearby villages,[92] few Ducklington inhabitants described themselves as weavers or factory workers, and almost all the labourers were agricultural.[93] Witney's importance to Ducklington increased in the 20th century as numbers employed in agriculture declined. In the 1920s most Ducklington men who were not farm labourers, and many girls, worked in Witney's mills; married women worked as out-workers for gloving factories in the area.[94] Since the Second World

68 O.R.O., Hardwick tithe award and map, plot 4021; P.R.O., HO 107/1731.
69 O.R.O., Hardwick tithe award; P.R.O., HO 107/1731; ibid. RG 11/1515; *Oxf. Chron.* 1 Nov. 1851, 11 Sept. 1852.
70 O.R.O., Hardwick tithe award; P.R.O., HO 107/1731; ibid. RG 12/1176; C.O.S., *Sale Cat. Duckl. and Hardwick* (1919).
71 Wadham Coll. Mun., 86/71–3; St. John's Coll. Mun., EST. I. L.104.
72 St. John's Coll. Mun., XV.50; XVII.60, 65, 81–5; ibid. EST. I. A.16, pp. 452–3 and *passim*; Wadham Coll. Mun., 86/74.
73 St. John's Coll. Mun., XVII.68a; *Kelly's Dir. Oxon.* (1915 and later edns.).
74 O.R.O., Duckl. tithe award.
75 O.S. *Area Bk.* (1877). Orr, *Oxon. Agric.*, maps.
76 e.g. *Oxf. Chron.* 4 Aug. 1860; *P.O. Dir. Oxon.* (1877); *Kelly's Dir. Oxon.* (1883 and later edns.).
77 *Oxf. Chron.* 25 Dec. 1852, 24 Dec. 1853.
78 Orr, *Oxon. Agric.*, maps.
79 Bodl. MS. Top. Oxon. b 78, f. 236; C.O.S., *Sale Cat. Cokethorpe Estate* (1919).
80 C.O.S., *Sale Cat. Duckl.* (1937); *Kelly's Dir. Oxon.* (1939).

81 O.R.O., MS. Oxf. Archd. Oxon. b 40, f. 119.
82 St. John's Coll. Mun., XI.19, p. 173.
83 O.R.O., MS. Oxf. Archd. Oxon. b 40, f. 119.
84 J. I. Millard, 'Lower Windrush Valley: the Cultural Heritage' (TS. 1991 in possession of Oxf. Arch. Unit), map 5.
85 *Census,* 1801–31.
86 *Rep. Com. Poor Laws,* H.C. 44, p. 371 (1834), xxx–xxxiv.
87 *Rep. Com. on Children and Women in Agric.* [4202-I], p. 329, H.C. (1868–9), xiii. The report was by Walter Strickland, whose land lay mostly in Ducklington, although many of his comments relate to Standlake: ibid. pp. 346, 350.
88 P.R.O., HO 107/1731.
89 Ibid. RG 9/906; O.R.O., MS. d.d. Par. Duckl. c 4, 25 May 1866; Magd. Coll. Mun., MS. 799 (iii), poster 16 Oct. 1891.
90 P.R.O., HO 107/1731.
91 e.g. *Witney Ct. Bks.* 145; below, this section.
92 A. Plummer and R. E. Early, *The Blanket Makers,* 8.
93 P.R.O., RG 9/906; RG 10/1452; RG 11/1515; RG 12/1176.
94 M. Harris, *A Kind of Magic, passim.*

War most of the greatly enlarged population has been employed outside the parish.

MILLS AND FISHERIES. In 1044 there was a mill weir at Ducklington at the point where Witney's boundary left the river Windrush to cross the Moors north of Ducklington;[95] the mill was probably that which, until the early 19th century, stood near the footbridge on the north side of the village.[96] Presumably it was the manorial mill which in 1086 rendered 12s. a year.[97] By 1279 freeholders on Ducklington manor held New mill, with a house and 2 a., and a mill with unspecified land; a third freeholder, John Miller, may also have held a mill with his house and yardland. At Cokethorpe, but held of Ducklington manor, was a fulling mill with a house and ½ yardland.[98] In 1311 Ducklington manor contained two corn mills and a fulling mill, the last perhaps Cokethorpe mill, mentioned in 1318, when its site was on the river Windrush apparently between Ducklington and Hardwick.[99] New mill was still so called in 1328, when it marked the limit of a fishery on the Windrush, and in 1601 when it was next to Ducklington's Upper Meadow and therefore presumably on the site of the surviving Ducklington mill, south-east of the village.[1] By the early 15th century there were 3 mills on the divided Ducklington manor.[2] From the later 16th century the reunited Ducklington manor contained only 2 mills,[3] probably those north and south-east of the village.

In 1587 both manorial water mills were let by Sir Christopher Brome on 2,000-year leases, one to Edward Harris, the other to Roger Wilshire; the lands attached to Harris's mill included New Mill close, implying that his was the later Ducklington mill.[4] It was still held by Harrises in the mid 17th century and may have passed later to the Quinneys,[5] who certainly acquired the other mill, of which they were tenants, in 1694.[6] In the 1750s the Quinneys were succeeded in one or both mill leases by William Leake and before 1785 by John Leake.[7] At inclosure in 1839 Charles Leake held both Ducklington mill and the site of the mill on the north side of the village.[8] That mill, demolished by 1838, was known variously as Coxeter's, after a mid 18th-

century mortgager,[9] and Smith's and Knipe's after late 18th- and early 19th-century lessees or millers.[10] It was a fulling mill in the later 18th century, and was described as a tucking mill in 1823; it was presumably the watermill, for sale in 1828, which was used for spinning in connexion with blanket manufacture.[11]

Ducklington mill, a water corn mill with 2 pairs of stones in 1838, had been worked for much of the later 18th century by the Hudson family and later by William Wright.[12] Non-resident owners sublet the mill with attached cottages and c. 80 a. of land until 1894,[13] when it was sold to G. H. Holtom, miller there since 1867.[14] Flax-processing equipment was said to have been installed c. 1838, but in 1853 the machinery comprised only 3 pairs of stones powered by an iron water wheel.[15] In 1885 the mill was partly converted for flour rolling, and in 1898 Holtom & Sons built a large 3-storeyed rolling plant, with a steam engine to supplement the water-power; the old mill remained in use for grinding barley and maize.[16] Holtom & Sons continued at the mill until the 1950s, when W. J. Oldacre Ltd. converted it for the processing of animal feeds.[17] The old mill and the building of 1898 were demolished in 1983 and a new feed mill and warehousing (extended in 1985) built for the storage of E.C. grain. In the 1980s the firm employed c. 40 people. The feed mill closed in 1992 but grain storage continued. The mill house, of unknown date but built before 1839 on a site immediately north of the mill, was demolished in the mid 20th century.[18]

By 1279 there were two mills on Hardwick and Brighthampton manor;[19] one, Beard or Under-down mill, came to belong to Standlake parish,[20] the other was presumably the later Hardwick mill. In 1295 the manor contained two water corn mills and a fulling mill, in 1312 one corn mill and a fulling mill, and in 1423 two water mills;[21] the respective functions of Hardwick and Beard mills at that date are not known.

By the 16th century Hardwick mill was a copyhold of the manor, held with 1 yardland and some meadows.[22] St. John's College, Oxford, owners from 1571, changed the tenure to lease-hold in 1743.[23] In the 1560s the miller was presented in the manorial court for excessive

95 *P.N. Oxon.* (E.P.N.S.), ii. 490.
96 O.R.O., incl. award and map, plot 65.
97 *V.C.H. Oxon.* i. 414.
98 *Bampton Hund. R.* 59–60, 62.
99 P.R.O., C 134/21, no. 2; *Cal. Close,* 1307–13, 312; D. & C. Exeter, MS. 2865.
1 *Cal. Close,* 1327–30, 377; O.R.O., MS. Oxf. Archd. Oxon. b 40, f. 119.
2 P.R.O., C 139/6, no. 51; ibid. E 142/84, no. 6.
3 e.g. P.R.O., CP 25/2/197/29 Eliz. I/Mich.; ibid. CP 25/2/957/11 Anne Mich.
4 Bodl. MS. Ch. Oxon. c 24, no. 3630; P.R.O., C 5/408/165.
5 P.R.O., C 5/408/165; C 5/625/62.
6 Bodl. MS. Ch. Oxon. c 24, no. 3630.
7 Ibid.; Bodl. MS. d.d. Harcourt c 133/2, leasehold quitrents 1754–5; ibid. c 263, leasehold quitrents 1757; O.R.O., land tax assess. 1785–1831.
8 O.R.O., incl. award and map, plots 65, 82.
9 Ibid. incl. award, schedule s.v. Chas. Leake (description of plot 265); Bodl. MS. Ch. Oxon. c 24, no. 3630.
10 O.R.O., incl. award, plot 65 and schedule s.v. Chas. Leake; ibid. Welch. XI/i/2.

11 *Oxf. Jnl.* 4 Dec. 1773, 9 Jan. 1790, 13 Sept. 1828; Bryant, *Oxon. Map* (1823).
12 Ibid. incl. award and map, plot 82; ibid. MS. Wills Oxon. 135/2/39; ibid. land tax assess. 1785 and later.
13 O.R.O., Welch XI/i/1–15; LV/7; XXXVIII/7: *Sale Cat.* (1894), including plan of estate.
14 *Oxf. Times,* Suppl. 12 Mar. 1898.
15 W. Foreman, *Oxon. Mills,* 67; O.R.O., Welch XI/i/2.
16 *Oxf. Times,* Suppl. 12 Mar. 1898; *Milling,* 24 Dec. 1904, p. 522.
17 Cf. *West Oxon. Standard,* 23 Sept. 1983; *Witney Gaz.* 12 Mar. 1992. For deeds and surveys 1894–1925, O.R.O., Welch XI/iii/1–10.
18 *West Oxon. Standard,* 23 Sept. 1983, 10 Aug. 1984; *Oxf. Mail,* 23 May 1985; *Witney Gaz.* 12 Mar. 1992. For mill site, cf. O.R.O., incl. map; O.S. Map 1/2,500, Oxon. XXXII.13 (1876 and later edns.); ibid. 1/2,500, SP 3607–3707 (1971, 1990 edns.).
19 *Bampton Hund. R.* 64.
20 Below, Standlake, econ. hist. (mills).
21 P.R.O., C 133/72, no. 6; C 134/29, no. 11; C 139/12, no. 36.
22 e.g. St. John's Coll. Mun., XVII.14.
23 Ibid. ADMIN. I. A.7, p. 141; ADMIN. I. A.8–10, *passim.*

tolls, but in 1577 his monopoly of grinding the corn of college tenants was confirmed.[24] The Bullock family held the mill by the mid 16th century and until the 1630s;[25] it passed to John Franklin (d. 1682),[26] whose son-in-law William Grove and his descendants, prosperous yeomen, held the mill until the mid 18th century.[27] The Hawkinses were lessees until 1827, and the Stricklands of Cokethorpe Park until the 1880s.[28] The mill estate comprised c. 34 statute acres in the later 18th century, and 48 a. after inclosure in the mid 19th.[29] The Stricklands' undertenants were sometimes both farmers and millers,[30] but others sublet the mill separately from the house and farm.[31] The college lessee from 1890 was G. H. Holtom;[32] his large-scale enterprise at Ducklington mill presumably made Hardwick mill redundant and it ceased operation in the early 20th century.[33] Later it was held with the adjacent Mill Farm, sold by St. John's College in 1964.[34]

The surviving mill building is mostly 18th-century with earlier masonry, including a late-medieval stone doorway. Most of the machinery was sold c. 1940 and the undershot wheel has been removed; the main stream of the river has been diverted through the mill leet and wheel chamber, and its earlier course is silted up. There are indications that there were once 2 wheels, the surviving second chamber perhaps used for fulling.[35] The mill floor contains pieces of a large gravestone with a monastic indent of c. 1300, perhaps from Eynsham abbey.[36] The mill house, of ashlar and coursed rubble, has an 18th-century symmetrical 3-window front range and an early 17th-century rear wing, which retains internal evidence of original timber-framing. The central doorway and windows probably date from a rebuilding by Richard Hawkins in 1801, commemorated by a datestone. West of the house is a late 18th-century granary, its first floor timber-framed with later brick infill.

By the later 18th century the Cokethorpe estate was conveyed with three mills,[37] of which two were presumably those acquired with Ducklington manor and the third perhaps the early 18th-century water-house (Fish House), which seems to have been used also as a corn mill.[38] An

earlier 'fish house' on the site, not apparently counted as a mill when acquired by the Harcourts in the early 18th century,[39] may have been the successor of the medieval Cokethorpe mill.

A fishery on the river Windrush was attached to Ducklington manor in the 14th century and probably earlier.[40] In the 16th century it seems to have extended southwards along the west branch of the river into Cokethorpe and Hardwick,[41] and to have included the brook (then called Cogges River) which ran south from the eastern Windrush at Shilton ham, east of Ducklington mill.[42] The fishery descended with Ducklington manor and most was merged with the Harcourts' Cokethorpe estate from 1712;[43] part, separated from the manor and granted c. 1693 with the Barley park estate, was acquired with that estate by the Harcourts in the 1750s.[44] In 1587 the lease of one Ducklington mill, and probably of the other, included an attached fishery.[45]

In 1279 Hardwick manor included a fishery allegedly on the river Thames,[46] but the fishery later attached to the manor was on the Windrush. In 1571 most of the Hardwick fishery passed with the manor from John Herle to St. John's College;[47] part, attached to Underdown mill and granted by Herle in 1569 to Peter Ranckell, was sold to Joseph Mayne in 1604–5 and to Sir David Williams of Cokethorpe in 1610.[48] Williams had acquired another fishery on the Windrush, probably in Standlake, with Golofers or Giffards (later Cokethorpe) manor.[49] Williams seems also to have leased the St. John's College fishery in Hardwick from 1610.[50] The fisheries owned by Williams descended with the Cokethorpe estate,[51] whose owners from 1710 or earlier continued to lease the college fishery.[52]

LOCAL GOVERNMENT. In 1279 the lord of Ducklington manor had view of frankpledge conducted by the bailiff of Bampton, presumably a franchise acquired from the lord of Bampton manor.[53] The lord of Ducklington was exempted from the biannual view at Bampton which his freeholders were expected to attend; presumably, therefore, the Ducklington view was for

24 St. John's Coll. Mun., XI.9 (81, 86); XI.10 (137).
25 Ibid. XI.10 (152, 160); XI.12, p. 79.
26 Ibid. XI.12, p. 98; XI.13, p. 15; O.R.O., MS. Wills Oxon. 23/3/23.
27 St. John's Coll. Mun., XI.15, p. 123; ibid. ADMIN. I. A.7, p. 141; O.R.O., MS. Wills Oxon. 207, f. 25v.
28 St. John's Coll. Mun., ADMIN. I. A.7–10, passim.
29 Ibid. XVII.45; O.R.O., tithe award and map 202.
30 e.g. O.R.O., Hardwick tithe award and map; P.O. Dir. Oxon. (1864).
31 e.g. P.R.O., RG 10/1452; RG 11/1515; RG 12/1176; St. John's Coll. Mun., XVII.62.
32 Ibid. XVII.89.
33 Kelly's Dir. Oxon. (1904 and later edns.).
34 St. John's Coll. Mun., XVII. 74, 90–2
35 C.O.S., PRN 844, including a plan; W. Foreman, Oxon. Mills, 109.
36 W. J. Blair, 'Early Monastic Indent at Hardwick, Oxon.', Trans. Monumental Brass Soc. xi (5), 308–11; E. Gordon, 'Adventure at Hardwick mill', Eynsham Record, i (1984), 10–13: copy in C.O.S.
37 e.g. P.R.O., CP 25/2/1391/45 Geo. III Trin.
38 Above, manors (Cokethorpe).
39 e.g. Bodl. MS. d.d. Harcourt c 262 (R); ibid. b 5, ff. 2v.–4:

surveys of Harcourt estate at Cokethorpe before and after purchase of Ducklington's mills.
40 P.R.O., C 135/1, no. 27; C 139/6, no. 51 (18); Cal. Close, 1327–30, 377–8.
41 P.R.O., C 66/1369, mm. 37–8.
42 O.R.O., Peake II/i/1. For identification of field names, ibid. Ducklington incl. award and map.
43 e.g. P.R.O., C 142/333, no. 24; Gooch MSS., deed of 1649; above, manors.
44 e.g. P.R.O., CP 25/2/865/12 Wm. III Mich.; CP 25/2/1649/3 Geo. I Trin.; above, other estates.
45 Bodl. MS. Ch. Oxon. c 24, no. 3630.
46 Bampton Hund. R. 63.
47 Above, manors (Hardwick).
48 St. John's Coll. Mun., XVII.5; P.R.O., CP 25/2/339/2 Jas. I Mich., 8 Jas I Hil.; Bodl. MS. d.d. Harcourt c 109/6.
49 P.R.O., CP 25/2/339/8 Jas. I East.; above, manors (Cokethorpe).
50 St. John's Coll. Mun., XVII.46.
51 e.g. P.R.O., CP 25/2/473/11 Chas. I Trin., Hil.
52 e.g. Bodl. MSS. d.d. Harcourt b 5, ff. 2v.–4; c 14, items 1–2; c 263, rentals 1737 sqq.
53 Bampton Hund. R. 59, where the text is obscure because of MS. omissions. For a similar franchise, above, Bampton: Bampton and Weald, local govt.

unfree tenants.[54] In 1423 the two Ducklington views were held with the manor by service of suit to the hundred court.[55] In the 17th century Ducklington retained, within the Bampton frankpledge, a 'law day of itself',[56] and in the 1670s Bampton's steward was holding the residual annual view in Ducklington at Michaelmas; a constable, and tithingmen for Ducklington, Claywell, and Cokethorpe, were appointed and field orders issued.[57] The annual court continued into the 19th century.[58]

In 1279 both free and unfree tenants of Ducklington manor owed suit to the lord's three-weekly court.[59] Perquisites of Ducklington manor courts were mentioned in the earlier 16th century,[60] and when Sir Christopher Brome turned all his copyholds into leaseholds in 1587 he agreed to maintain one court baron a year near Lady Day, presumably chiefly to regulate the fields.[61] Courts both baron and leet continued to be conveyed with Ducklington manor, but few references to sittings have been found: in the 1740s courts baron of Elizabeth, Dowager Lady Harcourt, held in October, appointed grass stewards and a hayward,[62] and in 1876 Catherine Strickland as lady of Ducklington held what seems to have been an annual court leet, baron, and view, to which all residents were expected to pay suit.[63] In the 18th century ancient freehold quitrents payable at Michaelmas, and leasehold quitrents payable then and at Lady Day,[64] were presumably paid in Ducklington manor courts. It was claimed in 1912 that payment of quitrents had long ceased.[65]

In 1279 the Claywell tenants of Eynsham abbey held of Ducklington manor but owed hidage to Bampton, a payment presumably reserved when that part of Claywell was first separated from the royal manor.[66] Eynsham abbey may have held separate courts for Claywell in the 13th century but by the early 14th the homage attended the abbot's Shifford court.[67]

In 1279 the Greys' manor of Hardwick, Brighthampton, and Yelford was said to be ancient demesne and claimed large liberties, notably view of frankpledge, gallows, and tumbrel, and probably then, as later, the assize of bread and of ale.[68] In the 1540s the view was usually held biannually in April and near Michaelmas,[69] but in the later 16th century the few April courts seem to have been courts baron only. By the 17th century there was only a combined court leet and baron at Michaelmas. The manor was divided into three tithings, Hardwick, Brighthampton, and Yelford, which paid certainty money of 3s. 9d., 3s., and 3d. respectively. The court elected one tithingman for each, and constables for Hardwick and Brighthampton; by the late 16th century no tithingman for Yelford was elected. Freehold suitors were fined for non-appearance and the jury made regular presentments of woundings, breaking the lord's park, and neglect of butts and archery practice. Punitive instruments, notably stocks and cucking stool, were frequently lacking or ruinous. In 1579, 'for the confirmation of the liberties and royalty' of the manor, the lord gave an elm for a gallows, to be built by the tenants and erected in the 'old place' near Knight Bridge on the Shifford brook, where the Aston–Brighthampton road entered the liberty.[70] Repair of highways and watercourses was ordered regularly. Two fieldsmen (sometimes called wardens of the Great Moor) and a hayward were appointed, and bylaws were issued regulating the commons and common fields; there was an autumn meeting in the fields to set merestones and decide other matters. Copyhold transfers provided much of the court's business until the 18th century, when St. John's College turned much to leasehold. After inclosure separate haywards were appointed for Hardwick and Brighthampton and a few heriots were paid, but at the last recorded court in 1867 no jury was impanelled because of lack of business.[71]

Parish officers appointed annually in Ducklington's vestry in the 17th century included 2 churchwardens, 2 overseers of the poor, and 2 surveyors of the highways. In 1668 the vestry agreed to pay a hayward at the rate of 2s. a yardland, and 'parishioners' made decisions about the seasonal fencing of roads through the open fields.[72] Hardwick was separately responsible for its poor, and later had its own churchwardens.

Poor-relief expenditure in Ducklington rose steeply from c. £30 a year in the 1780s to almost £240 in 1803, or 15s. per head of the population; almost all was spent on out relief. During the Napoleonic wars expenditure per head on the poor rose to over 17s., falling thereafter to only 10s. in 1825; there was another sharp rise to 18s. 3d. in 1827, but by 1832, when £263 was spent, the cost was only 13s. per head.[73] In 1803 regular out relief was given to only 8 adults and 9 children, and 43 persons received occasional relief. In 1815 there were 27 persons on out relief.[74] The outcome of a plan of 1817 to farm out the poor of Ducklington, Witney, and Curbridge to a single contractor is not known.[75] In the 1830s labourers were said to have sufficient

54 *Bampton Hund. R.* 59–61.
55 P.R.O., C 139/6, no. 51.
56 B.L. Add. MS. 27535, f. 45.
57 Longleat Ho., NMR 3315: ct. bk. 1667–73.
58 B.L. Map C 7 e 16 (3); Arundel Castle, MS. TP 100.
59 *Bampton Hund. R.* 59–61.
60 e.g. P.R.O., E 318/15/725; ibid. SC 6/Hen. VIII/7247–50.
61 O.R.O., Peake II/v/1.
62 Bodl. MS. d.d. Harcourt b 4/1, ff. 41, 45.
63 Ibid. MS. Top. Oxon. b 78, f. 65.
64 Ibid. MS. d.d. Harcourt b 5, ff. 2–4v.
65 Ibid. G.A. Oxon. b 90 (23).
66 *Bampton Hund. R.* 62; above, manors (Claywell).
67 Above, Bampton: Shifford, local govt.

68 *Bampton Hund. R.* 63, where tumbrel (? cucking stool) is rendered as stocks; J. A. Giles, *Hist. Bampton*, 132.
69 The rest of this para. is based on P.R.O., SC 2/179/43: ct. rolls 1541–6; Bodl. MS. Top. Oxon. b 21: ct. rolls 1561–9; St. John's Coll. Mun., XI.9–22: ct. rolls 1550, 1555–1867.
70 St. John's Coll. Mun., XI.10 (139).
71 Ibid. XI.22, p. 124. An out-of-court surrender was recorded in 1878: ibid. pp. 127–8.
72 C.O.S., par. reg. transcripts.
73 *Poor Abstract, 1777*, p. 140; *1787*, p. 188; *1804*, pp. 398–9; *1818*, pp. 352–3; *Poor Rate Returns*, H.C. 556, p. 135 (1822), v; H.C. 334, p. 170 (1825), iv; H.C. 83, p. 157 (1830–1), xi; H.C. 444, p. 153 (1835), xlvii.
74 *Poor Abstract, 1804*, pp. 398–9; *1818*, pp. 352–3.
75 O.R.O., MS. d.d. Par. Witney b 14, 7 Apr. 1817.

summer work, but in winter many required relief.[76] Although in 1804 no workhouse was recorded £48 worth of flax was spun into thread by the poor and sold for £73 which was shared among the ratepayers.[77] A group of church houses rented to the poor may have included a short-lived workhouse before 1831, but again in 1834 no workhouse was recorded.[78] The church houses continued to be used as poor houses until sold in 1872.[79]

Hardwick in the 1780s was spending c. £21 a year on the poor, and a similar amount in 1803 when four adults and four children were on regular out relief, and 19 were occasionally relieved. Expenditure per head rose from 3s. 4d. in 1803 to over 12s. in 1818, falling sharply in the early 1820s but again over 8s. in the 1830s.[80]

After 1834 Ducklington and Hardwick belonged to Witney union. Ducklington's vestry continued to appoint officers, including the parish churchwarden, 2 overseers, 2 highway surveyors, a constable, and later a waywarden. It approved accounts, set rates, regulated church matters, and made orders for road repair, payments for sparrows, and the impounding of strays; meetings in the mid 19th century were in the Strickland Arms, but later in the church and from 1869 in the National school. By the later 19th century business was almost entirely confined to church matters.[81] In the mid 19th century a Hardwick vestry was meeting in Cokethorpe chapel, usually only to elect an overseer and waywarden; later it met in the parish room at Hardwick. In 1873 the rector chose a churchwarden to assist a parish warden who had served for many years. Thereafter the vestry was concerned largely with church rates, church repair, and charitable administration.[82]

In 1894 the residual secular powers of Ducklington's vestry were taken over by a parish council. Ducklington and Hardwick became part of Witney rural district, and in 1974 of West Oxfordshire district.[83]

CHURCHES. In 958 the 'old church of East Lea' stood on the site of Cokethorpe chapel on the periphery of the Ducklington estate.[84] The antiquity of Cokethorpe chapel presumably accounts for the tradition that it was the 'mother church' of Ducklington;[85] its possible origin in the period of the conversion is discussed above.[86] By 958 there may have been a church in the principal settlement of the estate, although the fabric of the surviving Ducklington church contains no dateable features earlier than the 12th century. That the later parish included Claywell, partly separated from the Ducklington estate by the mid 11th century,[87] suggests that Ducklington church was established early enough to retain the tithes of most of the estate described in 958. Cokethorpe was a dependent chapelry by the 13th century and remained so until the 20th.[88] Before Claywell was deserted in the later Middle Ages there may have been a dependent chapel there, though none was mentioned in comprehensive lists of local chapels over which Bampton church claimed rights.[89] In 1601, however, Ducklington's glebe included what was thought to have been a churchyard at Claywell, for which the tenants of Claywell farm continued to pay 2s. 6d. a year to the churchwardens into the 20th century.[90]

Niel, chaplain or rector of Ducklington, was mentioned c. 1170, and in 1195 witnessed a grant by the manorial lord Guy de Dive, who, like later Dives, was probably patron of the living.[91] The advowson was held with the manor until the later 17th century.[92] In 1222 the bishop of Lincoln collated during the minority of William de Dive, and other minorities led to royal presentations in 1295 and 1331.[93] The last recorded presentation by a Dive was in 1348. When the manor was divided in the later 14th century the advowson remained with the Lovels, despite a challenge by Edmund, earl of March, lord of the other part of the manor, who made a rival presentation in 1422.[94] In 1467 Richard Neville, earl of Warwick, presented as guardian of Francis Lovel.[95] In 1568 the rector Lewis Evans was presented by kinsmen who had purchased a turn.[96] In 1585 Robert Harrison was presented by Sir Christopher Brome and also later by the Crown, perhaps because a delay had caused the presentation to lapse to the then vacant see of Oxford.[97] In 1610 Bartholomew and Thomas Harris presented as grantees of William Bayley (d. 1613).[98] In 1684 William Bayley (d. 1688), during the incumbency of his brother Walter (d. 1695), sold the advowson to Magdalen College, Oxford, of which both brothers were *alumni*.[99] The college retained the advowson until 1951 when it was conveyed to the Diocesan Board of Patronage.[1]

The living was a rectory, assessed for tax in 1291 on £14 (including £2 for Cokethorpe chapelry) less £1 6s. 8d. payable to Osney abbey

76 *Rep. Com. Poor Laws*, H.C. 44, p. 371 (1834), xxx–xxxiv.
77 *Poor Abstract, 1804*, 398–9.
78 O.R.O., MS. d.d. Par. Duckl. b 9, terrier 1831; *Rep. Com. Poor Laws*, H.C. 44, p. 371 (1834), xxx–xxxiv.
79 Below, church.
80 *Poor Abstract, 1777*, p. 140; *1787*, p. 188; *1804*, pp. 398–9; *1818*, pp. 352–3; *Poor Rate Returns*, H.C. 556, p. 135 (1822), v; H.C. 334, p. 170 (1825), iv; H.C. 83, p. 157 (1830–1), xi; H.C. 444, p. 153 (1835), xlvii.
81 O.R.O., MSS. d.d. Par. Duckl. c 4, e 6.
82 Ibid. b 8, e 7.
83 O.R.O., RO 3251, pp. 201–3; RO 3267.
84 Above, intro.
85 e.g. *Hearne's Colln.* xi (O.H.S. lxii), 67.
86 Above, intro.   87 Above, manors.
88 Below, this section [Cokethorpe].
89 e.g. D. & C. Exeter, MS. 2865.
90 O.R.O., MS. Oxf. Archd. Oxon. b 40, f. 119; O.R.O., MS. d.d. Par. Duckl. b 7, *passim*; above, intro. [Claywell].

91 *Oseney Cart.* iv, pp. 466, 524; cf. *Eynsham Cart.* i, p. 104, where he is Niel the deacon.
92 For list of rectors, W. D. Macray, *Our Parish Church*: copy in Bodl. G.A. Oxon. 8° 469 (6), annotated in Bodl. MS. Top. Oxon. b 78, ff. 147v.–148v. Medieval institutions are noted in Bodl. MS. Top. Oxon. c 55, later institutions in Oldfield, 'Clerus Oxf. Dioc.'; O.R.O., TS. Cal. Presentation Deeds.
93 *Rot. Welles*, ii (L.R.S. vi), 8; *Cal. Pat.* 1292–1301, 141; 1330–4, 231; *Reg. Sutton*, viii (L.R.S. lxxvi), 189.
94 P.R.O., C 137/207, no. 29; Bodl. MS. Top. Oxon. c 55, f. 141; ibid. b 78, ff. 147v.–148v.; *Cal. Pat.* 1422–9, 88.
95 Bodl. MS. Top. Oxon. c 55, f. 153.
96 Ibid. b 78, ff. 147v.–148v.
97 Lambeth Palace Libr., Reg. Whitgift, i, f. 300; *Cal. Pat.* 1584–5 (L. & I. Soc. ccxli), 20.
98 O.R.O., TS. Cal. Presentation Deeds, ser. II, f. 32.
99 Bodl. MS. Top. Oxon. b 78, ff. 168, 180; *Reg. Magd. Coll.* v. 196; ibid. N.S. iv. 35–6, 98.
1 O.R.O., MS. Oxf. Dioc. c 1801.

for tithes.[2] For the tax of 1341, which excluded glebe and certain tithes, Ducklington's earlier assessment was reduced to £8 and Cokethorpe's to £1 13s. 4d.[3] In the early 16th century the value of the living was stated variously to be £16 and £25 gross; a curate was paid £5 6s. 8d. in 1526.[4] Post-Reformation estimates of value, which presumably included Cokethorpe, rose from £120 in the early 17th century to over £160 in 1684 and nearly £200 in the early 18th century.[5]

Allegedly in 1074 Robert d'Oilly granted two thirds of his demesne tithes in Ducklington to the canons of St. George's in Oxford castle, a grant later confirmed to their successors, the canons of Osney.[6] In the 1170s, after a dispute between Ducklington's incumbent Niel and Osney abbey, Ralph de Chesney also confirmed the abbey's right to two thirds of all tithes from some additional demesne.[7] The abbey defended its rights against the rector's tithe farmer in the early 14th century,[8] and its portion was still valued at £1 6s. 8d. in the 16th century.[9]

Eynsham abbey's right to the tithes of 40 a. in Claywell, confirmed in 1239, may have derived from Ralph de Chesney's grant to the abbey of a hide of land there in the late 12th century; the abbey's tithe there was not recorded later.[10] In the early 15th century the dean and chapter of Exeter were claiming that tithes in Ducklington manor were being withheld by the Lovels, perhaps from Claywell where some demesne tithes were said in 1317 to belong to Bampton rectory,[11] or from Barley Park where some land was later thought to be tithable to Bampton.[12]

Recurrent post-Reformation tithe disputes[13] included one of 1588 over an alleged modus payable by Walter Bayley for the tithes of Barley Park.[14] In 1601, however, it was affirmed that the rector received tithes in kind from almost all Ducklington and Hardwick, even from parishioners' holdings in Lew meadow (presumably outside the parish boundary), the only modus being one of 2s. from each of three mills.[15] Later moduses included several from the Harcourt estate which in the 1720s paid £2 14s. for its Ducklington tithes and 15s. 3d. for those of Hardwick. By the 1740s the Hardwick payment had risen to £2 15s. 6d. and in the 1750s, after further acquisitions, the Harcourts paid £5 1s. for 'Cokethorpe', presumably the Ducklington

part of Cokethorpe Park, £7 10s. for Barley Park, and £2 5s. for other Ducklington land;[16] for some 125 a. of Cokethorpe Park they paid a modus to the rector of Standlake.[17]

In the early 19th century the rector was letting the tithes and glebe to local farmers.[18] In 1819 compositions for the tithes of Ducklington and Hardwick were yielding c. £455, reduced by the 1830s to an average of c. £400.[19] Formal commutation, considered from the early 19th century,[20] was partly achieved in 1839 when Ducklington township was inclosed and its rectorial tithes replaced by a rent charge of £475.[21] A field attached to Claywell Farm was charged with a modus of 1s. 8d. payable to the vicars of Bampton, possibly related to the tithes payable from Claywell to Bampton in the 14th century, although those were rectorial, not vicarial tithes; a payment from Claywell farm to Aston vicarage survived in the 20th century.[22] In 1842 the rector of Ducklington was awarded £6 a year for the tithes of a few acres in Standlake.[23] The tithes of Hardwick chapelry, valued at c. £68 in 1821,[24] were formally commuted in 1852 when 422 a. of the 670 a. in the newly inclosed and redefined township were deemed to be tithable to Ducklington, the rest to Yelford or Bampton; the rector was awarded a rent charge of c. £83.[25] Tithe income, c. £564 gross in the 1850s, was altered slightly when rent charges were adjusted in 1887 to take account of boundary changes.[26] In the later 19th century the value of the living declined steadily to c. £320 net, but tithe income later recovered to c. £520 in 1922.[27]

In 1601 the glebe comprised the rectory house and gardens (c. 2 a.), 2 yardlands of arable in Ducklington and Hardwick, c. 7 a. of meadow, and the churchyards of Ducklington, Cokethorpe, and Claywell.[28] A later 17th-century terrier listing less arable may have excluded Hardwick.[29] At inclosure in 1839 the rector had c. 10 a. of closes and was awarded 22½ a. for his openfield glebe; in 1852 his Hardwick glebe comprised c. 5 a.[30] The glebe was unchanged in the later 19th century,[31] and until 1895 rectors also had the use of land near the rectory house garden, acquired on their behalf by Magdalen College in 1812 and 1836.[32]

In 1520 the churchwardens reported that the rectory house was let to a layman and in need of

2 *Tax. Eccl.* (Rec. Com.), 32.
3 *Inq. Non.* (Rec. Com.), 141.
4 *Subsidy, 1526*, 261; *Valor Eccl.* (Rec. Com.), ii. 178.
5 B.L. Harl. MS. 843, f. 4; *Reg. Magd. Coll.* N.S. iv. 35–6; *Par. Colln.* iv. 128.
6 *Facsimiles of Early Chart.* ed. H. E. Salter, no. 58; *Oseney Cart.* iii, pp. 345, 353, 369; iv, pp. 3, 7, 46–51.
7 *Oseney Cart.* iv, pp. 524–5.
8 *Abbrev. Plac.* (Rec. Com.), 246; *Oseney Cart.* iv, pp. 525–6.
9 e.g. *Oseney Cart.* vi, pp. 242.
10 *Eynsham Cart.* i, pp. 4, 82–3; ii, pp. lxv–lxvi.
11 D. & C. Exeter, MS. 2931.
12 Ibid. MS. 5100: Bampton Deanery bailiff's acct. 1416–17; Bodl. MS. d.d. Harcourt c 134/2, p. 43; above, econ. hist. [Barley Pk.].
13 e.g. O.R.O., MS. Oxf. Archd. Oxon. c 9, f. 271v.; Bodl. MS. Top. Oxon. b 78, ff. 205–6.
14 O.R.O., MS. Oxf. Archd. Oxon. c 9, ff. 35, 101, 127; Bodl. MS. Top. Oxon. b 78, ff. 202–3.
15 O.R.O., MS. Oxf. Archd. Oxon. b 40, f. 119. For a copy with some variants, ibid. c 142, f. 155.
16 Bodl. MSS. d.d. Harcourt b 5–6, *passim*; c 133/1–2;

c 134/2; c 144/1, p. 37.
17 O.R.O., Standlake tithe award.
18 e.g. ibid. Misc. Druce VI/v/1.
19 Ibid. MS. d.d. Par. Duckl. b 9, tithe pps. 1819–38.
20 e.g. Bodl. MS. Top. Oxon. b 78, f. 168.
21 O.R.O., Duckl. tithe award and map.
22 Ibid.; Bodl. G.A. Oxon. b 90 (25).
23 O.R.O., Standlake tithe award.
24 Ibid. Misc. Pe. VII/1.
25 Ibid. Hardwick tithe award.
26 *P.O. Dir. Oxon.* (1847 and later edns.), which ignore the £6 rent charge from Standlake, confirmed in 1887; O.R.O., Duckl. and Standlake tithe awards (1887); ibid. MS. d.d. Par. Duckl. b 9, corresp. 1885–7.
27 *Kelly's Dir. Oxon.* (1883 and later edns.); O.R.O., MS. d.d. Par. Duckl. b 9, tithe pps. 1900–26.
28 O.R.O., MS. Oxf. Archd. Oxon. b 40, f. 119.
29 Ibid. f. 118: undated but c. 1689. For a copy, with some variants, ibid. c 142, ff. 151–3.
30 Ibid. Duckl. incl. award; ibid. Hardwick tithe award.
31 Bodl. MS. Top. Oxon. b 78, f. 211.
32 Ibid. ff. 166, 168, 188; Magd. Coll. Mun., modern deeds 14.3.27; O.R.O., Duckl. incl. map, plot 19.

repair.[33] In 1552 the rector let his whole estate for 30 years, reserving only a single chamber for himself and his successors; c. 1574 a later rector was in dispute over the rent.[34] In 1601 the rectory house was described as a 'fair mansion', comprising a 2-storeyed entrance porch, hall, parlour, buttery, kitchen, brewhouse, and other offices, all with chambers over, built round a courtyard and set in gardens of c. 2 a.; there was a large barn and a dovecot.[35] For much of the 17th century rectors were resident, and the house, assessed for tax on 12 hearths in 1665, was much the largest in the village; during the Civil War troops were billeted there regularly.[36] In 1679 the patron and rector obtained a faculty to pull down a ruinous brewhouse and other parts of a south range, to provide materials for the repair of the main building.[37] In the late 17th century the 'very convenient' house comprised 10 bays of building, a 2-bayed brewhouse and washhouse, and a 6-bayed tithe barn with porch.[38] James Hawkins, rector from 1798, claimed that he had been obliged to rebuild 'almost the whole'; the work, which included demolishing the 'old hall' and the 'cellar part', was still in progress in 1802.[39] There were substantial additions by the rectors Thomas Farley in 1843–4 and W. D. Macray in 1870–1.[40]

The range which forms the north-west front is 17th–century, probably rebuilt by Thomas Wyatt, rector 1610–52, much altered internally in the earlier 18th century, and achieving its present form in the rebuilding of c. 1800. Behind it the two staircase halls and the rooms on the south-east are probably early 19th-century, incorporating older walls around the staircases. Later, probably in 1870–1, they were extensively remodelled and a south-west porch added. The north-east service wing, incorporating a carriage house and loose box, is work of c. 1800, although the vaulted half-cellars may be earlier.

Re-used timbers in the early 19th-century rear range include 15th-century painted beams with shields of arms of Grey and Deincourt[41] and heraldic emblems associated with the Sydenham and Holand families.[42] To all those arms the Lovels became entitled through marriages to

heiresses, culminating in that of William, Lord Lovel and Holand (d. 1455), to Alice Deincourt, coheir, and from 1454 sole heir, to the baronies of Deincourt and of Grey of Rotherfield.[43] Assertions that the beams were brought from Minster Lovell are unfounded:[44] the Lovels were lords and patrons of Ducklington, and the beams were probably re-used when the older parts of the rectory house were demolished c. 1800. A similar roof beam survives in the parish room, formerly the tithe barn, also largely rebuilt c. 1800.[45] In 1977 the rectory house was sold and the living provided with a house on Standlake Road.[46]

Many of Ducklington's early rectors were educated men,[47] and some were probably non-resident beneficiaries of the well endowed living. Robert de Askeby, rector 1295–1304, a royal presentee, was a prominent royal envoy.[48] Philip of Hanbury, rector in 1363, belonged to an armigerous family and held estates in Worcestershire and elsewhere.[49] Thomas Raysaker, rector 1447–67, and his successor John Pereson were considerable pluralists; both were wardens of St. Katherine's chantry in Wanborough (Wilts.), which, like Ducklington, was in the patronage of the Lovels.[50]

The wealth of the living is reflected by Pereson's acquisition in 1501 of a pension of £10 for life from his successor at Ducklington, another pluralist.[51] In the 1520s the non-resident rector paid curates,[52] and Sir Thomas More's presentee in 1533, William Leson, Chancery master and considerable pluralist, was probably also non-resident.[53] In 1552 his successor, William Wright, archdeacon of Oxford and vicar of Bampton,[54] let the rectory house for 30 years,[55] presumably encouraging further non-residence.

Both Ducklington's rectors in the period 1558–85 subscribed to the Elizabethan settlement;[56] Lewis Evans, rector from 1568, and his curate appeared frequently in ecclesiastical courts, both as litigants and to answer for alleged misconduct.[57] Robert Harrison, rector 1585–1610, was resident.[58] He seems to have been the former fellow of Corpus Christi College, Oxford,[59] a 'zealous Catholic' whose election in 1568 as president of the college was annulled after royal

---

33 *Visit. Dioc. Linc.* (L.R.S. xxxiii), 132.

34 P.R.O., REQ 2/210/99.

35 O.R.O., MS. Oxf. Archd. Oxon. b 40, f. 119.

36 *Hearth Tax Oxon.* 220; Bodl. MS. Top. Oxon. c 378, *passim*.

37 Bodl. MS. Top. Oxon. b 78, f. 209.

38 Ibid. f. 160; O.R.O., MS. Oxf. Archd. Oxon. b 40, f. 118.

39 O.R.O., MS. Oxf. Dioc. d 566, ff. 113–14; Bodl. MS. d.d. Fitt c 4/2; ibid. MS. Top. Oxon. b 78, f. 198.

40 C.O.S., PRN 11207: archit. notes, including drawing of dated rainwaterhead; Bodl. MS. Top. Oxon. b 78, ff. 172, 174.

41 C.O.S., PRN 11207. The shield mistakenly attributed to Poynings is that of Grey (barry of six argent and azure a bend gules) in which the silver and blue pigments have corrupted respectively to yellow/gold and green.

42 e.g. for Sydenham, padlocks; for Holand, silver fleur-de-lys on a blue ground and silver leopards (corrupted on one beam to yellow/gold).

43 *Complete Peerage*, s.v. Deincourt, Grey, Holand, and Lovel. For the heraldry cf. E. A. Greening Lamborn, 'Lovel Tomb at Minster', O.A.S. *Rep.* (1937), 13–20.

44 C.O.S., PRN 11207, corresp. files.

45 Bodl. MS. d.d. Fitt c 4/2.

46 O.R.O., MS. Oxf. Dioc. c 1801.

47 e.g. *Rot. Welles*, ii (L.R.S. vi), 8; Emden, *O.U. Reg. to 1500*, i, s.v. Abberbury, John.

48 e.g. *Cal. Pat.* 1292–1301, 141; 1301–7, 72; P.R.O., SC 1/38/158.

49 B.L. Harl. Ch. 50.H.26; P.R.O., SC 8/14995; *Genealogist*, N.S. xxiv. 242–3.

50 Emden, *O.U. Reg. to 1500*, 1463–4, 1547; *Cal. Papal Reg.* x. 135; *V.C.H. Wilts.* ix. 177–8, 184.

51 Emden, *O.U. Reg. to 1500*, 939; Bodl. MS. Top. Oxon. b 78, ff. 147v.–148v.

52 *Visit. Dioc. Linc.* i (L.R.S. xxxiii), 132; ibid. ii (L.R.S. xxxv), 49; *Subsidy, 1526*, 261.

53 Emden, *O.U. Reg. 1501–40*, 352; *Cal. Pat.* 1548–9, 158.

54 Emden, *O.U. Reg. 1501–40*, 641; O.A.S. *Rep.* (1914), 191–2.

55 P.R.O., REQ 2/210/99.

56 O.A.S. *Rep.* (1914), 187, 197–8.

57 e.g. Bodl. MS. Top. Oxon. b 78, ff. 199, 201; O.R.O., MS. Oxf. Archd. Oxon. c 5, f. 71; *Archdeacon's Ct.* ii (O.R.S. xxiv), 139–40.

58 He signs many contemporary documents in the parish: e.g. O.R.O., Peake II/i/1; II/iii/1.

59 No other M.A. of that name and those dates is known. W. D. Macray identifies Harrison as the Corpus Christi fellow, citing no source: cf. Bodl. G.A. Oxon. 8° 469 (6), 8; O.A.S. *Rep.* (1913), 150. For Harrison's presentation cf. Lambeth Palace Libr., Reg. Whitgift, i, f. 300; *Cal. Pat.* 1584–5 (L. & I. Soc. 241), 20.

intervention because of his alleged Romanist views.[60] At Ducklington Harrison may have been concerned in a belated effort to continue the veneration of St. Mary the Virgin.[61]

Harrison was the first of a succession of remarkably long-serving resident rectors: between 1585 and 1947 there were only 11 rectors, of whom only two served for fewer than 20 years. Thomas Wyatt, D.D., rector 1610–52, negotiated the perils of the Civil War with tact, as the rectory house became a billet for successive waves of troops from both factions;[62] although evidently mildly Royalist, and once threatened with arrest by passing Parliamentary soldiers, he was described by William Lenthall in 1649 as 'an honest and grave divine'.[63] William Burley (? 1652–71) was kinsman of the patron, William Bayley,[64] and Walter Bayley, rector 1671–95, a former fellow of Magdalen College, was the patron's brother.[65] When the Bayleys sold the living to the college in 1684 they reported that the duty expected was only moderate, comprising one service and sermon each Sunday, alternately at Ducklington and Cokethorpe.[66]

The churchwardens reported satisfactorily on Ducklington for most of the 18th century.[67] Mainwaring Hammond, rector 1695–1731, was one of the fellows ejected from Magdalen College by James II in 1687;[68] he left much of the duty to his curate, a Witney schoolmaster.[69] On Sundays in 1738 there was a morning service at Ducklington and an evening service at Cokethorpe, but only one sermon each week at alternate churches.[70] John Pinnell, resident rector for over 50 years from 1747, performed the duty himself and increased the number of services at Ducklington.[71] By contrast James Hawkins, rector 1798–1836, although resident was never known to preach or to read prayers; he reduced the number of services, and, claiming ill health throughout a long life, relied wholly on non-resident curates.[72]

His successor Thomas Farley (1836–70), at first an assiduous incumbent, annoyed his bishop by quarrelling with Walter Strickland of Cokethorpe and by conducting services from a 'reading pen' instead of from the altar; he also resisted pressure for additional services.[73] In 1851 average attendances at Ducklington of 60 in the morning and 100 in the afternoon were

reported, but in fact there was only one service there each Sunday, the other being at Cokethorpe for which separate figures were given.[74] In the 1860s, when most of the duty was carried out by curates, some of them highly regarded, a second service was held at Ducklington in the summer.[75] Under W. D. Macray, rector 1870–1912, the duty was increased to two full services weekly at Ducklington and one at Cokethorpe. The living evidently could not support curates until, from 1899, the rector's income was increased by holding Yelford in plurality.[76] Macray, a distinguished archivist and librarian,[77] was also a model parish priest whose family played a large part in village life for over 40 years.[78] His successor Christopher Tristram, rector 1912–47, was similarly influential, his contribution including the creation of a parish room in the former tithe barn.[79]

The church of ST. BARTHOLOMEW,[80] built of rubble with ashlar dressings, comprises chancel, aisled nave, west tower, and north and south porches. There is a late 12th-century south arcade, of which the plain, single-chamfered western arch was presumably the earliest part. Flat buttresses supporting the west wall on each side of the later tower probably indicate the length and width of the nave c. 1200. In the early to mid 13th century the long, narrow chancel was built and a tower, of which the entrance arch from the nave survives, was added at the west end. The late 12th-century south aisle was probably narrower than the surviving aisle, of which the scale and fenestration indicate rebuilding in the later 13th century.[81] The small, plain south doorway is probably also of that date.

In the earlier 14th century a large window with geometrical tracery was inserted in the south wall of the chancel, and later, perhaps c. 1340, the chancel arch was rebuilt and a north arcade and lavish north aisle added or rebuilt. The work was distinctive, with tall, sharply pointed windows containing flowing tracery similar to work at Cogges and in the north transept at Witney; the aisle buttresses, with pack-saddle heads and ogee-headed niches, also have close parallels at Witney. Features such as the continuous exterior string course suggest that aisle and buttresses were of one build, an impression confirmed by examination of the footings in 1994.[82] The con-

60 T. Fowler, *Hist. Corpus Christi Coll.* (O.H.S. xxv), 98, 125–9; *Cal. Pat.* 1566–9, 329; *Reg. Univ. Oxf.* i (O.H.S. i), 230; ibid. ii (2) (O.H.S. xi), 14.
61 Below, this section.
62 Bodl. MS. Top. Oxon. c 378, *passim*.
63 e.g. ibid. p. 399; ibid. b 78, f. 149.
64 Burley (d. 1671) was certainly rector by 1654: *Cal. S.P. Dom.* 1654, 248; cf. Bodl. G.A. Oxon. 8° 469 (6), 8, wrongly dating his incumbency. For relationship of Burley and Bayley, O.R.O., MS. Wills Oxon. 6/4/23; *Oxon. Visit. 1634*, 3; *Wilts. Visit.* (Harl. Soc. cv/cvi), 200.
65 Magd. Coll. Mun., EP/109/53; *Reg. Magd. Coll.* v. 196; ibid. N.S. iv. 98; Bodl. MS. Top. Oxon. b 78, f. 168.
66 *Reg. Magd. Coll.* N.S. iv. 35–6.
67 O.R.O., MS. Oxf. Archd. Oxon. c 65, *passim*.
68 *Reg. Magd. Coll.* N.S. iv. 121–2; *V.C.H. Oxon.* iii. 198–9. For a hostile judgment of him, *Par. Colln.* ii. 128.
69 Bodl. MS. Top. Oxon. b 78, ff. 147v.–148v. For curates, ibid. f. 162 and v.
70 *Secker's Visit.* 55–6.
71 O.R.O., MSS. Oxf. Dioc. d 555, d 558, d 561, d 564; Bodl. MS. Top. Oxon. b 78, ff. 161, 163; *Reg. Magd. Coll.* N.S. v. 70–1.

72 e.g. O.R.O., MSS. Oxf. Dioc. d 566, d 574; ibid. b 38; Bodl. MS. Top. Oxon. b 78, f. 164; *Reg. Magd. Coll.* N.S. v. 133.
73 O.R.O., MSS. Oxf. Dioc. d 178, p. 191; d 550, f. 59v.; ibid. MS. Oxf. Archd. Oxon. c 38, f. 87; *Wilb. Letter Bks.* pp. 151, 286–7, 289, 293–4; *Reg. Magd. Coll.* vii. 263–4; ibid. N.S. vi. 81–2; McClatchey, *Oxon. Clergy*, 88; *Oxf. Chron.* 10, 17 Mar. 1860.
74 *Ch. and Chapel*, nos. 145, 203.
75 e.g. O.R.O., MS. Oxf. Dioc. c 335; *Oxf. Chron.* 3 Mar. 1860.
76 O.R.O., MS. Oxf. Dioc. c 338.
77 Bodl. MS. Top. Oxon. d 89, pp. 1–5; E. Craster, *Hist. Bodl. Libr. 1845–1945*, 33, 52, 96–8, 104; *Reg. Magd. Coll.* N.S. vii. 53–9.
78 Magd. Coll. Mun., MS. 799 (i–vi): misc. Ducklington pps., including par. mags.
79 M. Harris, *A Kind of Magic*, 168.
80 Recorded in 1546: O.R.O., MS. Wills Oxon. 179, f. 131.
81 Footings at the east end of the south aisle indicated an aisle earlier than the chancel, and those at the west end a possibly narrower structure: C.O.S., PRN 3889, Oxf. Archaeol. Unit report, 1994.   82 Ibid.

tinuation of the string course inside the north porch makes it unlikely that a porch formed part of the original design,[83] while the elaborate treatment of the north doorway suggests that it was by then the principal entrance to the church.

The interior of the aisle[84] is united by a string-course with ballflower running round the wall plate on the north and south sides and forming the window hoods on the east and west. The arcade piers are decorated with crowned heads, possibly of Edward III and Philippa, and coiled serpents, of which that on the east was added or recarved in 1873.[85] Apparently out of keeping with the high quality of much of the work is the setting of the windows, which have wide, flat splays below the level of the rear arches. Suggestions that the splays were retained from an earlier, presumably 13th-century, aisle[86] may be discounted on the ground of style and scale. The splays, in existence by the early 19th century, may have been cut to provide more light when galleries were added, but it seems unlikely that galleries occupied the length of the aisle. One possibility, though implying unusual ambition for a village church, is that the jambs formed part of the 14th-century design, and were prepared for niches or other decorations which were never completed.

The east end of the north aisle, heavily decorated with carved masonry, has the appearance of a private chapel and it has been suggested that the aisle's donors, probably members of the manorial family, the Dives, were entombed there in the surviving recesses in the north wall.[87] The recesses have cusped, ogee-headed arches decorated with carved heads and foliage arranged along a branching vine which, though incomplete, evidently issued from the reclining figure of Jesse in the central spandrel; the composition is set in a rectangular frame of plain roll moulding. The western recess contains a medieval grave slab, and a similar slab lies in the churchyard near the north aisle; both were once decorated with a raised floriated cross, and in 1805 an axe was visible on the slab in the recess.[88] The slabs, however, probably had no original connexion with the recesses, which they appear to pre-date. Other signs of later alteration include the clumsy setting of some parts into the frame, and the absence of a plinth. The craftmanship of the composition, though vigorous, is inferior to that of the aisle and its location across the lower part of an original window suggests that it was not a memorial to the aisle's founders. Even so most of the masonry is of the 14th century and the frame, in parts at least, is integral with the carving of the arches; a comparably framed 14th-century double recess, complete with effigies, survives in the north transept at Witney.[89] The Ducklington

recesses are probably the remains of a sepulchral monument of the 14th century, although much altered and possibly wholly reset.

Other decorative masonry in the supposed chapel may be re-used. High on the walls in deep, rectangular recesses are mutilated statues depicting scenes from the life of St. Mary the Virgin, notably, on the north, the Salutation, at the north-east corner the Nativity and the Madonna and Child, and on the south the Annunciation; the upper recess on the south-east contains vestiges of an Ascension. The centrepiece of the group, relatively undamaged, is a depiction of the Coronation of the Virgin set into the east window.[90] The statues were in their present arrangement and condition by the early 18th century, having perhaps been mutilated during or after the Civil War. In 1815 J. C. Buckler described their 'rude execution' and location as a 'puzzle',[91] and in 1891 scholarly visitors debated whether or not the Coronation scene was part of the 14th-century tracery design or (as surmised in 1871) a recent insertion.[92] The statues, although probably 14th-century, may have been reset; their frames have ill-fitting corners and are placed randomly and adapted crudely to accommodate the available figures. Yet the central tracery of the east window is carved out of the rear stonework of the Coronation scene, and parts of the outer moulding of the window arch are integral with the flanking recesses. The evidence for resetting is therefore inconclusive, although if the statues are *in situ* their location so high above the ground seems inexplicable. One possibility is that they were brought to Ducklington from Cokethorpe chapel, which before its partial destruction at the Reformation had attracted pilgimages to an 'image' of the Virgin, possibly in the form of carvings.[93] The controversial nature of such material after the Reformation might explain the obscure positioning of the statues. A possible instigator of a revived cult of the Virgin was the late 16th-century rector, Robert Harrison.[94]

In the 15th century or early 16th the three-stage west tower was rebuilt, perhaps from ground level except for the nave arch; an east window was inserted and the chancel heightened, and a window was inserted in the south aisle. The north porch, which incorporates a wide 13th-century doorway with attached shafts and moulded capitals, was perhaps added at that time. The re-used doorway may have been an earlier north entrance, although its retention seems implausible if, as argued above, no porch was planned at the time that the north aisle was added: perhaps the doorway was moved from the west end when the tower was rebuilt. Beneath the north porch, and

---

83 Footings at the junction of the aisle and west side of the porch showed a northern projection contemporary with the aisle wall, probably a former buttress balancing that further east.

84 Above, plate 21.

85 Bodl. MS. Top. Oxon. b 78, f. 170.

86 e.g. O.A.S. *Rep.* (1891), 5; Pevsner, *Oxon.* 588–9.

87 e.g. *Gent. Mag.* lxxxv (2), 491–2; Bodl. MS. Top. Oxon. b 256, f. 3; O.A.S. *Rep.* (1872), 33–5; ibid. (1891), 11.

For the recesses, above plate 21.

88 O.A.S. *Rep.* (1872), 33–5; Bodl. MS. Top. Oxon. b 78, f. 132.

89 Illust. in Skelton, *Antiq. Oxon.* Bampton hund. pl. 5.

90 Above, plate 21.

91 *Par. Colln.* iv. 128–9; *Gent. Mag.* lxxxv (2), 491–2.

92 O.A.S. *Rep.* (1891), 10–11; ibid. (1871), 5.

93 Below, this section [Cokethorpe].

94 Above, this section.

probably built at the same time, is a plain vault, evidently a charnel house.[95]

The south porch, described in 1815 as modern,[96] is possibly 17th-century. In 1824–6 extensive repairs, which included restoration of the aisle roofs, were aided by a donation of £120 from Walter Strickland.[97] Thomas Farley, rector from 1836, in his early years restored the tower, tiled the sanctuary, and replaced much furniture with the help of grants and gifts from Magdalen College.[98] The principal 19th-century restoration took place in 1871–2 to plans by Edward Bruton: the work included partial reflooring, repewing the nave and north aisle, moving the font from the south aisle to the centre of the nave and the pulpit and reading desk from the north side of the nave to the chancel arch, and removing a singers' gallery from the west end and a men's gallery from the west end of the north aisle; a vestry was created by installing part of the former chancel screen in the tower arch, and blocked windows in the north aisle were opened up and whitewash removed from the 'curious sculptures'. The chancel was restored, reseated, and its roof repaired.[99] A second phase of restoration in 1883–4 included replastering both aisles and repewing the south.[1]

The drum font, decorated with intersecting round arches and roll moulding, is of the 12th century.[2] On the south side of the chancel are a piscina and sedilia and on the north an aumbry and credence, all 13th-century, as is a piscina in the south aisle. Traces of early 14th-century wall paintings were uncovered in both aisles in 1884, but only a depiction of the Trinity in a window jamb in the south aisle and some script over the south door were preserved.[3] By 1805 there seems to have been none of the medieval heraldic glass recorded at Ducklington in the 17th century, notably the coats of Dive, Holand, and Deincourt;[4] birds reported to be in the glass may have been from the arms of Bayley, the 17th-century manorial family after which the north aisle was once named.[5] There are fragments of 14th-century glass in the east window of the north aisle, which was damaged by vandalism in the 19th century.[6]

The medieval church had several altars and

lights;[7] a house and half yardland given by an unknown donor for an obit was seized by the Crown at the Reformation.[8] Surviving epitaphs are of the 18th century and later, and include those of several rectors.[9] Stained glass of the late 19th century and early 20th commemorates members of the Macray family.[10] The pulpit includes late 17th-century panels and, like that at Cokethorpe, may have been made up from redundant woodwork from Magdalen College chapel given to Thomas Farley. A cartouche of the college arms, given at the same time, is in the north aisle.[11] The oak reredos incorporates 17th-century panels, possibly Flemish, given by Farley,[12] whose family in 1871 gave the oak eagle lectern in his memory.[13] In the early 19th century music was provided by 'an instrumental choir' and there was a small harmonium, replaced by organs from 1891.[14]

Of the ring of six bells four date from 1708; the tenor was recast in 1829 and a treble added in 1889. The saunce of 1633 is by James Keene of Woodstock.[15] The church plate includes a silver chalice of 1578, a silver paten given by the rector Mainwaring Hammond in 1707, and an alms dish given by Thomas Farley in 1841.[16] The registers date from 1579, with a few earlier entries, and are complete except for a gap in the burial register in the 1670s.[17]

An additional burial ground was provided in 1878 on land in Court Close north of the church given by Catherine Strickland; it was extended in 1926.[18]

By the early 19th century the parish held property independent of the rectorial glebe: it included a few strips of arable in the open fields, a small piece of pasture within the north boundary of Cokethorpe Park, a garden near Ducklington pond, and church houses in Ducklington on the site of the surviving brick terrace on the north-west side of the Square.[19] The open field land, 1 a. after inclosure in 1839,[20] and the other church land was still let by the church-wardens in the mid 20th century.[21] In the early 19th century the church houses, two in 1831 and three by 1839, were rented to the poor, although one was thought to have been used as a work-house.[22] After 1834 that house, still owned by

95 Magd. Coll. Mun., MS. 799 (vi), *Par. Mag.* July 1910: rep. of excavation. For a fanciful interpretation of the vault, F. S. Thacker, *Stripling Thames*, 219.
96 *Gent. Mag.* lxxxv (2), 491–2.
97 Bodl. MS. Top. Oxon. b 78, ff. 165v., 174; O.R.O., MS. d.d. Par. Duckl. b 7, endpps.
98 *Reg. Magd. Coll.* N.S. vi. 10, 81–2; Bodl. MS. Top. Oxon. b 78, f. 174; O.R.O., MS. d.d. Par. Duckl. b 7, s.a. 1837, 1841.
99 Bodl. MS. Top. Oxon. b 78, ff. 94v.–97 (plans), 107–108v., 134; ibid. c 103, ff. 404–12; O.R.O., MS. d.d. Par. Duckl. c 1801 (plan); Magd. Coll. Mun., MS. 799 (vi), s.a. 1871–6; *Oxf. Jnl.* 27 July 1872.
1 Bodl. MS. Top. Oxon. b 78, ff. 99–106, 110v.; O.R.O., MS. Oxf. Dioc. c 1801: faculty 1883; ibid. c 2205, no. 33.
2 For illust. of 1819, Bodl. MS. Top. Oxon. c 532, f. 37.
3 Ibid. b 78, ff. 105–6, 110v.; O.A.S. *Rep.* (1891), 11.
4 Bodl. MS. Top. Oxon. b 256, f. 3; *Par. Colln.* iv. 128; O.A.S. *Rep.* (1871), 6.
5 Bodl. MS. Top. Oxon. b 256, f. 3; *Par. Colln.* iv. 128–9. For Bayley arms, Bodl. MS. Top. Oxon. d 271, f. 13.
6 Bodl. MS. Top. Oxon. b 78, f. 165.
7 e.g. O.A.S. *Rep.* (1871), 6.
8 P.R.O., E 315/67, f. 240.

9 Listed in Bodl. MS. Top. Oxon. b 78, f. 164 and v.
10 Magd. Coll. Mun., MS. 799 (iii–v), Nov. 1888, Oct. 1901, Apr. 1909.
11 *Reg. Magd. Coll.*, N.S. vi. 81–2. For photo. of cartouche, Bodl. MS. Top. Oxon. c 486.
12 Bodl. MS. Top. Oxon. b 78, f. 170v.
13 Ibid. ff. 171, 177–8; cf. *Reg. Magd. Coll.* N.S. vi. 81–2, which erroneously gives date 1873.
14 e.g. Bodl. MS. Top. Oxon. b 78, f. 175; Magd. Coll. Mun., MS. 799 (ii, v), Jan. 1885, Feb. 1904, Feb. 1905; O.R.O., MS. d.d. Par. Duckl. b 9, s.a. 1948.
15 Bodl. MS. Top. Oxon. b 78, ff. 169 and v, 209v.; *Ch. Bells Oxon.* 123–4.
16 Evans, *Ch. Plate*, 58–9; cf. O.A.S. *Rep.* (1890), 8–9.
17 O.R.O., MSS. d.d. Par. Duckl. b 1–5, 10–11, c 1, d 1–2, e 1. There are transcripts in C.O.S., O.R.O., and Bodl. MS. Eng. c 2030; cf. also W. D. Macray, 'Index of Duckl. Par. Regs.', O.A.S. *Rep.* (1880).
18 O.R.O., MS. Oxf. Dioc. c 1801, s.a. 1878, 1926; ibid. MS. d.d. Par. Duckl. e 6, s.a. 1914; ibid. b 7, s.a. 1926.
19 Ibid. MS. d.d. Par. Duckl. b 9, terrier 1831.
20 Ibid. incl. award and map, plot 257.
21 Ibid. MS. d.d. Par. Duckl. b 7, *passim*.
22 Ibid. b 9, terrier 1831; ibid. tithe award and map, plot 239; above, local govt.

the parish, was administered by the guardians of Witney union, while the rent of the others supplemented church rates. In 1872 all three were sold and rebuilt.[23]

The origins of Cokethorpe chapel as the Anglo-Saxon church at East Lea are discussed above.[24] William, parson of East Lea, witnessed a grant of *c.* 1195 × 1218, but in 1212–13 reference was made to Robert, chaplain of Cokethorpe.[25] In 1290 it was alleged that the little church or chapel (*ecclesiola seu capella*) of Cokethorpe[26] had been dependent beyond memory and had usually been served by a resident chaplain or parson appointed and removed by Ducklington's rector. The rector was paid in cash or incense by the chaplain, who served Cokethorpe and Hardwick with all offices and sacraments except burials. Others claimed, however, that William de Dive (d. 1261) had directly presented a chaplain to Cokethorpe who had held it for forty years as an independent living without episcopal or papal sanction. On the chaplain's death in 1290 Philip de Dive, rector of Ducklington, secured episcopal confirmation of his rights over Cokethorpe on condition that he supplied a resident and honest curate.[27] The chapel's status was again in dispute in the later 14th century: the Crown made and revoked several presentations[28] until in 1376 an examination of the bishops' registers confirmed that Cokethorpe had never been a separate benefice.[29] In the 15th century presentations to Ducklington usually included reference to the annexed chapel of Cokethorpe.[30]

Hardwick lay outside the Ducklington estate granted in 958, but its inhabitants came to attend Cokethorpe chapel: references to Hardwick chapelry reflect the concentration of the congregation in that hamlet. Hardwick, unlike Ducklington, was claimed as ancient demesne,[31] in which by charter Bampton church had tithes, perhaps strengthening, in the case of Hardwick, Bampton's persistent claims to parochial rights throughout Ducklington parish.[32] In 1290 the dead of Hardwick were still buried at Bampton, but by then Cokethorpe burials were at Ducklington.[33] As late as 1405–6 the dean and canons of Exeter were claiming for Bampton all Hardwick burials, some of which were taking place illicitly at Ducklington.[34] By the 16th century, however, when it was confirmed that there were no burials at Cokethorpe,[35] Hardwick people

were evidently buried at Ducklington without challenge.[36] Later, although some residents in Cokethorpe House were buried at Ducklington,[37] most were buried at Standlake, of which technically they were parishioners.[38]

In 1520 Cokethorpe was served by a friar who in winter celebrated vespers only on festival days. In 1540 the churchwardens complained of a broken window in the chancel, the responsibility of the rector.[39] In the early 16th century there were pilgrimages to the image or picture of the Blessed Mary of Cokethorpe; wax images were sold to pilgrims from shops or stalls near the chapel.[40] The pilgrimages ceased in the late 1530s after Henrician legislation; allowances for decayed rents from shops associated with the cult were made to the bailiff of Ducklington manor from 1539.[41] A deponent in the 1590s remembered pilgrimages taking place for eight or nine years before the suppression of the monasteries;[42] the practice was presumably much older, although a claim in 1549 that the chapel owed its existence to the cult was evidently unfounded.[43] In the 18th century there was a memory of a curative well at Cokethorpe.[44]

In 1549, although it was conceded that Ducklington's curate celebrated Mass weekly at Cokethorpe, the chapel was suppressed as a chantry; its fabric was sold to Francis Chesildon and *c.* 9 a. of land, including the chapel yard, was sold to Richard Venables and John Maynard.[45] Chesildon pulled down much of the building and sold the materials to Leonard Yate and William Box. Local men successfully argued that the chapel should not have been suppressed, since it provided parochial functions for Cokethorpe and Hardwick as a chapel-of-ease, and in July 1549 Yate and Box were ordered to return the materials and to repair the defaced chapel. By 1553–4, however, there had been little progress beyond the return of the bells.[46] In 1584 the rector denied responsibility for repairing Cokethorpe on the ground that it was only a chapel-of-ease, but he was censured for his neglect.[47] The chapel was still decayed in the 1590s.[48]

There are hints that in the later 16th century the chapel provided a centre for covert Roman Catholic worship in the area. Money for its upkeep was given by John Holyman (d. 1558), rector of Hanborough and formerly bishop of Bristol, a 'zealous Romanist'.[49] The move to

---

23 Ibid. MS. d.d. Par. Duckl. c 4, s.a. 1868–72; ibid. Welch LXI/1, LXII/1; ibid. Peake II/xiii/4; Bodl. MS. Top. Oxon. b 78, ff. 252–4.
24 Above, intro.; above, this section.
25 *Eynsham Cart.* i, p. 157; B.L. Harl. Ch. 45.D.18.
26 Misread as the 'church of La, otherwise the chapel of Cokethorpe': Bodl. MS. Top. Oxon. d 271, ff. 3, 31.
27 *Reg. Sutton,* viii (L.R.S. lxxvi), 173–5.
28 Bodl. MS. Top. Oxon. b 78, ff. 288v.–290v.; *Cal. Pat.* 1364–7, 101, 112.
29 Bodl. MS. Top. Oxon. b 78, ff. 290–2; *Cal. Pat.* 1370–4, 254, 287, 451.
30 e.g. Bodl. MS. Top. Oxon. c 55, ff. 153, 169; *Liber de Antiquis Legibus* (Camd. Soc. [1st ser.], xxxii), pp. ccxxvii sqq.
31 Above, manors (Hardwick).
32 D. & C. Exeter, MS. 2865; J. Blair, 'Parish versus village: the Bampton-Standlake tithe conflict of 1317–19', *Oxon. Local Hist.* ii (2), 34–47.
33 *Reg. Sutton,* viii (L.R.S. lxxvi), 173–5.
34 D. & C. Exeter, MS. 648.

35 Bodl. MS. Top. Oxon. b 78, f. 291v.
36 C.O.S., Duckl. par. reg. transcripts.
37 e.g. ibid. Agnes Carew, s.a. 1633.
38 Ibid. Standlake par. reg. transcripts.
39 *Visit. Dioc. Linc.* i (L.R.S. xxxiii), 132; ibid. ii (L.R.S. xxxv), 51; O.A.S. *Rep.* (1930), 299.
40 Bodl. MS. Top. Oxon. b 78, f. 291v., citing a Particular for Grant not traced in P.R.O.
41 P.R.O., SC 6/Hen. VIII/7248–9. The allowances were not claimed in 1537–8: ibid. SC 6/Hen. VIII/7247.
42 O.R.O. MS. Oxf. Dioc. c 22, f. 67.
43 Above, this section; Bodl. MS. Top. Oxon. b 78, f. 291v.
44 *Hearne's Colln.* xi (O.H.S. lxxii), 67.
45 Bodl. MS. Top. Oxon. b 78, f. 291v.; P.R.O., E 318/37/2025; *Cal. Pat.* 1549–51, 89.
46 P.R.O., E 321/25/11; ibid. STAC 4/4/53.
47 *Archdeacon's Ct.* (O.R.S. xxiv), 139.
48 O.R.O., MS. Oxf. Dioc. c 22, f. 67 and v.
49 Bodl. MS. Top. Oxon. b 78, f. 294v. The alleged bequest is not mentioned in Holyman's will: P.R.O., PROB 11/42A.

Cokethorpe by the Easts, noted recusants, in the 1570s, despite the probable lack of a house of gentry status, may have been connected with the chapel.[50] Both Ducklington and Yelford churches had incumbents who were suspected Romanists.[51]

In the later 17th century the rector was entertained, presumably at Cokethorpe House, when he used the chapel on alternate Sundays for the parish's one Sunday service and sermon.[52] In the 18th century the Harcourts attended Cokethorpe chapel, which by mid century stood isolated in their park.[53] There was a weekly service, but sermons only on alternate Sundays, and communion services four times a year.[54] In the 19th century there was usually a single service with sermon, and average congregations were stated to be 50 in the mornings and 90 in the afternoons.[55] The chapel continued to provide services not only for Hardwick but also for some 25 residents of Cokethorpe Park;[56] that they were not parishioners may have contributed to the friction between the rector, Thomas Farley, and Walter Strickland, which included quarrels over pew rents and churchyard fencing.[57] By the 1880s services had been reduced to only one evening a month, the day of the monthly communion service, but there was an increase to alternate Sundays in 1899 when W. D. Macray acquired a curate.[58] From the 1950s the chapel was used chiefly by Cokethorpe School. Damage caused by a falling elm in 1976 hastened the decision to declare it redundant; it was presented to the school by the old boys in 1979.[59]

The chapel of *ST. MARY* was probably dedicated originally to St. Michael, whose feast day was still observed as Hardwick's wake in the 19th century.[60] By 1365 the dedication was to St. Mary, and in the 16th century, reflecting the importance there of the cult of the Virgin, the chapel was called Our Lady of Cokethorpe.[61] In the 18th century a dedication feast on 22 July was noted, indicating (if not an error) a post-Reformation change of invocation to St. Mary Magdalen which had been reversed by the 19th century.[62] The building comprises chancel, nave, north aisle, and north-west tower.[63] The older masonry is of coursed limestone rubble, additions made in 1873–4 are of dressed stone, and the roof is of 20th-century tiles. The earliest dateable features include a reset plain 12th-

century tympanum inside the south doorway,[64] a notable 12th-century font, and a fragment of carved masonry, probably part of a late 11th-century windowhead, discovered in the demolished east wall in 1873 and adapted as a piscina.[65] The lower stages of the tower, which include on the west side a 13th-century two-light lancet and signs of a gable, and on the north a blocked early window close to the eastern corner, suggest that the largely post-medieval tower was built up on the walls of a probably 13th-century north aisle.[66] The plain western arch of the surviving north arcade also belonged to an earlier aisle, of which the foundations were discovered in the 1870s; until then a crude diagonal wall created a passage through the arch into the east side of the tower.[67] There may have been a large reredos in the medieval chancel: a blocked, probably 14th-century, window was revealed in the blank east wall in 1873, and until that date the east end was lit by a large, probably 14th-century, window at the east end of the south wall.[68] The image of the Virgin, the focus of Cokethorpe's medieval cult, may have formed part of such a reredos.

The surviving plain late-Perpendicular work perhaps dates from an unrecorded rebuilding in the late 16th century or early 17th, after the chapel had been ruinous from 1549 until at least 1590.[69] The tower, with blocked round-headed apertures, presumably bell-openings, in the second stage, probably belongs to that phase of building. In the early 18th century work sponsored by the Harcourts included timber flooring,[70] new bells and plate, perhaps the blocking of a late-Perpendicular priest's doorway in the south chancel wall (re-opened in 1873–4),[71] and perhaps the addition of the surviving south porch, certainly built before 1824 and for long housing chained books given in the early 18th century.[72] The tower's surviving belfry stage, of rendered brick, and low pointed roof were added before 1824, probably between 1807 and 1811 when there was much repair and refitting and the bells were rehung.[73]

Repaving and refurnishing were carried out by the rector Thomas Farley in 1840–3.[74] His successor W. D. Macray instigated a major restoration in 1873–4 to plans by E. G. Bruton;[75] the chief additions were a north aisle for the use of the Cokethorpe Park residents, donated in memory of Walter Strickland (d. 1870) by his relict

50   Above, manors; below, nonconf.
51   Above, this section; below, Yelford, church.
52   *Reg. Magd. Coll.* N.S. iv. 35–6.
53   e.g. O.R.O., MS. Oxf. Dioc. d 555; Bodl. MS. Top. Oxon. b 78, f. 212v.
54   *Secker's Visit.* 55–6; O.R.O., MSS. Oxf. Dioc. d 555, d 558, d 561, d 564.
55   O.R.O., MSS. Oxf. Dioc. b 38, c 335, c 338, c 344, d 572, d 580; *Ch. and Chapel*, no. 203; *Wilb. Visit.* 51.
56   O.R.O., MS. Oxf. Dioc. c 2205, no. 33.
57   *Wilb. Letter Bks.* pp. 286–7, 289, 293–4.
58   Magd. Coll. Mun., MS. 799 (i–vi): par. mags.
59   O.R.O., MS. Oxf. Dioc. c 1801; plaque in chap.; C.O.S., PRN 11202: notes by James Cartland.
60   Bodl. MS. Top. Oxon. b 78, f. 301b, *verso*.
61   *Cal. Pat.* 1364–7, 101; Bodl. MS. Top. Oxon. b 78, f. 291v.
62   Bodl. MS. Top. Oxon. b 78, f. 301b, *verso*; O.R.O., MS. d.d. Par. Duckl. b 8, f. 1.
63   Above, plate 23.

64   It was in that position in 1823: Skelton, *Oxon. Antiq.* Bampton hund., p. 8 and n.
65   Bodl. MS. Top. Oxon. b 78, f. 302.
66   For a different view of the antiquity of tower and gable cf. C.O.S., PRN 11202: Cartland's notes.
67   Bodl. MS. Top. Oxon. d 271, f. 27c; *Oxf. Jnl.* 17 Oct. 1874; O.A.S. *Rep.* (1871), 16.
68   Bodl. MS. Top. Oxon. d 271, f. 27c; above, plate 23; O.A.S. *Rep.* (1871), 16.
69   Above, this section. For a different dating of many features, D.o.E., *Revised Hist. Bldg. List* (1988).
70   *Hearne's Colln.* xi (O.H.S. lxxii), 67.
71   Bodl. MS. Top. Oxon. b 78, f. 301b.
72   W. J. Monk, *By Thames and Windrush*, 46; O.A.S. *Rep.* (1872), 32–5.
73   C.O.S., PRN 11202: Cartland's notes; O.R.O., MS. d.d. Par. Duckl. b 8, *passim*.
74   O.R.O., MS. d.d. Par. Duckl. b 8.
75   Bodl. MS. Top. Oxon. b 78, f. 305v.; O.R.O., MS. d.d. Par. Duckl. b 8, s.a. 1873.

Catherine,[76] an east window, a replacement of the medieval window at the east end of the south wall, heightened chancel and nave walls, and a new roof. The pulpit, font, and large pews for the rector and the owners of Cokethorpe Park were removed from the chancel, which was given a raised floor; the harmonium and singers were moved there from the demolished west gallery. There was a shortfall in subscriptions, notably because St. John's College considered the building inconvenient for Hardwick and not worth restoring.[77]

The 12th-century font has an elaborate intersecting arcade with spiral-fluted columns and rose decoration.[78] The credence shelf and piscina are medieval fragments found in the east wall in 1873.[79] The pulpit, lectern, and reredos, incorporating 17th-century woodwork from Magdalen College, were constructed by the rector Thomas Farley c. 1842.[80] Bosses bearing the arms of Sydenham and Lovel were brought in from the exterior of the building during the restoration of 1873–4.[81] There are several memorials to the Stricklands and their successors at Cokethorpe House, including stained glass by Usher & Kelly in the east window, given in 1874 by Frances Cottrell-Dormer daughter of Walter Strickland (d. 1839).[82] The three bells include one of 1732 by Henry Bagley.[83] The plate includes a chalice of 1575 and another, with paten cover, of 1727 given by Elizabeth, Lady Harcourt.[84]

A chapel yard said to be 1 a. in 1549[85] was reduced in 1712 when Simon, Viscount Harcourt (d. 1727) leased some of it to lay out an avenue.[86] It was later merged with the park; it measured less than ¼ a. in 1761 and remained unfenced until 1875 when Mrs. Strickland gave iron railings, removed in modern times.[87] The base of an ancient cross stood near the south porch until destroyed in 1873.[88]

NONCONFORMITY. The possibility that Roman Catholic worship was maintained after the Reformation in Ducklington church and Cokethorpe chapel is discussed elsewhere.[89] The principal known recusant was Edward East who moved from Bledlow (Bucks.) before 1577, making his house a Catholic centre where masses

were said.[90] East's daughter and heir Dorothy married Thomas Fitzherbert (d. 1640), who later fled the country, became a Jesuit, and Rector of the English College at Rome.[91] Among other recusants at Cokethorpe in the late 16th century and early 17th was the gentry family of Heywood which included a Benedictine monk and probably a secular priest.[92] The Cokethorpe group seems to have dispersed in the earlier 17th century, and only isolated Roman Catholics were recorded in the parish thereafter.[93]

In 1678 there were 3 Quaker women and 2 other dissenters in the parish, and 5 dissenters were listed in 1683.[94] Two Anabaptists were attending Cote chapel (in Bampton parish) in 1738 and a Ducklington farmer and his wife regularly attended there in the later 18th century.[95] By 1802 there were said to be no dissenters, but a few years later the rector admitted that a few parishioners probably attended 'conventicles' at Witney.[96] In 1817 several families were attending meetings there, mostly Methodist, and Wesleyans were reported regularly in Ducklington thereafter.[97] In 1827 Witney's Wesleyan minister registered a meeting house in Ducklington;[98] the meeting was briefly included in Witney's local preaching plan but was given up in 1832.[99] In 1854 a few reported dissenters of unstated denomination included two farming families.[1] Congregationalists from Ducklington were attending Witney chapel at that time, and in 1861 an inhabitant was a Wesleyan preacher.[2] Primitive Methodists from Witney were active in Ducklington in the 1860s, and occasionally later.[3]

In 1868 a Baptist chapel was built on the Witney road on land provided by the Cook family and under the auspices of Cote chapel.[4] Ducklington remained part of the Cote circuit despite efforts to make it independent in 1914. In 1901 the congregation was large enough to be expected to contribute £10 to circuit funds. In the mid 20th century there were 20–30 adult members and a flourishing Sunday school.[5] In 1990 the chapel had a resident minister and a membership of 17 adults and 26 children.[6] The chapel, to a design by H. Lee of Bristol, was built of limestone in Gothic style; it was renovated in 1901.[7]

76 Plaque in chapel.
77 Bodl. MS. Top. Oxon. b 78, f. 305v.; Oxf. Jnl. 17 Oct. 1874; O.R.O., MS. Oxf. Dioc. c 2205, no. 33.
78 Bodl. MS. Top. Oxon. d 271, ff. 29–30.
79 Ibid. b 78, f. 302.
80 Ibid. ff. 168, 305v.; Reg. Magd. Coll. N.S. vi. 81–2; C.O.S., PRN 11202: J. Cartland's notes.
81 Bodl. MS. Top. Oxon. b 78, f. 305v.; B.L. Add. MS. 36372: drawing of 1825. For the Sydenham/Lovel marriage, Complete Peerage, viii. 215.
82 Oxf. Jnl. 17 Oct. 1874; plaque in chapel.
83 Ch. Bells Oxon. i, p. 98.
84 Evans, Ch. Plate, 59–60.
85 Cal. Pat. 1549–51, 89.
86 Hearne's Colln. xi (O.H.S. lxxii), 67; Bodl. MS. d.d. Harcourt c 14/1.
87 O.R.O., MSS. d.d. Par. Duckl. c 1, f. 1v.; e 7, s.a. 1875; ibid. MS. Oxf. Archd. Oxon. c 61, ff. 410, 423, 425; N.M.R., photo. of chap. (1943).
88 Bodl. MS. Top. Oxon. b 78, f. 302.
89 Above, church.
90 Above, manors; Cath. Rec. Soc. xxii. 110; lvii. 122; Bodl. MS. Top. Oxon. d 602, ff. 283–4, 411.
91 Bodl. MS. Top. Oxon. d 602, ff. 380–1; D.N.B.

92 Bodl. MS. Top. Oxon. d 602, ff. 284, 291; H. E. Salter, 'Oxon. Recusants', O.A.S. Rep. (1924), 17, 25, 40, 46, 53–4, 56, 58; Stapleton, Cath. Miss. 181.
93 e.g. Compton Census, 423; Bp. Fell and Nonconf. 66, n. 229; W. O. Hassall, 'Papists in Early 18th-cent. Oxon.', Oxoniensia, xiii. 80.
94 O.R.O., BOQM I/ii/1, s.a. 1676–7, 1683; O.R.O., MS. Oxf. Dioc. d 708, ff. 95v.–96; Bp. Fell and Nonconf. 38.
95 e.g. O.R.O., MSS. Oxf. Dioc. d 555, 558, 561.
96 Ibid. d 566, d 570.
97 Ibid. d 576.
98 Ibid. c 645, f. 86; ibid. Cal. Q.S. viii. 84.
99 Ibid. Acc. 1060, I/i/6 a, ff. 5–6, 10, 16, 34, 43.
1 Wilb. Visit. 51.
2 e.g. O.R.O., WCC I/1, f. 55; I/2, s.a. 1861; P.R.O., RG 9/906, s.v. Dix, Chas.
3 O.R.O., Acc. 1060, II/1 b, 1 c.
4 Baptist Union Corpn., file 1367/4; J. Stanley, Ch. in the Hop Garden, 209; Baptist Mag. (1868), 732; Bodl. MS. Top. Oxon. b 78, ff. 68–9.
5 Regent's Park Coll., Oxf., Cote Ch. Bk. 1882–1972.
6 Baptist Union Dir. (1990–1), 111.
7 Baptist Mag. (1868), 732; Regent's Park Coll., Cote Ch. Bk. s.a. 1901.

From the 1890s Baptists attached to the Cote circuit met in a rented room in Hardwick. A chapel was being planned in 1912, but disagreements reduced support; in 1913 members walked to Ducklington for evening services. In 1917 the Hardwick meetings ceased.[8]

EDUCATION. In 1759 some 'well-disposed persons' were paying a schoolmaster in Ducklington to teach a few children;[9] similar support for teaching reading was noted in the 1770s, but in 1802 there was no school of any kind, the 'principal parishioners' sending their children to Witney schools.[10] The accessibility of Witney National school for older children was blamed for the failure to provide Ducklington schools.[11] In 1808 there was a dame school in Ducklington with c. 30 children,[12] and by 1815 there was a school with 12 boys, another with 22 girls.[13] In 1819 two young women taught 40–50 children, probably infants, at the parents' expense, and in 1831 some 30 or 40 children 'of the poor' were similarly taught.[14] In 1835 a Sunday school, begun by the rector in 1832, was attracting c. 75 children.[15]

Although an approach was made to the National Society in the 1830s the parish was said to have been unable to raise subscriptions to meet a grant.[16] For the Sunday school the Stricklands of Cokethorpe offered a schoolroom in a disused mansion (probably the 'Great House' demolished c. 1840), but declined the expense of fitting it out.[17] Ducklington's day and Sunday schools, supported chiefly by the rector, Thomas Farley, continued until the 1850s.[18] The day school, an infants' school run in her cottage by Hannah Fisher, continued on a small scale long after a National school was opened.[19] Another small school, remembered for teaching reading and arithmetic but not writing, was held in a cottage west of the Strickland Arms in the 1830s or 1840s.[20]

A National school and attached teachers' house overlooking Ducklington green were built in 1857–8 on a site given by the Stricklands. The cost was met by subscriptions and a parliamentary grant.[21] In 1869 there were c. 40 pupils from the age of four, but the rector noted that numbers were low because 'the old dame school system lingers'; an attempt to establish an evening school failed.[22]

W. D. Macray, rector from 1870, immediately opened an evening school, which attracted a government grant, and placed the day school's finances on a sound footing. Profits from a sale of parish houses were used for school improvements in 1872.[23] In the later 19th century about half the school's income of £100–£120 came from subscriptions, school pence, and an annual contribution by the rector,[24] the rest from parliamentary grants. In the 1870s there were two mistresses but from 1884 one certificated teacher, usually aided by assistants or monitors who received nominal payments.[25] In 1872 there were 38 infants and 47 older pupils, and winter evening classes were attended by 15.[26] Accommodation was increased and by 1883 average attendance was 92; the rector's son continued to provide evening classes.[27] The infants' classroom was enlarged in 1896 and a third room added in 1901.[28]

The school was reorganized as a junior school in 1930. Senior children continued to attend Witney schools. Average attendance at Ducklington in 1939 was only 36, but numbers increased sharply as the village expanded in modern times; in 1970 the roll was 159. New school buildings on the opposite side of the green, opened in 1962, were extended in the 1970s. In 1994 the school roll was 144. In that year, to finance extensions, it was agreed to sell the old school buildings, which had continued in use for infants' classes after strong local resistance to closure.[29]

At Hardwick there was a mixed school with 11 pupils in 1815 and 20 in 1835, of whom 12 were supported by Frances Strickland of Cokethorpe.[30] The school survived until 1894, supported chiefly by the Stricklands with small contributions from St. John's College.[31] The pupils, usually fewer than 20, were taught in the teacher's house.[32]

CHARITIES. Richard Lydall of Northmoor, by will proved 1721, left 2 adjacent cottages and 8½ a. in Hardwick, his birthplace, for a bread charity, which was distributed at Cokethorpe chapel.[33] One cottage was later demolished and in the later 18th century and early 19th the estate was rented for between £7 and £14 10s. a

8 Stanley, *Ch. in the Hop Garden*, 215; Regent's Park Coll., Cote Ch. Bk. 1882–1972.
9 O.R.O., MSS. Oxf. Dioc. d 555, f. 181; d 558, f. 196.
10 Ibid. d 561, f. 187; d 564, f. 156; d 566, f. 113.
11 e.g. ibid. d 574, ff. 104–5.
12 Ibid. d 707, f. 57.
13 Ibid. c 433, f. 81.
14 *Educ. of Poor Digest*, H.C. 224, p. 723 (1819), ix (2); O.R.O., MS. Oxf. Dioc. b 38, f. 78.
15 *Educ. Enq. Abstract*, H.C. 62, p. 746 (1835), xlii.
16 O.R.O., MS. Oxf. Dioc. b 38, f. 78; Magd. Coll. Mun., MS. 799 (v), Dec. 1903: brief hist. of sch. by W. D. Macray.
17 O.R.O., MS. Oxf. Dioc. b 38, f. 78. For the house, above, other estates.
18 *Wilb. Visit.* 51.
19 Cf. Bodl. MS. Top. Oxon. b 78, f. 157v.; Magd. Coll. Mun., MS. 799 (v), Dec. 1903.
20 Bodl. MS. Top. Oxon. b 78, f. 157v.
21 Magd. Coll. Mun., MS. 799 (i), Nov. 1888; ibid. MS. 799 (v), Dec. 1903.
22 O.R.O., MS. Oxf. Dioc. c 335.
23 Ibid. c 344; ibid. MS. d.d. Par. Duckl. c 4, Mar. 1872.

24 For the contribution, below, charities.
25 Bodl. G.A. Oxon. 8° 622: printed sch. accts. 1871–96.
26 O.R.O., MS. Oxf. Dioc. c 338, ff. 144–5; *Returns Relating to Elem. Educ.* H.C. 201, p. 324 (1871), lv.
27 *Returns Relating to Elem. Educ.* p. 324; *Public Elem. Schs. 1875–6* [C. 1882], pp. 214–15, H.C. (1877), lxvii; *Rep. of Educ. Cttee. of Council, 1882–3* [C. 3706-I], pp. 717–19, H.C. (1883), xxv; Magd. Coll. Mun., MS. 799 (i), June 1886.
28 Bodl. G.A. Oxon. 8° 622, s.a. 1896; *Return of Non-Provided Schs.* H.C. 178 (1906), lxxxviii; Magd. Coll. Mun., MS. 799 (iv), Dec. 1900, Sept. 1901.
29 Inf. from L.E.A.
30 O.R.O., MS. Oxf. Dioc. c 433, f. 81; *Educ. Enq. Abstract*, H.C. 62, p. 746 (1835), xlii.
31 Magd. Coll. Mun., MS. 799 (v), Sept. 1904; Bodl. G.A. Oxon. 8° 622; *Gardner's Dir. Oxon.* (1852).
32 O.R.O., MS. Oxf. Dioc. b 70, f. 292; *Returns Relating to Elem. Educ.* H.C. 201, p. 324 (1871), lv.
33 *10th Rep. Com. Char.* 359; O.R.O., MS. Wills Oxon. 139/4/48. Lydall was born in 1642: C.O.S., par. reg. transcripts.

year. In 1824 bread was distributed to *c.* 16 poor Hardwick families.[34] At inclosure in 1853 the churchwardens of Hardwick were awarded *c.* 4½ a. for Lydall's land, which was turned into allotments.[35] In the later 19th century the rent of cottage and allotments was *c.* £15[36] and was not raised substantially until 1967. Bread distributions continued, but the charity was also deflected at the rector's discretion to chiropody and other purposes.[37]

Anne Sammon (d. 1832), daughter of Ducklington's rector John Pinnell, left £200 for a bread and coal charity. After prolonged litigation the charity, in operation by the 1870s, was endowed with *c.* £105, which in the later 19th century and in 1969 was yielding *c.* £3 a year.[38]

On the death of Catherine Strickland of Cokethorpe House in 1892 her relatives provided a memorial fund of £60 to ensure continuation of her regular charitable donations to the parish, which from 1873 or earlier had been £5 a year used for coal. In the 1960s the fund was yielding £5 a year.[39]

Kenneth Macray, son of the rector W. D.

Macray, by will proved 1941 left £300 for general alms with no religious distinction. The income was *c.* £16 10s. in 1968.[40]

A weekly bread charity for Ducklington intended by the will of James Leverett of Witney dated 1783 seems never to have been implemented.[41] Under a Scheme of 1972 the charities of Lydall, Sammon, Strickland, and Macray were amalgamated and the income (*c.* £150 in 1979) was used for general relief in need.[42]

In the late 18th century, following a long-established practice referred to as the 'Easter custom', the rector provided an Easter feast for his parishioners at the rectory house; the traditional fare was pies of veal or apple. In 1798, during a vacancy in the living, Magdalen College agreed to provide £10 worth of bread instead of the 'custom', and bread of that value was provided thereafter, divided equally between the inhabitants of Hardwick and Ducklington. Thomas Farley (rector 1826–70) transferred the customary payment to the support of the village school, a practice followed by his successor W. D. Macray.[43]

NORTHMOOR

NORTHMOOR, a secluded rural parish between the rivers Thames and Windrush, lies 6 miles (9.75 km.) south-west of Oxford and 6¾ miles (10.8 km.) east of Bampton.[44] In the 11th century part of it formed an outlier to an estate at Taynton in Chadlington hundred, and the parish remained a detached part of that hundred.[45] The ancient parish, compact in shape, included the hamlet of Moreton, and in 1877 comprised 2,048 a.; 1 a. was transferred from Stanton Harcourt under the Divided Parishes Act in 1886, and 3 a. were transferred to Standlake in 1932, creating a civil parish of 2,046 a. (828 ha.).[46]

The eastern and southern boundaries mostly followed the river Thames, and the western boundary the river Windrush, small deviations presumably representing the rivers' earlier courses. Most of Achim or Eacham mead west of the Windrush, and Gaingey mead south of the Thames, were included from an early date. The sinuous northern boundary followed small streams between Northmoor's and Stanton Harcourt's open fields, and in the extreme north-east followed the perimeter of inclosed meadow.[47]

Sections of those boundaries were ancient: in 1059 the bounds of the estate attached to Taynton ran down the Windrush to meet the Thames at 'beafolces ears' (i.e. arse), probably ¼ mile west of Newbridge where traces survive of a relict river channel roughly on the line of the modern parish boundary. They then followed the Thames eastwards, turning up a stream or ditch to *wilstede*, and continuing to cattle (*rythera*) ford and *wireneges* thorn, apparently near the Windrush in the north-western part of the later parish.[48] The points between the Thames and *wireneges* thorn are unidentified, but it is likely that that estate represented only the south-western part of the later parish, corresponding with a part of Northmoor then included in Bampton's *parochia*: in 1318 deponents claimed, probably anachronistically, that Bampton's eastern boundary still ran down a stream called Wirlak' or Wytherlak', which flowed south or south-eastwards into the Thames apparently from the Linch hill area of Stanton Harcourt, and which may have been the boundary ditch of 1059.[49] The later parish's north-eastern part may have belonged in the

34 *Char. Don.* 968–9; *10th Rep. Com. Char.* 359; cf. Magd. Coll. Mun., MS. 799 (ii), June 1885: notes on char.
35 O.R.O., Standlake incl. award, where the charity's open-field land was also measured at only 4½ a.
36 *Gardner's Dir Oxon.* (1852); Magd. Coll. Mun., MS. 799 (i), printed par. accts. 1873–9.
37 O.R.C.C., Kimber files.
38 Magd. Coll. Mun., MS. 799 (v), Aug. 1904: notes on char.; ibid. MS. 799 (i–iii), char. accts. 1873–90; O.R.C.C., Kimber files.
39 O.R.C.C., Kimber files; Magd. Coll. Mun., MS. 799 (i–iii), char. accts. 1873–90.
40 O.R.C.C., Kimber files.
41 Bodl. MS. Top. Oxon. b 78, f. 28; ibid. G.A. Oxon. 8° 364: printed copy of will.
42 O.R.C.C., MS. Rep. on Oxon. Chars. 1979.

43 *10th Rep. Com. Char.* 359; Bodl. MS. Top. Oxon. b 78, ff. 63, 211v.; ibid. G.A. Oxon. 8° 622: sch. accts. 1871–95.
44 The principal maps used were O.R.O., tithe and incl. maps; ibid. Misc. Ch. II/1–2 (pre-incl. maps 1839); O.S. Map 1/2,500, Oxon. XXXVIII. 7, XXXVIII. 10–11 (1876 and later edns.); ibid. 6", Oxon. XXXVIII (1883 and later edns.); ibid. 1/25,000, SP 40/50 (1980 edn.). This article was written in 1995.
45 *Census,* 1841; *Kelly's Dir. Oxon.* (1883); below, manors.
46 O.S. *Area Bk.* (1877); *Census,* 1881–1991.
47 O.R.O., tithe award; *V.C.H. Oxon.* xii. 268; below, econ. hist.; below, Standlake, intro.
48 *P.N. Oxon.* (E.P.N.S.), ii. 367, 488–9.
49 D. & C. Exeter, MS. 2865; *V.C.H. Oxon.* xii. 267; cf. Bodl. MS. d.d. Harcourt c 47/4; ibid. b 4, item 2; O.R.O., MS. Wills Oxon. 51/4/10, mentioning Wivelake and Wivell or Wyfolde ditch near Linch hill.

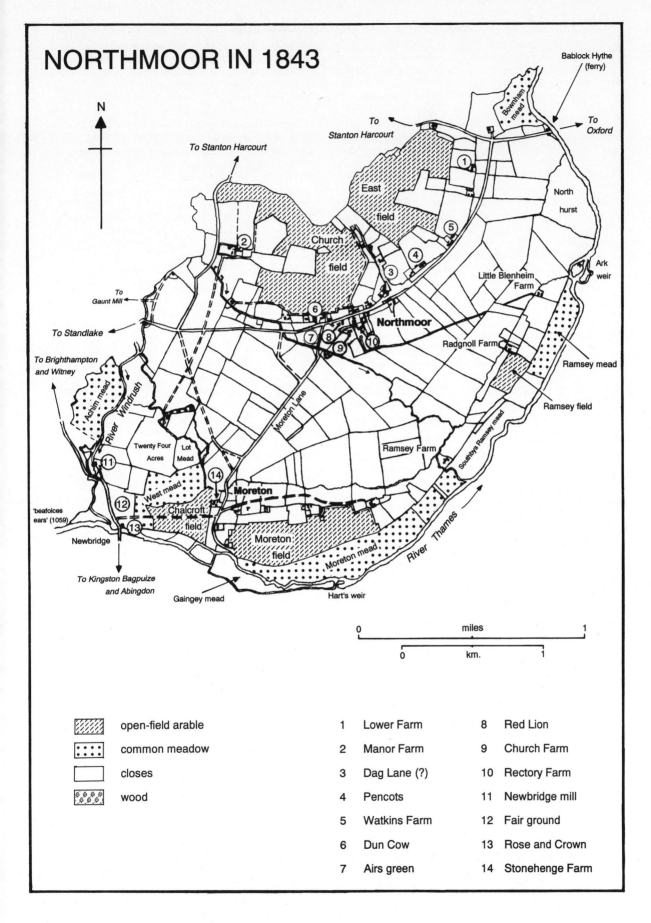

NORTHMOOR IN 1843

N

Bablock Hythe (ferry)

To Stanton Harcourt

To Oxford

To Stanton Harcourt

Bownham mead

East field

North hurst

Church field

Ark weir

Little Blenheim Farm

To Gaunt Mill

To Standlake

Northmoor

Radgnoll Farm

Ramsey mead

To Brighthampton and Witney

Ramsey field

River Windrush

Achim mead

Moreton Lane

Ramsey Farm

Southbys Ramsey mead

Twenty Four Acres

Lot Mead

Moreton

West mead

Chalcroft field

'beafolces ears' (1059)

Newbridge

Moreton field

River Thames

To Kingston Bagpuize and Abingdon

Gaingey mead

Moreton mead

Hart's weir

0   miles   1

0   km.   1

open-field arable	1 Lower Farm	8 Red Lion
common meadow	2 Manor Farm	9 Church Farm
closes	3 Dag Lane (?)	10 Rectory Farm
wood	4 Pencots	11 Newbridge mill
	5 Watkins Farm	12 Fair ground
	6 Dun Cow	13 Rose and Crown
	7 Airs green	14 Stonehenge Farm

11th century to Stanton Harcourt, which claimed parochial rights until the mid 12th century and pasture rights much later. By the later 12th century Northmoor formed a single estate with its own church,[50] and, notwithstanding Bampton's persistent claims, its later boundaries were probably already established: in 1318 another deponent asserted that the parochial division was partly by fee, and that all land belonging to the prior of Deerhurst as lord of Northmoor lay within Northmoor parish.[51]

The parish lies chiefly on river gravels of the First Flood Plain terrace, fringed by a wide band of alluvium in the east and south which includes the site of Moreton.[52] It is notably flat and low-lying, c. 62 m. in the north-east, c. 64 m. near Northmoor village, and c. 65 m. in the extreme north-west. Flooding occurred frequently and although there was good-quality meadow there was much inferior pasture.[53] The name More or Moor, meaning marsh, was recorded from the 11th century; the prefix North, distinguishing it from Southmoor then in Berkshire, was added intermittently from the late 13th century.[54]

The main Gloucester–London road, crossing the Thames at Newbridge, cut across the parish's south-west corner.[55] It was partly re-routed in 1782, prompting disputes over liability for repairs.[56] Cropmarks indicate an early but undated east–west trackway south of Manor Farm, which curved south-westwards towards the river Windrush, and which also branched northwards towards Manor Farm itself;[57] further south, the existing east–west road along which Northmoor village stands, called Oxford way in 1666,[58] formed part of an early route from Standlake to Oxford via the Thames crossing at Bablock Hythe, where a ferry operated by 1212.[59] Then and later the ferry was held freely of Northmoor manor for rent, suit, and the service of ferrying the prior of Deerhurst or his servants;[60] a causeway to the ferry was mentioned from 1320, when it was said to be frequently damaged by floods and was repaired from alms.[61] A 'great boat' to ferry carts and coaches was mentioned in 1693.[62] A private attempt in 1855 to build a road bridge under Act of Parliament failed following opposition from, among others,

the earl of Abingdon, who feared losing tolls at Swinford bridge in Eynsham,[63] and a bridge rebuilt in 1883 was evidently only part of the causeway across a small stream.[64] In the early 20th century no ferry ran at night or during the frequent high floods, and harness horses were sometimes drowned, but despite repeated local appeals for a bridge the ferry continued until the 1960s, when the crossing was abandoned.[65] Thereafter the nearest crossings were at Newbridge and Swinford. A ferry attached apparently to Fyfield manor (then Berks.) in the 15th century[66] was perhaps that at Hart's weir south-east of Moreton, recorded from the 17th century when access was across Moreton meadow; the ferry was not mentioned in the 19th century, and a footbridge was built in 1879.[67] A ferry across the Thames was attached to a Northmoor freehold in 1279,[68] and the 'ferry place' west of Newbridge was mentioned in the mid 16th century.[69]

The road southwards from Stanton Harcourt past Manor Farm may have formed part of an ancient pattern,[70] and was perhaps that called the Broadway in the 14th century.[71] The modern name Cow Lane may have derived from its use as a droveway to Stanton Harcourt's West moor, where Northmoor's inhabitants had grazing rights.[72] Dag Lane, apparently a track running north-westwards from Northmoor's main street,[73] was mentioned from the 15th century,[74] and a predecessor of Chapel Lane, beginning opposite the church and running closely parallel to Dag Lane at its northern end, seems to have existed by the mid 18th.[75] Moreton Lane, running southwards across the common, was recorded from the 17th century and was presumably medieval, and field tracks and bridges or fords crossing small streams were mentioned frequently in the 16th century and the 17th.[76] At inclosure c. 1844 most of the chief roads were confirmed, though Dag Lane was superseded by the later Chapel Lane, which became a 25-foot carriage road and was extended to the parish's northern boundary. A new 30-foot road running westwards from Moreton to Newbridge replaced an earlier track,[77] and in the 1860s new brick bridges were built over some

50 Below, manors; econ. hist.; church.
51 D. & C. Exeter, MS. 2865.
52 Geol. Surv. Map 1/25,000, solid and drift, sheet 236 (1982 edn.).
53 Below, econ. hist.
54 Oseney Cart. iii, p. 116; P.N. Oxon. (E.P.N.S.), ii. 366.
55 O.S. Map 6", Oxon. XXXVIII (1883 edn.); below, Standlake, intro.
56 O.R.O., Cal. Q.S. viii. 631–2; St. John's Coll. Mun., ADMIN. I. A.7, p. 548.
57 C.O.S., PRN 8320; D. Benson and D. Miles, Upper Thames Valley, 48–9.
58 Bodl. MS. Rawl. B. 250, f. 11.
59 P.N. Oxon. (E.P.N.S.), ii. 366; above, plate 29; below, Standlake, intro.
60 Cal. Pat. 1317–21, 43, 430–1; Rot. Hund. (Rec. Com.), ii. 733; cf. Bodl. MS. d.d. Harcourt c 122/1; ibid. b 10, p. 14.
61 Cal. Pat. 1317–20, 430–1; cf. Bodl. MS. Rawl. B. 250, f. 7.
62 B.L. Harl. MS. 4716, f. 16; cf. O.R.O., Cal. Q.S. ix, p. 403.
63 Berks. R.O., D/EM B31/1–2.
64 Ibid. D/TC 185, s.a. 1883–5; Ch. Ch. Arch., MS. Estates 80, f. 144.
65 Bodl. G.A. Oxon. c 317/12, appeals 1910; J. Stowell,

Glimpses of Northmoor through 800 Yrs. (priv. print. c. 1930), 1, 34: copy in Bodl. G.A. Oxon. 8° 1055 (17); O.S. Map 6", SP 40 SW. (1960 edn.); local inf.
66 Cal. Close, 1447–54, 38–9; Cat. Anct. D. v, A 10957.
67 Bodl. MSS. d.d. Harcourt c 123/8, c 123/11; St. John's Coll. Mun., II.36; Jefferys, Oxon. Map (1767); Davis, Oxon. Map (1797); F. S. Thacker, Thames Highway (1968 edn.), ii. 80, 83.
68 Rot. Hund. (Rec. Com.), ii. 733.
69 St. John's Coll. Mun., II.5, p. 10; XV.16.
70 V.C.H. Oxon. xii. 269.
71 Bodl. MSS. d.d. Harcourt c 68/20, c 68/22.
72 V.C.H. Oxon. xii. 268; below, econ. hist.
73 Jefferys, Oxon. Map (1767); O.S. Map 1", sheet 13 (1830 edn.); cf. St. John's Coll. Mun., XV.40; Bodl. MS. d.d. Harcourt c 76/6; Magd. Coll. Mun., D-Y 5; Ch. Ch. Arch., Standlake A 48; O.R.O., tithe and incl. awards.
74 Bodl. MS. d.d. Harcourt c 68/36.
75 St. John's Coll. Mun., XV.10A, mentioning a road belonging to Ric. Kent; cf. O.R.O., Misc. Ch. II/2.
76 Bodl. MS. Rawl. B. 250, ff. 7, 11; ibid. MSS. d.d. Harcourt c 122/5, c 123/5, c 123/14; Ch. Ch. Arch., Standlake A 48.
77 O.R.O., incl. award and map; Bodl. (R) C 17:49 (99); Jefferys, Oxon. Map (1767).

watercourses.[78] In 1870 Northmoor was said to have been 'almost unapproachable' in winter before improved drainage in the 1860s,[79] and incumbents throughout the 19th century commented on the poor roads.[80] A wharf at Newbridge, later a coal wharf, was mentioned from the late 17th century,[81] but in 1871 trade was thought to have declined since the opening in 1861 of the Witney railway;[82] the wharf closed in the early 20th century.[83] Northmoor lock, in the east on the river Thames between the former Hart's and Ark weirs, was opened in 1896 and remained in 1995.[84]

Numerous cropmarks indicating prehistoric activity survive south, south-west, and north-west of Northmoor village, and earthworks noted south-east of the village may have been remains of Bronze-Age round barrows.[85] A Middle Iron-Age enclosed settlement near Watkins Farm, occupied c. 250 B.C.–c. 50 B.C., had a predominantly pastoral economy perhaps with an emphasis on horse-breeding,[86] and there was probably Iron-Age settlement near Stonehenge Farm further south.[87] An Iron-Age sword was dredged from the Thames at Newbridge.[88] The Iron-Age settlements were re-used in the Roman period, that at Watkins Farm apparently after a brief abandonment,[89] and there is evidence of further Romano-British settlement west and south-west of Northmoor village;[90] a Roman altar was found in the Thames at Bablock Hythe,[91] and Roman coins on the flood-plain south of the village and at Northmoor lock.[92] Occupation near Watkins Farm seems to have ended by the 3rd century, perhaps because of wetter conditions, though farming presumably from another site continued until the 4th century.[93] No evidence has been found of early or middle Anglo-Saxon occupation,[94] and in 1059 the estate at Northmoor granted with Taynton was described as marsh or moor.[95] Pottery probably of the 11th or 12th century found near Watkins Farm nevertheless suggests nearby settlement by that date,[96] and a few of the 51 tenants noted on Taynton manor in 1086[97] may have lived at Northmoor.

In 1279 there were 22 recorded tenants at Northmoor, but several other inhabitants and landholders were mentioned in contemporary sources,[98] and in all there may have been 30 or more households. At least 55 taxpayers were listed in 1306, 44 in 1316, and 43 in 1327, not all of them resident,[99] and in 1377 poll tax was paid by 140 people over 14,[1] implying that the impact of plague had been limited. The population may have fallen by the 16th century when only 11–20 taxpayers were noted,[2] but was probably considerably higher than the 63 people claimed in 1548:[3] in the mid 17th century there were at least 120–30 adults,[4] and 43 houses were taxed in 1662.[5] From the mid 17th century and particularly from c. 1700 baptisms usually outnumbered burials,[6] and most 18th-century curates estimated c. 50 houses;[7] in 1801 there were 53 houses occupied by 334 people. The population rose, with intermissions, until 1851, when it was 375, of whom c. 74 lived in Moreton; thereafter it fell to 212 by 1901, rising gradually to 292 in 1961 and to 363 in 1991.[8]

Northmoor village lies loosely scattered chiefly along the north side of the Standlake–Bablock Hythe road, on the south side of which stands the church, founded in the mid 12th century.[9] Thirteenth- and 14th-century references to houses with fields on the north, the moor on the south, and adjoining tenements to east and west[10] suggest a similar but perhaps slightly denser medieval pattern. Most older houses stand well back from the modern road behind drainage ditches, with a wide belt of former common in front,[11] perhaps the green plot or place (*viridis placee*) lying by one house's gate in 1393.[12] The rectory house, mentioned from the 14th century,[13] stands immediately south of the church jutting into the former common; traces survive of a wide access road running alongside the churchyard's southern edge, which connected with the main road north of the church, and, apparently, with Moreton Lane.[14] Two houses immediately west of the rectory house, presumably on or near the site of Church Farm, were mentioned in 1381,[15] and perhaps fronted a small triangular green

78 Berks. R.O., D/TC 184, pp. 39, 51.
79 *Jnl. R. Agric. Soc.* 2nd ser. vi. 374.
80 O.R.O., MSS. Oxf. Dioc. c 359, ff. 297–8; d 573, f. 21.
81 Bodl. MS. Rawl. D. 384, ff. 110–11; O.R.O., Cal. Q.S. i, f. 35b.
82 Bodl. MS. d.d. Harcourt c 266, p. 46; E. T. MacDermot and C. R. Clinker, *Hist. G.W.R.* i. 289.
83 *Kelly's Dir. Oxon.* (1903 and later edns.); *Sale Cat., Harcourt Settled Estates* (1924), lot 53: copy in Bodl. G.A. Oxon. c 226.
84 F. S. Thacker, *Thames Highway* (1968 edn.), ii. 84; O.S. Map 1/25,000, SP 40/50 (1980 edn.).
85 C.O.S., PRN 1670; Benson and Miles, *Upper Thames Valley*, 48–50; *Oxoniensia*, viii/ix. 92.
86 *S. Midlands Arch.* xiv. 106–8; xv. 98–100; xvi. 106; T. G. Allen, *Iron Age and Romano-British Settlement at Watkins Fm., Northmoor*, pp. xiii, 73 sqq.
87 *S. Midlands Arch.* xx. 79; cf. C.O.S., PRN 8318.
88 C.O.S., PRN 2362.
89 *S. Midlands Arch.* xx. 79; Allen, *Watkins Fm.* pp. xiii, 79 sqq.
90 C.O.S., PRN 1665, 8312–20, 15051; *Oxoniensia*, xvii/xviii. 218.
91 *Oxoniensia*, xi/xii. 181–2.
92 *Berks. Bucks. and Oxon. Arch. Jnl.* iv. 23–4; C.O.S., PRN 1671.
93 Allen, *Watkins Fm.* pp. xiii, 83.
94 For a late Anglo-Saxon spearhead found at Northmoor lock, *V.C.H. Oxon.* i. 369, 371; cf. *Berks. Bucks. and Oxon. Arch. Jnl.* iv. 23.
95 *P.N. Oxon.* (E.P.N.S.), ii. 366, 489.
96 Allen, *Watkins Fm.* pp. xiii, 31, 51, 83.
97 *V.C.H. Oxon.* i. 409.
98 Below, econ. hist.
99 P.R.O., E 179/161/8–10; below, econ. hist. The 1306 list is damaged.
1 P.R.O., E 179/161/42.
2 Ibid. E 179/161/170; E 179/161/179; E 179/162/320; L. & P. Hen. VIII, xvii, p. 506.
3 *Chant. Cert.* 35.
4 *Protestation Rtns. and Tax Assess.* 94; *Compton Census*, ed. Whiteman, 418, 422.
5 P.R.O., E 179/255/4, pt. ii, f. 153.
6 C.O.S., par. reg. transcripts.
7 O.R.O., MSS. Oxf. Dioc. b 13, ff. 33–4; c 327, p. 145; d 559, ff. 141–4; d 562, ff. 159–62; *Secker's Visit.* 110.
8 *Census*, 1801–1991.
9 Below, church.
10 Bodl. MSS. d.d. Harcourt c 68/4–6, c 68/23, c 68/27.
11 O.R.O., tithe and incl. maps; cf. Bodl. MS. Rawl. B. 250, ff. 5–11.
12 Bodl. MS. d.d. Harcourt c 68/27.
13 Ibid. c 68/23.
14 Cf. O.R.O., incl. award and map.
15 Bodl. MS. d.d. Harcourt c 68/23.

bounded by Moreton Lane, the main road, and a watercourse running south-eastwards; the name Airs green survived in the 19th century.[16] A predecessor of the moated Manor Farm, on the parish's western edge, existed probably in the 13th century and certainly by the 14th;[17] a cottage on Dag Lane was mentioned in 1432, and others there from the 17th century.[18]

Moreton (i.e. *tūn* in swampy ground) was mentioned from the early 13th century, and in the 18th comprised a straggling line of houses along the southern edge of the large central common.[19] There may formerly have been a small green with houses on its west and south sides at the southern end of Moreton Lane, though by 1721 the site seems to have been closes held with adjoining tenements.[20] The hamlet's size altered little between the late 18th century and the late 19th, when there were c. 16 dwellings, some dilapidated, and most occupied by labourers.[21] Moreton Farm at the hamlet's eastern end included only farm buildings in the 1920s, and by the later 20th century the only houses were Stonehenge Farm and a few nearby cottages, some of them modern.[22]

Ramsey (O.E. *hramsa-īeg*, probably meaning island with ramsons), by the Thames on the east, was mentioned in the earlier 13th century, and gave its name to a local family mentioned until the early 14th.[23] Ramsey field and meadow stretched from the later Ramsey Farm on the south to Ark weir on the north, but the settlement was probably never more than a short-lived farmstead or small group of farmsteads, and there were no buildings in the 18th century.[24] Ramsey Farm, built by 1830, was demolished c. 1900, and associated farm buildings by the 1950s;[25] Radgnoll and Little Blenheim Farms, near Ramsey mead further north, were apparently also built in the early 19th century and were demolished in the later 20th.[26] Other outlying sites were Newbridge mill, recorded from the 13th century, and the Rose Revived public house and its wharf at Newbridge, recorded from the 17th;[27] in the north, some houses attached to West End in Stanton Harcourt parish lay south of the parish boundary in Northmoor.[28]

Most older buildings are of limestone rubble with stone-slated roofs, but a few retain timber framing, in most cases now rendered, and in the 19th century several farmhouses were 'half-timbered' and thatched.[29] Brick was used occasionally in the 19th century. The most significant domestic buildings, described below, are Manor and Rectory Farms, respectively the houses for a substantial medieval freehold and for the rectory estate,[30] and there are a few moderately sized yeoman houses of the 17th and 18th centuries. Lower Farm at Northmoor's northern end, owned in the 16th and 17th centuries by the prominent Fairbeards,[31] incorporates on the south a substantial part of a two-storeyed, timber-framed house of the early 17th century; in 1798 it comprised 8 bays and was said to be of stone and thatch,[32] implying that it had already been rendered and was longer than the surviving building. A wing west of the central stack had apparently been demolished by the later 18th century, and in the 20th the house was extended northwards. Pencots, further south, named from 17th- and 18th-century tenants of Northmoor manor,[33] incorporates at its north-east end an early 17th-century stone-walled house of one storey and attics, with three rooms arranged on an **L**-plan, and has original four-centred stone fireplaces. A two-roomed addition, perhaps a separate dwelling, was added on the south-west probably in the 18th century, and in the 19th the whole was divided into cottages.[34] In Moreton, Stonehenge Farm, so named from the early 20th century[35] and owned from the 16th to the earlier 18th by the Harrises,[36] probably incorporates part of a large 17th-century house in its central part, the gabled east front of which is of ashlar with stone hoodmoulds. On either side are nearly symmetrical 18th-century additions each of one room with attics, and there is a short, 19th-century kitchen wing at the rear. Smaller houses include Willow Tree Cottage on Northmoor's main street, a 16th-century timber-framed house of one storey with attics whose eastern bay, mostly occupied by a large stack, retains smoke-blackened roof timbers indicating an open hall; both the stack and the upper floor in the central bay were inserted apparently in the 17th century.

Church Farm near the rectory house, of coursed limestone rubble, retains the outer walls and roof of an 18th-century house with an almost

16 O.R.O., incl. and tithe maps.
17 Below, manors.
18 Bodl. MS. d.d. Harcourt c 68/36; Magd. Coll. Mun., D-Y 28; *8th Rep. Com. Char.* 491.
19 *P.N. Oxon.* (E.P.N.S.), ii. 366; Jefferys, *Oxon. Map* (1767); below, econ. hist.
20 Jefferys, *Oxon. Map* (1767); cf. O.R.O., Mor. VIII/v/1, s.v. Lyfords close; ibid. incl. award and map.
21 P.R.O., RG 11/1513; Ch. Ch. Arch., MS. Estates 80, f. 130; O.S. Map 1/2,500, Oxon. XXXVIII. 11 (1876 edn.).
22 *Sale Cat., Harcourt Settled Estates* (1924), lot 50: copy in Bodl. G.A. Oxon. c 226; O.S. Map 1/2,500, SP 4001-4101, SP 4201-4301 (1970 edn.).
23 P.R.O., E 179/161/8-10; O.R.O., incl. and tithe maps; *P.N. Oxon.* (E.P.N.S.), ii. 367; below, econ. hist.
24 O.R.O., Misc. Ch. II/1-2; Jefferys, *Oxon. Map* (1767); Davis, *Oxon. Map* (1797).
25 O.R.O., Misc. Ch. II/1-2; O.S. Map 1", sheet 13 (1830 edn.); ibid. 6", SP 40 SW (1960 edn.); Magd. Coll. Estates Bursary, survs. 1892-1912, pp. 364-5.
26 Davis, *Oxon. Map* (1797); O.S. Map 1", sheet 13 (1830 edn.); ibid. 6", SP 40 SW (1960 edn.); cf. O.R.O., Mor. XLIV/iii/6; Stowell, *Glimpses of Northmoor,* 6.

27 Below, this section; below, econ. hist. (mills).
28 O.R.O., tithe and incl. maps; Jefferys, *Oxon. Map* (1767); *Census,* 1871.
29 Bodl. MS. d.d. Harcourt c 281, ff. 2 sqq.; cf. D.o.E., *Revised Hist. Bldgs. List: Northmoor* (1988): copy in C.O.S.
30 Below, manors.
31 Traceable partly through 3s. 2d. quitrent: Magd. Coll. Mun., D-Y 5, D-Y 10-11; ibid. Estates Bursary, ledger K, pp. 80-1; Bodl. MS. d.d. Harcourt c 123/13; St. John's Coll. Mun., XV.36.
32 Magd. Coll. Mun., D-Y 226, s.v. Jos. Morris; cf. ibid. MP/2/Oxon./1.
33 Bodl. MS. d.d. Harcourt c 74/4; ibid. c 282, partics. of estate late J. Blewitt, pp. 4-5; ibid. MS. Rawl. B. 250, f. 8.
34 O.R.O., tithe award, no. 45; *Sale Cat., Harcourt Settled Estates* (1924), lot 44: copy in Bodl. G.A. Oxon. c 226. Cf. C.O.S., PRN 14080, suggesting 16th-century origins.
35 *Kelly's Dir. Oxon.* (1924 and later edns.).
36 Traceable partly through 5s. quitrent: Magd. Coll. Mun., D-Y 69-88; ibid. Estates Bursary, ledger K, pp. 80-1; Bodl. MS. d.d. Harcourt c 123/13; St. John's Coll. Mun., XV.36.

square main block, which was remodelled in the later 19th century; perhaps then the central stack was reconstructed with a passage between the formerly back-to-back fireplaces. A short kitchen wing at the rear, perhaps part of an earlier house, retains a possibly re-used fireplace beam with the date 1679 and the initials probably of Thomas and Katherine Martin, implying that this was the chief house of the Martins' large freehold before its sale to the Harcourts in 1719.[37] Other houses attached to larger freeholds in the 17th and 18th centuries[38] included Moreton House or Farm, which stood *c.* 270 yd. east of Stonehenge Farm and in 1671, when part of the chief manor, was two-storeyed with a symmetrical three-bayed front, projecting gables, and three ridge stacks. It was demolished before 1844.[39] Notable agricultural buildings, besides a late medieval cruck-framed barn at Rectory Farm,[40] include 18th-century timber-framed barns in Northmoor village[41] and at Lower Farm.

The later Red Lion was rebuilt *c.* 1741[42] and the single-storeyed Dun Cow *c.* 1800, the latter retaining a 17th-century stack and, on the east, a late 18th-century timber-framed annexe of two storeys. Parish cottages (later Greystones) between Dag and Chapel Lane were rebuilt in 1797[43] by the prominent farmer John Nalder, who may also have built a terrace of one-room-and-attic cottages, with timber-framed walls infilled with red brick, north of the Red Lion.[44] Another cottage row was built near Willow Tree Cottage before 1844,[45] and a pair of brick-built cottages at the southern end of Chapel Lane bear the inscription RE 1873, probably for the prominent farmer Richard Eagle.[46] Most farmhouses on Northmoor manor were in reasonable repair in 1816 and 1871,[47] and inclosure in 1844 prompted little if any new building, though Watkins Farm was substantially rebuilt in the later 19th century. A Primitive Methodist chapel (later demolished) was built in 1843, and a National school *c.* 1873.[48] Houses in the village were reportedly damp and unhealthy, but in 1870 Northmoor's appearance was said to have completely changed following recent drainage works,[49] and dilapidated wattle-and-daub cottages

north of the church and at Moreton were demolished in the later 19th century.[50]

About 1930 Northmoor was said to have been 'slowly decaying for generations',[51] and during the 20th century there was little new building, though a few council houses were erected at Chapel Lane's southern end and private houses were built by the Standlake road and north of the main street in Windrush Place.[52] A small, timber-built village hall, erected north of church before 1970, was replaced in 1995 by a more substantial building on the same site.[53] Park Farm, a large complex adjoining the Standlake road near the parish's western edge, was begun in 1955 by Oxford university for breeding and maintaining laboratory animals,[54] and in 1995 there was a large park for mobile homes near Bablock Hythe. Electricity was introduced before 1939,[55] mains water after 1945,[56] and main drainage in the 1970s.[57] A postal service through Witney existed by the 1850s,[58] and a post office near the church was opened *c.* 1880 and closed in the 1960s.[59]

There were four inns or alehouses by the later 18th century.[60] The Rose Revived (formerly the Rose or the Rose and Crown) at Newbridge was an alehouse by the later 17th century;[61] the Dun Cow in Northmoor village, perhaps briefly licensed *c.* 1677–89 when it was owned by a local victualler, opened under its later name *c.* 1793,[62] but probably never provided accommodation. The Chequers alehouse at Bablock Hythe existed by the 1750s, was 'much frequented by the lower class' in the 1850s, and in the 1930s was rebuilt as an hotel,[63] later renamed the Ferryman. The Red Lion in Northmoor, formerly a church house and evidently not the house of that name mentioned in 1715, was opened probably in the 1770s.[64] Three of those public houses remained in 1995, the Dun Cow having closed *c.* 1990.[65]

The village stocks stood near the later Red Lion in the mid 18th century.[66] A custom of throwing apples into the churchyard on Easter Sunday, followed by a procession to the rectory house where bread, cheese, and beer were provided, was noted reportedly in the early 19th century, and was revived in modified form in the

---

37 Bodl. MSS. d.d. Harcourt c 69/28, c 70/12; C.O.S., par. reg. transcripts, s.v. Martin; below, econ. hist.

38 Below, econ. hist.

39 Bodl. MS. d.d. Harcourt c 123/17; ibid. MS. Ch. Oxon. 2845; O.R.O., tithe and incl. maps.

40 Below, manors [other estates].

41 *S. Midlands Arch.* xv. 90–1.

42 O.R.O., MS. d.d. Par. Northmoor c 3, item a, lease 1741; below, local govt.

43 Datestone.

44 *8th Rep. Com. Char.* 491; O.R.O., tithe award and map, nos. 115, 140; C.O.S., par. reg. transcripts, s.v. Nalder.

45 O.R.O., tithe map, no. 131.

46 Magd. Coll. Estates Bursary, survs. 1892–1912, pp. 522–3; below, econ. hist.

47 Bodl. MSS. d.d. Harcourt c 281, *passim*; c 266, pp. 45–56.

48 Below, nonconf.; educ.

49 *Jnl. R. Agric. Soc.* 2nd ser. vi. 374.

50 Ch. Ch. Arch., MS. Estates 80, f. 130; below, church [vic. ho.].

51 Stowell, *Glimpses of Northmoor*, 34.

52 O.S. Map 6", SP 40 SW (1960 edn.); ibid. 1/2,500, SP 4001–4101, 4002–4102, 4201–4301, 4202–4302 (1970 edn.); *Social Services in Oxf. District*, ed. A. F. C. Bourdillon, i. 302.

53 O.S. Map 1/2,500, SP 4202–4302 (1970 edn.); C.O.S., OPA 80/13231; local inf.

54 Inf. from fm. manager, Park Fm.

55 *Kelly's Dir. Oxon.* (1939)

56 *Sale Cat., Watkins Fm.* (1945): microfilm in C.O.S.; *Social Services in Oxf. District*, ed. Bourdillon, i. 302.

57 *Oxf. Times*, 17 Nov. 1972.

58 P.O. Arch., POST 35/186, p. 241; POST 35/245, p. 439.

59 P.R.O., RG 11/1513, no. 25; *P.O. Dir. Oxon.* (1877); O.S. Map 6", SP 40 SW. (1960 edn.); ibid. 1/2,500, SP 4202–4302 (1970 edn.).

60 O.R.O., QSD V/1–4.

61 Bodl. MS. Rawl. D. 384, f. 110; ibid. MSS. d.d. Harcourt c 281, f. 1v.; c 282, partics. of estate late J. Blewitt, p. 3; *Kelly's Dir. Oxon.* (1883 and later edns.).

62 Berks. R.O., D/EM T226.

63 Ibid. D/EM B 31/2, letter 4 June 1855; Bodl. MS. d.d. Harcourt c 282, partics. of estate late J. Blewitt, p. 10, s.v. T. Ridge; O.R.O., QSD V/1; *Sale Cat., Chequers Hotel* (1952): copy in O.R.O., Adkin V/1.

64 Bodl. MS. d.d. Harcourt c 78/3; O.R.O., MS. d.d. Par. Northmoor c 3, item a, *passim*; ibid. f 1, *passim*; ibid. QSD V/1–2.   65 Local inf.

66 O.R.O., MS. d.d. Par. Northmoor c 3, item a, lease 1741; cf. *Oxon. Justices in 17th Cent.* (O.R.S. xvi), 24.

1970s;[67] presumably it was associated with an annual payment of 40s. by the lay rector for entertainment of the parish at Easter, recorded in 1648 but discontinued by the lessee before 1830.[68] Northmoor steeplechases, held near Bablock Hythe, were mentioned in 1870,[69] and a cricket club existed until 1922 when it merged with Standlake's.[70]

In the earlier 15th century William, Lord Lovel (d. 1455) allegedly came from Minster Lovell with 'great power and might' during a dispute over Newbridge mill and forced its partial demolition.[71] During a further dispute over the mill c. 1651 the sheriff met armed resistance.[72] During the Civil War Newbridge was strategically important, and was forcibly crossed by the parliamentarians in 1644.[73] Sir Edmund Warcupp, lord from 1671, was a nephew of William Lenthall and was a former parliamentary captain.[74]

MANORS AND OTHER ESTATES. In 1059 land probably in the south-west of Northmoor was included in Edward the Confessor's grant of Taynton to St. Denis abbey, Paris.[75] The rest of Northmoor, included probably in the later Stanton Harcourt manor, was acquired by the abbey apparently before the mid 12th century,[76] and by the early 13th the combined estate, later the manor of MORE (or NORTHMOOR) ST. DENNIS or ABBOTS MORE, was administered by the abbey's cell at Deerhurst (Glos.).[77] As an alien priory Deerhurst was seized repeatedly during the 14th and 15th centuries by the Crown, which in 1345 and 1389 let it with its estates and c. 1447 granted it to Eton College. The Crown recovered the priory in 1461, and in 1467 granted it to Tewkesbury abbey, which retained Northmoor until the Dissolution.[78]

In 1554 the Crown granted the manor for life to a royal equerry, John Herle (d. 1581), who may have resided,[79] and in 1590 sold it to Walter Bayley (d. 1592), the queen's physician.[80] Bayley's son William, lord in 1596,[81] seems to

have sold it after 1600 to James Stone (d. 1617) of Northmoor, lord in 1604 and 1609.[82] Before 1619 it passed to Henry Greenway (d. c. 1640) of Northmoor, who bought an additional farm from Francis Yate of Standlake, and Manor farm, formerly part of an estate owned by the More family, from Sir Simon Every.[83] In 1645 Greenway's son Henry sold the manor to Edward Twyford of London and later of Northmoor, retaining Manor farm and other lands, which were sold to Twyford in 1647.[84] From c. 1664 Twyford mortgaged the manor, and in 1671 sold it to Edmund (later Sir Edmund) Warcupp of Durham Yard (Mdx.) and later of Northmoor, together with a Moreton farm bought in 1662 from Thomas Greenway. Warcupp made several small sales, and died in 1712 leaving the manor in trust to be sold.[85] His daughter Anna Maria Pryce, the surviving trustee, sold it in 1718 to John Blewitt, later of Northmoor and Salford and a high sheriff of the county, who made small additions but mortgaged the estate from 1737; in 1755 trustees under his will sold it to Simon Harcourt (d. 1777), Earl Harcourt,[86] whose grandfather Simon (d. 1727), 1st Viscount Harcourt, had made piecemeal acquisitions in the parish.[87] The estate, c. 1,240 a. in 1844,[88] descended with Stanton Harcourt and Nuneham Courtenay until 1924 when most was sold,[89] and in 1979 the Harcourts retained only Manor farm, then 232 a.[90]

A house owned by the prior of Deerhurst in 1239 may have been a homestead for the demesne.[91] No later references have been found, and in the 17th century there seems to have been no manor house until Manor Farm was adopted after 1640,[92] Henry Greenway (d. c. 1640) living in a freehold farmhouse called Clarks, apparently by the Standlake road.[93]

The reputed manor of MORE, centred on Manor Farm and owned from the 13th century to the 17th by the More family, was an ordinary freehold held of the chief manor,[94] though owners in the 16th century may have laid claim to a court.[95] After 1608 John More sold the

[67] Witney Gaz. 26 Sept. 1974; Woman's Realm, Aug. (?) 1976: cuttings in C.O.S.
[68] St. John's Coll. Mun., ADMIN I. A.3, pp. 385–8; ibid. XV.44.
[69] Witney Express, 10 Mar. 1870.
[70] Below, Standlake, intro.
[71] Magd. Coll. Mun., EP 146/33; below, econ. hist. (mills).
[72] B.L. Add. MS. 34326, f. 34.
[73] Below, Standlake, intro.
[74] Wood's Life, i. 311; Collectanea, iii (O.H.S. xxxii), 277 and n.; below, manors.
[75] Early Chart. of Thames Valley, ed. M. Gelling, no. 300; above, intro.
[76] Above, intro.; below, church; cf. V.C.H. Oxon. xii. 267, 274, where Northmoor's inclusion in Stanton manor is not made explicit.
[77] Rot. Hund. (Rec. Com.), ii. 732–3; Cur. Reg. R. xii, pp. 378–9.
[78] Cal. Pat. 1467–77, 66–7; Cal. Papal Reg. xiii (1), 367–8; Valor Eccl. (Rec. Com.), ii. 472; V.C.H. Glos. ii. 104–5; cf. P.R.O., CP 40/934, m. 108d.
[79] Cal. Pat. 1554–5, 313; O.R.O., MS. Wills Oxon. 186, f. 189; P.R.O., C 2/Eliz. I/H 11/53.
[80] P.R.O., C 66/1342, mm. 16–18; ibid. PROB 11/79, ff. 179v.–180.
[81] Bodl. MSS. d.d. Harcourt c 122/6–7.
[82] O.R.O., Misc. Su. XXXVI/i/1; P.R.O., C 2/Jas. I/S 23/45; ibid. C 142/311, no. 111.

[83] Bodl. MSS. d.d. Harcourt c 73/1–3, c 122/8–9; ibid. MS. Ch. Oxon. 5303; O.R.O., MSS. Wills Oxon. 26/2/40, 59/3/14; below, this section (More).
[84] Bodl. MS. d.d. Harcourt c 73/2–11.
[85] Ibid. c 74/4–29; Bodl. MS. Ch. Oxon. 2845.
[86] Bodl. MSS. d.d. Harcourt c 75/1–6, c 76/4–7; C. Peters, Lord Lieutenants Oxon. 146; Salford Hist. Group, Salford, More Hist. of a Cotswold Village (priv. print. 1985), 7.
[87] Bodl. MSS. d.d. Harcourt c 61/7, c 63/10, c 63/18, c 65/13–16, c 70/11–12, c 72/2.
[88] O.R.O., tithe award.
[89] Sale Cat., Harcourt Settled Estates (1924), pp. 42 sqq.: copy in Bodl. G.A. Oxon. c 226; V.C.H. Oxon. v. 242; xii. 276.
[90] Probate valuation 3 Jan. 1979: copy in Old Estate Office, Stanton Harcourt Manor Ho. (1988).
[91] Oxon. Eyre, 1241 (O.R.S. lvi), no. 1008; Rot. Hund. (Rec. Com.), ii. 732.
[92] Below, this section (More).
[93] O.R.O., MS. Wills Oxon. 26/2/40; Bodl. MSS. d.d. Harcourt c 59/1, c 73/2; ibid. MS. Rawl. B. 250, f. 6, s.v. Pleydell. Not to be confused with later Clarks Fm. E. of the church.
[94] Rot. Hund. (Rec. Com.), ii. 733; Cal. Inq. p.m. Hen. VII, i, p. 399; Bodl. MS. d.d. Harcourt c 123/13; P.R.O., C 142/66, no. 60; C 142/133, no. 90; C 142/311, no. 111; Lincs. R.O., episc. regs. v, f. 167v.; vii, f. 164v. For descent, above, Bampton: Lower Haddon, manor.
[95] Below, local govt.

estate piecemeal,[96] the larger part, including Manor (or More) Farm, passing apparently to John Every (d. 1618) of Oxford University, whose son Sir Simon sold it to Henry Greenway before 1640.[97] Presumably Manor Farm was the 'manor house' at Northmoor in which Thomas de la More was licensed to have an oratory in 1333 and 1343,[98] and it remained the reputed manor house in the 16th century.[99] Though some Mores lived chiefly at Lower Haddon in Bampton family members lived at Northmoor until the later 16th century,[1] and successive lords of More St. Dennis occupied the house from 1640 until Blewitt's departure for Salford after 1730; thereafter it was let to tenant farmers.[2]

The existing, irregularly-planned house,[3] within a large rectangular moat near the parish's western edge, is built mostly of limestone rubble; it retains, however, some timber-framed first-floor walls and a short length of jettying, suggesting that the house's south-west corner originated as a 16th-century timber-framed cross wing abutting a main range on its east side. If so that house was curtailed in or before the late 17th century, when the building was reconstructed with a new roof above a prominent cornice and a more or less regular south entrance front, and at the same time several rooms were panelled and a new staircase with turned balusters was installed. The inscription EW 1672, presumably for Edmund Warcupp, was noted on a barn,[4] and the house was called new-built c. 1697.[5] Timber framing remained visible in the early 19th century, but had been rendered probably by the later 19th.[6] There was further refitting of the interior in the early 19th century, and renovations were carried out c. 1924 and in the early 1960s, when the house was dilapidated and some windows were replaced; c. 1990 the house was extended northwards, and an eastern service wing partly of red brick was replaced by a larger two-storeyed range, retaining a short stretch of earlier rubble walling on the north. The moat was cleared about the same time.[7] There was a separate house, within the moated area, for the tenant of the farmland in the early

18th century, when shared outbuildings included stables, a coach house with a room above, a newly built brewhouse, and a dovecot.[8]

In 1555 the rectory estate, comprising a house, tithes, and c. 40 a. of glebe, was appropriated to St. John's College, Oxford, at the instigation of its founder Sir Thomas White.[9] The college acquired a further 60 a. of meadow and a farm in Moreton as part of Fyfield manor (then Berks.),[10] and in 1569, after protracted litigation, acquired a second Moreton farm bought by White from Christopher Ashton of Fyfield.[11] At the inclosure of Northmoor's commons c. 1666 the college received 16 a. for common rights attached to the glebe and c. 60 a. for those attached to its Moreton land,[12] and in 1843 the estate totalled c. 236 a.;[13] piecemeal additions in the late 19th century and the 20th, notably the Harcourts' Moreton farm (116 a.) in 1927 and c. 50 a. from Christ Church, Oxford, c. 1964, increased it to over 400 a.[14] Quitrents to Northmoor manor were redeemed in 1932,[15] and in 1970 the estate and rectory house were sold to the tenant.[16]

Until 1840 the tithes were let with the glebe, early lessees including the vicar William More (d. 1612),[17] and in the 17th century and earlier 18th members of the Champneys family and their successors the Pleydells, most of whom occupied the rectory house.[18] Moduses c. 1600 included 10d. for every 20 sheep sold before Holy Rood day and 20d. for those sold after, 1½d.–2½d. for milch cows, and 1d. for colts;[19] others agreed in the mid 17th century included 1s. for calves, 2s. 6d. for lambs, and 1d. for garden produce, though for twenty years previously most tithes had been paid in kind, and calf and lamb tithes were usually still so paid. Half tithe was paid for sheep pastured in Northmoor for part of the year.[20] At the inclosure of the commons rent charges were agreed, despite opposition,[21] of 1s. 6d. per acre in the former common, 13¾d. per acre in West mead, and 2s. for every acre of arable or meadow converted to pasture;[22] those payments continued until 1811

[96] Bodl. MSS. d.d. Harcourt c 62/1–2, c 69/11–12; O.R.O., D.Y. V/i/3; P.R.O., CP 25/2/339/7 Jas. I East.; below, econ. hist. (mills).

[97] Bodl. MS. d.d. Harcourt c 73/2; cf. O.R.O., Misc. Su. XXXVI/ii/1; P.R.O., PROB 11/132, ff. 353–4.

[98] Lincs. R.O., episc. regs. v, f. 167v.; vii, f. 164v.

[99] O.R.O., D.Y. V/i/1–5; cf. ibid. tithe award and map; Bodl. MSS. d.d. Harcourt c 73/1–6.

[1] O.R.O., MS. Wills Oxon. 184, ff. 232v.–234; ibid. D.Y. V/i/1; P.R.O., PROB 11/81, f. 12 and v.; Magd. Coll. Mun., Standlake 7A, 23A; above, Bampton: Lower Haddon, manor.

[2] Bodl. MSS. d.d. Harcourt c 73–6, passim; ibid. c 282, partics. of estate late J. Blewitt; O.R.O., tithe award; C.O.S., par. reg. transcripts.

[3] Above, plate 26.

[4] J. Stowell, Glimpses of Northmoor through 800 Yrs. (priv. print. c. 1930), 12.

[5] Bodl. MS. Rawl. D. 384, f. 110; ibid. MS. d.d. Harcourt c 282, partic. of Northmoor [n.d.].

[6] Ibid. MS. d.d. Harcourt c 281, f. 6; cf. ibid. c 266, p. 47.

[7] Sale Cat., Harcourt Settled Estates (1924), 59: copy in Bodl. G.A. Oxon. c 226; N.M.R., Northmoor file, AA75/470–2; inf. from Mr. W. Gascoigne, Manor Fm. For ho. before repair, Bodl. MS. Top. Oxon. c 495, nos. 9856–9; above, plate 26.

[8] Bodl. MS. d.d. Harcourt c 282, partic. of Northmoor 1718;

ibid. MSS. c 75/2, c 75/5; ibid. MS. Rawl. D. 384, ff. 110, 111.

[9] St. John's Coll. Mun., XV.1; ibid. ADMIN. I. A.1, f. 147; below, church.

[10] St. John's Coll. Mun., II.2–3, 5, 29, 36; Cal. Pat. 1553–4, 493; Early Hist. St. John's Coll. (O.H.S. N.S. i), 115, 379. Fyfield manor, including the Northmoor land, was let to the Whites until 1738: Early Hist. St. John's Coll. 250 n., 501.

[11] St. John's Coll. Mun., XV.17–35; cf. ibid. XV.11–16.

[12] Bodl. MS. Rawl. B. 250, ff. 8–9, incl. 21 a. for the fm. held of Fyfield manor.

[13] O.R.O., tithe award, s.v. St. John's Coll. and glebe.

[14] St. John's Coll. Mun., XV.42, 45, 51–2, 58, 62–9, 71–2; ibid. EST. III.x.14, pp. 19–22.

[15] Ibid. XV.57; cf. ibid. XV.36.

[16] Inf. from Mr. P. Florey, Rectory Fm.

[17] St. John's Coll. Mun., XV.6, XV.8i; ibid. ADMIN. I. A.1, ff. 98, 247v., 270; below, church.

[18] St. John's Coll. Mun., XV.43–4; ibid. ADMIN. I. A.3, pp. 54–7, 94, 385–8, 474, 580, 764–6; ADMIN. I. A.7, pp. 30, 60, 102, 143, 178; O.R.O., MSS. Wills Oxon. 121/3/12, 145/1/25, 145/2/49.

[19] St. John's Coll. Mun., XV.5A.

[20] P.R.O., E 134/1658/East. 2; E 134/13 Chas. II/Mich. 41; E 134/15 Chas. II/Mich. 21.

[21] St. John's Coll. Mun., XV.9i (h).

[22] Bodl. MS. Top. Oxon. b 265, ff. 53, 74.

when St. John's found that Chancery decrees initiating them were not binding, and resolved to collect all tithes in kind or impose new compositions.[23] All the tithes were commuted in 1840–4 for a rent charge of c. £514, excluding £10 from the glebe, and thereafter the rectory farm was let without the tithes.[24] In the 1950s tithe redemption annuities were still paid to the college.[25]

Rectory Farm[26] lies immediately south-east of the church within a partly moated enclosure, evidently the site of the medieval rectory house.[27] Surviving medieval buildings are the lower part of a timber-framed gatehouse, later converted into a pigeon house, and the central cruck-framed part of a large, possibly 14th-century barn.[28] Repairs to the earlier house were recorded in 1572[29] and c. 1612–14, when stone walls were rebuilt in the hall, parlour, and old kitchen, and slates and roof tiles were bought; some 'old houses' were too dilapidated to be easily repaired, however,[30] and the existing house seems to have been built c. 1629[31] on a site probably a little way to the south of its predecessor, since the gatehouse is not aligned on it. The house is two-storeyed with attics, and is rubble-walled; its main range has a near-central doorway leading to a lobby built against the side of the main stack, and a long east wing incorporates, among other rooms, a parlour, and a newel stair. The parlour and a room above it retain moulded plaster cornices and decorative plasterwork along the beams, and the fireplaces have four-centred heads with sunk spandrels. The windows are stone-mullioned, and most lights have four-centred heads. The main range's west gable is timber-framed, implying that a symmetrical west wing may have been planned, but in the early 19th century there was apparently only a low, single-storeyed service wing of similar dimensions to the existing wing,[32] which is of the later 19th century. A barn north-west of the house was converted for domestic use c. 1990.[33]

In the later 16th century Edward Walwyn (fl. 1544–92), owner of Gaunt House in Standlake, acquired Orpwoods farm in Northmoor and c. 5 smaller holdings in Northmoor and Moreton.[34] The combined Northmoor estate, c. 158 a. in the 19th century,[35] owed quitrents to Northmoor manor, a liability unsuccessfully challenged by George Walwyn in 1604.[36] In 1686 the estate passed with Gaunt House to Christ Church, Oxford, which let much of it with Gaunt House farm;[37] the Northmoor part was sold piecemeal in the 1950s and 1960s.[38]

From 1741 to 1745 Magdalen College, Oxford, acquired c. 86 a. including the later Stonehenge farm in Moreton and Ark weir and Lower farm in Northmoor.[39] Between 1899 and 1904 the college bought Radgnoll, Ramsey, and Pinnocks farms from the trustees of Richard Eagle (d. 1899), increasing its freehold to c. 240 a., and rented a further 47 a. from an Abingdon charity.[40] Quitrents for Stonehenge and Lower farms were redeemed in 1889[41] and the estate was sold in 1920, chiefly to tenants.[42]

Land bought in 1638 to augment the perpetual curacy of St. Michael at the Northgate, Oxford, c. 22 a. in the 19th century, was treated sometimes as the curate's property and sometimes as that of Lincoln College, Oxford. Though the college was rector of St. Michael's it was, however, one of several trustees for the Northmoor land,[43] which seems to have remained with the curacy in the later 19th century.[44] Seven acres bought c. 1750 to augment the rectory of St. Martin's, Oxford, were sold in 1954.[45]

ECONOMIC HISTORY. Northmoor and Moreton seem to have had separate fields from an early date. Northmoor's West (later Church) and East fields, both north of the village, were mentioned from the 13th century,[46] and in the 19th were estimated at c. 77 a. and 49 a. respectively.[47] Holdings were rarely balanced between them, and lay often in one field only.[48] A third field, More field, was mentioned in 1648.[49]

23 Bodl. MS. d.d. Harcourt c 282, legal opinion 7 Oct. 1811; ibid., St. John's Coll. to Lord Harcourt, 28 Feb. 1812; ibid., formal notice 17 Mar. 1812.
24 O.R.O., tithe award; St. John's Coll. Mun., ADMIN. I. A.9, pp. 71, 113, 158, 163.
25 St. John's Coll. Mun., XV.53, XV.79.
26 Above, plate 27; cf. Pevsner, Oxon. 723; D.o.E., Revised Hist. Bldgs. List: Northmoor, 101–2: copy in C.O.S.; Bodl. MS. Top. Oxon. d 218, f. 200.
27 O.R.O., tithe award and map, no. 149; Bodl. MS. d.d. Harcourt c 68/23.
28 S. Midlands Arch. xvi. 137–40; for repairs 1612–14, St. John's Coll. Mun., XV.8i, XV.8v.
29 St. John's Coll. Mun., ADMIN. I. A.1, f. 98.
30 Ibid. XV.8, also mentioning carpenters' work.
31 Datestone; cf. St. John's Coll. Mun., ADMIN. I. A.3, pp. 54, 94.
32 B.L. Add. MS. 36373, f. 219; Bodl. MSS. Top. Oxon. a 68, nos. 403, 407; d 218, f. 200.
33 Inf. from Mr. P. Florey, Rectory Fm.
34 Ch. Ch. Arch., Standlake A 7, A 36; Abstracts of Glos. Inq. p.m. i (Index Libr. ix), 188; cf. Bodl. MS. d.d. Harcourt c 123/13; St. John's Coll. Mun., XV.36.
35 O.R.O., tithe award, schedule s.v. Christ Church; cf. Ch. Ch. Arch., MS. Estates 80, ff. 41v.–42v.
36 Ch. Ch. Arch., Standlake A 36; P.R.O., C 2/Jas. I/S 23/45.
37 Ch. Ch. Arch., Standlake A 7–57; ibid. MS. Estates 80, ff. 35v.–36v., 43–4, 142; below, Standlake, other estates.
38 St. John's Coll. Mun., XV.53, XV.69, XVII.79; Bodl.

MS. Top. Oxon. c 768/1, no. 76.
39 Magd. Coll. Mun., D-Y 5–11, 28–9, 31–3, 59–88; ibid. MP/2/Oxon./1; O.R.O., tithe award.
40 Magd. Coll. Estates Bursary, survs. 1892–1912, pp. 302–5, 364–5, 522–3, 548; ibid. ledger M, pp. 467–9; ledger O, p. 18; Magd. Coll. Mun., MP/2/Oxon. 35–6; for the charity estate, V.C.H. Berks. iv. 450.
41 Magd. Coll. Estates Bursary, ledger K, pp.80–1; cf. above, intro. [bldgs.].
42 Magd. Coll. Estates Bursary, survs. 1913–23, pp. 77, 83–4; ledger P, pp. 388–90, 399–403; St. John's Coll. Mun., XV.47; Sale Cat. (1920), lots 2, 15–16: copy in Bodl. G.A. Oxon. b 92* (11).
43 Linc. Coll. Mun., D/NOR/1–6; O.R.O., MS. Oxf. Dioc. c 446, f. 152; ibid. QSD L.211; ibid. incl. and tithe awards; Bodl. MS. Rawl. B. 250, ff. 5, 8; V.C.H. Oxon. iv. 394–5.
44 e.g. V. Green, Commonwealth of Lincoln Coll. app. VI, listing no Northmoor land.
45 O.R.O., MS. Oxf. Dioc. c 446, f. 146; ibid. incl. award; St. John's Coll. Mun., XV.52, wrongly calling it All Saints' glebe; Hodgson, Q.A.B. cccxxiv.
46 Balliol Coll. Arch., A.19.3a, A.19.7; Berks. R.O., D/EM T226, deeds of 1573 and 1673; O.R.O., Misc. Ch. II/1–2; Cat. Anct. D. i, C 618.
47 St. John's Coll. Mun., XV.44; cf. ibid. XV.40; O.R.O., incl. award and map, suggesting slightly larger acreages.
48 e.g. Bodl. MSS. d.d. Harcourt c 68/24–8; c 281; c 282, partics. of estate late John Blewitt; Magd. Coll. Mun., MP/2/Oxon./1; Ch. Ch. Arch., Standlake A 18.
49 Bodl. MS. d.d. Harcourt c 69/15.

Moreton's West (later Chawcroft or Chalcroft) field and East (later Moreton) field, occupying a narrow band across the parish's southern part, were also mentioned from the Middle Ages.[50] In the 19th century Moreton field was *c.* 41 a. but Chalcroft field only 12½ a.,[51] and as in Northmoor most holdings were unequally divided.[52] Ramsey field near the river Thames in the east, *c.* 7 a. in the 19th century,[53] was by the 17th century associated usually with Moreton, and presumably never formed part of a separate field system.[54] Very few farms included land in both Northmoor's and Moreton's fields.[55]

Meadows, some perhaps among 170 a. recorded on Taynton manor in 1086,[56] lay chiefly in the south and east by the river Thames, and were estimated in 1672 at over 480 a.[57] West mead (*c.* 139 a. in 1672) and the adjoining Chalcroft mead (*c.* 20 a.), near Newbridge, with Moreton mead (*c.* 139 a.) in the south, seem to have belonged chiefly to Moreton,[58] though some Northmoor farms included small parcels of meadow notably in West mead.[59] Ramsey mead by the eastern boundary (*c.* 95 a. in 1672, probably including inclosed meadow),[60] Bownham meadow (*c.* 35 a.)[61] in the north-east, and Achim mead (20–30 a.) west of the river Windrush,[62] belonged chiefly to Northmoor.[63] All included common meadow until inclosure in 1844, and Bownham and some others remained lot meadows.[64] Large several meadows included 18½ a. (later 25 a.) in Ramsey mead, attached to Appleton manor (formerly Berks.) from the 13th century to the 19th,[65] 24 a. in West mead attached in the 17th century to Manor farm,[66] and North hurst (*c.* 32 a.) in the north-east, attached in the 14th century to Eaton manor in Appleton and later to Fyfield manor (then Berks.).[67] Gaingey (earlier Kadengeye or Cangay) by the Thames was mentioned from the Middle

Ages,[68] and some small hams were also held in severalty.[69] In 1832 Ramsey mead was 'good Thames meadow', but holdings dispersed in Moreton common mead were 'of little value in their present state', and meadows flooded often.[70]

The moor from which the parish was named[71] ran between the two villages from the river Windrush on the west to near Bablock Hythe in the north-east, and in the 17th century was estimated at 1,000 a. It was then divided into Dedwick, Horseleaze, or Outer common in the south-west, mentioned from the 15th century, and Cowleaze or Inner common apparently in the north-east,[72] though North moor, the over and nether moors, and Moreton Lake were also sometimes mentioned.[73] Common rights attached to individual holdings varied: in the earlier 17th century the rectory estate, *c.* 40 a. including 15 a. of open-field arable, had commons for 8 cattle and 32 sheep at full stint,[74] while Gaunt House's estate, with *c.* 55 a. in Northmoor including 37 a. of arable, had rights for 21 cattle, 14 horses, and 100 sheep,[75] and a holding of 12 a. of arable and meadow had rights for 5¾ cattle, 3 horses, and 20 sheep, recently reduced to 12.[76] In all, there were commons for 1,600 sheep, 435 cattle, and 217 horses at full stint and for 800 sheep, 335 cattle, and an unreduced number of horses at half-stint,[77] though waterlogging caused rot and reduced the pasture's value.[78] Additional winter commons were claimed in North hurst,[79] and pigs were allowed in the common fields after harvest.[80] Standlake's inhabitants had commons in Dedwick in the 16th century,[81] as did the lord of Stanton Harcourt in the early 15th, when Thomas at More was impleaded for obstructing the droveway from Stanton Harcourt with a ditch and hedge;[82] Stanton Harcourt's claims prompted frequent litigation in the earlier 17th

50 Balliol Coll. Arch., A.19.5, A.19.11b, A.19.46; St. John's Coll. Mun., XV.35; O.R.O., Misc. Ch. II/1–2.

51 St. John's Coll. Mun., XV.44; cf. O.R.O., incl. award, suggesting slightly larger acreages.

52 e.g. St. John's Coll. Mun., XV.35; Bodl. MSS. d.d. Harcourt c 281, ff. 11v.–13v.; c 64/16; c 64/19–20; c 64/27.

53 St. John's Coll. Mun., XV.44; O.R.O., tithe map; ibid. incl. award and map.

54 Bodl. MS. Top. Oxon. b 265, f. 57; ibid. MS. d.d. Harcourt c 123/1; cf. Linc. Coll. Mun., D/NOR/1; St. John's Coll. Mun., XV.10A; above, intro.

55 e.g. Balliol Coll. Arch., A.19.11b, A.19.50; Bodl. MS. d.d. Harcourt c 282, partics. of estate late John Blewitt, pp. 6–7; St. John's Coll. Mun., XV.10A, describing glebe.

56 *V.C.H. Oxon.* i. 409; above, manors.

57 O.R.O., tithe map; ibid. incl. award and map; for acreages, Bodl. MS. d.d. Harcourt c 123/18; cf. St. John's Coll. Mun., XV.44.

58 Bodl. MSS. d.d. Harcourt c 64/16; c 281, *passim*; c 282, partic. of estate late J. Blewitt; St. John's Coll. Mun., XV.35; Magd. Coll. Mun., D-Y 73; Ch. Ch. Arch., Standlake A 55–6.

59 Bodl. MSS. d.d. Harcourt c 59/1, c 61/7, c 69/11–12; Ch. Ch. Arch., Standlake A 18.

60 Bodl. MS. d.d. Harcourt c 123/18; cf. St. John's Coll. Mun., XV.40, XV.44 (which say 21 a.); below, this section.

61 Apparently including Southbys, which was later inclosed: O.R.O., incl. award and map.

62 Bodl. MS. d.d. Harcourt c 123/18; cf. O.R.O., incl. award.

63 Bodl. MSS. d.d. Harcourt c 122/6; c 123/5; c 281, *passim*; c 282, partic. of estate late J. Blewitt; Magd. Coll. Mun., MP/2/Oxon./1; P.R.O., C 3/229/28.

64 Bodl. MS. d.d. Harcourt c 265; ibid. e 5; Ch. Ch. Arch., MS. Estates 80, f. 61; O.R.O., incl. award and map.

65 Bodl. MS. d.d. Harcourt c 68/2; Berks. R.O., D/EM T33, conveyance 11 Feb. 1882; O.R.O., tithe award; *Abbrev. Plac.* (Rec. Com.), 331. For another 18½ a., Bodl. MSS. d.d. Harcourt c 68/41–5, c 69/18.

66 Bodl. MSS. d.d. Harcourt c 73/2, c 123/18; O.R.O., incl. award and map.

67 St. John's Coll. Mun., II.2, II.95–9; O.R.O., incl. award; *Cal. Close*, 1360–4, 245; cf. *V.C.H. Berks.* iv. 338–9, 346–7.

68 O.R.O., incl. map; Bodl. MS. d.d. Harcourt c 123/18; *Oxon. Fines*, p. 145; *Cal. Close*, 1364–8, 397.

69 e.g. Bodl. MSS. d.d. Harcourt c 68/25, c 68/34, c 69/18; St. John's Coll. Mun., XV.16.

70 Bodl. MS. d.d. Harcourt c 265, ff. 25–7; ibid. e 5; below, this section.

71 Above, intro.

72 Bodl. MS. Rawl. B. 250, ff. 5–11; ibid. MS. Top. Oxon. b 265, ff. 42–3, 45–9; ibid. MSS. d.d. Harcourt c 40/2, c 73/2, c 73/4; P.R.O., C 5/426/84; for Dedwick's location, Berks. R.O., D/EM T226, conveyance 14 May 1638; O.R.O., tithe map; *V.C.H. Oxon.* xii. 295.

73 Bodl. MSS. d.d. Harcourt c 64/12, c 122/5; Linc. Coll. Mun., D/NOR/1; O.R.O., Misc. Su. XXXVI/i/1.

74 St. John's Coll. Mun., XV.9i (e); ibid. ADMIN. I. A.1, f. 147.

75 Ch. Ch. Arch., MS. Estates 80, f. 41v.

76 Linc. Coll. Mun., D/NOR/1.

77 Bodl. MS. d.d. Harcourt c 123/18; cf. St. John's Coll. Mun., XV.9i (e).

78 Bodl. MS. Top. Oxon. b 265, f. 42; Ch. Ch. Arch., Standlake A 48.

79 Bodl. MS. Top. Oxon. b 265, f. 53.

80 e.g. ibid. MS. d.d. Harcourt c 123/3.

81 Magd. Coll. Mun., ct. bk. 6, ct. 8 Mar. 4 & 5 Phil. and Mary.

82 Bodl. MS. d.d. Harcourt c 40/2.

century, and in 1677 Sir Philip Harcourt sold to the lord of Northmoor commons for 400 sheep and other animals in Dedwick and Cowleaze.[83] Northmoor evidently retained common rights in Stanton Harcourt's West moor in the 18th century.[84] Small pasture closes were mentioned frequently from the 16th century,[85] and leys in some of the common fields from the earlier 17th.[86]

In 1581 eight tenants were presented to the manor court for inclosing 37 a. of land formerly lying in common,[87] and a new close in Moreton was mentioned in 1597.[88] A farm in 1654 included 20 a. of grass ground, presumably inclosed, in East field,[89] and by then over 40 a. of inclosed pasture adjoined Manor Farm and there were apparently consolidated blocks of arable nearby in Church field.[90] In 1666 the lord, Edward Twyford, secured agreement for inclosing Dedwick and Cowleaze, and work began soon after; owners' allotments, awarded for cow commons only, ranged from 2 a. for a labourer's single common to c. 160 a. for the lord, who received a further 5 a. as owner of the waste.[91] Disagreement over allotments and tithes led to protracted litigation and to intimidation and fence-breaking, organized by a local group dubbed the Jovial Crew; prominent agitators included the gentry John Pleydell and John Heron, who allegedly gathered supporters 'at common alehouses' and persuaded labourers and other commoners to join in their lawsuits.[92] A Chancery decree of 1673 ratified inclosure of the commons and of c. 25 a. of lot meadow in West mead,[93] and though plans to inclose the arable and the remaining common meadows[94] were abandoned, in the earlier 19th century only c. 430 a. (c. 20 per cent of the parish) remained uninclosed.[95] Winter commons in North hurst were extinguished for 30s. a year paid to the poor by the lord of the manor,[96] but common rights continued in the common fields and meadows, where in the late 17th century and early 18th those mowing once had commons not exceeding 2 cows per acre from Michaelmas to 2 February, and those mowing twice had a quarter rate.[97] Lammas meadows were noted in the 19th century.[98] The decree of 1673 required all landholders to clean watercourses passing

through their land at least once a year,[99] and in the late 17th century floodgates allowed most inclosed meadows and pastures to be flooded if required.[1]

A wood of 6 a., attached apparently to Fyfield manor, was mentioned in 1448,[2] and coppices of ½–2 a. and sometimes more were noted on Manor farm and other freeholds from the 16th century.[3] In 1586 two inhabitants were presented to the manor court for cutting trees on the waste, though the court ruled that windfall oaks belonged to tenants.[4] About 1700 there were allegedly several thousand trees worth up to £5,000 on Northmoor manor, besides c. 3 a. thick-planted with fast-growing abeles (white poplars) which were expected to yield large profits,[5] and in 1768 Magdalen College's three small farms included over 370 trees, chiefly ash and elm, presumably in hedgerows.[6] In the 19th century the only recorded woodland was c. 2 a. of coppice in the south-west, let with Manor farm, and c. 1 a. on the rectory estate.[7]

In 1086 Northmoor was presumably surveyed with Taynton manor, on which 17 *villani* and 30 *bordarii* were noted with 17 ploughteams. Though some may have lived in Northmoor, the demesne, on which 4 *servi* worked another 4 ploughteams, was presumably in Taynton,[8] and Northmoor's unusual social structure in 1279 may reflect comparatively recent colonization. Only 10 villeins were then recorded, holding a total of 39½ a.; individual tenants held between ½ a. and 10 a. for varying rents and services, and one house was held apparently without land. The holdings suggest irregular encroachments on the waste, and none was described in terms of yardlands.[9] Far more land (188 a.) was occupied by freeholders, of whom 12 held between 2 a. and 30 a. for rents of between 1s. 9d. and 53s. 4d.; the largest rent was for John de la More's 30 a., mill, and ferry, a reputed manor by the early 14th century.[10] Holdings not listed in 1279 included 97 a. claimed as freehold by the Ramsey family of Ramsey in the 1220s, but proved to have been held earlier in villeinage,[11] and since rents in 1294 were valued at c. £10 more than in 1279[12] there may have been other unrecorded holdings. There was an active land market and complex subletting, and other families omitted

83 Bodl. MS. Ch. Oxon. 5167; P.R.O., C 5/44/83.
84 Bodl. MS. d.d. Harcourt c 23/6; cf. ibid. MS. Rawl. D. 384, f. 110.
85 e.g. Bodl. MS. d.d. Harcourt c 122/6; St. John's Coll. Mun., XV.5A, XV.35; Ch. Ch. Arch., Standlake A 7.
86 e.g. Ch. Ch. Arch., Standlake A 7, A 17, A 55–6; St. John's Coll. Mun., XV.5A, XV.35, XV.38.
87 Bodl. MS. d.d. Harcourt c 122/2.
88 Ibid. c 64/4.
89 Ch. Ch. Arch., Standlake A 43.
90 Bodl. MSS. d.d. Harcourt c 73/2, c 73/6, c 73/12; cf. O.R.O., Misc. Ch. II/1–2; ibid. incl. award and map.
91 Bodl. MS. Rawl. B. 250, ff. 5–11; ibid. MS. Top. Oxon. b 265, ff. 40–50.
92 Ibid. MS. Top. Oxon. b 265, ff. 40 sqq.; ibid. MS. d.d. Harcourt c 282, envelope marked 'MSS. purchased by Ld. Harcourt 1913'; Berks. R.O., D/ELl L1; St. John's Coll. Mun., XV.9i.
93 Bodl. MS. Top. Oxon. b 265, ff. 63–86.
94 Ibid. f. 54; St. John's Coll. Mun., XV.9i (b).
95 O.R.O., incl. award. For a small intake in the earlier 18th century, Bodl. MS. d.d. Harcourt c 70/12.
96 Bodl. MS. Top. Oxon. b 265, ff. 53, 68, 82; O.R.O., Mor. XXIX/i/1; ibid. MS. Oxf. Dioc. d 577, f. 23.

97 Bodl. MS. Top. Oxon. b 265, f. 82; ibid. MS. d.d. Harcourt c 123/11.
98 St. John's Coll. Mun., XV.44; Magd. Coll. Mun., D-Y 231.
99 Bodl. MS. Top. Oxon. b 265, f. 77.
1 Ibid. MS. Rawl. D. 384, f. 110v.; ibid. MS. d.d. Harcourt c 282, partics. of Northmoor (n.d.).
2 Cal. Close, 1447–54, 38–9.
3 e.g. Bodl. MSS. d.d. Harcourt c 64/5–6, c 64/11, c 72/11, c 72/18, c 73/1, c 74/14; St. John's Coll. Mun., ADMIN. I. A.1, f. 147; ibid. XV.26; Ch. Ch. Arch., Standlake A 7.
4 Bodl. MS. d.d. Harcourt c 122/4.
5 Ibid. c 282, partics. of Northmoor (n.d.); cf. ibid. MS. Rawl. D. 384, ff. 110v.–111. The figure of 50–100,000 trees is not credible.   6 Magd. Coll. Mun., MP/2/Oxon./1.
7 O.R.O., tithe award and map; St. John's Coll. Mun., XV.44; O.S. Area Bk. (1877).
8 V.C.H. Oxon. i. 409; above, intro.; manors.
9 Rot. Hund. (Rec. Com.), ii. 732–3; cf. ibid. 742–3.
10 Ibid. 733; above, manors (More).
11 Cur. Reg. R. xi, pp. 194–5, 493; xii, pp. 288, 378–9; cf. ibid. vi. 174–5; ix. 306.
12 B.L. Add. MS. 6164, f. 15; Rot. Hund. (Rec. Com.), ii. 732–3.

in 1279 were possibly subtenants:[13] a freeholder with 20 a. in 1279 had earlier manumitted a servile tenant and regranted his house and 2 a. for 12d. rent,[14] and all or part of the More family's freehold was sublet in the earlier 13th century.[15] A ploughland in demesne in 1279 was valued at 100s.[16]

Labour services for the 10-a. villein holding in 1279 included mowing, haymaking, and carriage, worth 12d. in all, and one tenant of ½ a. owed services valued at 17d. Most labour services were worth less, and two small tenants owed only rent and 4 hens. The Mores performed the lord's suit at the hundred and county courts presumably as part of the service for their freehold, and tenants at Taynton and Northmoor collectively owed 20s. hidage and 10d. wardpenny, besides payments at the sheriff's tourn and 4d. cert money.[17] Farming, as later, was presumably mixed: former pasture in East field near the later Watkins Farm had apparently been ploughed by the late 12th century,[18] and an inhabitant's piggery was mentioned in 1203.[19]

Total wealth taxed in the early 14th century fell from c. £115 in 1306 to c. £94 in 1327, but average personalty rose from c. 42s. to 44s., placing Northmoor locally among parishes of middling prosperity. Some high payments were from freeholders recorded in 1279, among them John Laurence (alias de la More) who was assessed on £7 in 1306, but there was little consistency, and several prosperous taxpayers were otherwise unrecorded.[20] Hugh of Standlake, one of a prominent Witney family, was assessed in 1316 on over £33, by far the largest assessment in any year,[21] and John of Ducklington, the highest taxpayer in 1327, was a prominent Oxford clothier to whom a Northmoor freeholder had recently mortgaged some of his property.[22] The lowest payment in 1306, on goods worth 10s., was from one of a villein family with ½ a. or less in 1279.[23]

Northmoor seems to have escaped serious depopulation during the Black Death.[24] Buying, selling, and leasing by prominent families continued in the 14th century and the 15th;[25] no especially large freeholds had been created by the mid 16th century, however, when c. 15

tenants owed quitrents of between 12d. and 20s., excluding the More family's rent and 29s. from St. John's College, Oxford.[26] Among the more notable freeholders were the Martins, who later called themselves gentry and whose estate, after early 17th-century additions, included a mansion house (later Church Farm) and c. 80 a. of arable and meadow, to which 53 a. of new inclosure was added in 1666;[27] a smaller freehold, including a mansion house occupied in the 1630s by the lord of the manor, passed c. 1655 to the Pleydells.[28] Non-resident freeholders included the Yates and Walwyns of Standlake and the Seacoles of Stanton Harcourt, whose land passed later to the local Ferrymans.[29]

Eleven copyholders in 1568 owed rents ranging from 4d. for a cottage recently built on the waste to 55s. for 3 houses, 6 closes, and 52 a. of arable, meadow and pasture,[30] sublet by the Stones in the 1590s and bought by them in 1600.[31] Another copyholder had 11 a. of arable and 35½ a. of meadow, but most holdings were smaller, and 3 tenants were cottagers. Only one copyholder was also a notable freeholder.[32] All holdings were still measured in acres rather than yardlands and showed little uniformity,[33] though in the early 17th century yardlands were claimed variously to include 30 a., 35 a., or 40 a.[34]

Twelve taxpayers paid a total of 20s. 4d. in 1524, implying that Northmoor was relatively impoverished, though in 1576 fourteen inhabitants paid a total of £3 14s., a higher sum than in neighbouring Standlake with its larger population.[35] The wealthiest taxpayers included both freeholders and copyholders, often assessed on goods rather than land, and in 1524 one inhabitant was taxed on wages.[36] Few medieval surnames survived.[37] John More (d. 1566) was taxed c. 1558 on goods worth £10, and in 1576 John Herle, then lord, was taxed on lands worth £20;[38] a cottager twice paid on goods worth £5 and left personalty of c. £67,[39] and a copyholder taxed in 1610 on land worth £1 left personalty of £265.[40] During the 17th century Northmoor's prosperity and social structure remained similar to that of neighbouring parishes, most testators leaving goods worth between £11 and £60, and only a few leaving less than £10 or more than

[13] Balliol Coll. Arch., A.19, passim; Bodl. MSS. d.d. Harcourt c 68/1–52; P.R.O., E 179/161/8–10; Cur. Reg. R. v. 163, 231; Oxon. Fines, pp. 145, 221, 227.
[14] Balliol Coll. Arch., A.19.3b–c; Rot. Hund. (Rec. Com.), ii. 733.
[15] Cur. Reg. R. v. 163, 231.
[16] Rot. Hund. (Rec. Com.), ii. 732.
[17] Ibid. ii. 732–3, 743.
[18] T. G. Allen, Watkins Fm., Northmoor (Thames Valley Landscapes: Windrush Valley, vol. i), pp. xiii, 83.
[19] Cur. Reg. R. ii. 310.
[20] P.R.O., E 179/161/8–10; Rot. Hund. (Rec. Com.), ii. 733. The total was incorrectly given in the 1306 roll.
[21] P.R.O., E 179/161/8; cf. Cal. Pat. 1330–4, 194.
[22] P.R.O., E 179/161/9; Balliol Coll. Arch., A.19.23–4, 29–30, 32; V.C.H. Oxon. iv. 38, 277, 374.
[23] P.R.O., E 179/161/10; Rot. Hund. (Rec. Com.), ii. 732–3.
[24] Above, intro.
[25] Bodl. MS. d.d. Harcourt c 68, passim; Balliol Coll. Arch., A.19, passim.
[26] Bodl. MS. d.d. Harcourt c 123/13; cf. above, manors. Another 4d. was owed for a church ho.
[27] Bodl. MSS. d.d. Harcourt c 69/7–18, c 122/6, c 123/13; ibid. MS. Rawl. B. 250, f. 9; O.R.O., MS. Wills Oxon. 83/4/26; above, intro.

[28] Bodl. MSS. d.d. Harcourt c 59, passim; cf. ibid. c 123/13, s.v. J. Clarke; above, manors.
[29] Bodl. MS. d.d. Harcourt c 123/13; P.R.O., C 2/Eliz. I/S.s. 5/35; V.C.H. Oxon. xii. 283; below, Standlake, other estates.
[30] Bodl. MSS. d.d. Harcourt c 122/6, c 123/13.
[31] Ibid. c 122/7; O.R.O., Misc. Su. XXXVI/i/1.
[32] Bodl. MSS. d.d. Harcourt c 122/1, c 122/4, c 122/6, c 123/13.   [33] e.g. ibid. c 122/6.
[34] O.R.O., MS. Oxf. Archd. Oxon. b 25, f. 304; cf. P.R.O., C 2/Jas. I/K 7/18; Bodl. MS. d.d. Harcourt c 122/12.
[35] P.R.O., E 179/161/179; E 179/162/341, including 26s. 8d. from the lord.
[36] P.R.O., E 179/161/179; E 179/162/320; E 179/162/331; E 179/162/341; E 179/163/398; cf. Bodl. MS. d.d. Harcourt c 123/13.
[37] For exceptions, P.R.O., E 179/161/10; Bodl. MS. d.d. Harcourt c 68/48.
[38] P.R.O., E 179/162/320; E 179/162/341; O.R.O., MS. Wills Oxon. 184, f. 234 and v.; above, manors.
[39] Bodl. MS. d.d. Harcourt c 123/13; P.R.O., E 179/162/320; E 179/162/331; O.R.O., MS. Wills Oxon. 185, ff. 407v.–408.
[40] O.R.O., MS. Wills Oxon. 83/3/37; P.R.O., E 179/163/435; Bodl. MS. d.d. Harcourt c 122/7.

£100;[41] exceptionally, Thomas Harris (d. 1639), probably of later Stonehenge Farm in Moreton, left chattels worth c. £319, including a lease worth £100 and £90 in money.[42] Twenty-eight taxpayers (65 per cent) paid on 1 or 2 hearths in 1662, and only six (14 per cent) on 5 hearths or more, among them the lord (11 hearths), the lay rector (9 hearths), and members of the Pleydell, Martin, and Stone families (5 hearths). Eight inhabitants were exonerated through poverty in 1665.[43]

The chief crops in the 17th century and early 18th were wheat, barley, and pulses.[44] Maslin was mentioned in 1611, hops in 1671, and rye in 1688.[45] A few testators left malt or malt mills, several left hemp, and a few left apples;[46] many left hay, sometimes in large quantities.[47] A wealthy freeholder in 1550 had 2 yoke of oxen.[48] Cattle, cheese, and cheese-making equipment were mentioned frequently, and some wealthy farmers had herds of up to 15 cattle;[49] Manor Farm included a well-furnished dairy for 50 cows c. 1713,[50] and Northmoor cheesemongers evidently attended Oxford market in the 1750s.[51] Sheep were recorded less often and there were few large flocks, presumably because of the low, wet commons, though two freeholders in the 1560s were fined for exceeding their stints by 60 sheep,[52] and another in 1632 left 36 adult sheep besides cattle and crops.[53] Several testators owned a few sheep or left wool or fleeces, and some inventories itemized dung.[54] Pigs and bacon were mentioned frequently, several testators owned poultry, and a few kept bees.

A leasehold tenant was recorded on Northmoor manor in 1622.[55] Manor farm was let at rack rent on 10- and later 21-year leases from the 1640s, though in the later 17th century and early 18th it seems sometimes to have been kept in hand.[56] In the mid 18th century it comprised 270 a., mostly ancient and 17th-century inclosures,[57] and it remained the largest farm in the earlier 19th century.[58] Leasehold gradually superseded copyhold in the later 17th century and early 18th, though most early leases were lifehold grants of customary holdings let for small rents and large entry fines,[59] and some rack rents were

reduced before 1755 'on account of the badness of the times'.[60] After 1755 the Harcourts systematically replaced lifeholds with short leases at rack rent, the last lifehold expiring in 1806.[61] Six freeholds totalling c. 300 a., bought by the Harcourts in the earlier 18th century, became part of Northmoor manor and were also let at rack rent.[62] By c. 1809 four out of nine farms on the manor exceeded 100 a., two exceeded 200 a., and at least one smaller farm was occupied with other lands.[63]

Rents to St. John's College were demanded partly in corn or its market equivalent under the Corn Rent Act of 1576. That for the rectory farm was increased to £100 before 1629 and so remained in the earlier 19th century, with large entry fines payable every 3½ years,[64] though in the mid 17th century the rent was not always paid and fines were sometimes waived.[65] Christ Church's farms were let at rack rent by the mid 17th century,[66] and Magdalen's by the later 18th.[67] Of those only Christ Church's Gaunt House farm exceeded 50 a.,[68] but in the later 18th century many larger farmers held more than one farm, often combining freehold and leasehold; a freeholder who in 1785 paid over £42 land tax was tenant under five owners, and another who paid c. £22 held under three.[69] In all c. 40 proprietors were recorded, half of them owing less than 20s. land tax.[70]

Some parts of the former common were arable by the earlier 19th century,[71] but on Northmoor manor most farms in the later 18th century and early 19th were predominantly pastoral,[72] and in 1844 c. 1,414 a. (73 per cent of the parish) was meadow or pasture, much of it of inferior quality.[73] Flooding still occurred frequently, causing serious losses in 1829.[74] The best-quality arable was that in the common fields, which was potentially good turnip land, and in 1832 the Harcourts' agent claimed never to have seen a place where inclosure and drainage would bring greater benefit.[75] The remaining common land was inclosed c. 1844, when the award was inrolled; the Harcourts received c. 1,044 a. including c. 193 a. of new inclosure, 41 other owners or tenants received new allotments ranging

41 O.R.O., MSS. Wills Oxon., Northmoor wills and inventories.
42 Ibid. 298/1/46; above, intro.
43 P.R.O., E 179/255/4, pt. ii, f. 153; *Hearth Tax Oxon.* 183.
44 O.R.O., MSS. Wills Oxon., Northmoor wills and inventories, on which rest of para. based.
45 Ibid. 43/3/51, 86/3/12, 141/2/16.
46 e.g. ibid. 43/3/4, 43/3/5, 141/2/16, 296/4/16.
47 e.g. ibid. 298/2/8.   48 Ibid. 180, f. 6.
49 e.g. ibid. 172/1/45, 298/1/46.
50 Bodl. MS. d.d. Harcourt c 262, undated partics. of Northmoor 'delivered when my lord was lord chancellor'.
51 Oxf. Jnl. Synopsis, 10 Jan. 1756.
52 Bodl. MS. Top. Oxon. b 21, ff. 8v., 29.
53 O.R.O., MS. Wills Oxon. 31/3/28; cf. ibid. 172/1/45.
54 e.g. ibid. 172/1/45.
55 Bodl. MS. d.d. Harcourt c 122/9.
56 Ibid. c 73/6, c 73/10, c 74/29, c 75/2, c 75/5; ibid. c 282, partics. 1718; Bodl. MS. Rawl. D. 384, ff. 110–11.
57 Bodl. MS. d.d. Harcourt c 282, partics. of estate late John Blewitt, p. 1; cf. ibid. c 73/2, c 74/14; Bodl. MS. Rawl. D. 384, f. 110v.
58 O.R.O., tithe award, s.v. Rachel Eagle.
59 Bodl. MS. Rawl. D. 384, ff. 110–11; ibid. MSS. d.d. Harcourt c 77/28–34, c 123/5–12.
60 Bodl. MS. d.d. Harcourt c 282, partics. of estate late

John Blewitt, p. 2.
61 Ibid., *passim*; ibid., rental 1780; ibid. MS. d.d. Harcourt b 35, *passim*.
62 Bodl. MSS. d.d. Harcourt c 61/7, c 63/16–18, c 65/13–14, c 70/11–12, c 72/2–7; ibid. c 262 (R); ibid. c 282, terrier of Lapworths fm.
63 Bodl. MS. d.d. Harcourt b 35; cf. O.R.O., QSD L.211.
64 St. John's Coll. Mun., ADMIN. I. A.1, ff. 147, 207v.–208; ADMIN. I. A.3, pp. 54–7, 383–4, 580, 764–6, 806, 812–14; ADMIN. I. A.9, pp. 27, 71, 163.
65 Ibid. ADMIN. I. A.3, pp. 94, 385, 474; ibid. XV.9i (a).
66 Ch. Ch. Arch., Standlake A 41, A 43, A 57; ibid. MS. Estates 80, ff. 35–6.
67 Magd. Coll. Mun., D-Y 31–3; ibid. ES 6/4, pp. 43–4.
68 Ch. Ch. Arch., MS. Estates 80, f. 41 and v.
69 O.R.O., QSD L.211, s.v. N. Kent, C. Watkins; cf. ibid. MS. Wills Oxon. 40/3/11; Bodl. MS. d.d. Harcourt b 35; Ch. Ch. Arch., MS. Estates 80, f. 47.
70 O.R.O., QSD L.211.
71 Ibid. tithe award.
72 Bodl. MS. d.d. Harcourt c 282, partics. of estate late John Blewitt; ibid. b 35, c 281.
73 O.R.O., tithe award; St. John's Coll. Mun., XV.44.
74 St. John's Coll. Mun., XV.44; Bodl. MS. d.d. Harcourt c 5; cf. O.R.O., MS. d.d. Par. Northmoor c 2, f. 46.
75 Bodl. MS. d.d. Harcourt c 265, f. 32.

from less than an acre to *c.* 67 a. for St. John's College's open-field land, and a total of 39 a. of old and new inclosure was exchanged. Achim mead was separately inclosed with Standlake *c.* 1853.[76]

Immediately after inclosure there were (excluding cottagers) 37 occupiers of land, of whom 20, many of them non-resident, had 15 a. or less. Eight farmers had over 100 a., frequently held under several owners, and Rachel Eagle of Manor farm and John Nalder of Rectory farm had over 200 a.[77] By 1861 there were 6 farms over 100 a. and two of 300 a. or more, in all employing 56 men and boys; *c.* 80 agricultural labourers and plough boys were recorded, by far the largest occupational group.[78] All the farms were worked from earlier homesteads, and in the 1870s and later some large farms were worked from outside the parish.[79] Flooding remained serious, and in 1866, on the initiative of local farmers and landowners, the Northmoor and Stanton Harcourt Drainage Board was established under the Land Drainage Act of 1861. Several miles of embankments and cuttings were constructed along the river Thames and a short stretch of the river Windrush, the cost met by levies on those likely to benefit; as a result land which had supplied only rough summer pasture for cattle was ploughed, producing spring corn (usually barley), Italian rye grass, and root crops which provided good sheep feed. Pastures on the newly drained land remained poor, and conversion to arable was recommended.[80] By 1877 arable in the parish had been increased to *c.* 49 per cent,[81] though most farms remained mixed; the Harcourts' Moreton farm (157 a.) was in 1871 a 'useful small dairy farm', and most homesteads included cattle sheds and piggeries.[82]

Such improvements did not offset the effects of agricultural depression, and in 1881 the tenants of Watkins and Brook farms, both members of the prominent Walter family, were granted rent reductions following losses caused by excessively wet seasons. Some newly cultivated land had produced poor-quality straw but no corn, and grassland had suffered.[83] Most rents had been reduced by 1886 when John Walter, who in 1881 had the best herd on the estate, received notice to quit, though several other prominent farmers continued into the 1890s or later.[84] Most notable was Richard Eagle (d. 1899), who by the 1880s held Manor, Moreton, and Rectory farms (*c.* 700 a.) besides freehold land and other farms in Stanton Harcourt and Standlake.[85]

In 1896 Manor farm was scattered, of uneven quality, and expensive to cultivate,[86] and in 1920 scattered fields, wet and unproductive arable, and continued flooding near the Thames prompted Magdalen College to sell its estate.[87] River meadows yielded good hay crops and arable in the north-west on Pinnocks farm was 'fairly productive',[88] but poor communications with Oxford adversely affected the parish's economy.[89] In 1914 the parish was 61 per cent permanent pasture, and cattle were kept in relatively large numbers, though many fewer sheep were kept than elsewhere in the region and their numbers were falling. Pigs were kept also. The chief crops were wheat (24 per cent), barley (15 per cent), and oats (11 per cent), with swedes and turnips (6 per cent) and mangolds (5 per cent).[90] Most farms remained mixed in the 1920s, when there was some dairying and poultry farming, though the proportion of arable varied from 23 per cent on Watkins farm (229 a.) to over 75 per cent on the much smaller Brooks and Pinnocks farms.[91] In 1939 there were 9 chief farms, of which Church, Watkins, and the combined Rectory and Brook farms exceeded 150 a.;[92] in 1979 Manor farm was 232 a. (94 ha.), of which 16 per cent was permanent pasture, 43 per cent was under wheat or barley, 36 per cent was leys, and 5 per cent was fallow and stubble.[93] Rectory farm remained mixed in 1995, livestock including beef cattle and some sheep.[94] Land belonging to Stonehenge farm in Moreton was alleged in 1960 to be 'little more than a bog', though adjacent land was of good quality.[95]

Medieval surnames included Tailor, Draper, Weaver, and Carpenter, though none was recorded frequently.[96] Rural tradesmen recorded occasionally from the later 16th century included a butcher, baker, tailor, carpenter, cordwainer, and wheelwright;[97] several tanners were noted in the late 16th century and earlier 17th,[98] and some other testators left bark mills.[99] An apprentice tucker with Witney connections lived at New-

76   O.R.O., incl. award; ibid. Standlake incl. award.
77   Ibid. incl. award; ibid. tithe award; P.R.O., HO 107/879.
78   P.R.O., RG 9/904; cf. Bodl. MS. d.d. Harcourt c 282, list of labourers 1832.
79   P.R.O., RG 9/904; ibid. RG 11/1513; Bodl. MS. d.d. Harcourt c 266, p. 54; ibid. c 282, lease to J. Walter 29 Sept. 1881.
80   Bodl. MS. d.d. Harcourt c 266, pp. 42, 60; *Jnl. R. Agric. Soc.* 2nd ser. vi. 367–74; O.S. Map 6", Oxon. XXXVIII (1883 edn.). For mins., Berks. R.O., D/TC 184–5.
81   O.S. *Area Bk.* (1877).
82   Bodl. MS. d.d. Harcourt c 266, pp. 45–60; Magd. Coll. Estates Bursary, survs. 1883–91, p. 348.
83   Bodl. MS. d.d. Harcourt c 282, note on J. and W. Walter's farms, 1881; cf. ibid. c 266, pp. 51, 54; O.R.O., tithe map.
84   Bodl. MS. d.d. Harcourt c 266, pp. 38, 40–2, 48–9, 65, 71, and unpaginated surv. 1895; ibid. c 282, note on J. Walter's farm, 1881; *P.O. Dir. Oxon.* (1877); *Kelly's Dir. Oxon.* (1883 and later edns.).
85   Bodl. MSS. d.d. Harcourt c 266, p. 47; e 25, pp. 6, 38, and unpag. surv. 1895; St. John's Coll. Mun., EST. III.x.14, pp. 19–22; Magd. Coll. Mun., modern deeds box 98.
86   St. John's Coll. Mun., XV.50, referring perhaps to college land worked from Manor Farm.

87   Magd. Coll. Estates Bursary, survs. 1913–23, pp. 83–4; cf. ibid. 1892–1912, p. 522.
88   Ibid. 1913–23, p. 77.
89   Bodl. MS. d.d. Harcourt c 266, p. 45; ibid. G.A. Oxon. c 317/12, appeals for Bablock Hythe bridge, 1910; Stowell, *Glimpses of Northmoor*, 34; above, intro.
90   Orr, *Oxon. Agric.*, statistical plates.
91   *Sale Cat., Harcourt Settled Estates* (1924), pp. 45–60: copy in Bodl. G.A. Oxon. c 226.
92   *Kelly's Dir. Oxon.* (1939); cf. *Sale Cat., Watkins Fm.* (1945): microfilm in C.O.S.
93   Probate Valn. 3 Jan. 1979: copy in Old Estate Office, Stanton Harcourt Manor Ho. (1988).
94   Inf. from Mr. P. Florey, Rectory Fm.
95   St. John's Coll. Mun., XV.54.
96   P.R.O., E 179/161/8–10; *Rot. Hund.* (Rec. Com.), ii. 733; *Oxon. Eyre, 1241* (O.R.S. lvi), no. 1008.
97   O.R.O., MSS. Wills Oxon. 35/4/40, 39/1/9, 56/1/32, 132/2/16, 135/3/23; P.R.O., C 3/64/46.
98   O.R.O., MS. Wills Oxon. 170/2/2; *Witney Ct. Bks.* 105, 176.
99   O.R.O., MSS. Wills Oxon. 4/1/22, 141/1/16.

bridge mill *c.* 1559,[1] and a moderately prosperous clothier and weaver died in 1688, though he was also a substantial mixed farmer.[2] Several inhabitants, some of them prominent yeomen, left linen or woollen wheels,[3] and in 1814 many poor children worked at home for Witney blanketeers rather than enter service.[4] Nineteenth-century tradesmen included a few carpenters and shoemakers, sawyers employed presumably on the Harcourts' estates in Stanton Harcourt or Ducklington, and coal dealers at Newbridge, and several women were seamstresses or dress- or trousermakers; in 1813 there was a blacksmith, in 1841 a weaver and a basketmaker, and in 1861 a thatcher and a gloveress.[5] There were grocers' shops at the Red Lion and Dun Cow public houses by 1861, and in 1881 there was a baker.[6] In 1903 there was a machinist and boot repairer, in 1904 a blacksmith, and in 1911 a road contractor and a wheelwright, but traditional crafts had disappeared by 1939. The village shop closed presumably with the post office in the 1960s.[7]

FAIRS. Two annual fairs at Newbridge on 20 March and 20 August were granted to Edmund Warcupp as lord of Northmoor in 1675.[8] The first fair was moved to 31 March (20 March old style) presumably after the calendar change of 1753, and the second to 28 September before 1768.[9] Both were held in an inclosed meadow of *c.* 10 a. adjoining the Standlake road north-east of Newbridge,[10] and in 1768 the September fair was postponed because of flooding.[11] A 'fair house' was let with the Rose and Crown (later the Rose Revived) public house and its wharf from the later 17th century to the early 19th;[12] the tolls were let separately for £16 *c.* 1697 and for £13 in the earlier 18th century, at first with Manor farm, and in the 1750s to another local farmer.[13] 'Some little sage cheese' was sold in the later 17th century, and cattle and horses in the early 18th, when buyers came from Buckinghamshire and Wiltshire;[14] in the mid 18th century one or both of the fairs was evidently large, with 40 booths and stalls, 3 or 4 house boats from Oxford and Binsey, and tradesmen

from Witney and presumably elsewhere.[15] From the later 18th century tolls were collected apparently by the lord's bailiff, but profits fell from *c.* £13 in 1780 to 9*s.* in 1798, when there may have been only one fair, and no income was recorded from 1799 to 1803.[16] In 1806 the tolls were let for 30*s.* to the tenant of the Rose and Crown,[17] but though the fair house was mentioned in 1816[18] the fair itself had lapsed possibly by 1819 and certainly by the later 1840s.[19]

MILLS AND FISHERIES. One of two mills recorded on Taynton manor in 1086 may have been in Northmoor.[20] In 1279 a predecessor of Newbridge (earlier Moreton) mill on the river Windrush belonged to the More family's freehold, with which it descended until 1608 when John More sold it to Thomas Webley;[21] the Loggins of Swalcliffe and Butlers Marston (Warws.) acquired it before 1635, but following disputes sold or released it to Henry Webley of Northmoor in 1653.[22] Like their predecessors the Webleys let it to resident millers,[23] and in 1719 sold it to John Blewitt, lord of Northmoor.[24] It remained part of Northmoor manor until 1924.[25]

In the mid 15th century it was a corn mill, to which Robert More (fl. 1445) added a fulling mill presumably at its western end, encroaching on land belonging to Standlake manor. The fulling mill was demolished after intervention by a lord of Standlake, though the corn mill was allowed to remain.[26] That, too, encroached on Standlake lordship,[27] implying either that the mill stood on a different branch of the river Windrush west of its later site, or, more likely, that the boundary there was adjusted later.[28] Another fulling mill was built onto the mill's west end *c.* 1548 and continued *c.* 1556, when the tenant gave 2 bu. of malt a year to Standlake parish in acknowledgement of his encroachment.[29] In 1608 there were two fulling mills and a corn mill, and in 1637 two corn mills and a fulling mill;[30] in 1682 there were two grist mills under one roof, to which two more were added *c.* 1719,[31] and the mill remained a corn grist mill thereafter.[32] In 1832 it was 'of great power', and

[1] O.R.O., MS. Wills Oxon. 183, f. 93.
[2] Ibid. 141/2/16.
[3] Ibid. 71/2/43, 124/4/22, 127/2/28, 138/3/14, 299/1/20.
[4] Bodl. MSS. d.d. Harcourt b 35; b 37, p. 12.
[5] O.R.O., Cal. Q.S. ii, f. 191; P.R.O., HO 107/879; ibid. RG 9/904; RG 11/1513.
[6] P.R.O., RG 9/904; RG 11/1513.
[7] Magd. Coll. Estates Bursary, survs. 1892–1912, p. 522; *Kelly's Dir. Oxon.* (1903 and later edns.); above, intro.
[8] *Cal. S.P. Dom.* 1675–6, 368.
[9] D. and S. Lysons, *Magna Britannia et Hibernia: Berks.* (1806, facsimile edn. 1978), 307; *Oxf. Jnl. Synopsis,* 11 Oct. 1768.
[10] Bodl. MS. Rawl. D. 384, f. 110; O.R.O., incl. award and map, s.v. Fair ground.
[11] *Oxf. Jnl. Synopsis,* 11 Oct. 1768.
[12] Berks. R.O., D/ELl T39; Bodl. MS. Rawl. D 384, f. 110; ibid. MSS. d.d. Harcourt c 75/1, schedule of leases; c 282, partic. of estate late J. Blewitt, p. 3; c 281, ff. 1v.–2; cf. O.R.O., QSD V/1–4; above, intro.
[13] Bodl. MS. Rawl. D. 384, f. 110; ibid. MS. d.d. Harcourt c 282, partic. of Northmoor 1718; ibid. partic. of estate late J. Blewitt, p. 3.
[14] B.L. Harl. MS. 4716, f. 8v.; O.R.O., QS/1708 Trin./11.
[15] O.R.O., P4/2/MS 1/5, p. 11.
[16] Bodl. MSS. d.d. Harcourt b 10, b 16, c 182, s.v. Northmoor.

[17] Ibid. b 16, p. 340; b 17, pp. 13, 67, 199 sqq.; cf. ibid. c 281, f. 1v.
[18] Ibid. c 281, f. 2.
[19] *Hist. and Topog. Oxon.* (Pinnock's Co. Histories, 1819), 68–9; *P.O. Dir. Oxon.* (1847 and later edns.); cf. *Lewis's Topog. Dict. of Eng.* (1840), iii. 381.
[20] *V.C.H. Oxon.* i. 409; above, manors.
[21] P.R.O., C 1/941/46; ibid. CP 25/2/339/6 Jas. I East; Magd. Coll. Mun., ct. bk. 6, Standlake cts. 15 Mar. 3 & 4 Phil. and Mary, 2 Aug. 2 Eliz.; *Rot. Hund.* (Rec. Com.), ii. 733; O.S. Map 1/2,500, Oxon. XXXVIII. 10 (1876 edn.).
[22] P.R.O., C 142/735, no. 124; Bodl. MS. d.d. Harcourt c 72/11, schedule of deeds; B.L. Add. MS. 34326, f. 34.
[23] O.R.O., MS. Wills Oxon. 154/1/41; cf. P.R.O., C 1/941/46; Magd. Coll. Mun., EP 146/4; ibid. ct. bk. 9, Standlake ct. 26 July 14 Eliz.
[24] Bodl. MSS. d.d. Harcourt c 72/11–22.
[25] *Sale Cat., Harcourt Settled Estates* (1924), lot 54: copy in Bodl. G.A. Oxon. c 226.
[26] Magd. Coll. Mun., EP 146/33.
[27] Ibid.
[28] O.R.O., incl. map; below, Standlake, intro.
[29] Magd. Coll. Mun., EP 146/4.
[30] P.R.O., CP 25/2/339/6 Jas. I East.; ibid. C 142/735, no. 124.
[31] Bodl. MSS. d.d. Harcourt c 72/11–19.
[32] e.g. ibid. c 76/6; O.S. Map 1/2,500, Oxon. XXXVIII. 10 (1876 edn.).

in 1871 it had 3 pairs of stones driven by 2 undershot wheels.[33] Milling ceased apparently between 1915 and 1920, and in 1924 the mill was a storeroom;[34] it was demolished during the earlier 20th century.[35] The surviving millhouse, formerly attached to the mill's east end, is of the 18th century,[36] and incorporates an originally symmetrical, 3-bayed front of squared limestone blocks, to which a matching fourth bay was added on the west after 1950.[37] Service ranges at the rear are probably 19th-century.

A freehold mill in Northmoor or Standlake, mentioned in the early 14th century, has not been identified.[38] A mill in Northmoor by the Thames, called Thames mill, was recorded in 1687 but had been demolished by 1704.[39]

The name *wilstede*, recorded in 1059, may indicate a fishtrap.[40] The surname Fisher (*Piscator*) was recorded from the 13th century,[41] and two 17th-century yeomen left fishing tackle.[42] Common waters apparently in a tributary of the river Thames were mentioned in 1394 and 1424,[43] but in the mid 15th century Standlake parishioners vindicated their common rights in much of the river Windrush against Robert More, perhaps to the exclusion of Northmoor's parishioners.[44] Lords of Northmoor claimed royalty of fishing (as of hunting and fowling) throughout the parish,[45] and in 1696 a tenant was fined for appropriating and leasing a pond or watercourse stocked with fish near Dag Lane.[46] Courts in the later 17th century repeatedly fined those erecting weirs or fishtraps in a stream called Flexneys Lake.[47]

A several fishery in the Thames at 'Widewere', near Gaingey meadow, was mentioned in 1247,[48] and a fishpond in a freeholder's garden about the same date.[49] Freehold fisheries mentioned later included one from west of Newbridge to south of Moreton, acquired by St. John's College, Oxford,[50] and Newbridge mill carried fishing rights in tributaries of the Windrush.[51] The moat around Manor Farm was well stocked with fish *c.* 1700, and manorial fisheries in both rivers were let in the later 17th century,[52] though one

of the Thames fisheries was sold in 1704 to the lord of Appleton (then Berks.).[53] A fishery in the Thames at Noah's Ark weir, so named by the mid 18th century, was detached from Northmoor manor in 1600 and was bought in 1741 by Magdalen College, Oxford, which let it to local fishermen.[54] The attached house, new-built in 1768, was in disrepair in 1798,[55] and in the 1850s the weir was unused and decayed; its remains were cleared after 1866.[56] Hart's, Ridge's, Cock's, or Langley weir further upstream, within the parish but with buildings on the south bank in Berkshire, belonged to Fyfield manor,[57] and was perhaps associated with a fishery mentioned from the 15th century.[58] The weir was working but dilapidated in 1879 and was removed in 1880, leaving only a newly built footbridge.[59]

In the 1880s Edward Harcourt complained that crayfish could no longer live in the Windrush because of pollution from Witney factories,[60] but in 1924 there was 'first class' trout fishing near Newbridge mill. Fishing in the Thames was by then let to the Oxford Angling and Preservation Society and non-resident sportsmen.[61]

LOCAL GOVERNMENT. Courts were held for Northmoor manor by 1279.[62] In the earlier 16th century there were reportedly two courts a year,[63] but from the later 16th only one was recorded every two or three years.[64] Annual views of frankpledge were held in 1279 by the bailiff of the earl of Gloucester, then lord of Chadlington hundred, who received the fines and 4*d.* cert money.[65] In 1590, however, the Crown sold Northmoor manor including its court leet and view of frankpledge,[66] and though only courts baron were recorded in the later 16th century and earlier 17th, views were held regularly from 1661.[67] Seventeenth-century lords also claimed waifs, strays, and felons' goods, certainty, and royalties of hunting, hawking, and fishing.[68] No courts are known after 1712,

33 Bodl. MSS. d.d. Harcourt c 265, f. 13; c 266, p. 53.
34 *Kelly's Dir. Oxon.* (1915 and later edns.); *Sale Cat., Harcourt Settled Estates* (1924), lot 54.
35 N.M.R., Northmoor file, unref. photo. (1950). C.O.S., PRN 2305 wrongly says demolished 1920.
36 Cf. Bodl. MS. d.d. Harcourt c 282, rental 1780, recording a rent increase 'for building'.
37 Illust. in Bodl. MS. Top. Oxon. d 218, f. 238; N.M.R., Northmoor file, unref. photo.
38 P.R.O., CP 25/1/189/14, no. 134; CP 25/1/189/15, no. 105.
39 Bodl. MS. Ch. Oxon. 5306; ibid. MS. d.d. Harcourt c 74/25.
40 *P.N. Elements* (E.P.N.S.), ii. 147, 265; above, intro.
41 P.R.O., E 179/161/10; *Rot. Hund.* (Rec. Com.), ii. 732-3.
42 O.R.O., MSS. Wills Oxon. 79/3/24, 86/3/12.
43 Bodl. MSS. d.d. Harcourt c 68/26, c 68/33.
44 Magd. Coll. Mun., EP 146/33.
45 e.g. Bodl. MS. Rawl. D. 384, f. 110; St. John's Coll. Mun., XV.36.
46 Bodl. MS. d.d. Harcourt c 123/8; for Dag Lane, above, intro.
47 Bodl. MSS. d.d. Harcourt c 123/1, c 123/4-6, c 123/8.
48 *Oxon. Fines,* p. 145; cf. O.R.O., incl. map, s.v. Gaingey.
49 Balliol Coll. Arch., A.19.11c.
50 St. John's Coll. Mun., XV.35; cf. P.R.O., CP 25/2/198/38 Eliz. I East.; Ch. Ch. Arch., Standlake A 7.
51 Bodl. MS. d.d. Harcourt c 76/6.
52 Ibid. MS. Rawl. D. 384, ff. 110-11.
53 Ibid. MS. d.d. Harcourt c 74/25.

54 Magd. Coll. Mun., D-Y 5, 33, 90, 92; ibid. MP/2/Oxon./1; cf. P.R.O., C 3/229/28.
55 Magd. Coll. Mun., MP/2/Oxon./1; ibid. D-Y 226.
56 F. S. Thacker, *Thames Highway* (1968 edn.), ii. 87; O.S. Map 6", Oxon. XXXVIII (1883 edn.).
57 St. John's Coll. Mun., II.36, s.v. Cottmore and Cocke; Thacker, *Thames Highway,* ii. 79-84; O.S. Map 1", sheet XIII (1830 edn.); ibid. 6", Oxon. XXXVIII (1883 edn.); A. Bryant, *Oxon. Map* (1824).
58 *Cal. Close,* 1447-54, 38-9; *Cat. Anct. D.* v, A 10957; cf. *V.C.H. Berks.* iv. 346-7.
59 Thacker, *Thames Highway,* ii. 83. For Northmoor lock, above, intro.
60 Bodl. MS. d.d. Harcourt c 282, letter 12 Aug. 1887.
61 *Sale Cat., Harcourt Settled Estates* (1924), pp. 2, 58; cf. Magd. Coll. Estates Bursary, ledger M, pp. 331-3.
62 *Rot. Hund.* (Rec. Com.), ii. 733; *Tax. Eccl.* (Rec. Com.), 44; cf. *Cal. Pat.* 1317-21, 430-1, mentioning suit at the prior of Deerhurst's court of Taynton.
63 *Valor Eccl.* (Rec. Com.), ii. 472; cf. P.R.O., SC 2/197/20-1; ibid. SC 6/Hen. VIII/1260, m. 45d.
64 Bodl. MS. Top. Oxon. b 21, ff. 4v. sqq.; ibid. MSS. d.d. Harcourt c 122/1-14; c 123/1-12.
65 *Rot. Hund.* (Rec. Com.), ii. 733, 736.
66 P.R.O., C 66/1342, m. 17; ibid. C 142/233, no. 89; cf. ibid. SC 2/197/20-1.
67 Bodl. MS. Top. Oxon. b 21, ff. 4v. sqq.; ibid. MSS. d.d. Harcourt c 122/6-14, c 123/1-12.
68 Ibid. c 74/14; ibid. MS. Rawl. D. 384, ff. 110-11.

though in 1741 trustees of the church house reserved the lord's right to hold courts leet and law days there.[69] In the 16th century the Mores may have held separate courts for their reputed manor, since they reportedly granted a copy in 1574.[70]

Recorded courts for Northmoor manor dealt primarily with copyholds and agricultural affairs. Two field wardens were appointed in 1564, and courts in the later 17th century elected a constable, mentioned from the 14th century, and tithingmen for Moreton, West or Upper, East or Lower, and Middle tithings.[71] Other 17th-century officers, chosen apparently by the vestry, were a hayward, 4 grass stewards, and 2 surveyors of highways.[72] In the 19th century the vestry appointed or nominated a constable and 2 surveyors or, later, a waywarden; in 1850 it fixed parishioners' carriage duties towards road repairs, and in 1859 resolved to contract out repairs.[73]

There were two churchwardens by 1530[74] and still in 1995. From the early 17th century and probably in the mid 16th their income included rent from the church house, later the Red Lion, and from nearby cottages,[75] and from the mid 18th century they received rent from land and cottages left by Richard Lydall (d. 1721) towards upkeep of the church tower and bells.[76] The Red Lion was sold in 1908.[77]

There were two collectors or overseers by 1653.[78] A deputy overseer was noted in 1784 and a salaried overseer in 1817,[79] but a proposal in 1790 to farm the poor[80] was evidently abandoned. Expenditure on poor relief rose irregularly from c. £5 in the mid 17th century to c. £25 in the early 18th, and to sometimes over £100 in the later 18th; by the 1790s it sometimes exceeded £300, and in 1801 was c. £700, c. 42s. per head.[81] Expenditure remained exceptionally high, 73s. per head in 1819, c. 38s. in the mid 1820s, and 69s. by 1834,[82] and high poor rates attracted comment.[83] In 1803 there were 29 adults and over 100 children receiving regular out relief, 23 children in schools of industry apparently outside the parish, and 21

people receiving occasional relief;[84] the proportion of casual relief gradually increased, chiefly because of rising unemployment, and 25 adults received occasional and 21 regular relief in 1815.[85] Regular payments were from c. 1812 related to weekly bread prices.[86] A rented workhouse with accommodation for 20 inmates was noted from 1776 to 1799, when it housed 1 man, 4 women, and 6 children;[87] it had closed by 1803, but continued to be rented as pauper accommodation.[88]

In the 1750s and later some poor were employed spinning hemp, flax, and sometimes wool, carding, and, less frequently, weaving.[89] Spinning wheels were occasionally supplied or repaired, and in 1799 the workhouse contained cards, cardboards, and 4 spinning wheels.[90] Roundsmen were mentioned frequently in the early 19th century, and in 1816–17 some poor were employed on the roads.[91] Occasionally paupers' children were apprenticed or put into service.[92] In 1705 the overseers built a house on the waste near Newbridge,[93] and from the mid 18th century paid rent for several houses, including, in the 1760s, the church house, and in the early 19th century cottages between Dag and Chapel Lane belonging to the tower and bells estate.[94] Medical expenses were paid frequently, and from c. 1812 an Appleton doctor was contracted for c. £20 a year.[95]

After 1834 Northmoor belonged to Witney union.[96] The vestry continued to appoint 2 overseers and to regulate rating, and in 1854 it apprenticed a Northmoor child then in the union workhouse. A salaried assistant overseer was appointed in 1867.[97] From 1894 the parish belonged to Witney rural district, and from 1974 to West Oxfordshire district.[98]

CHURCH. A dispute over parochial rights in Northmoor between Reading abbey, owner of Stanton Harcourt church, and the abbey of St. Denis in Paris, whose church of Taynton professed an ancient claim, was settled in 1145 × 1148 in favour of the French house. North-

69 O.R.O., MS. d.d. Par. Northmoor c 3, item a, lease 1741.
70 Bodl. MS. d.d. Harcourt c 69/15; above, manors.
71 Bodl. MS. Top. Oxon. b 21, f. 8v.; ibid. MSS. d.d. Harcourt c 122/1–14, c 123/1–12; for earlier constables, P.R.O., E 179/161/42; E 179/161/177.
72 Bodl. MSS. d.d. Harcourt c 122/10–12, c 123/4, c 123/11; O.R.O., MS. d.d. Par. Northmoor e 1, pp. 61, 144, 309, and passim.
73 O.R.O., Acc. 3878, vestry bk. 1847–1959.
74 Visit. Dioc. Linc. ii. 49.
75 Bodl. MS. d.d. Harcourt c 123/13; St. John's Coll. Mun., XV.36; O.R.O., MS. d.d. Par. Northmoor c 3, item a; ibid. e 2, passim; ibid. f 1, passim.
76 O.R.O., MSS. d.d. Par. Northmoor c 3, item d; e 1, pp. 103–4; e 2, passim; f 1, passim; ibid. MS. Wills Oxon. 139/4/48; ibid. tithe award, mistakenly listing the Red Lion under the tower estate.
77 Courage Arch., Bristol, C 163, p. 125; Sale partics. (1908) in Red Lion, 1995.
78 O.R.O., MS. d.d. Par. Northmoor e 1, p. 1a.
79 Ibid. pp. 435, 451 sqq.; O.R.O., MS. d.d. Par. Northmoor c 2, f. 176.
80 Oxf. Jnl. Synopsis, 27 Mar. 1790.
81 O.R.O., MSS. d.d. Par. Northmoor e 1, passim; b 1, items a–b; cf. Census, 1801.
82 O.R.O., MS. d.d. Par. Northmoor c 2, passim; Poor Abstract, 1804, pp. 402–3; ibid. 1818, pp. 354–5; Poor Rate

Returns, H.C. 556, pp. 136–7 (1822), v; H.C. 334, p. 171 (1825), iv; H.C. 83, p. 159 (1830–1), xi; H.C. 444, p. 154 (1835), xlvii; cf. Census, 1801–41.
83 Bodl. MSS. d.d. Harcourt b 35; c 265, f. 32.
84 Poor Abstract, 1804, pp. 402–3.
85 O.R.O., MS. d.d. Par. Northmoor c 2, passim; Poor Abstract, 1818, pp. 354–5; D. Eastwood, Governing Rural Eng. 140.
86 O.R.O., MS. d.d. Par. Northmoor c 2, ff. 54v. sqq.
87 Ibid. b 1, item e; e 1, p. 430; O.R.O., Cal. Q.S. ii, f. 4; Poor Abstract, 1777, p. 141.
88 O.R.O., MS. d.d. Par. Northmoor c 2, ff. 19, 157; Poor Abstract, 1804, pp. 402–3.
89 O.R.O., MSS. d.d. Par. Northmoor b 1, item a; c 2, passim.
90 Ibid. b 1, item a, s.a. 1768; item e, inventory 1799; ibid. c 2, ff. 19, 36, 162–3.
91 Ibid. c 2, f. 144 and passim.
92 Ibid. f. 93v.; ibid. e 1, p. 33.
93 Ibid. e 1, pp. 96, 147; ibid. b 1, item b, quitrent receipt 1762.
94 Ibid. b 1, item a, passim; c 2, passim and s.v. new hos.; cf. ibid. c 3, item a, leases; 8th Rep. Com. Char. 491.
95 O.R.O., MSS. d.d. Par. Northmoor b 1, item b; c 2, ff. 66 sqq. and passim.
96 O.R.O., RO 3251, pp. 201–3.
97 Ibid. Acc. 3878, vestry bk. 1847–1959.
98 Ibid. RO 3251, pp. 201–3; RO 3267.

moor was created a separate parish, and a church was built shortly after. A pension due to Stanton Harcourt as part of the settlement was still paid in the 18th century.[99] The benefice was a rectory until appropriated by Sir Thomas White in 1555 on behalf of his college, St. John's, Oxford. A vicarage was then ordained, taking effect in 1558 on the death of the incumbent.[1] The college appropriated the vicarage in 1711, establishing a perpetual curacy to be served by a senior fellow.[2] The benefice, styled a vicarage from 1868,[3] was in 1959 united with that of Stanton Harcourt, which in 1976 joined, with Standlake and Yelford, in the united benefice of Lower Windrush.[4]

The advowson of the rectory belonged to the abbey of St. Denis whose daughter house, Deerhurst priory (Glos.), exercised the patronage.[5] The Crown presented in 1347 and regularly thereafter following Deerhurst's seizure as an alien priory,[6] until in 1467 Edward IV granted the advowson with Deerhurst to Tewkesbury abbey.[7] An exceptionally prolonged incumbency was already under way,[8] and the abbey sold the next turn, in 1502, to Richard Croft,[9] so it can rarely have exercised its right before the Dissolution. The advowson seems to have been granted to Charles Brandon (d. 1545), duke of Suffolk, but reverted to the Crown, which in 1554 sold it to Sir Thomas White.[10] Although Sir Thomas gave the advowson of the vicarage to St. John's College he exercised the right of patronage personally until his death in 1567.[11] The college remained patron of the vicarage, and from 1711 of the perpetual curacy, after 1976 sharing the right to present to the united benefice with the dean and chapter of Exeter cathedral, the bishop of Oxford, and the Oxford Diocesan Board of Patronage.[12]

The living was valued in 1254 at only £5,[13] but in 1291 and 1341 at £14, including £10 of glebe, hay tithe, and small tithes, and excluding a pension of 13s. 4d. to Stanton Harcourt.[14] In 1535 the net value was £18 17s. 6¼d.[15] Under the terms of appropriation in 1555 the vicar was

to receive £12 a year,[16] which St. John's increased to £30 in 1612.[17] From the later 18th century the living was several times augmented by Queen Anne's Bounty, meeting benefactions of £800 in total from St. John's, of £200 in 1764 from the Revd. Samuel Dennis, and of £200 in 1821 from the trustees of J. Marshall.[18] In 1808 the benefice's clear annual value was £68,[19] rising by 1851 to £123, at which level it remained at the end of the century.[20]

Although the settlement of 1145 × 1148 gave the tithes of Northmoor to the church,[21] Eynsham abbey seems to have received, allegedly 'ab antiquo', the corn tithes of certain tenements, valued at 30s. in 1254.[22] In 1555 glebe of 40 a. was appropriated with the tithes.[23] Bounty money was used in 1808 to buy a 'piece' of land for the incumbent.[24] In 1883 the vicar's glebe comprised 42 a., worth £46; it seems to have been sold in 1920.[25]

There was a rectory house by 1381, on or near the site of Rectory Farm.[26] St. John's seems to have provided or built a cottage for the vicar's use after appropriation.[27] The cottage, with garden, orchard, and small close adjoining, stood north of the church across Church Road.[28] It was described in 1805 as a thatched, lath-and-plaster building,[29] and dismissed in 1814 as comprising two 'miserable' rooms.[30] A drawing of 1873 shows a long single-storeyed row with attics, modest in appearance but evidently comprising more than two rooms.[31] It is likely that in 1814 the building was divided into two dwellings, used by 1831 as the parish school and teacher's house. Their demolition was urged in 1879 but apparently not carried out until 1891.[32] Incumbents lodged at Rectory Farm,[33] then rented the house later known as Ferryman Farm.[34] In 1892-3 a new vicarage, designed by John Oldrid Scott, was built on land provided by E. W. Harcourt and with financial assistance from the Bounty and St. John's.[35] It was sold c. 1960 to raise funds for a house at Stanton Harcourt to serve the united benefice.[36]

John of More, presented in 1229, and Thomas

99 *Reg. Regum Anglo-Norm.* iii, no. 680; *Reading Cart.* i (Camd. 4th ser. xxxi), pp. 130, 408-9; *Letters and Charters of Gilb. Foliot*, ed. A. Morey and C. N. L. Brooke, pp. 100-1; F. M. Stenton, 'Acta Episcoporum', *Camb. Hist. Jnl.* iii. 3-4; *V.C.H. Oxon.* xii. 289.
1 St. John's Coll. Mun., XV.1-3; ibid. ADMIN. I. A.1, f. 46; O.R.O., MS. Wills Oxon. 181, ff. 244-5.
2 *Par. Colln.* iii. 233-4.
3 Tithes Act Amendment Act, 31-2 Vic. c. 117.
4 O.R.O., MS. Oxf. Dioc. c 1713/2, Order in Council 12 Apr. 1976.
5 e.g. *Rot. Gravesend* (L.R.S. xx), 222.
6 *Cal. Pat.* 1345-8, 274, 283; 1350-4, 38, 486; 1354-8, 364; 1370-4, 317; 1377-81, 8, 14, 292, 297; 1391-6, 382, 611; 1416-22, 149; above, manors.
7 *Cal. Pat.* 1467-77, 66-7; *V.C.H. Glos.* ii. 104.
8 Below.
9 'Manor of Taynton', *O.A.S. Rep.* (1935), 82.
10 *Cal. Pat.* 1553-4, 493; *V.C.H. Berks.* iv. 348.
11 St. John's Coll. Mun., XV.1; O.R.O., MS. Oxf. Dioc. d 105, p. 189; W. H. Stevenson and H. E. Salter, *Early Hist. St. John's Coll.* (O.H.S. N.S. i), 115, 122, 379.
12 *Crockford's Clerical Dir.* (1963 and later edns.).
13 Lunt, *Val. Norw.* 309.
14 *Tax. Eccl.* (Rec. Com.), 32; *Inq. Non.* (Rec. Com.), 141.
15 *Valor Eccl.* (Rec. Com.), ii. 177.
16 St. John's Coll. Mun., XV.1.
17 O.R.O., MS. Oxf. Dioc. c 1913, letter of 4 Apr. 1881; *Par. Colln.* iii. 233.

18 Hodgson, *Q.A.B.* clxxi, clxxxi, cxcvi-cxcvii, ccxiii.
19 O.R.O., MS. Oxf. Dioc. c 446, f. 134.
20 Bodl. MS. Top. Oxon. c 105, ff. 136-7; O.R.O., MS. Oxf. Dioc. c 359, f. 298; *Ch. and Chapel, 1851*, no. 320.
21 *Camb. Hist. Jnl.* iii. 3-4.
22 *Rot. Welles*, ii (L.R.S. vi), 31; *Eynsham Cart.* i, p. 3; Lunt, *Val. Norw.* 488.
23 St. John's Coll. Mun., ADMIN. I. A.1, f. 147. For hist. of glebe and tithes, above, manors [other estates].
24 O.R.O., MS. Oxf. Dioc. c 446, f. 134.
25 St. John's Coll. Mun., ADMIN. I. A.10, p. 545; *Kelly's Dir. Oxon.* (1883).
26 Bodl. MS. d.d. Harcourt c 68/23; above, manors [other estates].
27 St. John's Coll. Mun., ADMIN. I. A.1, f. 98.
28 Ibid. XV.43; O.R.O., MS. Oxf. Archd. Oxon. b 41, f. 55; O.R.O., tithe map.
29 O.R.O., MS. Oxf. Dioc. c 449, f. 15a.
30 Ibid. b 33, ff. 90-1.   31 Above, plate 24.
32 O.R.O., MS. Oxf. Dioc. c 1914, petition 1879; St. John's Coll. Mun., ADMIN. I. A.9, p. 118; A.10, pp. 292, 294.
33 O.R.O., MS. Oxf. Dioc. b 38, ff. 152-3.
34 Ibid. c 341, ff. 308-9; O.S. Map 1/2,500, Oxon. XXXVIII. 11 (1876 edn.).
35 Bodl. MSS. Top. Oxon. c 105, ff. 134-7; d 42, ff. 91-2; O.R.O., MSS. Oxf. Dioc. c 359, f. 297; c 1914, plans and accts., 1891-3; Ch. Ch. Arch., Estates 80, ff. 148-151v.
36 O.R.O., MS. Oxf. Dioc. c 2020, copy of Order in Council, 20 Oct. 1959; *V.C.H. Oxon.* xii. 290.

More, ejected in 1418,[37] were presumably local men. Few of 28 rectors traced before 1555 appear to have held the living for more than a year or two, and three who held it for more than 30 years each were exceptional also in dying in office.[38] Several were graduates and some had noteworthy careers, usually as non-resident pluralists. Richard of Chaddesley (1312–15) later served as a royal envoy.[39] William Cogyn (c. 1439), said to be 'of noble race', was chaplain to Richard Beauchamp, earl of Warwick.[40] John Hale (1530), who was executed in 1535 with the London Carthusians,[41] employed an allegedly unintelligible Irish curate.[42]

Simon Walkelin of Northmoor c. 1300 gave a rent of 10d. from ½ a. of land in Moreton to support a light dedicated to the Assumption of the Virgin Mary.[43] In 1508 twelve lights were recorded.[44]

Sir Thomas White's first presentee, Leonard Stopes, was almost immediately deprived of the living and of his fellowship of St. John's at the visitation of the university in 1559. He later died in prison as a Catholic missionary priest.[45] His successor, William More, presumably that family's third incumbent, was vicar for 53 years until his death in 1612. Although licensed in 1564 to hold an additional living he probably resided at Northmoor, where he rented the rectory estate.[46] Thereafter St. John's appointed a succession of its own fellows, who usually resigned within a few years. Edmund Tillesley was suspended by Parliamentary Visitors in 1648, though he seems to have been reinstated by 1653.[47] From 1711 the living was reserved to senior fellows, suggesting that it was seen, in what was then a poor college, more as a financial opportunity than an obligation.[48]

Although few of the transient college fellows can have established close links with parishioners, they rode out weekly to maintain services. In 1738 the vice-president of St. John's, William Walker, held two services and preached a sermon each Sunday, and catechized children during Lent; there were six communion services a year, with 20–30 communicants.[49] In 1748 the president, William Holmes, left £10 a year to incumbents who spent three nights a week in the parish;[50] most remained in college. Though two Sunday services remained the norm, reputedly

with only 'four or five of the lowest class' absent, communion services, reduced to four a year, were said in 1802 seldom to attract more than 16 communicants.[51] The incumbent in 1831 claimed an average congregation of 150–160 and 40 communicants,[52] but other estimates, and the religious census of 1851, put the totals much lower.[53] The long and, for Northmoor, unsatisfactory succession of St. John's men ended with the appointment in 1872 of John Coen, who initiated a belated religious revival. Coen took up residence nearby at Appleton (then Berks.), introduced weekly communion services, daily prayers, and a Sunday recitation of the Litany, and established a religious guild.[54] The quickening of church life did not survive his departure in 1879, and in 1882 its debility in the face of nonconformist vigour prompted newspaper comment. Criticism was levelled unfairly at Lewis Tuckwell, rector of Standlake, serving Northmoor at the bishop's request after a year-long vacancy.[55] The building of a new vicarage house allowed incumbents to reside constantly after 1893, but revitalization of church life in the late 19th century and earlier 20th was slow.[56]

The church of ST. DENIS comprises chancel, nave with north and south transepts, south porch, and integral west tower. It is built of limestone rubble which, apart from the chancel and the upper part of the tower, is rendered, and the roofs are covered with natural and artificial stone slate.

Except for the cylindrical font with its carved sprig of stylized leaves nothing survives from the 12th-century church. The almost total rebuilding may have begun with the chancel c. 1300 and finished when the transepts were completed in the mid 14th century.[57] The long chancel has a piscina and a triple sedilia in the south wall, and above them is a window, presumably re-used, with 13th-century plate tracery. The unusually wide nave is lit by two-light windows with rere-arches supported by crudely carved foliage capitals, and by a large west window. The matching transepts have windows with reticulated tracery in their gable walls. The north transept, which was long known as the More aisle, has twin tomb recesses containing 14th-century effigies of a knight and a lady, probably Sir Thomas de la More (fl. 1330 × 1357) and his wife Isabel;[58] the

37 Rot. Welles, ii (L.R.S. vi), 31; Reg. Repingdon, iii (L.R.S. lxxiv), 231; O.A.S. Rep. (1935), 76.
38 Balliol Coll. Mun., A.19.22, 26, 28; Bodl. MS. d.d. Harcourt c 68/10; P.R.O., PROB 11/13, f. 62; Cart. Hosp. St. John (O.H.S. lxvi), p. 160; Rot. Grosseteste (L.R.S. xi), 465; Rot. Gravesend (L.R.S. xx), 22; Emden, O.U. Reg. to 1500.
39 Cal. Papal Reg. ii. 103; Emden, O.U. Reg. to 1500.
40 Cal. Papal Reg. ix. 64.
41 Emden, O.U. Reg. to 1500; J. Gairdner, Lollardy and the Reformation in Eng. 430–1.
42 Visit. Dioc. Linc. ii, pp. xxxvi, 49.
43 O.R.O., Warner III/i/1.
44 Some Oxon. Wills (O.R.S. xxxix), 96; Chant. Cert. 35.
45 O.R.O., MS. Oxf. Dioc. d 105, p. 189; O.A.S. Rep. (1914), 186–7, 198–9; A. Wood, Fasti Oxon. 154.
46 O.R.O., Cal. Presentation Deeds, ser. 1; O.A.S. Rep. (1914), 186–7; above, manors [other estates].
47 O.R.O., MS. d.d. Par. Northmoor e 1, p. 1a; Walker Revised, 300; W. H. Sutton, St. John Baptist Coll. 159.
48 Par. Colln. iii. 233.
49 Secker's Visit. 111.

50 W. C. Costin, Hist. St. John's Coll. 1598–1860 (O.H.S. N.S. xii), 188. The £10 payment was still available in the later 19th cent.: O.R.O., MS. Oxf. Dioc. c 1913, letter of 4 Apr. 1881.
51 O.R.O., MSS. Oxf. Dioc. b 13, ff. 33–4; c 327, p. 145; d 559, ff. 141–4; d 562, ff. 159–62; d 567, ff. 29–30.
52 Ibid. b 38, ff. 152–3.
53 Ibid. c 332, ff. 308–9; Ch. and Chapel, no. 320; Wilb. Visit. 104.
54 O.R.O., MSS. Oxf. Dioc. c 341, ff. 308–9; c 344, ff. 285–6.
55 Ibid. c 1913, presentation pps., 1881; Bodl. G.A. Oxon. c 317/12; Oxf. Times, 26 Aug., 23 Sept. 1882.
56 O.R.O., MSS. Oxf. Dioc. c 359, ff. 297–8; c 362, ff. 288–9.
57 Descriptions in Bodl. MS. Top. Oxon. d 218, ff. 187–206; Pevsner, Oxon. 722–3; W. Hobart Bird, Old Oxon. Chs. 117–18. Views (19th-cent.) in B.L. Add. MS. 36373, ff. 215–18; Bodl. MSS. Top. Oxon. a 68, nos. 402, 404–8; b 89, f. 128; b 90, f. 75; b 91, f. 310; b 220, f. 155; ibid. MS. Don. c 90, pp. 321, 323.
58 Pevsner, Oxon. 722. For identification, cf. Cal. Pat. 1330–4, 88, 115; above, Bampton: Lower Haddon, manor; this article, manors (More).

transept was the property of the Mores and later of the lords of Northmoor manor, who remained liable for its repair in the 17th century.[59] It retains a piscina in the east wall. The south transept has a piscina in its south wall and, on the east wall, a 15th-century canopied niche containing a statue of 1959.[60] In the 15th century the tower was built into the nave, to which it had open arches on the north, east, and south. The 14th-century nave roof was probably then left in place, but was replaced soon afterwards by a tie-beam roof. The barrel-shaped plaster roofs of the north, and, presumably, of the south, transept were apparently built by Edmund Warcupp soon after he acquired Northmoor manor in 1671;[61] the rough tie-beams in the transepts are probably of the same period. The chancel roof appears to be 19th-century. The timber-framed porch is of the 16th or 17th century.

Richard Lydall gave a bell loft in 1701.[62] Its rail, which has turned balusters, was originally across the tower arch. It was reset in an extended gallery erected in front of the arch later in the 18th century. Painting and gilding of the gallery, recorded in 1827 and 1829, has since been removed.[63] The lavishly carved 17th-century altar rails were until 1843 in St. John's College chapel.[64]

A heating system installed in 1854 has since been removed.[65] Bishop Wilberforce in 1855 recommended the church's restoration, to include removal of the 'hideous' gallery and 'little stone altar'; the latter, put up by Dr. Thomas Silver, incumbent 1819–22, was presumably that which still stands against the chancel's east wall.[66] In 1887 the church was said to be in a 'miserable, dilapidated' state, with a collapsed vault, perhaps in the nave.[67] A conservative restoration that year under the direction of Clapton Crabb Rolfe included renewing part of the nave plaster ceiling, reflooring with wooden blocks, installing new pews, and fitting a new north door. A pulpit on a stone base was erected north of the chancel arch, and a matching lectern was provided; plans to preserve tracery in the existing pulpit and lectern, thought to be from a rood screen, seem to have been abandoned.[68] The chancel was apparently excluded from the restoration since it was in disrepair in the 1890s.[69] In 1948 electric lighting was installed using existing, presumably oil lamp, fittings. A

high altar made of oak was installed in 1957, and in 1958 the chancel ceiling was repaired and the chancel and nave limewashed.[70] The south transept, designated the Lady Chapel in 1959, was restored between 1955 and 1961.[71] The tower was re-roofed in 1960, and the nave in the 1970s.[72] In 1993 new north and south doors were fitted.[73]

Remains of 14th-century wall paintings associated with the More tombs survive on the north and west walls of the north transept. Descriptions of the 17th century and later record More family heraldry, little of which survives, on the walls and on the knight's shield.[74] Still visible in the north-west corner is a depiction of two angels raising a soul to heaven before Christ in majesty. The paintings were restored in 1932 by E. T. Long, who uncovered in the recesses paintings of the Virgin Mary and of the Virgin and Child flanked by kneeling figures, which by 1990 were no longer visible.[75] Some medieval floor tiles remain in the chancel.[76] Fragments of medieval glass survive in the east window of the south transept. The chancel has a notable east window of 1866 given by Sarah Nalder of Rectory Farm; there is a window of 1871 in the south wall of the nave.

The More effigies were moved to the chancel in the earlier 19th century,[77] but by 1850 had been returned to the north transept.[78] A photograph of c. 1930 shows them on tall stone bases, the lady in the western recess, the knight by her side.[79] The bases were removed in 1932 when the knight was placed in the eastern recess. A medieval tomb slab was moved to the chancel in 1932 from the north transept, where another remains.[80] Later monuments include, in the north transept, the tomb chest of Sir Edmund Warcupp (d. 1712), a floor tablet to Sir John Stone (d. 1719), and a bust of Richard Lydall (d. 1721). Lost monuments include several of the More family recorded in the south transept in the early 18th century.[81] The war memorial tablet on the south wall of the nave was designed by F. E. Howard in 1919; it was extended in 1948.[82] In the churchyard, east of the chancel, is the base of a 14th-century stone cross.

There is a 17th-century parish chest in the blocked south doorway of the nave, and a parish chest dated 1721 in the south transept. An organ apparently of the late 19th century stands at the

59 Bodl. MS. Rawl. D. 384, ff. 44–68v.; ibid. MS. Top. Oxon. b 75, f. 138; O.R.O., MS. Oxf. Archd. Oxon. c 120, ff. 123–7; ibid. MS. Oxf. Dioc. c 455, ff. 115–16; Par. Colln. iii. 233.
60 Oxf. Times, 3 Apr. 1959.
61 O.R.O., MS. Oxf. Dioc. c 455, f. 115; above, manors.
62 Inscription on rail. The year 1693 in Pevsner, Oxon. 722, is the date of a bell given by Lydall: below.
63 O.R.O., MS. d.d. Par. Northmoor f 1, ff. 74v., 76v.
64 V.C.H. Oxon. iii. 263 and n.
65 O.R.O., MS. Oxf. Dioc. d 178, p. 346b; St. John's Coll. Mun., ADMIN. I. A.9, p. 229.
66 O.R.O., Acc. 3878, vestry bk. 1847–1959, 10 Apr. 1855; ibid. MS. Oxf. Dioc. d 178, p. 346b; V. Sillery, St. John's Coll. Biog. Reg. 1775–1875, 20–1. The altar was c. 1873 thought to be pre-Reformation: Bodl. MS. Top. Oxon. d 218, f. 189.
67 Ch. Ch. Arch., MS. Estates 80, ff. 174–175v.
68 O.R.O., MSS. Oxf. Dioc. c 353, f. 289; c 1914, faculty and plans, 1886–7; A. Saint, 'Three Oxf. Archits.', Oxoniensia xxxv. 101.
69 O.R.O., MSS. Oxf. Dioc. c 359, ff. 297–8; c 362, f. 289.

70 Ibid. c 1914, faculties, 1948, 1957, 1958; St. John's Coll. Mun., ADMIN. I. A.11, p. 402.
71 O.R.O., MS. Oxf. Dioc. c 1914, faculties, 1957, 1958; Oxf. Times, 3 Apr. 1959; plaque in chapel.
72 O.R.O., MS. Oxf. Dioc. c 2020, faculty of 1960; local inf.
73 Dedication plaque.
74 Bodl. MS. Top. Oxon. b 75, ff. 138–9; Par. Colln. iii. 233–4; Bodl. G.A. Oxon. c 317/12; Wood's Life, i. 271–2.
75 Bodl. MS. Top. Oxon. a 75, 139; O.R.O., MS. Oxf. Dioc. c 1914, faculty, 1932; Oxf. Times, 1 Apr. 1932; 17 Feb. 1933; J. Edwards, 'Lost Medieval Wall-Paintings', Oxoniensia, lv. 89–90.
76 L. Haberly, Medieval Eng. Pavingtiles, passim.
77 Bodl. MS. Top. Oxon. b 220, f. 155; Skelton, Antiq. Oxon. Chadlington Hund. 12.
78 Parker, Eccl. Top. 197.
79 C.O.S., OPA 19699N.
80 Oxf. Times, 17 Feb. 1933.
81 Par. Colln. iii. 233. Description of monuments in 1873 in Bodl. MS. Top. Oxon. d 218, ff. 190v.–203.
82 O.R.O., MS. Oxf. Dioc. c 1914, faculties, 1919, 1948.

entrance to the north transept. Church plate includes a silver chalice of 1646, a silver paten of 1684 inscribed D. C., probably Dorothy Champneys (d. 1705), lessee of the rectory estate, and a silver paten of 1776 given by William Kent.[83] A 17th-century Spanish painting of Christ carrying the cross hangs above the chancel south door. In the late Middle Ages the tower apparently carried a ring of four bells, increased to six in the 17th century. Richard Lydall gave a new tenor bell in 1693. The fifth was recast in 1717 at the Gloucester foundry of Abraham Rudhall, and the others, including Lydall's, in 1764 by Thomas Rudhall. The bells, rehung in 1966, are praised as 'one of the best light rings in the country'. Lydall also gave, by will proved 1721, money for a clock in the tower.[84] The present mechanism is inscribed Hawting of Oxford 1785. The clock face, extensively repaired in 1827,[85] had only an hour hand until 1863 when a minute hand was added.[86] The registers begin in 1654.[87]

NONCONFORMITY. Six recusants listed in 1577 included John Hearbes, presumably John Herle (d. 1581), the lord of Northmoor, and two members of the More family.[88] No papists were noted later. In 1768 there were said to be two or three Anabaptists in Northmoor, without a meeting place of their own.[89] In 1821 Ephraim Dix, later a prominent Primitive Methodist, registered a meeting at his house,[90] and in 1826 Northmoor joined the Faringdon Primitive Methodist circuit. Membership fluctuated between 14 in 1826 and 26 in 1835.[91] Since many 'Ranters' were said in 1834 to attend the parish church and even to take the sacrament,[92] relations at that time were presumably amicable. About 1841, however, a hostile farmer bought the 'chapel' and turned the congregation out; some members were even dismissed and evicted from their cottages. A temporary building erected in 1842 was replaced the following year by a brick chapel built north of the village on the east side of the later Chapel Lane. Local Baptists, notably the Gileses of Standlake, gave substantial assistance, and the preachers at the opening service were all Baptist ministers.[93]

Despite its modest size,[94] the new chapel re-portedly provided 140 free sittings. On census day in 1851 90 people attended in the morning and 150 in the evening, a marked contrast to the 50 and 60 respectively attending the parish church.[95] The curate in 1854 estimated that there were 12 or 13 families of Primitive Methodists, presumably meaning subscribers.[96] Membership in 1867 was drawn from at least 14 local families.[97] Two members of the Taylor family (a carpenter and a sawyer) were recorded in 1861 as local preachers, and the chapel steward (an agricultural labourer), also a local preacher, had as a visitor on census day that year the minister of Faringdon chapel.[98]

In the later 19th century nonconformity continued to benefit from the non-residence of Northmoor's vicars. In 1878 the vicar asserted that there were only 20 'professed dissenters',[99] but it was more credibly claimed that most parishioners were either Primitive Methodists or Salvationists.[1]

The chapel was transferred to the Witney Circuit in 1916.[2] It was closed and sold in 1920, the proceeds being used to support evangelistic services during the winter; by c. 1930 it had been demolished.[3] Thereafter local nonconformists went to Witney.

EDUCATION. In the earlier 17th century children were taught in the church.[4] There was no school from the earlier 18th century to the early 19th, and by 1808 a Sunday school held 'some time back' had also ceased.[5] An unendowed day school taught 8 boys and 6 girls in 1815.[6] Another school, established in 1829, was by 1831 housed in the incumbent's cottages north of the church, which were refitted as a schoolroom and mistress's house. It had 50 pupils in 1831 and 20–30 in 1854; it received pence and £5 a year from St. John's College, Oxford, but in 1854 was supported chiefly by the incumbent. In 1834 some children attended dame schools in Standlake.[7]

A National school was opened in 1873 in a new, stone-and-slated schoolroom on former glebe north-east of the incumbent's cottages,[8] which may have remained part of the school until 1891.[9] The register rose from 32 to 53 within a year, though in 1876 over half the pupils were from a short-lived orphanage in Northmoor

83 Bodl. MS. Top. Oxon. b 265, f. 59; O.R.O., MS. Wills Oxon. 123/3/12; Evans, Ch. Plate, 114.
84 O.R.O., MS. Oxf. Dioc. c 2020, faculty of 1966; Ch. Bells Oxon. ii. 220–2.
85 O.R.O., MS. d.d. Par. Northmoor f 1, f. 74v.
86 Inscription.
87 C.O.S., par. reg. transcripts.
88 Recusant Roll, 1577 (Cath. Rec. Soc. xxii), 113–14; cf. above, Bampton: Lower Haddon, nonconf.
89 O.R.O., MS. Oxf. Dioc. d 559, f. 141.
90 Ibid. c 644, f. 233.
91 O.R.O., NM2/B/A5/1.
92 Ibid. MS. Oxf. Dioc. b 39, f. 275.
93 O.S. Map 6" Oxon. XXXVIII (1883 edn.); Primitive Methodist Mag. (1853), 618.
94 Drawing of 1873 in Bodl. MS. Top. Oxon. d 218, f. 201.
95 Ch. and Chapel, nos. 320–1.
96 Wilb. Visit. 104.
97 O.R.O., NM2/23/F1/1.
98 P.R.O., RG9/904.
99 O.R.O., MS. Oxf. Dioc. c 344, f. 285.

1 Oxf. Times, 26 Aug. 1882.
2 O.R.O., NM2/B/A5/8. The statement in trade dirs. that a new chapel was built in 1891 has not been verified: Kelly's Dir. Oxon. (1893 and later edns.); cf. O.R.O., NM2/B/A5/8; ibid. NM2/23/F1/1.
3 O.R.O., NM2/B/A5/8; J. Stowell, Glimpses of Northmoor Through 800 Yrs. (priv. print. c. 1930), 13: copy in Bodl. G.A. Oxon. 8° 1055 (17).
4 Bodl. MS. Rawl. D. 384, ff. 47–8.
5 O.R.O., MSS. Oxf. Dioc. d 559, ff. 141–4; d 562, ff. 159–62; d 707, f. 119; Secker's Visit. 111.
6 O.R.O., MS. Oxf. Dioc. c 433, f. 153.
7 Ibid. b 38, f. 152; b 39, f. 275; b 70, p. 154; St. John's Coll. Mun., ADMIN. I. A.9, p. 118; Wilb. Visit. 104; Educ. Enq. Abstract, H.C. 62, p. 750 (1835), xliii; above, church.
8 O.R.O., T/SL 38i, p. 1; ibid. MS. Oxf. Dioc. c 1913, conveyance 1869; O.S. Map 1/2,500, Oxon. XXXVIII. 7 (1876 edn.); illust. in Bodl. MS. Top. Oxon. d 218, f. 198.
9 St. John's Coll. Mun., ADMIN. I. A.10, pp. 292, 294; above, church.

where children had been trained for occupations.[10] A new room was added in 1902 to meet government requirements,[11] and in 1907 the register was 47.[12] Reports were often critical, and in 1890 E. W. Harcourt withheld his annual subscription;[13] the school was 'admirably conducted' in 1904 but in 1919 was acknowledged to have 'special difficulty', and pupils were often judged backward. It became an infant and junior school in 1929, when 11 children were transferred to Standlake school, leaving 28 at Northmoor. The roll was 38 (many of them evacuees) in 1940, 12 in 1945, and 35 in 1955, when the school was 'happy' and efficient; in 1957 it was forced to become a single-class school and several children were transferred elsewhere, but by 1971 the roll was 26. The school closed in 1981, when children and equipment were transferred to Standlake.[14]

A successful night school was noted in 1872.[15]

CHARITIES FOR THE POOR.[16] Thomas Weale, by will proved 1658, left land in Standlake, a quarter of the rent to benefit the Northmoor poor;[17] in 1738 Northmoor's share was £1. Sir Edmund Warcupp left £20 by will proved 1712, and Thomas Martin £5 by will proved 1714, together used c. 1719 to buy c. 1 a.,[18] which in 1738 yielded 25s. Francis White of Fyfield (then Berks.), by will proved 1737, left £100 to the Northmoor poor, used c. 1743 with a bequest to Fyfield to buy land then worth £12 a year, of which one third went to Northmoor.[19] St. John's College, Oxford, paid 40s. a year to the poor by the earlier 17th century, perhaps the 40s. awarded to the bishops of Oxford and Salisbury at its appropriation of the rectory,[20] and from 1673 lords of the manor paid 30s. a year in lieu of extinguished common rights.[21] A Scheme of 1897, confirming all those charities as eleemosynary, was revised in 1917, when the lord's 30s. was no longer mentioned. Total income from eleemosynary charities in 1979 was £40.[22]

STANDLAKE

STANDLAKE, a rural parish between the rivers Thames and Windrush, lies c. 4¼ miles (7 km.) south-east of Witney and 7½ miles (12 km.) south-west of Oxford.[23] The ancient parish, whose western and northern boundaries remained ill defined until inclosure in 1853, included part of Brighthampton, the rest of which belonged to Bampton parish, and in the north Boys and Home woods and the western part of Cokethorpe Park, all formerly part of a large block of ancient woodland which extended southwards to the area around Breach Farm.[24] The history of the whole of Brighthampton and of the early woodland is treated below, but the later history of Cokethorpe Park under Ducklington. In 1844 the parish was reckoned at 2,487 a.,[25] and in 1877, after inclosure, it contained 2,346 a., of which 30 a. lay in four newly created detached areas near Brighthampton and near Hardwick in Ducklington parish.[26] Transfers from Hardwick and Bampton in 1886 under the Divided Parishes Act, notably the incorporation of a large detached part of Hardwick in the north-west, increased the civil parish to 2,624 a., from which 3 a. were transferred to Yelford before 1901.[27] The part of Brighthampton in Bampton parish was ill defined until artificially delineated at inclosure; thereafter it formed a separate township and later civil parish of 665 a., reduced in 1886 to 626 a. through transfers to and from Hardwick and Standlake. In 1932 it was merged with Standlake, which lost c. 640 a. (including the land in Cokethorpe Park) to Hardwick-with-Yelford, creating a civil parish of 2,606 a. (1,055 ha.) which was unaltered in 1981.[28]

In the Anglo-Saxon period Standlake formed part of a large *parochia* centred on Bampton minster,[29] and its independent boundaries only gradually emerged during the Middle Ages. The eastern boundary ran in the earlier 19th century down Standlake and Medley brooks, tributaries of the river Windrush running between the river's two main streams, before turning along small watercourses east of the main stream to include the site of Gaunt House and its adjacent closes. It then followed the main stream southwards to the river Thames.[30] The southern part of that boundary corresponded with the bounds of an estate in neighbouring Northmoor described in 1059,[31] and the site of Gaunt House was included in Standlake probably in the 15th

[10] O.R.O., T/SL 38i, pp. 1, 8, 33; Bodl. G.A. Oxon. c 317/12, appeal re St. Denys's Orphanage.
[11] O.R.O., T/SL 38i, pp. 255, 288, 321 sqq.; Ch. Ch. Arch., MS. Estates 80, ff. 160–161v.; *Kelly's Dir. Oxon.* (1903).
[12] O.R.O., T/SL 38i, p. 431.
[13] Ibid. *passim*; St. John's Coll. Mun., XV.46.
[14] O.R.O., T/SL 38i–iii, *passim*.
[15] Ibid. MS. Oxf. Dioc. c 338, f. 287.
[16] Based, except where stated, on *Char. Don.* 980–1; *8th Rep. Com. Char.* 491–2; *Secker's Visit.* 111.
[17] P.R.O., PROB 11/283, f. 401.
[18] Bodl. MSS. d.d. Harcourt c 74/29, c 74/39; O.R.O., MS. Wills Oxon. 208, f. 54v.; ibid. MS. d.d. Par. Northmoor c 3, item b.
[19] O.R.O., MS. d.d. Par. Northmoor c 3, item c.
[20] St. John's Coll. Mun., XV.1; ibid. ADMIN. I. A.3, pp. 385–8.

[21] Above, econ. hist. [agric.].
[22] O.R.C.C., Kimber files.
[23] The chief maps used were O.R.O., Standlake and Brighthampton tithe and incl. maps; Magd. Coll. Mun., CP 3/16, ff. 178v.–179; O.S. Maps 6", Oxon. XXXVIII (1883 edn.); 1/25,000, SP 20/30 (1977 edn.), SP 40/50 (1980 edn.). This article was written in 1994 and revised in 1995.
[24] Below, econ. hist. (agric.).
[25] O.R.O., tithe award (1844).
[26] O.S. *Area Bk.* (1877); O.R.O., incl. award.
[27] *Census*, 1881–1901; O.S. Map 6", Oxon. XXXVIII (1883 edn.).
[28] O.S. *Area Bk.* (1877), s.v. Bampton; *Census*, 1881–1981.
[29] Above, Bampton, gen. intro.; below, church.
[30] O.R.O., Standlake tithe and incl. maps; cf. *V.C.H. Oxon.* xii. 240, 268.
[31] Above, Northmoor, intro.

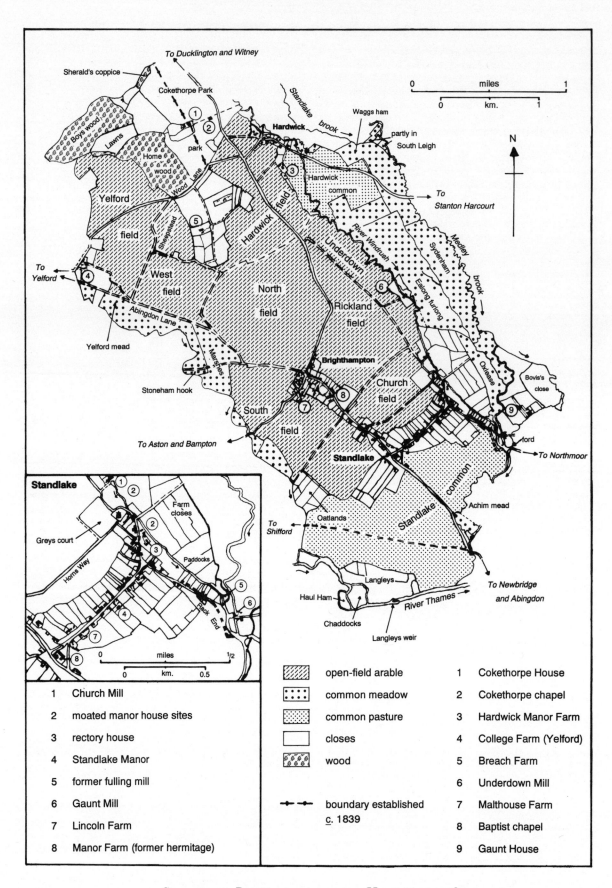

STANDLAKE, BRIGHTHAMPTON, AND HARDWICK *c.* 1850

century and certainly by the 16th, when perambulations included a gospel-reading at Bovis's (or Brice's) close north-east of the house on the modern boundary.[32] In 1318 local deponents nevertheless claimed that the boundary of Bampton's residual *parochia*, including Standlake, lay further east, running down the Windrush to Beard Mill in Stanton Harcourt parish, then following a path running probably south-eastwards, and a stream called Wirlak' or Wytherlak' which flowed southwards to the Thames through the later Northmoor parish.[33] In the 15th and 16th centuries the boundary near Newbridge mill, which later followed the Windrush's westernmost channel, may have followed the eastern channel on which the mill stands, and where there was a merestone; disputes over boundaries near there erupted *c.* 1564 after part of the river's main channel was diverted during work on the Newbridge causeway.[34] Most of Achim or Eacham mead, north-west of Newbridge mill on the Windrush's west bank, was in Northmoor, though Standlake commoners had rights there.[35] At inclosure *c.* 1853 Medley brook was straightened, but remained part of the eastern boundary.[36] The Thames formed the southern boundary in 1318 and later.[37]

On the west there was, except within Brighthampton village, no distinct boundary until inclosure between those parts of Brighthampton in Bampton and those in Standlake, the shared fields of Brighthampton and Standlake extending undifferentiated as far as the brook marking Shifford's eastern boundary.[38] The boundary through Brighthampton village, however, corresponded with that between holdings of Hardwick and Brighthampton manor, in the village's western part, and of Standlake manor, in its eastern part, and was evidently tenurial in origin: Hardwick and Brighthampton manor had remained part of the royal estate in Bampton until probably the 12th century and was classed as ancient demesne, and in the 14th century Bampton church explicitly claimed jurisdiction over ancient demesne formerly part of the royal manor.[39] Within the fields blocks of furlongs, chiefly in the west and north-west and in a band across the middle of the parish, remained tithable to Bampton, presumably representing strips originally held by tenants of Hardwick and Brighthampton

manor.[40] Underdown Mill on the river Windrush, held with Hardwick and Brighthampton manor from the Middle Ages, remained a detached part of Bampton parish.[41]

In 958 Standlake's northern boundary seems to have followed approximately the southern edge of the later Cokethorpe Park, thus excluding not only the later park but also Home and Boys woods, all of which then formed part of a large estate centred on Ducklington.[42] By the early 13th century, however, woodland covering the area of the two woods and the western part of the later park was attached to Standlake manor and belonged thereafter to Standlake parish.[43] The transfer from the Ducklington estate to Standlake may have occurred before 1086, when the Ducklington hidation seems to have been lower than in 958, though woodland was noted in neither Standlake nor Brighthampton at that date.[44] By the early 18th century the area around Cokethorpe House comprised assarted closes, of which some, chiefly west of the house, lay in Standlake, and the remainder in Ducklington; a straight parish boundary through the park was established at or before the inclosure of Ducklington in 1839.[45] Elsewhere Standlake's northern boundary followed the division between its open fields and those of Hardwick, but intermixture of holdings blurred parochial distinctions and in the 19th century some strips in Hardwick's fields remained tithable to Bampton or to Standlake.[46] At inclosure the northern and western boundaries were redrawn to follow newly created closes, though the existing boundaries through Brighthampton hamlet and Cokethorpe Park were retained.[47] In 1932 the northern and western boundaries were completely redrawn.[48]

The parish is flat and low-lying, rising gently from *c.* 65 m. near the rivers to *c.* 90 m. near Home wood, where there are some slightly steeper slopes. Its southern part, including the village sites and most of the former open fields, lies chiefly on gravels of the Thames Flood Plain, Summertown–Radley, and Wolvercote terraces, though alluvium in the west and south and along the Windrush in the east provided plentiful meadow and pasture. Standlake's northern part around Breach Farm and Cokethorpe House lies chiefly on Oxford Clay, a tongue of which extends southwards across the former open fields towards Underdown Farm.[49] Gravel pits were

32   Magd. Coll. Mun., EP 99/2; *Wood's Life*, i. 272.
33   D. & C. Exeter, MS. 2865; *V.C.H. Oxon.* xii. 267; above, Northmoor, intro.
34   Magd. Coll. Mun., EP 146/6, EP 146/33; O.R.O., tithe map (1844).
35   O.R.O., Standlake tithe award.
36   Ibid. incl. maps; O.S. Map 6", Oxon. XXXVIII (1883 edn.).
37   D. & C. Exeter, MS. 2865; O.R.O., Standlake tithe map. For rerouting of the Thames at Haul Ham *c.* 1675, Magd. Coll. Mun., EP 147/7.
38   O.R.O., Standlake tithe map; ibid. incl. map B; below, econ. hist. (agric.).
39   O.R.O., Standlake tithe award (1844); ibid. Brighthampton tithe award (1852); cf. D. & C. Exeter, MSS. 2865, 2867; ibid. MS. 2931, s.v. *decima*; *Oxon. Local Hist.* ii (2), 36–7, 42–6.
40   O.R.O., Standlake tithe award (1844); cf. ibid. incl. award, schedule s.v. Brighthampton.
41   P.R.O., PROB 11/283, f. 401; O.S. Map 6", Oxon.

XXXVIII (1883 edn.); below, econ. hist. (mills).
42   Grundy, *Saxon Oxon.* 29–30, which misinterprets the boundary; above, Ducklington, intro.
43   O.R.O., tithe award (1844); below, econ. hist. (agric.).
44   *V.C.H. Oxon.* i. 405, 414, 423, 425–6; Grundy, *Saxon Oxon.* 28. The woodland may have been briefly re-attached to Bampton manor: above, Bampton: Bampton and Weald, manors.
45   Bodl. MS. d.d. Harcourt c 13/2; B.N.C. Mun., Room B ser., 534, terrier 11 Feb. 1761, terrier and map 1 Oct. 1765; above, Ducklington.
46   O.R.O., tithe award (1844); ibid. incl. award, schedule s.v. Brighthampton, Hardwick; below, econ. hist. (agric.).
47   O.R.O., incl. award; O.S. Map 6", Oxon. XXXVIII (1883 edn.).
48   *Census*, 1931; O.S. Map 1/25,000, SP 20/30 (1977 edn.).
49   O.S. Maps 1/25,000, SP 20/30 (1977 edn.), SP 40/50 (1980 edn.); Geol. Surv. Map 1/50,000, solid and drift, sheet 236 (1982 edn.).

mentioned from the 18th century,[50] and commercial extraction in the 20th century created several large lakes near the Windrush and in the south-west, some landscaped for recreation.[51]

The parish's development may have been influenced by a network of early roads or tracks running from north-west to south-east and from north-east to south-west, reflected in the later road pattern. Several Iron-Age and Romano-British sites at Stanton Harcourt, Standlake, and Shifford are strung out along the alignment of Standlake High Street and of Horn's Way to the north,[52] and lost routes on similar alignments include a putative Roman track running south of Gaunt Mill, where fragmentary stone surfaces have been noted,[53] and a path running south of and parallel to the road from Brighthampton to Aston across the site of an early Anglo-Saxon burial ground.[54] North–south routes included a continuation of Abingdon Lane from Yelford to Brighthampton, and a branch road cutting across Shifford's northern edge, both of which were suppressed in 1629 because of frequent flooding but survived as green lanes until 19th-century inclosure.[55]

The chief north–south route by the later Middle Ages was from Witney through Ducklington and Brighthampton to Newbridge in Northmoor parish, part of the Gloucestershire–London road.[56] Parts of that route, which crosses early settlement sites on Standlake Downs west of Underdown Farm,[57] may also be ancient, though no positive evidence has been found for a river crossing at Newbridge before the surviving bridge was built in the late 14th century or early 15th: the surname 'at bridge', recorded on Standlake manor in 1279, may refer only to a crossing of the Windrush or its tributaries.[58] In the 16th century and later a stone causeway raised the road between Standlake and Newbridge above the level of the floodplain;[59] bridge hermits living at the causeway's northern end were recorded in the 15th century, and one was licensed c. 1462 to collect alms for repairs.[60] The causeway was rebuilt in the early 16th century, when winter flooding sometimes made the crossing impassable,[61] and from the later 17th century

both the causeway and the northern half of the bridge were repaired frequently by the county.[62] A scheme in 1766 to turnpike the road, linking it with the Kingston Bagpuize turnpike south of the Thames, was evidently abandoned.[63]

The Brighthampton–Cote road, crossing Shifford's boundary brook at Knight Bridge, was a bridlepath until c. 1629 when it became a highway.[64] The chief route eastwards from Standlake in the 18th century and presumably earlier seems to have been along Rack End to a ford just south of the later Broad Bridges, then continuing through Northmoor to cross the Thames at Bablock Hythe, and so to Oxford.[65] Several lesser crossings of the Windrush[66] perhaps included an unidentified stone bridge built by a local farmer in 1761.[67]

At inclosure c. 1853 the Northmoor road was rerouted across the newly-built Broad Bridges, other principal roads were confirmed, and some lesser ones were upgraded. A lane past the church to the Witney road became a 30-foot carriageway, later called Downs Road, and Wood Lane, from Yelford to Hardwick, was replaced by a new 30-foot road further south. Other new roads included a 30-foot carriageway, later a lane, from Standlake High Street to Shifford, replacing an earlier track across Standlake common, and a road from Broad Bridges to the Witney–Newbridge road running south of Standlake High Street. Several tracks were replaced by new occupation roads, though Horn's Way, north of Standlake High Street, was retained.[68]

In the mid 19th century the nearest railway stations were those at Witney and South Leigh, opened in 1861, and Faringdon Road station in Faringdon (then Berks.) on the G.W.R., opened in 1840.[69] Carriers to Oxford, Witney, and Abingdon were noted in 1847.[70] A post office run by the schoolmaster, presumably from the schoolhouse near the church, existed by 1847.[71] It was at the Green in the 1860s, in Bracken Cottage on High Street before 1887, and on its present site next to the Bell Inn by 1960; it was a money order and telegraph office before 1907.[72]

Palaeolithic axes have been found west of

50 Magd. Coll. Mun., CP 3/16, f. 182; *Oxoniensia*, xxxviii. 233–4.
51 O.S. Map 1/25,000, SP 20/30 (1977 edn.); cf. *Stanton Harcourt Area Minerals Plan, Consultative Doc.* (Oxon. C.C. 1978): copy in C.O.S.; *Oxoniensia*, xi/xii. 27.
52 D. Benson and D. Miles, *Upper Thames Valley, an Arch. Survey of the River Gravels*, 44, 46–7; C.B.A. Group 9, *Newsletter*, ix (1979), 37; *S. Midlands Arch.* xix (1989), 47; below.
53 C.O.S., PRN 5355.
54 *Archaeologia*, xxxvii. 393; not shown on O.R.O., tithe map.
55 Bodl. MS. Top. Oxon. c 118, f. 7 and v.; O.R.O., Ducklington incl. map; ibid. Standlake incl. map B; O.S. Map 1", sheet 13 (1830 edn.); above, Bampton: Lew, intro.
56 Leland, *Itin.* ed. Toulmin Smith, v. 73; *Wood's City of Oxf.* ii (O.H.S. xvii), 499; St. John's Coll. Mun., XVII.45, f. 22, mentioning 'London road'.
57 Below, this section.
58 M. R. Toynbee, 'Radcot Bridge and Newbridge', *Oxoniensia*, xiv. 49–50; *Bampton Hund. R.* 69; cf. *Oxoniensia*, xxxvii. 249.
59 Leland, *Itin.* ed. Toulmin Smith, v. 73; *Oxoniensia*, xxxvii. 250.
60 Bodl. MS. Twyne 4, p. 243; R. M. Clay, *Hermits and Anchorites of England*, 61, 242–3; *Wood's City of Oxf.* ii. 499; below, this section. No enrolled licence has been found.

61 Magd. Coll. Mun., EP 146/6; cf. O.R.O., P4/2/MS 1/5, f. 9.
62 e.g. O.R.O., Cal. Q.S. iii, pp. 348, 404, 413, 415; *Oxoniensia*, xiv. 50–1; *List of County and other Bridges* (1845): copy in Bodl. G.A. Oxon. Fol. A. 137.
63 Oxf. Jnl. Synopsis, 27 June 1766; cf. O.S. Map 6", Oxon. XXXVIII (1883 edn.).
64 Bodl. MS. Top. Oxon. c 118, f. 7 and v.; above, Bampton: Shifford, intro.
65 O.R.O., tithe award and map (1844); A. Bryant, *Oxon. Map* (1824); cf. O.R.O., P4/2/MS 1/5, f. 9; above, Northmoor, intro.
66 O.R.O., P2/2/MS 3/1, f. 5; *V.C.H. Oxon.* xii. 269–70.
67 *Oxf. Jnl.* 28 Nov. 1761.
68 O.R.O., incl. award; cf. ibid. tithe award (1844); O.S. Map 1", sheet 13 (1830 edn.).
69 St. John's Coll. Mun., XVII.52; E. T. MacDermot and C. R. Clinker, *Hist. G.W.R.* i. 53–4, 286, 452, 461; *V.C.H. Oxon.* xii. 239.
70 *P.O. Dir. Oxon.* (1847).
71 Ibid.; cf. P.R.O., HO 107/872; ibid. RG 9/905; P.O. Arch., POST 35/103, p. 230.
72 Bodl. MS. Top. Oxon. c 768/1, nos. 33, 43, 50; O.S. Maps 1/2,500, Oxon. XXXVIII. 6 (1876 and later edns.); SP 3903 (1971 edn.); ibid. 6", SP 30 SE. (1960 edn.); *Kelly's Dir. Oxon.* (1883 and later edns.).

Standlake village and north-east of Brighthampton, and Neolithic implements north of Standlake village.[73] Ring ditches north of Brighthampton on Standlake Downs contained late Bronze-Age urn burials, though the ditches had been re-used and were evidently of earlier origin.[74] Extensive Iron-Age settlement nearby, much discussed in the mid 19th century,[75] respected some of the Bronze-Age features; remains included round huts and storage pits, but settlement in the area may have been shifting, and the site was not palisaded.[76] Cropmarks north and west of Standlake village may relate to Iron-Age settlement,[77] and an exceptionally fine Iron-Age sword was dredged from the Thames near Langley's weir.[78] Evidence of Romano-British settlement west, north, and north-east of Standlake village and perhaps on Standlake Downs does not necessarily indicate continuous occupation, though the sites north and north-east of Standlake were occupied apparently by the mid 1st century A.D. and still in the late 2nd.[79]

There was settlement near Brighthampton in the 5th and 6th centuries, indicated by a large pagan burial ground discovered south of Malthouse Farm with grave goods displaying mixed Roman, British, and Saxon influences.[80] The Bronze-Age burial ground on Standlake Downs was re-used for burials in the 7th century, and there may have been sunken huts nearby.[81] In 984 Brighthampton (i.e. Beorhthelm's tūn) formed an outlier within the large royal manor of Bampton, and in 1086 the only estates identifiably within the parish were recorded under Brighthampton;[82] no evidence has been found of Anglo-Saxon occupation at Standlake village, which was evidently a secondary settlement, not recorded by name until the mid 12th century.[83] That Standlake became the centre of, and gave its name to, a new parish was presumably due to its inclusion in an estate granted before 1086 to the Grey family, which in or before the 12th century built a manor house and church by the river Windrush at the northern end of the later village. That site may have been intentionally chosen for its distance from the older settlement at Brighthampton, which was on the fringes of

the Greys' lands and which remained partly attached to Bampton.[84]

The name Standlake, meaning 'stone stream',[85] reflects the village's low-lying position among a network of tributaries of the Thames. In the 18th century the village was described as 'situate upon a damn'd standing puddle, long, deep and dirty',[86] and the main street occasionally flooded even in the 19th century.[87] The place name's first element refers presumably to the nearby Devil's Quoits stone circle, from which Stanton Harcourt was also named.[88] The name Brittenton, for that part of Brighthampton within Standlake parish, represents an alternative corruption of the original place name and was established by the early 16th century, by which time the two halves of the hamlet were becoming more sharply defined for civil as well as parochial purposes.[89] In the 19th century and presumably earlier the name denoted both the eastern part of Brighthampton hamlet and the farmsteads by Abingdon road as far south as its intersection with Standlake High Street.[90]

In 1086 a total of 37 villani and bordarii and 5 servi were recorded on two estates, some of them perhaps already living at or near Standlake.[91] Other Brighthampton inhabitants were probably included among those noted on Bampton manor.[92] The population may have risen significantly by 1279 when c. 95 free and customary tenants were noted in Standlake and Brighthampton; of those, perhaps 30 or more lived at Brighthampton.[93] Numbers fell only slightly if at all in the earlier 14th century: over 84 landholders in both villages were taxed in 1306, at least 94 in 1316, and c. 80–87 in 1327.[94] In 1377 poll tax was paid by 288 people over 14, suggesting that even if the figure represented both villages[95] the impact of the Black Death had been limited, notwithstanding occasional references to vacant holdings.[96] The population may have declined during the later 15th century,[97] and between 55 and 77 inhabitants were taxed in the earlier 16th;[98] from the mid 16th century baptisms usually outnumbered burials,[99] and in 1642 the Protestation was subscribed by 147 men from both villages,[1] indicating an adult

73 C.O.S., PRN 3264, 11479, 12943.
74 D. N. Riley, 'A Late Bronze Age and Iron Age Site on Standlake Downs', Oxoniensia, xi/xii. 27–35.
75 Archaeologia, xxxvii. 363–70; Proc. Soc. Antiq. [1st ser.], iv. 92–100; L. S. Tuckwell, Reminiscences of Thirty Happy Years ... in Standlake (priv. print. c. 1918), 46–7: copy in C.O.S.; cf. Oxf. Jnl. 9 July 1859.
76 Oxoniensia, xi/xii. 33, 35 sqq.; Antiq. Jnl. xxii. 202–14.
77 C.B.A. Group 9, Newsletter, ix (1979), 35–7.
78 O.A.S. Rep. (1949), 7–8; C.O.S., PRN 2448.
79 C.B.A. Group 9, Newsletter, ix. 35–7; S. Midlands Arch. xvii (1987), 96–7; Antiq. Jnl. xxii. 208; cf. C.O.S., PRN 3369, 4470, 5690.
80 Archaeologia, xxxvii. 391–8; xxxviii. 84–97; V.C.H. Oxon. i. 360–2; J. Blair, A.-S. Oxon. 8–9, 12.
81 T. M. Dickinson, 'Excavations at Standlake Down in 1954', Oxoniensia, xxxviii. 239–57; V.C.H. Oxon. i. 362–3; Blair, A.-S. Oxon. 48, 70–1.
82 Early Chart. of Thames Valley, ed. M. Gelling, no. 282; V.C.H. Oxon. i. 405, 426; P.N. Oxon. (E.P.N.S.), ii. 329–30; below, manors.
83 P.N. Oxon. ii. 329; cf. Medieval Villages, ed. D. Hooke, 105.
84 Above, this section; below, manors; church.
85 P.N. Oxon. ii. 329.
86 Par. Colln. iii. 287.

87 e.g. Standlake Par. Mag. no. 61 (Nov. 1882), 254: copy in Bodl. G.A. Oxon. c 317/13; Magd. Coll. Estates Bursary, survs. 1883–91, p. 33.
88 V.C.H. Oxon. xii. 267, 270.
89 P.R.O., E 179/161/172, E 179/162/320; ibid. HO 107/872; P.N. Oxon. ii. 329–30; below, local govt.
90 P.R.O., HO 107/872; cf. O.R.O., tithe award (1844).
91 V.C.H. Oxon. i. 405, 426; below, manors.
92 V.C.H. Oxon. i. 400; above, Bampton: Bampton and Weald, intro.; manors.
93 Bampton Hund. R. 64, 66–71. Standlake manor included houses in Brighthampton: Magd. Coll. Mun., CP 3/16, ff. 178v.–179.
94 P.R.O., E 179/161/8–10. The 1306 list is damaged, in 1316 Brighthampton was taxed with Hardwick and Yelford, and the 1327 Brighthampton list includes Yelford names: cf. Bampton Hund. R. 64; Oxon. Local Hist. ii (2), 42–6.
95 P.R.O., E 179/161/42; no separate return for Brighthampton has been found.
96 Cf. below, econ. hist. (agric.). For abandoned tofts by Abingdon road, C.O.S., SMR air photos. SP 3903 A–B.
97 Below, econ. hist. (agric.).
98 P.R.O., E 179/172–3, E 179/162/234; cf. ibid. E 101/60/11; Chant. Cert. 47.
99 C.O.S., par. reg. transcripts.
1 Protestation Rtns. and Tax Assess. 9, 26–7.

population of c. 300. Building and subdivision of houses in the early 17th century allegedly encouraged an influx of poor.[2] Hearth tax in 1662 was paid on 39 houses in Standlake and on 16 in Brittenton; another nine houses in Brighthampton were assessed in 1665,[3] probably well below the actual number existing, and 365 adults were noted in the three townships in 1676.[4] Most 18th-century rectors estimated that there were 100–120 houses excluding the western part of Brighthampton,[5] and in 1801 Standlake, Brighthampton, and Brittenton together contained 117 houses occupied by 663 people. The population rose to 827 in 1841, when roughly a third lived in Brighthampton and Brittenton, and to 911 in 1851 and 1861, falling to 555 by 1921 partly through emigration. Between 1961 and 1981 population rose sharply from 666 to 1,257, falling to 1,247 by 1991.[6]

The early nucleus of Standlake village was presumably the church, manor house, and rectory house at its northern end,[7] near which there were several tenements, some later abandoned, in 1354.[8] Expansion south-westwards along High Street may have been associated with a market grant in 1230:[9] the Green, a triangular space at High Street's north-eastern end, was presumably laid out as a market place at that date, and High Street itself, called the market street in the 15th century,[10] was of notable width before encroachment at its north-eastern end in the 17th century or earlier.[11] Rack End, a lane leading from the Green to the river crossing near Gaunt Mill, derived its name from fullers' racks near its southern end, and was settled by the later 15th century.[12]

Brighthampton developed possibly around an intersection of north–south and east–west routes.[13] Brittenton or Brighthampton cross was mentioned in the early 17th century,[14] and in 1857 the base of an 'ancient' stone cross survived at the central cross roads.[15] There was straggling settlement along Abingdon road between Brighthampton and Standlake by the 17th century and probably much earlier.[16] Gaunt House, a substantial late-medieval house on the parish boundary east of the river Windrush, originated allegedly as a cottage tenement on Standlake manor, and until the 16th century two

or more cottages with small adjacent crofts survived nearby at 'Moor end'. They owed quitrent to Standlake manor and perhaps formed a small outlying group of cottages associated with nearby fulling mills.[17] Breach Farm, in the north of the parish, existed by 1767,[18] but apart from the mills there were no other outlying houses before inclosure.

The medieval part of Standlake Manor on Standlake High Street is timber-framed, and some stone-built houses retain evidence of former timber construction,[19] among them Gaunt House, Lincoln Farm on High Street, the post-medieval Cheswell, Rose, and Blenheim[20] Cottages on Abingdon road, and Cedar Cottage on Lancot Lane. Most surviving buildings are of local limestone rubble, with thatched or stone-slated roofs. In the 14th century rough stone for one of the manor houses came from Witney and some thatching straw from South Leigh, and in the 16th century freestone was said to be available within ten miles;[21] in the 19th century limestone blocks and Welsh slate became common, and a few houses and cottages were built or refaced in brick.[22] Among early buildings, Forge Cottage in Brighthampton incorporates at its north-west end a small, two-bayed open hall of the 16th century, with smoke-blackened roof timbers and a central cruck truss; an upper floor and a fireplace with a timber-framed smoke hood were inserted probably in the 17th century. A back wing, demolished c. 1990 when the house was restored and extended, had a cruck truss in one gable.[23] Lincoln Cottage at Church End, of the late 15th or early 16th century, is of similar construction and was originally thatched with reed,[24] and cruck construction was noted at Brasenose Farm in Brighthampton, demolished c. 1970,[25] and possibly at Sadlers on Standlake High Street.[26] Larger late-medieval buildings, besides Gaunt House, are Standlake Manor, Lincoln Farm, and the high-quality stone-built rectory house, all described below. The first three were the focus of sizeable freeholds by the later Middle Ages, and perhaps reflect commercial wealth derived from the cloth trade.[27] A leading inhabitant in 1406 was licensed to have an oratory in another, presumably substantial house.[28]

[2] Bodl. MS. Top. Oxon. c 118, f. 2; below, econ. hist. (agric.).

[3] P.R.O., E 179/255/4, pt. i, ff. 23, 27; Hearth Tax Oxon. 213, 228–9. No Brighthampton return for 1662 has been found.

[4] Compton Census, ed. Whiteman, 417–18.

[5] O.R.O., MSS. Oxf. Dioc. d 557, f. 57; d 560, f. 77; d 563, f. 77; Secker's Visit. 143.

[6] Census, 1801–1991; J. Goadby, 1228 and All That (priv. print. 1978), 48: copy in C.O.S.

[7] Below, manors; church; above, plate 31.

[8] Lincs. R.O., episc. reg. ix, ff. 263v.–264.

[9] Below, econ. hist. (market and fair).

[10] e.g. Magd. Coll. Mun., EP 15/12, EP 31/10 (in vico mercati); cf. ibid. EP 14/23 ('le market place').

[11] O.S. Map 1/2,500, Oxon. XXXVIII. 6 (1876 edn.); Bodl. MS. Top. Oxon. c 768/1, no. 47, asserting that one of the encroaching cottages existed by 1553.

[12] P.R.O., SC 2/209/57; Magd. Coll. Mun., EP 31/14; below, econ. hist. (trade and ind.).

[13] Above, this section; map on p. 172.

[14] Bodl. MS. Top. Oxon. c 118, f. 7v.

[15] Archaeologia, xxxvii. 393; not marked on O.S. Map 1/2,500, Oxon. XXXVIII. 5 (1876 edn.).

[16] Below, this section; cf. Bodl. MS. Top. Oxon. c 768/1, nos. 12–26; D.o.E., Hist. Bldgs. List: Standlake (1988), 114–18, 127: copy in C.O.S.

[17] Magd. Coll. Mun., EP 85/22, EP 99/2, EP 99/12–13; cf. ibid. EP 85/30, s.v. Wal. Huytheward; EP 14/22, s.v. John Brese; below, other estates; econ. hist. (mills).

[18] Jefferys, Oxon. Map (1767).

[19] S. J. Stradling, 'Vernacular Archit. of the Parish of Standlake' (Univ. of Manchester M.A. thesis, 1979), 27–8; below, other estates.

[20] Substantially rebuilt after 1978.

[21] New Coll. Arch., 9161–4; Linc. Coll. Mun., D/STA/30.

[22] e.g. Stradling, 'Vernacular Archit. Standlake', 28–9.

[23] Oxoniensia, xxxiii. 82, 85; misidentified in Stradling, 'Vernacular Archit. Standlake', 89–90.

[24] S. Midlands Arch. xv (1985), 83–5; cf. Bodl. MS. Top. Oxon. c 768/1, no. 55.

[25] N.M.R., Standlake file, s.v. Old Fm.; Bodl. MS. Top. Oxon. c 768/1, no. 12.

[26] Stradling, 'Vernacular Archit. Standlake', 88–9, 120.

[27] Below, other estates; econ. hist. (trade and ind.); church.

[28] Reg. Repingdon, i (L.R.S. lvii), 64; ii (L.R.S. lviii), 249.

Few later houses are notable, though some solid farmhouses reflect the parish's status as a community of moderately prosperous yeomen, rural tradesmen, and cottagers. Manor Farm (Floreys) at Brighthampton,[29] a substantial stone-built house with mullioned windows, dripmoulds, and steep-pitched roofs, was built in the early 17th century on a two-room plan, with a rear stair turret and outshut and a symmetrical west front; it was extended southwards soon after, perhaps c. 1659,[30] and in the 19th century the outshut was continued along the entire length of the back and raised to two storeys. A rough inscription TB 1721 on the door jamb refers perhaps to Thomas Brown (d. 1764), one of a prominent yeoman family which owned the house for much of the 18th century[31] but who was non-resident in 1754.[32] Glebe Farm on Abingdon road, rebuilt in the later 18th century and early 19th apparently for another family of yeoman freeholders, incorporates a symmetrical south-facing front of three bays, and retains a fine Adam-style fireplace in the principal bedroom. Yew Tree Farm on Abingdon road has a nearly symmetrical front with central doorway and brick quoining, and in 1867 may have been entirely brick-fronted; a datestone inscribed TSA 1745 commemorates building probably by members of the Spiers family, prominent farmers and Baptists, and another inscribed RFM 1811 may refer to the building of a conservatory by Richard and Mary Francis.[33] Building work by small yeomen or cottagers is commemorated by inscriptions at 2 Lancot Lane (EBX 1673 for Edward and Christian Bennett), the Black Horse public house (WBS 1673 for William and Susannah Baston), and Bracken Cottage on High Street (IKA 1717 for John and Katherine Alder).[34] Some rebuilding followed fires: in Brighthampton c. 1621 three 'poor neighbours ... near dwelling together' lost houses totalling 8 or 9 bays and all their household possessions, and two mills were burnt during the 18th century.[35]

Between 1801 and 1871 the number of houses rose from 117 to 219,[36] partly through subdivision[37] but also through erection of new cottages. Among them were Longwood Cottage Row opposite Standlake High Street, built in stages between c. 1789 and 1847, and nos. 31–7 Rack End, built probably in the 1850s.[38] The Limes, a tall, three-storeyed house east of Manor Farm on the edge of the former common, with a

fanlight and hood over a central doorway, was built evidently before 1841 when it housed a small private school, and from 1877 was occupied by a prominent farmer.[39] Inclosure prompted little new building, though the outlying Westfield Farm was erected apparently as labourers' accommodation before 1860,[40] and some dilapidated farmhouses were rebuilt, notably Malthouse Farm in Brighthampton (c. 1888)[41] and Manor Farm in Standlake (1889).[42] During the 1890s the Cavendish Land Co. of Westminster (Mdx.) planned a group of riverside holiday chalets in the former common, but the scheme was abandoned leaving only Bankside Lodge and an embanked access road dubbed Manor Avenue.[43] New institutional buildings were the Baptist chapel on Abingdon road, built in 1832, the parish school, built in 1846, and the Primitive Methodist chapel at the Green, built c. 1865.[44]

Longwood House, a large, eclectic building of brick, roughcast, timber, and concrete, was erected on Abingdon road during the 1920s, incorporating two detached cottages at the northern end of Longwood Cottage Row. Attached grounds were adapted for market gardening in the later 1920s, and both the house and cottages later formed part of the Mulberry Bush school for severely disturbed children, established c. 1948 by Stephen and Barbara Dockar-Drysdale. The school, which achieved wide recognition, acquired purpose-built accommodation to the west c. 1971, when there were 36 residential pupils, and Longwood House was demolished, leaving only the six cottages to the south.[45] Expansion north of Standlake village along Downs Road, begun c. 1929 when Witney R.D.C. built four labourers' cottages, accelerated during the 1960s, and by 1974 there were over 100 houses, bungalows, and flats.[46] Manor Crescent and Woodlands, north of Standlake High Street, were laid out in the late 1960s and early 1970s, and during the same period there was extensive infilling along the main streets,[47] mostly in untraditional materials. By 1994 the emergence of the Witney–Newbridge road as a trunk route had radically altered the character of much of the parish, though Standlake High Street, Rack End, and Church Lane remained as comparatively quiet side roads. An army hut refurbished as a village hall was erected on Standlake High Street near Manor Farm c. 1921, and was re-

[29] Cf. Stradling, 'Vernacular Archit. Standlake', 49–51, claiming earlier origins.

[30] Reset datestone.

[31] Bodl. MS. Top. Oxon. c 768/1, no. 2, making unsubstantiated assertions regarding the ho.'s earlier history.

[32] *Oxon. Poll, 1754.*

[33] Stradling, 'Vernacular Archit. Standlake', 104–8; Bodl. MS. Top. Oxon. c 768/1, nos. 11, 14; cf. O.R.O., QSD L.260; ibid. Misc. Stand. Hist. S. I/2; Bodl. G.A. Oxon. b 92 (1).

[34] Cf. Stradling, 'Vernacular Archit. Standlake', 70–1, 83–4, 86–7, 95–7, 100–1; Bodl. MS. Top. Oxon. c 768/1, nos. 7, 17, 18, 29, 33 (wrongly giving JAK).

[35] Bodl. MS. Top. Oxon. c 118, f. 4; below, econ. hist. (mills).

[36] *Census,* 1801–71.

[37] e.g. Bodl. MS. Top. Oxon. c 768/1, nos. 17–18, 20, 48, 63–4, 68–70.

[38] Ibid. nos. 28, 65–6; Stradling, 'Vernacular Archit.

Standlake', 117–19.

[39] P.R.O., RG 9/905; O.R.O., tithe award (1844), s.v. Rob. Hanks; deeds in private possession, calling it 'new built' in 1846.

[40] *Sale Cat., Manor Ho. and Fm.* (1860): copy in C.O.S.

[41] Bodl. MS. Top. Oxon. c 768/1, no. 5.

[42] Datestone on bldg.

[43] O.R.O., P2/2/MS 3/1, f. 3; ibid. P2/2/MS 6/34; O.S. Map 1/2,500, Oxon. XXXVIII. 10 (1899 and later edns.).

[44] Below, nonconf., educ.

[45] Bodl. MS. Top. Oxon. c 768/1, no. 28; *Sale Cats., Longwood* (1925 and 1939): copies in C.O.S. For the school, B. Dockar-Drysdale, *Therapy in Child Care* (1968), xiii–xvii; *Witney Gaz.* 8 Apr. 1971.

[46] O.R.O., P4/1/MS 3/4, f. 26Q; *Witney Gaz.* 4 July 1974: copy in C.O.S.; cf. Goadby, *1228 and All That,* 65, 68.

[47] *Residential Bldg. Land, Standlake* (1972): copy in C.O.S.; O.S. Map 6", SP 30 SE (1960 edn.); ibid. 1/2,500, SP 3802–3902 (1971 edn.).

placed by a purpose-built community centre at Rack End in 1989. A second army hut was erected as a youth club near the rectory house in 1954, and was replaced by a new concrete-built centre on the same site in 1963.[48]

A single street lamp near the church was maintained in the early 20th century through private donations.[49] The Wessex Electric Co. supplied electricity from 1937.[50] Mains water was introduced in 1957, replacing polluted wells, and mains drainage in 1970.[51]

There were three or four small inns and ale-houses on the Witney–Newbridge road by the early 17th century, patronized by travellers to and from London.[52] Of those the Chequers, in the former hermitage at the west end of Standlake High Street, was the scene of 'notorious disorders' c. 1630 and continued as an inn until c. 1776, after which the sign may have been briefly transferred to the former Red Lion in Forge Cottage at Brighthampton.[53] In the later 18th century there were usually 7–11 licensed houses, but by the early 19th century there were 3–4.[54] The Black Horse on Standlake High Street[55] and the Bell at Rack End, transferred to High Street before 1804,[56] remained open in 1994; the Golden Balls at Brighthampton, licensed probably by 1753[57] and largely rebuilt in the early 20th century, closed c. 1992 and was demolished in 1994.

The Standlake and Brighthampton Association for the Protection of Persons and Property was established at the Black Horse by 1785 and continued at the Bell in 1790.[58] A friendly society established at the Black Horse in 1761 was refounded c. 1795 and dissolved in 1844, when it had 60 members; a new society then founded at the Bell continued until c. 1890.[59] A friendly society based at the Chequers by 1781, with club feasts in June, continued probably until the Chequers' closure, and a friendly society was established at the Golden Balls in 1837.[60] A Lodge of Oddfellows established at the Bell in 1893 and a Court of Foresters established at the Black Horse in 1895 continued until 1951 and 1965 respectively; in the 1890s the Oddfellows

held Bank holiday fêtes, and until the 1930s both societies held annual processions from Northmoor to Brighthampton, collecting for the Radcliffe Infirmary and Oxford Eye Hospital.[61] A coal club established by the curate before 1849 continued into the early 20th century,[62] a clothing fund existed by 1877, and in 1878 the rector established a clothing club for Sunday school children.[63]

The rector encouraged musical and other entertainments in the late 19th century, and for several years there was also a brass band of mixed reputation.[64] A library was mentioned in 1877,[65] and a coffee room and lending library established by the rector in a cottage on High Street in 1882 continued, with intermissions, into the 20th century. Another lending library, financed partly from an educational charity, was established in the school in 1924 and continued until superseded by a mobile county service in 1964.[66] A cricket team, with a ground at Rack End provided by Magdalen College at inclosure,[67] existed by 1869, and in 1922 merged with Northmoor's team to form the Oxford Downs cricket club, still active in 1994. A women's institute was founded in 1933, a youth club, at first for girls only, in 1934, and a football club in 1948.[68]

Perambulations of the parish were mentioned in 1602. Then and later the gospel was read at certain points on the boundary, marked in the 18th century by crosses cut in the ground, and at Cokethorpe House a cross was chalked in the parlour.[69] Standlake Feast, celebrated apparently in the mid 18th century, was held in the 19th century in September, following immediately on Witney Feast; it was later a pleasure fair, with stalls along Standlake High Street, and continued into the 1950s. An annual flower show established in 1881 continued, with intermissions, until 1940, and by the 1920s had acquired the character of a village fête with stalls and sideshows.[70]

The medieval hermitage, occupied by bridge hermits in the 15th century,[71] stood on the site of Manor Farm.[72] Only two hermits are known,

48 O.R.O., P2/2/MS 11/12; Goadby, *1228 and All That*, 65, 70; O.S. Map 1/2,500, SP 3802–3902 (1971 edn.); local inf.

49 O.R.O., P4/1/MS 3/4, ff. 33T, 43T.

50 *Sale Cat., Longwood* (1939): copy in C.O.S.; C.O.S., PRN 11403.

51 Goadby, *1228 and All That*, 68; cf. O.R.O., T/SL/98 ii, s.a. 1962.

52 Bodl. MS. Top. Oxon. c 118, ff. 1v., 2v., 5v., 6v.; for breaches of assize of ale, Longleat House (Wilts.), NMR 3315, s.a. 1670.

53 Bodl. MS. Top. Oxon. c 118, f. 5v.; ibid. MS. Top. Oxon. c 768/1, no. 10; O.R.O., QSD V/1–3; ibid. P2/2/MS 2/1; *Wood's Life*, i. 273.

54 O.R.O., QSD V/1–4; cf. ibid. tithe award (1844); Bodl. MS. Top. Oxon. c 768/1, nos. 10, 15, 29, 42–3, 62; *P.O. Dir. Oxon.* (1847 and later edns.).

55 Cf. Bodl. MS. Top. Oxon. c 768/1, no. 29; Linc. Coll. Mun., C/STA/6, docs. *re* Black Horse.

56 Bodl. MS. Top. Oxon. c 768/1, nos. 42, 62.

57 O.R.O., QSD V/1–4; Oxf. Jnl. Synopsis, 3 Nov. 1786.

58 Oxf. Jnl. Synopsis, 15 Nov. 1785, 9 Mar. 1787, 12 Nov. 1790.

59 O.R.O., Misc. Coll. I/1 (missing 1994); *Oxf. Chron.* 20 Jan. 1844; Goadby, *1228 and All That*, 35, 47, 57, citing registration of a soc. at the Bell in 1866.

60 O.R.O., MS. Wills Oxon. 64/4/4; *Oxf. Jnl.* 9 June

1781; Goadby, *1228 and All That*, 47.

61 O.R.O., P4/4/PR 1/6, p. 598; Goadby, *1228 and All That*, 57–8, 66.

62 *Wilb. Letter Bk.* p. 173; *Standlake Par. Mag. 1877–9*, p. 49: copy in Bodl. Per. G.A. Oxon. 8° 666; Goadby, *1228 and All That*, 57.

63 *Standlake Par. Mag. 1877–9*, pp. 3, 49, 53, 100.

64 Bodl. G.A. Oxon. c 317/13, programmes 1880, 1882; O.R.O., PAR 248/17/M 52/1, pp. 5–6; Goadby, *1228 and All That*, 60.

65 *Standlake Par. Mag. 1877–9*, p. 3.

66 Bodl. MS. Top. Oxon. c 768/1, no. 40; O.R.O., P4/4/PR 1/7, p. 608; Goadby, *1228 and All That*, 52, 66.

67 O.R.O., incl. award; O.S. Map 6", Oxon. XXXVIII (1883 edn.).

68 Bodl. MS. Top. Oxon. c 768/1, no. 42; *Witney Express*, 29 July 1869, 16 June 1870; *Witney Gaz.* 8 Apr. 1971; Goadby, *1228 and All That*, 60–1, 66.

69 Magd. Coll. Mun., EP 99/2, deposition of Hen. Bantinge; O.R.O., P4/2/MS 1/5, f. 11.

70 O.R.O., P4/2/MS 1/5, f. 6; ibid. P4/5/A 1/1; *Witney Express*, 22 Sept. 1870; Goadby, *1228 and All That*, 58, 60, 67.

71 Above, this section [roads].

72 Linc. Coll. Mun., L/STA/84; Magd. Coll. Mun., ct. bk. 58, p. 93; ibid. CP 3/16, ff. 178v.–179, 263; ibid. CP 3/27, no. 60 (Standlake); *Oxoniensia*, xxxvii. 250–1.

of whom the earlier was noted for sayings on sin and temptation *c.* 1434.[73] By 1555 the building was a copyhold cottage held of the four quarters of Standlake manor and, later, of Magdalen and Lincoln Colleges;[74] in 1659 it was a 'little old stone building',[75] and in 1873, when the site was a farmstead,[76] buildings included a large, probably 17th- or 18th-century house, presum-

Raids probably on one of the manor houses in 1343 and on the rectory house *c.* 1350 involved local people.[81] During the Civil War, Gaunt House, then owned by the royalist Samuel Fell,[82] was garrisoned successively by royalists and parliamentarians, reflecting Newbridge's strategic importance: a royalist garrison existed perhaps by June 1644, when Waller forcibly crossed the

STANDLAKE HERMITAGE IN 1873

ably part of the former Chequers inn, and a smaller detached range of two storeys with a large chimney stack and a pointed doorway, perhaps part of the hermitage itself.[77] All the buildings were demolished *c.* 1889 when Manor Farm was rebuilt.[78] In 1677 Robert Plot reported that during parish processions on or near Holy Thursday the rector read a gospel 'at a barrel head in the cellar of the Chequer Inn', thought then to have been the site of either a hermitage or an ancient cross.[79] The practice may have reflected religious functions fulfilled from the hermitage before the Reformation, but in the mid 18th century it was associated rather with parish (and presumably township) perambulations, and by the early 19th century it had lapsed.[80]

bridge with 5,000 horse and foot,[83] and certainly by May 1645, when after a two- or three-day siege the house was surrendered to Col. Thomas Rainsborough, who took over 50 prisoners. Canon balls found in the moat in the 19th century suggest a violent engagement, though contemporary accounts were contradictory and artillery was not explicitly mentioned.[84] A Parliamentary garrison placed in the house soon after supplied 200 horse for a successful sortie at Kidlington in October, and footsoldiers for the containment of Radcot in April 1646, but was removed presumably soon after the fall of Oxford in June.[85] A carved ivory ball depicting Strafford's and Laud's executions and found in an unidentified Standlake gravel pit may date from the Civil War period.[86]

73 *Loci e Libro Veritatum: Passages from Gascoigne's Theological Dictionary*, ed. J. E. Thorold Rogers, 105–6; above, this section [roads].

74 Magd. Coll. Mun., Standlake 2; ibid. EP 1/3, EP 31/6; Linc. Coll. Mun., D/STA/38, L/STA/13–14; cf. ibid. partics. of estates 1853–4, p. 316; ibid. C/STA/6, corresp. 1884–7, 1920.

75 *Wood's Life*, i. 273; cf. O.A.S. *Rep.* (1871), 27.

76 e.g. O.R.O., tithe awards (1844 and 1847), schedule s.v. Magdalen College.

77 Bodl. MS. Top. Oxon. d 218, ff. 244v.–245; this section [inns]. Bodl. MS. Top. Oxon. c 768/1, no. 26a asserts that the drawings relate to Fletcher's Fm., but cf. O.S. Map 1/2,500, Oxon. XXXVIII. 6 (1876 edn.).

78 Datestone; O.S. Map 1/2,500, Oxon. XXXVIII. 6

(1876 and later edns.).

79 Plot, *Nat. Hist. Oxon.* (1677), 203; cf. *Par. Colln.* iii. 288.

80 O.R.O., P4/2/MS 1/5, f. 11; Brewer, *Oxon.* 482–3.

81 *Cal. Pat.* 1343–5, 181, 398, 388; 1348–50, 447, 463–4; 1350–4, 2, 43; below, manors.

82 Below, other estates.

83 *Oxoniensia*, xiv. 51.

84 *Oxf. Jnl.* 28 May 1892; cf. J. Sprigge, *Anglia Rediviva* (1647), 22; *W. Dugdale's Life, Diary, and Corresp.* ed. W. Hamper, 79–80; B. Whitelocke, *Memorials of Eng. Affairs* (1732), 148; below, other estates.

85 Sprigge, *Anglia Rediviva*, 27; Whitelocke, *Memorials* (1732), 166, 174; *Cal. S.P. Dom.* 1645–7, 165, 406; *Cal. Cttee. for Money*, ii. 1028, 1132; *V.C.H. Oxon.* iv. 80.

86 *Oxoniensia*, xiv. 77.

There were no resident lords after the later Middle Ages, though in the 19th century the Stricklands of Cokethorpe House were active in parish affairs and achieved some popularity.[87] The antiquary and naturalist Stephen Stone (d. 1866), who made pioneering use of crop marks in his excavations in the parish, lived in Brighthampton from the 1840s, for a time in Manor Farm (Floreys).[88] Dr. Kofi Busia, prime minister of Ghana, lived in Brighthampton while in exile during the 1960s and maintained a home there in 1971. The childbirth expert Sheila Kitzinger lived in Standlake Manor from c. 1966.[89]

MANORS. In the late Anglo-Saxon period Standlake and Brighthampton formed part of the royal manor of Bampton, which was later diminished by piecemeal grants. Aethelred gave 3 cassati at Brighthampton to his 'minister' Aelfwine in 984,[90] and in 1086 Wadard held 1½ hide there under Odo, bishop of Bayeux. That estate was apparently forfeited on Wadard's and Odo's fall, and was probably included in Henry I's grant to Sées priory (Orne) in 1131 of land at Brighthampton and Hardwick, later Hardwick and Brighthampton manor.[91] A 6-hide estate, recorded under Brighthampton in 1086 and held by Anketil de Grey of William FitzOsbern, earl of Hereford, was probably the later manor of STANDLAKE, which was assessed in 1220 at 5½ carucates, and which unlike Hardwick and Brighthampton manor was not claimed later as ancient demesne.[92] By 1242 the overlordship was held with the Isle of Wight by Baldwin (II) de Rivers (d. 1245), earl of Devon, and it descended with the Isle to the Crown in 1293.[93] Thereafter Standlake was usually said to be held of the honor of Carisbrooke or that of Aumâle,[94] which remained in the king's hands. The overlordship passed with life grants of the Isle to Edward III's daughter Isabel in 1355–6,[95] and to William Montagu (d. 1397), earl of Salisbury, in 1385;[96] its inclusion among possessions of Sir Robert de Lisle of Rougemont in 1368 arose probably from confusion with other estates inherited from Isabel de Forz.[97] In 1388 the overlord was said to be John of Gaunt (d. 1399),

duke of Lancaster,[98] and from the early 15th century Standlake was consistently said to be held of the duchy of Lancaster, sometimes as of the honor of Aumâle. The overlordship was last recorded in the early 16th century.[99]

In 1242–3 and later the manor was reckoned usually at 1 knight's fee[1] but in 1279 and 1346 at 1½ fee, perhaps through inclusion of land at Brize Norton held of the manor by the 13th century, and for which quitrent remained due in the 16th.[2] An apparently separate fee or half-fee, held of the same overlord by Roger Foliot (fl. 1243?) and by Laurence de Broke (fl. 1368), was reported in the 14th century, but though both held former FitzOsbern lands elsewhere in the county neither is otherwise known to have been associated with Standlake,[3] and the fee was not mentioned later.

The Greys' mesne tenancy descended presumably through Anketil's son Richard to his grandson Anketil (fl. 1150) and great-grandson John (d. by 1192), both of whom granted meadows and common rights in Standlake to Eynsham abbey.[4] John's daughter and heir Eve married the royal judge Ralph Murdac, who was lord in 1192 but whose lands were forfeited in 1194 for rebellion.[5] A claim was evidently made by Guy de Dive, Murdac's great nephew through marriage, who that year confirmed the grants to Eynsham abbey, but the Crown restored the manor to Eve c. 1197,[6] soon after Murdac's death. In 1200 her second husband Andrew de Beauchamp paid 50 marks for seisin of Murdac's former lands in Northamptonshire,[7] and in 1214 he received custody of Standlake wood, which by 1230 was attached to the manor.[8] On Eve's death c. 1246 the manor was divided into four parts, three passing to her daughters Beatrice (relict of Robert Mauduit), Joan (wife of Ernald de Boys), and Alice (wife of Ralph Hareng and formerly of Alan of Buckland), and the fourth to Jolland de Neville, son of her daughter Maud.[9] It descended in quarters until the 16th century, the Boys, Hareng, and Neville quarters being held apparently of the Mauduit quarter.[10]

The de Boys quarter passed to Joan's son and grandson, both called Ernald, to the younger Ernald's brother John (fl. 1279–85), who leased

87 O.R.O., PAR 248/2/A 1/1, passim; L. S. Tuckwell, Reminiscences of Thirty Happy Years ... in Standlake (priv. print. c. 1918), 2–4, 27–30: copy in C.O.S.; Goadby, 1228 and All That, 43, 61.
88 P.R.O., HO 107/1731; ibid. RG 9/905; Tuckwell, Reminiscences, 46–7; Oxf. Chron. 6 Oct. 1866; cf. Archaeologia, xxxvii (1857), 363–70; Proc. Soc. Antiq. [1st ser.], iv. 92–100.
89 Witney Gaz. 8 Apr. 1971; local inf.
90 Early Chart. of Thames Valley, ed. M. Gelling, no. 282.
91 V.C.H. Oxon. i. 405; above, Ducklington, manors.
92 V.C.H. Oxon. i. 426; Bk. of Fees, i. 316; Bampton Hund. R. 63, 66–71; above, intro.
93 Bk. of Fees, ii. 823, 834; Cal. Inq. p.m. i, p. 290; iv, p. 102; Complete Peerage, iv. 309–33; cf. V.C.H. Hants v. 222.
94 Cal. Inq. p.m. iv, p. 102; ix, p. 16; xii, p. 378; Cal. Pat. 1324–7, p. 164; 1330–4, p. 452.
95 V.C.H. Hants v. 222; Cal. Inq. p.m. xi, p. 193; xiv, p. 134.
96 V.C.H. Hants v. 222; Cal. Inq. p.m. xvii, p. 323; cf. ibid. xix, p. 229.
97 Cal. Close, 1364–8, 496; Complete Peerage, viii. 71, 76–7; cf. V.C.H. Oxon. vi. 136–7.
98 Cal. Inq. p.m. xvi, p. 222.

99 e.g. Cal. Close, 1413–19, 403; 1441–7, 242; Cal. Inq. p.m. Hen. VII, ii, p. 272.
1 Bk. of Fees, ii. 823, 834; Cal. Inq. p.m. ix, p. 16; x, p. 66; xvii, p. 323; Abbrev. Rot. Orig. (Rec. Com.), 299.
2 Bampton Hund. R. 37, 66–70; Feud. Aids, iv. 183; Magd. Coll. Mun., EP 31/6; cf. Oxon. Fines, p. 2.
3 Cal. Close, 1364–8, 496; Cal. Inq. p.m. xvii, p. 323; xix, p. 229; Farrer, Honors, 234–7; V.C.H. Oxon. vi. 136–7.
4 Eynsham Cart. i, pp. 87–9; Misc. Gen. et Her. 5th ser. v. 161–2, 164.
5 Eynsham Cart. i, p. 84; Misc. Gen. et Her. 5th ser. v. 164; Pipe R. 1194 (P.R.S. N.S. v), 15–16, 92; Chanc. R. 1196 (P.R.S. N.S. vii), 71, 75, 203.
6 Eynsham Cart. i, pp. 89–91; Pipe R. 1197 (P.R.S. N.S. viii), 35, 40; cf. V.C.H. Oxon. xi. 91.
7 Rot. de Ob. et Fin. (Rec. Com.), 48; Misc. Gen. et Her. 5th ser. v. 162, 164.
8 Rot. Litt. Pat. (Rec. Com.), i. 170; Cal. Chart. R. 1226–57, 121.
9 Cal. Inq. p.m. i, p. 290; for date, cf. Ex. e Rot. Fin. (Rec. Com.), i. 455. Mauduit may have had some right by 1230: Pipe R. 1230 (P.R.S. N.S. iv), 246.
10 e.g. Bampton Hund. R. 66, 68–70; Oxon. Fines, 170–1.

it to Nicholas Sifrewast,[11] and before 1296 to John's brother Master William, who after 1309 sold it to Sir Roger Corbet (d. c. 1349) of Hadley (Salop.).[12] Roger settled most of it in 1335 on his daughter Eleanor for life,[13] and in 1347 on his son and heir John,[14] dead by 1350 when Roger's daughter Amice (d. 1361) and her husband John d'Oddingseles (d. 1352) held the quarter for their lives.[15] In 1357 John Corbet's son Sir Robert granted the reversion for their lives to Edmund Giffard of Standlake, his wife Margaret, and their son Robert, but on Corbet's death in 1404 the quarter passed under a settlement of 1390 to his relict Maud, with reversion to their son Robert (d. 1417).[16] He settled it in 1415 on his daughter Sibyl, who married John Greville, the owner in 1428; on John's death in 1444 it passed with Hadley under earlier settlements to Robert's nephew Robert (d. 1495), son of his brother Guy.[17] From the 1460s or earlier Robert mortgaged the quarter, and in 1464 sold it to Sir John Leynham or Plummer (d. 1479), a London grocer.[18] In 1482 executors of Leynham's relict Margaret sold it to William Waynflete, bishop of Winchester, who in 1483 gave it to the newly founded Magdalen College, Oxford.[19]

Jolland de Neville's quarter had been let by 1254 to Maud's cousin Sir Walter de Grey (d. 1268), whose rent was remitted that year.[20] Though Jolland's brother Andrew claimed the advowson in 1284[21] the Nevilles' interest was not mentioned later, and the quarter descended until 1474 with the Greys' manor of Cogges.[22] In 1316 it was held in dower by the first Sir John Grey's relict Margaret and her husband Robert Morby,[23] from the 1330s to 1360s all or part was held by Sir Ralph de Grey, presumably a relative,[24] and in the later 1360s the 2nd Lord Grey leased the quarter for their lives to Edmund Giffard and his wife;[25] a small part was held by the Quatremayns family in the late 14th century and early 15th.[26] In 1474 the quarter passed under a family settlement to William Lovel (d. 1476), Lord Morley, second son of the Greys' heir Alice Boteler, Lady Sudeley; it passed to William's son

Henry (d. 1489), Lord Morley, and to Henry's sister Alice (d. 1518), suo jure Baroness Morley, who married William Parker (d. after 1504) and Sir Edward Howard (d. 1513).[27] Her son and heir Henry Parker, Lord Morley, conveyed it in 1532 to Edward Lee, archbishop of York, and others, apparently by sale, but in 1538 sold it to Magdalen College.[28]

Alice Hareng's quarter passed on her death in 1247 to her grandson Osbert (II) Giffard,[29] who came of age c. 1255. In 1284 he abducted a nun of Wilton (Wilts.) and took her overseas, having given custody of his lands to his son Osbert III (d. 1290); the king nevertheless seized his estates, which were briefly restored to the younger Osbert in 1285 and were recovered by his father in 1290.[30] All or part of the quarter was granted in dower to the younger Osbert's relict Sarah, still lady in 1302;[31] after disputes in 1291–2 it was agreed that she should have additional rent from lands in Standlake bought by the elder Osbert from John of Hadenham, and that on Osbert's death his granddaughter and heir Alice should have land in Standlake and Deddington also formerly John of Hadenham's.[32] The elder Osbert died before 1312,[33] and by 1316 the lord was Richard Darcy,[34] whose son John and relict Alice, presumably Alice Giffard, seem to have sold the quarter c. 1338 to William Casse and his wife Maud.[35] Thomas Souwy, lord in 1346,[36] was perhaps only a lessee, and in 1364 rents and homages formerly belonging to him and to Maud Casse were conveyed to Thomas Tirrell and his wife Alice, who conveyed them to Thomas Spigurnel and his wife Catherine.[37] Edmund Giffard of Standlake, mentioned from 1353,[38] bought or recovered the quarter from the Spigurnels in 1367,[39] and in 1381 his relict Margaret granted it to William of Wykeham, bishop of Winchester.[40] A claim by a descendant of Richard Darcy was defeated the following year.[41]

In 1381 Wykeham gave the quarter to New College, Oxford,[42] but recovered it c. 1392 and settled it on himself, with reversion to his great-nephew Thomas (later Sir Thomas) Wykeham

11 P.R.O., CP 40/55, m. 79d.; ibid. KB 27/90, m. 33; *Bampton Hund. R.* 68; cf. *Cal. Inq. p.m.* ii, pp. 134–5. For Sifrewast, C. Peters, *Lord Lieutenants Oxon.* 39–40.

12 Magd. Coll. Mun., Standlake 17B; *Cal. Pat.* 1292–1301, 184; cf. Lincs. R.O., episc. reg. ii, f. 155; *V.C.H. Berks.* iv. 379; *V.C.H. Salop.* xi. 256.

13 Magd. Coll. Mun., Standlake 12C, 24–5; P.R.O., CP 25/1/190/18, calling Eleanor William Corbet's daughter.

14 Magd. Coll. Mun., Standlake 12B.

15 B.L. Harl. Ch. 54 D. 28; *Cal. Inq. p.m.* x, p. 66; xi, p. 193; cf. Magd. Coll. Mun., Standlake 20C.

16 Magd. Coll. Mun., Standlake 14C, 18A, 20A, 32A; *Cal. Close,* 1413–19, 402–3.

17 Magd. Coll. Mun., Standlake 3A, 15B; *Feud. Aids,* iv. 194; *Cal. Close,* 1441–7, 242; *V.C.H. Salop.* xi. 256.

18 Magd. Coll. Mun., Standlake 6B, 7B, 10C, 12–13, 16A, 20, 28A, 29A; P.R.O., C 140/73, no. 74.

19 Magd. Coll. Mun., Standlake 1A, 2A, 6C, 10–11, 18C, 27A.

20 *Oxon. Fines,* 170–1; cf. *Misc. Gen. et Her.* 5th ser. v. 164; *Complete Peerage,* vi, pedigree between pp. 128–9.

21 P.R.O., CP 40/55, m. 79d.

22 e.g. *Feudal Aids,* iv. 183, 194; *Cal. Inq. p.m.* xvi, pp. 221–2; P.R.O., C 139/159, no. 34. For descent, *V.C.H. Oxon.* xii. 59–60.

23 *Feud. Aids,* iv. 162, giving Margery de Grey; *Complete Peerage,* vi. 145; P.R.O., E 179/161/8–9.

24 Magd. Coll. Mun., Standlake 11A, 20A; *Edington Cart.* (Wilts. Rec. Soc. xlii), no. 503; below [manor hos.].

25 *Cal. Inq. p.m.* xiv, p. 134; *Cal. Close,* 1364–8, 471.

26 *Cal. Inq. p.m.* xvii, p. 473; xviii, p. 178; xix, p. 190; *Cal. Inq. p.m.* (Rec. Com.), iv. p. 8.

27 *Cal. Fine R.* 1485–1509, pp. 125–6; P.R.O., C 142/34, no. 77; *Complete Peerage,* ix. 219–21.

28 Magd. Coll. Mun., Standlake 1C, 4C, 5A, 19A; an implicit claim by the abbot of Westminster in 1532 is unexplained.

29 *Cal. Inq. p.m.* i, pp. 26–7; *Misc. Gen. et Her.* 5th ser. v. 149, 163.

30 *Complete Peerage,* v. 649–53 and nn.; *Rot. Parl.* (Rec. Com.), i. 30; cf. *Reg. G. Giffard* (Worcs. Hist. Soc. xv), ii. 278–9.

31 P.R.O., KB 27/131, m. 42d.; *Cal. Inq. p.m.* iv, p. 102.

32 P.R.O., KB 27/131, m. 42 and d.; *Complete Peerage,* v. 652–3 and n.; cf. *Oxon. Fines,* 195.

33 *Year Bk.* 5 Edw. II (Selden Soc. xxxiii), 189, 191.

34 *Feud. Aids,* iv. 162; P.R.O., E 179/161/8–9.

35 P.R.O., KB 27/315, m. 25; ibid. CP 25/1/287/39; CP 25/1/190/19; cf. P.R.O., CP 40/486, m. 117.

36 *Feud. Aids,* iv. 183.

37 *Cal. Close,* 1364–8, 44–5; P.R.O., CP 25/1/190/22; cf. *Cal. Pat.* 1343–5, 181, 398.

38 P.R.O., CP 40/374, m. 202d.

39 Ibid. CP 25/1/190/22; cf. *Cal. Close,* 1369–74, 336.

40 New Coll. Arch., 13921.

41 P.R.O., CP 40/486, m. 117.

42 *Cal. Pat.* 1381–5, 63; New Coll. Arch., 9161–4.

alias Perrot (d. 1443), in possession by 1402.[43] Thomas's son William (d. 1457) settled it in 1448 on his daughter Margaret (d. 1477) and her husband William Fiennes (d. 1471), Lord Saye and Sele,[44] who settled it on their son Henry (d. 1476) and his wife Anne (fl. 1491).[45] It descended to Henry and Anne's son Richard (d. 1501), Lord Saye and Sele, and to Richard's son Edward (d. 1528),[46] whose relict Margaret, with her second husband Thomas Neville of Holt (Leics.), retained a life interest, prompting disputes in the 1540s with Edward's son Richard Fiennes, *de jure* Lord Saye and Sele.[47] Before 1555 Richard sold all or part to Francis Fettiplace of Standlake and others, who in that year conveyed a part to Cuthbert Temple of Standlake, clothier. Temple sold his estate soon after to Robert Radborne (d. 1557) of Standlake, miller, who in 1556 sold most of it to Magdalen College,[48] to which Fettiplace made additional small sales in 1557.[49]

Beatrice Mauduit's quarter passed on her death after 1250 to Sir John Mauduit (d. 1302) of Somerford (Wilts.), her son or grandson. It descended with Somerford to his nephew Sir John Mauduit (d. 1347), who briefly forfeited it c. 1322–3, to John's relict Agnes (d. 1369), who married Sir Thomas de Bradeston (d. 1360), Lord Bradeston, and to John's and Agnes's grandson William de Moleyns (d. 1381), son of their daughter Gilles.[50] Thereafter it descended until the 16th century with Aston Pogges in Bampton,[51] passing by 1532 to George Hastings (d. 1544), earl of Huntingdon, who in 1537 sold it to Thomas Cromwell, later earl of Essex.[52] On Cromwell's fall in 1540 the quarter escheated to the Crown, and in 1541 was granted for her life to Anne of Cleves (d. 1557);[53] the reversion was granted with other lands in 1552 to Henry Grey, duke of Suffolk, and Thomas Duport, who the same year sold it to Cuthbert Temple, Anne of Cleves's lessee.[54] In 1555 Temple sold the reversion of the demesne to Francis Fettiplace[55] and the rest, with some exceptions, to Robert Radborne; Radborne sold most of it to Magdalen College,[56] thereafter lord of the reunited, if diminished, manor. The college's estate, over 650

a. in 1887,[57] was enlarged in the late 19th century and early 20th[58] and was sold in parcels c. 1920, chiefly to tenants.[59]

The demesne lands acquired by Fettiplace, including closes and woodland adjoining Cokethorpe in the north of the parish, passed on his death in 1558 to his infant daughter Cecily, who married Edward East of Bledlow (Bucks.).[60] The estate was by then known usually as Golofers, presumably from an unrecorded medieval tenant or from confusion with the Moleyns's submanor of Golofers in Bampton parish.[61] Though Fettiplace was alleged in 1558 to hold no other land in Standlake[62] the family seems also to have retained part of the Fiennes quarter, since in 1573 Cecily and Edward settled the manors of Golofers and Giffards, the latter also called Standlake Fiennes, on themselves and their heirs.[63] That combined estate, sometimes known later as Cokethorpe manor and forming the core of later Cokethorpe Park, descended independently thereafter;[64] attached open-field land in Standlake was sold piecemeal during the 18th century.[65]

Eve de Grey had a demesne farm and presumably a house in Standlake at her death c. 1246.[66] It passed probably with the Mauduit quarter,[67] which in 1302 included a house and garden, an adjoining close, and a dovecot.[68] John Mauduit (d. 1347) witnessed a local charter c. 1309,[69] but the family resided chiefly at Somerford (Wilts.) and by c. 1370 leased the demesne,[70] and in 1425 the site of the house was worth only 4d. a year.[71] The house stood probably east of the river Windrush, north-east of the church: traces survive there of a moated rectangular inclosure with a causewayed entrance,[72] and in 1558 an inquisition referring apparently to the Mauduit quarter mentioned a manor house formerly there.[73]

The Giffard quarter presumably included a house in the later 13th century, when a son of Osbert (II) Giffard was allegedly born in Standlake.[74] William Casse was licensed to have an oratory in his house, perhaps the manor house, in 1340.[75] Between 1387 and 1391 New College, Oxford, embarked on major repairs to manorial buildings: stone, lime, laths, nails, and roof tiles were bought for repair of the

43 B.L. Add. Roll 41642; *Cal. Chart. R. 1341–1417*, 419; *Complete Peerage*, xi. 482 and n.
44 P.R.O., CP 25/1/293/71; *V.C.H. Oxon.* ix. 88.
45 P.R.O., C 140/62, no. 45; *Cal. Pat. 1485–94*, 345.
46 P.R.O., C 142/50, no. 91; *Cal. Inq. p.m. Hen. VII*, ii, p. 272; cf. ibid. p. 401.
47 P.R.O., C 1/1121/47–9; ibid. C 78/1, no. 88.
48 Magd. Coll. Mun., Standlake 2, 22C.
49 Ibid. Standlake 1.
50 Ibid.; P.R.O., CP 40/55, m. 79d.; ibid. SC 6/1146/15; *Cal. Inq. p.m.* iv, p. 102; ix, p. 16; x, p. 479; xii, p. 378; *Feud. Aids*, vi, p. 626; *V.C.H. Wilts.* xiv. 207; *Complete Peerage*, viii. 551–4.
51 Above, Bampton: Aston and Cote, manors.
52 *L. & P. Hen. VIII*, v, p. 582; xii (2), p. 353.
53 Ibid. xvi, p. 242; B.L. Harl. Roll I. 15, B. 20.
54 *Cal. Pat. 1550–3*, 242, 416; Magd. Coll. Mun., Standlake 3.
55 *Cal. Pat. 1554–5*, 138–9.
56 Ibid. 138; ibid. 1555–7, 328; Magd. Coll. Mun., Standlake 22C.
57 O.R.O., tithe award (1887).
58 Magd. Coll. Mun., modern deeds, boxes 37, 39, 41, 59, 88–9, 92–3; ibid. map of 1897 (Group II).
59 *Sale Cat.* (1920): copy in Bodl. G.A. Oxon. b 92* (11); Magd. Coll. Estates Bursary, Ledger P.

60 P.R.O., C 142/115, no. 32.
61 Above, Bampton: Aston and Cote, manors; cf. Magd. Coll. Mun., Standlake 11A, 12B, 14C, 15B, 17B, 18A, 20A, 20C, witnessed by members of the Golafre family.
62 P.R.O., E 150/822, no. 1.
63 Ibid. CP 25/2/196/15 & 16 Eliz. I Mich.; cf. ibid. CP 25/2/339/4 Jas. I East; CP 25/2/339/8 Jas. I East.
64 Above, Ducklington, manors.
65 e.g. Bodl. MS. Ch. Oxon. 4459; O.R.O., P 4/1/MS 3/4, ff. 29R–30R; Magd. Coll. Mun., LMR Add. Deeds 2, docs. re Farm closes.
66 *Cal. Inq. p.m.* i, p. 290; cf. *Reg. W. de Gray* (Surtees Soc. lvi), 233.
67 Above, this section.
68 P.R.O., C 133/108, no. 6.
69 Magd. Coll. Mun., Standlake 17B.
70 *Cal. Pat. 1324–7*, 164; *Cal. Inq. p.m.* ix, p. 16; P.R.O., SC 6/961, no. 19.
71 P.R.O., C 139/17, no. 29.
72 C.O.S., PRN 4127; C.B.A. Group 9, *Newsletter*, ii (1972), 30; viii (1978), 68–9; above, plate 31.
73 P.R.O., E 150/822, no. 1, perhaps also referring to former Giffard lands, however.
74 *Year Bk.* 5 Edw. II (Selden Soc. xxxiii), 189, 191.
75 Lincs. R.O., episc. reg. v, f. 176; cf. *Cal. Pat. 1343–5*, 398.

hall and chamber; other buildings were strengthened or underpinned in stone; timber framing, thatch, wattle, daub, and plaster were renewed; and gates were replaced and fitted with new locks.[76] The house, apparently moated,[77] may have stood in a close east of the Windrush near the rectory house, where earthworks suggest a second, L-shaped moated inclosure.[78] The quarter continued to be called 'Giffardscourt' or 'Wykehamscourt', but 15th-century owners were non-resident and no buildings were noted later.[79]

The Greys presumably had a house or home farm in 1279 when land was in demesne, but no owners are known to have resided and by the 1360s the demesne was leased.[80] Manorial buildings stood probably in or near Greys court, a large square inclosure north-west of the church which seems to have descended with the Greys' quarter.[81] Numerous cropmarks have been noted in the vicinity, though none are identifiably medieval.[82] In 1338 Ralph de Grey was licensed to alienate 1 rood of land to enlarge the churchyard, which later jutted into the close's south-east corner,[83] and by the 16th century there were apparently no buildings.[84]

The Boys quarter included a manor house probably in 1279 and certainly in the earlier 14th century, when it was let with the demesne. By 1361 it had no net value, and in 1394 the site, which is unidentified, was a garden.[85]

OTHER ESTATES. Wallingford priory acquired land in Standlake before 1247, when it was apparently let to the four owners of Standlake manor.[86] In 1528, following the priory's suppression, unspecified lands or rents in Standlake passed to Thomas Wolsey, archbishop of York, who gave them to Cardinal College, Oxford;[87] the college's successor, Christ Church, seems, however, to have had no interest in Standlake before acquiring separate estates there in the 17th century.[88] Meadows by the Thames granted in the late 12th century to Eynsham abbey by Anketil and John de Grey were retained as part of the abbey's Shifford manor until the Dissolution.[89]

An estate centred on Standlake Manor, a house on the south side of High Street so called from c. 1860,[90] was built up from the later Middle Ages by the Cornewell or Cornwall family and by their successors the Yates, following the marriage before 1487 of Margaret, daughter and heir of John Cornwall (fl. 1480), to Edmund Yate (d. c. 1516) of Charney Bassett in Longworth (then Berks.). Edmund Yate's estate, not all of it derived from the Cornwalls, descended to John (d. 1545), Robert (d. 1554), James (d. 1608), and Francis Yate (fl. 1613);[91] he or another Francis sold it in 1647 to Richard Hyde (d. 1665), gentleman, from whom it passed to William Hyde (d. 1717) and his relict Mary (d. 1733), to their son Richard (d. 1741), and to Richard's relict Elizabeth and son Richard.[92] Most Yates and some Hydes seem to have resided,[93] though the resident Mary Hyde let the estate and may have occupied a different house.[94] Ownership passed to the non-resident Newmans before 1785 and c. 1792 to the Tomkinses of Abingdon, who let the house and land to farmers.[95] In 1860 executors of William Tomkins's son-in-law G. W. Anstie sold it with 228 a. as the 'Manor House and farm', and it remained a farmhouse until 1896 when most of the land was sold.[96] Quitrents to Standlake manor remained due in 1860.[97]

The house's timber-framed main range, aligned along the street, is of the 15th century, and was built perhaps by John Cornwall.[98] Though of three bays in the 20th century it formerly extended further west, the surviving end bay having apparently formed part of a larger hall which was open to the roof. The roof itself has intermediate curved scissor trusses similar to those at the rectory house, and its western bay, above the former open hall, is wind-braced. An evidently re-used ceiling, to which a badge with part of the Yate family arms[99] was nailed, was inserted into the hall in

76   New Coll. Arch., 9161–4.

77   Ibid. 9162, mentioning hedges *infra motam*; ibid. 9163, apparently mentioning a bridge.

78   C.O.S., PRN 4128; C.B.A. Group 9, *Newsletter*, viii. 68; *Medieval Villages*, ed. D. Hooke, 104; above, plate 31.

79   e.g. P.R.O., C 140/62, no. 45; ibid. C 2/Eliz. I/M 8/46; *Cal. Pat. 1485–94*, 345; *Cal. Inq. p.m. Hen. VII*, ii, p. 272.

80   *Bampton Hund. R.* 69; below, econ. hist.

81   Magd. Coll. Mun., CP 3/16, ff. 178v.–179, 189; cf. ibid. CP 3/34, f. 29.

82   C.O.S., PRN 8255; D. Benson and D. Miles, *Upper Thames Valley* (1974), 46.

83   *Cal. Pat. (1338–40)*, 32; *Inq. ad quod damnum* (Rec. Com.), 304; Magd. Coll. Mun., CP 3/16, ff. 178v.–179; O.R.O., tithe award (1844).

84   Magd. Coll. Mun., EP 85/34; Linc. Coll. Mun., D/STA/31.

85   *Bampton Hund. R.* 68; Magd. Coll. Mun., Standlake 13B, 17B, 23; ibid. EP 123/16; P.R.O., C 135/120, no. 11; C 135/165, no. 31.

86   *Oxon. Fines*, p. 143.

87   *L. & P. Hen. VIII*, iv (2), p. 1957; *V.C.H. Berks.* ii. 79; Bodl. MS. d.d. Ch. Ch. MM1.

88   *Valor Eccl.* (Rec. Com.), ii. 250–3; Ch. Ch. Arch., Treasury Bks. lvi. c. 1–2; below, this section (Gaunt Ho.).

89   *Eynsham Cart.* i, pp. 87–90; Bodl. MSS. d.d. Harcourt c 109/10.

90   *Sale Cat., Manor Ho. and Fm.* (1860): copy in C.O.S.,

o   STANb 631.2.

91   Magd. Coll. Mun., ct. bk. 4, cts. 8–9 Hen. VIII; ct. bk. 6, ct. 3 July 1 Mary; ct. bk. 5, cts. 20 Sept. 10 Eliz., 19 Sept. 12 Eliz.; ibid. EP 15/10, EP 31/6, EP 31/10; Bodl. MSS. d.d. Harcourt c 113/4–5; O.R.O., MS. Wills Oxon. 179, f. 38; P.R.O., PROB 11/111, ff. 295v.–296v.; *Oxon. Visit.* 158–9.

92   Magd. Coll. Mun., ct. bk. 43, p. 58; ct. bk. 55, ct. 2 July 3 Geo. I; Bodl. MS. Ch. Oxon. 2906; O.R.O., MS. Oxf. Dioc. d 557, ff. 57–60; C.O.S., par. reg. transcripts.

93   e.g. P.R.O., PROB 11/111, f. 295v.; O.R.O., MS. Wills Oxon. 179, f. 38; ibid. MS. Oxf. Dioc. d 557, ff. 57–60; Bodl. MS. d.d. Harcourt c 113/4; Magd. Coll. Mun., MS. 427, f. 56 and v.; *Secker's Visit.* 143.

94   O.R.O., QSD E.1, pp. 45–6, 205; cf. P.R.O., PROB 11/660, f. 99.

95   O.R.O., QSD L.260; Bodl. MS. Top. Oxon. c 768/1, no. 35.

96   *Sale Cat.* (1860): copy in C.O.S.; *Sale Cat.* (1896): copy in Bodl. G.A. Oxon. b 92 (1); Bodl. MS. Top. Oxon. c 768/1, no. 35.

97   Magd. Coll. Mun., ct. bk. 15, p. 200; *Sale Cat.* (1860), lot 5: copy in C.O.S.

98   Magd. Coll. Mun., ct. bk. 9, ct. 20 Sept. 10 Eliz. For the bldg., Pevsner, *Oxon.* 778; D.o.E., *Revised Hist. Bldgs. List: Standlake* (1988), 125: copy in C.O.S.; Bodl. MS. Top. Oxon. c 499/2; ibid. c 768/2, no. 35.

99   Cf. *Oxon. Visit.* 158.

the later 16th century or early 17th; about the same time a stack was built into the north-west corner of the surviving central bay, the rest of which became a cross passage, and a two-storeyed porch was added against the northern doorway. The overmantel of the ground-floor fireplace to the former hall is also re-used and is decorated with quatrefoils enclosing heraldic shields of arms, among them the Tudor rose and crown and other, unidentified, devices.[1] On the first floor, the two eastern bays appear to have formed one large room. The gable created by the removal of the western end of the hall was long exposed to the weather before a rubble-built wing was added in front of it in the earlier 19th century; timber framing on the street front-age, presumably rendered by 1860 when the house was said to be of brick and tile, was exposed and restored in the mid 20th century.[2]

A freehold centred on Gaunt House was built up apparently from the later 15th century by the Gaunt family and their descendants the Walwyns. Spurious claims in the late 16th century and early 17th that the estate was a manor were successfully challenged by Magdalen College, which asserted that Gaunt House was a cottage held of Standlake manor for quitrent and suit of court. Though quitrents were owed for lands then attached to the estate there seems, however, to have been no rent payable explicitly for the house.[3] The earliest known owner was John Gaunt, who in 1461 held a different house and half yardland of the Corbets' manor,[4] and whose wife Joan (d. 1465/6) was commemorated by a brass formerly in Standlake church;[5] the surname was not recorded in Standlake earlier, and may indicate Flemish origin.[6] The name Tirletts Court, recorded, as an alternative for Gaunt House, from the 16th century,[7] may refer to an earlier owner.

From John (d. c. 1473) the estate passed to his son Simon (d. c. 1506),[8] perhaps to Simon's relict Alice,[9] and to his son George (d. s.p. c. 1516) and daughter Ann. Ann married George Walwyn and in 1544 settled it on their son Edward Walwyn.[10] He sold some of the land[11] and settled the rest c. 1580 on his son George (d. 1609), whose relict Mary (d. 1626) was in 1623 leasing it to George's son and heir Edward.[12]

Edward's brother John (d. 1628) left it to his sister Dorothy Gascoigne with reversion to her son Stephen Gascoigne,[13] who sold it in 1638, including lands in Standlake, Northmoor, and Shifford, to Samuel Fell (d. 1649), dean of Christ Church, Oxford;[14] from him it passed to his relict Margaret and son John (d. 1686), later bishop of Oxford, who left it to Christ Church to found a bursary for poor students.[15] Small additions were made in 1715 and 1889, when the Standlake part of Christ Church's estate totalled 67 a.[16] From the mid 17th century the estate was let to local farmers, notably the Marchants and their descendants the Burfords and Gileses;[17] Christ Church sold it in 1955.[18]

The surviving house,[19] within a large L-shaped moat, is of coursed limestone rubble, and comprises a central hall range with cross-passage doorways at its eastern end, and two cross wings. That plan, together with the survival of a main post from a timber-framed wall at the house's north-west corner and of a section of timber-framed wall in the west wing, suggests an early, probably late-medieval origin, and the hall fireplace, located on the northern, outside wall, may be a later addition. Replacement, in stages, of timber walling by stone appears to have been substantially complete by the early 17th century, the date of several doorways and of windows and plasterwork in the west, parlour, wing; since both Ann Walwyn and her son Edward leased the house[20] those features may reflect remodel-ling by George Walwyn, resident from c. 1580, or his successors.[21] During the Civil War the house was garrisoned and besieged,[22] but though musket loops were cut in the main door there is no evidence of major damage or rebuilding, and in 1649 and 1654 the Fells reserved for their occasional use the hall and parlour, both with chambers over, the kitchen, and a stable.[23] Some minor work may have been carried out c. 1669,[24] and the causeway crossing the moat to the main door is dated 1718, but the house seems to have undergone no further structural alteration. There were two restorations in the later 20th century.[25]

A freehold of 2¼ yardlands centred on the later Lincoln Farm was sold in 1545 by William Tyrling (d. 1546) to Humphrey Bostocke of

[1] Bodl. MS. Top. Oxon. c 499/2, no. 170A; ibid. c 768/1, no. 35, suggesting identification with the Boys family, which was, however, unconnected with Standlake after the early 14th cent.
[2] Sale Cat. (1860); Country Life, 25 Feb. 1939, p. xv; Bodl. MS. Top. Oxon. c 768/1, no. 35.
[3] P.R.O., REQ 2/181/27; Magd. Coll. Mun., EP 85/22, 99/2, 99/12–13, 99/16, 146/8, 146/22; cf. ibid. EP 31/6.
[4] Magd. Coll. Mun., EP 85/39.
[5] Wood's Life, i. 272.
[6] P. Hanks and F. Hodges, Dictionary of Surnames, 206
[7] e.g. P.R.O., REQ 2/181/27.
[8] O.R.O., Warner IV/ii/1; Bodl. MS. d.d. Harcourt c 127/4.
[9] Cf. Magd. Coll. Mun., EP 88/16, 85/22.
[10] P.R.O., C 1/1503/22–4; Bodl. MS. d.d. Harcourt c 127/4; ibid. MS. Ch. Oxon. 3753.
[11] Magd. Coll. Mun., EP 99/2, deposition of Jas. Somer; O.R.O., MS. Wills Oxon. 1/5/8.
[12] P.R.O., REQ 2/181/27; ibid. C 142/394, no. 41; ibid. C 2/Jas. I/G 10/10; ibid. PROB 11/116, ff. 39v.–41; PROB 11/149, ff. 190 and v.
[13] Abstracts of Glos. Inq. p.m. i (Index Libr. ix), 187–9; cf. Ch. Ch. Arch., Standlake A 27; C.O.S., par. reg. tran-

scripts, s.v. Walwyn.
[14] Ch. Ch. Arch., Standlake A 3–7, 20–7.
[15] Ibid. A 39–46; ibid. MS. Estates 80, ff. 6 sqq.; P.R.O., PROB 11/165, f. 95v.; D.N.B.
[16] Ch. Ch. Arch., Standlake C 1–14, D 1–2; O.R.O., tithe award (1887).
[17] Ch. Ch. Arch., Standlake A 41–2, A 71–2, A 75; ibid. MS. Estates 80, ff. 30 sqq.; ibid. Treasury Bk. lv. b. 30; O.R.O., tithe awards; C.O.S., par. reg. transcripts.
[18] Bodl. MS. Top. Oxon. c 768/1, no. 76.
[19] Cf. ibid. c 768/2, no. 76; ibid. d 218, ff. 227v.–228; B.L. Add. MS. 36377, f. 71; Country Life, 27 June 1903, 870–3; Pevsner, Oxon. 778; above, plate 32.
[20] Bodl. MS. Ch. Oxon. 3753; P.R.O., PROB 11/51, f. 27v.; Magd. Coll. Mun., EP 99/2, deposition of Thos. Bennett.
[21] Magd. Coll. Mun., EP 99/12; cf. ibid. EP 146/22; Ch. Ch. Arch., Standlake A 2 (b), A 3; C.O.S., par. reg. transcripts, s.v. Walwyn, Gascoigne.
[22] Above, intro.
[23] Ch. Ch. Arch., Standlake A 41–2.
[24] Country Life, 27 June 1903, 872; Bodl. MS. Top. Oxon. c 768/1, no. 76.
[25] C.O.S. PRN 5875, letter of 1967; local inf.

Abingdon (then Berks.), draper, who leased it to Tyrling for life and in 1548 sold it to Robert Radborne (d. 1557).[26] Radborne's son Robert, a London stationer, sold it in 1567 to Lincoln College, Oxford, with scattered cottages and tenements formerly part of Standlake manor, and other small freeholds acquired since the 1540s.[27] Quitrents to Magdalen College for the former manor lands were compounded for in 1905,[28] and in 1918 the entire estate, c. 110 a. after inclosure,[29] was sold piecemeal to tenants.[30]

Lincoln Farm, formerly Tyrlings,[31] includes a late medieval hall range parallel to Standlake High Street and a western cross wing, and is two-storeyed throughout. The hall, which has a smoke-blackened roof, was formerly timber-framed, but much of the framing has been replaced by rubble walls. A stack was inserted in front of the present cross passage presumably c. 1564, when the lessee was to build a chimney, flue, and freestone mantel in the 'hall house' partly at the owner's expense; there was then a chamber over the parlour, and by 1582 there was a storage chamber over the hall,[32] though the existing beamed ceiling is of early 17th-century character. The cross wing, also rubble-walled, includes a two-light window of the later 16th century and has an added chimney gable on its west side; traces of ochre paintwork survived on its roof timbers in 1970.[33] Rooms in 1582 included a buttery and milkhouse evidently beyond the cross passage, storage within a timber pentice at the rear, an apparently free-standing kitchen, and agricultural buildings around a 'court'; most windows were glazed, though one, in the chamber over the parlour, had shutters only, and the parlour had been recently refitted.[34] The house's east end, beyond the cross passage, was rebuilt in the 17th century. Both Tyrling and the Radbornes apparently occupied the house,[35] but from 1564 the estate was let to prominent farmers and others, among them Walter Bayley (d. 1592), the queen's physician, who presumably sublet it, Nicholas Dixon (d. 1627), a local man and servant to the earl of Salisbury, who resided, and relatives of the minister Nicholas Shorter (fl. 1650).[36] The house continued as a farmhouse following the college's sale to its tenant in 1918, but was later separated from the estate.[37]

A small estate in Brighthampton and Standlake passed from John Fettiplace (d. 1510) of Charney Bassett (then Berks.) to his son Philip,[38] who in 1524 sold it to Simon Starkey, bursar of Brasenose College, Oxford. In 1529 Starkey conveyed it to John Elton or Baker who granted it to Brasenose, and in 1624 the college acquired an additional tenement in Cokethorpe.[39] The estate, let to tenant farmers and totalling c. 76 a. after inclosure,[40] was sold in two parcels in 1911 and 1918.[41]

Land and cottages belonging to a chantry in Standlake church passed on its suppression to the Crown, which in 1590 sold the estate, much decayed in 1569, to its lessee Walter Bayley.[42] Bayley's son William sold some parts piecemeal,[43] and the rest was absorbed into his manor of Northmoor.[44]

ECONOMIC HISTORY. AGRICULTURE. In the early Middle Ages Standlake and Brighthampton may have had separate fields. Standlake's East field was mentioned in 1318,[45] and in 1354 a holding was divided between the Down in Standlake's fields and South field in Brighthampton.[46] There was presumably a single system by 1480, when Standlake manor's demesne arable lay in the Down and in South, North, Standlake, and Little fields,[47] and Standlake and Brighthampton had shared fields thereafter. In the 17th century the principal fields were South and North fields, west of Brighthampton village, Church or Little field immediately north of Standlake village, and Rickland (earlier Richland) field north of Church field. Some holdings included small acreages in West field, south-west of Breach Farm, and Underdown, a subdivision of Church field, was sometimes counted as a separate field.[48] Hardwick, in Ducklington parish, had its own fields to the north, but some holdings in Hardwick, Standlake, and Brighthampton fields were so intermixed that for inclosure in the 19th century it was found convenient to treat all the fields as a unit.[49]

Extensive meadows, estimated in 1086 at 106 a. on Wadard's and the Greys' estates, bordered the rivers Thames and Windrush and the Shifford boundary brook.[50] Farm, Underdown,

[26] Linc. Coll. Mun., D/STA/1–6; O.R.O., MS. Wills Oxon. 179, f. 184.
[27] Linc. Coll. Mun., D/STA/38; cf. ibid. D/STA/1–37; V. Green, *Commonwealth of Lincoln College.* 130; above, manors.
[28] Linc. Coll. Mun., D/STA/48–9; ibid. C/STA/6, release 12 Aug. 1905.
[29] Ibid. *Reg. Estates, 1898,* 5.
[30] Ibid. C/STA/6, docs. *re* sale; ibid. bursar's corresp., letters *re* estates 1880–1926, ff. 611, 613–14.
[31] Ibid. D/STA/52 [misnumbered 53 on MS.]; illust. in Bodl. MS. Top. Oxon. c 768/2, no. 31.
[32] Linc. Coll. Mun., D/STA/30, D/STA/52.
[33] Inf. from C. R. J. Currie.
[34] Linc. Coll. Mun., D/STA/52.
[35] Ibid. D/STA/30; O.R.O., MSS. Wills Oxon. 179, f. 184; 182, f. 162v.
[36] Linc. Coll. Mun., D/STA/30, D/STA/52, L/STA/10, L/STA/16–18, L/STA/26–7, L/STA/43, L/STA/53, L/STA/68, L/STA/95; cf. ibid. Z/STA/4–5; O.R.O., QSD L.260; *D.N.B.* s.v. Bayley, wrongly dating his death to 1593.
[37] Linc. Coll. Mun., C/STA/6, valn. and rep. 1917; ibid. bursars' corresp., letters *re* estates 1880–1926, f. 614; local inf.

[38] P.R.O., C 142/25, no. 60.
[39] B.N.C. Mun., Standlake 7–15, Cokethorpe 6; *B.N.C. Quatercentenary Monographs,* iv (O.H.S. lii), 10; ix (O.H.S. liii), 139; cf. below, econ. hist. (mills).
[40] B.N.C. Mun., B 10.13: survey 1850.
[41] Ibid. B 3c. 14, pp. 198–9, 347–8.
[42] P.R.O., E 310/22/119, f. 14; ibid. E 318/46/2473; ibid. C 66/1342, m. 17; below, church.
[43] e.g. Bodl. MS. d.d. Harcourt c 64/4.
[44] Ibid. c 73/2, c 74/14; above, Northmoor, manors. For the former priest's ho., below, church.
[45] *Oxon. Local Hist.* ii (2), 41.
[46] Lincs. R.O., episc. reg. ix, f. 264; cf. St. John's Coll. Mun., XVII.21.
[47] Magd. Coll. Mun., EP 31/10.
[48] O.R.O., MS. Oxf. Archd. Oxon. c 142, pp. 181–8 [of repeated pagination]; Linc. Coll. Mun., Z/STA/1–2; B.N.C. Mun., Room B ser., 534, terrier of land occ. T. Coles; Magd. Coll. Mun., D-Y 420; cf. ibid. CP 3/16, ff. 178v.–265; O.R.O., incl. award and maps.
[49] Magd. Coll. Mun., D-Y 447; ibid. CP 3/16, ff. 182, 191; St. John's Coll. Mun., XVII.45; below, this section.
[50] *V.C.H. Oxon.* i. 405, 426; O.R.O., tithe award (1844).

and Up meadows, the last of which included Ealong furlong, Middle Dole, and Sydenham, lay by the Windrush; in the 15th century and the mid 18th they were apparently distributed by lot,[51] and in the 19th they were Lammas meadows.[52] Some intermixed parcels of meadow, chiefly in the north-east near Hardwick common, belonged to Hardwick.[53] Larger several meadows by the Thames were recorded from the early Middle Ages, when they formed part of Standlake manor's demesne. Langhurst (later Langleys), granted to Eynsham abbey with nearby Chaddocks or Chattoksham in the late 12th century, comprised 29 a. of meadow and pasture c. 1360, and in the later Middle Ages both meadows were usually farmed to local tenants.[54] Hasses (24 a.), probably an adjacent meadow bordering Langley's weir, was granted to Cold Norton priory before 1246 but was recovered c. 1260, and remained part of the Corbets' demesne.[55] In the 15th century and later demesne parcels of up to 8 a. were recorded in Oxlease by the Windrush, in Standlake 'perrockes', perhaps the later Paddocks east of Rack End, and in Oatlands in the south-west, though the demesnes also included lot meadow.[56] A meadow near Gaunt Mill was said in 1804 to lie on rich, deep soil, though some meadows flooded frequently.[57]

Pasture 10 furlongs by 4 recorded on Anketil de Grey's estate in 1086[58] presumably included the later Standlake common, c. 458 a. occupying much of the parish's southern part.[59] Sixteenth- and 17th-century references to Cowleaze and to the moor, presumably adjoining Northmoor, suggest that it was internally divided.[60] Additional pasture was available in the fields after harvest, and in most of the meadows, including those held in severalty, after Lammas.[61] In 1361 a demesne ploughland (4 yardlands) carried common rights for 10 cattle and 160 sheep;[62] in the 16th century the stint for each yardland on Standlake manor was usually 6–8 cattle, 3–4 horses, and 40–50 sheep, and landless cottagers were allowed 2 cow commons. The miller was allowed an extra horse common in 1552.[63] Sheep were excluded from the moor in 1536 from 3 May to 1 August, and in 1541 from Cowleaze before Michaelmas, and in 1562 pigs were forbidden from Pentecost until the end of the harvest.[64] The stint remained similar on both

manors in the 18th century and early 19th, when in addition most tenants of Hardwick and Brighthampton manor held up to 5 a. in the Marsh, a Lammas ground near the Shifford boundary.[65] In the mid 19th century Standlake common was open usually from 21 May to Lady Day or, latterly, to Candlemas.[66]

In the 14th century the townships of Standlake, Brighthampton, Hardwick, and Shifford intercommoned from Lammas to Martinmas.[67] In 1447–8 Hardwick's rights in Addehurst meadow in Standlake were challenged by the lord and tenants of Shifford, to which manor it belonged;[68] in the 16th century commons in Standlake Down and in a meadow called Volnhurst were disputed between Hardwick and Standlake,[69] and in 1558 Northmoor's inhabitants challenged Standlake's rights in a common in Northmoor.[70] An apportionment of intermixed meadow among the townships of Standlake, Ducklington, Stanton Harcourt, and South Leigh was proposed in 1620,[71] and in the 19th century Standlake commoners retained feeding rights after 1 August in Achim or Eacham mead (30 a.) by the Thames, and in part of Upper Sydenham (8 a.) by the Windrush, included in Northmoor and South Leigh parishes respectively.[72] Standlake and Brighthampton inhabitants were by the 19th century excluded from Hardwick's common pastures, though Brighthampton tenants of Hardwick and Brighthampton manor shared rights in Standlake common, prompting disputes between the respective lords in 1852 over rights in the waste.[73]

Though no woodland was recorded in 1086[74] much of the northern part of the parish, including Home and Boys woods, the site of Cokethorpe House, and the area around Breach Farm, seems to have been wooded in the early Middle Ages. Presumably that was the Standlake or 'East Lea' wood of which custody was granted to Andrew de Beauchamp in 1214, and in which Eve de Grey granted pannage for 20 swine to Standlake church.[75] Following the manor's partition c. 1246[76] the woods were divided among the four quarters, all of which included woodland into the later Middle Ages. Boys wood, c. 70 a. in 1844,[77] was let by the Corbets to the Yelford and Hastings families of Yelford and later to the Mores of Northmoor for

51 Magd. Coll. Mun., EP 31/10; ibid. D-Y 420; Bodl. MS. Ch. Oxon. 4457; O.R.O., Misc. Go. I/1.
52 Magd. Coll. Mun., D-Y 447; O.R.O., tithe award (1844).
53 Magd. Coll. Mun., D-Y 447; O.R.O., incl. award.
54 O.R.O., tithe award and map (1844), s.v. Chadocks and Langleys; Bodl. MSS. d.d. Harcourt c 128/4–7; Eynsham Cart. i, pp. 87–90; ii, pp. 4–6.
55 B.N.C. Mun., Standlake 2–3; Magd. Coll. Mun., EP 31/10; ibid. CP 3/16, f. 183, s.v Langleys.
56 Magd. Coll. Mun., EP 31/10; ibid. CP 3/16, f. 183; Cal. Pat. 1554–5, 138–9.
57 Ch. Ch. Arch., MS. Estates 80, ff. 55–6; below, this section.
58 V.C.H. Oxon. i. 426.
59 O.R.O., tithe award (1844).
60 e.g. Magd. Coll. Mun., EP 85/43, EP 85/35; St. John's Coll. Mun., XI.15, p. 67; ibid. XVII.18 (4).
61 e.g. Magd. Coll. Mun., D-Y 447; ibid. ct. bk. 6, s.a. 4 Aug. 4 Eliz.; P.R.O., C 135/165, no. 31; Eynsham Cart. ii, p. 4.
62 P.R.O., C 135/165, no. 31.
63 Ibid. REQ 2/181/27; Magd. Coll. Mun., EP 85/36, EP 146/9–10.

64 Magd. Coll. Mun., EP 85/35, EP 85/43; ibid. ct. bk. 6, s.a. 1562.
65 Ibid. CP 3/16, ff. 179v.–265; Linc. Coll. Mun., Z/STA/7; St. John's Coll. Mun., XVII.45; O.R.O., PAR 248/8/L 1/1; ibid. incl. award.
66 Magd. Coll. Mun., D-Y 447.
67 Eynsham Cart. ii, p. 6.
68 P.R.O., SC 6/961/20; cf. Eynsham Cart. i, no. 411; ii, p. 5; Bodl. MS. d.d. Harcourt c 127/3; O.R.O., tithe award and map (1844), s.v. Adsworth; ibid. incl. award.
69 P.R.O., E 321/11/25.
70 Magd. Coll. Mun., ct. bk. 6, ct. 8 Mar. 4 & 5 Phil. and Mary.
71 St. John's Coll. Mun., XI.11, p. 151.
72 O.R.O., tithe award (1844), s.v. wastes and roads.
73 Magd. Coll. Mun., D-Y 447.
74 Cf. above, intro. [boundaries].
75 Rot. Litt. Pat. (Rec. Com.), i. 170; Cal. Pat. 1334–8, p. 23. For the name East Lea, above, Ducklington, intro.
76 Above, manors.
77 O.R.O., tithe award (1844).

much of the 14th and 15th centuries, prompting disputes over ownership in the later 15th century and early 16th.[78] It subsequently descended with Yelford, and was let in the early 17th century to the Medhopps of Cote in Bampton, and in the early 19th to the Stricklands of Cokethorpe House, who kept it in hand.[79] In 1949 it comprised chiefly oak.[80] Home or Cokethorpe wood, c. 68 a. in 1844,[81] was evidently the Greys wood owned by the Greys and Lovels in the 14th and 15th centuries,[82] and hedging and sale of underwood was recorded in the 1380s when it was briefly held by New College, Oxford, presumably on lease.[83] It did not pass to Magdalen College with the rest of the Lovels' manor, and by the early 17th century was attached to the later Cokethorpe estate.[84] Woods adjoining Sherald's Copse north-east of Boys wood passed chiefly with the Mauduits' quarter of Standlake manor until the 16th century, when they too were leased, and in 1538 the lord's agent remarked that there was sufficient timber to maintain the lord's houses for a hundred years. In 1555 those woods were sold with other demesne lands to Francis Fettiplace, and thus also became part of the later Cokethorpe estate.[85] Over 750 elms and ashes recorded on farms held of Standlake manor in 1768 were evidently in or around closes near the villages.[86]

In 1230 Eve de Grey was licensed to impark her wood and to have a deer leap.[87] Henry III gave 4 does and a buck in 1232, and in 1279 the park was attached to the Mauduits' quarter.[88] It was not mentioned later, and the surname Parker, recorded in the 14th century, seems by then to have been hereditary.[89] Presumably the park included only a small proportion of the total woodland: the curving northern and western boundaries of Home wood have been suggested as possible park pales,[90] but since the Mauduits' woodland lay mostly further east the park perhaps occupied the area north-west of the later Cokethorpe House, subsequently coppiced and, in the 18th century, landscaped.[91]

Woodland on all four quarters of Standlake manor was being assarted by the 14th century. Boysbreach (later the Lawns), between Boys wood and Greys wood, was mentioned with the adjoining Mauduitsbreach in 1355, and the 'breach towards Cokethorpe', probably near

later Breach Farm, in 1480.[92] By the early 18th century Cokethorpe House was surrounded by small coppices and assarted closes extending into Ducklington.[93] Further demesne closes totalling c. 75 a. lay east of Standlake village around the putative moated manor houses,[94] and closes in the south-east, totalling c. 60 a. and attached to Gaunt House, Gaunt Mill, and the adjacent fulling mill by the early 17th century, were probably also medieval;[95] Church mill was held with a small adjoining close by the 15th century.[96] In 1480 it was alleged that a ham adjoining Hasses meadow would increase in value from 6d. to 5s. if inclosed.[97]

Yardlands on Standlake manor were reckoned in the Middle Ages at 30 a. of arable and c. 6 a. of meadow,[98] measured probably in customary acres. On Hardwick and Brighthampton manor some 14th-century yardlands seem to have included only 15 a. of arable, possibly also customary,[99] though in the 16th century all yardlands on the manor in Brighthampton were traditionally reckoned at 35 a.[1] In the later 18th century Standlake manor's yardlands included c. 23 statute acres of arable, and some of those on Hardwick and Brighthampton manor over 30 statute acres besides 5–11 a. of meadow.[2]

In 1086 land for 7 ploughs was reported on Anketil de Grey's estate, probably the later Standlake manor. Nine teams were recorded, 2 of them worked by 4 servi on the demesne, and 7 of them held by 15 villani and 16 bordarii. The estate's value had risen from £5 in 1066 to £6. Wadard's 1½-hide estate in Brighthampton, worth 40s. as in 1066, had 1 plough in demesne, and a servus, a villanus, and 5 bordarii were mentioned. Other lands and tenants were probably surveyed with Bampton.[3]

Two ploughlands were in demesne in the earlier 13th century[4] and four by 1279, one attached to each of the quarters into which the manor had been divided, and each variously reported during the 14th century to contain between 60 a. and 100 a. of arable.[5] The Corbets' demesne was farmed to the rector and others from the early 14th century,[6] and by the 1380s the Mauduits', Giffards', and probably the Greys' demesnes were also being farmed.[7] A demesne ploughland on the Greys' Hardwick and Brighthampton manor, 100 a. in 1295,[8] may

78 Magd. Coll. Mun., Standlake 7A, 8C, 9A, 14–16, 18B, 23A, 24A, 26A, 30A; ibid. EP 146/15; P.R.O., C 1/849/1–2.
79 O.R.O., QS/Epiph. 1708/19; ibid. tithe award (1844); P.R.O., PROB 11/107, ff. 282–3.
80 O.R.O., Adkin I/641, lot 3.
81 Ibid. tithe award (1844).
82 Magd. Coll. Mun., Standlake 11A; Berks. R.O., D/ELl T41; St. John's Coll. Mun., XVII.39 (v); P.R.O., C 139/158, no. 28; cf. O.R.O., tithe award and map (1844).
83 New Coll. Arch., 9162–3.
84 P.R.O., C 142/346, no. 80; O.R.O., tithe award (1844).
85 P.R.O., C 142/115, no. 32; O.R.O., tithe award and map; L. & P. Hen. VIII, xiii (2), p. 31; Cal. Pat. 1554–5, 138–9; above, manors; cf. Magd. Coll. Mun., Standlake 11A.
86 Magd. Coll. Mun., CP 3/16, ff. 178v.–265.
87 Cal. Chart. R. 1226–57, 121.
88 Close R. 1231–4, 37; Bampton Hund. R. 66.
89 P.R.O., E 179/161/8–9; ibid. SC 6/961/19; Bampton Hund. R. 67, 70.
90 C.O.S., PRN 11680.
91 Above, Ducklington.
92 Magd. Coll. Mun., Standlake 11A; ibid. EP 31/10; cf. O.R.O., tithe award (1844).

93 Bodl. MS. d.d. Harcourt c 13/2; cf. B.N.C. Mun., Room B ser., 534, terrier 1761 and map 1765.
94 O.R.O., tithe award and map (1844); cf. Magd. Coll. Mun., EP 31/10; P.R.O., C 142/115, no. 32; Cal. Pat. 1554–5, 138–9; above, manors.
95 O.R.O., tithe award and map (1844); Ch. Ch. Arch., MS. Estates 80, f. 41; Magd. Coll. Mun., EP 99/2, EP 146/5.
96 Magd. Coll. Mun., EP 31/10. 97 Ibid.
98 Bampton Hund. R. 67, s.v. Wm. Follare; Magd. Coll. Mun., EP 31/6, EP 85/39, EP 123/16; O.R.O., MS. Wills Oxon. 159/4/18.
99 Oxon. Local Hist. ii. (2), 43–6, implying varying yardlands of 15–30 a.
1 St. John's Coll. Mun., XVII.14.
2 Ibid. XVII.45; Magd. Coll. Mun., CP 3/16, ff. 178v.–265; cf. O.R.O., Standlake tithe award.
3 V.C.H. Oxon. i. 405, 426; above, manors.
4 Cal. Inq. p.m. i, p. 290.
5 Bampton Hund. R. 66–70; P.R.O., C 133/108, no. 6; C 135/120, no. 11; C 135/165, no. 31; ibid. E 142/70, m. 5.
6 Magd. Coll. Mun., Standlake 13B, 23; ibid. EP 14/20.
7 P.R.O., SC 6/961/19; New Coll. Arch, 9161–4.
8 Bampton Hund. R. 63 and n.

have been farmed or absorbed into tenant holdings, since only 60 a. of demesne arable were mentioned in 1312, and 22 a., with 8 a. of meadow, in 1423.[9] Demesne farming was evidently mixed: hay and grain was sold from Standlake manor's demesne in 1195, and 16 oxen, 20–30 cattle, and over 100 swine were allegedly driven from probably the Giffard demesne in 1343.[10]

Tenant holdings on Standlake manor had undergone much subdivision by 1279.[11] Twenty-eight villeins then held half yardlands, another held two half yardlands of different quarters of the manor, and one held a house and 7½ a., apparently ¼ yardland. Eight cottagers[12] had holdings of 5–8 a., one of them divided between a father and son. On Hardwick and Brighthampton manor 6 Brighthampton villeins held yardlands and 10 held half yardlands, and 2 cottagers had 5 a. each. Large numbers of freeholders perhaps reflected expansion and assarting since the 11th century: 35 were recorded on Standlake manor[13] with holdings ranging from 2 a. to a yardland or more, mostly occupied with houses.

Unfree half yardlands on Standlake manor in 1279 owed rent of 22½d. and exceptionally heavy works valued at 8s. 5d., though obligations had perhaps been reduced since 1247 when total income from 7 half-yardlanders on the Giffards' quarter exceeded that in 1279.[14] Services in 1303, allegedly 3 days' work per week from 1 August to 29 September and 2 days' work per week for the rest of the year, were valued at c. 5s. 11d., suggesting further reductions.[15] Tenants of Hardwick and Brighthampton manor, held as ancient demesne,[16] owed heavier rents but lighter services, including weeding, mowing, harvesting, and carting, and tenants in 1295 paid aid and churchscot.[17] Cottagers on Standlake manor owed varying rents and services in 1279, though in 1303 those on the Mauduits' quarter seem to have been counted as ¼-yardlanders owing proportionate rents and services; cottagers on Hardwick and Brighthampton manor in 1279 owed rent of 21d. and works valued at 9d.[18] Freeholders' rents, between 5d. and 9s. 10d. in 1279, did not consistently reflect size of holdings, and one free yardland owed light labour services.[19]

In 1322–3 a keeper of the Mauduits' quarter claimed that 100 a. lay uncultivated through lack of buyers and animals,[20] but between 1306 and 1327 the average value of movables assessed for taxation rose from c. 46s. to c. 62s. in Standlake and to c. 64s. in Brighthampton, putting both places among the more prosperous rural settlements in the area.[21] The wealthiest contributors in 1316 were the four lords of Standlake manor, together taxed on goods worth over £37; others were assessed on goods worth from 9s. 4d. to £5 12s., some large assessments being on villeins.[22]

On both manors holdings remained markedly stable in the early 14th century.[23] A few vacant tenements were recorded from the 1350s,[24] but the long-term effects of the Black Death seem to have been relatively limited: more tenants and houses were recorded on the Corbets' quarter in the late 14th century than in 1279, and of four tofts mentioned in 1385, all were let and two apparently had houses on them by 1394. Most of the 13th-century half yardlands remained identifiable, and at least one was held by the same family as in 1279.[25] By the later 14th century many labour services had been commuted,[26] and in 1385, as in the 16th century, most half-yardlanders on the Corbets' quarter owed only heriot, suit of court, and 10s. rent; light harvest services remained for a mill, a cottage, and the free yardland, by then divided into two, but had been commuted by the 1440s.[27] Entry fines in the 15th century were generally low, sometimes less than the annual rent, and in 1445 a fine was waived on account of the tenant's poverty.[28]

The four demesne farms totalled possibly 100 a. each in the 15th century including closes and meadow,[29] but there seems to have been little amalgamation of other holdings before the 16th century. No tenant held more than half a yardland of the Corbets' quarter in the 1480s, and few held a yardland in 1569, though some may have held of other lords or owned freehold.[30] On Hardwick and Brighthampton manor two Brighthampton copyholders occupied 2 and 1¼ yardlands respectively by the later 16th century, while 6 occupied yardlands and 3 occupied half yardlands.[31] Some late-medieval freeholders may have owned land elsewhere or derived income from commerce. The resident Marshalls, recorded from the 13th century, had property and commercial links in Woodstock,[32] while Thomas Stephens (fl. 1416), licensed to have an oratory in his house in Standlake, owned lands in Northmoor and probably elsewhere,[33] and two other 15th-century residents called

9 P.R.O., C 134/29, no. 11; C 139/12, no. 36.
10 *Pipe R.* 1195 (P.R.S. N.S. vi), 60; *Cal. Pat.* 1343–5, 181, 398.
11 Following two paras. based on *Bampton Hund. R.* 63–4, 66–71; the survey omitted Wallingford priory's estate and Cold Norton priory's mill.
12 Excluding the miller and a half-yardlander entered in error.
13 Excluding Robert of Yelford's holding outside the parish and the tenant of Gaunt Mill.
14 P.R.O., C 132/6, no. 11; that only 6 half-yardlanders were listed in 1279 does not fully account for the discrepancy.
15 P.R.O., C 133/108, no. 6.
16 *Bampton Hund. R.* 63.
17 P.R.O., C 133/72, no. 6; ibid. C 134/29, no. 11.
18 Ibid. C 133/108, no. 6; *Bampton Hund. R.* 64, 67–71.
19 *Bampton Hund. R.* 66–70; cf. Magd. Coll. Mun., EP 85/30, s.v. Freeman.
20 P.R.O., SC 6/1146/15.
21 Ibid. E 179/161/8–10; cf. Glasscock, *Subsidy 1334*, 237.

22 Cf. *Oxon. Local Hist.* ii (2), 42–6; *Bampton Hund. R.* 63–4, 66–71.
23 *Oxon. Local Hist.* ii (2), 42–6; P.R.O., C 133/108, no. 6; C 135/165, no. 31.
24 Lincs. R.O., episc. reg. ix, ff. 263v.–264; New Coll. Arch., 9162–3.
25 Magd. Coll. Mun., EP 85/30, EP 123/16, s.v. Thos. Fisher, John Bush, John Walker; cf. *Bampton Hund. R.* 68–9.
26 P.R.O., C 135/165, no. 31; ibid. C 139/12, no. 36; ibid. SC 6/961/19; New Coll. Arch., 9161–2.
27 Magd. Coll. Mun., EP 14/22, EP 31/6, EP 85/30, EP 123/16.
28 Ibid. EP 85/31, EP 85/41.
29 Ibid. EP 31/10.
30 Ibid. EP 31/6, EP 31/10, EP 85/39, EP 123/16.
31 St. John's Coll. Mun., XVII.14.
32 *Bampton Hund. R.* 67; below, this section (trade and ind.).
33 *Cat. Anct. D.* i, C 183, C 593; *Reg. Repingdon*, i (L.R.S. lvii), 64; ii (L.R.S. lviii), 249.

themselves gentlemen.[34] By the early 16th century resident families such as the Yates, Gaunts, and Tyrlings had assembled notable estates within the parish.[35]

Some rents were reduced before the later 15th century when a few holdings remained unlet, and on the Corbets' quarter fewer tenants were recorded than earlier.[36] Arrears on the same quarter rose from c. 23s. in 1487–8 to over £18 in 1506–7, reducing thereafter.[37] During the 16th century Standlake seems nevertheless to have been among the more prosperous rural settlements in the area: 32 inhabitants paid a total of £4 14s. 10d. to the first subsidy of 1524, and 36 payed £2 14s. 6d. in 1542, while in Brighthampton 23 inhabitants paid £1 16s. in 1524 and 41 paid £1 6s. 6½d. in 1542.[38] Among freeholders and gentry, John Yate was assessed in 1524 on goods worth £40, Richard Harcourt on £16, Edward or Edmund Yate and Alice Gaunt on over £13 each, and John Fettiplace on £10;[39] moderately prosperous yeomen included John Bennett (d. 1551) of Brighthampton, assessed in 1524 on goods worth £10, who held 1 or 2 yardlands of Hardwick and Brighthampton manor and probably one of Standlake's demesne farms, and at his death left 10 oxen and over 80 sheep.[40] Richard Stone (d. 1577), who paid the second highest assessment in 1576, held c. 3 leasehold yardlands.[41] Three quarters of the taxpayers of 1524 were nevertheless assessed on less than £4 and almost a quarter on only 20s., while three, including a servant, were assessed on wages.

During the later 16th century and the 17th both villages remained predominantly agricultural communities with some moderately prosperous farmers, over half those for whom inventories survive leaving personalty of between £10 and £59, and only a few, c. 15 per cent in Standlake and 9 per cent in Brighthampton, leaving over £100.[42] Exceptionally, Nicholas Dixon (d. 1627) of Standlake and John Tanner (d. 1647) of Brighthampton left goods worth over £300, chiefly furnishings, money owed, and agricultural items.[43] A labourer left personalty of only 35s.,[44] and in the early 17th century inhabitants accused landlords of creating a 'multitude' of poor by deliberately crowding two or more families into single dwellings, alleging that as a result corn, poultry, and fuel could no longer be left unattended overnight.[45] In the 1660s most householders were taxed on between 1 and 3 hearths, the chief exceptions being Cokethorpe House (14 hearths), Gaunt House (8 hearths), and the rectory house (7 hearths); 12 inhabitants from the two settlements were exonerated through poverty in 1665.[46]

A two-course rotation was followed in 1361 when half of one demesne was sown and half lay fallow,[47] but in 1636 there was a four-course rotation of (1) wheat, maslin, or rye, (2) pulse, (3) barley, and (4) fallow, and in 1644 an 8-a. holding included 2 a. 'in every field'.[48] A valuation made about that time allowed for either a three- or a four-course rotation.[49] The chief crops were then wheat and barley, followed by pulses; rye, hops, hemp, maslin, dill, and oats were mentioned occasionally,[50] and an illegal tobacco crop of c. 26 a. was destroyed in the late 17th century.[51] Several testators left apples and other fruit, and some left malt, among them a yeoman who in 1627 left 36 qr. worth £30.[52] Most owned one or more cows and horses and a few pigs, though few had a full yoke of oxen;[53] a prosperous yeoman in 1676 was owed £40 from several inhabitants for corn, malt, money lent, and 'work done' with his team of horses, which he presumably hired out.[54] Flocks were generally small, though a Standlake farmer left 130 sheep and lambs in 1632, and another at Brighthampton left 103 in 1707.[55] Most testators seem to have had sufficient hay, one in 1690 leaving hay worth £29, his most valuable single item.[56] Several inhabitants owned poultry,[57] a few kept bees, and cheese and cheese-making equipment were mentioned frequently.

A tenant of Gaunt House farm and of former demesne held at least 200 a. c. 1650,[58] and by the later 18th century a few farmers seem to have occupied comparable estates combining freeholds, leaseholds, and copyholds, often under several owners. Six farmers in 1785, among them the tenants of Malthouse, Lincoln, and probably Breach farms, paid land tax of between £10 and over £37,[59] and by 1844 at least 7 farms exceeded 100 a., among them the Standlake Manor House

34 *Cat. Anct. D.* ii, C 1978; vi, C 5559; *Cal. Fine R.* 1430–7, 248–9; 1445–52, 59; *Cal. Pat.* 1446–52, 395.
35 Magd. Coll. Mun., EP 15/10, EP 31/3; above, other estates.
36 Magd. Coll. Mun., EP 14/23, EP 15/10, EP 31/10, EP 85/39; P.R.O., SC 2/209/57.
37 Magd. Coll. Mun., EP 15/2, EP 15/9, EP 88/16, EP 13/18–19.
38 P.R.O., E 179/161/172, E 179/162/234; Brighthampton totals include Brittenton.
39 Cf. *Oxon. Visit.* 135–6; *Cat. Anct. D.* v, A 13007; Magd. Coll. Mun., EP 31/3; O.R.O., MS. Wills Oxon. 179, ff. 38, 183 and v.; above, other estates.
40 P.R.O., E 179/161/172; St. John's Coll. Mun., XVII.14; Magd. Coll. Mun., EP 31/4; O.R.O., MS. Wills Oxon. 180, ff. 88v.–89.
41 P.R.O., E 179/162/341; Linc. Coll. Mun., D/STA/30; Magd. Coll. Mun., EP 31/6; O.R.O., MS. Wills Oxon. 185, f. 530 and v.
42 O.R.O., MSS. Wills Oxon., Standlake and Brighthampton inventories, indexed in D. M. Barratt, *Oxon. Probate Records 1516–1732* (British Record Soc. xciii–xciv).
43 O.R.O., MSS. Wills Oxon. 17/4/31, 66/2/59.
44 Ibid. 44/2/24.

45 Bodl. MS. Top. Oxon. c 118, f. 2.
46 P.R.O., E 179/255/4, pt. i, ff. 23, 27, apparently omitting the part of Brighthampton in Bampton parish; *Hearth Tax Oxon.* 213, 228–9.
47 P.R.O., C 135/165, no. 31.
48 Magd. Coll. Mun., ct. bk. 37, p. 30; O.R.O., MS. Wills Oxon. 115/4/23.
49 Wadham Coll. Mun., 4/59.
50 O.R.O., MSS. Wills Oxon., Standlake and Brighthampton wills and inventories, on which rest of para. based.
51 J. Kibble, *Hist. Notes on Wychwood* (priv. print. 1928), 115.
52 O.R.O., MS. Wills Oxon. 17/4/31.
53 e.g. ibid. 184, f. 204v.; ibid. 50/4/32, 51/4/25.
54 Ibid. 34/1/8.
55 Ibid. 51/2/31, 67/3/34; cf. ibid. 34/1/8, 81/3/2.
56 Ibid. 295/1/85.
57 For a poulterer, O.R.O., Coz. II/1.
58 Ch. Ch. Arch., Standlake A 35, A 41–2; Magd. Coll. Mun., LE/55, lease 1649; cf. P.R.O., E 179/255/4, pt. i, f. 23.
59 O.R.O., QSD L.260–1; for their fms., ibid. MS. Wills Oxon. 119/3/34; ibid. Pickford I/ii/2; St. John's Coll. Mun., XVII.45; Magd. Coll. Mun., CP 3/16, ff. 180–5, 189–94; ibid. ES/6/2, p. 1; Linc. Coll. Mun., Z/STA/5, L/STA/93.

estate (175 a.) and an amalgamation of 229 a. which included Lincoln farm and former demesne. Many inhabitants farmed 30 a. or less, however, and in 1849 two farms of *c.* 53 a. and 49 a. were combined for a tenant's benefit since alone they were 'not tenable ... to support a team'.[60] Many cottagers, some of them freeholders, had little or no land; a few were tradesmen, though most in the early 19th century were agricultural labourers, by far the largest occupational group. Others dependent on agriculture in 1841 included 4 cattle- or corn dealers, 4 gardeners, a calfman, and a castrator.[61]

Gaunt House farm was let at rack rent by the early 17th century.[62] On other college estates long leases at the old quitrents, often including heriot, persisted until inclosure,[63] and although under the Corn Rent Act of 1576[64] a third of the rent was demanded in wheat and malt or their cash equivalents and a part sometimes in poultry, producing substantial increments by the 19th century, rents nevertheless remained well below the farms' true values.[65] Entry fines, in contrast, were sometimes heavy.[66] On the manors copyholds survived inclosure, though by then leasehold was predominant[67] and several Hardwick manor copyholders sublet their farms.[68] Short leases at rack rent became usual in the later 19th century.[69]

Four-course rotation persisted probably in the mid 19th century, when the quarters were perhaps represented by an otherwise unrecorded division of the arable among North, South, and Rickland fields, and 'Brighthampton land'.[70] Inclosure, considered in the 17th century, *c.* 1805, and in 1836,[71] was eventually carried out in Standlake, Brighthampton, and Hardwick between 1848 and 1853, when the award was sealed.[72] Magdalen College and its tenants received *c.* 530 a. in Standlake, and St. John's College and its tenants *c.* 670 a. in Standlake and Brighthampton; the colleges received a further 22 a. and 14 a. respectively for manorial rights. Lincoln College received *c.* 79 a., Brasenose College 55 a., and Christ Church 15 a. for its open-field land, and awards were made to the rector for glebe (25 a.), to the poor of Standlake, Brighthampton, Hardwick, and Northmoor (*c.* 17 a. in all), and to the parish clerk. Another 41 freeholders received allotments ranging from 197 a. for the Standlake Manor estate to less than an acre. A further 569 a. were awarded in Hardwick, whose boundaries were redrawn, and other boundary adjustments necessitated small awards to proprietors in neighbouring parishes.

In 1861 there were 12 farmers with over 100 a., and two, at Lincoln Farm and Standlake Manor, with over 200 a.[73] Most farms were worked from earlier homesteads, though the newly built Westfield Farm had its own land perhaps by 1876.[74] During the 1860s and 1870s John Perry (d. 1895), one of a local family, accumulated several freeholds and leaseholds, among them Yew Tree farm where he eventually lived, Glebe farm, and the Standlake Manor estate, and by 1881 farmed 650 a. directly and employed 21 labourers and 6 boys. The estate was broken up after his death,[75] and though Percival Pinnock and D. C. Hosier each held *c.* 300 a. in the 1880s, most farms were under 200 a.[76] A few included large, consolidated blocks of land, but others were more scattered, and in 1917 the distance of Lincoln farm's lands from the village was said to undermine its efficiency.[77]

In 1877 the parish was *c.* 60 per cent arable and 25 per cent pasture,[78] but the balance on individual farms varied, and in the 1880s some were predominantly pastoral.[79] Livestock included sheep, dairy cattle, and pigs, and inhabitants in 1881 included several cattle- and pig dealers and at least two shepherds.[80] By then some meadows in the east of the parish had been converted to arable,[81] and free-working loams elsewhere were judged capable of producing heavy crops of corn and roots; stiffer clays in the north were well adapted for wheat and beans, drainage problems notwithstanding, though in 1917 gravelly soils on Lincoln farm were thought unlikely to produce 'more than ordinary crops in a good season'.[82] The chief markets, as earlier,

60 O.R.O., Standlake tithe award (1844); ibid. Brighthampton tithe award; ibid. incl. award; B.N.C. Mun., Room B ser., 42, T. S. Hellier to B.N.C. 30 Nov. 1849.
61 O.R.O., Standlake tithe award (1844); P.R.O., HO 107/872.
62 Ch. Ch. Arch., Standlake A 41–2; ibid. MS. Estates 80, f. 35v.–36v.
63 B.N.C. Mun., Standlake, Brighthampton, and Cokethorpe leases; Linc. Coll. Mun., Standlake leases, listed in 'Linc. Coll. Archive', vol. 2, pt. ii, pp. 391–6 (copy in Linc. Coll. Library); Magd. Coll. Mun., LE/55–6; O.R.O., Mor. XLIII/iv/1.
64 Act for the Maintenance of Colleges, 18 Eliz. I, c. 6.
65 e.g. Linc. Coll. Mun., rental 1821–57; ibid. bursar's day bk. 1827; cf. ibid. Z/STA/7.
66 V. Green, *Commonwealth of Linc. Coll.* 197 n., 388; cf. Linc. Coll. Mun., L/STA/93.
67 Magd. Coll. Mun., ct. bk. 82, *passim*; St. John's Coll. Mun., XI.22, *passim*; ibid. EST. III.x.7, pp. 26–35; O.R.O., incl. award.
68 O.R.O., Brighthampton tithe award; cf. B.N.C. Mun., Room B ser., 42, T. S. Hellier to B.N.C. 30 Nov. 1849.
69 e.g. Magd. Coll. Mun., LE/56; Linc. Coll. Mun., *Reg. Estates 1898*, p. 5.
70 Magd. Coll. Mun., D-Y 447; cf. O.R.O., incl. award.
71 St. John's Coll. Mun., XVII.18 (4); ibid. ADMIN. I. A.9; O.R.O., MS. Oxf. Dioc. d 569, f. 99; Linc. Coll. Mun., C/STA/1.
72 Second Annual Incl. Act, 11 & 12 Vic. c. 109; O.R.O.,

incl. award.
73 P.R.O., RG 9/905; cf. O.R.O., Brighthampton tithe award (1852); ibid. Standlake tithe award (1887).
74 O.S. Map, 1/2,500, Oxon. XXXVIII. 1 (1876 edn.); *Sale Cat., Manor and Yew Tree Fms.* (1896), lot 5: copy in Bodl. G.A. Oxon. b 92 (1); above, intro.
75 Magd. Coll. Mun., modern deeds box 98, *Sale Cat., Manor and Yew Tree Fms.* (1896); ibid. conveyance 4 Nov. 1890; P.R.O., RG 11/1514; Bodl. MS. Top. Oxon. c 768/1, nos. 11, 14, 22, 35.
76 P.R.O., RG 11/1514; O.R.O., Standlake tithe award (1887).
77 O.R.O., Brighthampton tithe award; ibid. Standlake tithe award (1887); Linc. Coll. Mun., C/STA/6, valuation 1917.
78 *O.S. Area Bk.* (1877); 10 per cent was woodland and ornamental parkland.
79 O.R.O., Standlake tithe award (1887); Magd. Coll. Mun., modern deeds, box 98, *Sale Cat., Manor and Yew Tree Fms.* (1896); ibid. conveyance of Eagle fm. 2 Oct. 1899.
80 *Sale Cat., Manor and Yew Tree Fms.* (1896); P.R.O., RG 11/1514; cf. *Oxf. Chron.* 24 Apr. 1852, 25 Dec. 1852, 22 Oct. 1853.
81 O.R.O., Standlake tithe award (1887).
82 *Sale Cat., Manor and Yew Tree Fms.* (1896); St. John's Coll. Mun., XVII.56; Linc. Coll. Mun., C/STA/6, valuation 1917; cf. Magd. Coll. Estates Bursary, survs. 1913–23, pp. 54–5, 57–8, 79.

were Witney and to a lesser extent Abingdon and Oxford; very little produce was then taken to Great Faringdon.[83]

Agricultural depression affected the parish during the 1870s and 1880s, allegedly halving land values and prompting conversion of some poorer land to pasture.[84] The subtenant on Brasenose College's principal farm, granted a rent reduction in 1881, surrendered his lease *c.* 1882, leaving the buildings in disrepair,[85] and some larger farmers, including members of the long-established Pinnock family, were apparently bankrupted.[86] Most larger farmers nevertheless survived into the 1890s or beyond,[87] despite wrangles over 'exorbitant' rents during the 1880s.[88] A branch of the National Agricultural Labourers' Union existed in Standlake by 1873–4,[89] and in 1891 the Fabians Sidney Webb and William Hines addressed a meeting of farm labourers at the Black Horse.[90] In 1905 the tenant of Lincoln farm sought further rent reductions, citing 'ruinous' rain and floods in 1903 which had effectively lost him two years' crops; the college met some of his requests,[91] and he continued as tenant.[92] There was no unemployment in the parish in 1908.[93]

Flooding remained a problem despite expensive new watercourses constructed at inclosure.[94] Landowners carried out some piecemeal drainage,[95] and in 1866 a small part of Standlake adjoining the river Windrush was incorporated into the Northmoor and Stanton Harcourt drainage district, established under the Land Drainage Act of 1861.[96] Immediate works included embankments, new cuts, and cleaning of the river, which near Gaunt Mill was particularly neglected. Despite the scheme's success, however,[97] poor drainage elsewhere in the parish prompted both Magdalen and St. John's Colleges to sell their estates in the early 20th century.[98] In 1917 pasture in the former common could not be ploughed up for the war effort because it flooded in winter.[99]

By 1914 permanent pasture in the parish had increased to 49 per cent. Sheep, cattle, pigs, and horses were kept in average numbers for the area, though sheep farming was declining as elsewhere. The chief crops were wheat (26 per cent) and barley (18 per cent), followed by oats (11 per cent), swedes and turnips (10 per cent), mangolds (4 per cent), and a few potatoes (0.3 per cent).[1] Most farms remained mixed, and a few were predominantly pastoral: Old Manor farm (344 a.) in Brighthampton, a dairy and stock holding producing high-quality milk, was *c.* 70 per cent under grass in 1924, much of it on former arable north-west of the hamlet, and its buildings included pigstyes and a cowhouse for 68 head of cattle.[2] Poultry-raising was important, notably at Church Farm and Church Mill.[3] In 1939 there were 6 farms over 150 a. and at least 5 smaller ones; in 1978 there were 5 principal and 2 smaller farms, all mixed, besides a factory poultry farm and a pig farm. Store cattle had by then replaced sheep and dairy cattle, and it was estimated that no more than 10 per cent of pasture ploughed up during wartime had been returned to grass.[4]

MARKET AND FAIR. A Friday market and an annual fair on the eve, feast, and morrow of St. Giles (31 August–2 September) were granted to Eve de Grey in 1230.[5] Of Eve's coheirs only the Mauduits were expressly said to have income from the market and fair in 1279, but late-medieval owners of the Corbets' quarter of the manor had rents from market stalls, and presumably the tolls were among the franchises shared by all four lords.[6] The fair, held on only two days by 1279,[7] may have lapsed soon after, and though Wednesday and Thursday markets at Bampton and Witney may initially have attracted trade to the area, Standlake's market seems to have suffered from local competition:[8] in 1303 the Mauduits' income from tolls was estimated at only 20d.,[9] in 1317 demesne produce from nearby Chimney (in Bampton) was to be sold at Oxford,[10] and in 1370–1, when

83   St. John's Coll. Mun., XVII.52; cf. Magd, Coll. Mun., EP 146/6, deposition of J. Stone; O.R.O., P4/2/MS 1/5, ff. 7–9; ibid. Cal. Q.S. iii, p. 463; Oxf. Jnl. Synopsis, 19 Nov. 1774, 22 Sept. 1776.

84   Magd. Coll. Estates Bursary, survs. 1883–91, p. 293; 1892–1912, p. 150.

85   B.N.C. Mun., Room B ser., 42, T. S. Hellier to B.N.C. 4 May 1881, 16 Jan., 14 Mar. 1883.

86   St. John's Coll. Mun., EST. I. L.104, note of fm. bldg. 30 June 1885; Magd. Coll. Estates Bursary, survs. 1883–91, p. 364; Bodl. MS. Top. Oxon. c 768/1, nos. 3, 21, 26a.

87   P.R.O., RG 11/1514; O.R.O., Standlake tithe award (1887); Kelly's Dir. Oxon. (1883 and later edns.).

88   Linc. Coll. Mun., bursars' corresp., letters *re* estates 1880–1926, ff. 95, 125; B.N.C. Mun., Room B ser., 42, J. Giles to B.N.C. 9 Dec., 14 Dec. 1887.

89   *Agric. Trade Unionism in Oxon.* (O.R.S. xlviii), 23.

90   Bodl. G.A. Oxon. c 317/13, poster for meeting 9 Nov. 1891.

91   Linc. Coll. Mun., C/STA/6, letter 23 Jan. 1905; ibid. bursars' corresp., letters *re* estates 1880–1926, ff. 181, 193, 197.

92   Bodl. MS. Top. Oxon. c 768/1, no. 31.

93   O.R.O., P4/1/MS 3/4, f. 43T.

94   Ibid. incl. award; B.N.C. Mun., Room B ser., 42, T. S. Hellier to B.N.C. 23 Aug. 1850; Magd. Coll. Estates Bursary, survs. 1883–91, pp. 99–100; cf. below, local govt.

95   e.g. St. John's Coll. Mun., XVII.56; Magd. Coll. Estates Bursary, survs. 1883–91, p. 293.

96   Land Drainage Supplemental Act, 1866, Number 2,

29 & 30 Vic. c. 80.

97   B.N.C. Mun., 2nd ser., 467, rep. to Northmoor Drainage Board 26 Apr. 1867; *Jnl. Royal Agric. Soc.* 2nd ser. vi (1870), 367–76; for mins. 1866–1936, Berks. R.O., D/TC 184–5.

98   Magd. Coll. Estates Bursary, survs. 1913–23, pp. 43, 54–5, 57–8, 61–2, 70–1, 79; St. John's Coll. Mun., XVII.70.

99   B.N.C. Mun., Room B ser., 43, War Agric. Cttee. enquiry 25 July 1917.

1   Orr, *Oxon. Agric.* statistical plates.

2   *Sale Cat., Brighthampton Manor Estate* (1924): copy in Bodl. G.A. Oxon. c 224 (16); cf. *Sale Cat., Manor Fm.* (1935), *Sale Cat., Eagle and Church Fms.* (1941): copies in C.O.S.; Magd. Coll. Estates Bursary, Ledger P, pp. 381–5, 392–3, 416–17; Linc. Coll. Mun., C/STA/6, valuation 1917.

3   Bodl. G.A. Oxon. c 317/13, advertisement for sale of 'Bullock's' [Church Fm.] 19 May 1904; Kelly's Dir. Oxon. (1915 and later edns.).

4   Kelly's Dir. Oxon. (1939); J. Goadby, *1228 and All That* (priv. print. 1978), 67–8: copy in C.O.S.; cf. O.R.O., P2/2/MS 11/1, f. 5.

5   *Cal. Chart. R. 1226–57*, 121; for the market place, above, intro.

6   *Bampton Hund. R.* 66–70; below.

7   *Bampton Hund. R.* 66.

8   Above, Bampton: Bampton and Weald, econ. hist. (markets and fairs); cf. *Midland Hist.* xii (1987), 14–25. Witney is reserved for treatment in a later vol.

9   P.R.O., C 133/108, no. 6.

10   D. & C. Exeter, MS. 2931.

the Mauduits' tolls were leased, a 4*d.* rent reduction was recorded for the half year.[11] On the Corbets' manor rent of 2*s.* for market stalls was paid in 1394 and the 1440s, but the stalls were unlet in 1461, and some or all of them for several years in the early 1480s, when the rent may have been only 10*d.* a year.[12] An attempt to revive the market was made *c.* 1488–9 when 20*d.* was allowed towards repair of stalls and workshops,[13] but in 1500 a stall remained unlet at an annual rent of 20*d.*,[14] and market income was not mentioned later.

The existence of a market and fair may account for early 14th-century surnames such as Merchant, Chapman, and Iremonger,[15] but there is no evidence for marketing of goods other than agricultural produce. A man from Sutton in Stanton Harcourt parish took geese to sell at Standlake market in 1389,[16] and in 1461 market stalls were said to be for sale of victuals.[17]

A 'place formerly called the pig market' near Standlake church was mentioned in 1839,[18] but no references to an institutionalized market in modern times have been found.

TRADE AND INDUSTRY. Woollen textile manufacture, dependent perhaps on Witney's wool and cloth trade and later on its blanket industry, was mentioned from the 13th century to the early 18th.[19] At least two fulling mills existed by the early 13th century,[20] and in the late 13th and early 14th the surnames Fuller, Weaver, and Webber, borne by villeins, cottagers, and small freeholders, were recorded frequently.[21] A chaloner was mentioned in 1348,[22] and members of the Trilling family, lessees of Gaunt Mill in the late 14th century, were fullers in the mid 15th.[23] In 1394 four tenants, of whom three were named Fuller, paid small rents for four racks on the lord's waste, presumably at Rack End, though they themselves seem not to have held local fulling mills.[24] The racks were unlet in 1461,[25] but in the 16th century and later tenants of Gaunt Mill and an adjacent fulling mill owed 4*d.* a year for the right of tentering on the lord's land,[26] and two clothworkers in the early 17th

century left fullers' racks in the common.[27] From the 16th century the most frequently recorded textile workers were broad- and narrow weavers,[28] of whom some were moderately prosperous and, since they owned more than one loom, perhaps employed assistants.[29] Several shearmen were recorded from the mid 15th century to the mid 17th,[30] and in 1756 a dyer with an apprentice;[31] a tilt-weaver was noted in 1743 and a clothworker in 1751,[32] but by then the industry was in decline, and no textile workers were recorded in the 19th century. The remaining fulling mill had closed by 1770.[33]

William Marshall of Standlake, gentleman, who owned property fronting the market place in New Woodstock, in 1469 apprenticed his son to a leading Woodstock mercer to learn the trades of mercer, wax chandler, and cap maker,[34] and some other leading 15th-century families may have had commercial interests.[35] Cuthbert Temple (d. by 1558) of Standlake, who in the 1550s bought much of Standlake manor as an investment, was a clothier with strong Witney connexions and may have lived at Gaunt House.[36] Henry Wheeler (d. 1721), also a clothier, had a 'mansion and dwelling house' in Standlake.[37] Mercers, recorded from the 16th century to the early 18th, included Arthur Yate (d. 1633), whose personalty of nearly £190 clear was chiefly in debts and obligations, and Joseph Huckwell, lessee in 1709 of Brasenose College's fulling mill.[38]

Other medieval surnames included Smith, Baker, Taylor, and Turner,[39] and the usual rural crafts and trades were recorded later, among them blacksmiths, wheelwrights, carpenters, masons, coopers, and shoemakers.[40] A Standlake corviser in 1433 owed debts in Coventry and in Stratford-on-Avon.[41] Butchers, recorded from the 15th century,[42] included some moderately prosperous men by local standards, one in 1567 owning a house in Woodstock, and another in 1684 leaving personalty of nearly £75 including money and book debts.[43] Glaziers were recorded in 1604 and 1720, and a mason in 1756.[44] There

11 P.R.O., SC 6/961/19.
12 Magd. Coll. Mun., EP 14/22, EP 14/23, EP 85/39, EP 123/16.
13 Ibid. EP 15/12.
14 Ibid. EP 15/9, EP 15/23.
15 P.R.O., E 179/161/8–10; *Cat. Anct. D.* vi, C 5120.
16 P.R.O., JUST 2/136.
17 Magd. Coll. Mun., EP 85/39, mentioning *stall' vitellar'*.
18 O.R.O., Mor. XLIII/ii/5–6; cf. ibid. P4/1/MS 3/4, f. 14Q.
19 Cf. *V.C.H. Oxon.* iv. 40. Witney is reserved for treatment in a later volume.
20 Below, this section (mills).
21 P.R.O., E 179/161/8–10; *Bampton Hund. R.* 64, 67–8.
22 *Cal. Pat.* 1348–50, 241.
23 Magd. Coll. Mun., EP 14/22, EP 85/30; *Cat. Anct. D.* i, C 1125.
24 Magd. Coll. Mun., EP 123/16; for tenants of fulling mills, ibid.; B.N.C. Mun., Standlake 5.
25 Magd. Coll. Mun., EP 85/39.
26 Ibid. EP 18/1, EP 31/6, EP 86/8.
27 O.R.O., MSS. Wills Oxon. 25/4/23, 26/1/55; cf. *Witney Ct. Bks.* 69.
28 e.g. O.R.O., MSS. Wills Oxon., indexed in D. M. Barratt, *Oxon. Probate Recs.* (Brit. Rec. Soc. xciii–xciv); ibid. Cal. Q. Sess., *passim*.
29 e.g. *Protestation Rtns. and Tax Assess.* 27, s.v. Gerring;

30 O.R.O., MSS. Wills Oxon. 26/1/55, 66/3/5, 87/4/10; ibid. 184, ff. 56v.–57; P.R.O., E 179/162/320, s.v. Quelch.
30 O.R.O., MS. Wills Oxon. 17/2/26; B.N.C. Mun., Standlake 27, 37; *Cat. Anct. D.* ii, C 1978.
31 Oxf. Jnl. Synopsis, 11 July 1756.
32 O.R.O., MSS. d.d. Par. Bampton c 16, nos. 21, 23–4.
33 Below, this section (mills).
34 *Cat. Anct. D.* i, C 812, C 1127, C 1129; vi, C 7450; *Cal. Close,* 1447–54, 43, 49; *V.C.H. Oxon.* xii. 348–9, 360.
35 Cf. above, this section (agric.).
36 *Witney Ct. Bks.* lxii and n., lxxxi; P.R.O., PROB 11/51, f. 27v.; above, manors. For the fam., cf. Magd. Coll. Mun, EP 85/31; *Cat. Anct. D.* ii, C 2680.
37 O.R.O., MS. Wills Oxon. 208, f. 314 and v.; cf. ibid. QS/1714 Epiph./42–8.
38 Ch. Ch. Arch., Standlake B 7; O.R.O., MS. Wills Oxon. 159/4/18; cf. ibid. MS. Wills Oxon. 184, f. 355 and v.; ibid. Costar II/i/1.
39 *Bampton Hund. R.* 69; *Pipe R.* 1176 (P.R.S. xxv), 33; P.R.O., E 179/161/8–10.
40 O.R.O., MSS. Wills Oxon., index s.v. Standlake.
41 *Cal. Pat.* 1429–36, 239.
42 e.g. *Cat. Anct. D.* i, C 1537; *Witney Ct. Bks.* 54.
43 O.R.O., MS. Wills Oxon. 184, f. 269v.; ibid. 34/2/35.
44 *Witney Ct. Bks.* 183; O.R.O., MS. Wills Oxon. 157/1/26; ibid. Cal. Q.S. iii, p. 509.

were higglers and badgers from the 17th century to the early 19th, some of whom evidently frequented Oxford market.[45] A gunmaker lived in Standlake in the early 18th century,[46] and in the mid 18th the clockmaker John Nethercott (d. 1763).[47]

Small-scale gloving and light leather working was recorded in the 16th and 17th centuries.[48] Several members of the Hewes or Calcott family, chiefly farmers and millers and some of them prosperous, called themselves glovers,[49] and fellmongers were mentioned in 1686 and 1719.[50] Collarmakers were noted in 1622 and 1694 and a currier in 1701.[51]

A few maltsters included Joseph Huckwell (d. 1682) of Standlake, whose personalty of £97 included large debts owed him in Oxford,[52] and George Grafton (d. 1770), lessee of the Chequers, who malted for farmers in Cote and possibly Shifford from the 1740s to 1760s.[53] In 1773 either his or another malthouse in Standlake was able to produce up to 30 qr. a week.[54] There was a malthouse at Malthouse Farm, Brighthampton, by 1740 when George Brown (d. 1761) obtained the copyhold, and both he and his son Thomas (d. 1799) called themselves maltsters as well as being substantial farmers.[55] Before 1855 a later Thomas Brown allowed part of the malthouse to fall down, and the building was demolished soon after.[56]

In 1811 only 41 families out of 146 were employed in trade, craft, or manufacture,[57] and many trades remained agriculturally based. In 1841 there were 3 smiths, 2 wheelwrights, 2 millwrights, and a saddler, besides several carpenters, shoemakers, and tailors, a grocer, 2 butchers, 2 bakers, 3 shopkeepers, and a cooper. At least 30 women were employed as domestic servants, and throughout the century a few worked as laundresses, dressmakers, or seamstresses.[58] In the late 19th century and early 20th several of the Cantwell family were stonemasons and builders.[59]

There was a cycle maker in 1907 and a wireless repairer in 1924, and a motor repair garage was opened on Abingdon road in 1927. Traditional crafts and trades surviving in 1939 included those of blacksmith, wheelwright, thatcher, baker and butcher.[60] Most had gone by the 1970s, when many inhabitants were newcomers employed in Witney, Oxford, or elsewhere.[61] In 1993 there was a general store and post office, besides two antiques shops, the motor garage, an engineering and electrical company, and a computer software firm. A brick factory on Witney road, opened in 1949, continued possibly into the 1960s,[62] and in 1994 there was a large industrial estate on the site which accommodated several businesses.

MILLS AND FISHERIES. In 1086 a mill rendering 11s. a year was recorded on Anketil de Grey's estate, probably the later Standlake manor.[63] Three water mills were attached to the manor in the early 13th century, of which one, a fulling mill at Rack End on the westernmost channel of the river Windrush, was granted to Cold Norton priory by Eve de Grey between 1228 and 1246.[64] The priory was seized by the Crown in 1496, and the mill passed with its possessions in 1507 to the free chapel of St. Stephen in Westminster Palace, c. 1512 to William Smith, bishop of Lincoln, and in 1513 to Brasenose College, Oxford,[65] which from the late 17th century to the 19th leased it to Christ Church, Oxford, owner of nearby Gaunt House.[66] In 1405 there was an inner and an outer mill held by different tenants,[67] but by the 16th century there was one mill only.[68] Early tenants included probably John the fuller in the mid 13th century, and in 1651 a Witney clothier.[69] In 1685 the lessee agreed to carry out repairs,[70] and the fulling mill was still so described in 1709 and 1764; by 1770, however, it had apparently ceased to function.[71] By 1849 it had 'long been in ruins',[72] and it was demolished soon after.[73]

The two other 13th-century mills were divided among the quarters of Standlake manor at its partition c. 1246, but were each held by single tenants presumably by agreement. Gaunt Mill was called the new mills in the earlier 13th century, when it was a double corn and fulling mill.[74] Payments

45 Bodl. MS. Top. Oxon. c 118, ff. 4v., 6v.; O.R.O., MSS. Wills Oxon. 5/4/32, 67/4/17; P.R.O., HO 107/872; Oxf. Jnl. Synopsis, 19 Nov. 1774.
46 Ch. Ch. Arch., Standlake C 6–14.
47 Oxon. Clockmakers (Banbury Hist. Soc. iv), 131; Oxf. Jnl. Synopsis, 27 Apr. 1763; C.O.S., par. reg. transcripts.
48 Witney Ct. Bks. 79; O.R.O., MS. Wills Oxon. 183, f. 183v.; ibid. 3/2/58; Linc. Coll. Mun., D/STA/11–12.
49 O.R.O., MS. Wills Oxon. 181, ff. 212v.–213; ibid. 132/1/28, 296/3/11; cf. P.R.O., E 179/162/234; below, this section (mills).
50 O.R.O., MS. Wills Oxon. 34/3/11; ibid. Cal. Q.S. i, f. 199.
51 Ibid. MSS. Wills Oxon. 17/4/2, 165/3/33; ibid. Cal. Q.S. i, f. 56.
52 Ibid. MS. Wills Oxon. 167/2/38.
53 Linc. Coll. Mun., L/STA/84; Bodl. MS. Top. Oxon. e 632, f. 15 and v.; ibid. MS. d.d. Harcourt c 133/3, p. 19; Oxf. Jnl. 20 Oct. 1770.
54 Oxf. Jnl. 26 June 1773.
55 St. John's Coll. Mun., ADMIN. I. A.7, pp. 110, 411; ibid. XVII.45; O.R.O., MSS. Wills Oxon. 118/2/52, 119/3/34.
56 St. John's Coll. Mun., XI.22, pp. 66, 73; Archaeologia, xxxvii. 391; cf. C.O.S., PRN 13124.
57 Census, 1811, including separate figs. for that part of Brighthampton in Bampton par.
58 P.R.O., HO 107/872; cf. ibid. RG 9/905, RG 11/1514.

59 P.R.O., RG 9/905, RG 11/1514; Magd. Coll. Mun., CP 3/26, f. 10v.; ibid. Estates Bursary, survs. 1883–91, pp. 3, 308; Kelly's Dir. Oxon. (1883 and later edns.).
60 Kelly's Dir. Oxon. (1907 and later edns.); sign at Standlake Garage 1993.
61 J. Goadby, 1228 and All That (priv. print. 1978), 68.
62 Sale Cat., Cotswold Brick and Tile Co. Ltd. (1951): copy in C.O.S. STANb 666.7; O.S. Map 6", SP 30 SE. (1960 edn.).
63 V.C.H. Oxon. i. 426; above, manors.
64 B.N.C. Mun., Standlake 3; cf. O.R.O., tithe award and map (1844); Bodl. MS. Top. Oxon. d 218, f. 242v.; Jefferys, Oxon. Map (1767); Top. Oxon. (1971), 1–5.
65 Cal. Inq. p.m. Hen. VII, iii, pp. 536, 539–40; Cal. Pat. 1494–1509, p. 544; B.N.C. Mun., Cold Norton 38, 41–2.
66 B.N.C. Mun., Standlake 63, 69, 74, 85, 91, 99; Ch. Ch. Arch., Standlake B 1–6; ibid. MS. Estates 80, f. 6.
67 B.N.C. Mun., Standlake 5.
68 Ibid. 40, 54, 99; ibid. Cold Norton 32.
69 Magd. Coll. Mun., Standlake 19C; B.N.C. Mun., Standlake 40.
70 B.N.C. Mun., Standlake 54.
71 Ch. Ch. Arch., Standlake B 7, B 9; Oxf. Jnl. 25 Feb. 1764.
72 Ch. Ch. Arch., MS. Estates 80, ff. 98–9; cf. ibid. ff. 55–6, 64.
73 O.R.O., tithe map (1844); cf. ibid. incl. map.
74 B.N.C. Mun., Standlake 3; Magd. Coll. Mun., Standlake 19C; cf. above, this section (trade and ind.).

by the lessee for the right of tentering were recorded in the 16th century and the 17th,[75] and two mills, presumably meaning wheels or stones, were mentioned in the 18th,[76] but from the early 17th century the mill was consistently described as a corn or grist mill.[77] In 1279 it was said to be freely held with 10 a. for 16s. 9½d. to the lords of each quarter, but in the 15th and 16th centuries it was a copyhold owing heriot and suit of court.[78] It became leasehold before 1617.[79] The rent to each lord, 12s. 6d. in 1394 and 13s. 4d. in 1445, was by 1480 only 10s.,[80] and in the earlier 1480s the mill lay vacant and unrepaired for two years.[81] Magdalen College, Oxford, acquired two quarters with parts of the manor in 1483 and 1538, and in 1617 bought the rest from Thomas Radborne, miller;[82] the college leased the mill from 1743 until the 19th century to tenants of nearby Gaunt House, who sublet it.[83] Following a fire in 1770 William Marchant of Gaunt House rebuilt both the mill and mill house,[84] and a separate house was built to the south in the early 19th century.[85] In the 1860s weeds were impeding the mill's operation,[86] and in 1883 it was in poor repair;[87] in 1920 the college sold it to the tenant, on whose death in 1928 it ceased to function except for occasional production of cattle feed and to generate electricity. It was converted for domestic use in stages during the 1940s and early 1950s.[88]

Church Mill, formerly Collins mill after a late 14th-century tenant,[89] was in 1279 a customary cottage tenement, held with 10 a. for total rent of 20s. and works valued at 15d.[90] The rent was unaltered in the 16th century, though in the 15th the amount for which works were commuted varied greatly.[91] The mill may always have been a corn mill, and in the late 18th century and the 19th there was a bakehouse.[92] Two quarters passed with parts of the manor to Magdalen College, which retained them in 1636;[93] the other quarters were acquired c. 1555 by the Hewes or Calcott family, copyhold tenants of the mill under Magdalen College into the 17th century.[94]

They seem to have conveyed their freehold c. 1598 to Andrew Yate,[95] and Edmund Hodgkins, miller, acquired the entire freehold before 1723.[96] Later resident owners included Edward Harris (d. 1791), Thomas Witley (1791–3), and Edward's relict Margaret (d. 1853), whose family through her second husband William Hemming (d. 1806) continued as millers and corn merchants until 1908;[97] James Hemming was running 'a first rate little business' in 1897, though major repairs were needed to the mill roof.[98] The mill was disused by 1911,[99] but the wheel and machinery were repaired in the 1920s and used to generate electricity until 1968; in the Second World War some corn milling was carried out.[1] The mill was restored to working order in the early 1980s. The surviving mill and attached mill house were built in 1726 by the Hodgkinses,[2] and in the early 19th century an additional domestic block with a symmetrical north front was built at the rear. A detached bakehouse survives on the west.

Underdown Mill, formerly Beard or Berry Mill, belonged until the 16th century to Hardwick and Brighthampton manor, and in 1279 was a customary tenement occupied with a house and 5 a. for 40s. rent and works valued at 12d.[3] It remained copyhold in the 16th century, owing suit, heriot, and rent of 30s.[4] A fulling mill on the manor in the 13th and 14th centuries may have been in Hardwick,[5] and though Underdown Mill was briefly owned by a Witney clothier in the later 16th century[6] it was a corn mill in 1660 and later.[7] Three mills, presumably pairs of stones rather than wheels, were mentioned in 1728, along with a boulting or sieving mill.[8] In 1569 John Herle, then lord, sold the mill to Peter Ranckell of Witney, whose son Henry sold it in 1604 to Joseph Mayne, lord of Shifford;[9] Mayne's son Edward sold it to Thomas Weale (d. 1658), the first of several owner-occupiers and millers who included Henry Hewes (c. 1657–60), members of the Harris family (1660–c. 1766), Samuel Clack

---

75 Magd. Coll. Mun., EP 1/3, EP 18/1, EP 31/6.

76 Ibid. Standlake 23C; ibid. LE/55, leases 1680–1821.

77 e.g. ibid. Standlake 23C; ibid. CP 3/16, f. 186; Ch. Ch. Arch., Standlake C 1. A lease to a Witney dyer cited in Bodl. MS. Top. Oxon. c 768/1, nos. 74–5, has not been found.

78 *Bampton Hund. R.* 66–70, s.v. John de Flexeneye; Magd. Coll. Mun., EP 14/22, EP 85/31; ibid. ct. bk. 6, 26 June 6 Eliz.

79 Magd. Coll. Mun., CP 3/34, f. 26v.

80 Magd. Coll. Mun., EP 14/22, EP 31/10, EP 123/16.

81 Ibid. EP 14/23.

82 Ibid. EP 31/6; ibid. Standlake 23C; cf. ibid. Standlake 22C; above, manors.

83 Magd. Coll. Mun., ledger Z, p. 560; ibid. LE/55; O.R.O., tithe award (1844).

84 Datestone inscribed WM 1770; beam inscribed 1770 (?)RD; *Oxford Jnl.* 5 May 1770.

85 Cf. datestone of 1828(?) on mill gable.

86 B.N.C. Mun., 2nd ser., 467, rep. to Northmoor Drainage Board 26 Apr. 1867.

87 Magd. Coll. Estates Bursary, survs. and estimates 1883–91, p. 33.

88 Ibid. ledger P, pp. 416–17; Bodl. MS. Top. Oxon. c 768/1, nos. 74–5; above, plate 33.

89 Magd. Coll. Mun., EP 14/22, EP 85/30, EP 123/16.

90 *Bampton Hund. R.* 67–9, s.v. John Simond.

91 Magd. Coll. Mun., EP 14/22, EP 31/6, EP 85/39.

92 Ibid. Standlake 3; O.R.O., Misc. Coll. II/4, II/20, II/31; C.O.S., PRN 1895.

93 Magd. Coll. Mun., ct. bk. 6, 14 July 6 Edw. VI; ct.

bk. 37, p. 29; above, manors.

94 Magd. Coll. Mun., Standlake 3; ibid. ct. bks. 6, 9, 15, 37; O.R.O., MS. Wills Oxon. 181, f. 212v.; ibid. 132/1/28.

95 P.R.O., CP 25/2/198/40 Eliz. I Trin.; ibid. C 142/379, no. 68.

96 O.R.O., P4/1/MS 3/4, f. 27R; ibid. Misc. Coll. II/1, 6–7; Bodl. MS. d.d. Harcourt c 300, lease 23 Oct. 1732.

97 O.R.O., P4/1/MS 3/4, ff. 24R–27R; ibid. Misc. Coll. II/1–32; Bodl. MS. Top. Oxon. c 768/1, no. 53; C.O.S., par. reg. transcripts.

98 O.R.O., Misc. Coll. II/31.

99 Magd. Coll. Estates Bursary, survs. 1892–1912, pp. 676–7.

1 C.O.S., PRN 1895; Bodl. MS. Top. Oxon. c 768/1, no. 53; inf. from owner.

2 Datestone inscribed IHE 1726, though the owners seem to have been Edmund and Elizabeth Hodgkins: O.R.O., Misc. Coll. II/1, 6–7; ibid. P4/1/MS 3/4, f. 27R; C.O.S., par. reg. transcripts.

3 *Bampton Hund. R.* 64, listing it under Hardwick; cf., however, *Oxon. Local Hist.* ii (2), 46.

4 P.R.O., SC 2/197/43.

5 Ibid. C 133/72, no. 6; C 134/29, no. 11; above, Ducklington, econ. hist. (mills).

6 Bodl. MS. d.d. Harcourt c 109/7.

7 O.R.O., Costar I/i/1; O.S. Map 6", Oxon. XXXVIII (1883 edn.).

8 O.R.O., QS/Epiph. 1728.

9 St. John's Coll. Mun., XVII.5; P.R.O., C 142/242, no. 59; ibid. CP 25/2/339/2 Jas. I Mich.; Bodl. MS. d.d. Harcourt c 109/7.

(1810–20), and the Swingburn family (1829–1911).[10] From 1766 to 1810 it was owned and let by the Wrights of Hailey in Witney,[11] and from c. 1850 the Swingburns sometimes let it to their relatives the Mountains.[12] Like Church Mill it was heavily mortgaged during the 18th century and early 19th, and several sales were prompted apparently by mounting debt.[13] From Mary Swingburn (d. 1911) the mill passed to Mary Cook and to her son B. D. Costar. It continued to operate, primarily as a grist mill, until c. 1933, and later the wooden wheels and machinery were removed.[14]

The surviving house, which replaced one of 7 bays burnt in 1727,[15] incorporated a small attached mill at its eastern end. After the mill ceased working a part was demolished, and c. 1990 the remains were taken into the house.

Fishing rights were attached to all four mills by the 17th century.[16] The name Fisher was recorded in the late 13th century,[17] and fishermen were mentioned occasionally from the 16th;[18] four were noted in Standlake in 1861.[19] Free fisheries in the Thames were recorded on both manors in 1279,[20] though that on Hardwick and Brighthampton manor, reportedly worth 6s. a year, was not mentioned later. The other, worth 7s. 8d. to each of the four lords of Standlake,[21] was presumably that near Haul Ham in the south-west, held by copy with adjacent meadows from the 14th century to the 19th for 6s. 8d. to each lord.[22] Two weirs held with it in 1558[23] were presumably on the site of later Langley's weir, recorded under various names from the late 18th century and held with the fishery in the 19th. Earlier 19th-century subtenants included local fishermen, but there seems to have been no house or resident keeper, and the weir, by then evidently much neglected, was removed c. 1872.[24]

In the 15th century and early 16th common fishing rights in the river Windrush were defended by lords of Standlake against encroachments from Northmoor.[25] In 1536 the manor court ordered that the waters should be fished only once a week, and in 1602 that no-one should fish at night.[26] From the 17th century manorial fishing and fowling rights in the Wind-rush and elsewhere, excepting those held by copy, were let en bloc to local landowners,[27] and in the early 20th century Magdalen College let all its fishing to non-resident sportsmen.[28]

LOCAL GOVERNMENT. A court for the Mauduits' quarter of Standlake manor was mentioned in 1254, when the lord of one of the other quarters owed suit there.[29] In 1279 all four lords claimed pillory, tumbrel, and assize of bread and ale, and in 1285 gallows,[30] but no such liberties were recorded later, and in the 17th century the lord of Bampton, as lord of the hundred, held a Michaelmas court and view of frankpledge at Standlake in September or October and enforced the assize of ale.[31] Separate courts baron, held by lords of each of the quarters throughout the Middle Ages and by Magdalen College following the manor's reunification, met in the 14th and 15th centuries once or twice a year, in the later 16th century usually every other year, and in the 18th century sometimes less frequently; in the 15th and 16th centuries they issued field orders, but from the mid 17th century they dealt almost exclusively with copyholds, sometimes at special interim sessions.[32] A general court baron was recorded in 1847, but thereafter individual copyhold grants only, the last in 1882.[33] The lord of Bampton's Michaelmas court and view, which issued field orders in the later 17th century,[34] continued probably until the earlier 19th century.[35] A court house, apparently on Standlake High Street, was mentioned from the 15th century to the 17th, but all or part was usually let to tenants,[36] and in the late 18th century courts were said to have met formerly in the Chequers inn.[37]

Tenants in Standlake and Brittenton, the part of Brighthampton within Standlake manor and parish,[38] formed a single homage. In 1536 a court baron appointed officers to enforce fishing and field orders,[39] but officers in the mid 17th century were elected at the lord of Bampton's

---

[10] O.R.O., Costar I/i/1–23, I/iii/1–13, III/i/1–11; P.R.O., PROB 11/283, ff. 401–402v.
[11] O.R.O., Costar I/i/19–23, I/iii/1–2.
[12] e.g. O.R.O., Brighthampton tithe award (1852); ibid. Standlake incl. award; P.R.O., RG 11/1514.
[13] O.R.O., Costar I/i/1–23, I/iii/1–13, III/i/1–11; ibid. Misc. Coll. II/1–32.
[14] Ibid. Costar I/i/10–11; Bodl. MS. Top. Oxon. c 768/1, no. 52; cf. Kelly's Dir. Oxon. (1883 and later edns.).
[15] O.R.O., QS/Epiph. 1728.
[16] B.N.C. Mun., Standlake 40; St. John's Coll. Mun., XVII.5; Magd. Coll. Mun., D-Y 421; P.R.O., C 142/379, no. 68.
[17] Bampton Hund. R. 68; P.R.O., E 179/161/8.
[18] e.g. B.N.C. Mun., Standlake 16; O.R.O., MSS. Wills Oxon. 7/3/23, 77/3/26; Ch. Ch. Arch., Standlake B 9.
[19] P.R.O., RG 9/905.
[20] Bampton Hund. R. 63, 66–70.
[21] Cf. P.R.O., C 133/108, no. 6, valuing one quarter at 20d. in 1302.
[22] Magd. Coll. Mun., EP 31/6, EP 85/30, EP 250/14; ibid. CP 3/16, ff. 178v., 202; O.S. Map 6″, Oxon. XXXVIII (1883 edn.).
[23] Magd. Coll. Mun., ct. bk. 6, 8 Mar. 4 & 5 Phil. and Mary.
[24] O.R.O., tithe award and map (1844), no. 2240; Magd. Coll. Mun., ES/6/2, p. 6; F. S. Thacker, Thames Highway (1968 edn.), ii, 67, 75–7.

[25] Magd. Coll. Mun., EP 146/33.
[26] Ibid. EP 85/43; ibid. ct. bk. 15, p. 99; cf. St. John's Coll. Mun., XVII.17.
[27] Magd. Coll. Mun., CP 3/34, f. 27v.; ibid. LE/55, lease 6 Dec. 1757; Bodl. MSS. d.d. Harcourt c 14/1–2.
[28] Magd. Coll. Estates Bursary, ledger M, pp. 331–3; ledger O, pp. 566–8; cf. Ch. Ch. Arch., MS. Estates 80, f. 159.
[29] Oxon. Fines, 170–1.
[30] Bampton Hund. R. 66–70 (translating tumberellum as stocks); Giles, Hist Bampton, 132; Rot. Hund. (Rec. Com.), ii. 702.
[31] Longleat House (Wilts.), NMR 3315; cf. B.L. Add. MS. 27535, f. 45; P.R.O., E 317/Oxon./1, f. 2; above, Bampton hundred.
[32] For lists of ct. rolls, C. M. Woolgar, 'Cat. Estate Archives of Magd. Coll.' (TS. 1981), i. 261 sqq., 337–8: copy in Bodl. R. Top. 680a; cf. Magd. Coll. Mun., EP 14/22, EP 15/10, EP 15/12; P.R.O., SC 2/209/57, SC 6/961/19; ibid. C 133/108, no. 6; C 135/120, no. 11; B.L. Harl. Roll I.15.
[33] Magd. Coll. Mun., ct. bk. 82, ff. 75 sqq.
[34] Longleat House, NMR 3315.
[35] Arundel Castle, MS. TP 100; above, Bampton hundred.
[36] Magd. Coll. Mun., EP 18/1, EP 25/12, EP 31/6, EP 88/19; cf. ibid. EP 31/10, s.v. Rob. Harres.
[37] O.R.O., P4/2/MS 1/5, f. 11.
[38] Above, intro.
[39] Magd. Coll. Mun., EP 85/43.

Standlake court, when they included a constable for Standlake and another for Brittenton, tithingmen for each of the quarters of the manor, a field warden, and two inspectors of carcasses.[40] In 1622 the constable of Standlake received 15s. rent towards highway repairs, apparently a temporary expedient.[41]

Brighthampton tenants of Hardwick manor attended that manor's courts and views of frankpledge from the Middle Ages to the later 19th century; by the 16th century they belonged to a different tithing from the Hardwick tenants. Officers included a constable for the part of Brighthampton within Hardwick manor and Bampton parish, elected annually until 1842, and a hayward with shared jurisdiction over Standlake common, whose office continued after inclosure.[42]

For civil and parochial purposes the part of Brighthampton within Bampton parish was administered independently, raising its own rates and presumably electing its own officers, though no overseer was mentioned in 1642. Probably in the 15th century and still in the late 19th Brighthampton appointed a chapelwarden for Shifford chapel.[43] Brittenton was administered with Standlake.[44] Two churchwardens for Standlake were recorded from 1530 and two collectors or overseers from 1642,[45] and in the earlier 19th century there were two surveyors of highways, who seem usually to have contracted out road repairs.[46] In the later 19th century Standlake vestry appointed a waywarden, 2 overseers, 2 churchwardens, 3 allotment wardens, and 2 assessors, and nominated constables to the magistrates.[47] Grass stewards, recorded from c. 1775 until inclosure, were said in 1852 to be appointed annually at parish meetings; there were then 4 for Standlake, presumably including Brittenton, and 2 for Brighthampton, with shared responsibility for Standlake common. Duties included repair of gates and fences, drainage, provision of powder and shot for bird-scaring, and provision, with the rector, of town bulls; their income included rents from small meadows and commons, and profits from sale of bushes and scrub after haining. Occasionally the grass stewards appointed herdsmen.[48]

At inclosure responsibility for cleaning ditches and watercourses and maintaining some private roads passed to the newly established Standlake Drainage Board, financed by annual rates.[49] In 1938 chief responsibility for the area passed

under the Land Drainage Act of 1930 to the Thames Conservancy Catchment Board, though in the 1940s the Standlake Board retained limited powers over roads, bridges, and minor ditches.[50] A resident police constable was recorded from 1861, and c. 1930 a police office was built near the school.[51] A pair of 'parish' stocks remained at the Green until c. 1927, when their use was still remembered.[52]

Claims in the early 17th century that the parish was overburdened with poor prompted a petition to the justices of assize.[53] In 1775–6 Standlake spent £104 on poor relief, in 1783–5 an average of £158, and in 1803 £267 or c. 9s. per head of population, a relatively low figure. By 1813 expenditure was £579 or c. 20s. per head, rising to c. 29s. in 1819. It fell to 12s. in 1824, rose again in the later 1820s, and in 1834 was 19s. per head. A rented workhouse with accommodation for 14 inmates in 1775 was re-established in 1781, when the poor were chiefly employed spinning wool for a Witney factory; it had closed by 1803, when 31 adults and 4 children received permanent out relief and 12 received occasional relief. Under £2 was spent on setting the poor to work in 1775–6, and c. £5 in 1802–3. By 1813 there were 36 adults on permanent and 10 on occasional relief, and 18 adults were relieved permanently and 14 occasionally in 1815.[54]

A select vestry to oversee poor relief, established in 1819, continued until 1834, with 8–10 annually elected members usually including the curate and leading farmers.[55] Besides authorizing weekly and extraordinary payments in money, clothing, or kind it confronted rising unemployment, ruling in 1819 that all inhabitants should employ labourers in proportion to their rates, and the same year distributing 20 labourers among the ratepayers by ballot.[56] A supervisor of those put to work on the roads received 6s. a week, and in 1820 action was taken against labourers allegedly leaving the roads or gravel pits to purloin firewood.[57] Inhabitants supplementing their income by spinning hemp were to be employed by the overseers whenever hemp could not be supplied, and were to receive additional allowances for carriage of hemp.[58] A new workhouse was established c. 1820 at the south of Rack End, adjoining or incorporating existing parish cottages, and a governor and two guardians were appointed; nothing is known of its operation and at its sale in 1840 it had long

40 Longleat House, NMR 3315, cts. 1670–2; cf. *Protestation Rtns. and Tax Assess.* 1, 27.

41 Bodl. MS. Top. Oxon. c 118, f. 10 and v.

42 P.R.O., SC 2/197/43; St. John's Coll. Mun. XI.11–22 (ct. bks. 1606–1878); Magd. Coll. Mun., D-Y 447; *Protestation Rtns. and Tax Assess.* 9; above, Ducklington, local govt.

43 D. & C. Exeter, MS. 6016/8, notes *re* division of Bampton par. c. 1845; *Protestation Rtns. and Tax Assess.* 9; above, Bampton: Shifford, local govt.

44 e.g. O.R.O., PAR 248/2/A 1/1; PAR 248/5/A 4/1.

45 *Visit. Dioc. Linc.* ii. 49; *Protestation Rtns. and Tax Assess.* 1, 27.

46 O.R.O., QS/1813 Mic.; ibid. PAR 248/2/A 1/1, ff. 43 and v., 45 sqq.

47 Ibid. PAR 248/2/A 1/1, ff. 59v. sqq.; *Standlake Par. Mag. 1877–9, passim*: copy in Bodl. Per. G.A. Oxon. 8° 666.

48 O.R.O., PAR 248/8/A 1/1, *passim*; Magd. Coll. Mun., D-Y 447.

49 St. John's Coll. Mun., XVII.58, XVII.69; cf. Act to Extend Provisions of the Act for Incl. of Commons, 11 & 12 Vic. c. 99.

50 St. John's Coll. Mun., EST. I. N, various subjects III, 126 (corresp. 1921–49), ff. 26 sqq.

51 P.R.O., RG 9/905, no. 128; O.R.O., P4/1/MS 3/4, f. 18Q; *Kelly's Dir. Oxon.* (1899 and later edns.); O.S. Map 1/2,500, SP 3803–3903 (1971 edn.).

52 O.R.O., P4/1/MS 3/4, f. 24Q.

53 Bodl. MS. Top. Oxon. c 118, ff. 2, 4.

54 *Poor Abstract, 1777*, p. 140; *1787*, p. 188; *1804*, pp. 398–9; *1818*, pp. 352–3; *Poor Rate Returns*, H.C. 556, p. 135 (1822), v; H.C. 334, p. 170 (1825), iv; H.C. 83, p. 157 (1830–1), xi; H.C. 444, p. 153 (1835), xlvii; Oxf. Jnl. Synopsis, 1 Dec. 1781, 20 July 1782.

55 O.R.O., PAR 248/2/A 1/1, *passim*.

56 Ibid. f. 4v.

57 Ibid. ff. 4v.–5; cf. ibid. ff. 7, 38v.

58 Ibid. f. 9v.

been let as 5 separate cottages.[59] In 1824 the vestry appointed an assistant overseer on a salary of £20, and the same year vaccinated those potentially chargeable to the parish.[60] From 1820 the vestry ceased paying rents or supplying beer at pauper funerals,[61] and weekly allowances, then 7s. a week for a man and wife and 1s. 6d. for each child, were reduced to 5s. 6d. and 1s. 3d. respectively by 1824.[62] From 1825 relief was denied to anyone keeping a dog.[63]

Brighthampton spent only £16 on poor relief in 1775–6 and an average of c. £18 in 1783–5. In the earlier 19th century capitation was usually lower than in Standlake and Brittenton, 14s. in 1814 and, exceptionally, 6s. in 1815. By 1819 it had risen to c. 26s. but declined during the early 1820s, rising again to c. 20s. in 1828. In 1834 it was 14s., and total expenditure was £78. Eight adults and 6 children received regular out relief in 1802–3, and between 8 and 10 adults in 1813–15; there was no occasional relief, and no workhouse.[64]

After 1834 Standlake and Brighthampton belonged to Witney union, and from 1894 to Witney rural district. In 1974 they became part of West Oxfordshire district.[65]

CHURCH. In the late Anglo-Saxon period Standlake and Brighthampton formed part of an extensive *parochia* centred on Bampton minster.[66] A church or chapel was established presumably by the lords of Standlake before the late 12th century, the date of the earliest surviving fabric;[67] a priest and clerk of Standlake who witnessed a grant by the lord before 1192, and a chaplain who witnessed another before 1196, may have served it.[68] Eve de Grey presented to the church in 1227 or 1228,[69] and thereafter the living was treated usually as a rectory with its own advowson.[70] The church had baptismal rights probably from the 12th century, the date of the former font,[71] but conflicts with Bampton over burial rights, tithes, and boundaries persisted into the later Middle Ages. Between 1317 and c. 1319 several tenants of Hardwick and Brighthampton manor, regarded as Bampton parishioners, attended Standlake church and paid their tithes and offerings there in league

with the rector, James de Boys, who illegally buried some Brighthampton people in his churchyard; judgement was given against Standlake, and the manor's tenants in Brighthampton remained fully subject to Bampton until the 19th century and attended Shifford chapel.[72] In 1338 the rector of Standlake enlarged his churchyard, allegedly to accommodate burial of large numbers of parishioners and 'others choosing burial there'.[73] By the 15th century burial was explicitly allowed in return for an annual pension,[74] converted by the 17th century into a 'pension tithe' to the vicars of Bampton, and payable in the 19th as a modus of £2 2s. 6d.[75] In 1976 the benefice was absorbed with Yelford, Stanton Harcourt, and Northmoor into the united benefice of Lower Windrush, part of a group ministry with the benefice of Bampton with Clanfield, and in 1993 it was served from Stanton Harcourt.[76]

The advowson descended with Standlake manor, after whose partition c. 1246 each of the four lords presented in turn,[77] prompting disputes in 1284 and 1309.[78] From c. 1367 the Greys' right was held, though not exercised, with the Giffards' quarter, with which it briefly passed to New College, Oxford,[79] but by 1423 the Greys had recovered it.[80] In the late 15th century and the early 16th both the Greys' and the Corbets' rights passed with their respective shares of the manor to Magdalen College, Oxford;[81] the Mauduit and Giffard rights were included in sales c. 1555 to Francis Fettiplace, who sold them to Magdalen in 1557,[82] though in 1602 the college repurchased the Mauduit share of the advowson from Fettiplace's daughter Cecily and her husband Edward East, presumably following disputes over title.[83] Thereafter the college retained the patronage until 1953 when it was vested in the Diocesan Board of Patronage, joint patron of the united benefice in 1993.[84] Nicholas Sifrewast presented in the right of Osbert Giffard in 1284,[85] and the king during the minority of Eleanor, daughter of William Moleyns (d. 1429), in 1431.[86] Wadham College presented by agreement in 1635 and Charles II in 1660.[87]

The rectory, of middling value, was estimated in 1254 at £13 6s. 8d., in 1291 at £15 6s. 8d.,

59 Ibid. ff. 7v.–8, 9v., 41v.–42v.; Bodl. MS. Top. Oxon. c 768/1–2, no. 73; cf. below, charities, s.v. Crouch.
60 O.R.O., PAR 248/2/A 1/1, f. 18 and v.
61 Ibid. ff. 6v.–7.   62 Ibid. ff. 7v., 17v.
63 Ibid. f. 20.
64 *Poor Abstract, 1777*, p. 140; *1787*, p. 188; *1804*, pp. 398–9; *1818*, pp. 352–3; *Poor Rate Returns*, H.C. 556, p. 135 (1822), v; H.C. 334, p. 170 (1825), iv; H.C. 83, p. 157 (1830–1), xi; H.C. 444, p. 153 (1835), xlvii.
65 O.R.O., RO 3251, pp. 201–3; RO 3267.
66 Above, Bampton, intro.; Bampton and Weald, church.
67 Below, this section.
68 *Eynsham Cart.* i, p. 89; *Oseney Cart.* iv, p. 337.
69 *Rot. Welles*, ii (L.R.S. vi), 28.
70 e.g. *Tax. Eccl.* (Rec. Com.), 32; *Inq. Non.* (Rec. Com.), 141; *Cal. Pat.* 1327–30, 197; cf. D. & C. Exeter, MS. 2865, claiming subjection to Bampton.
71 Below, this section [ch. archit.].
72 D. & C. Exeter, MSS. 486, 645, 647–9, 2865, 2867; *Oxon. Local Hist.* ii (2), 34–47; above, Bampton: Shifford, church; this article, intro.
73 Lincs. R.O., episc. reg. v, f. 556; *Cal. Pat.* 1338–40, 32.
74 D. & C. Exeter, MS. 648.

75 O.R.O., Standlake tithe award (1844); above, Bampton: Bampton and Weald, church.
76 O.R.O., MS. Oxf. Dioc. c 1713/2, Order in Council 12 Apr. 1976; *Oxf. Dioc. Yr. Bk.* (1976 and later edns.).
77 e.g. Magd. Coll. Mun., EP 146/34; J. Goadby, *1228 and All That* (priv. print. 1978), 71–2, which contains errors.
78 P.R.O., CP 40/55, m. 79d.; Lincs. R.O., episc. reg. ii, f. 155.
79 New Coll. Arch., 9161, 13921; *Cal. Close*, 1364–8, 471–2, 474; *Cal. Pat.* 1381–5, 63.
80 P.R.O., C 139/12, no. 36; C 139/158, no. 28.
81 Magd. Coll. Mun., Standlake 4C, 10.
82 *Cal. Pat.* 1554–5, 138–9; Magd. Coll. Mun., Standlake 1, 6A, 13C.
83 Magd. Coll. Mun., Standlake 17C; ibid. EP 146/27. The college exercised the Mauduit advowson in 1581: O.A.S. *Rep.* (1914), 197.
84 O.R.O., MS. Oxf. Dioc. c 2017, Order in Council 1 Aug. 1953; *Oxf. Dioc. Yr. Bk.* (1993), 83.
85 P.R.O., CP 40/55, m. 79d., reading Oyfrewast; cf. ibid. KB 27/90, m. 33.
86 *Cal. Pat.* 1429–36, 143.
87 O.R.O., Cal. Presentation Deeds, 1st ser. p. 84; ibid. 2nd ser. f. 80.

and in the early 16th century at *c.* £16 gross.[88] Roughly a third of the total was attributed to glebe and to hay and small tithes in 1341.[89] Pasture for 6 oxen and 2 cows and pannage for 20 swine, granted by Eve de Grey in the early 13th century, was not mentioned after the early 14th,[90] but in the 17th century and presumably earlier there was a yardland (29 a.) of glebe with appurtenant meadow and commons,[91] and from the later 18th *c.* 50 a. were held of Magdalen College under a beneficial lease.[92] About 1520

tithes and 5*s.* for each acre of glebe not in hand.[96] Total income in 1851 was estimated at *c.* £594, including £50 for glebe, £70 for the land held under Magdalen, and £8 for fees and offerings; at inclosure in 1853 *c.* 25 a. were awarded for glebe and *c.* 62 a. for the Magdalen land, all of it sublet.[97]

The rectory house, on its site south-east of the church by 1246,[98] is of notable size and quality. It is rubble-built, and incorporates a central hall range with north and south wings projecting in

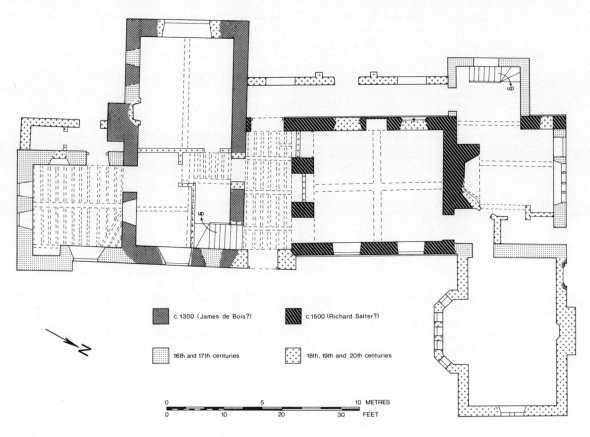

c.1300 (James de Bois?)   c.1500 (Richard Salter?)

16th and 17th centuries   18th, 19th and 20th centuries

0   5   10 METRES
0   10   20   30   FEET

STANDLAKE RECTORY HOUSE

the estate was held by a layman,[93] and from the 17th century all or part, including tithes, oblations, and, in 1635, rooms in the house, was let frequently to local farmers.[94] Moduses for hay, sheep, and milk tithes were established by 1685,[95] and in the early 19th century 13*s.* 4*d.* was paid for Cokethorpe Park and 1¼*d.* an acre for some meadows. Other tithes may have been collected in kind until commutation in 1842–4, when the rector was awarded *c.* £460 a year for

opposite directions.[99] Though subdivided in the 1950s, it remained the rectory house for Standlake until 1976 and for the united benefice until sold in 1980.[1] The two-storeyed south wing retains a tall lancet window of *c.* 1300 in its east gable, a possibly original stack near the centre of its south wall, and an original roof constructed with exceptionally small rafters. A cross passage separates the wing from the later 15th-century hall range built possibly for Richard Salter,

88 Lunt, *Val. Norw.* 308; *Tax. Eccl.* (Rec. Com.), 32; *Subsidy 1526*, 261; *Valor Eccl.* ii. 179.
89 *Inq. Non.* (Rec. Com.), 141.
90 *Cal. Pat.* 1334–8, 23.
91 O.R.O., MS. Oxf. Archd. Oxon. c 142, pp. 181–8 [of repeated pagination].
92 Magd. Coll. Mun., ES/6/2, pp. 2, 10; ibid. LE/56, lease 9 Oct. 1833; O.R.O., QSD L.260; ibid. tithe awards (1844, 1887); *Ch. and Chapel, 1851*, no. 408.
93 *Visit. Dioc. Linc.* i. 133.
94 Magd. Coll. Mun., LE/55, lease 28 May 11 Chas. I;

O.R.O., PAR 248/13/6D/3; PAR 248/10/D1/1–2; ibid. QSD L.260; ibid. tithe awards (1844, 1887).
95 O.R.O., MS. Oxf. Archd. Oxon. b 41, f. 111.
96 Ibid. tithe award (1844).
97 Ibid. incl. award; *Ch. and Chapel, 1851*, no. 408.
98 B.N.C. Mun., Standlake 3.
99 C.B.A. Group 9, *Newsletter*, xi (1981), 81; xii (1982), 94–5; Vernacular Archit. Group Spring Conference 1987 (TS. 1987), 52–3: copy in C.O.S.
1 Goadby, *1228 and All That*, 71; *Oxf. Dioc. Yr. Bk.* (1975 and later edns.); *Sale Cat.* (1980): copy in O.R.O., P2/2/M 55/60.

rector 1473–1509,[2] which seems to have been two-storeyed from the outset and which includes remains of an original stack against the cross passage. The hall range's roof incorporates unusual curved scissor trusses similar to those at Standlake Manor. The northern cross wing, altered and extended at various times, may also be 15th-century in origin, and a two-storeyed porch or stair tower, whose roof incorporates re-used cusped timbers, was built against its west end perhaps in the 17th century. Rooms in 1626 included chambers over the parlour and 'dark entry' (presumably the cross passage), middle and outer chambers perhaps over the hall, and a closet chamber with another chamber above, perhaps at the house's north or south end. Detached outbuildings, presumably to the north, west, and south as in the 19th century, included a kitchen and brewhouse which apparently survived in 1685, butteries, a malthouse, a woodhouse, and stabling.[3] Two 'new', presumably refitted, chambers over the hall were mentioned in 1635.[4] A new block was added against the south wing in the later 17th century perhaps by John Dale, rector 1660–84, who carried out renovations at his own expense[5] and whose initials, with the date 1661, survive on a chimney stack at the hall's north end. Further alterations were carried out c. 1745 and c. 1803,[6] perhaps the date of an early 19th-century remodelling of the south wing. In the mid 19th century the north wing's eastern end was reconstructed, and an outshot, linking the north and south wings and incorporating a central main entrance, was added.[7] Dilapidated outbuildings, including a large tithe barn and granary south of the house, were demolished c. 1868.[8] Wall paintings, probably of the early 17th century, were uncovered c. 1981 in a room over the hall;[9] panelling in the study on the south wing's ground floor was reportedly brought from Magdalen College's ante-chapel c. 1833[10] but seems to be *in situ*.

A chapel founded in honour of the Virgin, St. John the Evangelist, and other saints was mentioned c. 1235, but may have been only a side chapel in one of the transepts of the church.[11] The medieval hermitage, mentioned from the 15th century, is not known to have fulfilled any pastoral functions despite the 17th-century practice of reading a gospel on the site on Holy

Thursday.[12] Simon of Evesham, rector 1320–61, founded a chantry in the church in 1354 at the altar of the Holy Cross, St. John the Evangelist, St. Thomas the martyr, St. Nicholas, and St. Catherine for the benefit of relatives, the lords of Standlake, and the king and queen.[13] Successive rectors presented chantry priests until the 16th century: at least one was a graduate, and Thomas Gaunt (1484–1502) was of a prominent local family.[14] The endowment comprised rents and tenements in Standlake and Brighthampton and small rents in Worcestershire, valued in all at c. 80s., and in the 16th century gross income was reportedly £5 6s. 8d. or more.[15] A priest's house stood probably south of the churchyard on the site of Church Farm, called the 'chantry house' in the earlier 19th century and evidently one of the tenements given to the chantry at its foundation;[16] in 1473 a rector left half a year's rectorial income for the priest to build a dovecot.[17] At the suppression of chantries ornaments worth 6s. 8d. were recorded, but no jewels or plate. A tenement worth 4s. a year, given at an unknown date for an obit, was evidently unconnected.[18]

Thirteenth-century rectors may have resided,[19] as did James de Boys (1309–20), a university graduate and a dominant figure in local life, who probably rebuilt the rectory house.[20] From the early 14th century most medieval rectors were graduates and several were pluralists, administrators, and academics who presumably had little direct influence on the parish;[21] others may have resided occasionally, among them the royal clerk Simon of Evesham (rector 1320–61), whose house was robbed in 1350,[22] the episcopal official and proctor at Rome William Symond (1431–43), who bequeathed furnishings at Standlake and was involved in local land transactions,[23] and the civil lawyer Richard Salter (1473–1509), precentor of Lichfield, who repaired the chancel and possibly remodelled the rectory house.[24] Unbeneficed chaplains, of whom several were recorded in the 14th and 15th centuries,[25] presumably served the parish on a daily basis, and from 1379 to 1431 three successive rectors, none of them known to have been graduates,[26] perhaps served it themselves. In the 16th century some non-resident pluralists employed resident curates, the fee in 1526 being

2 Vernacular Archit. Group Spring Conference, 52; cf. Emden, *O.U. Reg. to 1500*, s.v. Ric. Salter.

3 O.R.O., MS. Wills Oxon. 37/3/17; cf. ibid. MS. Oxf. Archd. Oxon. b 41, f. 111; ibid. MS. Oxf. Dioc. c 2017, faculty petition 29 June 1868; Magd. Coll. Mun., LE/55, lease 28 May 11 Chas. I.

4 Magd. Coll. Mun., LE/55, lease 28 May 11 Chas. I.

5 *Cal. S.P. Dom.* 1664–5, 181.

6 *Secker's Corresp.* 130; O.R.O., MS. Oxf. Archd. Oxon. c 154, f. 25; ibid. MS. Oxf. Dioc. d 569, ff. 99–100.

7 L. S. Tuckwell, *Reminiscences of Thirty Happy Years ... in Standlake* (priv. print. c. 1918), 7–8: copy in C.O.S.

8 O.R.O., MS. Oxf. Dioc. c 2017, faculty petitions 29 June 1868.

9 C.B.A. Group 9, *Newsletter*, xii (1982), 94–5.

10 Bodl. MSS. Top. Oxon. c 551, f. 18; c 768/1, no. 56, giving 1893.   11 Below, this section [ch. archit.].

12 Above, intro.

13 Lincs. R.O., episc. reg. ix, ff. 262–4; *Cal. Pat.* 1350–4, 226, 478, 482.

14 Bodl. MS. Top. Oxon. c 551, ff. 41–2; B.L. Add. Ch. 42577; Emden, *O.U. Reg. to 1500*, s.v. Rob. Pegge.

15 Lincs. R.O., episc. reg. ix, ff. 263v.–264; *Subsidy 1526*,

261; *Val. Eccl.* ii. 179; *Chant. Cert.* 18, 47–8.

16 Magd. Coll. Mun., box 89, deeds re Bullocks 1826–1905; Lincs. R.O., episc. reg. ix, f. 263v., s.v. Brounesplace; Bodl. MS. Top. Oxon. c 768/1, no. 54.

17 *Some Oxon. Wills* (O.R.S. xxxix), 31.

18 *Chant. Cert.* 18; for later history, above, other estates.

19 e.g. John de Limesey: B.N.C. Mun., Standlake 3. For incumbents, Bodl. MS. Top. Oxon. c 551, ff. 39–40, 48; Oldfield, 'Clerus Oxf. Dioc.'; Goadby, *1288 and All That*, 71–2.

20 Emden, *O.U. Reg. to 1500*, i. 238; *Oxon. Local Hist.* ii (2), 38–41; above, this section.

21 Cf. Emden, *O.U. Reg. to 1500*, *passim*.

22 Ibid. iii. 657; *Cal. Pat.* 1317–21, 572; 1338–40, 32; 1348–50, 447, 463–4.

23 O.R.O., Warner IV/i/1–2; Emden, *O.U. Reg. to 1500*, vii. 1841; *Cat. Anct. D.* i, C 102, C 812; *Some Oxon. Wills* (O.R.S. xxxix), 16–17.

24 Emden, *O.U. Reg. to 1500*, vii. 1633; *Par. Colln.* iii. 287; Bodl. MS. d.d. Harcourt c 113/5; above, this section.

25 Magd. Coll. Mun., EP 31/10; P.R.O., C 146/9539; *Cat. Anct. D.* i, C 885; ii, C 2680; *Cal. Close, 1364–8*, 471; *Cal. Pat.* 1370–4, 438.

26 Bodl. MS. Top. Oxon. c 551, ff. 39, 48; cf. Emden, *O.U. Reg. to 1500*.

£6 a year,[27] though other rectors, notably William Pettifer (1562–81) and Roger Inkforbye (1581–1626), both former fellows of Magdalen College, were closely involved in local life and probably resided.[28] Long-serving curates included a former chantry chaplain, and Thomas Napkyn (1616–39), who from 1626 served the cure alone under non-resident pluralists.[29] All later 16th-century rectors and curates conformed.[30]

Accepted Frewen, rector from 1635, president of Magdalen College, and later archbishop of York, was a prominent High Church royalist who presumably had little contact with Standlake.[31] Following his deprivation c. 1646 his curate Nicholas Shorter, a Witney man and graduate of Balliol College, was presented under the Great Seal;[32] he resided, but had been deprived by 1660 when Frewen resigned the rectory,[33] and c. 1662 he apparently left the parish for a benefice elsewhere.[34] John Dale, rector 1660–84, allegedly 'kept pace with the ... presbyterians and independents' during the Interregnum, but at the Restoration won immediate royal approval and conformed thereafter.[35]

From the Restoration to the early 19th century all rectors seem to have resided, all were former fellows of Magdalen, and all remained for life, some serving long incumbencies.[36] Dale, a licensed pluralist, repaired the chancel and rectory house;[37] his successor John Chambers (rector 1685–1721) endowed a school and probably donated church plate, and like Dale left a large library in his house at Standlake.[38] Matthew Horbery (rector 1756–73), noted as a fine preacher and theologian, at first lived partly at Lichfield where he was a canon, but by 1768 seems usually to have resided and to have served the parish alone.[39] There were two Sunday services with one sermon throughout the 18th century, and the sacrament was administered four times a year usually to 20–40 communicants. 'Too many' neglected services in favour of fishing, idleness, or the alehouse, but none were habitually absent and by 1805 parishioners were said to be 'constant' in their devotions. Attempts at weekly catechizing c. 1738 met with apathy, and in 1759 Horbery catechized at Lent.[40]

From 1806 until 1868 rectors lived elsewhere and the parish was served by curates occupying the rectory house, notably James Stopes (1808–37) and Frank Burges (1837–55). The stipend, £50 in 1808, was £75 by 1814 and £100 by 1838.[41] Parishioners in 1807 were 'perfectly satisfied',[42] but in 1841 Burges was said so to displease them that 'he will soon have empty pews to preach to',[43] and his hunting and 'unclerical conduct' prompted episcopal censure and complaints from local churchmen and landowners. In other respects he seems, however, to have been conscientious,[44] and by 1854 there were two Sunday sermons and a monthly sacrament administered to some 60 communicants.[45] Average attendance, c. 230 in 1851 and c. 280 in 1866, rose slightly in relation to the population, though the curate claimed that many attended the morning service only to receive charity loaves, distribution of which fuelled resentment.[46]

Joseph West (rector 1868–76), though resident and formerly a noted preacher and evangelical, was remembered as 'an elderly rector who could do little'.[47] Lewis Tuckwell (1876–1907), like West a former chaplain of Magdalen College,[48] resided and served the cure alone. Under him church attendance increased and the building was restored, musical life, including a church choir, was cultivated, and a churchmen's union, bellringers' club, and other societies were formed.[49] Conflict over tithe and other issues during the 1880s, culminating in a tithe reapportionment in 1887, was promoted chiefly by the querulous farmer John Perry, whose produce was distrained and who apparently enjoyed little support.[50]

In the earlier 20th century only Thomas Lovett (rector 1908–32), who in 1911 completed

[27] *Subsidy 1526*, 261; A. H. Thompson, *Hist. Newarke Hosp.* 237 and n.; O.A.S. *Rep.* (1914), 196, 201.

[28] *Alum. Oxon. 1500–1714*, ii. 788 (wrongly stating that Inkforbye d. 1599), iii. 1152; O.R.O., MSS. Wills Oxon. 37/3/17, 50/1/13; C.O.S., par. reg. transcripts, s.v. Inkforbye.

[29] O.A.S. *Rep.* (1914), 181, 201; F. Goadby, 'Thomas Napkyn', *Top. Oxon.* xix (1973/4); *Alum. Oxon. 1500–1714*, s.v. Fras. Bradshaw, Thos. Napkyn; *V.C.H. Oxon.* v. 316. For other curates, O.R.O., MSS. Wills Oxon. 155/2/23, 295/2/56; ibid. 179, ff. 114, 183–4.

[30] O.A.S. *Rep.* (1914), 181, 196–7, 201.

[31] *D.N.B.*; cf. Magd. Coll. Mun., LE/55, lease 28 May 11 Chas. I, reserving part of the rectory ho.

[32] *Protestation Rtns. and Tax Assess.* 27; Hist. MSS. Com. 5, *6th Rep., H.L.*, p. 127; *L.J.* viii. 435; *Alum. Oxon. 1500–1714*, iv. 1353.

[33] O.R.O., Cal. Presentation Deeds, 2nd ser. f. 80; C.O.S., par. reg. transcripts; cf. Linc. Coll. Mun., L/STA/43.

[34] Linc. Coll. Mun., D/STA/53; *Progress Notes of Warden Woodward* (Wilts. Arch. and Nat. Hist. Soc., Rec. Branch, xiii), p. 7; cf. *Hearth Tax Oxon.* 229.

[35] A. Wood, *Athenae Oxonienses*, ed. P. Bliss, iv. 161; W. D. Macray, *Reg. Magd. Coll.* N.S. iii. 181–2; O.R.O., Cal. Presentation Deeds, 2nd ser. f. 80.

[36] O.R.O., Cal. Presentation Deeds, 2nd ser. ff. 80–1; cf. *Alum. Oxon. 1500–1714, 1715–1886*.

[37] *Cal. S.P. Dom. 1664–5*, 181.

[38] O.R.O., MS. Wills Oxon. 124/4/17; *Hearne's Colln.* vii (O.H.S. xlviii), 236; below, this section [ch. archit.]; educ.

[39] O.R.O., MSS. Oxf. Dioc. d 557, ff. 57–60; d 560, ff. 77–9; d 563, ff. 77–80; *D.N.B.*

[40] O.R.O., MSS. Oxf. Dioc. d 557, ff. 57–60; d 560, ff. 77–9; d 563, ff. 77–80; d 569, ff. 99–100; *Secker's Visit.* 143–4.

[41] O.R.O., MSS. Oxf. Dioc. b 38, ff. 186–7; b 41, f. 204; c 332, f. 403; c 428, f. 39; d 571, ff. 97–8; d 573, ff. 97–8; d 575, ff. 99–100; ibid. Cal. Presentation Deeds, 2nd ser. ff. 80–1; *Wilb. Visit.* 134.

[42] O.R.O., MS. Oxf. Dioc. c 658, f. 29.

[43] *Oxf. Chron.* 20 Mar. 1841.

[44] *Wilb. Letter Bks.* pp. 151–3, 163, 166–7, 173–4.

[45] *Wilb. Visit.* 134.

[46] O.R.O., MS. Oxf. Dioc. c 332, ff. 403–404v.; *Ch. and Chapel, 1851*, no. 408; cf. *Census, 1851–71*.

[47] O.R.O., PAR 248/17/MS 2/1, p. 1; ibid. MSS. Oxf. Dioc. c 338, f. 381; c 341, f. 400; J. S. Reynolds, *Evangelicals at Oxford 1735–1871*, 115, 186.

[48] *Alum. Oxon. 1715–1886*, iv. 1445, 1527.

[49] O.R.O., MSS. Oxf. Dioc. c 344, ff. 377–8; c 350, ff. 372–3; c 353, ff. 386–7; c 362, ff. 382–3; ibid. PAR 248/17/MS 2/1; PAR 248/9/J 1/1, pp. 71, 77; *Standlake Par. Mag. 1877–9, passim*: copy in Bodl. Per. G.A. Oxon. 8° 666; Tuckwell, *Reminiscences of Thirty Happy Years, passim*; above, intro.; below, this section [ch. archit.].

[50] O.R.O., PAR 248/9/J 1/1, pp. 75, 333, 343; Bodl. G.A. Oxon. c 317/13, cuttings etc. c. 1877–88.

the church restoration, served the living for a long period, and three rectors stayed for under five years. From 1912 all served Yelford also.[51] Church attendance reportedly increased after the First World War but declined in the 1930s;[52] Standlake was at that time a centre of anti-tithe agitation, and though farmers remained 'personally fairly friendly' most 'held aloof' from the Church.[53] George Dauglish (rector 1936–47), though deeply involved in village life, was at 'continual loggerheads' with some prominent parishioners notably over confirmation, and in 1945 appealed to the bishop for support.[54]

The church of *ST. GILES*, so called probably by 1230 and certainly by 1439,[55] comprises chancel, north and south transepts each formerly with an east chapel, aisled nave with south

lancets at its east end and a round-headed doorway in its north wall. The asymmetrical transepts, with east chapels or apses, were added about the same time, perhaps *c.* 1235 when indulgences were granted to those visiting a 'chapel' founded and built in Standlake;[57] the entrance to a rood loft survives high up in the south transept's north-east corner, and the outline of a piscina immediately south of the north transept's former east chapel. A small chapel was built soon after into the angle between the nave and the south transept, indicating that there was then no south aisle; since the north transept is longer than the south there may, however, have been a north aisle. Both aisles were either newly built or remodelled in the early 14th century, the date

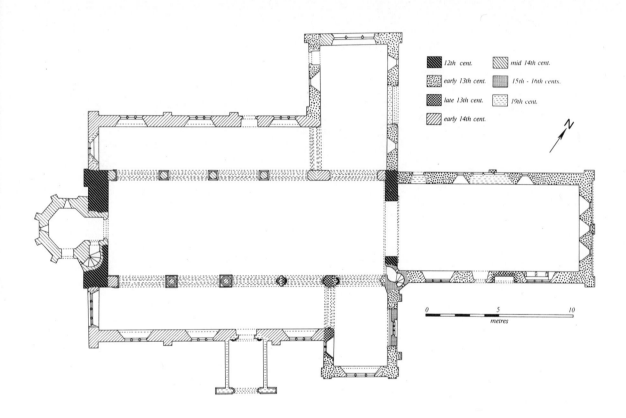

THE CHURCH OF ST. GILES, STANDLAKE

porch, and octagonal west tower with spire.[56] The chancel arch and the thick west wall of the nave, which has flat external buttresses, are of the late 12th century, and there may formerly have been a large west tower within the area of the later nave, which is of notable length. In the earlier 13th century the chancel was rebuilt on a large scale, with a triplet of

of their windows and of the surviving south arcade, and about the same time a window with a cusped rere-arch was inserted into the south transept's south wall. Similarities to the pier and tracery forms of Bampton church, remodelled *c.* 1317,[58] suggest that the same masons were employed. In the mid 14th century the north arcade was rebuilt, and the unusual, three-staged

[51] O.R.O., MS. Oxf. Dioc. c 2017, presentations etc.; below, this section [ch. archit.].

[52] Goadby, *1228 and All That*, 62; O.R.O., PAR 248/9/J 1/3, ff. 33v., 37v.

[53] O.R.O., PAR 248/9/J 1/3, f. 32v.

[54] Ibid. ff. 33v.–34, 40.

[55] *Cal. Papal Reg.* ix. 55–6; above, econ. hist. (mkt. and fair).

[56] Pevsner, *Oxon.* 776–8; for church before restoration, Bodl. MSS. Top. Oxon. a 68, no. 497; c 522, f. 27v.; ibid. MSS. Don. c 91, p. 165; e 108, ff. 12–15; J. Parker, *Eccl. Top.* no. 198; O.A.S. *Rep.* (1871), 17–19; above, plate 30.

[57] *Reg. W. Gray* (Surtees Soc. lvi), p. 72.

[58] Above, Bampton: Bampton and Weald, church.

octagonal tower and spire, reminiscent of the tower at Cogges, were added; also in the mid 14th century, windows with flowing tracery were inserted into the north walls of the chancel and of the north transept, the latter window perhaps associated with Simon of Evesham's chantry.[59] The south porch, rebuilt in the 19th century, was probably of similar date.

Indulgences were granted c. 1439 to those giving alms towards the church's conservation.[60] Perhaps at that time the chancel's east windows were blocked and replaced with external canopied niches,[61] implying that there was a substantial reredos. A nave clerestory was added c. 1500 and the roof pitch lowered, though the steeper gables at the nave's east end and against the tower were retained. About the same time two four-light, square-headed windows were inserted into the south wall of the chancel and the west end of the south aisle, the cill of the former being dropped to form double sedilia with arm rests. The work may have been instigated by the rector Richard Salter, who inserted or repaired one of the chancel windows in 1503.[62]

The chapels east of the transepts were demolished and their opening arches blocked presumably after the suppression of chantries; the former opening in the south transept includes a two-light window presumably of 16th-century date. The church was 'in decay' in the early 17th century when disputes arose over church rates levied for repairs,[63] and in the early 1660s the rector John Dale went to 'great expense' in restoring and wainscotting the chancel.[64] The nave roof was repaired c. 1787, reportedly re-using 16th-century timbers, and general repairs were undertaken from c. 1803.[65] Then or later the chancel was reroofed in 'meagre' fashion,[66] and before 1871 the blocked east windows were restored.[67]

In 1831 the church was said to be in good repair, but in 1854 the spire was 'ruinous'.[68] By the 1870s the roof leaked, the walls bulged and were disfigured by moss, and the floors were so rotten that in the chancel they had fallen through, exposing tombs beneath.[69] Restoration by the architect C. Clapton Rolfe was carried out in four stages between 1880 and 1891, financed chiefly from local fund-raising and private donations. The walls were repointed and in places rebuilt, the south doorway was replaced by one in 13th-century style, and the church was entirely reroofed, the new nave and chancel roofs

incorporating carved figures of angels. The porch was rebuilt in its former style re-using original stonework. Rediscovered lancets in the chancel's north wall and in the north transept and a late 13th-century two-light window in the north aisle's west end were reopened, and the mid 14th- and 15th-century windows in the chancel were blocked. A western gallery was removed, and the church was repewed and refurnished throughout, the south transept being refitted as a baptistry and the north as a choir vestry.[70] The tower was restored in 1911.[71] Substantial repairs to the nave roof were required c. 1950, a consequence partly of wartime bomb damage and partly of structural defects,[72] and general repairs were carried out in 1970–1.[73] A major restoration in the early 1990s included reroofing, and repair of stonework, timber, and glass.[74] Heating was by stove in 1880, and electric heating was introduced c. 1959; electric lighting replaced oil lamps c. 1949.[75]

New furnishings introduced between 1880 and 1891 included carved woodwork by Harry Hems of Exeter, notably an oak pulpit and lectern, oak pews with bench ends featuring representations of saints, an oak screen shutting off the north transept vestry, choir stalls with representations of the apostles, and an oak altar with a central figure of Christ, modelled on the altarpiece of Magdalen College chapel.[76] A carved oak cupboard was made from the 17th-century pulpit by a local craftsman.[77] The Norman font, then in the north aisle but behind the communion rail in the earlier 19th century,[78] was replaced in 1883 by a new one in the south transept, with an elaborately carved cover by Hems.[79] A pipe organ installed in the north transept in 1967 following local controversy was replaced by an electronic organ before 1978.[80]

Remains of red colouring survive on the south transept's blocked eastern arch, and remains of a red consecration cross on the lintel of an original cupboard behind the main altar. Fragments of medieval stained glass in the south transept's west window, of various dates between the 14th century and the 16th, include part of an inscription of 1503 to the rector Richard Salter, formerly in the chancel. A representation of St. Giles survived in one of the chancel's south windows in the 18th century.[81] Modern stained glass in the chancel, installed in 1892 and 1894, commemorates members of the Strickland and Cottrell-Dormer

59 Above, this section.
60 *Cal. Papal Reg.* ix. 55–6.
61 Bodl. MS. Top. Oxon. d 218, f. 225; Parker, *Eccl Top.* no. 198; above, plate 30.
62 *Par. Colln.* iii. 287; cf. Bodl. MS. Don. e 108, f. 14v.; O.A.S. *Rep.* (1871), 17.
63 Bodl. MS. Top. Oxon. c 118, f. 2v.
64 *Cal. S.P. Dom.* 1664–5, 181; *Par. Colln.* iii. 288.
65 O.R.O., MS. Oxf. Archd. Oxon. c 104, ff. 45–7, 72, 75–7; ibid. MS. Oxf. Dioc. d 569, ff. 99–100; *Standlake Par. Mag.* 1877–9, 136: copy in Bodl. Per. G.A. Oxon. 8° 666.
66 *Standlake Par. Mag.* 1877–9, 135.
67 O.A.S. *Rep.* (1871), 17 and n.
68 O.R.O., MS. Oxf. Dioc. b 38, ff. 186–7; ibid. MS. Oxf. Archd. Oxon. c 43, ff. 182v., 186v.; *Wilb. Visit.* 135.
69 Bodl. G.A. Oxon. c 317/13, concert programme 23 July 1879; Tuckwell, *Reminiscences*, 10, 13–14; cf. *Standlake Par. Mag.* 1877–9, 135–7.
70 O.R.O., MSS. Oxf. Dioc. c 2017, faculty petition

1880; c 2207, no. 4; ibid. PAR 248/9/J 1/1, pp. 133, 195, 333, 389; Bodl. G.A. Oxon. c 317/13, cuttings etc.; Tuckwell, *Reminiscences*, 10–16.
71 Tuckwell, *Reminiscences*, 18.
72 O.R.O., MS. Oxf. Dioc. c 2017, faculty petition 12 May 1950.
73 Ibid. faculty application 22 Dec. 1970; Goadby, *1228 and All That*, 68.
74 Display in church 1994.
75 O.R.O., MS. Oxf. Dioc. c 2017, faculty petitions.
76 Ibid. PAR 248/9/J 1/1, pp. 133, 195, 333, 389; Tuckwell, *Reminiscences*, 11–15.
77 O.R.O., P2/2/MS 1/3, listing other furnishings also.
78 Ibid. MS. Oxf. Dioc. c 2017, faculty petition 1880; Bodl. MS. Top. Oxon. a 68, no. 495; ibid. MS. Don. e 108, f. 12.
79 Tuckwell, *Reminiscences*, 11.
80 O.R.O., MS. Oxf. Dioc. c 2017, faculty application and corresp. 1966; Goadby, *1228 and All That*, 68–9.
81 *Par. Colln.* iii. 287; cf. O.A.S. *Rep.* (1871), 17.

families of Cokethorpe House, some or all of it by Burlison and Grylls of London.[82] A window in the south transept commemorates James Florey (d. 1882) of Brighthampton.

A small, 13th-century tomb recess survives in the chancel's external south wall. Headless statues of St. Thomas and St. John the Evangelist, discovered in the north aisle c. 1888,[83] are probably 14th-century, and were perhaps associated with Simon of Evesham's chantry; they were reset in the south transept in 1994. Later monuments include memorials to members of the Strickland and Western families of Cokethorpe House and to several rectors; lost monuments include a brass to Joan (d. 1465/6), wife of John Gaunt of Gaunt House.[84]

The plate includes an 'Elizabethan' chalice and paten cover, and a silver paten cover of 1697 inscribed I:C, presumably for John Chambers, rector 1684–1721.[85] Robert Radborne (d. 1557) bequeathed a 'large bell' to the church,[86] and from the 18th century there was a ring of five by Henry Bagley III, dated 1709, 1710, and 1730. The tenor, split by 1837, was replaced in 1843 by a bell by William Taylor, and in 1887 the bells were rehung and a treble by Mears & Stainbank added as a Jubilee offering, making a ring of six. The present fourth was recast in 1931, when a cast iron frame replaced the wooden one. The saunce, by Thomas Rudhall of Gloucester, is dated 1781.[87] The registers begin c. 1559.[88]

The churchyard was extended westwards in 1899 after plans for a separate cemetery were abandoned; it was further enlarged in 1953.[89]

NONCONFORMITY. Malyn and Mary Yate of the later Standlake Manor were fined for recusancy during the late 16th century and early 17th, though their husbands James (d. 1608) and Francis seem to have conformed. Two or three other women and two yeomen were also fined repeatedly.[90] Three recusants signed the Protestation in 1642,[91] among them Richard Hyde of Standlake Manor, whose family continued as Roman Catholics in the early 1770s. No other papists were recorded in 1738 or later.[92]

In 1521 members of the Brabant family of Standlake were accused of holding meetings at which scriptures were read in English, and of denouncing pilgrimages.[93] A few nonconformists recorded in the later 17th century were probably Anabaptists, of whom four families were noted in 1738 and 6–8 families in the later 18th century, all attending Cote chapel.[94] Meeting house licences in 1750, 1800, and 1817 related probably to Baptists,[95] and Standlake Manor, let by the Baptist Tomkins family of Abingdon to the Baptist farmer Thomas Peck, was registered in 1799.[96] Curates in the early 19th century reported no more than 10–12 dissenters and claimed that numbers were decreasing,[97] but a 'good congregation' of Baptists was noted in 1821,[98] and in 1832 a rubble and slate chapel with 180 sittings, served from Cote, was built on the Abingdon road between Standlake and Brighthampton, on land given by William Tomkins.[99] Those dissatisfied with Standlake's curate, Frank Burges, allegedly filled the chapel 'almost to suffocation' by 1841,[1] and in 1850–1 average attendance for evening services was over 160.[2] A gallery was added to the chapel in 1865.[3] Relations with the Established Church seem usually to have been amicable, and several prominent adherents, among them members of the Giles, Pinnock, Hosier, and Costar families, held parish offices sometimes including that of churchwarden.[4] An organ was acquired in 1903 and the chapel was repaired in 1911 and 1914, but its isolated position between the two villages contributed to falling attendance by the 1930s, and from 1937 to 1951 services were discontinued. In 1962 the Sunday school had 20 pupils, but the chapel was closed c. 1978, and ownership was transferred to a missionary society which in 1994 used it as offices.[5]

Primitive Methodists held a mission at Standlake in 1845,[6] and in the later 1850s a minister from Faringdon (then Berks.) preached and held meetings there regularly before a 'large congregation'.[7] A meeting house at the Green was licensed in 1857, and a chapel of variegated brick, with 150 sittings, was built on the same site c. 1864–5 and licensed in 1866.[8] It was transferred from the Faringdon to the Witney

[82] O.R.O., MS. Oxf. Dioc. c 2017, faculties; plaques in church.
[83] O.R.O., PAR 248/9/J 1/1, p. 333.
[84] Par. Colln. iii. 287; above, other estates.
[85] Evans, Ch. Plate, 156; above, this section.
[86] O.R.O., MS. Wills Oxon. 182, f. 165.
[87] Ibid. MS. Oxf. Archd. Oxon. c 43, ff. 166v., 170v.; Ch. Bells Oxon. iv. 384–5.
[88] C.O.S., par. reg. transcripts.
[89] O.R.O., MS. Oxf. Dioc. c 2018, conveyances; Oxf. Jnl. 4 Nov. 1899; Tuckwell, Reminiscences, 16, wrongly implying c. 1892.
[90] H. E. Salter, 'Oxon. Recusants', O.A.S. Rep. (1924), 21–2, 25, 30, 33, 35, 37, 43, 48–9, 51–2, 54–5, 58; Recusant Roll 1592–3 (Cath. Rec. Soc. xviii), 257; cf. P.R.O., PROB 11/111, ff. 295v.–296v.; above, other estates.
[91] Protestation Rtns. and Tax Assess. 27.
[92] O.R.O., MSS. Oxf. Dioc. d 557, f. 57v.; d 560, f. 77; d 563, ff. 77; ibid. QSD E.1, pp. 45–6, 205; Secker's Visit. 143; above, other estates.
[93] J. Foxe, Acts and Mons. ed. J. Pratt (4th edn.), iv. 235–9, 242.
[94] O.R.O., MSS. Oxf. Dioc. d 557, f. 57v.; d 560, f. 77; d 563, f. 77; Bp. Fell and Nonconf. 33, 35, 38, 61 n.; Secker's Visit. 143.
[95] O.R.O., QSR Easter 1750, Trin. 1800; ibid. MS. Oxf. Dioc.

c 644, f. 86; cf. 'Extracts from Cote Ch. Bks.' (TS. in C.O.S.), passim.
[96] O.R.O., MS. Oxf. Dioc. c 644, f. 48; cf. ibid. QSD L.260; V.C.H. Berks. iv. 450–1; above, other estates.
[97] O.R.O., MSS. Oxf. Dioc. d 569, f. 99; d 571, f. 97; d 573, f. 97; d 575, f. 99; d 581, f. 94.
[98] J. Hinton, Hist. Sketch of Assoc. Churches (1821), 8: copy in Bodl. 11135 e 90 (11).
[99] O.R.O., P2/2/MS 1/21; Ch. and Chapel, 1851, no. 409; J. Stanley, Church in the Hop Garden [c. 1936], 191–2.
[1] Oxf. Chron. 20 Mar. 1841.
[2] Ch. and Chapel, 1851, no. 409.
[3] O.R.O., P2/2/MS 1/21, f. 5.
[4] 'Extracts from Cote Ch. Bks.' (TS. in C.O.S.), passim; O.R.O., PAR 248/2/A1/1; Bodl. G.A. Oxon. c 317/13, open letter from D. C. Hosier 11 Apr. 1877; J. Goadby, 1228 and All That, 61.
[5] H. Eden, 'Cote Baptist Ch.' 18–19 (TS. c. 1957 in C.O.S.); Regent's Park Coll., Cote Ch. Bk. 1882–1972; Goadby, 1228 and All That, 69; local inf.
[6] O.R.O., NM2/B/A5/2, 15 Sept. 1845.
[7] Ibid. P 115/J/1, passim.
[8] Ibid. P2/2/MS 1/22, f. 1; ibid. NM2/B/A2/28; P.R.O., RG 9/905; P.O. Dir. Oxon. (1864); mutilated datestone 1865(?). For illust. of 1873, Bodl. MS. Top. Oxon. d 218, f. 230.

circuit *c.* 1917.[9] Dissent generally in the parish was said to be decreasing in the later 19th century,[10] though 40 Primitive Methodists were reported in Standlake in 1918 and still in 1932,[11] when they were absorbed into the United Methodist Church. By 1970 there was only one resident member, and Sunday services ceased; weekday evening meetings and a Sunday school continued, however, and there were ecumenical activities with Baptists and Anglicans.[12] The chapel remained in occasional use in 1994.

EDUCATION. A school in Standlake was mentioned in 1672.[13] William Plasterer of Stanton Harcourt, by will proved 1711, left £30 to be invested for educating poor children of Standlake,[14] and the rector John Chambers, by will proved 1721, left *c.* 12 a. towards teaching them to read.[15] In 1738 fifteen children were taught reading and writing under the endowment, and 5 more at the rector's expense, but the income of £6 a year was insufficient to attract licensed masters: the rector had dismissed three unlicensed masters since 1724 and was contemplating dismissing a fourth.[16] By 1805, however, 12 children were taught by a long-serving master of 'great repute'.[17] In 1808 the endowed pupils learned reading only, but 33 others, supported from parental contributions, learned writing and accounts also;[18] 20 boys and 10 girls were taught in 1815, though many were removed for harvest work.[19] In 1834 there were 42 pupils, of whom 16 were taught free.[20] The endowment yielded £7–8 *c.* 1820, when not all the rent was received, and £20 *c.* 1846.[21]

Until 1846 the school was held in the church, but in that year a master's house and a stone-built schoolroom for around 60 boys were erected opposite the rectory house on land donated by Magdalen College, the cost met by subscriptions and donations.[22] Children from Brighthampton were admitted then if not earlier.[23] In 1854 there were *c.* 40 pupils[24] but in 1863 *c.* 18, inefficiently taught by a long-serving but neglectful master.[25] An additional room was built *c.* 1865, and in 1866 the school had room

for 47 pupils of both sexes and 47 infants;[26] further locally-financed enlargements were made *c.* 1874 and *c.* 1894,[27] the government having refused aid unless the school accepted dissenters.[28] Average attendance rose from 43 in 1875 to 109 by 1890.[29] Income of *c.* £114 in 1877 included £22 from the endowment, *c.* £17 from government grant (increased to £43 in 1878), £21 from children's pence, £28 from a voluntary rate, and £23 from the chief landowners; outgoings were *c.* £113, including £80 for salaries.[30] Weekly fees, 2*d.* or 4*d.* in 1867, were increased in 1882 to 3*d.* for children of tradesmen and 6*d.* for those of farmers.[31] The voluntary rate in 1883 was allegedly higher than necessary because two leading farmers, one a dissenter, refused to contribute.[32]

By 1867 there was a certificated master sometimes assisted by a mistress. Thereafter the school was usually judged satisfactory,[33] though in the early 1920s inadequate heating and sanitation allegedly reduced it to 'minding children generally and teaching them occasionally'.[34] In 1939 the seniors were transferred to the Batt school in Witney despite local opposition, leaving 57 pupils and 2 teachers in the junior and infant school;[35] the school was granted controlled status *c.* 1947 and Northmoor children were admitted in 1957.[36] During the 1960s experiments with out-of-class work prompted interest from educationalists, though in the later 1960s there was controversy over facilities and academic standards.[37] The buildings were extended in 1969, when the roll was 112, and in 1974; the roll was 164 in 1975 and 159 in 1977.[38] From 1906 John Chambers's endowment, under a Charity Commission Scheme, funded prizes for pupils entering higher education or apprenticeships.[39]

There were 2 or 3 private day schools for much of the 19th century, supported by parental contributions and usually with 30–60 pupils between them. Three in 1808, teaching reading and sewing, had closed by 1815 chiefly because of parental apathy, and in 1831, when three other schools taught 36 pupils, over 60 children had no access to education. In 1835 two day and four

9 O.R.O., NM2/B/A2/27–8.
10 Ibid. MSS. Oxf. Dioc. c 332, f. 404; c 344, f. 377v.; c 347, f. 389v.
11 Ibid. NM2/B/A2/28–42.
12 Ibid. NM2/26/A1/1, s.a. 1970–6.
13 O.R.O., MS. Oxf. Dioc. e 22, p. 14.
14 Ibid. MS. Wills Oxon. 145/2/3.
15 Ibid. MS. Wills Oxon. 122/1/30; cf. ibid. PAR 248/13/6 D/1–3. 16 *Secker's Visit.* 144.
17 O.R.O., MS. Oxf. Dioc. d 569, ff. 99–100v.
18 Ibid. d 707, f. 164.
19 Ibid. c 433, f. 186.
20 Ibid. b 39, f. 312.
21 Ibid. c 433, f. 186; Ch. Ch. Arch., MS. Estates 80, f. 105; *10th Rep. Com. Char.* 360; *Educ. of Poor*, H.C. 224, p. 730 (1819), ix (2); cf. *Digest Schs. and Chars. for Educ.* [435], p. 221, H.C. (1843), xviii.
22 O.R.O., MS. Oxf. Dioc. d 569, f. 101 and v.; ibid. PAR 248/14/L 1/1; Ch. Ch. Arch., MS. Estates 80, ff. 105–6; O.S. Map 1/2,500, Oxon. XXXVIII. 6 (1876 edn.).
23 Magd. Coll. Mun., EP 220/39, letter 7 Dec. 1874; *Returns relating to Elem. Educ.* H.C. 201, p. 324 (1871), lv.
24 *Wilb. Visit.* 135.
25 Linc. Coll. Mun., C/STA/3; cf. *P.O. Dir. Oxon.* (1847 and later edns.).
26 Ch. Ch. Arch., MS. Estates 80, ff. 135–137v.; O.R.O.,

MS. Oxf. Dioc. c 332, f. 403v.
27 Magd. Coll. Mun., EP 220/39; Linc. Coll. Mun., C/STA/6, corresp. 1893; O.R.O., PAR 248/14/D 1/1; Tuckwell, *Reminiscences*, 17–18.
28 Ch. Ch. Arch., MS. Estates 80, ff. 135–6.
29 *Return of Public Elem. Schs. 1875–6* [C. 1882], pp. 216–17, H.C. (1877), lxvii; *Public Elem. Schs. Return*, H.C. 403, pp. 212–17 (1890), lvi.
30 *Standlake Par. Mag. 1877–9*, pp. 44, 77, 127: copy in Bodl. Per. G.A. Oxon. 8° 666; cf. *Return of Public Elem. Schs. 1875–6*, pp. 216–17.
31 *Schs. Inquiry* [3966-XI], pp. 308–9, H.C. (1867–8), xxviii (10); O.R.O., PAR 248/2/A 1/1, f. 70v.
32 Magd. Coll. Mun., EP 224/8, letter 21 May 1883; cf. Ch. Ch. Arch., MS. Estates 80, ff. 135–6.
33 *Schs. Inquiry*, pp. 308–9; *Standlake Par. Mag. 1877–9*, pp. 44, 49, 81, 128; O.R.O., PAR 248/9/J 1/1, pp. 355, 371, 373, 387, 407.
34 O.R.O., T/SL/98 i, s.a. 1919 sqq.
35 Ibid. s.a. 1939; O.R.O., PAR 248/9/J 1/3, ff. 33v., 38 and v.
36 O.R.O., T/SL/98 ii, s.a. 1957.
37 Ibid. s.a. 1964–70; *Oxf. Times*, 8 Sept. 1967.
38 O.R.O., T/SL/98 ii, s.a. 1969–77.
39 Ibid. T/SL/98 i, s.a. 1907; ibid. P4/4/A 2/1, copy of Scheme 9 Oct. 1906; J. Goadby, *1228 and All That* (priv. print. *c.* 1978), 70.

infant schools taught over 100 pupils in all, and some in the 1840s and 1850s took a few boarders. Three or four nonconformist schools, charging pupils between 3d. and 6d. weekly, were reported in 1864, and one continued until 1890.[40] A night school run successfully by the curate in 1866 was revived in the later 1870s but had closed by 1884.[41] L. S. Tuckwell, rector 1876–1907, taught private pupils.[42]

CHARITIES FOR THE POOR.[43] William Allen, by will proved c. 1632 or c. 1686,[44] bequeathed a 10s. rent charge on a house and land for yearly distribution in bread. After the sale of the property in parcels in 1811 nothing was received until 1823 when the purchasers were found to be liable, and three years' arrears were distributed in bread. The charity was mentioned by name in 1852[45] but not after 1878, when it was perhaps represented by 10s. rent administered with another charity and distributed yearly in bread to schoolchildren.[46]

Elizabeth West, by will dated 1638, and her brother John Walter, by will proved 1640, gave land in Appleton (then Berks.) to the poor of Standlake, Witney, and Eynsham. Standlake's share, one quarter, was c. £11 in 1786 and over £18 in 1878, distributed weekly in bread.[47] Thomas Weale, by will proved 1658,[48] left a cottage and land for the poor of Standlake, Brittenton, Brighthampton, and Northmoor, in equal portions; Standlake and Brittenton's share, £2 in 1738 and 1786 and £9 10s. in 1878, was distributed twice yearly in bread and money. Robert Wyatt, by will proved 1676,[49] left a £2 rent charge distributed yearly in money.

In 1694 charitable bequests including those of Dame Elizabeth Stonehouse (£5 by will proved 1655),[50] one Allen (£5), John Jones (£3), and William Farr (£10 by will proved 1691)[51] were used to buy a cottage and land later called Yatemans,[52] the rents to benefit the poor. In the early 18th century the cottage was held rent-free, and c. £1 was received for the land; cottage and land together yielded £4 by 1824 and £6 by 1878, distributed yearly in bread and money.

Susannah Crouch, by will dated 1713, left £300, used in 1715 to buy land in Stanford-in-the-Vale (then Berks.). The rent, c. £16 in 1786 and £48 in 1878, was distributed weekly in bread.[53] In 1808 accumulated rents of c. £64 were used to build or rebuild cottages for the parish poor at Rack End, and interest of £3 4s. from the overseers was carried to the bread account. In 1866 £36 undistributed income was used to buy two other cottages,[54] the rent from which, £5 4s. in 1878, was also distributed in bread.

Thomas Weston, by will proved 1757, left a house and close,[55] the rents to be distributed twice a year in bread. The charity yielded c. £4 10s. in 1786 and £16 in 1878, then distributed in bread and money. A bequest by James Leverett of Witney, by will dated 1783,[56] seems not to have been received.

A Charity Commission Scheme of 1908, when income, excluding the West and Walter charity, was c. £67, amalgamated the surviving charities, and separately vested the poor allotment of 10 a. granted at inclosure. The Scheme was amended in 1937. A further Scheme of 1976 reorganized the charities as Standlake Welfare Trust for the benefit of Standlake and that part of Hardwick-with-Yelford formerly within the parish. Brighthampton's share of Weale's charity became part of Bampton Consolidated Charities and later of Bampton Welfare Trust under Schemes of 1888 and 1972; a two-acre close in Bampton thought to belong to the Brighthampton poor was sold in 1967 for £450, interest from which was administered by the Trust for the benefit of the Brighthampton poor.[57]

YELFORD

YELFORD, one of Oxfordshire's smallest rural parishes until it was included in 1932 in the civil parish of Hardwick-with-Yelford,[58] lies 3 miles (4.75 km.) south of Witney and 3 miles east of Bampton.[59] The village, noted for its seclusion,[60] is accessible by a single narrow lane. In 1876 the parish contained 336 a.,[61] but its medieval extent was greater, the eastern part being lost to

[40] O.R.O., MSS. Oxf. Dioc. d 707, f. 164; c 433, f. 186; d 579, f. 73; b 38, f. 187; Ch. Ch. Arch., MS. Estates 80, ff. 135–6; Educ. Enq. Abstract, H.C. 62, p. 754 (1835), xlii; Goadby, 1228 and All That, 46–7, 57; cf. Educ. of Poor, H.C. 224, p. 730 (1819), ix (2); Returns relating to Elem. Educ. H.C. 201, p. 324 (1871), lv.

[41] O.R.O., MSS. Oxf. Dioc. c 332, f. 404; c 341, f. 401; c 344, f. 378; c 350, f. 373; cf. Standlake Par. Mag. 1877–9, pp. 65, 81, 90, 137.   [42] O.R.O., PAR 248/17/MS 2/1, p. 8.

[43] Based, except where stated, on Secker's Visit. 144; Char. Don. 970–1; 10th Rep. Com. Char. 360–3, 402–3; Standlake Par. Mag. no. 15 (Mar. 1878), 60–1: copy in Bodl. Per. G.A. Oxon. 8° 666.

[44] Char. Don. 970–1; 10th Rep. Com. Char. 360; no will has been found.

[45] Gardner's Dir. Oxon. (1852).

[46] Cf. J. Goadby, 1228 and All That (priv. print. c. 1978), 70.

[47] For deeds, O.R.O., PAR 248/13/2D1/1–2, PAR 248/13/2D2/1–2, PAR 248/13/2D3/1, PAR 248/2D4/1–2; cf. V.C.H. Oxon. xii. 158.

[48] P.R.O., PROB 11/283, ff. 401–402v.; for deeds, O.R.O., PAR 248/13/4D/1–4.

[49] P.R.O., PROB 11/351, f. 24.

[50] Ibid. PROB 11/243, f. 369.

[51] Ibid. PROB 11/403, f. 184v.

[52] Cf. O.R.O., PAR 248/13/3D/1–10; C.O.S., PRN 11403; Oxoniensia, xliii. 194.

[53] For deeds, O.R.O., PAR 248/13/1D/1–25.

[54] Bodl. MS. Top. Oxon. c 768/1, no. 72; cf. Standlake Par. Mag. no. 15 (Mar. 1878), 61.

[55] O.R.O., MS. Wills Oxon. 158/4/15; cf. Bodl. MS. Top. Oxon. c 768/1, no. 24.

[56] Copy in Bodl. G.A. Oxon. 8° 364.

[57] O.R.C.C., Kimber files; Magd. Coll. Estates Bursary, ledger o, pp. 477–80; cf. Goadby, 1228 and All That, 70.

[58] Census, 1931; M.O.H. Order 76241.

[59] The chief maps used were Berks. R.O., D/ELl P2: map of Yelford, 1625, reproduced above, plate 39; O.S. Map 1", sheet 13 (1830 edn.); ibid. 1/25,000, SP 20/30 (1978 edn.); ibid. 1/10,000, SP 30 SE., NE. (1975 edn.); 6", Oxon. XXXVII (1884), XXXVIII (1883); for the village ibid. 1/2,500, Oxon. XXXVII. 4, 8; XXXVIII. 1, 5 (1876 and later edns.).

[60] e.g. W. J. Monk, By Thames and Windrush, 42.

[61] O.S. Area. Bk. (1877).

Hardwick (then in Ducklington parish) for reasons discussed below. This article treats the history of the area covered by the medieval parish.

Before the mid 16th century, probably in response to severe depopulation in the later Middle Ages, Yelford's west part became an inclosed estate in single ownership, leaving other holdings to the east in open fields cropped with the fields of Hardwick. That reorganization seems to have been forgotten by the early 17th century when there was confusion over parish boundaries, including assertions that there were two Yelfords, West and East, the former belonging in some way to Bampton, the latter to Hardwick.[62] Evidently the tenants of Yelford's residual open fields, for taxation and other purposes, had become the responsibility of Hardwick's officers, while the inclosed estate, held entirely by the Hastings family, was assessed independently; disputes with Hardwick's officers seem to have arisen after John Hastings, usually taxed only for his inclosed estate, acquired some open-field land with the Walwyn family's Yelford estate in the mid 16th century.[63]

The division of Yelford for civil purposes persisted: the inclosed estate, which in 1625, excluding land outside the parish, comprised *c.* 310 a. worked from Yelford Manor,[64] came to be regarded as the whole parish, and although much of the open-field land immediately to the east continued to be worked from the only other farmhouse in the village (later College Farm)[65] both the house and attached estate were regarded as 'in another district', that is Hardwick.[66] Early 19th-century censuses and Yelford's tithe award of 1848 maintained that distinction,[67] so Yelford's boundaries in 1848 were those of the inclosed estate of 1625.[68] Although in 1852 the tithe commissioners declared *c.* 213 a. of Hardwick tithable to Yelford[69] no changes were made to parish boundaries. Minor discrepancies between Yelford's boundaries in 1876 and those of the inclosed estate of 1625 resulted from an agreement at the inclosure of Hardwick in 1853 that some old inclosures should be re-allotted.[70]

The medieval parish probably comprised some 550 a., its eastern part largely represented in later times by a section of Hardwick's open fields called Yelford field:[71] most strips there were attached to holdings in Yelford,[72] and after

inclosure in the mid 19th century the new fields in that area remained tithable to Yelford.[73] Yelford field, and probably the ancient parish, was bounded on the north and north-east by Boys wood and Home wood on a line which in 958 seems to have marked the limits of an important estate centred on Ducklington, and was later a boundary of Standlake.[74] On the east the boundary of Yelford field and perhaps of the early parish ran from the southern tip of Home wood probably down the shallow declivity west of Westfield Farm;[75] it met, near the beginning of Brighthampton Cut, the small stream which, bisecting Yelford, formed the eastern edge of the inclosed estate of 1625, and of Yelford as defined in the 19th century.[76] The southern and western boundaries of the ancient parish were those of the inclosed estate, and of the surviving Hardwick-with-Yelford. Westward from Brighthampton Cut the boundary with Shifford and Aston follows a watercourse which once bordered an ancient road or 'way', mentioned as Shifford's boundary in 1005;[77] the road, surviving in 1625, was suppressed shortly afterwards.[78] Yelford's north-western boundary with Ducklington, from a point on Aston's boundary south of Claywell Farm to Boys wood, is marked by a ditch, probably the dyke on Ducklington's boundary in 958 which led towards the boundary with Aston. On the north Yelford's boundary followed the southern edge of Boys wood, probably the Ducklington boundary in 958 and later that of Standlake.[79]

The southern part of the early parish, including the village site, lies on river alluvium at a height of *c.* 65 m.; gravel deposits cover the higher ground in the north of the parish at Rickless Hill (87 m.) and near Home wood (*c.* 90 m.), and Oxford clay the hill slopes.[80] The problem of flooding, not entirely solved by extensive drainage works in the area in the mid 19th century,[81] probably accounted in part for the two early moated sites in the village.[82] Water was obtained from shallow wells, and in a field north of the village there was an unfailing spring, Taberwell or Taperwell, reputedly both holy and medicinal, which from the 1950s was piped to Yelford Manor and the adjacent farm buildings.[83] Isolated cottages on the Hardwick road were similarly supplied from another ancient spring, Stockwell, in a field to the north.[84]

A lane links Yelford with Hardwick to the east

62 e.g. P.R.O., E 134/3 Jas. I/Mich. 22; E 134/4 Jas. I/Mich. 7; E 134/ 8 Jas. I/Trin. 3; E 134/1350/Misc. East Yelford tithing was mentioned in Hardwick court rolls in the 1580s: St. John's Coll. Mun., XI.10 (152, 154).

63 Below, econ. hist.

64 Above, plate 39. The acreage there given includes Boys wood and the Lawns, both in Standlake.

65 Below, econ. hist.

66 *Secker's Corresp.* 288.

67 *Census,* 1801–51; O.R.O., tithe award and map 451. Cf. Bryant, *Oxon. Map* (1823), which creates a fanciful boundary for this detached part of Hardwick.

68 Yelford was not resurveyed: the tithe map is a tracing of the estate map of 1625 with minor amendments.

69 O.R.O., Hardwick tithe award and map.

70 O.S. Map 6", Oxon. XXXVII, XXXVIII (1883–4 edns.); O.R.O., Hardwick and Yelford tithe maps; ibid. Standlake incl. award.

71 O.R.O., Standlake incl. award and map B.

72 e.g. Wadham Coll. Mun. 86/121, 123: terriers 1649, 1715.

73 O.R.O., Standlake incl. award and map A; ibid. tithe

award and map 202.

74 O.R.O. Standlake incl. map B; *Cart. Sax.* ed. Birch, iii, pp. 239–40, discussed above, Ducklington, intro.

75 Cf. O.R.O., Standlake incl. map B; O.S. Map 1/25,000, SP 20/30. For signs of former furlong divisions in that area cf. also C.O.S., SMR air photo. SP 3605 D.

76 Cf. above, plate 39; O.S. Map 6", Oxon. XXXVII, XXXVIII (1883–4 edns.).

77 Grundy, *Saxon Oxon.* 54–5; above, Bampton: Shifford, intro.

78 Above, plate 39; Bodl. MS. Top. Oxon. c 118, f. 7 and v.

79 *Cart. Sax.* ed. Birch, iii, pp. 239–40; Grundy, *Saxon Oxon.* 30; above, Ducklington, intro.

80 Geol. Surv. Map 1/50,000, solid and drift, sheet 236 (1982 edn.).

81 e.g. above, Standlake, econ. (agric.).

82 Below, manors.

83 Inf. from Mrs. H. Babington Smith. For Taberwell, Wadham Coll. Mun., 86/88, 121, 1234. For its site, C.O.S., SMR air photo. SP 2605 AS.

84 Inf. from Mrs. H. Babington Smith. For Stockwell, Wadham Coll. Mun., 86/121, 123–4.

and the Witney–Aston road to the west. Until the inclosure of Hardwick in 1853 the route to Hardwick ran further north, following the line of the surviving bridleway from the north end of the village towards Ducklington before branching north-eastwards to skirt the southern edge of Home wood.[85] An ancient lane from Brighthampton to Yelford, crossing the open fields between the later Westfield Farm and Brighthampton Cut, was abandoned at inclosure in 1853. In 1629 it joined the village street roughly opposite Rectory Cottage, although a section near that junction seems to have been realigned before the 19th century.[86] The lane formed part of an ancient route running south-eastwards to the river Thames, and a section south-east of Yelford was still called Abingdon Lane in 1839, although by then reduced to a fieldpath.[87] The lane leading west from Yelford in the early 17th century joined another ancient lane from Brighthampton which formed Yelford's south-west boundary; both lanes were dangerous and unsuitable for carts in 1629, and that on the boundary seems to have fallen out of use.[88] Perhaps in the later 18th century the village street seems to have been replaced or supplemented, at least for carts, by an east-west road which passed north of Yelford Manor and along the lower slopes of Rickless Hill before turning south to join the old route at the parish boundary.[89] By 1876, presumably after drainage work, the old route had been restored.[90] By then the village street south of College Farm had been realigned slightly to the west, perhaps destroying part of Yelford Manor's moat.[91] At inclosure in 1853 a straight road to Hardwick was laid out, and an occupation road from Boys wood to Brighthampton provided access to the newly inclosed fields.[92]

In fields immediately south-west of Home wood, within the bounds of the probable ancient parish, there are abundant signs of undated prehistoric settlements; crop marks and pottery finds indicate Romano-British settlement, and early-Saxon huts have been identified.[93] Romano-British pottery was also found on the north side of Rickless Hill.[94] An Anglo-Saxon burial ground, probably of the 7th century, was discovered in 1857 west of Westfield Farm on the

perimeter of the ancient parish.[95] An indication of early settlement in Yelford village was 12th-century pottery found beneath the hall of Yelford Manor.[96]

The place name, of which the early forms included Aieleforde, Eleford, and Eilesford, incorporates the Saxon personal name Aegel,[97] also associated with Elm Bank ditch on Ducklington's western boundary, which in 958 was *Aeglesuuillan broce* (the brook of Aegel's spring).[98] The ford was perhaps on the small, unnamed stream which, rising on the edge of Boys wood, runs through the village towards the river Thames; an early 14th-century inhabitant was Ralph at Ford.[99]

The village comprises only the church, the former rectory house (Rectory Cottage), a notable timber-framed manor house (Yelford Manor), a large 19th-century stone farmhouse (College Farm),[1] and a few modern houses. In the 1920s Yelford was noted for its setting 'in the midst of giant trees',[2] but most were elms which perished in the 1970s. In the early Middle Ages some 10–12 households were recorded in Yelford and in 1327 there were 16 taxpayers.[3] Depopulation, probably the result of plague, reduced Yelford to two or three taxable households by the 16th century. There are signs of abandoned house sites in a field on the north side of the village,[4] and others in fields west of the church.[5] The complete rebuilding of Yelford Manor and, unusually, of the church in the later 15th century may reflect extensive dereliction. In 1542 five men were mustered and six (in three families) were assessed for subsidy.[6] In the early 17th century usually two families were assessed,[7] and in the 18th century there were only the three houses mentioned above and perhaps, as later, a cottage attached to College Farm.[8] Yelford's recorded early 19th-century population of 16 or 17 people excluded the College Farm site.[9] On census day in 1851 the recorded population (17) was artificially high because both the departing tenant of Yelford Manor and his successor were present with their families; enumerated with Hardwick were the inhabitants of College Farm and its cottage, and an isolated cottage (Clarke's cottage) in a field towards Home wood, bringing Yelford's population effectively to over 30.[10]

85 O.R.O., Standlake incl. maps A and B; O.S. Map 1" (1830 edn.), sheet 13.
86 O.R.O., Standlake incl. map B; Bodl. MS. Top. Oxon. c 118, f. 7 and v.; O.S. Map 1" (1830 edn.), sheet 13.
87 O.R.O., Ducklington tithe map, plan of detached meadow near Yelford.
88 Above, plate 39; Bodl. MS. Top. Oxon. c 118, f. 7 and v.; above, Bampton: Shifford, intro.
89 O.S. Map 1" (1830 edn.), sheet 13; pencilled 19th-century amendments to map of 1625: above, plate 39. Cf. Jefferys, *Oxon. Map* (1767) and Davis, *Oxon. Map* (1797), which respectively show the road passing south and north of Yelford church.
90 O.S. Map 1/2,500, Oxon. XXXVII. 4 (1876 edn.).
91 Cf. above, plate 39; O.S. Map 1/2,500, Oxon. XXXVII. 4 (1876 edn.); below, manors.
92 O.R.O., Standlake incl. map A; O.S. Map 6", Oxon. XXXVIII (1883 edn.). The road was mistakenly referred to as a turnpike in 1871: O.A.S. *Rep.* (1871), 28.
93 C.O.S., SMR air photos. SP 3605 A–AS; ibid. PRN key map, and espec. 1535, 3978, 8209, 8677–9, 12526; D. Benson and D. Miles, *Upper Thames Valley*, 42–3; *V.C.H. Oxon.* i. 363–4.

94 Inf. from Mrs. H. Babington Smith.
95 C.O.S., PRN 1599; *V.C.H. Oxon.* i. 363; *Proc. Soc. Antiq.* 1st ser. iv. 97, 213–19; *Archaeologia*, xxxvii. 97; *Oxoniensia*, xxxvi. 112.
96 C.O.S., PRN 11977, esp. P. Gilman and others, 'Yelford Manor' (TS.), 6. A collection of finds from Yelford is housed in the Oxfordshire Museum Store, Standlake.
97 *P.N. Oxon.* (E.P.N.S.), 324.
98 Grundy, *Saxon Oxon.* 31.
99 P.R.O., E 179/161/9.
1 Below, church, manors.
2 W. J. Monk, *By Thames and Windrush*, 42.
3 *V.C.H. Oxon.* i. 421; *Bampton Hund. R.* 50–1, 63–4, 69; P.R.O., E 179/161/9.
4 There were buildings in the field in 1625: above, plate 39.
5 C.O.S., PRN 1101; ibid. SMR air photo. SP 3504 A–C.
6 *L. & P. Hen. VIII*, xvii, p. 507; P.R.O., E 179/162/234.
7 e.g. P.R.O., E 179/163/398, 435, 443.
8 *Secker's Corresp.* 288; P.R.O., HO 107/1731.
9 *Census*, 1801–51; P.R.O., HO 107/872, 1731.
10 P.R.O., HO 107/1731. For identification of Clarke's Cottage, O.R.O., Hardwick tithe map, plot 5007a.

Before 1871 a pair of cottages was built for College farm on the Hardwick road;[11] Clarke's cottage was abandoned in the late 19th century or early 20th when the well failed.[12] In 1891 there were 12 people in Rectory Cottage and Yelford Manor, and a further 14 in College Farm and the cottages.[13] There was no expansion until, from the 1970s, a few detached houses were built in the village.

MANORS AND OTHER ESTATES. In 1086 Walter son of Ponz held of the king 3 hides in *YELFORD*, together with estates in Westwell and Alwoldsbury (in Alvescot or Clanfield) and a piece of land belonging to the royal manor of Bampton, probably the 40 a. given before 1279 to Robert Pogeys by the lord of Yelford.[14] Walter also held Eaton Hastings (Berks.) and estates in Gloucestershire, notably Southrop.[15] Later Walter's Domesday estate, sometimes described as the honor of Hastings, was held by the Hastings family for 5 knights' fees, of which the Oxfordshire portion comprised 1½ fee.[16] Walter was probably a direct ancestor of the Hastings family,[17] of which, in Yelford, the earliest recorded representative was Philip, patron of the living in 1221.[18]

The overlordship of Yelford, held by William of Hastings in the 1240s,[19] passed on his death c. 1278 to a daughter Joan, wife of Benet of Blakenham,[20] and in 1279 Benet held Yelford in chief as ½ knight's fee.[21] By 1285 he had been succeeded by a minor son,[22] presumably the Benet who in 1297 conveyed the overlordship of the honor to his sister Alice, wife of Hugh de St. Philibert.[23] Their son John, a minor, held Yelford in 1305;[24] John de St. Philibert died in 1333 and was succeeded by his son John, a minor, who was recorded as lord of Yelford in 1346.[25] In 1428 the rector of Edington (Wilts.) was recorded as the holder by writ of John de St. Philibert's former estates in Westwell, Alwoldsbury, and Yelford.[26] John had sold Westwell in 1351 to William of Edington, founder of Edington monastery, but Yelford was not mentioned in that or other conveyances of the

St. Philibert lands in Oxfordshire.[27] In 1401–2 Yelford was not listed among the possessions of Edington,[28] and it seems that the overlordship had effectively ended.

Philip of Hastings, patron of the living and presumably lord of the manor in 1221, was apparently of a junior branch of the family: certainly his successor Miles, probably his son, held Yelford as an undertenant of the main line represented by William of Hastings (d. c. 1278) and Joan of Blakenham. Miles, a supporter of Simon de Montfort, suffered temporary confiscation of his estate after the battle of Evesham in 1265.[29] In 1279 he held Yelford of Benet of Blakenham, and in 1281 granted it to his son Thomas, retaining a life interest.[30] On Miles's death c. 1305 it therefore passed not to his heir, his grandson Miles, son of Philip, but to his son Thomas.[31] Thomas may have been dead by 1306 when Reynold (probably an error for Roland) of Hastings was listed as the principal taxpayer in Yelford.[32] In 1310, when Thomas's relict Agnes held a life interest in Yelford, Roland, probably their son, conveyed the reversion to Hugh Golafre.[33] Roland, however, seems to have retained or recovered the property, and was lord in 1316 and 1333;[34] he died c. 1335.[35] His heir, Thomas, died in 1361 leaving a son, Bartholomew, who came of age in 1368; both Thomas and Bartholomew seem to have made their principal residence at Daylesford (Worcs.), although retaining Yelford.[36]

A Thomas Hastings, holding Yelford in the early 15th century and said to be Bartholomew's son,[37] was presumably the Thomas who held Daylesford by 1408.[38] Before 1455 Thomas was succeeded by his son Edward who remained patron of Yelford rectory in 1498.[39] Edward witnessed a conveyance at Northmoor in 1461[40] but there is no firm evidence that the Hastings family was resident at Yelford until later. In the 1490s Edward was still lord but his son John appears to have settled in Yelford, his father perhaps remaining at Daylesford.[41] Yelford's manor house and church seem to have been rebuilt about that time, and John was certainly 'of Yelford' in the early 16th century.[42] He was listed as the only taxpayer there in 1523–4.[43] He

11 P.R.O., RG 10/1451, preamble to Hardwick schedule; O.S. Map 1/2,500, Oxon. XXXVIII (1876 edn.).
12 Local information. It was depicted unhatched (? uninhabited) in O.S. Map 1/2,500, Oxon. XXXVIII. 1 (1921 edn.).
13 P.R.O., RG 12/1175.
14 *V.C.H. Oxon.* i. 400, 421; *Bampton Hund. R.* 21.
15 *V.C.H. Berks.* i. 354; *V.C.H. Glos.* vii. 130; *Dom. Bk.* (Rec. Com.), i. 164, 168; *Dom. Bk. Glos.*, ed. J. S. Moore, nos. 2.8, 55.1.
16 e.g. *V.C.H. Berks.* iv. 528; *Red. Bk. Exch.* (Rolls Ser.), i. 24; *Bk. of Fees*, i. 50, 438, 448, 459; ii. 822, 841, 844, 857.
17 *V.C.H. Berks.* iv. 528.
18 *Rot. Welles*, ii (L.R.S. vi), 6.
19 *Bk. of Fees*, ii. 822, 841. For William's probable predecessors, *V.C.H. Glos.* vii. 130.
20 *Cal. Inq. p.m.* ii, p. 153.
21 *Bampton Hund. R.* 50.
22 *Feud. Aids*, ii. 237.
23 *V.C.H. Berks.* iv. 528; *Cal. Pat.* 1292–1301, 390–1; *Cal. Inq. Misc.* i, p. 491; *Edington Cart.* (Wilts. R.S. xlii), nos. 620–3, where no mention is made of Yelford among Benet's estates, although soon afterwards Yelford was held of the St. Philiberts: ibid. no. 592.
24 *Cal. Inq. p.m.* iv, pp. 208–9.
25 Ibid. vii. pp. 366–8; *Feud. Aids* iv. 183.

26 *Feud. Aids* iv. 195.
27 *Edington Cart.*, pp. xxxiii–xxxiv.
28 Ibid. no. 668.
29 *Cal. Inq. Misc.* i, p. 261.
30 *Bampton Hund. R.* 50; *Oxon. Fines*, 211.
31 *Cal. Inq. p.m.* iv, p. 208; *Cal. Close*, 1302–7, 284–5. For Miles and his fam., *V.C.H. Bucks.* iv. 467.
32 P.R.O., E 179/161/10.
33 Ibid. CP 25/1/189/14/38. An unreferenced statement that Thomas was rector of Yelford seems mistaken: O.A.S. *Rep* (1871), 30.
34 *Feud. Aids*, iv. 163; P.R.O., E 179/161/8; *Cal. Inq. p.m.* vii, p. 368.
35 Bodl. G.A. Oxon. b 96 (40): list of presentations; *V.C.H. Worcs.* iii. 336.
36 *Cal. Inq. p.m.* xi, p. 203; xii, p. 245. Cf. *Cal. Close*, 1364–8, 447.
37 Magd. Coll. Mun., Standlake 14; P.R.O., C 1/849/1–2.
38 *V.C.H. Worcs.* iii. 336.
39 Bodl. G.A. Oxon. b 96 (40).
40 Bodl. MS. d.d. Harcourt c 68/45.
41 Magd. Coll. Mun., Standlake 14: dispute over treefelling by John in Boys wood.
42 e.g. P.R.O., C 1/324/6; C 1/528/28.
43 Ibid. E 179/161/172.

died in 1542, having bequeathed *YELFORD HASTINGS* to his son John.[44]

John enlarged his Yelford estate in or after 1554 by purchase of the Walwyn manor there.[45] On his death in 1585 he was succeeded by his son Simon.[46] Simon (d. 1628) later lived at Daylesford,[47] and by 1610 Yelford was occupied by his son John.[48] Under a settlement of 1618–19 parts of Yelford were granted as portions for the use of Simon's younger sons and daughters,[49] an arrangement which caused prolonged dispute. John succeeded Simon and died in 1629, leaving an infant son John, child of his third wife Mary (Pudsey).[50] During John's minority, which did not end until 1648, Yelford was held for a time by Mary and her second husband John Berrow.[51] By 1651 John Hastings, living at Daylesford but allegedly owing the Berrows for costs incurred during his minority, was raising money by mortgaging Yelford. In October of that year he sold it to William Lenthall, Speaker of the Commons, to whom he was related by marriage.[52] A later tradition that Hastings, ruined by fines imposed on him as a royalist, was taken advantage of by Lenthall remains unsubstantiated; it ignores evidence that the estate was heavily encumbered as a result of earlier settlements.[53]

Yelford descended in the Lenthall family for almost three centuries, the owners living at Burford Priory and later at Bessels Leigh (then Berks.).[54] William (d. 1662) was succeeded by his son Sir John (d. 1681), John's son William (d. 1687), and William's infant son John. In 1727 John seems to have settled Yelford on his son William, although occasionally acting as lord or patron thereafter.[55] John died in 1763 and William, unmarried, in 1781.[56] He was succeeded by his brother John (of Burford), after whose death in 1783 Yelford descended to John's second son William John (of Bessels Leigh).[57] During his lifetime W. J. Lenthall (d. 1855) conveyed Yelford to his son Kyffin John William Lenthall, lord by 1840,[58] on whose death in 1870 it passed to his son Edmund Kyffin Lenthall. He enlarged his Yelford estate by acquiring Wadham College's farm there,[59] and died unmarried in 1907. Yelford passed to a cousin Edmund Henry Lenthall, great grandson of John (d. 1783), who died in 1909 leaving Yelford to a sister Katherine (d. 1915). She was succeeded by her sister Edith, whose husband Henry Ball

adopted the surname and arms of Lenthall by royal licence in 1916.[60] Edith Lenthall sold her Yelford property in 1949, Manor farm being purchased by F. E. Parker of Barley Park, Ducklington, who sold the manor house to B. Babington Smith in 1952.[61] Of the Lenthalls' tenants at Yelford from the mid 17th century few were long-established except for the Bakers, who farmed the manorial estate for some sixty years from the 1760s.[62]

Yelford Manor, 'the best and certainly the most picturesque large timber-framed house in the county',[63] stands on a partly moated site some 100 m. east of the church.[64] It was built in the later 15th century by Edward or John Hastings on the site of an earlier house.[65] It has a central 3-bay range flanked by cross wings (originally 3-bayed) projecting on the east and jettied on the west; the principal, west, front measures *c.* 21 m. Originally the central range comprised a 2-bayed hall, open to the roof and with a central hearth, at the north end a screens passage, and above it a gallery room extending into the hall and lit by an oriel window. The wings were 2-storeyed, the northern, service, wing having an original stone stack, presumably for a kitchen, and retaining external signs, near the north-west corner, of a timber-framed extension, probably a garderobe. The southern, solar wing, much rebuilt and lacking its eastern bay, probably had similar features. The three main ranges of building were not tied together structurally. Wall timbers were close-studded throughout, resting on a coursed limestone plinth. Roofs were of arch-braced tie-beam construction with no ridge piece, and there were two rows of arched wind braces between double purlins; the central truss of the open hall was arch-braced to the collar, presumably for decorative effect. Almost the entire construction was of elm. Roof timbers in both cross wings retain vestiges of painted decoration up to the level of the lower purlins. Externally the solar wing was more ornate than its counterpart, and there are indications on its west front of former barge boards, decorated bressumers, and oriel windows to both floors; that on the upper floor survived in 1825.[66]

In the later 16th century or early 17th the plan of the house was substantially altered by flooring over the open hall at gallery level, adding a timber-framed staircase turret, originally entered

44   Ibid. C 142/64, no. 177; C 142/210, no. 121; *Oxon. Visit.* (Harl. Soc. v), 5–6.

45   *Cal. Pat.* 1554–5, 210; below.

46   P.R.O., C 142/210, no. 121; cf. ibid. PROB 11/88, ff. 7v.–8.

47   e.g. Berks. R.O., D/ELl T42, deed of 9 May 1619.

48   P.R.O., E 179/163/435.

49   Ibid. C 142/440, no. 75; ibid. CP 25/2/386/Trin. 16 Jas. I; ibid. CP 43/142, rot. 72; Berks. R.O., D/ELl T42, deed of 9 May 1619.

50   P.R.O., C 142/440, no. 75; C 142/452, no. 60. For Hastings pedigree, *Oxon. Visit.* (Harl. Soc. v), 262–3. For disputes, e.g. Berks. R.O., D/ELl T42, deed of 29 Mar. 1652; P.R.O., C 3/446/129.

51   e.g. Berrow was of Yelford in 1634: *Oxon. Visit.* 262.

52   Berks. R.O., D/ELl T42–3, *passim*; P.R.O., CP 25/2/587/Mich. 1651. For the relationship to Lenthall, Berks. R.O., D/ELl F18/6, notes on deed of 29 Mar. 1652.

53   e.g. Berks. R.O., D/ELl F18/6: notes by E. K. Lenthall on article on Warren Hastings in *Times*, 10 May 1873.

54   For the Lenthalls, Burke, *Land Gent.* (1894 and later edns.), corrected in some details by this account.

55   Berks. R.O., D/ELl T42, deed of 1727: cf. ibid. T43, leases of 1731, 1738, 1753; Bodl. G.A. Oxon. b 96 (40).

56   C.O.S., Burford par. reg. transcripts.

57   Ibid.; Berks. R.O., D/ELl T2/1; ibid. T43, leases of 1797 and later.

58   *Lewis's Topog. Dict. of Eng.* (1840), 640.

59   Below, this section.

60   For the date, incorrect in Burke, *Land. Gent.*, see O.R.O., MS. Oxf. Dioc. c 2086, deed of 1949, second schedule.

61   O.R.O., Adkin I/641; ibid. MS. Oxf. Dioc. c 2086, conveyance of 1949; C.O.S., PRN 11977.

62   e.g. O.R.O., MSS. Oxf. Dioc. d 560, c 449; Berks. R.O., D/ELl T43, leases of 1793, 1803; ibid. E 3.

63   Pevsner, *Oxon.* 869; above plates 36–8.

64   C.O.S., PRN 11977 contains large colln. of drawings, photos., and surveys, including P. Gilman and others, 'Yelford Manor' (TS.), based on a detailed survey (1984) by Oxon. County Mus.

65   e.g. for arch. finds on site, Gilman, 'Yelford Manor', 5–6.

66   Above, plate 37.

from the hall, in the re-entrant angle between central and service range, and building in the centre of the rear wall a massive stone chimney with fireplaces on both floors; a 2-storeyed hexagonal bay window was added on the west front. The surviving chimney overshadows windows in the staircase wing, and presumably post-dates it, but there was probably an earlier, narrower chimney to which the staircase turret related more easily; the chimney may have been rebuilt because of the structural problems mentioned below. A door frame between the staircase and gallery room bears the initials of John Hastings, suggesting that the instigator of the rebuilding was either John, lord from 1542 to 1585, or his grandson John, resident by 1610 and dying in 1629.[67] The latter was responsible for the fine carved overmantel in the parlour in the south wing; it bears his initials, those of his third wife Mary Pudsey, and a shield of arms with the Hastings maunche impaling a cat and a stag's head, punning allusions to Pudsey (pussy) and to Rowe, the surname of John's earlier wife.[68] John's house, as depicted on a map of 1625, seems to have had a courtyard on the front, approached through a central gatehouse on the west and flanked by buildings on the north and south; that on the south, possibly a dovecot, survived in 1825.[69]

Later structural repairs included bracing the central truss of the hall, which had been cut through on the east side when the upper fireplace was inserted; that had caused serious damage to the chimney stack and probably to the lower fireplace, and the whole central range had tilted to the west.[70] Probably in the earlier 19th century the south wing, presumably after a collapse, was partially rebuilt in stone, losing its eastern bay.[71] In the later 19th century the house was usually occupied by farm bailiffs and labourers, and in the earlier 20th century was subdivided to provide for three families.[72] From 1952 the derelict house was extensively restored by the Babington Smiths. Roger Rosewell, owner from 1984, restored the roof, removed modern partitions, planted formal gardens, and created an enclosed courtyard with a cloister linking outbuildings to the house.[73] A plaque in the courtyard commemorates the bicentenary of the acquittal in 1795 of Warren Hastings (d. 1818), governor-general of India, descendant of the John Hastings who sold Yelford in 1651.[74]

South-west of the house is a water-filled moat or ditch of unknown date, its main section

running north and opening westwards into a small irregular pond. In 1876 the pond was sharply rectangular, the ditch broad and straight-edged, and a narrow ditch ran north from the pond along the edge of the lawn fronting the house; the whole had the appearance of an ornamental garden feature.[75] The stream running south through the village was evidently diverted at various dates, and there may once have been a complete circuit of water around the house. Arguments that the moat formed part of a single design with a ditch or moat around College Farm (on land historically quite separate) are unpersuasive, although both houses were depicted in 1830 with at least a 3-sided moat.[76] An eastern section of Yelford Manor's moat seems to have been largely filled in when the road between the house and College Farm was realigned to the west.[77] The uncertainty about the moat's extent suggests that it was never a substantial defensive feature, and perhaps provided drainage and protection for a garden or orchard.

Part of Yelford, attached to the royal manor of Bampton and centred on Brighthampton or Hardwick, was granted in 1131 by Henry I to the priory of Sées (Orne) and was regranted by the priory c. 1245 to Walter de Grey, archbishop of York; the estate, later usually called Hardwick manor, was held by the Greys as $\frac{1}{20}$ knight's fee.[78] In 1279 its Yelford portion, described as 'Yelford de Grey', comprised some 5 yardlands held of Robert de Grey, and at least another $\frac{1}{2}$ yardland held of him by Robert of Yelford; other land in Yelford held of Isabel de Grey belonged to a separate, Standlake, manor.[79] The Greys' Yelford estate followed the descent of Hardwick manor, passing to the Lovels in the 15th century, to Thomas Howard, duke of Norfolk in 1514, and to his son Thomas, who sold it to the Crown in 1540.[80]

In 1544 part of the manor, centred on Yelford, was among lands sold to a speculator, Alexander Unton;[81] when Unton sold in 1545 to the tenant, Richard Edwards, the estate comprised a house and 3 yardlands in Yelford, together with two other houses and a total of $2\frac{1}{2}$ yardlands formerly occupied by John Thurward and William Hyatt in Yelford and Hardwick.[82] In 1570 William Edwards, son of Richard, added two houses and 2 yardlands in Hardwick, acquired from Peter Ranckell.[83] On the death of William's grandson William in 1613[84] an infant daughter

67 Above, this section.
68 *N. & Q.* 21 June 1941, 442.
69 Above, plates 37, 39.
70 Pevsner, *Oxon.* 869 mistakenly interprets the brace as a cruck; cf. note by A. Pacey in C.O.S., PRN 11977. The lower fireplace was also damaged by the insertion of a range c. 1904.
71 A newspaper of 1848 was beneath the south bedroom floor: inf. from Mrs. H. Babington Smith.
72 e.g. P.R.O., RG 9/905; RG 11/1514; RG 12/1125; *Oxf. Times*, 2 Nov. 1901; *Kelly's Dir. Oxon.* (1903 and later edns.); O.R.O., Adkin I/641.
73 [R. Rosewell], 'Guide to Yelford Manor' (TS.): copy in C.O.S., PRN 11977.
74 *D.N.B.*; *V.C.H. Worcs.* iii. 336–7.
75 O.S. Map 1/2,500, Oxon. XXXVII. 4.
76 Ibid. 1", sheet 13 (1830 edn.). Gilman, 'Yelford

Manor', 6–14 and fig. 1 describes surviving features but misinterprets the map of 1625: Berks. R.O., D/ELl P2, reproduced above, plate 39.
77 Cf. above, plate 39; Gilman, 'Yelford Manor', fig. 1; O.S. Map 1/2,500, Oxon. XXXVII. 4.
78 Above, Ducklington, manors.
79 *Bampton Hund. R.* 63–4. For Robert of Yelford, below.
80 Above, Ducklington, manors.
81 *L. & P. Hen. VIII*, xix (2), p. 471. Yelford is missing from the associated particulars for the grant: P.R.O., E 318/22/1162.
82 Wadham Coll. Mun., 86/1, 17.
83 Ibid. 86/3–4; *Cal. Pat.* 1569–72, p. 180. For Ranckell's acquisition of the property, St. John's Coll. Mun., XVII.5; *Cal. Pat.* 1569–72, p. 137.
84 For the relationship, cf. P.R.O., C 142/307, no. 64; C 142/340, no. 211.

Elizabeth became a ward of the Crown since part of the estate was thought to be held in chief; wardship was granted to Elizabeth's mother, Elizabeth, and her second husband Edward Smith.[85] In 1633 the daughter Elizabeth and her husband Ambrose Sheppard were granted livery of Yelford, which they sold to Wadham College in 1636, although, following disputes between the college and its warden, the conveyance seems to have required confirmation as late as 1642.[86]

The Wadham estate was later let in two portions, a Yelford farm, and a smaller Hardwick farm.[87] In 1904 the college sold the Yelford farm to E. K. Lenthall, owner of Yelford manor.[88] When the Lenthall estate was sold in 1949 College farm was bought by its tenant, A. G. Weeks.[89]

The chief house of the estate was depicted on a map of 1625 as Mr. Smith's house, immediately east of Yelford Manor on the site of the surviving College Farm; Smith was Edward Smith, guardian of Elizabeth Edwards.[90] The 17th-century house, perhaps that of which the roof was derelict in 1863,[91] seems to have been entirely rebuilt thereafter, certainly before 1898.[92] The garden south of the house was edged on three sides by a moat or ditch of pre-19th-century date, similar in character to that at Yelford Manor; there is no indication that it continued on the north side of the house.[93] The moat was backfilled in the 1980s.

A prominent local family taking its name from Yelford but by the 13th century having its principal holdings in Lew and Cote[94] held land freely at Yelford from three lords. In 1279 Robert of Yelford, also called the forester, held ½ yardland and 9 a. (later reckoned to be ⅔ yardland) of the Hastings manor, a house and ½ yardland of Robert de Grey's Hardwick manor, and a house and yardland of Isabel de Grey's Standlake manor.[95] At his death in 1293 Robert of Yelford was succeeded by his son Robert,[96] principal taxpayer in Yelford in 1306 and perhaps the Robert the woodward assessed to pay tax there in 1316.[97] In 1328 Robert died holding the same Yelford estate of three lords.[98] His son Robert, prominent in the service of the Black Prince,[99] was found in 1367 to have granted his estates without royal licence to Edmund of Yelford: Edmund's property in Yelford was reported to be a house and ½ yardland held

of the Greys' Hardwick manor and 1½ yardland held of Standlake manor.[1]

Its descent thereafter has not been traced directly, but in or before 1373 Edmund of Yelford, clerk, and Philip Walwyn were acting jointly over rent from Boys wood in Standlake,[2] and the bulk of the Yelford family's estates elsewhere passed to the Walwyns. Land in Shilton (then Berks.), for example, granted in 1347 to Robert of Yelford by Robert at Hall was evidently the Hall Place in Shilton attached to the Walwyns' Yelford manor in the 16th century;[3] the Walwyns' manor also included the Lawns, south of Boys wood and in Standlake, which as Boys breach had been granted in 1355 to Robert of Yelford by Robert Corbet.[4] An Edmund Walwyn was of Yelford in 1433[5] and at his death in 1439 his son Edward was a minor. The Walwyn estates were said variously to be held of William and Alice Lovel, as of Hardwick, or to be held in chief as 1/20 knight's fee. William and Alice Lovel were disturbed in their wardship of Edward Walwyn by Crown grantees, but in 1446 successfully counter-claimed that Yelford was held of them for ¼ fee; perhaps the confusion arose because the Walwyns, like the Yelford family, held Yelford land attached to both Hardwick and Standlake manors, which by then were both held by the Lovels.[6]

In 1545 Nicholas Walwyn died holding what was described as Yelford manor, later *YELFORD WALWYN*, again reckoned to be held in chief for a knight's fee.[7] No mention was made of any holding from Hardwick manor, and suit paid to Hardwick's court from the mid 16th century 'for Walwyn's land' by the Edwards family, owners of the Yelford estate formerly part of Hardwick manor, suggests that there had been a recent sale.[8] The Walwyns were not resident, but their tenants the Moseleys were one of the three families paying tax in Yelford in 1542–3.[9] Until 1554 Nicholas Walwyn's son John was a minor, and the king committed his wardship to Roger More.[10] In 1554 John was licensed to sell the site of his Yelford manor, the closes called the Lawns, and all his demesne in Yelford and Standlake to John Hastings.[11] It seems that John Walwyn, who married Hastings's daughter Dorothy, retained an interest in the estate for

85 Wadham Coll. Mun. 86/8–11; P.R.O., C 142/340, no. 211. Smith was named as owner or occupant in 1625: above, plate 39.
86 Wadham Coll. Mun., 86/12–21.
87 Below, econ. hist. For the Hardwick portion, above, Ducklington, manors.
88 Wadham Coll. Mun., 2/4, pp. 307, 315, 328. For completion date, ibid. 86, unnumbered copy of item 19.
89 O.R.O., Adkin I/641.
90 Above, plate 39.
91 Wadham Coll. Mun., 86/46E.
92 O.S. Map 1/2,500, Oxon. XXXVII. 4 (1899 edn.); ibid. (1876 edn.) appears to show a different building. No ref. to rebuilding was found in Wadham Coll. Mun.
93 O.S. Map 1", sheet 13 (1830 edn.).
94 e.g. *Oxon. Eyre 1241*, p. 140; *Bampton Hund. R.* 22–4. Cf. *Bk. of Fees*, ii. 830, where Robert of Yelford's serjeanty (in Lew) in 1242–3 is mistakenly located at Yelford.
95 *Bampton Hund. R.* 50–1, 63, 69.
96 *Cal. Inq. p.m.* iii, p. 65.
97 P.R.O., E 179/161/8, 10.
98 *Cal. Inq. p.m.* vii, p. 113.

99 *Black Prince's Reg.* ii–iv, *passim*.
1 P.R.O., C 143/362, no. 1, printed in Giles, *Hist. Bampton*, 139–40.
2 Magd. Coll. Mun., Standlake 26A.
3 *Cal. Pat.* 1345–8, 295; P.R.O., C 142/75, no. 42; ibid. C 1/1378/1–5. For other Walwyn acquisitions from the Yelford family, above, Bampton: Aston and Cote, manors [other estates].
4 Magd. Coll. Mun., Standlake 11A, 20C; *Cal. Pat.* 1554–5, 210. For the Lawns, above, plate 39.
5 O.R.O., Warner IV/i/1.
6 P.R.O., C 139/113, no. 14; *Cal. Pat.* 1441–6, 461; above, Ducklington, manors [Hardwick]; Standlake, manors.
7 P.R.O., C 142/75, no. 42.
8 e.g. St. John's Coll. Mun., XVII. 16–17. Suit paid by John Walwyn in the later 16th century was for a small cottage only.
9 P.R.O., E 179/162/223, 234. For the Moseleys' tenancy, ibid. E 134/3 Jas. I/Mich. 22; *Cal. Pat.* 1554–5, 210.
10 P.R.O., C 60/368, no. 29; *Cal. Pat.* 1557–8, 299–300.
11 *Cal. Pat.* 1554–5, 210; cf. P.R.O., CP 25/2/76/650/1 & 2 Phil. and Mary Hil.

some years,[12] but John Hastings at his death in 1585 held both Yelford Hastings and Yelford Walwyn manors, the latter said to be held in chief for ⅙ knight's fee.[13] Thereafter the manor followed the descent of Yelford Hastings, although the Lawns seem to have been separated in 1651, let by Edmund Montfort on a 99-year lease, but held by the Lenthalls in 1710;[14] by the mid 18th century they had been acquired by the Harcourts and thereafter formed part of their Cokethorpe estate.[15]

There seems to have been no manor house on the Walwyn manor in 1554.[16] The site presumably formed part of the Hastings estate mapped in 1625, perhaps the close north of Yelford Manor containing scattered buildings, of which none survived by the 19th century.[17]

ECONOMIC HISTORY. Yelford's medieval open fields probably covered much of the area of the Hastings family's inclosed estate depicted in 1625,[18] together with Yelford field to the east which formed part of Hardwick's fields until inclosure in 1853.[19] In 1086 Yelford manor had land for 3 ploughs,[20] and there may have been other, unrecorded, land in the parish: in 1279 various estates there comprised a ploughland, 10½ yardlands, and some odd acres, a total of perhaps 15 yardlands.[21] In the 17th century the former Walwyn estate comprised 2 yardlands[22] and the Edwards (later Wadham College) estate c. 5 yardlands;[23] thus unless the Hastings manor had changed greatly from the ploughland and 4 yardlands recorded in 1279, there were probably still c. 15 yardlands in Yelford. The 11 yardlands on which the parish was rated for poor-relief in 1708 presumably excluded much of the open-field land, certainly the college estate, which by then was regarded as part of Hardwick.[24] In 1305 a yardland on the Hastings manor was said to contain only 24 a.,[25] but Wadham College's estate in 1649 comprised 162 estimated acres, implying a yardland of 30 a. or more.[26]

The valuation of a ploughland in 1305 as only 60 a. of arable worth 4d. an acre suggests that half the land then lay fallow.[27] Change to a three-field rotation of crops before the mid 17th century may be indicated by the fairly even distribution of Wadham College's arable between three major subdivisions of Yelford field.[28] In 1086 Yelford manor contained 36 a. of meadow and 15 a. of pasture; the meadow was worth 1s. 6d. an acre in 1305 when the manor included 10 a., together with common pasture worth 3s.[29] At that time the inhabitants of

Yelford intercommoned with those of Shifford, Cote, and Aston between Michaelmas and Martinmas, probably in the meadows along Shifford brook.[30] No early woodland was recorded in Yelford, but in the later Middle Ages the Hastings family acquired Boys wood (c. 72 a.) on the northern edge of the parish, and it descended thereafter with Yelford manor.[31] Within the parish in 1625 there were only a few small coppices, covering c. 5 a.[32]

In 1086 Yelford manor's demesne was worked by 4 *servi* with 2 ploughs, while the tenants (3 villeins and 3 bordars) had ½ plough; undercultivation may have accounted for a fall in value from 60s. to 50s. since the Conquest.[33] By 1279 Yelford men were tenants of three manors. The Hastings manor, its demesne reduced to 1 ploughland, supported 4 freeholders, 1 villein yardlander, and 2 cottars, the tenant land amounting to perhaps 4 yardlands; rents yielded £1, and the villein's works were valued at 9s. By 1305 there were 6 free tenants paying a total of 12s., 1 yardlander paying no rent but providing works worth 6s. 11½d., and 6 cottars with works worth 4s. 2d.[34] In 1279 the Grey manor, of which the demesne lay in Hardwick, supported 5 villein yardlanders in Yelford, each paying 6s. 7d. rent and works worth 4s. 2½d.; one of them held additional land for 2s. 6d. A freeholding of ½ yardland and ½ a. on the Grey manor, for which Robert of Yelford paid 3s., probably lay in Yelford. Robert also paid 2s. for a house and yardland in Yelford attached to Isabel de Grey's Standlake manor.[35] In 1328 the Yelford family's estate in Yelford, of which parts belonged to three different manors, included 40 a. of demesne arable and 6 a. of meadow, and supported 3 cottars paying total rent of 4s. 1d. and works worth 10d.[36] Tenants of the Greys' Hardwick manor, of whom some presumably lived at Yelford, continued to provide works in the early 14th century.[37]

In 1306 Yelford's assessment of 17s. 3d. for a thirtieth was payable by c. 10 persons, of whom the highest assessed were Robert of Yelford (6s.) and Reynold (? Roland) of Hastings (2s.).[38] In 1327 an assessment of 48s. for a twentieth was payable by 16 persons, of whom 8 were assessed at 2s. or below, while 3, including John de Grey, were assessed at 5s. 6d.[39] For later medieval taxes Yelford seems to have been included with Hardwick and its members.[40] Yelford's only contributor to the subsidy of 1523–4 was John Hastings, resident lord of Yelford manor, assessed on goods worth £40.[41] By then much of Yelford was an inclosed farm in single ownership,

12 e.g. P.R.O., E 179/162/320; ibid. C 2/Jas. I/H 2/53.
13 Ibid. C 142/210, no. 121.
14 Berks. R.O., D/ELl T41, deeds 1651–1710.
15 Above, Ducklington, manors [Cokethorpe].
16 *Cal. Pat.* 1554–5, 210.
17 Above, plate 39; O.R.O., Yelford tithe map.
18 Above, plate 39.   19 Above, intro.
20 *V.C.H. Oxon.* i. 421.
21 *Bampton Hund. R.* 50–1, 63–4, 69.
22 Cf. P.R.O., E 134/3 Jas. I/Mich. 22; *Cal. Pat.* 1554–5, 210.
23 Above, manors.
24 O.R.O., QS/1708 Epiph./20; above, intro.
25 P.R.O., C 133/118, no. 14.
26 Wadham Coll. Mun., 86/121.
27 P.R.O., C 133/118, no. 14.

28 Below, this section.
29 *V.C.H. Oxon.* i. 421; P.R.O., C 133/118, no. 14.
30 *Eynsham Cart.* ii, p. 6.
31 Above, Standlake, econ. hist. (agric.).
32 Above, plate 39.
33 *V.C.H. Oxon.* i. 421.
34 *Bampton Hund. R.* 50; P.R.O., C 133/118, no. 14.
35 *Bampton Hund. R.* 63–4, 69.
36 P.R.O., E 152/16, mm. 2d., 3.
37 e.g. P.R.O., C 134/29, no. 11; above, Ducklington, econ. hist. (agric.).
38 P.R.O., E 179/161/10.
39 Ibid. E 179/161/9.
40 e.g. Glasscock, *Subsidy 1334*, 237.
41 P.R.O., E 179/161/172.

but a few other substantial residents were included in later subsidies: in 1542–3, when Hastings paid on land worth £30, three members of the Edwards family, tenants of the former Grey manor, were assessed on goods worth a total of £15, and two members of the Moseley family, tenants of the Walwyn estate, on goods worth £5.[42]

The transformation of the west part of the parish into pasture and meadow closes[43] probably followed depopulation through plague in the mid 14th century, which elsewhere in the area caused widespread abandonment of arable.[44] The retention of open fields east of the stream which bisected the parish, and their incorporation into the fields of Hardwick, may have resulted from a deliberate exchange of holdings, creating an integrated inclosed estate wholly owned by the Hastings family,[45] and leaving the former Grey manor, centred on Hardwick, with most of the open-field land to the east. Existing closes near the village may have been shared out, since in the 17th century some closes attached to the former Grey manor duplicated the names of closes on the Hastings estate.[46] A third Yelford estate, that of the Walwyns, may have retained land on both sides before it was absorbed into the Hastings estate in the mid 16th century: the site of its chief house seems to have been on the west,[47] while there are hints that the open-field strips on the east held by the Hastings family in the 17th century had only been acquired with the Walwyn estate.[48]

From that time Yelford's division effectively into two farms was reflected in subsidy returns in which only the Hastings and Edwards families were assessed. In 1576 John Hastings paid on land worth £18 and William Edwards, assessed under Hardwick, on goods worth £4; in 1600 the Hastings land was valued at £10 and the Edwards assessment was unchanged.[49] That the Edwardses were substantial yeomen is indicated by the will of Richard Edwards (d. 1609) which included cash bequests of c. £250.[50]

In 1625 the inclosed Hastings estate, later Manor farm, comprised 218 a. of pasture, 109 a. of meadow, 4 a. of 'old leys', and 75½ a. of wood and coppice, a total of 407 a.;[51] Boys wood and the Lawns, c. 29 a. of pasture acquired with the Walwyn estate, though contiguous with the Yelford estate, lay in Standlake.[52] In the mid 17th century the Hastings family also held a small quantity of arable in Yelford field (presumably 2 yardlands if it was the former Walwyn land).[53] The inclosed farm as let by the Lenthalls

from the mid 17th century was resurveyed in 1811 as 316½ a., which excluded the Standlake land and a coppice (c. 3½ a.) kept in hand;[54] after small adjustments in the mid 19th century Manor farm comprised c. 336 a., the entire civil parish.[55]

At least one pasture close depicted in 1625 was ploughed before 1629[56] and, although the Lenthalls imposed the standard penalties on lessees for converting established grassland,[57] by the mid 19th century a third of the farm, chiefly its higher, northern part, was arable.[58] Before 1876 most of the southern part of the farm was ploughed, increasing the arable proportion to two thirds.[59] The farm without its woodland was reckoned to be worth c. £250 a year in the mid 17th century, reflecting the high valuation of inclosed land.[60] Leases were usually for 7 years or fewer until the mid 18th century when the Bakers, tenants for several generations, acquired leases of 20 years or more. Annual rents doubled from £101 in 1674 to £220 and 100 'good milk cheeses' in 1726, falling steadily thereafter until, during the Napoleonic wars, there was a sharp increase to £360; in 1822 the rent was still £340 with penalties as high as £40 an acre for conversion to arable.[61] In the agricultural depression of the later 19th century it may have been difficult to let the farm, and in 1881 and 1891 the house was occupied by farm managers.[62]

The Edwards (later Wadham College) farm remained largely uninclosed until the mid 19th century. In the 1630s its roughly calculated value, on the basis of 5s. an acre for open-field land and twice that for closes, was c. £81 a year.[63] When surveyed in 1649 it comprised, in addition to a house and farmstead on the site of College Farm, c. 36 a. of meadow and pasture, much of it in closes around the farmstead, and 162 a. of open-field arable.[64] The arable lay chiefly in Lawn, Middle, and Stockwell fields (45 a., 42 a., and 58 a. respectively), evidently subdivisions of the area depicted as Yelford field in 1853. Small quantities of arable lay in Sheepstead (16 a.) and Brighthampton West field (1½ a.), which were probably never part of Yelford's early fields.[65] Within the main fields there had been much union of strips; pieces of 5 a. or more were commonplace, and some of c. 18 a. were recorded.[66] When the college's Yelford farm was resurveyed in 1715 it comprised c. 168 statute acres, of which some 48 a. were grass.[67] In 1772 another survey mentioned only c. 148 a., made up of 22½ a. of meadow and pasture closes, 19 a. in Brighthampton's meadows, and c. 107 a. of open-field arable

42   Ibid. E 179/162/234.
43   Above, plate 39.
44   e.g. V.C.H. Oxon. xii. 115–16.
45   Above, plate 39.
46   e.g. Bodl. MS. Top. Oxon. c 118, f. 7 and v., mentioning both Mr. Smith's Great Linthorn and Mr. Hastings's Linthorn. Cf. also Wadham Coll Mun. 86/121, mentioning Mead corner and Cott mead.
47   Above, manors.
48   Above, intro.
49   P.R.O., E 179/162/341; E 179/163/398.
50   O.R.O., MS. Wills Oxon. 20/3/1.
51   Above, plate 39.
52   For the Lawns, above manors; for Boys wood, above, Standlake, econ. hist. (agric.).
53   Wadham Coll. Mun., 86/121.
54   Berks. R.O., D/ELl E3.

55   Above, intro.
56   Berks. R.O., D/ELl T43, deed of 1629.
57   Ibid. D/ELl T43 passim.
58   O.R.O., Yelford tithe award and map.
59   O.S. Map 1/2,500, Oxon. XXXVII. 4, 8; XXXVIII. 1, 5 (1876 edn.); O.S. Area. Bk. (1877).
60   Berks. R.O., D/ELl T42, deed of 8 Aug. 1651.
61   Ibid. T43 passim. The first lease to the Bakers has not been found, but they were tenants by 1768: O.R.O., MS. Oxf. Dioc. d 560.
62   Cf. P.R.O., RG 9/906; RG 10/1451; RG 11/1514; RG 12/1175.
63   Wadham Coll. Mun., 4/59.
64   Ibid. 86/121.
65   For the fields, O.R.O., Standlake incl. map B.
66   Notably in Middle field: Wadham Coll. Mun., 86/121.
67   Ibid. 86/123.

distributed as before.[68] At inclosure in 1853 Wadham College and its lessee Thomas Pinnock, in return for 152 a. of land and 160 sheep commons, were awarded 138 a. of new closes adjacent to the farm's existing old inclosures, which, including the house and farmstead, comprised c. 25 a.[69] In 1863 the farm, still 163 a., comprised 130 a. of arable land, described as strong loam on clay above a substratum of gravel; the grass, of good quality, was chiefly in the old closes.[70] By 1876 the arable area had increased to c. 139 a.[71]

From the 17th century Wadham College's leases were for 20 years.[72] At first the whole estate was let for £40 a year, but from 1715 it was divided into Yelford and Hardwick farms, let respectively for £32 2s. and £8 18s. The rent for Yelford farm was unchanged until the mid 19th century, but substantial renewal fines were payable: in 1834 the tenant successfully appealed to the college to reduce his fine to £200,[73] and in 1848 he paid £198 on renewal. From 1868 the farm, with 22 a. of newly purchased land in Hardwick, was let year to year for £274; from 1879 it was let without the extra land for only £200, but with a fine of £50 an acre for new tillage. Many of Wadham's nominal lessees, such as Mary Mountford of Oxford in the later 17th century and the Groves of Woodstock or Maximilian Western of Cokethorpe in the 18th, were intermediaries. Farmers long-established at College farm included the Terrys from the 1680s,[74] the Mountains in the earlier 18th century, and the Pinnocks for much of the 19th.

The residence of a shepherd in Yelford's small farming community in 1584[75] reinforces the indications given by field names and land use in 1625 that sheep farming and probably cattle grazing were dominant, at least on the inclosed land. Conversion from arable to pasture is suggested by field names such as Linthorn, probably once an enclosure for flax, but by the 17th century applied to pasture closes on both the Hastings and Wadham estates.[76] Specialization seems to have been reduced by the later 17th century: the tenant of Manor farm in 1683 had cattle worth c. £44, hay worth £46 10s., and wheat, barley, oats, and pulse worth c. £60; there were a few pigs and only 4 sheep.[77] The inclusion of cheeses in the annual rent of Manor farm in 1726 and 1731 suggests that dairy farming was of particular importance there.[78] Until inclosure the lessees of College farm carried on the mixed

farming practised elsewhere in Hardwick's open fields.[79] Yelford's principal crops in the mid 19th century were wheat, barley, beans, and turnips,[80] and many livestock were grazed: in 1852 the departing tenant of Manor farm sold over 30 cattle, 30 sheep, 25 pigs, and 2 ricks of wheat, and in 1862 another sale at Yelford included 68 dairy cattle and 100 Oxford Down ewes.[81] Despite the enlarged arable area there was continued interest in stock and dairy farming, with particular emphasis on cheese-making.[82] In 1851 Yelford's two farms employed 12 labourers.[83]

After the Lenthalls acquired both farms in 1904 they rearranged their estate so that Manor farm (302 a.) comprised all the fields north of the Aston–Hardwick road, and College farm (196 a.) all those to the south.[84] The Weeks family held both farms in the earlier 20th century, and continued at College farm after J. F. Florey took on Manor farm on a yearly tenancy in the 1940s. In 1937 a 'Danish' pig house for 300 pigs was built near the Brighthampton–Boys wood lane.[85] When Manor farm was sold in 1949 only a third (107 a.) of the land was arable. In modern times the farm formed part of a larger unit worked from Barley Park farm in Ducklington. In 1949, when the Weekses bought College farm, over four-fifths (165 a.) of the land was arable, but in the later 20th century much was converted to pasture.

LOCAL GOVERNMENT. In 1279 there was a twice-yearly view of frankpledge for the Hastings manor, and the Greys' manor in Hardwick, Brighthampton, and Yelford had view of frankpledge and other liberties, including gallows.[86] Courts for the Hastings manor presumably ceased when the estate came into single ownership,[87] but in the early 17th century a tithingman was allegedly still nominated for that part of Yelford, and suit was paid to Bampton manor, whose lord had waifs, strays, and felons' goods in Yelford: there may have been confusion with the hundred court.[88] Sixteenth-century tenants of the former Grey manor paid suit to Hardwick's courts,[89] which until the 1580s nominated a separate tithingman for what was sometimes called East Yelford,[90] namely the holdings, mostly open-field, east of the Hastings estate.[91] In the 1840s, and presumably until inclosure in 1853, tenants of Wadham College's Yelford estate, descended from the Grey manor, were

---

68 Wadham Coll. Mun., 86/124, completed by ibid. 35/27–8.
69 O.R.O., Standlake incl. award and maps.
70 Wadham Coll. Mun., 86/46 E.
71 O.S. *Area. Bk.* (1877).
72 Except where stated otherwise this para. based on leases in Wadham Coll. Mun., 86/22 sqq.
73 Ibid. 2/4, p. 21.
74 For their relationship to an earlier lessee Humphrey Slater (d. 1688), MS. Wills Oxon. 62/3/8.
75 Ibid. 69/1/36.
76 Cf. Bodl. MS. Top. Oxon. c 118, f. 7 and v.; Berks. R.O., D/EL1 T42, s.a. 1651, 1652; above, plate 39, where the form Lenthall for Linthorn is a later alteration. For derivation, *P.N. Oxon.* (E.P.N.S.), ii. 457.
77 O.R.O., MS. Wills Oxon. 86/4/15.
78 Berks. R.O., D/EL1 T43.
79 Above, Ducklington, econ. hist. (agric.).

80 *P.O. Dir. Oxon.* (1869).
81 *Oxf. Chron.* 22 Jan. 1852.
82 Inf. from Mrs. H. Babington Smith.
83 P.R.O., HO 107/1731.
84 Except where stated otherwise this para. based on O.R.O., Adkin I/641: sale cat. 1949; ibid. Adkin VIII/23: valuation, 1930s; *Kelly's Dir. Oxon.* (1903 and later edns.); inf. from Mrs. H. Babington Smith.
85 The building was derelict in 1994.
86 *Bampton Hund. R.* 50, 63. For Hardwick manor, above, Ducklington, local govt.
87 Above, intro., econ. hist.
88 P.R.O., E 134/8 Jas. I/Trin. 3.
89 For court rolls 1541–7, 1561–9, and 1533–1878, P.R.O., SC 2/197/43; Bodl. MS. Top. Oxon. b 21; St. John's Coll. Mun., XI.9–22.
90 e.g. St. John's Coll. Mun., XI.10 (152, 154).
91 Above, intro.

still attending Hardwick's courts.[92] Mid 16th-century courts held nominally for Yelford Walwyn manor, but apparently serving other small Walwyn estates in the area, presumably ceased when Yelford Walwyn was absorbed into the Hastings estate.[93]

The distinction between the Hastings (later Lenthall) inclosed estate and the rest of Yelford persisted in later parochial arrangements, tenants of the open-field land being taxed with Hardwick and in the care of its officers[94] while the Lenthall estate was governed from Bampton. In 1708 rates payable to Bampton for the Lenthall estate, assessed at 11 yardlands and by then regarded as the whole of Yelford, were reduced on appeal: it was found that Yelford had paid poor-rates to Bampton for at least 50 years, had called occasionally upon the services of Bampton's overseers, but paid for its own highway maintenance and incurred few other costs.[95] Bampton's overseers continued to serve Yelford until 1758 when, after a dispute, responsibility seems to have been placed on the Lenthalls.[96] The Yelford for which poor-relief expenditure was recorded in the early 19th century was only the Lenthall estate: sometimes *c.* £8 was spent, but in several years no poor were recorded.[97] From 1834 Yelford belonged to Witney union, from 1894 to Witney rural district, and from 1974 to West Oxfordshire district.[98]

CHURCH. Masonry of the 12th century or earlier re-used in the church porch may be from the chapel in existence at Yelford by 1221.[99] In the later 13th century Yelford's incumbents were called rectors[1] and the living remained a rectory until 1976, when it was absorbed with Northmoor, Standlake, and Stanton Harcourt in the united benefice of Lower Windrush.[2] Bampton, to whose large pre-Conquest *parochia* Yelford belonged, evidently surrendered certain parochial rights in return for a pension[3] but was still claiming Yelford as a dependent chapel in 1318.[4] That residual dependency probably concerned burial rights, for, although Yelford was not named when the mother church claimed such rights over a wide area in 1405–6,[5] there

were no known medieval burials in Yelford;[6] in the 16th century the Hastings family, despite rebuilding Yelford church, had its tomb at Bampton and at least one resident rector was also buried there.[7] In the 18th century Bampton was the usual burial place,[8] but there were also burials at Shifford, Standlake, and Ducklington, the last becoming the favoured place in the 19th century.[9] An isolated burial at Yelford, recorded in the Bampton registers in 1700, apparently caused controversy because of fears that the ground might be unconsecrated.[10] In the 20th century most Yelford burials were at Standlake.

The advowson, held by Philip Hastings in 1221, descended in the Hastings family with Yelford manor until 1651;[11] John Bablake, who presented in 1368, was an associate and possibly guardian of Bartholomew Hastings, a minor,[12] and a Crown presentation in 1637 was also during a minority. The Lenthalls held the advowson with the Hastings manor from 1651 until 1949, when it was sold to F. E. Parker.[13] In 1952 Parker sold it with the manor house to B. Babington Smith, whose family retained it when the house was sold in 1984.[14]

In 1254 the living was valued at 20s. (corrected to 26s. 8d.),[15] in 1291 at £2, and in 1341 at only 24s. after allowance for the exempt glebe and hay tithe.[16] In 1535 the net value was £4 3s. 5d. after deductions which included a pension of 5s. to Bampton;[17] a 'pension tithe' of 20d., possibly related to the pension, was still paid from Yelford in 1848.[18] In the early 18th century Yelford was a discharged living valued at £29 10s. net and its stated value changed little until it was augmented from the Bounty in 1793.[19] In 1808 its value was £103 and in 1831 £108, which rose after commutation of tithes in mid century to nearer £150.[20] By the late 19th century it had fallen below £100.[21]

The tithes from ½ a. of demesne corn and from 3 a. and another piece of land in Yelford field were payable to Bampton parish in the Middle Ages.[22] The rector had the remaining tithes, which in 1818 comprised those from W. J. Lenthall's estate (estimated at 315 a.), from Wadham College's Yelford farm (160 a.), and from another 80 a. in the open fields of Hardwick.[23]

92 e.g. St. John's Coll. Mun., XI.22, pp. 6, 23.
93 B.L. Add. MS. 38961; above, manors.
94 Above, intro.
95 O.R.O., QS/1708 Epiph./20.
96 Ibid. MS. d.d. Par. Bampton b 10, ff. 21v.–22; ibid. b 11–13, *passim.*
97 *Poor Abstract, 1818*, pp. 352–3; *Poor Rate Returns*, H.C. 556, p. 135 (1822), v; H.C. 334, p. 170 (1825), iv; H.C. 83, p. 157 (1830–1), xi; H.C. 444, p. 153 (1835), xlvii.
98 O.R.O., RO 3251, pp. 201, 203; RO 3267.
99 *Rot. Welles*, ii (L.R.S. vi), 6.
1 e.g. *Bampton Hund. R.* 51.
2 O.R.O., MS. Oxf. Dioc. c 1713/2, Order in Council, 12 Apr. 1976.
3 e.g. *Valor Eccl.* (Rec. Com.), ii. 178.
4 D. & C. Exeter, MS. 2865.
5 Ibid. MS. 648.
6 A will of 1408 stipulating burial in the church related to Elford (Staffs.): below, this section.
7 P.R.O., PROB 11/88, ff. 7v.–8; C.O.S., Bampton par. reg. transcripts: John Latham, 1567.
8 *Secker's Visit.* 182.
9 C.O.S., par. reg. transcripts, preface; *Kelly's Dir. Oxon.* (1883).
10 C.O.S., par. reg. transcripts, preface; ibid. Bampton

par. reg. transcripts.
11 *Rot. Welles*, ii (L.R.S. vi), 6; Bodl. G.A. Oxon. b 96 (40).
12 e.g. Magd. Coll. Mun., Standlake 25A. For Bartholomew's minority, *Cal. Inq. p.m.* xii, p. 245.
13 O.R.O., MS. Oxf. Dioc. c 2086, deed of 1949.
14 C.O.S., PRN 11977; *Crockford's Clerical Dir.* (1952 and later edns.).
15 *Val. Norw.* ed. Lunt, 309.
16 *Inq. Non.* (Rec. Com.), 141. Yelford is absent from the 1291 valuation in *Tax. Eccl.* (Rec. Com.); elsewhere a value in 1291 of £3 3s. was recorded: Bodl. MS. Top. Oxon. d 218, f. 179.
17 *Valor. Eccl.* (Rec. Com.) ii. 178.
18 Giles, *Hist. Bampton*, 31.
19 e.g. J. Ecton, *Liber Valorum* (1711), 290; *Secker's Corresp.* 288; O.R.O., MS. Oxf. Dioc. d 577; Hodgson, *Q.A.B.* cccxxii.
20 McClatchey, *Oxon. Clergy*, 62; O.R.O., MSS. Oxf. Dioc. c 446, ff. 214–15; c 2086, note on presentation deed of 1869.
21 e.g. *Kelly's Dir. Oxon.* (1895 and later edns.).
22 D. & C. Exeter, MSS. 2931, 5100. The payment to Bampton in 1848, mentioned above, may relate to tithe.
23 O.R.O., MS. Oxf. Dioc. c 449, ff. 81–2: terrier, partly illegible.

In 1708 part of Combe hill in Lew was said to be tithable to Yelford, but no later reference to that connexion has been found.[24] In 1848 the rector was awarded a rent charge of £65 for tithes of Lenthall's land, and in 1852 a further £50 rent charge for the tithes of *c.* 213 a. in Hardwick's fields.[25]

A house and yardland held from the lord by the rector in 1279 as a freeholder for 10*d.* a year was probably additional to the glebe.[26] In 1625 the rectory house stood south of the church on the site of the surviving Rectory Cottage, surrounded by a small piece of glebe.[27] The house was in disrepair in 1742,[28] and the rector's intention to rebuild in 1811 was presumably unfulfilled, since it was later declared unfit for clerical residence.[29] In 1818 it was a cottage with two ground-floor rooms, and the glebe comprised its garden and a 4½ a. close let to a farmer.[30] In the mid 19th century the glebe was claimed to be *c.* 7 a., but only the cottage garden remained in the mid 20th.[31] From the 18th century Rectory Cottage was usually let; the tenant for much of the later 19th century was a farm labourer who also served as parish clerk and in 1869 held an alehouse licence.[32] One room was used as a vestry until 1958 when the cottage was sold by the Church Commissioners. The building is mostly 18th-century with earlier features, including a fireplace with a 4-centred head. There are foundations, perhaps of the medieval rectory house, immediately to the south.[33]

After the parish was depopulated in the 14th century the living offered an income and few duties, and many rectors were probably non-resident. No presentations have been found between 1382 and 1455.[34] Distinguished late-medieval incumbents included Nicholas West (1489–98), later a prominent royal envoy and bishop of Ely.[35] John Latham (d. 1567) seems to have been resident for some forty years, and his bequests to the poor of many neighbouring parishes suggest that he had been active in a wide area.[36] His will implies acceptance of Reformation changes, but his successor Gregory Gunnis (resigned 1579) was later arrested at Henley and imprisoned as a suspected Roman Catholic priest.[37] William Wyatt, rector 1579–

1624, described as 'sufficient' in 1593, was a local man, probably resident.[38] His successor Charles Hastings (d. 1637) was a younger son of the patron.[39]

The rectors presented by the Lenthalls from the later 17th century were almost all Oxford graduates and few, if any, were resident. Henry Newcome (d. 1750), rector for 42 years, resided elsewhere and seems to have neglected the fabric of both church and rectory house.[40] In the later 18th century and the 19th there was a sustained connexion with Jesus College, of which several rectors were fellows and two were principals; W. J. Lenthall, patron 1783–1855, had been educated at the college.[41] Yelford was served by curates, not always local.[42] One of them, the vicar of Burford, serving as curate at the patron's request, was allowed the whole profits of the living; he argued with the bishop over the need for weekly services in view of Yelford's remoteness, lack of population, and proximity to other churches.[43]

From the 1760s the principal farming family in Yelford for several generations was nonconformist, reducing the average number of communicants to 6; services for long continued fortnightly, becoming weekly in the early 19th century, by which time curates were paid 30 gns. or more.[44] In 1834 there were two Sunday services, but later in the century only one, with congregations of fewer than 20, and communion services at the principal festivals.[45] From 1899 W. D. Macray, rector of Ducklington, was licensed to hold Yelford in plurality, which enabled him to afford an assistant curate to serve both those churches and Cokethorpe.[46] From 1912 the living was held with Standlake.[47] Services were still held twice monthly in the 1990s.

The church is dedicated to *ST. NICHOLAS AND ST. SWITHUN.*[48] The former dedication was recorded regularly from 1334;[49] the latter was first appended *c.* 1740[50] on the evidence of the will of Sir John Ardern (d. 1408) which stipulated burial in St. Swithun's church, Elford, in fact Elford (Staffs.) but wrongly identified as Yelford.[51] The building, only *c.* 52 ft. long and 16 ft. wide in the interior, comprises a nave and

24 O.R.O., QS/1708 Epiph./20.
25 Ibid. Yelford tithe award and map; ibid. Hardwick tithe award, where the preamble refers to *c.* 217 a. tithable to Yelford.
26 *Bampton Hund. R.* 51.
27 Berks. R.O., D/ELl P2, reproduced above, plate 39, which marks the glebe as 'gleer'.
28 O.R.O., MSS. Oxf. Archd. Oxon. c 115, p. 279; cf. ibid. b 27, ff. 458–9: action for dilapidations.
29 e.g. O.R.O., MSS. Oxf. Dioc. c 659, ff. 183–4; b 39.
30 Ibid. c 449, ff. 81–2.
31 *Kelly's Dir. Oxon.* (1883 and later edns.); inf. from Mrs. H. Babington Smith.
32 P.R.O., HO 107/1731; ibid. RG 11/1514; *P.O. Dir. Oxon.* (1869).
33 Inf. from Mrs. H. Babington Smith.
34 Bodl. G.A. Oxon. b 96 (40).
35 Emden, *O.U. Reg. to 1500*; ibid. *C.U. Reg. to 1500*.
36 O.R.O., MS. Wills Oxon. 184, f. 248v. Latham was rector by 1530: *Visit. Dioc. Linc.* ii. 51.
37 Bodl. MS. Top. Oxon. d 602, ff. 377–9; P.R.O., SP 12/179, no. 7; *Miscellanea II* (Cath. Rec. Soc. ii), 240; T. Hadland, *Thames Valley Papists* (priv. print 1992), 42. For his earlier career, *Alum. Oxon. 1500–1714*.
38 O.A.S. *Rep.* (1914), 196; O.R.O., MS. Wills Oxon. 70/2/36.
39 *Oxon. Visit.* (Harl. Soc. v), 262–3; P.R.O., PROB 11/174, f. 151.

40 Bodl. G.A. Oxon. b 96 (40); O.R.O., MS. Oxf. Archd. Oxon. b 27, ff. 458–9; *Secker's Visit.* 182.
41 *Alum. Oxon. 1715–1886*, s.v. Hughes, David; Foulkes, Hen.; Lenthall, Wm. J.   42 e.g. *Secker's Visit.* 182.
43 O.R.O., MS. Oxf. Dioc. d 557; *Secker's Corresp.* 288.
44 e.g. O.R.O., MSS. Oxf. Dioc. c 327, p. 154; d 549; d 560; d 563; d 571; d 573.
45 e.g. ibid. b 39; *Ch. and Chapel*, no. 507; *Wilb. Visit.* 171.
46 Magd. Coll. Mun., MS. 799 (iv), Ducklington par. mags. Feb., Apr. 1899.
47 O.R.O., MS. Oxf. Dioc. c 2086, presentation deeds.
48 The oddity of the conjuncture was regularly noted: e.g. O.A.S. *Rep.* (1904), 53; W. J. Monk, *By Thames and Windrush*, 44.
49 Lincs. R.O., bps. reg. iv, f. 271v.; *Cal. S.P. Dom.* 1637–8, 288.
50 J. Ecton, *Thesaurus Rerum Ecclesiarum* (1742), 479, using inf. from Browne Willis.
51 For the mistake, Bodl. MSS. Willis 52 (a), f. 3; 62, f. 108. For the will, P.R.O., PROB 11/2A, f. 129v., printed in *Some Oxon. Wills* (O.R.S. xxxix), 9; cf. *Cal. Inq. p.m.* xix, p. 195. For the Arderns and Elford, S. Shaw, *Hist. and Antiq. of Staffs.* 380–7. The attribution to Yelford in *P.C.C. Wills 1383–1558* (Index Libr. x), 17 presumably arose because the St. Swithun dedication adopted at Yelford had been lost at Elford.

chancel of coursed limestone rubble with ashlar dressings, and a south porch of ashlar; the roofs are stone slated. A carved relief with beaded arcs reset in the east wall of the porch may be 12th-century or earlier. Otherwise the nave, chancel, and porch seem to have been rebuilt in the late 15th century or early 16th, probably after a period of decay caused by depopulation, and probably soon after the Hastings family had returned to residence in the parish.[52] The uniform thickness of the walls and standardised form of window suggest that nave and chancel were of one build, and the porch was probably added soon afterwards. A pair of blocked pointed apertures in the west wall, wrongly identified as 13th-century lancets,[53] were bell-openings, probably post-medieval, protected in the 19th century by a weather-boarded structure on the exterior. An open bellcote was built over the west gable in the late 19th century.[54] The church, in 'sad disrepair within' in 1869, was restored and re-seated by 1873; the roofs were reslated in the 1950s.[55]

The windows, font, piscina, south door, and carved wooden screen are all of c. 1500. The high-pitched roofs of both nave and chancel retained low-pitched ceilings in 1850;[56] the nave ceiling is of c. 1500, oak, with moulded purlins and cambered tiebeams, and there is a similar ceiling in the porch; the chancel's higher, barrel-shaped ceiling was presumably inserted during the restoration of c. 1870. The lectern was given in the 1950s and a new pulpit in 1965. Until 1965 the church was lit by candles or oil lamps.[57] There are two bells, one given by Elizabeth Lenthall in the 1660s, the other, perhaps originally of the same date, recast for E. K. Lenthall in 1891.[58] In 1759 the curate complained of the lack of communion plate and in 1792 the rector David Hughes presented a chalice, which was stolen in recent times.[59] There were no burials in the church and the sole memorial is to B. Babington Smith (d. 1993). The register dates from 1813; another, dating from 1745, was lost before 1907.[60] The churchyard shows no sign of interments, despite the recorded burial there in 1700. A church repair fund of £80, given by will of E. K. Lenthall (d. 1907), was augmented with £500 given by Mrs. E. M. M. Parker (d. 1969).[61]

NONCONFORMITY. Gregory Gunnis, rector 1567–79, was imprisoned in 1585 as a suspected seminary priest, but no later reference to Roman Catholicism has been found.[62] Several generations of the Baker family, tenants of Manor farm from the 1760s to c. 1820, were Baptists attending Cote chapel.[63]

EDUCATION. No evidence.

CHARITIES. None known.

52 Above, manors.
53 W. H. Bird, *Old Oxon. Chs.* 173; D.o.E., *Historic Bldgs. List.*
54 Cf. above, plate 37; O.A.S. *Rep.* (1871), 31.
55 *P.O. Dir. Oxon.* (1869, 1877); *Kelly's Dir. Oxon.* (1891); O.R.O., MS. Oxf. Dioc. c 2086, faculties.
56 Parker, *Eccl. Top.*, no. 205.
57 O.R.O., MS. Oxf. Dioc. c 2086, faculties.
58 *Ch. Bells Oxon.* p. 465. The date on the treble has been read as 1661: C.O.S., PRN 11977, TS. ch. guide.
59 O.R.O., MS. Oxf. Dioc. d 557; Evans, *Ch. Plate*, 189.
60 C.O.S., par. reg. transcripts.
61 Bodl. G.A. Oxon. c 317 (15); inf. from Mr. P. Rogers, churchwarden.
62 Above, church.
63 O.R.O., MSS. Oxf. Dioc. d 560, d 563, d 571, d 573; above, econ. hist.

INDEX

NOTE. Page numbers in bold-face type indicate the substantive account of a subject. A page number in italic denotes an illustration on that page. A page number followed by *n* is a reference only to the footnotes on that page. Among the abbreviations used in the index the following may require elucidation: abp., archbishop; adv., advowson; agric., agriculture; And., Andrew; Ant., Anthony; Bart., Bartholomew; bdy., boundary; Benj., Benjamin; bp., bishop; Cath., Catherine, Catholic; ch., church; chap., chapel; char., charity; Chas., Charles; Chris., Christopher; chwdns., churchwardens; ct., court; ctss., countess; d., died; Dan., Daniel; dau., daughter; dchss., duchess; dom. archit., domestic architecture; Edm., Edmund; Edw., Edward; Eliz., Elizabeth; est., estate(s); fam., family; fl., flourished; Fm., Farm; Fred., Frederick; Geo., George; Geof., Geoffrey; Gilb., Gilbert; grds., grandson; Hen., Henry; Herb., Herbert; ho., house; hosp., hospital; Humph., Humphrey; hund., hundred; inc., inclosure; ind., industry; Jas., James; Jos., Joseph; Laur., Laurence; Lawr., Lawrence; ld., lord; libr., library; m., married; man., manor(s); Marg., Margaret; Mat., Matthew; mkt., market; Max., Maximilian; Mic., Michael; Nat., Nathaniel; Nic., Nicholas; nonconf., nonconformity; par., parish; pk., park; Phil., Philip; pop., population; prehist., prehistoric; rem., remains; Ric., Richard; riv., river; rly., railway; Reg., Reginald; Rob., Robert; Rog., Roger; Rom., Roman; s., son; Sam., Samuel; sch., school; Sim., Simon; Steph., Stephen; Thos., Thomas; Tim., Timothy; univ., university; vct., viscount; w., wife; Wal., Walter; Wm., William.